Course	Global Finance: Investing and Managing Across Nations & Markets
Course Number	**FINC 360** **International Finance**
Professor	Dr. Malcolm C. Harris, Sr. Friends University **Business and Information Technology**

http://create.mheducation.com

ISBN-10: 1121238823   ISBN-13: 9781121238824

Contents

Credits

I. The International Environment

CHAPTER

2 International Monetary System

THIS CHAPTER EXAMINES the **international monetary system**, which defines the overall financial environment in which multinational corporations and international investors operate. As mentioned in Chapter 1, the exchange rates among major currencies, such as the U.S. dollar, British pound, Swiss franc, and Japanese yen, have been fluctuating since the fixed exchange rate regime was abandoned in 1973. Consequently, corporations nowadays are operating in an environment in which exchange rate changes may adversely affect their competitive positions in the marketplace. This situation, in turn, makes it necessary for many firms to carefully measure and manage their exchange risk exposure. Similarly, international investors face the problem of fluctuating exchange rates affecting their portfolio returns. As we will discuss shortly, however, many European countries have adopted a common currency called the **euro**, rendering intra-European trade and investment much less susceptible to exchange risk. The complex international monetary arrangements imply that for adroit financial decision making, it is essential for managers to understand, in detail, the arrangements and workings of the international monetary system.

The international monetary system can be defined as the *institutional framework within which international payments are made, movements of capital are accommodated,* and *exchange rates among currencies are determined.* It is a complex whole of agreements, rules, institutions, mechanisms, and policies regarding exchange rates, international payments, and the flow of capital. The international monetary system has evolved over time and will continue to do so in the future as the fundamental business and political conditions underlying the world economy continue to shift. In this chapter, we will review the history of the international monetary system and contemplate its future prospects. In addition, we will compare and contrast the alternative exchange rate systems, that is, fixed versus flexible exchange rates. For astute financial management, it is important to understand the dynamic nature of international monetary environments.

Evolution of the International Monetary System

The international monetary system went through several distinct stages of evolution. These stages are summarized as follows:

1. Bimetallism: Before 1875.

2. Classical gold standard: 1875–1914.

3. Interwar period: 1915–1944.

4. Bretton Woods system: 1945–1972.

5. Flexible exchange rate regime: Since 1973.

We now examine each of the five stages in some detail.

Bimetallism: Before 1875

Prior to the 1870s, many countries had **bimetallism**, that is, a double standard in that free coinage was maintained for both gold and silver. In Great Britain, for example, bimetallism was maintained until 1816 (after the conclusion of the Napoleonic Wars) when Parliament passed a law maintaining free coinage of gold only, abolishing the free coinage of silver. In the United States, bimetallism was adopted by the Coinage Act of 1792 and remained a legal standard until 1873, when Congress dropped the silver dollar from the list of coins to be minted. France, on the other hand, introduced and maintained its bimetallism from the French Revolution to 1878. Some other countries such as China, India, Germany, and Holland were on the silver standard.

The international monetary system before the 1870s can be characterized as "bimetallism" in the sense that both gold and silver were used as international means of payment and that the exchange rates among currencies were determined by either their gold or silver contents.[1] Around 1870, for example, the exchange rate between the British pound, which was fully on a gold standard, and the French franc, which was officially on a bimetallic standard, was determined by the gold content of the two currencies. On the other hand, the exchange rate between the franc and the German mark, which was on a silver standard, was determined by the silver content of the currencies. The exchange rate between the pound and the mark was determined by their exchange rates against the franc. It is also worth noting that, due to various wars and political upheavals, some major countries such as the United States, Russia, and Austria-Hungary had irredeemable currencies at one time or another during the period 1848–79. One might say that the international monetary system was less than fully *systematic* up until the 1870s.

Countries that were on the bimetallic standard often experienced the well-known phenomenon referred to as **Gresham's law**. Since the exchange ratio between the two metals was fixed officially, only the abundant metal was used as money, driving more scarce metal out of circulation. This is Gresham's law, according to which "bad" (abundant) money drives out "good" (scarce) money. For example, when gold from newly discovered mines in California and Australia poured into the market in the 1850s, the value of gold became depressed, causing overvaluation of gold under the French official ratio, which equated a gold franc to a silver franc 15½ times as heavy. As a result, the franc effectively became a gold currency.

Classical Gold Standard: 1875–1914

Mankind's fondness for gold as a storage of wealth and means of exchange dates back to antiquity and was shared widely by diverse civilizations. Christopher Columbus once said, "Gold constitutes treasure, and he who possesses it has all he needs in this world." The first full-fledged **gold standard**, however, was not established until 1821 in Great Britain, when notes from the Bank of England were made fully redeemable for gold. As previously mentioned, France was effectively on the gold standard beginning in the 1850s and formally adopted the standard in 1878. The newly emergent German empire, which was to receive a sizable war indemnity from France, converted to the gold standard in 1875, discontinuing free coinage of silver. The United States adopted the gold standard in 1879, Russia and Japan in 1897.

[1]This does not imply that each individual country was on a bimetalic standard. In fact, many countries were on either a gold standard or a silver standard by 1870.

One can say roughly that the *international* gold standard existed as a historical reality during the period 1875–1914. The majority of countries got off gold in 1914 when World War I broke out. The classical gold standard as an international monetary system thus lasted for about 40 years. During this period, London became the center of the international financial system, reflecting Britain's advanced economy and its preeminent position in international trade.

An *international* gold standard can be said to exist when, in most major countries, (1) gold alone is assured of unrestricted coinage, (2) there is two-way convertibility between gold and national currencies at a stable ratio, and (3) gold may be freely exported or imported. In order to support unrestricted convertibility into gold, banknotes need to be backed by a gold reserve of a minimum stated ratio. In addition, the domestic money stock should rise and fall as gold flows in and out of the country. The above conditions were roughly met between 1875 and 1914.

Under the gold standard, the exchange rate between any two currencies will be determined by their gold content. For example, suppose that the pound is pegged to gold at six pounds per ounce, whereas one ounce of gold is worth 12 francs. The exchange rate between the pound and the franc should then be two francs per pound. To the extent that the pound and the franc remain pegged to gold at given prices, the exchange rate between the two currencies will remain stable. There were indeed no significant changes in exchange rates among the currencies of such major countries as Great Britain, France, Germany, and the United States during the entire period. For example, the dollar–sterling exchange rate remained within a narrow range of $4.84 and $4.90 per pound. Highly stable exchange rates under the classical gold standard provided an environment that was conducive to international trade and investment.

Under the gold standard, misalignment of the exchange rate will be automatically corrected by cross-border flows of gold. In the above example, suppose that one pound is trading for 1.80 francs at the moment. Since the pound is undervalued in the exchange market, people will buy pounds with francs, but not francs with pounds. For people who need francs, it would be cheaper first to buy gold from the Bank of England and ship it to France and sell it for francs. For example, suppose that you need to buy 1,000 francs using pounds. If you buy 1,000 francs in the exchange market, it will cost you £555.56 at the exchange rate of Fr1.80/£. Alternatively, you can buy 83.33 = 1,000/12 ounces of gold from the Bank of England for £500:

$$£500 = (1,000/12) \times 6$$

Then you could ship it to France and sell it to the Bank of France for 1,000 francs. This way, you can save about £55.56.[2] Since people only want to buy, not sell, pounds at the exchange rate of Fr1.80/£, the pound will eventually appreciate to its fair value, namely, Fr2.0/£.

Under the gold standard, international imbalances of payment will also be corrected automatically. Consider a situation where Great Britain exported more to France than the former imported from the latter. This kind of trade imbalance will not persist under the gold standard. Net export from Great Britain to France will be accompanied by a net flow of gold in the opposite direction. This flow of gold will lead to a lower price level in France and, at the same time, a higher price level in Great Britain. (Recall that under the gold standard, the domestic money stock is supposed to rise or fall as the country experiences an inflow or outflow of gold.) The resultant change in the relative price level, in turn, will slow exports from Great Britain and encourage exports from France. As a result, the initial net export from Great Britain will eventually disappear.

---

[2]In this example, we ignored shipping costs. But as long as the shipping costs do not exceed £55.56, it is still advantageous to buy francs via "gold export" than via the foreign exchange market.

This adjustment mechanism is referred to as the **price-specie-flow mechanism**, which is attributed to David Hume, a Scottish philosopher.[3]

Despite its demise a long time ago, the gold standard still has ardent supporters in academic, business, and political circles, which view it as an ultimate hedge against price inflation. Gold has a natural scarcity and no one can increase its quantity at will. Therefore, if gold serves as the sole base for domestic money creation, the money supply cannot get out of control and cause inflation. In addition, if gold is used as the sole international means of payment, then countries' balance of payments will be regulated automatically via the movements of gold.[4]

The gold standard, however, has a few key shortcomings. First of all, the supply of newly minted gold is so restricted that the growth of world trade and investment can be seriously hampered for the lack of sufficient monetary reserves. The world economy can face deflationary pressures. Second, whenever the government finds it politically necessary to pursue national objectives that are inconsistent with maintaining the gold standard, it can abandon the gold standard. In other words, the international gold standard per se has no mechanism to compel each major country to abide by the rules of the game.[5] For such reasons, it is not very likely that the classical gold standard will be restored in the foreseeable future.

Interwar Period: 1915–1944

World War I ended the classical gold standard in August 1914, as major countries such as Great Britain, France, Germany, and Russia suspended redemption of banknotes in gold and imposed embargoes on gold exports. After the war, many countries, especially Germany, Austria, Hungary, Poland, and Russia, suffered hyperinflation. The German experience provides a classic example of hyperinflation: By the end of 1923, the wholesale price index in Germany was more than 1 trillion times as high as the prewar level. Freed from wartime pegging, exchange rates among currencies were fluctuating in the early 1920s. During this period, countries widely used "predatory" depreciations of their currencies as a means of gaining advantages in the world export market.

As major countries began to recover from the war and stabilize their economies, they attempted to restore the gold standard. The United States, which replaced Great Britain as the dominant financial power, spearheaded efforts to restore the gold standard. With only mild inflation, the United States was able to lift restrictions on gold exports and return to a gold standard in 1919. In Great Britain, Winston Churchill, the chancellor of the Exchequer, played a key role in restoring the gold standard in 1925. Besides Great Britain, such countries as Switzerland, France, and the Scandinavian countries restored the gold standard by 1928.

The international gold standard of the late 1920s, however, was not much more than a façade. Most major countries gave priority to the stabilization of domestic economies and systematically followed a policy of **sterilization of gold** by matching inflows and outflows of gold respectively with reductions and increases in domestic money and credit. The Federal Reserve of the United States, for example, kept some gold outside the credit base by circulating it as gold certificates. The Bank of England also followed the policy of keeping the amount of available domestic credit stable by neutralizing the effects of gold flows. In a word, countries lacked the political will to abide by the "rules of the game," and so the automatic adjustment mechanism of the gold standard was unable to work.

---

[3]The price-specie-flow mechanism will work only if governments are willing to abide by the rules of the game by letting the money stock rise and fall as gold flows in and out. Once the government demonetizes (neutralizes) gold, the mechanism will break down. In addition, the effectiveness of the mechanism depends on the price elasticity of the demand for imports.

[4]The balance of payments will be discussed in detail in Chapter 3.

[5]This point need not be viewed as a weakness of the gold standard per se, but it casts doubt on the long-term feasibility of the gold standard.

Even the facade of the restored gold standard was destroyed in the wake of the Great Depression and the accompanying financial crises. Following the stock market crash and the onset of the Great Depression in 1929, many banks, especially in Austria, Germany, and the United States, suffered sharp declines in their portfolio values, touching off runs on the banks. Against this backdrop, Britain experienced a massive outflow of gold, which resulted from chronic balance-of-payment deficits and lack of confidence in the pound sterling. Despite coordinated international efforts to rescue the pound, British gold reserves continued to fall to the point where it was impossible to maintain the gold standard. In September 1931, the British government suspended gold payments and let the pound float. As Great Britain got off gold, countries such as Canada, Sweden, Austria, and Japan followed suit by the end of 1931. The United States got off gold in April 1933 after experiencing a spate of bank failures and outflows of gold. Lastly, France abandoned the gold standard in 1936 because of the flight from the franc, which, in turn, reflected the economic and political instability following the inception of the socialist Popular Front government led by Leon Blum. Paper standards came into being when the gold standard was abandoned.

In sum, the interwar period was characterized by economic nationalism, halfhearted attempts and failure to restore the gold standard, economic and political instabilities, bank failures, and panicky flights of capital across borders. No coherent international monetary system prevailed during this period, with profoundly detrimental effects on international trade and investment. It is during this period that the U.S. dollar emerged as the dominant world currency, gradually replacing the British pound for the role.

Bretton Woods System: 1945–1972

In July 1944, representatives of 44 nations gathered at Bretton Woods, New Hampshire, to discuss and design the postwar international monetary system. After lengthy discussions and bargains, representatives succeeded in drafting and signing the Articles of Agreement of the International Monetary Fund (IMF), which constitutes the core of the **Bretton Woods system**. The agreement was subsequently ratified by the majority of countries to launch the IMF in 1945. The IMF embodied an explicit set of rules about the conduct of international monetary policies and was responsible for enforcing these rules. Delegates also created a sister institution, the International Bank for Reconstruction and Development (IBRD), better known as the World Bank, that was chiefly responsible for financing individual development projects.

In designing the Bretton Woods system, representatives were concerned with how to prevent the recurrence of economic nationalism with destructive "beggar-thy-neighbor" policies and how to address the lack of clear rules of the game plaguing the interwar years. The British delegates led by John Maynard Keynes proposed an international clearing union that would create an international reserve asset called "bancor." Countries would accept payments in bancor to settle international transactions, without limit. They would also be allowed to acquire bancor by using overdraft facilities with the clearing union. On the other hand, the American delegates, headed by Harry Dexter White, proposed a currency pool to which member countries would make contributions and from which they might borrow to tide themselves over during short-term balance-of-payments deficits. Both delegates desired exchange rate stability without restoring an international gold standard. The American proposal was largely incorporated into the Articles of Agreement of the IMF.

Under the Bretton Woods system, each country established a **par value** in relation to the U.S. dollar, which was pegged to gold at $35 per ounce. This point is illustrated in Exhibit 2.1. Each country was responsible for maintaining its exchange rate within ±1 percent of the adopted par value by buying or selling foreign exchanges as necessary. However, a member country with a "fundamental disequilibrium" may be allowed to make a change in the par value of its currency. Under the Bretton Woods

EXHIBIT 2.1

The Design of the Gold-Exchange System

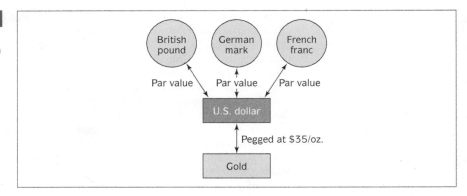

system, the U.S. dollar was the only currency that was fully convertible to gold; other currencies were not directly convertible to gold. Countries held U.S. dollars, as well as gold, for use as an international means of payment. Because of these arrangements, the Bretton Woods system can be described as a dollar-based **gold-exchange standard**. A country on the gold-exchange standard holds most of its reserves in the form of currency of a country that is *really* on the gold standard.

Advocates of the gold-exchange system argue that the system economizes on gold because countries can use not only gold but also foreign exchanges as an international means of payment. Foreign exchange reserves offset the deflationary effects of limited addition to the world's monetary gold stock. Another advantage of the gold-exchange system is that individual countries can earn interest on their foreign exchange holdings, whereas gold holdings yield no returns. In addition, countries can save transaction costs associated with transporting gold across countries under the gold-exchange system. An ample supply of international monetary reserves coupled with stable exchange rates provided an environment highly conducive to the growth of international trade and investment throughout the 1950s and 1960s.

Professor Robert Triffin warned, however, that the gold-exchange system was programmed to collapse in the long run. To satisfy the growing need for reserves, the United States had to run balance-of-payments deficits continuously. Yet if the United States ran perennial balance-of-payments deficits, it would eventually impair the public confidence in the dollar, triggering a run on the dollar. Under the gold-exchange system, the reserve-currency country should run balance-of-payments deficits to supply reserves, but if such deficits are large and persistent, they can lead to a crisis of confidence in the reserve currency itself, causing the downfall of the system. This dilemma, known as the **Triffin paradox**, was indeed responsible for the eventual collapse of the dollar-based gold-exchange system in the early 1970s.

The United States began to experience trade deficits with the rest of the world in the late 1950s, and the problem persisted into the 1960s. By the early 1960s the total value of the U.S. gold stock, when valued at $35 per ounce, fell short of foreign dollar holdings. This naturally created concern about the viability of the dollar-based system. Against this backdrop, President Charles de Gaulle prodded the Bank of France to buy gold from the U.S. Treasury, unloading its dollar holdings. Efforts to remedy the problem centered on (1) a series of dollar defense measures taken by the U.S. government and (2) the creation of a new reserve asset, **special drawing rights (SDRs)**, by the IMF.

In 1963, President John Kennedy imposed the Interest Equalization Tax (IET) on U.S. purchases of foreign securities in order to stem the outflow of dollars. The IET was designed to increase the cost of foreign borrowing in the U.S. bond market. In 1965, the Federal Reserve introduced the U.S. voluntary Foreign Credit Restraint

CHAPTER 2 | INTERNATIONAL MONETARY SYSTEM

31

Program (FCRP), which regulated the amount of dollars U.S. banks could lend to U.S. multinational companies engaged in foreign direct investments. In 1968, these regulations became legally binding. Such measures as IET and FCRP lent a strong impetus to the rapid growth of the Eurodollar market, which is a transnational, unregulated fund market.

To partially alleviate the pressure on the dollar as the central reserve currency, the IMF created an artificial international reserve called the SDR in 1970. The SDR, which is a basket currency comprising major individual currencies, was allotted to the members of the IMF, who could then use it for transactions among themselves or with the IMF. In addition to gold and foreign exchanges, countries could use the SDR to make international payments.

www.imf.org/external/fin.htm

Provides detailed information about the SDR, such as SDR exchange rates, interests, allocations, etc.

Initially, the SDR was designed to be the weighted average of 16 currencies of those countries whose shares in world exports were more than 1 percent. The percentage share of each currency in the SDR was about the same as the country's share in world exports. In 1981, however, the SDR was greatly simplified to comprise only five major currencies: U.S. dollar, German mark, Japanese yen, British pound, and French franc. As Exhibit 2.2 shows, the weight for each currency is updated periodically, reflecting the relative importance of each country in the world trade of goods and services and the amount of the currencies held as reserves by the members of the IMF. Currently, the SDR is comprised of four major currencies—the U.S. dollar (44 percent weight), euro (34 percent), Japanese yen (11 percent), and British pound (11 percent).

The SDR is used not only as a reserve asset but also as a denomination currency for international transactions. Since the SDR is a "portfolio" of currencies, its value tends to be more stable than the value of any individual currency included in the SDR. The portfolio nature of the SDR makes it an attractive denomination currency for international commercial and financial contracts under exchange rate uncertainty.

The efforts to support the dollar-based gold-exchange standard, however, turned out to be ineffective in the face of expansionary monetary policy and rising inflation in the United States, which were related to the financing of the Vietnam War and the Great Society program. In the early 1970s, it became clear that the dollar was overvalued, especially relative to the mark and the yen. As a result, the German and Japanese central banks had to make massive interventions in the foreign exchange market to maintain their par values. Given the unwillingness of the United States to control its monetary expansion, the repeated central bank interventions could not solve the underlying disparities. In August 1971, President Richard Nixon suspended the convertibility of the dollar into gold and imposed a 10 percent import surcharge. The foundation of the Bretton Woods system cracked under the strain.

In an attempt to save the Bretton Woods system, 10 major countries, known as the Group of Ten, met at the Smithsonian Institution in Washington, D.C., in December 1971. They reached the **Smithsonian Agreement**, according to which (1) the price of gold was raised to $38 per ounce, (2) each of the other countries revalued its currency against the U.S. dollar by up to 10 percent, and (3) the band within which the exchange rates were allowed to move was expanded from 1 percent to 2.25 percent in either direction.

The Smithsonian Agreement lasted for little more than a year before it came under attack again. Clearly, the devaluation of the dollar was not sufficient to stabilize the situation. In February 1973, the dollar came under heavy selling pressure, again prompting central banks around the world to buy dollars. The price of gold was further raised from $38 to $42 per ounce. By March 1973, European and Japanese currencies were allowed to float, completing the decline and fall of the Bretton Woods system. Since then, the exchange rates among such major currencies as the dollar, the mark (later succeeded by the euro), the pound, and the yen have been fluctuating against each other.

EXHIBIT 2.2	Currencies	1981–85	1986–90	1991–95	1996–2000	2001–2005	2006–
The Composition of the Special Drawing Right (SDR)ᵃ	U.S. dollar	42%	42%	40%	39%	45%	44%
	Euro	—	—	—	—	29	34
	German mark	19	19	21	21	—	—
	Japanese yen	13	15	17	18	15	11
	British pound	13	12	11	11	11	11
	French franc	13	12	11	11	—	—

ᵃThe composition of the SDR changes every five years.
Source: The International Monetary Fund.

The Flexible Exchange Rate Regime: 1973–Present

The flexible exchange rate regime that followed the demise of the Bretton Woods system was ratified after the fact in January 1976 when the IMF members met in Jamaica and agreed to a new set of rules for the international monetary system. The key elements of the **Jamaica Agreement** include:

1. Flexible exchange rates were declared acceptable to the IMF members, and central banks were allowed to intervene in the exchange markets to iron out unwarranted volatilities.

2. Gold was officially abandoned (i.e., demonetized) as an international reserve asset. Half of the IMF's gold holdings were returned to the members and the other half were sold, with the proceeds to be used to help poor nations.

3. Non-oil-exporting countries and less-developed countries were given greater access to IMF funds.

The IMF continued to provide assistance to countries facing balance-of-payments and exchange rate difficulties. The IMF, however, extended assistance and loans to the member countries on the condition that those countries follow the IMF's macroeconomic policy prescriptions. This "conditionality," which often involves deflationary macroeconomic policies and elimination of various subsidy programs, provoked resentment among the people of developing countries receiving the IMF's balance-of-payments loans.

As can be expected, exchange rates have become substantially more volatile since March 1973 than they were under the Bretton Woods system. Exhibit 2.3 summarizes the behavior of the dollar exchange rate since 1965. The exhibit shows the exchange rate between the U.S. dollar and a weighted basket of 21 other major currencies. The decline of the dollar between 1970 and 1973 represents the transition from the Bretton Woods to the flexible exchange rate system. The most conspicuous phenomena shown in Exhibit 2.3 are the dollar's spectacular rise between 1980 and 1984 and its equally spectacular decline between 1985 and 1988. These unusual episodes merit some discussion.

Following the U.S. presidential election of 1980, the Reagan administration ushered in a period of growing U.S. budget deficits and balance-of-payments deficits. The U.S. dollar, however, experienced a major appreciation throughout the first half of the 1980s because of the large-scale inflows of foreign capital caused by unusually high real interest rates available in the United States. To attract foreign investment to help finance the budget deficit, the United States had to offer high real interest rates. The heavy demand for dollars by foreign investors pushed up the value of the dollar in the exchange market.

The value of the dollar reached its peak in February 1985 and then began a persistent downward drift until it stabilized in 1988. The reversal in the exchange rate trend partially reflected the effect of the record-high U.S. trade deficit, about

http://cibs.sauder.ubc.ca

Provides a list of all the currencies of the world with information on each country's exchange rate regime. Also provides current and historical exchange rates.

CHAPTER 2 | INTERNATIONAL MONETARY SYSTEM

33

| EXHIBIT 2.3 | The Value of the U.S. Dollar since 1960[a] |

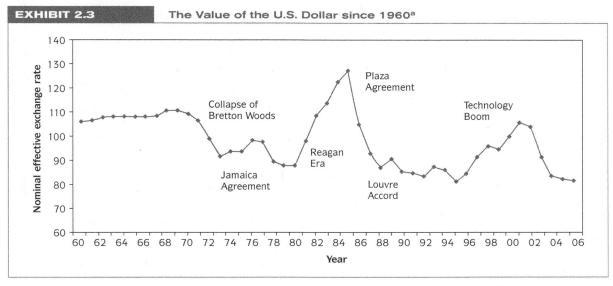

[a]The value of the U.S. dollar represents the nominal exchange rate index (2000 = 100) with weights derived from trade among 22 industrialized countries.
Source: International Financial Statistics.

$160 billion in 1985, brought about by the soaring dollar. The downward trend was also reinforced by concerted government interventions. In September 1985, the so-called G-5 countries (France, Japan, Germany, the U.K., and the United States) met at the Plaza Hotel in New York and reached what became known as the **Plaza Accord**. They agreed that it would be desirable for the dollar to depreciate against most major currencies to solve the U.S. trade deficit problem and expressed their willingness to intervene in the exchange market to realize this objective. The slide of the dollar that had begun in February was further precipitated by the Plaza Accord.

As the dollar continued its decline, the governments of the major industrial countries began to worry that the dollar may fall too far. To address the problem of exchange rate volatility and other related issues, the G-7 economic summit meeting was convened in Paris in 1987.[6] The meeting produced the **Louvre Accord**, according to which:

1. The G-7 countries would cooperate to achieve greater exchange rate stability.

2. The G-7 countries agreed to more closely consult and coordinate their macro-economic policies.

The Louvre Accord marked the inception of the **managed-float system** under which the G-7 countries would jointly intervene in the exchange market to correct over- or undervaluation of currencies. Since the Louvre Accord, exchange rates became relatively more stable for a while. During the period 1996–2001, however, the U.S. dollar generally appreciated, reflecting a robust performance of the U.S. economy fueled by the technology boom. During this period, foreigners invested heavily in the United States to participate in the booming U.S. economy and stock markets. This helped the dollar to appreciate. Since 2001, however, the U.S. dollar began to depreciate due to a sharp stock market correction, the ballooning trade deficits, and the increased political uncertainty following the September 11 attack.

---

[6]The G-7 is composed of Canada, France, Japan, Germany, Italy, the U.K., and the United States.

The Current Exchange Rate Arrangements

Although the most actively traded currencies of the world, such as the dollar, the yen, the pound, and the euro, may be fluctuating against each other, a significant number of the world's currencies are pegged to single currencies, particularly the U.S. dollar and the euro, or baskets of currencies such as the SDR. The current exchange rate arrangements as classified by the IMF are provided in Exhibit 2.4.

As can be seen from the exhibit, the IMF currently classifies exchange rate arrangements into eight separate regimes:[7]

Exchange arrangements with no separate legal tender: The currency of another country circulates as the sole legal tender or the country belongs to a monetary or currency union in which the same legal tender is shared by the members of the union. Examples include Ecuador, El Salvador, and Panama using the U.S. dollar and Montenegro and San Marino using the euro.

Currency board arrangements: A monetary regime based on an explicit legislative commitment to exchange domestic currency for a specified foreign currency at a fixed exchange rate, combined with restrictions on the issuing authority to ensure the fulfillment of its legal obligation. Examples include Hong Kong fixed to the U.S. dollar and Estonia fixed to the euro.

Other conventional fixed peg arrangement: The country pegs its currency (formally or de facto) at a fixed rate to a major currency or a basket of currencies where the exchange rate fluctuates within a narrow margin of less than 1 percent, plus or minus, around a central rate. Examples include Egypt, Nigeria, Saudi Arabia, and Ukraine.

Pegged exchange rates within horizontal bands: The value of the currency is maintained within margins of fluctuation around a formal or de facto fixed peg that are wider than at least 1 percent, plus or minus, around a central rate. Examples include Denmark, Slovak Republic, and Hungary.

Crawling pegs: The currency is adjusted periodically in small amounts at a fixed, preannounced rate or in response to changes in selective quantitative indicators. Examples are China, Iraq, and Nicaragua.

Exchange rates within crawling bands: The currency is maintained within certain fluctuation margins around a central rate that is adjusted periodically at a fixed preannounced rate or in response to changes in selective quantitative indicators. Costa Rica is an example.

Managed floating with no preannounced path for the exchange rate: The monetary authority influences the movements of the exchange rate through active intervention in the foreign exchange market without specifying, or precommitting to, a preannounced path for the exchange rate. Examples include Algeria, Colombia, Czech Republic, India, Russia, Singapore, and Thailand.

Independent floating: The exchange rate is market determined, with any foreign exchange intervention aimed at moderating the rate of change and preventing undue fluctuations in the exchange rate rather than at establishing a level for it. Examples include Australia, Brazil, Canada, euro area, Korea, Mexico, the U.K., Japan, Switzerland, and the United States.

As of April 2007, a large number of countries (35), including Australia, Canada, Japan, the United Kingdom, euro area, and the United States, allow their currencies to float independently against other currencies; the exchange rates of these countries are essentially determined by market forces. Forty-eight countries, including India,

---

[7]We draw on IMF classifications provided in *International Financial Statistics*.

Russia, and Singapore, adopt some forms of "managed floating" system that combines market forces and government intervention in setting the exchange rates. In contrast, 10 countries do not have their own national currencies. For example, Panama and Ecuador are using the U.S. dollar. Thirteen countries including Bulgaria, Hong Kong SAR, and Estonia, on the other hand, maintain national currencies but they are permanently fixed to such hard currencies as the U.S. dollar or euro. The remaining countries adopt a mixture of fixed and floating exchange rate regimes. As is well known, the European Union has pursued Europe-wide monetary integration by first establishing the European Monetary System and then the European Monetary Union. These topics deserve a detailed discussion.

European Monetary System

According to the Smithsonian Agreement, which was signed in December 1971, the band of exchange rate movements was expanded from the original plus or minus 1 percent to plus or minus 2.25 percent. Members of the European Economic Community (EEC), however, decided on a narrower band of ±1.125 percent for their currencies. This scaled-down, European version of the fixed exchange rate system that arose concurrently with the decline of the Bretton Woods system was called the **snake**. The name "snake" was derived from the way the EEC currencies moved closely together within the wider band allowed for other currencies like the dollar.

The EEC countries adopted the snake because they felt that stable exchange rates among the EEC countries were essential for promoting intra-EEC trade and deepening economic integration. The snake arrangement was replaced by the **European Monetary System (EMS)** in 1979. The EMS, which was originally proposed by German Chancellor Helmut Schmidt, was formally launched in March 1979. Among its chief objectives are:

1. To establish a "zone of monetary stability" in Europe.

2. To coordinate exchange rate policies vis-à-vis the non-EMS currencies.

3. To pave the way for the eventual European monetary union.

At the political level, the EMS represented a Franco-German initiative to speed up the movement toward European economic and political unification. All EEC member countries, except the United Kingdom and Greece, joined the EMS. The two main instruments of the EMS are the European Currency Unit and the Exchange Rate Mechanism.

The **European Currency Unit (ECU)** is a "basket" currency constructed as a weighted average of the currencies of member countries of the European Union (EU). The weights are based on each currency's relative GNP and share in intra-EU trade. The ECU serves as the accounting unit of the EMS and plays an important role in the workings of the exchange rate mechanism.

The **Exchange Rate Mechanism (ERM)** refers to the procedure by which EMS member countries collectively manage their exchange rates. The ERM is based on a "parity grid" system, which is a system of par values among ERM currencies. The par values in the parity grid are computed by first defining the par values of EMS currencies in terms of the ECU.

When the EMS was launched in 1979, a currency was allowed to deviate from the parities with other currencies by a maximum of plus or minus 2.25 percent, with the exception of the Italian lira, for which a maximum deviation of plus or minus 6 percent was allowed. In September 1993, however, the band was widened to a maximum of plus or minus 15 percent. When a currency is at the lower or upper bound, the central banks of both countries are required to intervene in the foreign exchange markets to keep the market exchange rate within the band. To intervene in the exchange markets,

EXHIBIT 2.4 Exchange Rate Regimes and Anchors of Monetary Policy (As of April 30, 2007)[1]

Exchange Rate Arrangements (Number of Countries)	Monetary Policy Framework				
	Exchange Rate Anchor	Monetary Aggregate Target	Inflation Targeting Framework	IMF-Supported or Other Monetary Program	Other[2]
Exchange arrangements with no separate legal tender (10)	Ecuador El Salvador[3] Kiribati Marshall Islands Micronesia, Fed. States of Montenegro Palau Panama[4] San Marino[15] Timor-Leste, Dem. Rep. of				
Currency board arrangements (13)	Bosnia and Herzegovina Brunei Darussalam Bulgaria Hong Kong SAR Djibouti Estonia[5] Lithuania[5] ECCU Antigua and Barbuda Dominica Grenada* St. Kitts and Nevis St. Lucia St. Vincent and the Grenadines				
Other conventional fixed peg arrangements (70)	**Against a single currency (63)** Angola[6] Argentina†[6] Aruba Bahamas, The[7] Bahrain, Kingdom of Barbados[6] Belarus[6] Belize Bhutan Bolivia[6] Cape Verde Comoros[8] Egypt[6,10] Eritrea Ethiopia[6] Guyana†[6,9] Honduras[6] Jordan[6] Kuwait Latvia[5] Nigeria[6,10] Oman Pakistan†[6] Qatar Rwanda*[6] Saudi Arabia Solomon Islands[6] Suriname†[6,7,9] Swaziland Syrian Arab Rep.[7] Trinidad and Tobago[6] Turkmenistan[6] Ukraine[6] United Arab Emirates Uzbekistan[6,7] Venezuela[7] Vietnam[6] Yemen, Rep. of[6] Zimbabwe[7]	Argentina†[6] Guyana[6,9] Suriname†[6,7,9]			Pakistan†[6]

Exchange rate regime	Exchange rate anchor — US dollar / single currency	Exchange rate anchor — Euro	Exchange rate anchor — Composite	Monetary aggregate target	Inflation-targeting framework	Other
(continued) Other conventional fixed peg arrangements	Lebanon[6], Lesotho, Macedonia, FYR*[6], Maldives, Malta[5], Mauritania*[6], Mongolia[6], Namibia, Nepal*[6], Netherlands Antilles	**CFA franc zone** — **WAEMU**[11]: Benin*, Burkina Faso*, Côte d'Ivoire, Guinea-Bissau, Mali*, Niger*, Senegal, Togo; **CAEMC**[11]: Cameroon*, Central African Rep.*, Chad*, Congo, Rep. of*, Equatorial Guinea, Gabon	**Against a composite (7)**: Fiji, Iran, I.R. of[6], Libyan Arab Jamahiriya, Morocco, Samoa, Seychelles, Vanuatu			
Pegged exchange rates within horizontal bands (5)[12]		**Within a cooperative arrangement (3)**: Cyprus[5], Denmark[5], Slovak Rep.†[5]	**Other band arrangements (2)**: Hungary†, Tonga	Iran, I.R. of†[6]	Hungary†, Slovak Rep.†[5]	
Crawling pegs (6)	Azerbaijan[6], Botswana[7], China[6]					Iraq*[6], Nicaragua, Sierra Leone*[6]
Crawling bands (1)						Costa Rica
Managed floating with no predetermined path for the exchange rate (48)				Bangladesh*, Gambia, The*[6], Haiti*, Jamaica[6], Lao P.D.R.[7], Madagascar*[6], Malawi[6], Mauritius*, Moldova*, Papua New Guinea[6], Sri Lanka[6], Sudan, Tajikistan, Tanzania, Tunisia, Uganda[6], Uruguay[6], Zambia*	Colombia, Czech Rep., Ghana, Guatemala†[6], Indonesia, Peru*, Romania, Serbia, Rep. of[13], Thailand	Algeria, Burundi*[6], Cambodia, Croatia, Dominican Rep.*, Guinea[6], India, Kazakhstan, Liberia[6], Malaysia, Myanmar[7], Paraguay*, Russian Federation, São Tomé and Príncipe*, Singapore; Afghanistan, I.R. of*[6], Armenia*[6], Georgia*, Kenya*, Kyrgyz Rep.*, Mozambique*[6]

(continued)

EXHIBIT 2.4	Exchange Rate Regimes and Anchors of Monetary Policy (As of April 30, 2007) (continued)				
	Monetary Policy Framework				
Exchange Rate Arrangements (Number of Countries)	**Exchange Rate Anchor**	**Monetary Aggregate Target**	**Inflation Targeting Framework**	**IMF-Supported or Other Monetary Program**	**Other**
Independently floating (35)		Albania* Congo, Dem. Rep. of	Australia Brazil Canada Chile Iceland Israel Korea Mexico New Zealand Norway Philippines Poland South Africa Sweden Turkey* United Kingdom		Japan Somalia[7,14] Switzerland United States Euro area Austria Belgium Finland France Germany Greece Ireland Italy Luxembourg Netherlands Portugal Slovenia Spain

Sources: IMF staff reports; and IMF staff estimates.

[1] This table incorporates additional changes made since the publication of the 2007 AREAER. Data generally refer to the 185 IMF members plus Aruba, Hong Kong SAR, and the Netherlands Antilles, and are as of end-April 2007.

[2] Includes countries that have no explicitly stated nominal anchor, but rather monitor various indicators in conducting monetary policy.

[3] The printing of new colones, the domestic currency, is prohibited, but the existing stock of colones will continue to circulate along with the U.S. dollar as legal tender until all colon notes wear out physically.

[4] The currency and unit of account of Panama is the balboa, the issue of which is limited to coins. The balboa is fixed at par to the U.S. dollar, which circulates freely.

[5] The member participates in the ERM II.

[6] The staff's assessment of the de facto arrangement in the country has been different from its de jure arrangements during the period under consideration.

[7] The country maintains an exchange arrangement involving more than one foreign exchange market. The arrangement shown is that maintained in the major market.

[8] Comoros has the same arrangement with the French Treasury as the CFA franc zone countries.

[9] There is no evidence of direct intervention by the authorities in the foreign exchange market.

[10] This classification is based on the exchange rate performance up to end-April 2007. The authorities have indicated that their current policy is to pursue a managed float.

[11] WAEMU = West African Economic and Monetary Union; CAEMC = Central African Economic and Monetary Community.

[12] The bands for these countries are as follows: Cyprus ±15%, Denmark ±2.25%, Hungary ±15%, Slovak Republic ±15%, and Tonga ±6%.

[13] The current monetary framework is anchored by core inflation objectives and the National Bank of Serbia is still in the process of transition towards full-fledged inflation targeting.

[14] Insufficient information on the country is available to confirm the classification; the classification of the last official consultation is used.

[15] San Marino has a monetary agreement with Italy, on behalf of the European Community, which allows for the use of the euro as official currency, the limited issuance of coins, and the access of its financial institutions to the euro area payment system.

the central banks can borrow from a credit fund to which member countries contribute gold and foreign reserves.

Since the EMS members were less than fully committed to coordinating their economic policies, the EMS went through a series of realignments. The Italian lira, for instance, was devalued by 6 percent in July 1985 and again by 3.7 percent in January 1990. In September 1992, Italy and the U.K. pulled out of the ERM as high German interest rates were inducing massive capital flows into Germany. Following German reunification in October 1990, the German government experienced substantial budget deficits, which were not accommodated by the monetary policy. Germany would not lower its interest rates for fear of inflation, and the U.K. and Italy were not willing to raise their interest rates (which was necessary to maintain their exchange rates) for fear of higher unemployment. Italy, however, rejoined the ERM in December 1996 in an effort to participate in the European monetary union. However, the U.K. still remains outside the European monetary union.

Despite the recurrent turbulence in the EMS, European Union members met at Maastricht (Netherlands) in December 1991 and signed the **Maastricht Treaty**. According to the treaty, the EMS will irrevocably fix exchange rates among the member currencies by January 1, 1999, and subsequently introduce a common European currency, replacing individual national currencies. The European Central Bank, to be located in Frankfurt, Germany, will be solely responsible for the issuance of common currency and conducting monetary policy in the euro zone. National central banks of individual countries then will function pretty much like regional member banks of the U.S. Federal Reserve System. Exhibit 2.5 provides a chronology of the European Union.

To pave the way for the European Monetary Union (EMU), the member countries of the European Monetary System agreed to closely coordinate their fiscal, monetary, and exchange rate policies and achieve a *convergence* of their economies. Specifically, each member country shall strive to: (1) keep the ratio of government budget deficits to gross domestic product (GDP) below 3 percent, (2) keep gross public debts below 60 percent of GDP, (3) achieve a high degree of price stability, and (4) maintain its currency within the prescribed exchange rate ranges of the ERM. Currently, "convergence" is the buzz word in such countries as the Czech Republic, Hungary, and Poland that would like to join the EMU in the near future.

The Euro and the European Monetary Union

On January 1, 1999, an epochal event took place in the arena of international finance: Eleven of 15 EU countries adopted a common currency called the euro, voluntarily giving up their monetary sovereignty. The original euro-11 includes Austria, Belgium, Finland, France, Germany, Ireland, Italy, Luxembourg, the Netherlands, Portugal, and Spain. Four member countries of the European Union—Denmark, Greece, Sweden, and the United Kingdom—did not join the first wave. Greece, however, joined the euro club in 2001 when it could satisfy the convergence criteria. Subsequently, Slovenia adopted the euro in 2007, and Cyprus and Malta did so in 2008.

The advent of a European single currency, which may potentially rival the U.S. dollar as a global currency, has profound implications for various aspects of international finance. In this section, we are going to (1) describe briefly the historical background for the euro and its implementation process, (2) discuss the potential benefits and costs of the euro from the perspective of the member countries, and (3) investigate the broad impacts of the euro on international finance in general.

A Brief History of the Euro

Considering that no European currency has been in circulation since the fall of the Roman Empire, the advent of the euro in January 1999 indeed qualifies as an epochal event. The Roman emperor Gaius Diocletianus, A.D. 286–301, reformed the coinage

EXHIBIT 2.5		
Chronology of the European Union	1951	The treaty establishing the European Coal and Steel Community (ECSC), which was inspired by French Foreign Minister Robert Schuman, was signed in Paris by six countries: France, Germany, Italy, Netherlands, Belgium, and Luxembourg.
	1957	The treaty establishing the European Economic Community (EEC) was signed in Rome.
	1968	The Custom Union became fully operational; trade restrictions among the EEC member countries were abolished and a common external tariff system was established.
	1973	The U.K., Ireland, and Denmark became EEC members.
	1978	The EEC became the European Community (EC).
	1979	The European Monetary System (EMS) was established for the purpose of promoting exchange rate stability among the EC member countries.
	1980	Greece became an EC member.
	1986	Portugal and Spain became EC members.
	1987	The Single European Act was adopted to provide a framework within which the common internal market can be achieved by the end of 1992.
	1991	The Maastricht Treaty was signed and subsequently ratified by 12 member states. The treaty establishes a timetable for fulfilling the European Monetary Union (EMU). The treaty also commits the EC to political union.
	1994	The European Community was renamed the European Union (EU).
	1995	Austria, Finland, and Sweden became EU members.
	1999	A common European currency, the euro, was adopted by 11 EU member countries.
	2001	Greece adopted the euro on January 1.
	2002	Euro notes and coins were introduced; national currencies were withdrawn from circulation.
	2004	EU expanded by admitting 10 new member countries: Cyprus, Czech Republic, Estonia, Hungary, Latvia, Lithuania, Malta, Poland, Slovak Republic, and Slovenia.
	2007	Bulgaria and Romania were admitted to the EU. Slovenia adopted the euro.
	2008	Cyprus and Malta adopted the euro.

and established a single currency throughout the realm. The advent of the euro also marks the first time that sovereign countries voluntarily have given up their monetary independence to foster economic integration. The euro thus represents a historically unprecedented experiment, the outcome of which will have far-reaching implications. If the experiment succeeds, for example, both the euro and the dollar will dominate the world of international finance. In addition, a successful euro may give a powerful impetus to the political unionization of Europe.

The euro should be viewed as a product of historical evolution toward an ever deepening integration of Europe, which began in earnest with the formation of the European Economic Community in 1958. As discussed previously, the European Monetary System (EMS) was created in 1979 to establish a European zone of monetary stability; members were required to restrict fluctuations of their currencies. In 1991, the Maastricht European Council reached agreement on a draft Treaty on the European Union, which called for the introduction of a single European currency by 1999. With the launching of the euro on January 1, 1999, the **European Monetary Union (EMU)** was created. The EMU is a logical extension of the EMS, and the European Currency Unit (ECU) was the precursor of the euro. Indeed, ECU contracts were required by EU law to be converted to euro contracts on a one-to-one basis.

As the euro was introduced, each national currency of the euro-11 countries was *irrevocably* fixed to the euro at a conversion rate as of January 1, 1999. The conversion rates are provided in Exhibit 2.6. On January 1, 2002, euro notes and coins were introduced to circulation while national bills and coins were being gradually withdrawn. Once the changeover was completed by July 1, 2002, the legal-tender status of national currencies was canceled, leaving the euro as the sole legal tender in the euro zone countries.

Monetary policy for the euro-12 countries is now conducted by the **European Central Bank (ECB)** headquartered in Frankfurt, Germany, whose primary objective is to maintain price stability. The independence of the ECB is legally guaranteed so that in conducting its monetary policy, it will not be unduly subjected to political pressure from any member countries or institutions. By and large, the ECB is modeled after the German Bundesbank, which was highly successful in achieving price stability in Germany. Willem (Wim) Duisenberg, the first president of the ECB, who previously served as the president of the Dutch National Bank, defined "price stability" as an annual inflation rate of "less than but close to 2 percent."

The national central banks of the euro zone countries will not disappear. Together with the European Central Bank, they form the **European System of Central Banks (ESCB)**, which is in a way similar to the Federal Reserve System of the United States. The tasks of the ESCB are threefold: (1) to define and implement the common monetary policy of the Union; (2) to conduct foreign exchange operations; and (3) to hold and manage the official foreign reserves of the euro member states. In addition, governors of national central banks will sit on the Governing Council of the ECB. Although national central banks will have to follow the policies of the ECB, they will continue to perform important functions in their jurisdiction such as distributing credit, collecting resources, and managing payment systems.

Before we proceed, let us briefly examine the behavior of exchange rate between the dollar and euro. Panel A of Exhibit 2.7 plots the daily dollar–euro exchange rate since the inception of the euro, whereas Panel B plots the rate of change of the exchange rate. As can be seen from Panel A, since its introduction at $1.18 per euro in January 1999, the euro has been steadily depreciating against the dollar, reaching a low point of $0.83 per euro in October 2000. The depreciation of the euro during this period reflects a robust performance of the U.S. economy and massive European investments in the United States. From the start of 2002, however, the euro began to appreciate against the dollar, reaching a rough parity by July 2002. This, in turn, reflects a slowdown of the U.S. economy and lessening European investments in the United States. The euro continued to strengthen against the dollar, reaching $1.49 per euro near the end of 2007 before it started to ease a bit. Panel B confirms that the dollar–euro exchange rate is highly volatile.

www.ecb.int/

Website of the European Central Bank offers a comprehensive coverage of the euro and links to EU central banks.

What Are the Benefits of Monetary Union?

The euro-15 countries obviously decided to form a monetary union with a common currency because they believed the benefits from such a union would outweigh the associated costs—in contrast to those eligible countries that chose not to adopt the single currency. It is thus important to understand the potential benefits and costs of monetary union.

What are the main benefits from adopting a common currency? The most direct and immediate benefits are reduced transaction costs and the elimination of exchange rate uncertainty. There was a popular saying in Europe that if one travels through all EU countries, changing money in each country but not actually spending it, one returns home with only half the original amount. Once countries use the same currency, transactions costs will be reduced substantially. These savings will accrue to practically all economic agents, benefiting individuals, companies, and governments. Although it is difficult to estimate accurately the magnitude of foreign exchange transaction costs, a consensus estimation is around 0.4 percent of Europe's GDP.

EXHIBIT 2.6

Euro Conversion Rates

1 Euro Is Equal to	
Austrian schilling	13.7603
Belgian franc	40.3399
Dutch guilder	2.20371
Finnish markka	5.94573
French franc	6.55957
German mark	1.95583
Irish punt	0.78756
Italian lira	1936.27
Luxembourg franc	40.3399
Portuguese escudo	200.482
Spanish peseta	166.386
U.S. dollar*	1.4635
Japanese yen*	156.39
British pound*	0.7455

*Represents the market exchange rates of February 12, 2008.
Source: *The Wall Street Journal.*

Economic agents should also benefit from the elimination of exchange rate uncertainty. Companies will not suffer currency loss anymore from intra–euro zone transactions. Companies that used to hedge exchange risk will save hedging costs. As price comparison becomes easier because of the common currency, consumers can benefit from comparison shopping. Increased price transparency will promote Europe-wide competition, exerting a downward pressure on prices. Reduced transaction costs and the elimination of currency risk together will have the net effect of promoting cross-border investment and trade within the euro zone. By furthering economic integration of Europe, the single currency will promote corporate restructuring via mergers and acquisitions, encourage optimal business location decisions, and ultimately strengthen the international competitive position of European companies. Thus, the enhanced efficiency and competitiveness of the European economy can be regarded as the third major benefit of the monetary union.

The advent of the common European currency also helps create conditions conducive to the development of continental capital markets with depth and liquidity comparable to those of the United States. In the past, national currencies and a localized legal/regulatory framework resulted in largely illiquid, fragmented capital markets in Europe, which prevented European companies from raising capital on competitive terms. The common currency and the integration of European financial markets pave the way for a European capital market in which both European and non-European companies can raise money at favorable rates. A study by Bris, Koskinen, and Nilsson (2004) indeed documents that the adoption of the euro as the common European currency has lowered firms' cost of capital in the euro zone and enhanced the firm value by about 17 percent on average. The increases in firm valuation are larger for firms that were exposed to intra-European currency risks, that is, those firms that were expected to benefit more from the common currency.

Last but not least, sharing a common currency should promote political cooperation and peace in Europe. The founding fathers of the European Union, including Jean Monnet, Paul-Henri Spaak, Robert Schuman, and their successors, took a series of economic measures designed to link European countries together. They envisioned a new Europe in which economic interdependence and cooperation among regions and countries replace nationalistic rivalries which so often led to calamitous wars in the past. In this context Helmut Kohl, a former German chancellor, said that the European Monetary Union was a "matter of war and peace." If the euro proves to be successful,

EXHIBIT 2.7   The Daily Dollar–Euro Exchange Rate since the Euro's Inception

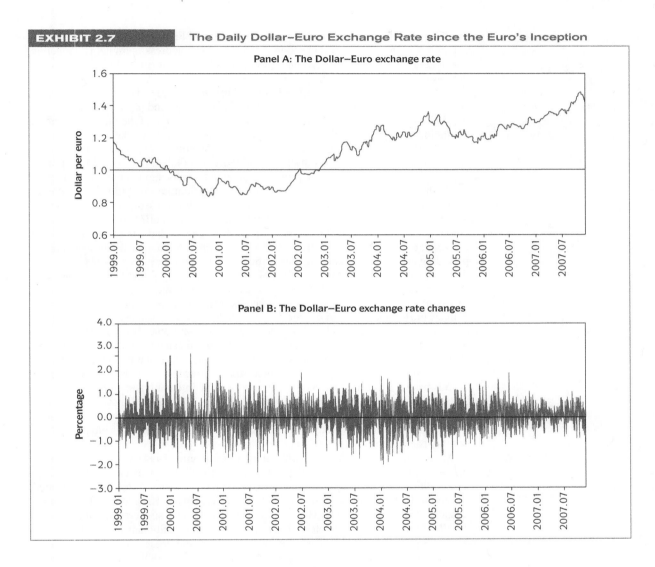

it will advance the political integration of Europe in a major way, eventually making a "United States of Europe" feasible.

Costs of Monetary Union

The main cost of monetary union is the loss of national monetary and exchange rate policy independence. Suppose Finland, a country heavily dependent on the paper and pulp industries, faces a sudden drop in world paper and pulp prices. This price drop could severely hurt the Finnish economy, causing unemployment and income decline while scarcely affecting other euro zone countries. Finland thus faces an "asymmetric shock." Generally speaking, a country would be more prone to asymmetric shocks the less diversified and more trade-dependent its economy is.

If Finland maintained monetary independence, the country could consider lowering domestic interest rates to stimulate the weak economy as well as letting its currency depreciate to boost foreigners' demand for Finnish products. But because Finland has joined the EMU, the country no longer has these policy options at its disposal. Further, with the rest of the euro zone unaffected by Finland's particular problem, the ECB is not likely to tune its monetary policy to address a local Finnish shock. In other words, a common monetary policy dictated in Frankfurt cannot address asymmetric economic shocks that affect only a particular country or subregion; it can only deal with euro zone–wide shocks.

If, however, wage and price levels in Finland are flexible, then the country may still be able to deal with an asymmetric shock; lower wage and price levels in Finland would have economic effects similar to those of a depreciation of the Finnish currency. Furthermore, if capital flows freely across the euro zone and workers are willing to relocate to where jobs are, then again much of the asymmetric shock can be absorbed without monetary adjustments. If these conditions are not met, however, the asymmetric shock can cause a severe and prolonged economic dislocation in the affected country. In this case, monetary union will become a costly venture. According to the theory of **optimum currency areas**, originally conceived by Professor Robert Mundell of Columbia University in 1961, the relevant criterion for identifying and designing a common currency zone is the degree of factor (i.e., capital and labor) mobility within the zone; a high degree of factor mobility would provide an adjustment mechanism, providing an alternative to country-specific monetary/currency adjustments.

Considering the high degree of capital and labor mobility in the United States, one might argue that the United States approximates an optimum currency area; it would be suboptimal for each of the 50 states to issue its own currency. In contrast, unemployed workers in Helsinki, for example, are not very likely to move to Milan or Stuttgart for job opportunities because of cultural, religious, linguistic, and other barriers. The stability pact of EMU, designed to discourage irresponsible fiscal behavior in the post-EMU era, also constrains the Finnish government to restrict its budget deficit to 3 percent of GDP at most. At the same time, Finland cannot expect to receive a major transfer payment from Brussels, because of a rather low degree of fiscal integration among EU countries. These considerations taken together suggest that the European Monetary Union will involve significant economic costs. Due to the sluggish economic conditions, France and Germany often let the budget deficit exceed the 3 percent limit. This violation of the stability pact compromises the fiscal discipline necessary for supporting the euro.

An empirical study by von Hagen and Neumann (1994) identified Austria, Belgium, France, Luxembourg, the Netherlands, and Germany as nations that satisfy the conditions for an optimum currency area. However, Denmark, Italy, and the United Kingdom do not. It is noted that Denmark and the United Kingdom actually chose to stay out of the EMU. Von Hagen and Neumann's study suggests that Italy joined the EMU prematurely. It is interesting to note that some politicians in Italy blame the country's economic woe on the adoption of the euro and argue for the restoration of Italian lira. The International Finance in Practice box, "Mundell Wins Nobel Prize in Economics," explains Professor Mundell's view on the monetary union.

Prospects of the Euro: Some Critical Questions

Will the euro survive and succeed in the long run? The first real test of the euro will come when the euro zone experiences major asymmetric shocks. A successful response to these shocks will require wage, price, and fiscal flexibility. A cautionary note is in order: Asymmetric shocks can occur even within a country. In the United States, for example, when oil prices jumped in the 1970s, oil-consuming regions such as New England suffered a severe recession, whereas Texas, a major oil-producing state, experienced a major boom. Likewise, in Italy, the highly industrialized Genoa–Milan region and the southern Mezzogiorno, an underdeveloped region, can be in very different phases of the business cycle. But these countries have managed their economies with a common national monetary policy. Although asymmetric shocks are no doubt more serious internationally, one should be careful not to exaggerate their significance as an impediment to monetary union. In addition, since the advent of the EMS in 1979, the EMU member countries have restricted their monetary policies in order to maintain exchange rate stability in Europe. Considering that intra–euro zone trade accounts for

www.columbia.edu/~ram15

This homepage of Professor Robert Mundell provides a synopsis of his academic works, Nobel lecture, etc.

EXHIBIT 2.8

Macroeconomic Data
for Major Economies[a]

Economy	Population (Million)	GDP ($ Trillion)	Annual Inflation	World Trade Share	International Bonds Outstanding ($ Billion)
United States	302.8	13.2	3.1%	12.2%	6,400.6
Euro zone	313.4	10.5	2.2%	13.9%	8,310.1
Japan	128.0	4.3	0.0%	5.1%	487.3
United Kingdom	60.5	2.3	3.0%	4.0%	1,450.0

[a]The inflation rate is the annual average from 2004 to 2006. The International bonds outstanding refer to internationalbonds and notes outstanding by December 2006 by currency of issue. The remaining data are 2006 figures.

Source: Datastream, *International Financial Statistics*; and *BIS Quarterly Review*, December 2007.

about 60 percent of foreign trade of the euro zone countries, benefits from the EMU are likely to exceed substantially the associated costs. Furthermore, leaders in political and business circles in Europe have invested substantial political capital in the success of the euro. It seems safe to predict that the euro will survive.

Will the euro become a global currency rivaling the U.S. dollar? The U.S. dollar has been the dominant global currency since the end of the First World War, replacing the British pound as the currency of choice in international commercial and financial transactions. Even after the dollar got off the gold standard in 1971, it retained its dominant position in the world economy. This dominance was possible because the dollar was backed by the sheer size of the U.S. economy and the relatively sound monetary policy of the Federal Reserve. Now, as can be seen from Exhibit 2.8, the euro zone is remarkably comparable to the United States in terms of population size, GDP, and international trade share. Exhibit 2.8 also shows that the euro is as important a denomination currency as the dollar in international bond markets. In contrast, the Japanese yen plays an insignificant role in international bond markets. As previously discussed, there is little doubt that the ECB will pursue a sound monetary policy. Reflecting both the size of the euro zone economy and the mandate of the ECB, the euro is emerging as the second global currency, challenging the dollar's sole dominance. A significant depreciation of the U.S. dollar in recent years seems to be precipitating the emergence of the euro as another global currency. The Japanese yen is likely to be a junior partner in the dollar–euro condominium. However, the emergence of the euro as another global currency may prompt Japan and other Asian countries to explore cooperative monetary arrangements for the region.

The Mexican Peso Crisis

On December 20, 1994, the Mexican government under new president Ernesto Zedillo announced its decision to devalue the peso against the dollar by 14 percent. This decision, however, touched off a stampede to sell pesos as well as Mexican stocks and bonds. As Exhibit 2.9 shows, by early January 1995 the peso fell against the U.S. dollar by as much as 40 percent, forcing the Mexican government to float the peso. As concerned international investors reduced their holdings of emerging market securities, the peso crisis rapidly spilled over to other Latin American and Asian financial markets.

Faced with an impending default by the Mexican government and the possibility of a global financial meltdown, the Clinton administration, together with the International Monetary Fund (IMF) and the Bank for International Settlement (BIS), put together a $53 billion package to bail out Mexico.[8] As the bailout plan was put together and

---

[8]The United States contributed $20 billion out of its Exchange Stabilization Fund, whereas IMF and BIS contributed, respectively, $17.8 billion and $10 billion. Canada, Latin American countries, and commercial banks collectively contributed $5 billion.

Mundell Wins Nobel Prize in Economics

Robert A. Mundell, one of the intellectual fathers of both the new European common currency and Reagan-era supply-side economics, won the Nobel Memorial Prize in Economic Science.

Mr. Mundell conducted innovative research into common currencies when the idea of the euro, Europe's new currency, was still a fantasy. The 66-year-old Columbia University professor, a native of Canada, also examined the implications of cross-border capital flows and flexible foreign-exchange rates when capital flows were still restricted and currencies still fixed to each other.

"Mundell chose his problems with uncommon—almost prophetic—accuracy in terms of predicting the future development of international monetary arrangements and capital markets," the selection committee said in announcing the prize.

An eccentric, white-haired figure who once bought an abandoned Italian castle as a hedge against inflation, Mr. Mundell later became a hero of the economic Right with his dogged defense of the gold standard and early advocacy of the controversial tax-cutting, supply-side economics that became the hallmark of the Reagan administration.

While the Nobel committee sidestepped his political impact in awarding Mr. Mundell the $975,000 prize for his work in the 1960s, his conservative fans celebrated the award as an endorsement of supply-side thinking.

"I know it will take a little longer, but history eventually will note that it was Mundell who made it possible for Ronald Reagan to be elected president," by providing the intellectual backing for the Reagan tax cuts, wrote conservative economist Jude Wanniski on his website.

Mr. Mundell's advocacy of supply-side economics sprang from his work in the 1960s examining what fiscal and monetary policies are appropriate if exchange

Mundell's View	
Great currencies and great powers according to Robert Mundell:	
Country	**Period**
Greece	7th–3rd C. B.C.
Persia	6th–4th C. B.C.
Macedonia	4th–2nd C. B.C.
Rome	2nd C. B.C.–4th C.
Byzantium	5th–13th C.
Franks	8th–11th C.
Italian city states	13th–6th C.
France	13th–18th C.
Holland	17th–18th C.
Germany (thaler)	14th–19th C.
France (franc)	1803–1870
Britain (pound)	1820–1914
U.S. (dollar)	1915–present
E.U. (euro)	1999

Source: The Euro and the Stability of the International Monetary System, Robert Mundell, Columbia University.

rates are either fixed—as they were prior to the collapse of the gold-based Bretton Woods system in the early 1970s—or floating, as they are in the U.S. and many other countries today.

One major finding has since become conventional wisdom: When money can move freely across borders, policy makers must choose between exchange-rate stability and an independent monetary policy. They can't have both.

Mr. Mundell's work has long had an impact on policy makers. In 1962, he wrote a paper addressing the

announced on January 31, the world's, as well as Mexico's, financial markets began to stabilize.

The Mexican peso crisis is significant in that it is perhaps the first serious international financial crisis touched off by cross-border flight of portfolio capital. International mutual funds are known to have invested more than $45 billion in Mexican securities during a three-year period prior to the peso crisis. As the peso fell, fund managers quickly liquidated their holdings of Mexican securities as well as other emerging market securities. This had a highly destabilizing, contagious effect on the world financial system. The same point is discussed in the International Finance in Practice box, "The New World Order of Finance" on page 48.

As the world's financial markets are becoming more integrated, this type of contagious financial crisis is likely to occur more often. Two lessons emerge from the peso crisis. First, it is essential to have a multinational safety net in place to

Kennedy administration's predicament of how to spur the economy while facing a balance-of-payments deficit. "The only correct way to do it was to have a tax cut and then protect the balance of payments by tight money," he recalled in a 1996 interview. The Kennedy administration eventually came around to the same way of thinking.

Mr. Mundell traces the supply-side movement to a 1971 meeting of distinguished economists, including Paul Volcker and Paul Samuelson, at the Treasury Department. At the time, most economists were stumped by the onset of stagflation—a combination of inflationary pressures, a troubled dollar, a worsening balance of payments and persistent unemployment. They thought any tightening of monetary or fiscal policy would bolster the dollar and improve the balance of payments, but worsen unemployment. An easing of monetary or fiscal policy might generate jobs, but weaken the dollar, lift prices and expand the balance-of-payments deficit.

Mr. Mundell suggested a heretical solution: Raise interest rates to protect the dollar, but cut taxes to spur the economy. Most others in the room were aghast at the idea, fearing tax cuts would lead to a swelling budget deficit—something many nonsupply-siders believe was exactly what happened during the Reagan years.

"I knew I was in the minority," he said in an 1988 interview. "But I thought my vote should count much more than the others because I understood the subject."

At the University of Chicago early in his career, Mr. Mundell befriended a student named Arthur Laffer, and together they were at the core of the supply-side movement. Even today, Mr. Mundell predicts similar policies will be necessary to keep the U.S. economic expansion going. "Monetary policy isn't going to be enough to stay up there and avoid a recession," he said in an interview yesterday. "We'll have to have tax reduction, too."

While in Chicago, he found himself constantly at odds with Milton Friedman, who advocated monetary rules and floating exchange rates. Mr. Mundell joined Columbia in 1974, two years before Mr. Friedman won the economics Nobel.

Ever the maverick, Mr. Mundell remains a fan of the gold standard and fixed exchange rates at a time when they're out of favor with most other economists. "You have fixed rates between New York and California, and it works perfectly," he said.

The Nobel committee also praised Mr. Mundell's research into common currency zones, which laid the intellectual foundation for the 11-country euro. In 1961, when European countries still clung to their national currencies, he described the circumstances in which nations could share a common currency.

"At the time, it just seemed like such a wacko thing to work on, and that's why it's so visionary," said Kenneth Rogoff, a Harvard economist.

In particular, Mr. Mundell argued that in any successful currency zone, workers must be able to move freely from areas that are slowing to areas that are booming. Some critics suggest the euro nations don't fit his description.

But Mr. Mundell believes the new currency will eventually challenge the dollar for global dominance. "The benefits will derive from transparency of pricing, stability of expectations and lower transactions costs, as well as a common monetary policy run by the best minds that Europe can muster," Mr. Mundell wrote last year. He began working on the euro project as a consultant to European monetary authorities in 1969.

Outside academia, Mr. Mundell has led a colorful life. Worried about the onset of inflation in the late 1960s, he bought and renovated a 16th century Italian castle originally built for Pandolfo Petrucci, the "Strong Man of Siena." Mr. Mundell has four children, who range in age from one to 40.

safeguard the world financial system from the peso-type crisis. No single country or institution can handle a potentially global crisis alone. In addition, in the face of rapidly changing market conditions, usually slow and parochial political processes cannot cope with rapidly changing market conditions. In fact, the Clinton administration faced stiff opposition in Congress and from foreign allies when it was working out a bailout package for Mexico. As a result, early containment of the crisis was not possible. Fortunately, the G-7 countries endorsed a $50 billion bailout fund for countries in financial distress, which would be administered by the IMF, and a series of increased disclosure requirements to be followed by all countries. The reluctance of the outgoing Salinas administration to disclose the true state of the Mexican economy, that is, the rapid depletion of foreign exchange reserves and serious trade deficits, contributed to the sudden collapse of the peso. Transparency always helps prevent financial crises.

INTERNATIONAL FINANCE IN PRACTICE

The New World Order of Finance

Global financial panics erupt every decade or so. But even by historical standards, Mexico's currency collapse ranks among the scariest. With the crisis stretching into its seventh week, investors were stampeding. Worse yet, the panic was spreading from Buenos Aires to Budapest. Even the dollar was taking an unexpected shellacking. Some were bracing for another 1987 crash—not just in Mexico City, but in New York, London, and Tokyo.

It took forceful action to stop the runaway markets before they dragged the world economy down with them: $49.8 billion in loans and guarantees for Mexico from the U.S. and its allies. Some bankers say the total could reach $53 billion or more. Certainly, this will go down as the largest socialization of market risk in international history.

Ambitious Labor

With the U.S. spreading the gospel of democracy and free-market economics throughout the developing world, Clinton and his cohorts had little choice but to assemble the megaplan. As the club of emerging-market nations expands, the rich nations' obligation to provide a safety net for poorer trading partners is growing exponentially. America and its allies must mount a collective drive to ensure global monetary and economic stability—much like their efforts to maintain geopolitical order in the post-cold-war era.

Such ambitious labor is needed because the nature of financial markets has changed since Latin America's last financial crisis in 1982. Back then, it was gunslinger bankers who lent to Latin America. Because banks could lend for the long haul and absorb losses, they were a valuable shock absorber for the financial system. When enough Latin loans eventually went bad, it still took years to craft and conclude their restructuring.

Since then, bankers have wised up. Now, others with a shorter time horizon make the emerging-market deals. This time, it was mutual-, hedge-, and pension-fund gunslingers who provided the capital. Mexico attracted $45 billion in mutual-fund cash in the past three years. And when the peso dived, fund managers bolted. In this global market, all it takes is a phone call to Fidelity to send money hurtling toward Monterey—or zooming back. And world leaders should be able to act with similar speed.

Clinton's $40 billion in loan guarantees for Mexico got nowhere because Congress objected to bailing out Wall Street. Legislators also did not like the U.S. shouldering most of the cost. They were right. Emerging markets will stay volatile, and countries and investors shouldn't expect a handout every time an economy hits a rough patch. And when a rescue is necessary, it should be global.

Bridge the Gap

Europe and Japan, after all, will benefit from a healthy Mexican economy and thus should bear the burden of supporting it in times of crisis. Likewise, Washington should be obliged to lend a hand to European or Asian allies if Poland or Indonesia come unglued. One way to keep the next crisis at bay: bridge the gap between short-term money and long-term investment needs.

In addition, emerging economies need to take steps to immunize themselves from the vagaries of a fund-dominated world. It would help a lot if more of them developed mandatory pension schemes to build up domestic savings. Along with that should come privatization. With capital so flighty, it may take hard decisions to make money stay put. But if the first world wants to encourage capitalism, it will have to underwrite it—even if the cost is huge.

Source: Reprinted from February 13, 1995 issue of *BusinessWeek* by special permission, © 1995 by The McGraw-Hill Companies, Inc.

Second, Mexico excessively depended on foreign portfolio capital to finance its economic development. In hindsight, the country should have saved more domestically and depended more on long-term rather than short-term foreign capital investments. As Professor Robert MacKinnon of Stanford University pointed out, a flood of foreign money had two undesirable effects. It led to an easy credit policy on domestic borrowings, which caused Mexicans to consume more and save less.[9] Foreign capital influx also caused a higher domestic inflation and an overvalued peso, which hurt Mexico's trade balances.

The Asian Currency Crisis

On July 2, 1997, the Thai baht, which had been largely fixed to the U.S. dollar, was suddenly devalued. What at first appeared to be a local financial crisis in Thailand quickly escalated into a global financial crisis, first spreading to other Asian

---

[9]See "Flood of Dollars, Sunken Pesos," *New York Times*, January 20, 1995. p. A2g.

CHAPTER 2 | INTERNATIONAL MONETARY SYSTEM   **49**

EXHIBIT 2.9

U.S. Dollar versus Mexican Peso Exchange Rate (November 1, 1994– January 31, 1995)

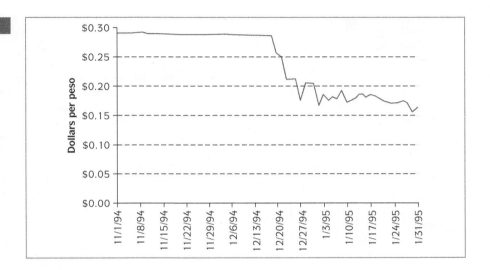

countries—Indonesia, Korea, Malaysia, and the Philippines—then far afield to Russia and Latin America, especially Brazil. As can be seen from Exhibit 2.10, at the height of the crisis the Korean won fell by about 50 percent in its dollar value from its precrisis level, whereas the Indonesian rupiah fell an incredible 80 percent.

The 1997 Asian crisis was the third major currency crisis of the 1990s, preceded by the crises of the European Monetary System (EMS) of 1992 and the Mexican peso in 1994–95. The Asian crisis, however, turned out to be far more serious than its two predecessors in terms of the extent of contagion and the severity of resultant economic and social costs. Following the massive depreciations of local currencies, financial institutions and corporations with foreign-currency debts in the afflicted countries were driven to extreme financial distress and many were forced to default. What's worse, the currency crisis led to an unprecedentedly deep, widespread, and long-lasting recession in East Asia, a region that, for the last few decades, has enjoyed the most rapidly growing economy in the world. At the same time, many lenders and investors from the developed countries also suffered large capital losses from their investments in emerging-market securities. For example, Long Term Capital Management (LTCM), one of the largest and, until then, profitable hedge funds, experienced a near bankruptcy due to its exposure to Russian bonds. In mid-August 1998, the Russian ruble fell sharply from 6.3 rubles per dollar to about 20 rubbles per dollar. The prices of Russian stocks and bonds also fell sharply. The Federal Reserve System, which feared a domino-like systemic financial failure in the United States, orchestrated a $3.5 billion bailout of LTCM in September 1998.

Given the global effects of the Asian currency crisis and the challenges it poses for the world financial system, it would be useful to understand its origins and causes and discuss how similar crises might be prevented in the future.

Origins of the Asian Currency Crisis

Several factors are responsible for the onset of the Asian currency crisis: a weak domestic financial system, free international capital flows, the contagion effects of changing market sentiment, and inconsistent economic policies. In recent years, both developing and developed countries were encouraged to liberalize their financial markets and allow free flows of capital across countries. As capital markets were liberalized, both firms and financial institutions in the Asian developing countries eagerly borrowed foreign currencies from U.S., Japanese, and European investors, who were attracted to these fast-growing emerging markets for extra returns for their portfolios. In 1996 alone, for example, five Asian countries—Indonesia, Korea, Malaysia, the Philippines,

EXHIBIT 2.10

Asian Currency Crisis

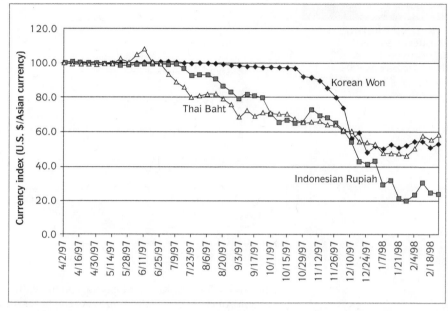

Exchange rates are indexed (U.S. $/Asian currency on 4/2/97 100). Exchange rates on 4/2/97: 0.00112 U.S. $/Korean won, 0.03856 U.S. $/Thai baht, and 0.00041 U.S. $/Indonesian rupiah.

and Thailand—experienced a new inflow of private capital worth $93 billion. In contrast, there was a net outflow of $12 billion from the five countries in 1997.

Large inflows of private capital resulted in a credit boom in the Asian countries in the early and mid-1990s. The credit boom was often directed to speculations in real estate and stock markets as well as to investments in marginal industrial projects. Fixed or stable exchange rates also encouraged unhedged financial transactions and excessive risk-taking by both lenders and borrowers, who were not much concerned with exchange risk. As asset prices declined (as happened in Thailand prior to the currency crisis) in part due to the government's effort to control the overheated economy, the quality of banks' loan portfolios also declined as the same assets were held as collateral for the loans. Clearly, banks and other financial institutions in the afflicted countries practiced poor risk management and were poorly supervised. In addition, their lending decisions were often influenced by political considerations, likely leading to suboptimal allocation of resources. However, the so-called crony capitalism was not a new condition, and the East Asian economies achieved an economic miracle under the same system.

Meanwhile, the booming economy with a fixed or stable nominal exchange rate inevitably brought about an appreciation of the real exchange rate. This, in turn, resulted in a marked slowdown in export growth in such Asian countries as Thailand and Korea. In addition, a long-lasting recession in Japan and the yen's depreciation against the dollar hurt Japan's neighbors, further worsening the trade balances of the Asian developing countries. If the Asian currencies had been allowed to depreciate in real terms, which was not possible because of the fixed nominal exchange rates, such catastrophic, sudden changes of the exchange rates as observed in 1997 might have been avoided.

In Thailand, as the run on the baht started, the Thai central bank initially injected liquidity to the domestic financial system and tried to defend the exchange rate by drawing on its foreign exchange reserves. With its foreign reserves declining rapidly,

EXHIBIT 2.11

Financial Vulnerability Indicators

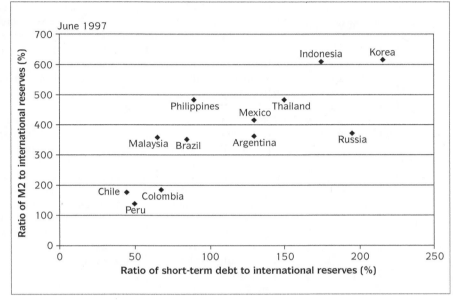

Source: The World Bank, International Monetary Fund.

the central bank eventually decided to devalue the baht. The sudden collapse of the baht touched off a panicky flight of capital from other Asian countries with a high degree of financial vulnerability. It is interesting to note from Exhibit 2.11 that the three Asian countries hardest hit by the crisis are among the most financially vulnerable as measured by (1) the ratio of short-term foreign debts to international reserve and (2) the ratio of broad money, M2 (which represents the banking sector's liabilities) to international reserve. Contagion of the currency crisis was caused at least in part by the panicky, indiscriminate flight of capital from the Asian countries for fear of a spreading crisis. Fear thus became self-fulfilling. As lenders withdrew their capital and refused to renew short-term loans, the former credit boom turned into a credit crunch, hurting creditworthy as well as marginal borrowers.

As the crisis unfolded, the International Monetary Fund (IMF) came to rescue the three hardest-hit Asian countries—Indonesia, Korea, and Thailand—with bailout plans. As a condition for the bailing out, however, the IMF imposed a set of austerity measures, such as raising domestic interest rates and curtailing government expenditures, that were designed to support the exchange rate. Since these austerity measures, contractionary in nature, were implemented when the economies had already been contracting because of a severe credit crunch, the Asian economies consequently suffered a deep, long-lasting recession. According to a World Bank report (1999), one-year declines in industrial production of 20 percent or more in Thailand and Indonesia are comparable to those in the United States and Germany during the Great Depression. One can thus argue that the IMF initially prescribed the wrong medicine for the afflicted Asian economies. The IMF bailout plans were also criticized on another ground: moral hazard. IMF bailouts may breed dependency in developing countries and encourage risk-taking on the part of international lenders. There is a sentiment that taxpayers' money should not be used to bail out "fat-cat" investors. Former U.S. senator Lauch Faircloth was quoted as saying: "Through the IMF we have privatized profits and socialized losses." No bailout, however, can be compared with the proposal to get rid of the only fire department in town so that people will be more careful about fire.

Lessons from the Asian Currency Crisis

www.adb.org/

Provides a broad coverage of Asian financial developments.

Generally speaking, liberalization of financial markets when combined with a weak, underdeveloped domestic financial system tends to create an environment susceptible to currency and financial crises. Interestingly, both Mexico and Korea experienced a major currency crisis within a few years after joining the OECD, which required a significant liberalization of financial markets. It seems safe to recommend that countries first strengthen their domestic financial system and then liberalize their financial markets.

A number of measures can and should be undertaken to strengthen a nation's domestic financial system. Among other things, the government should strengthen its system of financial-sector regulation and supervision. One way of doing so is to sign on to the "Core Principle of Effective Banking Supervision" drafted by the Basle Committee on Banking Supervision and to monitor its compliance with the principle. In addition, banks should be encouraged to base their lending decisions solely on economic merits rather than political considerations. Furthermore, firms, financial institutions, and the government should be required to provide the public with reliable financial data in a timely fashion. A higher level of disclosure of financial information and the resultant transparency about the state of the economy will make it easier for all the concerned parties to monitor the situation better and mitigate the destabilizing cycles of investor euphoria and panic accentuated by the lack of reliable information.

Even if a country decides to liberalize its financial markets by allowing cross-border capital flows, it should encourage foreign direct investments and equity and long-term bond investments; it should not encourage short-term investments that can be reversed overnight, causing financial turmoil. As Chile has successfully implemented, some form of **"Tobin tax"** on the international flow of hot money can be useful. Throwing some sand in the wheels of international finance can have a stabilizing effect on the world's financial markets.

A fixed but adjustable exchange rate is problematic in the face of integrated international financial markets. Such a rate arrangement often invites speculative attack at the time of financial vulnerability. Countries should not try to restore the same fixed exchange rate system unless they are willing to impose capital controls. According to the so-called "trilemma" that economists are fond of talking about, a country can attain only two of the following three conditions: (1) a fixed exchange rate, (2) free international flows of capital, and (3) an independent monetary policy. It is very difficult, if not impossible, to have all three conditions. This difficulty is also known as the **incompatible trinity**. If a country would like to maintain monetary policy independence to pursue its own domestic economic goals and still would like to keep a fixed exchange rate between its currency and other currencies, then the country should restrict free flows of capital. China and India were not noticeably affected by the Asian currency crisis because both countries maintain capital controls, segmenting their capital markets from the rest of the world. Hong Kong was less affected by the crisis for a different reason. Hong Kong has fixed its exchange rate permanently to the U.S. dollar via a currency board and allowed free flows of capital; in consequence, Hong Kong gave up its monetary independence. A currency board is an extreme form of the fixed exchange rate regime under which local currency is "fully" backed by the dollar (or another chosen standard currency). Hong Kong has essentially dollarized its economy.

The Argentine Peso Crisis

The 2002 crisis of the Argentine peso, however, shows that even a currency board arrangement cannot be completely safe from a possible collapse. Exhibit 2.12 shows how the peso–dollar exchange rate, fixed at parity throughout much of the 1990s,

EXHIBIT 2.12

Collapse of the Currency Board Arrangement in Argentina

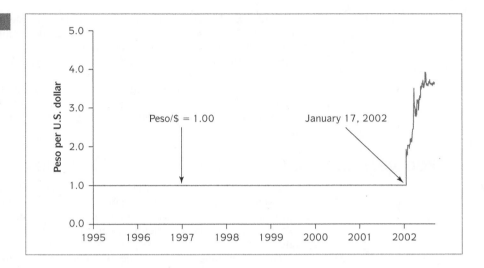

collapsed in January 2002. Short of a complete dollarization (as is the case with Panama, for example), a currency board arrangement can collapse unless the arrangement is backed by the political will and economic discipline to defend it.

When the peso was first linked to the U.S. dollar at parity in February 1991 under the Convertibility Law, initial economic effects were quite positive: Argentina's chronic inflation was curtailed dramatically and foreign investment began to pour in, leading to an economic boom. Over time, however, the peso has appreciated against the majority of currencies as the U.S. dollar became increasingly stronger in the second half of the 1990s. A strong peso hurt exports from Argentina and caused a protracted economic downturn that eventually led to the abandonment of the peso–dollar parity in January 2002. This change, in turn, caused severe economic and political distress in the country. The unemployment rate rose above 20 percent and inflation reached a monthly rate of about 20 percent in April 2002. In contrast, Hong Kong was able to successfully defend its currency board arrangement during the Asian financial crisis, a major stress test for the arrangement.

Although there is no clear consensus on the causes of the Argentine crisis, there are at least three factors that are related to the collapse of the currency board system and ensuing economic crisis: (1) the lack of fiscal discipline, (2) labor market inflexibility, and (3) contagion from the financial crises in Russia and Brazil. Reflecting the traditional sociopolitical divisions in the Argentine society, competing claims on economic resources by different groups were accommodated by increasing public sector indebtedness. Argentina is said to have a "European-style welfare system in a Third World economy." The federal government of Argentina borrowed heavily in dollars throughout the 1990s. As the economy entered a recession in the late 1990s, the government encountered an increasing difficulty in raising debts, eventually defaulting on its internal and external debts. The hard fixed exchange rate that Argentina adopted under the currency board system made it impossible to restore competitiveness by a traditional currency depreciation. Further, a powerful labor union also made it difficult to lower wages and thus cut production costs that could have effectively achieved the same real currency depreciation with the fixed nominal exchange rate. The situation was exacerbated by a slowdown of international capital inflows following the financial crises in Russia and Brazil. Also, a sharp depreciation of the Brazil real in 1999 hampered exports from Argentina.

While the currency crisis is over, the debt problem has not been completely resolved. The government of Argentina ceased all debt payments in December 2001 in the wake of persistent recession and rising social and political unrest. It represents the largest sovereign default in history. Argentina faces a complex task of restructuring over $100 billion borrowed in seven different currencies and governed by the laws of eight legal jurisdictions. In June 2004, the Argentine government made a 'final' offer amounting to a 75 percent reduction in the net present value of the debt. Foreign bondholders have rejected this offer and asked for an improved offer.

Fixed versus Flexible Exchange Rate Regimes

Since some countries, including the United States and possibly Japan, prefer flexible exchange rates, while others, notably the members of the EMU and many developing countries, would like to maintain fixed exchange rates, it is worthwhile to examine some of the arguments advanced in favor of fixed versus flexible exchange rates.

The key arguments for flexible exchange rates rest on (1) easier external adjustments and (2) national policy autonomy. Suppose a country is experiencing a balance-of-payments deficit at the moment. This means that there is an excess supply of the country's currency at the prevailing exchange rate in the foreign exchange market. Under a flexible exchange rate regime, the external value of the country's currency will simply depreciate to the level at which there is no excess supply of the country's currency. At the new exchange rate level, the balance-of-payments disequilibrium will disappear.

As long as the exchange rate is allowed to be determined according to market forces, external balance will be achieved automatically. Consequently, the government does not have to take policy actions to correct the balance-of-payments disequilibrium. With flexible exchange rates, therefore, the government can use its monetary and fiscal policies to pursue whatever economic goals it chooses. Under a fixed rate regime, however, the government may have to take contractionary (expansionary) monetary and fiscal policies to correct the balance-of-payments deficit (surplus) at the existing exchange rate. Since policy tools need to be committed to maintaining the exchange rate, the government cannot use the same policy tools to pursue other economic objectives. As a result, the government loses its policy autonomy under a fixed exchange rate regime.

Using the British pound as the representative foreign exchange, Exhibit 2.13 illustrates the preceding discussion on how the balance-of-payment disequilibrium is corrected under alternative exchange rate regimes. As is the case with most other commodities, the demand for British pounds would be downward sloping, whereas the supply of British pounds would be upward sloping. Suppose that the exchange rate is $1.60/£ at the moment. As can be seen from the exhibit, the demand for British pounds far exceeds the supply (i.e., the supply of U.S. dollars far exceeds the demand) at this exchange rate. The United States experiences trade (or balance of payment) deficits. Under the flexible exchange rate regime, the dollar will simply depreciate to a new level of exchange rate, $1.80/£, at which the excess demand for British pounds (and thus the trade deficit) will disappear. Now, suppose that the exchange rate is "fixed" at $1.60/£, and thus the excess demand for British pounds cannot be eliminated by the exchange rate adjustment. Facing this situation, the U.S. Federal Reserve Bank may initially draw on its foreign exchange reserve holdings to satisfy the excess demand for British pounds. If the excess demand persists, however, the U.S. government may have to resort to contractionary monetary and fiscal policies so that the demand curve can shift to the left (from D to D^* in the exhibit) until the excess demand for British pounds can be eliminated at the fixed exchange rate,

EXHIBIT 2.13

External Adjustment Mechanism: Fixed versus Flexible Exchange Rates

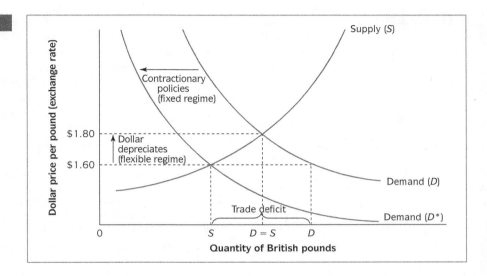

$1.60/£. In other words, it is necessary for the government to take policy actions to maintain the fixed exchange rate.

A possible drawback of the flexible exchange rate regime is that exchange rate uncertainty may hamper international trade and investment. Proponents of the fixed exchange rate regime argue that when future exchange rates are uncertain, businesses tend to shun foreign trade. Since countries cannot fully benefit from international trade under exchange rate uncertainty, resources will be allocated suboptimally on a global basis. Proponents of the fixed exchange rate regime argue that fixed exchange rates eliminate such uncertainty and thus promote international trade. However, to the extent that firms can hedge exchange risk by means of currency forward or options contracts, uncertain exchange rates do not necessarily hamper international trade.

As the above discussion suggests, the choice between the alternative exchange rate regimes is likely to involve a trade-off between national policy independence and international economic integration. If countries would like to pursue their respective domestic economic goals, they are likely to pursue divergent macroeconomic policies, rendering fixed exchange rates infeasible. On the other hand, if countries are committed to promoting international economic integration (as is the case with the core members of the European Union like France and Germany), the benefits of fixed exchange rates are likely to outweigh the associated costs.

A "good" (or ideal) international monetary system should provide (1) liquidity, (2) adjustment, and (3) confidence. In other words, a good IMS should be able to provide the world economy with sufficient monetary reserves to support the growth of international trade and investment. It should also provide an effective mechanism that restores the balance-of-payments equilibrium whenever it is disturbed. Lastly, it should offer a safeguard to prevent crises of confidence in the system that result in panicked flights from one reserve asset to another. Politicians and economists should keep these three criteria in mind when they design and evaluate the international monetary system.

SUMMARY

This chapter provides an overview of the international monetary system, which defines an environment in which multinational corporations and international investors operate.

1. The international monetary system can be defined as the institutional framework within which international payments are made, the movements of capital are accommodated, and exchange rates among currencies are determined.

2. The international monetary system went through five stages of evolution: (a) bimetallism, (b) classical gold standard, (c) interwar period, (d) Bretton Woods system, and (e) flexible exchange rate regime.

3. The classical gold standard spanned 1875 to 1914. Under the gold standard, the exchange rate between two currencies is determined by the gold contents of the currencies. Balance-of-payments disequilibrium is automatically corrected through the price-specie-flow mechanism. The gold standard still has ardent supporters who believe that it provides an effective hedge against price inflation. Under the gold standard, however, the world economy can be subject to deflationary pressure due to the limited supply of monetary gold.

4. To prevent the recurrence of economic nationalism with no clear "rules of the game" witnessed during the interwar period, representatives of 44 nations met at Bretton Woods, New Hampshire, in 1944 and adopted a new international monetary system. Under the Bretton Woods system, each country established a par value in relation to the U.S. dollar, which was fully convertible to gold. Countries used foreign exchanges, especially the U.S. dollar, as well as gold as international means of payments. The Bretton Woods system was designed to maintain stable exchange rates and economize on gold. The Bretton Woods system eventually collapsed in 1973 mainly because of U.S. domestic inflation and the persistent balance-of-payments deficits.

5. The flexible exchange rate regime that replaced the Bretton Woods system was ratified by the Jamaica Agreement. Following a spectacular rise and fall of the U.S. dollar in the 1980s, major industrial countries agreed to cooperate to achieve greater exchange rate stability. The Louvre Accord of 1987 marked the inception of the managed-float system under which the G-7 countries would jointly intervene in the foreign exchange market to correct over- or undervaluation of currencies.

6. In 1979, the EEC countries launched the European Monetary System (EMS) to establish a "zone of monetary stability" in Europe. The two main instruments of the EMS are the European Currency Unit (ECU) and the Exchange Rate Mechanism (ERM). The ECU is a basket currency comprising the currencies of the EMS members and serves as the accounting unit of the EMS. The ERM refers to the procedure by which EMS members collectively manage their exchange rates. The ERM is based on a parity grid that the member countries are required to maintain.

7. On January 1, 1999, eleven European countries including France and Germany adopted a common currency called the euro. Greece adopted the euro in 2001. Subsequently, three other countries—Cyprus, Malta, and Slovenia—adopted the euro. The advent of a single European currency, which may eventually rival the U.S. dollar as a global vehicle currency, will have major implications for the European as well as world economy. Euro zone countries will benefit from reduced transaction costs and the elimination of exchange rate uncertainty. The advent of the euro will also help develop continentwide capital markets where companies can raise capital at favorable rates.

8. Under the European Monetary Union (EMU), the common monetary policy for the euro zone countries is formulated by the European Central Bank (ECB) located in Frankfurt. The ECB is legally mandated to maintain price stability in Europe. Together with the ECB, the national central banks of the euro zone countries form

the European System of Central Banks (ESBC), which is responsible for defining and implementing the common monetary policy for the EMU.

9. While the core EMU members, including France and Germany, apparently prefer the fixed exchange rate regime, other major countries such as the United States and Japan are willing to live with flexible exchange rates. Under the flexible exchange rate regime, governments can retain policy independence because the external balance will be achieved by the exchange rate adjustments rather than by policy intervention. Exchange rate uncertainty, however, can potentially hamper international trade and investment. The choice between the alternative exchange rate regimes is likely to involve a trade-off between national policy autonomy and international economic integration.

KEY WORDS

bimetallism, *26*
Bretton Woods
  system, *29*
currency board, *34*
euro, *25*
European Central Bank
  (ECB), *41*
European Currency Unit
  (ECU), *35*
European Monetary
  System (EMS), *35*
European Monetary
  Union (EMU), *40*
Exchange Rate
  Mechanism (ERM), *35*

European System of
  Central Banks
  (ESCB), *41*
gold-exchange
  standard, *30*
gold standard, *26*
Gresham's law, *26*
incompatible trinity, *52*
international monetary
  system, *25*
Jamaica Agreement, *32*
Louvre Accord, *33*
Maastricht Treaty, *39*
managed-float
  system, *33*

optimum currency
  areas, *44*
par value, *29*
Plaza Accord, *33*
price-specie-flow
  mechanism, *28*
Smithsonian
  Agreement, *31*
snake, *35*
special drawing rights
  (SDRs), *30*
sterilization of gold, *28*
"Tobin tax," *52*
Triffin paradox, *30*

QUESTIONS

1. Explain Gresham's law.

2. Explain the mechanism that restores the balance-of-payments equilibrium when it is disturbed under the gold standard.

3. Suppose that the pound is pegged to gold at 6 pounds per ounce, whereas the franc is pegged to gold at 12 francs per ounce. This, of course, implies that the equilibrium exchange rate should be two francs per pound. If the current market exchange rate is 2.2 francs per pound, how would you take advantage of this situation? What would be the effect of shipping costs?

4. Discuss the advantages and disadvantages of the gold standard.

5. What were the main objectives of the Bretton Woods system?

6. Comment on the proposition that the Bretton Woods system was programmed to an eventual demise.

7. Explain how special drawing rights (SDR) are constructed. Also, discuss the circumstances under which the SDR was created.

8. Explain the arrangements and workings of the European Monetary System (EMS).

9. There are arguments for and against the alternative exchange rate regimes.

   a. List the advantages of the flexible exchange rate regime.

   b. Criticize the flexible exchange rate regime from the viewpoint of the proponents of the fixed exchange rate regime.

www.mhhe.com/er5e

c. Rebut the above criticism from the viewpoint of the proponents of the flexible exchange rate regime.

10. In an integrated world financial market, a financial crisis in a country can be quickly transmitted to other countries, causing a global crisis. What kind of measures would you propose to prevent the recurrence of an Asia-type crisis?

11. Discuss the criteria for a "good" international monetary system.

12. Once capital markets are integrated, it is difficult for a country to maintain a fixed exchange rate. Explain why this may be so.

13. Assess the possibility for the euro to become another global currency rivaling the U.S. dollar. If the euro really becomes a global currency, what impact will it have on the U.S. dollar and the world economy?

INTERNET EXERCISES

1. Using the data from http://cibs.sauder.ubc.ca, first plot the monthly exchange rate between the euro and the U.S. dollar since January 1999, and try to explain why the exchange rate behaved the way it did.

MINI CASE

Will the United Kingdom Join the Euro Club?

When the euro was introduced in January 1999, the United Kingdom was conspicuously absent from the list of European countries adopting the common currency. Although the current Labour government led by Prime Minister Tony Blair appears to be in favor of joining the euro club, it is not clear at the moment if that will actually happen. The opposition Tory party is not in favor of adopting the euro and thus giving up monetary sovereignty of the country. Public opinion is also divided on the issue.

Whether the United Kingdom will eventually join the euro club is a matter of considerable importance for the future of the European Union as well as that of the United Kingdom. If the United Kingdom, with its sophisticated finance industry, joins, it will most certainly propel the euro into a global currency status rivaling the U.S. dollar. The United Kingdom for its part will firmly join the process of economic and political unionization of Europe, abandoning its traditional balancing role.

Investigate the political, economic, and historical situations surrounding British participation in the European economic and monetary integration and write your own assessment of the prospect of Britain joining the euro club. In doing so, assess from the British perspective, among other things, (1) potential benefits and costs of adopting the euro, (2) economic and political constraints facing the country, and (3) the potential impact of British adoption of the euro on the international financial system, including the role of the U.S. dollar.

REFERENCES & SUGGESTED READINGS

Bris, Arturo, Yrjö Koskinen, and Mattias Nilsson. The Euro and Corporate Valuation. Working Paper (2004).

Chinn, Menzie, and Jeffrey Frankel. "The Euro May Over the Next 15 Years Surpass the Dollar as leading International Currency." Forthcoming in *International Finance* (2008).

Cooper, Richard N. *The International Monetary System: Essays in World Economics*. Cambridge, Mass.: MIT Press, 1987.

Eichengreen, Barry. *The Gold Standard in Theory and History*. Mathuen: London, 1985, pp. 39–48.

Friedman, Milton. *Essays in Positive Economics*. Chicago: University of Chicago Press, 1953.

Jorion, Philippe. "Properties of the ECU as a Currency Basket," *Journal of Multinational Financial Management* 1 (1991), pp. 1–24.

Machlup, Fritz. *Remaking the International Monetary System: The Rio Agreement and Beyond.* Baltimore: Johns Hopkins Press, 1968.

Mundell, Robert. "A Theory of Optimum Currency Areas." *American Economic Review* 51 (1961), pp. 657–65.

———. "Currency Areas, Volatility and Intervention," *Journal of Policy Modeling* 22 (2000), pp. 281–99.

Nurkse, Ragnar. *International Currency Experience: Lessons of the Interwar Period.* Geneva: League of Nations, 1944.

Solomon, Robert. *The International Monetary System, 1945–1981.* New York: Harper & Row, 1982.

Stiglitz, Joseph. "Reforming the Global Economic Architecture: Lessons from Recent Crisis." *Journal of Finance* 54 (1999), pp. 1508–21.

Tobin, James. "Financial Globalization," Unpublished manuscript presented at American Philosophical Society, 1998.

Triffin, Robert. *Gold and the Dollar Crisis.* New Haven, Conn.: Yale University Press, 1960.

II. Foreign Exchange Markets and FX Risk Management

A06-98-0021

TCAS, Inc.

On May 16, 1995, Mr. John Christopher, the assistant treasurer of TCAS, Inc., pondered several foreign exchange hedging alternatives that had been outlined by the account manager from his lead bank. Mr. Christopher had called his account manager, Judy Wright, to ask for her advice regarding a Canadian dollar contract Mr. Christopher had negotiated with a Canadian company. Ms. Wright, after first evaluating macroeconomic fundamentals and determining what her bank's lending rates were likely to be based on this outlook, was now ready to advise Mr. Christopher of the various alternatives to hedge the foreign currency risk.

Company Background

TCAS (Transnational Corporate Advisory Services), Inc. was founded in 1982 as a financial training and consulting firm incorporated in Delaware. Its primary assets and products were the knowledge and skills of the three founding partners. All three had worked for the Continental Illinois National Bank for about twelve years but left the bank before its problems in 1984. The expertise of the three founders was multinational business management including the financial, production, and marketing aspects of doing business globally.

In 1988, TCAS merged with Computer Software and Systems Company to extend its products to include management information systems. TCAS, Inc. was involved in developing specialized software and building custom-designed, local area personal computer networks for small- and medium-sized companies. Because of the dramatic changes in computer technology and communication during the decade of the 1980s, the deregulation of financial markets, and the increased emphasis on globalization, TCAS, Inc. experienced rapid growth in net income and assets. However, beginning in 1993, TCAS began to face sharply increased competition from much larger corporations that began to sell very competitively priced services. As a result of these developments, TCAS's net income narrowed dramatically in 1993 and 1994. The company was heavily in debt and had only a few contracts in hand. TCAS was headquartered in Phoenix, Arizona, and its customer base to date had been comprised totally of US companies. TCAS decided that it was time to "go international."

John Christopher recognized that the submission of the bid in Canadian dollars to a Canadian customer was fundamentally a risky step for TCAS. He also realized that, in order to survive, the company had to expand its traditional customer base. John Christopher was surprised when TCAS was awarded the bid. He knew that his foreign exchange worries had just begun and he was in need of expert help.

EXHIBIT 1TCAS, Inc.
Sales and Income Statement

Year Ended Dec. 31	Sales (US$ 000)	Net Income (US$ 000)
1987	1250.0	550.0
1988	1930.0	850.0
1989	2200.0	1120.0
1990	2270.0	1050.0
1991	2940.0	1640.0
1992	3150.0	1700.0
1993	2870.0	550.0
1994	2650.0	-250.0

1994 Balance Sheet

ASSETS

	(US$ 000)
Current assets:	
Cash and securities	250.0
Accounts receivable	620.0
Inventories	80.0
Total current assets	950.0
Property, plant and equipment	
Cost	2240.0
less Accumulated depreciation	(330.0)
Goodwill and intangibles	520.0
TOTAL ASSETS	3380.0

LIABILITIES

Current liabilities	
Bank loans	810.0
Accounts payable	480.0
Notes payable	120.0
Long-term liabilities	
Debt	620.0
TOTAL LIABILITIES	2030.0
Equity and retained earnings	1350.0
TOTAL LIABILITIES AND EQUITY	3380.0

The Bid

TCAS had bid Canadian dollar C$2,900,00 for the delivery and the installation of a new management information software system and an extensive local area network (LAN) computer system. The bid had been put together by the accounting department and accurately reflected costs. The bid was tendered on March 21 by FAX and was accepted on May 15. In accordance with the terms of the contract, the Canadian government agency (Canadian Crown Corporation) had telexed a letter of acceptance of the bid and wired 10% of the purchase price as a deposit on the morning of May 16. Also under the terms of the contract, TCAS would have to secure a performance bond from a third-party vender if awarded the bid. The performance bond would cost .75% of the outstanding contract value.

The remainder of the purchase price was due at the time the system was to be delivered and installed, which under the terms of the contract was to be within 90 days (the Canadian company had insisted on the 90 days and TCAS needed the extra time over the normal 45-day credit period) after the bid was accepted. The TCAS production manager had assured Mr. Christopher that there would be no problems in meeting this delivery schedule for the hardware, although the product was not currently in inventory. The software was already developed and available. Consequently, Mr. Christopher expected to receive a certified check for C$2,610,000 on August 16.

In preparing the bid, TCAS allowed for a tight mark-up of only 5% (see Exhibit 2) to improve the chances of winning the bid. Through past experience, TCAS knew that once it made the first sale, the quality of its product usually ensured additional purchases by the same company. Since the Canadian government agency had stipulated that the bid be in Canadian dollars, TCAS had used the opening spot rate existing on March 21, which was 1US$ = Canadian $1.4096.

EXHIBIT 2 Bid Preparation (US$)	
Design	300,000
Materials	779,287
Labor & installation	724,500
Shipping	32,466
Direct overhead	84,000
Allocation of indirect overhead	39,100
Sub-total	1,959,353
Mark-up (5%)	97,967
TOTAL BID	US$ 2,057,320
Conversion to C$ at March 21 spot rate of 1US$ = Canadian $1.4096	C$2,900,000

The US Dollar and the Canadian Dollar

On May 16, 1995, the day after the bid was accepted, the value of the US dollar closed at 1US$ = C$1.3594. The Canadian$/US$ exchange rate had moved erratically within a relatively narrow range over the past several months as reflected in the following table:

Month	Avg. C$/1US$
January 3	1.4027
February 7	1.3978
March 7	1.4168
April 4	1.4005
May 2	1.3553

The Canadian dollar had remained relatively stable against the US$ until mid-April 1995. It declined to the low registered on May 2 and recovered slightly by mid-May. Mr. Christopher was concerned that the Canadian dollar might depreciate against the US$ during the next 90 days before he received his final payment from the Canadian government agency. Mr. Christopher wanted to know what alternatives were available to him to reduce the foreign exchange risk associated with the outstanding Canadian dollar contract.

Foreign Currency Exposure Management

Judy Wright explained to Mr. Christopher the alternatives available to manage the foreign exchange risk brought about by the Canadian dollar contract. First, Mr. Christopher could do nothing. Over the 55 days since the bid was tendered, the US$ had depreciated by Canadian $0.0502 from Canadian dollar 1.4096 to Canadian dollar 1.3594, or 3.6% in absolute terms. This exchange rate change, if it held steady for the 90 days, would improve TCAS's mark-up from 5% to 8.6% when the Canadian dollars were converted into US dollars. Further depreciation of the US dollar could not be ensured, Judy explained, based on her review of macroeconomic fundamentals.

Foreign Currency Exposure Management Alternatives

The evaluation of expected macroeconomic developments confirmed Mr. Christopher's concerns about a possible depreciation of the Canadian dollar. Ms. Wright explained that a foreign currency hedge would be an appropriate response to the foreign exchange risk faced by TCAS, Inc. Since TCAS had an outstanding Canadian dollar contract, a hedge could be accomplished by any one of the following techniques:

1. *Forward contract*—This involved arranging to deliver Canadian $2,610,000 90 days in the future for conversion into US$ at a predetermined exchange rate. Thus, Mr. Christopher could contract today with Ms. Wright to deliver the Canadian dollar converted at today's quoted three-month forward rate of 1US$ = Canadian $1.3653.

2. *Foreign currency loan*—This created a Canadian $ obligation 90 days hence. TCAS could borrow Canadian $ from Ms. Wright's bank for 90 days and then use the proceeds on completion of the contract to repay the principal and accrued interest. The loan proceeds would be converted immediately into US$ at the prevailing spot rate of exchange. Any gains or losses on the receivable due to a change in the value of the Canadian $/US$ exchange rate would be offset by equivalent losses or gains on the loan itself. Ms. Wright thought that such a loan could be made at 2.25% above the present Canadian prime rate of 10.25% plus an arrangement fee of 0.125%. The US prime rate was at 8.875%. TCAS paid a spread of 2.125% over prime in the US market and would pay a similar spread in Canada

3. *Foreign currency options*—This instrument would give TCAS the right to either purchase (call) or sell (put) an asset at a specified price at a date in the future (European style) or anytime between the purchase date and a date in the future (American style). The buyer of an option has the right but not the obligation to exercise the option. The

buyer of an option has a choice whether to exercise the option and either receive the asset (call) or deliver the asset (put) or to allow the option to expire unexercised. The seller (writer) of the option must stand ready to fulfill an option obligation and surrender an asset on demand (call) or receive an asset on demand (put). Since TCAS had a Canadian dollar contract, it could hedge this foreign currency exposure by buying a Canadian dollar put or writing a Canadian dollar call. Buying a Canadian dollar put option would protect TCAS from an unfavorable downward movement in the Canadian dollar exchange rate while allowing the company to benefit from any further appreciation in the Canadian dollar . The purchase of a currency option would require that Mr. Christopher pay Ms. Wright an option premium at the time the contract was entered into. At the time, the 90-day currency options premium rates on a strike of 1 Canadian dollar = US$ .7200 (or implied 1USdollar = Canadian dollar 1.3888) were: call premium—US dollar 0.0356/Canadian dollar; put premium = US dollar 0.0225/ Canadian dollar. Note that the options are quoted as the US dollar price of one Canadian dollar which is the reciprocal of the Canadian dollar price of one US dollar. Writing a Canadian dollar call option would allow TCAS to benefit if there was little or no change in the value of the Canadian dollar. Instead of paying a premium, TCAS would receive the premium.

4. *Foreign currency futures*—A standardized obligation to purchase or sell a specific amount of currency at a specified date. The buyer or seller of the contract is obliged to take delivery or make delivery of the currency; the position could only be eliminated if the futures position was offset. Most futures positions are offset prior to the last day of trading, leaving the seller with a profit or loss. Ms. Wright explained that a futures contract could be arranged through the International Monetary Market (IMM) of the Chicago Mercantile Exchange. The August futures price was 1C = US$ 0.735. The cost of a round turn per contract (the purchase and subsequent sale of a futures contract) was US$ 50.00. Each Canadian dollar future contract represents Canadian $100,000.

5. *Pre-sale of foreign contract*—Ms. Wright explained that her bank had an export finance subsidiary that would purchase the short-term Canadian dollar contract from TCAS at a discount. The interest rate applicable was fixed for the term involved—90 days—at the cost of funding to the Export Finance Subsidiary, which was LIBOR currently at 7.375%, plus a premium based on normal credit criteria. At this time the credit spread for TCAS was 1.825% over LIBOR. TCAS would incur a flat up-front fee of 0.5%. The US dollar 90-day libor rate was 6.125%.

6. *Tunnel forwards*—A contractual agreement between the two parties which designates a specific exchange rate band within which TCAS would have to exchange currencies on a specific future date. It works like a forward exchange contract that fully protects the downside with no up-front premium paid, but the settlement rate falls within a range instead of at a specific rate. The upper and lower limits of the range act as contract settlement rates if the exchange rate exceed the limits of the range of the tunnel. Ms. Wright indicated that at the present time a zero cost tunnel or range forward (where the premium paid on the put is equal to the premium received) could be created with the

strike on the Canadian dollar put set at US dollar .7133 and the strike on the Canadian dollar call set at US$ .7533.

Canadadian Economic Performance

After finally gaining momentum in 1994, the economic recovery faltered in early 1995. After growing by more than 5-1/2% in 1994, real GDP increased only moderately in the first quarter of 1995 and was expected to decline in the second quarter, before rebounding in the third quarter of 1995. The economic slowdown in the United States dampened the demand for Canadian exports and the tighter monetary conditions moderated domestic demand in Canada. Fortunately, the economic slowdown also resulted in a significant drop in Canadian imports. The short-term interest spreads between Canada and the United States had increased from virtually zero in November 1994 to 2% in early April 1995. However, all indications were that the Canadian Central Bank would soon reverse policy direction and push interest rates lower in order to stimulate employment.

In its February 1995 budget, the federal government in Ottawa, Canada adopted drastic expenditure restraint in order to convince financial markets that deficit reduction targets would be met in spite of higher-than-expected hikes in short-term interest rates. The budget included proposals for major cuts in government employment, subsidies to business and agriculture, and transfers to the provinces.

The most interest-sensitive components of the domestic economy, durable goods and construction, declined markedly in the first quarter of 1995. The recent run-up in interest rates aborted the revival of residential investment. The impact of this weakening of final demand on the Canadian GDP was offset somewhat by a substantial accumulation of inventories.

The Canadian unemployment rate remained broadly stable in the 9-1/2% range. Persistent labor-market slack kept wage increases low, and unit labor costs hardly rose. Slower output growth has been associated with smaller productivity gains. Overall, the rate of inflation had begun to ease.

The Banker's Role

Judy Wright knew that she would need to assist John Christopher in the selection of the appropriate hedging alternative. She also knew that she should be able to talk intelligently about the likely movements in the Canadian dollar over the next three months. Judy Wright asked her bank's economic department to pull together a set of numbers that would help her explain the outlook for the Canadian dollar to Mr. Christopher.

What economic and financial data would she request from the economic department? What analytical framework would she use to interpret the data? How should she best explain the economic data to Mr. Christopher, and what would be her recommendation for the appropriate hedging strategy?

EXHIBIT 3 Marcoeconomic Data

	1989	1990	1991	1992	1993	1994	1995 Est
Real GDP Growth % Canada	2.4	-.2	-1.8	.8	2.2	4.6	2.4
Real GDP Growth % US	2.5	1.2	-.6	2.3	3.1	4.1	3.3
Inflation CPI % Canada	5.0	4.8	5.6	1.5	1.8	.2	1.9
Inflation CPI % US	4.8	5.4	4.2	3.0	3.0	2.6	2.8
Unemployment Rate % Canada	7.5	8.1	10.4	11.3	11.2	10.4	9.6
Unemployment Rate % US	5.3	5.5	6.7	7.4	6.8	6.1	5.6
Gov. Deficit as % GDP Canada	1.4	0.7	-2.0	-2.9	-2.6	-0.5	1.0
Current Account as % of GDP Canada	-3.9	-3.4	-3.7	-3.6	-3.9	-2.7	-0.5
Gross Savings as % of GDP Canada	19.4	16.4	14.3	13.2	13.7	15.4	
Investment as % of GDP Canada	21.9	19.1	20.0	19.7	20.2	18.6	
Current Account C$ dollar (billions)	-22.8	-21.6	-23.6	-21.4	-22.3	-16.3	-10.1
Capital Account C$ (billions)	24.1	23.2	22.1	16.8	22.9	12.3	9.9
Short-term Interest Rates Canada	12.2	13.0	9.0	6.7	5.0	5.4	7.1
Short-term Interest Rates US	8.1	7.5	5.4	3.4	3.0	4.2	5.5
Long-term Interest Rates Canada	9.9	10.8	9.8	8.8	7.9	8.6	8.3
Long-term Interest Rates US	8.5	8.6	7.9	7.0	5.9	7.1	6.6
C$/US$ Exchange Rate	1.184	1.167	1.146	1.209	1.290	1.366	1.370
Gov. Deficit as % GDP US	-1.5	-2.5	-3.2	-4.3	-3.4	-2.0	-1.6

Source: OECD Economic Outlook (June 1998).

THUNDERBIRD
THE AMERICAN GRADUATE SCHOOL
OF INTERNATIONAL MANAGEMENT

B06-03-0010

CURRENCY MARKETS AND PARITY CONDITIONS

In this Note, we examine one of the most pervasive and influential features of the international environment in which multinational enterprises (MNEs) operate: the market for national currencies, i.e., the foreign exchange market. Foreign exchange markets create a qualitatively new set of issues for MNEs to manage, including the different types of exchange rate exposure for its operations. This is so since currencies, and hence transactions denominated in them, do not have a fixed value across borders. Before a manager can start to grapple with the consequences of this fact, it is necessary to understand some of the underlying forces in the foreign exchange market and the concepts driving these forces. These concepts underpin much of what happens in both the theory and the practice of international finance.

We begin by defining some of the commonly used and necessary terminology. We will then discuss the theory of purchasing power parity (PPP), one of the most important ideas underlying the theory and practice of international finance and foreign exchange markets. The theory of PPP enables us to understand the distinction between nominal and real exchange rates, a distinction whose importance will become clear later in the discussion. These ideas will be integrated with those relating to the influence of interest rates, which will lead to two other crucial underpinnings of international finance theory, the covered interest parity theorem (CIP) and the uncovered interest parity theorem (UIP).

Using these ideas we will summarize the variables that influence the value of currencies in the medium term and examine the reasons why they are argued to do so. After providing brief descriptions of the key institutional features of currency markets, finally this Note briefly addresses the different types of exchange rate exposure that MNEs face—translation, transaction, and economic exposure.

Before going further it is important to keep one thing in mind: the role of an MNE manager is *not* to forecast exchange rates. Rather it is first, to appreciate the fact that the uncertainty induced by this aspect of the international environment is real and ubiquitous, and second, to manage and plan for the effects of this uncertainty on the operations and performance of the firm. This requires us to understand the different ways in which MNEs are exposed to exchange rates. That in turn requires us to understand the working of the foreign exchange markets, as well as the basic parity conditions, i.e., PPP, CIP, and UIP.

For the purposes of this discussion, and unless otherwise mentioned, the United States (U.S.) will be considered the home country and the U.S. dollar ($) the home currency. France will be considered the foreign country and the euro (€) the foreign currency. This discussion is, of course, generalizable to any pair of countries and currencies.

Basic Definitions

The foreign exchange rate is the nominal price of one nation's money in terms of another's, that is, the number of U.S. dollars it takes to buy each €.[1] The price of one currency in terms of another can be

---

[1] The "nominal" price is distinct from the "real" price, as will be made clear shortly.

quoted either directly or indirectly. A direct quote expresses the foreign exchange rate in terms of the number of units of home currency it takes to buy each unit of foreign currency (the same concept as, say, the number of dollars it takes to buy one hamburger). From the U.S. perspective, a direct quote would be written $/€. An indirect quote is the reverse—the number of units of foreign currency it takes to buy each unit of home currency (the number of hamburgers per dollar), which would be written €/$. To avoid confusion it is extremely important that we remember which of the two quotation methods is being used; otherwise, just about everything we do in international finance would become topsy-turvy. In our discussion of these basic ideas, we will use the direct quote ($/€) throughout. (The effects of using the indirect quote on all the formulae we develop are shown in the Appendix to this chapter.)

The two commonly observed foreign exchange rates are the *spot rate* (which we denote as e_0 or, when there is no scope for confusion, just e) and the T-period *forward rate* (which we denote as e_T). The spot rate is today's exchange rate, or the number of dollars you have to pay to buy each €.[2] In actuality, this transaction is formally settled two business days after the date on which the spot transaction is entered into.

The T-period forward rate is the exchange rate available today for transactions that we may wish to make at time T. That is, we can enter into an agreement today to, say, deliver €100 ninety days hence, at the 90-day forward rate known to us, or agreed upon today (no money changes hands until the ninetieth day). Thus, for example, we would pay $(100*e_{90})$, 90 days from now. Typically, maturities are 30, 90, 180, or 360 days. Forward rates are important for managing a problem that MNEs face known as "transaction exposure to exchange rates," which we will address later in the Note.

The forward rate is conceptually similar to the futures rate. Many of the differences between the two are institutional. Therefore, while actual forward rates may differ slightly from actual futures rates due to these institutional features (and because there are some valuation differences induced by the effects of interest rate uncertainty), for our purposes, we will use the two concepts interchangeably.

These two types of exchange rate, however, are different from the *expected future spot rate*, which we will express as $E(e_0^T)$. This rate reflects the expectation the market has about the price of a currency T days from now. $E(e_0^T)$ is, of course, only an expectation and is not known with certainty. We will see later that the forward rate and the expected future spot rate should be (in theory) closely related.

Depreciation, Appreciation, Premium, and Discount

Using the direct quote, the foreign currency is said to undergo an appreciation relative to the home currency when there is an increase in e, and the foreign currency is said to undergo a depreciation relative to the home currency when there is a decrease in e. That is:

e increases $\Rightarrow$ foreign currency appreciation
e decreases $\Rightarrow$ foreign currency depreciation

Using the example of hamburgers, if the price of hamburgers (€) goes up (the equivalent of an increase in e), we would say that the hamburger has become more expensive, i.e., it has appreciated vis-à-vis the dollar. To be more specific, suppose the initial exchange rate is $1.00/€ and this changes to $1.10/€. The number of dollars we need to buy each € has gone up (e has increased), and this means that € has become ten cents more expensive with respect to the dollar, that is, € has appreciated.

---

[2] In the real world, there are bid-offer (or bid-ask) spreads in currency quotations, that is, a rate at which the foreign exchange market will buy (bid) currencies from you and a rate at which it will sell (offer) currencies to you. Bid-offer spreads are quite small for the heavily traded currencies. In order to keep the development of ideas conceptually simple, we ignore bid-offer spreads.

A foreign currency is said to be at a forward premium if

$$e_T > e_0 \tag{1}$$

That is, if its forward rate is higher than the spot rate. If the inequality is reversed, the foreign currency is at a forward discount. The percentage annualized premium (or discount) is

$$\%FP = (100)\left(\frac{e_T - e_0}{e_0}\right)\left(\frac{360}{T}\right) \tag{2}$$

where T is the number of days forward.

Exchange Rates and Prices: Purchasing Power Parity

The theory of purchasing power parity (PPP), perhaps one of the most influential ideas in all of economics, establishes a formal link between a country's price level or inflation rates (relative to another country's) and the prevailing exchange rate between the two countries. There are two well-known versions of this theory, the absolute version and the relative version.

The absolute PPP relationship says that

$$P = eP^* \tag{3}$$

where P is the domestic price level, P^* is the foreign price level, and e is the spot exchange rate (direct quote). If we think about it for a moment, all that PPP is about is the absence of arbitrage opportunities in a frictionless (and undifferentiated) goods market—that is, it says that the exchange rate will adjust to eliminate discrepancies in price levels, or price levels will adjust to eliminate discrepancies in exchange rates, for similar commodities between two countries. Consider an example. Suppose a ton of widgets costs \$1 in the United States and €0.90 in France, and the exchange rate is \$1.00/€. For a U.S. buyer of widgets, the € price at the current exchange rate is only \$0.90 per ton and thus cheaper. This will increase the demand for French widgets and decrease the demand for U.S. widgets, raising their € price (P^*) and lowering their U.S. price (P). Further in the process of buying the French widgets, U.S. buyers will be supplying dollars and demanding euros, leading to appreciation of the euro and depreciation of the dollar (an increase in e). In equilibrium then, the theory says that U.S. and French widget prices and the \$/€ exchange rate will adjust, resulting in PPP .

A more commonly used definition of PPP is relative PPP (RPPP), which expresses this arbitrage relationship in terms of prices and exchange rates today (time 0) relative to our expectation for some future point in time (say, time 1). RPPP says that:

$$\left(\frac{P_1}{P_0}\right) = \left(\frac{e_1}{e_0}\right)\left(\frac{P_1^*}{P_0^*}\right) \tag{4}$$

where P, P^*, and e are as above, and the subscripts 1 and 0 refer to "tomorrow" and "today," respectively. Equation (4) can be rewritten as

$$1 + \Delta P = (1 + \Delta e)(1 + \Delta P^*) \tag{5}$$

or as,

$$\Delta e = \left(\frac{1 + \Delta P}{1 + \Delta P^*}\right) - 1 \tag{6}$$

where ΔP is the expected percentage change in domestic prices, i.e., the domestic inflation rate, Δe is the expected percentage change in exchange rates and ΔP^* is the expected percentage change in foreign prices, i.e., the foreign inflation rate.

What we have just seen is also a simple model for predicting future exchange rates. RPPP tells us that if the domestic inflation rate is expected to be higher than the foreign inflation rate, then Δe must be greater than zero, i.e., the foreign currency is expected to appreciate against the home currency by Δe percentage points. Specifically, if the inflation rate in the U.S. during the next year is expected to be 3%, and the inflation rate in the Euro-zone is expected to be 1%, RPPP predicts that $\Delta e = (1.03/1.01) - 1 = 0.0198 = 1.98\%$, or an approximately 2% appreciation of the € against the US$.[3]

Now we are ready to define real exchange rates, and more importantly *changes* in real exchange rates. Based on absolute PPP, the real exchange rate is defined as:

$$S = \left(\frac{eP^*}{P} \right) \qquad (7)$$

Note that if absolute PPP always holds, then S would be equal to 1. When S is different from 1, there has been a change in the real exchange rate. For instance if the nominal exchange rate, e, rises in value, i.e., the foreign currency appreciates and neither P nor P^* changes, then S would be greater than 1, implying that the foreign currency has appreciated (and the home currency has depreciated) in real terms. The intuition is as follows. If PPP held, an increase in e should have been the result of (or accompanied by) a decrease in foreign prices P^* or an increase in domestic prices P. The fact that they both stayed the same as before indicates that foreign goods have become more expensive in real terms and/or domestic goods have become cheaper in real terms. (Think about, and convince yourself that, in this situation, domestic exporters have become better off, and domestic importers have become worse off than before.)

The *change in the real exchange rate* is the nominal, i.e., actual exchange rate change minus the change in exchange rates predicted by RPPP:

$$\Delta S = [\text{Actual change}] - [\text{RPPP-predicted change}]$$
$$= \Delta e_{Actual} - \Delta e_{RPPP} \qquad (8)$$

where ΔS refers to the percentage change in the real exchange rate, Δe_{Actual} refers to the percentage change in the actual exchange rate, i.e., the new exchange rate minus the old change rate divided by the old exchange rate, and Δe_{RPPP} the RPPP-predicted change is as derived from equation (6) above.

There is also an effective exchange rate, which is a multilateral rate that measures the overall nominal value of the currency in the foreign exchange market. For example, the effective U.S. dollar exchange rate combines many bilateral exchange rates using a weighting scheme that reflects the importance of each country's trade with the United States. Several institutions (for example, the International Monetary Fund, the Federal Reserve Board) regularly calculate and report the effective exchange rates. There is also a real effective exchange rate, adjusting for multilateral PPP relationships.

Exchange Rates and Interest Rates

The relationship between exchange rates and nominal interest rates is captured in two simple propositions: (1) the covered interest parity theorem (CIP) which deals with a no-arbitrage equilibrium in international financial markets, and (2) the speculative efficiency hypothesis and the resulting uncovered parity theorem (UIP) which deals with a speculative equilibrium in international financial markets. Each of these is described below.

---

[3] The RPPP relationship is also sometimes expressed in its approximate form, as $\Delta e \approx \Delta P - \Delta P^*$, where $\approx$ means "approximately equal to." While this approximate form is a useful simplification when expected annual inflation rates are low (say, less than 5%), applying it in this way can lead to fairly large errors when inflation rates are high. In general, it is advisable to use the exact formula as given in (6) above, rather than the approximate formula.

Covered Interest Parity Theorem

Covered interest parity is the mechanism through which an equilibrium relationship is established between spot and forward exchange rates, and risk-equivalent domestic and foreign nominal interest rates. This relationship is also sometimes referred to as the interest rate parity theorem or the covered interest arbitrage condition.

In addition to the notation developed thus far, suppose r stands for the domestic (U.S.) T-period nominal interest rate, and r^* stands for the risk-equivalent foreign (French) T-period nominal interest rate. At any given point in time, we can observe e_0, e_T, r, and r^*. Is there an equilibrium relationship among these four variables? And if this equilibrium relationship is not met, is there an arbitrage opportunity? The answer to both questions is "yes."

Let us illustrate this issue with a simple example. Suppose that the $\$/€$ spot exchange rate (e_0) is $\$1.00/€$ and the 180-day forward rate (e_{180}) is $\$0.98/€$ (that is, the € is at a forward discount vis-à-vis the dollar). Let us also suppose that the relevant annual interest rate in the U.S., r, is 4% and that the corresponding French € interest rate, r^*, is 10% (that is, the 180-day interest rates are 2% and %, respectively).[4]

Suppose we did the following:

Borrow	$\$\left[\dfrac{X}{1.02}\right]$ in the U.S. markets for 180 days (so that we repay $\$X$ in 180 days);
Convert	it into $€\left[\dfrac{X}{1.02 \times 1.00}\right]$;
Invest	this in the € markets to get $€\left[\dfrac{X \times 1.05}{1.02 \times 1.00}\right]$ at the end of 180 days;
Sell Forward	this amount today to guarantee ourselves $\$\left[\dfrac{X \times 1.05 \times 0.98}{1.02 \times 1.00}\right]$ in the future, i.e., 180 days from now; and finally,
Repay	the $\$X$ we owe the U.S. bank that we originally borrowed from.

The profit from this transaction is:

$$X(1.00882) - X = X(0.00882)$$

For example, if we started with a borrowing of $\$10$ million, we would have netted a riskless profit of $\$88,200$—not bad for a day's work!

The profit relationship above can also be expressed in terms of our symbols as:

$$(X)\left[\frac{e_T(1 + r^*)}{e_0(1 + r)}\right] - X \tag{9}$$

---

[4] Note that the half-yearly rates are just one-half of the annualized quotes—this is, indeed, the correct way to calculate part-year rates, since that is the convention in foreign exchange markets. This convention arises from the interest rate/time-measure conventions used in the bond markets that foreign exchange markets use for their interest rate benchmarks, namely the eurobond markets. Thus the quarterly interest rate would be one-fourth of the annual rate, the monthly interest rate would be one-twelfth of the annual rate, etc.

However, if everybody else in the market started doing exactly the same thing, such arbitrage profits would be driven to zero. Why this would happen is easy to see. If everyone goes through the same set of transactions:

> r will increase because of increased demand for U.S. funds;
>
> r^* will decrease because of increased supply of euro funds,
>
> e_0 will rise, i.e., the foreign currency will appreciate because of the spot conversion demand for € (and supply of dollars) and
>
> e_T will fall because of the increased supply of forward € (and demand for forward dollars),

thereby driving the profit in expression (9) to zero.

Thus, in a no-arbitrage equilibrium, we can equate expression (9) to zero. Canceling out X and rewriting the expression in (9), we have the covered interest parity condition:

$$\left[\frac{e_T}{e_0}\right] = \left[\frac{1+r}{1+r^*}\right] \tag{10}$$

Empirical studies generally show that the covered interest parity relationship holds quite well, particularly when measured using eurobond interest rates. With increased global capital market integration, the relationship is becoming more true of pairs of domestic interest rates as well, at least in the industrialized countries. Indeed, bankers often use the CIP model to quote forward rates, a somewhat rare example of a model driving reality, rather than the other way around!

Speculative Efficiency Hypothesis

In this discussion of the theory of speculation in foreign exchange markets, we will assume risk-neutral speculators, by which we mean speculators who care only about expected returns and not about the standard deviation (risk) in returns. This theory could also be applied to risk averse cases, but with no significant gain in insights for our present purposes.

The idea behind all speculation is quite simple. If you expect a currency (or anything else) to appreciate in value, you want to buy into it (be long in it); if you expect it to depreciate, you want to get out of it (be short in it). Recall that $E(e_0^T)$ is the future spot rate you think will be realized at time T. Recall that this is an unknown variable. All we have today is an *expectation* of what the value of the currency is going to be when date T comes around.

The concept of speculation stated above translates more formally into the following:

>   If $e_T > E(e_0^T)$, get out of € (the foreign currency).

>   If $e_T < E(e_0^T)$, get out of $ (the domestic currency).

In the first case, our expectation is that the forward rate overpredicts the future spot rate for € and underpredicts the future spot rate for $. Thus, we want to buy into $ (and sell €).

An example will perhaps make this clearer. We know that the 180-day forward rate on € is $0.98/€. Suppose that we think that the actual future spot rate is going to be $0.99/€ (that is, we think that the forward rate known to us today underpredicts the expected future spot rate). Using the decision rule above, we want to get out of $ and into €. We buy € forward at $0.98/€; when the 180th day comes around, if our expectations are realized, we can sell these € for $0.99/€ cents. We would have made a profit of 1 cent on every € we bought. (As an exercise, work out what would happen if, instead, $e_T = 0.99$ and $E(e_0^T) = 0.98$.)

Now if others in the market also form the same expectation (there is no reason to assume that they aren't equally smart), they will start buying € forward and pushing up the forward price of the euro. In fact and even if no one else in the market shares our expectation, our going into an equilibrated market with a sudden and sizeable demand for forward € will have a similar effect. In the process, e_T will rise until there is a speculative equilibrium:

$$e_T = E(e_0^T) \tag{11}$$

Likewise, when the forward rate overpredicts the expected future spot rate, we will demand forward \$ (and supply forward €), so that e_T is driven down until the equality in expression (11) is again attained. This relationship—that the forward rate is the best unbiased predictor of the future spot rate in a speculative equilibrium—is called the speculative efficiency hypothesis (SEH).

Uncovered Interest Parity Theorem

If (11) is true, we can conceptually substitute $E(e_0^T)$ in place of e_T in the covered interest parity condition, with the interesting implication that

$$\frac{E(e_0^T)}{e_0} = \frac{(1+r)}{(1+r^*)}$$

or that

$$1 + \Delta e = \frac{(1+r)}{(1+r^*)}$$

or that

$$\Delta e = \frac{(1+r)}{(1+r^*)} - 1 \tag{12}$$

This relationship is called the uncovered interest parity theorem (UIP). Note that this formula, like RPPP, gives us an alternate means to predict exchange rates. It says that when domestic nominal interest rates are higher than the foreign nominal interest rates, the foreign currency is expected to appreciate, i.e., the domestic currency is expected to depreciate.

Empirical tests generally show that the forward rate is *not* a very good predictor of the level of the future spot rate (it explains about 10% of the change in the actual future exchange rates). However, evidence is strong that the forward rate does a better job of predicting at least the direction of changes to future spot rates than do about two-thirds of the better known foreign exchange forecasting services, making it one of the better predictors around.

An Implication: The International Fisher Effect

If we combine the insights from RPPP (equation (6)) and UIP (equation (12)), we obtain another interesting implication, known as the international Fisher effect. It says that:

$$\Delta e = \frac{(1+\Delta P)}{(1+\Delta P^*)} - 1 = \left(\frac{1+r}{1+r^*}\right) - 1$$

or that

$$\frac{(1+r)}{(1+\Delta P)} = \frac{(1+r^*)}{(1+\Delta P^*)} \tag{13}$$

or translated, that *real* interest rates, i.e., the nominal interest rates adjusted for inflation expectations, must be the same both at home and abroad. In other words, it implies the following: when goods markets are in equilibrium resulting from RPPP and capital markets are in equilibrium resulting from

UIP, real productivity of capital, i.e., the NPV of a similar project, must be the same across all countries where these two parity conditions hold!

The Foreign Exchange Market

The market for foreign exchange is the largest market in the world. Transactions in the foreign exchange market well exceed $1 trillion daily. The market operates almost twenty-four hours a day, so that somewhere in the world, at any given time, there is a market open in which you can trade foreign exchange. For example, trading starts in Sydney; before Sydney closes, trading opens in Tokyo, Hong Kong, and Singapore; before Singapore closes, trading opens in Bahrain; and so on.

Nearly nine-tenths of the trades across the world involve the U.S. dollar. The reasons for this are three-fold. One, the U.S. dollar is still the most heavily traded currency worldwide and is the reference currency for denominating the prices of a number of globally traded products such as oil, aircraft, gold, and so forth. Two, triangular arbitrage opportunities are rarely present in the foreign exchange markets for the heavily traded currencies. In other words, if the price of currency A is known with respect to B and C, the price of B in terms of C is automatically determined, otherwise there would be a costless arbitrage opportunity—traders quote prices as though such arbitrage opportunities are not present and thus, the arbitrage opportunity is non-existent in the first place. Three, the dollar-based quotation dramatically reduces information complexity. It is far easier for a trader to remember, say, eight currency quotes against the U.S. dollar and derive the rest by assuming absence of triangular arbitrage opportunities, rather than remember the $9*8/2 = 36$ pairwise currency quotes (including those for the U.S. dollar) that actually prevail.

Both direct and indirect quotes (against the U.S. dollar) are simultaneously used in foreign exchange markets, depending on the currency involved. For instance, the Euro and the British pound are quoted in direct terms (number of dollars per currency unit), while the Japanese yen is quoted indirectly (the number of yen per dollar).

The most important participants in the market are banks. Traders in the major money center banks are constantly buying from and selling to each other; in fact, deals between banks, so-called direct deals, account for nearly 85% of the activity in foreign exchange markets. Foreign exchange is traded "over-the-counter" via telephone and computer communications among banks, and not in organized exchanges such as stock exchanges.

The three common types of transactions in foreign exchange markets are spot, outright forward, and swap transactions. Spot transactions involve buying or selling at today's exchange rate (the actual deposit transfer between the buyer's bank and the seller's bank occurs two business days later). Outright forward transactions involve agreement on a price today for settlement at some date in the future. Swap transactions—which are really forward transactions in disguise, and the market's method to derive the quotation for forward rates—involve an agreement to buy (or sell) in the spot market, with a simultaneous agreement to reverse the trade in the outright forward market. Approximately 65% of trades take place in the spot markets, 33% in swap markets, and about 2% in the outright forward markets.

Determining the Value of Exchange Rates

There is a large volume of research on the underlying fundamentals that determine currency values. In the short run (hour to hour, or even over days), such fundamentals do not seem to matter much, since currency trading and speculation are driven almost entirely by technical considerations. This is consistent with the fact that direct deals account for a large proportion of foreign exchange transactions.

In the medium- to long-term (one to five years), however, there is general agreement that the following factors are determinants of the direction in which—if not the level to which—currency values move: a country's level of economic activity (GNP or GDP), its money supply and demand (M^s and M^d), its nominal and real interest rates (r^n and r^r), its economic productivity (η), its inflation rate (ΔP), and its trade or current account balances (the value of exports minus the value of imports, or $X - M$). In general, the effects of these variables on the future value of a currency (everything else remaining equal) and the reasons for these effects are hypothesized to be as follows:

- *GNP or GDP increase:* Increases a currency's value, since there is likely to be greater transaction demand for that country's currency.

- M^s *increase:* Decreases a currency's value, since there is greater supply of the currency; also, increased money supply could signal higher inflation.

- M^d *increase:* Opposite effect of M^s increase.

- r^n *increase:* Decreases a currency's value through uncovered interest parity and PPP; intuitively it signals an increase in the inflation rate.

- r^r *increase:* Opposite effect of r^n increase, since it increases the inflation-adjusted yield from securities denominated in that currency.

- η *increase:* Increases a currency's value because it signals GNP increase and r^r increase.

- ΔP *increase:* Decreases a currency's value through PPP.

- $X - M$ *increase:* Increases a currency's value, since it increases the demand for that currency (to pay for its exports) and decreases the demand for the other country's currency (because of reduced imports).

Of course, it is important to keep in mind that none of these variable changes occurs in isolation, and so the effect of an individual variable may be difficult to discern. In addition, actual changes in these variables are often not necessary for currency values to change—a credible expectation by the market that these changes will occur is sufficient (and it is difficult to pin down exactly when the expectations of market participants actually change). Finally, there may be significant currency movements even when expectations regarding a particular country's fundamentals do not change; all that is necessary is for expectations regarding a fundamental in the other country to change.

It is for these reasons that currency forecasting is an exercise that is, at best, tenuous and, at worst, somewhat pointless. Therefore, the list of variables and the effects indicated above should be used with a fair amount of caution. The role of an MNE manager is not to forecast exchange rates; rather, it is (a) to appreciate the fact that the uncertainty induced by this aspect of the international environment is real and ubiquitous, and (b) to manage and plan for the effects of this uncertainty on the operations and performance of the firm. This in turn requires us to understand the different ways in which MNEs are exposed to exchange rates.

Types of MNE Exchange Rate Exposure[5]

There are three types of impact of exchange rates on the operations and performance of MNEs: translation, transaction, and economic exposure (also sometimes called operating or real exposure) to exchange rates. A stylized graphical description of the three types of exchange rate exposure is shown in Figure 1.

---

[5] For a thorough discussion of the different types of exchange rate exposure defined in this section, and how managers of cross-border enterprises can and should deal with them, see the Thunderbird Case Series Note "A Global Manager's Guide to Currency Risk Management."

Translation exposure deals with the *ex post* impact of nominal exchange rate changes on the consolidated financial statements of MNEs. There are well-known accounting rules, e.g., the Financial Accounting Standards Board Rule 52, or "FAS 52" in the U.S., to deal with currency translation issues. In the most commonly used method in U.S. firms, translation effects are typically dealt with as follows: Income Statement items such as revenues and expenses are booked at the actual exchange rate at which transactions occur or some average exchange rate during the relevant period; Balance Sheet items are translated using the exchange rate that prevails on the date when the books are consolidated; currency translation gains and losses do not have any Income Statement impact, rather, they are simply entered as a "plug" item in the equity accounts in the Balance Sheet.[6]

The second type of exposure, transaction exposure, results from the fact that firms enter into transactions of known *ex ante* value (in domestic currency terms) prior to an exchange rate change, but are required to settle these transactions after an exchange rate change. These are exchange rate effects resulting from outstanding obligations across borders that have to be managed during the life of these obligations, rather than just recorded using accounting methods. The two common types of transaction exposure incurred by firms are (1) those relating to payables and receivables outstanding and (2) those relating to borrowing (debt issuance) or lending (debt investment) abroad. For instance, if a company has sold its products abroad and invoiced them in the foreign currency, it incurs a foreign currency receivable. During the life of the receivable, if the foreign currency were to depreciate, it would lower the home currency value of the sale. Similarly, for importers with foreign currency payables, an appreciation of the foreign currency will increase the amount of home currency required to pay for the purchase. This in turn raises the question of whether and how such transaction exposures should be hedged. Many commonly available financial instruments such as currency forwards, currency futures, and currency options contracts are used to manage this type of exposure.[7]

The third category, economic exposure, results from the fact that the firm's expected cash flows experience unexpected changes in the *real* exchange rate. More precisely, if we define a firm's cash flow as π, where π is the sum of domestic and foreign cash flows (and hence a function of the real exchange rate), then a firm is said to have economic exposure to exchange rates if $\partial\pi/\partial e$, that is the sensitivity of cash flows to real exchange rate changes is not equal to zero. While translation and transaction exposures often do not (and need not) affect real cash flows (since the *ex ante* domestic currency value of the exposure is known and hence can be hedged), economic exposure has to be dealt with typically through variables such as pricing, sourcing from different locations, diversifying the manufacturing base geographically, and so forth, rather than through financial hedging techniques. That is, these are exchange rate exposures that have to be planned for, rather than just managed or recorded. (Again, see Footnote 6 for reference to material that contains a detailed discussion of this issue.)

---

[6] The exception is when a foreign asset is liquidated. In that event, the actual loss or gain from the sale goes into the Income Statement. See the Note referred to in Footnote 6 for more details.

[7] It is beyond the scope of this Note to address the details of such hedging (but see Footnote 6). However, here is a summary of how forwards, futures, and options would be used. When a firm is attempting to hedge its expected foreign currency *receipts*, it is worried about putting a *floor* on the home currency value of such receipts, i.e., it is interested in protecting itself against a depreciation of the foreign currency. This in turn requires it to sell forward the foreign currency (if using forwards), or go short a foreign currency futures contract (if using futures), or to buy a foreign currency put option (if using options). On the other hand, when a firm is attempting to hedge its expected foreign currency *payments*, it is worried about putting a *ceiling* on the home currency value of such payments, i.e., it is interested in protecting itself against an appreciation of the foreign currency. This requires it to buy forward the foreign currency (if using forwards), or go long on a foreign currency futures contract (if using futures), or to buy a foreign currency call option (if using options).

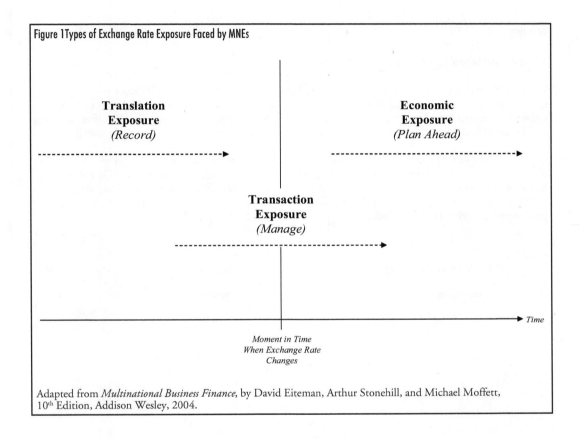

Figure 1 Types of Exchange Rate Exposure Faced by MNEs

Adapted from *Multinational Business Finance*, by David Eiteman, Arthur Stonehill, and Michael Moffett, 10th Edition, Addison Wesley, 2004.

APPENDIX

A Restatement of Some of the Key Relationships Using the Indirect Quote

It might be useful to see comparisons of some of the important formulae with direct versus indirect quotes. In the real world, you should have the ability to deal with both perspectives, since some currencies are quoted one way, e.g., € and others the opposite way, e.g., the Japanese Yen. Further, you will be confronted with these differences from one article to another, one text book to another, etc.

The best strategy, therefore, is not to try to memorize any of the formulae, but to develop the ability to derive them from first principles, given the particular currency quotation. Of course, the simplest approach is to just use one perspective—direct quotes—and if the situation requires you to switch perspectives, to pretend that the home currency is the foreign currency (and *vice versa*) for the purpose of applying the formulae!

	Direct Quote ($/€)	_Indirect Quote (€/$)_
Appreciation of FX:	e increases	e decreases
Depreciation of FX:	e decreases	e increases
Absolute PPP:	$P = eP^*$	$P^* = eP$
Relative PPP:	$\dfrac{P_1}{P_0} = \left(\dfrac{e_1}{e_0}\right)\left(\dfrac{P_1^*}{P_0^*}\right)$	$\dfrac{P_1^*}{P_0^*} = \left(\dfrac{e_1}{e_0}\right)\left(\dfrac{P_1}{P_0}\right)$
Forward Premium:	$e_T > e_0$	$e_T < e_0$
CIP:	$\dfrac{e_T}{e_0} = \dfrac{(1+r)}{(1+r^*)}$	$\dfrac{e_T}{e_0} = \dfrac{(1+r^*)}{(1+r)}$
UIP:	$\dfrac{E(e_0^T)}{e_0} = \dfrac{(1+r)}{(1+r^*)}$	$\dfrac{E(e_0^T)}{e_0} = \dfrac{(1+r^*)}{(1+r)}$

3 Balance of Payments

THE TERM **balance of payments** is often mentioned in the news media and continues to be a popular subject of economic and political discourse around the world. It is not always clear, however, exactly what is meant by the term when it is mentioned in various contexts. This ambiguity is often attributable to misunderstanding and misuse of the term. The balance of payments, which is a statistical record of a country's transactions with the rest of the world, is worth studying for a few reasons.

First, the balance of payments provides detailed information concerning the demand and supply of a country's currency. For example, if the United States imports more than it exports, then this means that the supply of dollars is likely to exceed the demand in the foreign exchange market, *ceteris paribus*. One can thus infer that the U.S. dollar would be under pressure to depreciate against other currencies. On the other hand, if the United States exports more than it imports, then the dollar would be likely to appreciate.

Second, a country's balance-of-payment data may signal its potential as a business partner for the rest of the world. If a country is grappling with a major balance-of-payment difficulty, it may not be able to expand imports from the outside world. Instead, the country may be tempted to impose measures to restrict imports and discourage capital outflows in order to improve the balance-of-payment situation. On the other hand, a country experiencing a significant balance-of-payment surplus would be more likely to expand imports, offering marketing opportunities for foreign enterprises, and less likely to impose foreign exchange restrictions.

Third, balance-of-payments data can be used to evaluate the performance of the country in international economic competition. Suppose a country is experiencing trade deficits year after year. This trade data may then signal that the country's domestic industries lack international competitiveness. To interpret balance-of-payments data properly, it is necessary to understand how the balance-of-payments account is constructed.

Balance-of-Payments Accounting

The balance of payments can be formally defined as *the statistical record of a country's international transactions over a certain period of time presented in the form of double-entry bookkeeping.* Examples of international transactions include import and export of goods and services and cross-border investments in businesses, bank accounts, bonds, stocks, and real estate. Since the balance of payments is recorded over a certain period of time (i.e., a quarter or a year), it has the same time dimension as national income accounting.[1]

---

[1]In fact, the current account balance, which is the difference between a country's exports and imports, is a component of the country's GNP. Other components of GNP include consumption and investment and government expenditure.

Generally speaking, any transaction that results in a receipt from foreigners will be recorded as a credit, with a positive sign, in the U.S. balance of payments, whereas any transaction that gives rise to a payment to foreigners will be recorded as a debit, with a negative sign. Credit entries in the U.S. balance of payments result from foreign sales of U.S. goods and services, goodwill, financial claims, and real assets. Debit entries, on the other hand, arise from U.S. purchases of foreign goods and services, goodwill, financial claims, and real assets. Further, credit entries give rise to the demand for dollars, whereas debit entries give rise to the supply of dollars. Note that the demand (supply) for dollars is associated with the supply (demand) of foreign exchange.

Since the balance of payments is presented as a system of double-entry bookkeeping, every credit in the account is balanced by a matching debit and vice versa.

EXAMPLE|3 .1

For example, suppose that Boeing Corporation exported a Boeing 747 aircraft to Japan Airlines for $50 million, and that Japan Airlines pays from its dollar bank account kept with Chase Manhattan Bank in New York City. Then, the receipt of $50 million by Boeing will be recorded as a credit (+), which will be matched by a debit (−) of the same amount representing a reduction of the U.S. bank's liabilities.

EXAMPLE|3 .2

Suppose, for another example, that Boeing imports jet engines produced by Rolls-Royce for $30 million, and that Boeing makes payment by transferring the funds to a New York bank account kept by Rolls-Royce. In this case, payment by Boeing will be recorded as a debit (−), whereas the deposit of the funds by Rolls-Royce will be recorded as a credit (+).

As shown by the preceding examples, every credit in the balance of payments is matched by a debit somewhere to conform to the principle of double-entry bookkeeping.

Not only international trade, that is, exports and imports, but also cross-border investments are recorded in the balance of payments.

EXAMPLE|3 .3

Suppose that Ford acquires Jaguar, a British car manufacturer, for $750 million, and that Jaguar deposits the money in Barclays Bank in London, which, in turn, uses the sum to purchase U.S. treasury notes. In this case, the payment of $750 million by Ford will be recorded as a debit (−), whereas Barclays' purchase of the U.S. Treasury notes will be recorded as a credit (+).

The above examples can be summarized as follows:

Transactions	Credit	Debit
Boeing's export	+$50 million	
Withdrawal from U.S. bank		−$50 million
Boeing's import		−$30 million
Deposit at U.S. bank	+$30 million	
Ford's acquisition of Jaguar		−$750 million
Barclays' purchase of U.S. securities	+$750 million	

Balance-of-Payments Accounts

Since the balance of payments records all types of international transactions a country consummates over a certain period of time, it contains a wide variety of accounts.

However, a country's international transactions can be grouped into the following three main types:

1. The current account.
2. The capital account.
3. The official reserve account.

The **current account** includes the export and import of goods and services, whereas the **capital account** includes all purchases and sales of assets such as stocks, bonds, bank accounts, real estate, and businesses. The **official reserve account**, on the other hand, covers all purchases and sales of international reserve assets such as dollars, foreign exchanges, gold, and special drawing rights (SDRs).

Let us now examine a detailed description of the balance-of-payments accounts. Exhibit 3.1 summarizes the U.S. balance-of-payments accounts for the year 2006 that we are going to use as an example.

The Current Account

Exhibit 3.1 shows that U.S. exports were $2,096.3 billion in 2006 while U.S. imports were $2,818.0 billion. The current account balance, which is defined as exports minus imports plus unilateral transfers, that is, (1) + (2) + (3) in Exhibit 3.1, was negative, −$811.3 billion. The United States thus had a balance-of-payments deficit on the current account in 2006. The current account deficit implies that the United States used up more output than it produced.[2] Since a country must finance its current account

EXHIBIT 3.1		Credits	Debits
A Summary of the U.S. Balance of Payments for 2006 (in $ billion)	*Current Account*		
	(1) Exports	2,096.3	
	(1.1) Merchandise	1,026.9	
	(1.2) Services	418.9	
	(1.3) Factor income	650.5	
	(2) Imports		−2,818.0
	(2.1) Merchandise		−1,861.4
	(2.2) Services		−342.8
	(2.3) Factor income		−613.8
	(3) Unilateral transfer	24.4	−114.0
	Balance on current account [(1) + (2) + (3)]		−811.3
	Capital Account		
	(4) Direct investment	180.6	−235.4
	(5) Portfolio investment	1,017.4	−426.1
	(5.1) Equity securities	148.5	−138.5
	(5.2) Debt securities	868.9	−287.6
	(6) Other investment	690.4	−400.0
	Balance on capital account [(4) + (5) + (6)]	826.9	
	(7) Statistical discrepancies		−18.0
	Overall balance		−2.4
	Official Reserve Account	2.4	

Source: IMF, *International Financial Statistics Yearbook, 2007.*

---

[2]The current account balance (BCA) can be written as the difference between national output (Y) and domestic absorption, which comprises consumption (C), investment (I), and government expenditures (G):

$$BCA = Y - (C + I + G)$$

If a country's domestic absorption falls short of its national output, the country's current account must be in surplus, for more detailed discussion, refer to appendix 3A.

www.bea.gov/

Website of the Bureau of
Economic Analysis, U.S.
Department of Commerce,
provides data related to the
U.S. balance of payments.

deficit either by borrowing from foreigners or by drawing down on its previously accumulated foreign wealth, a current account deficit represents a reduction in the country's net foreign wealth. On the other hand, a country with a current account surplus acquires IOUs from foreigners, thereby increasing its net foreign wealth.

The current account is divided into four finer categories: merchandise trade, services, factor income, and unilateral transfers. **Merchandise trade** represents exports and imports of tangible goods, such as oil, wheat, clothes, automobiles, computers, and so on. As Exhibit 3.1 shows, U.S. merchandise exports were $1,026.9 billion in 2006 while imports were $1,861.4 billion. The United States thus had a deficit on the **trade balance** or a trade deficit. The trade balance represents the net merchandise export. As is well known, the United States has experienced persistent trade deficits since the early 1980s, whereas such key trading partners as China, Japan, and Germany have generally realized trade surpluses. This continuous trade imbalance between the United States and her key trading partners set the stage for the relative decline of the dollar observed since 2001.

Services, the second category of the current account, include payments and receipts for legal, consulting, and engineering services, royalties for patents and intellectual properties, insurance premiums, shipping fees, and tourist expenditures. These trades in services are sometimes called **invisible trade**. In 2006, U.S. service exports were $418.9 billion and imports were $342.8 billion, realizing a surplus of $76.1 billion. Clearly, the U.S. performed better in services than in merchandise trade.

Factor income, the third category of the current account, consists largely of payments and receipts of interest, dividends, and other income on foreign investments that were previously made. If U.S. investors receive interest on their holdings of foreign bonds, for instance, it will be recorded as a credit in the balance of payments. On the other hand, interest payments by U.S. borrowers to foreign creditors will be recorded as debits. In 2006, U.S. residents paid out $613.8 billion to foreigners as factor income and received $650.5 billion, realizing a $36.7 billion surplus. Considering, however, that the United States has heavily borrowed from foreigners in recent years, U.S. payments of interest and dividends to foreigners are likely to rise sharply. This can increase the U.S. current account deficit in the future, *ceteris paribus*.

Unilateral transfers, the fourth category of the current account, involve "unrequited" payments. Examples include foreign aid, reparations, official and private grants, and gifts. Unlike other accounts in the balance of payments, unilateral transfers have only one-directional flows, without offsetting flows. In the case of merchandise trade, for example, goods flow in one direction and payments flow in the opposite direction. For the purpose of preserving the double-entry bookkeeping rule, unilateral transfers are regarded as an act of buying *goodwill* from the recipients. So a country that gives foreign aid to another country can be viewed as importing goodwill from the latter. As can be expected, the United States made a net unilateral transfer of $89.6 billion, which is the receipt of transfer payments ($24.4 billion) minus transfer payments to foreign entities ($114.0 billion).

The current account balance, especially the trade balance, tends to be sensitive to exchange rate changes. When a country's currency depreciates against the currencies of major trading partners, the country's exports tend to rise and imports fall, improving the trade balance. For example, Mexico experienced continuous deficits in its trade balance of about $4.5 billion per quarter throughout 1994. Following the depreciation of the peso in December 1994, however, Mexico's trade balance began to improve immediately, realizing a surplus of about $7 billion for the year 1995.

The effect of currency depreciation on a country's trade balance can be more complicated than the case described above. Indeed, following a depreciation, the trade balance may at first deteriorate for a while. Eventually, however, the trade balance will tend to improve over time. This particular reaction pattern of the trade balance to a depreciation is referred to as the **J-curve effect**, which is illustrated in Exhibit 3.2.

EXHIBIT 3.2

A Currency
Depreciation and the
Time-Path of the Trade
Balance: The J-Curve
Effect

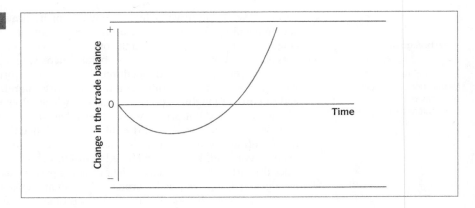

The curve shows the initial deterioration and the eventual improvement of the trade balance following a depreciation. The J-curve effect received wide attention when the British trade balance worsened after a devaluation of the pound in 1967. Sebastian Edwards (1989) examined various cases of devaluations carried out by developing countries in the 1960s through 1980s, and confirmed the existence of the J-curve effect in about 40 percent of the cases. (See the References and Suggested Readings at the end of this chapter for more information about this study.)

A depreciation will begin to improve the trade balance immediately if imports and exports are *responsive* to the exchange rate changes. On the other hand, if imports and exports are inelastic, the trade balance will worsen following a depreciation. Following a depreciation of the domestic currency and the resultant rise in import prices, domestic residents may still continue to purchase imports because it is difficult to change their consumption habits in a short period of time. With higher import prices, the domestic country comes to spend more on imports. Even if domestic residents are willing to switch to less expensive domestic substitutes for foreign imports, it may take time for domestic producers to supply import substitutes. Likewise, foreigners' demand for domestic products, which become less expensive with a depreciation of the domestic currency, can be inelastic essentially for the same reasons. In the long run, however, both imports and exports tend to be responsive to exchange rate changes, exerting positive influences on the trade balance.

The Capital Account

The capital account balance measures the difference between U.S. sales of assets to foreigners and U.S. purchases of foreign assets. U.S. sales (or exports) of assets are recorded as credits, as they result in *capital inflow*. On the other hand, U.S. purchases (imports) of foreign assets are recorded as debits, as they lead to *capital outflow*. Unlike trades in goods and services, trades in financial assets affect future payments and receipts of factor income.

Exhibit 3.1 shows that the United States had a capital account surplus of $826.9 billion in 2006, implying that capital inflow to the United States far exceeded capital outflow. Clearly, the current account deficit was offset by the capital account surplus. As previously mentioned, a country's current account deficit must be paid for either by borrowing from foreigners or by selling off past foreign investments. In the absence of the government's reserve transactions, the current account balance must be equal to the capital account balance but with the opposite sign. When nothing is excluded, a country's balance of payments must necessarily balance.

The capital account can be divided into three categories: direct investment, portfolio investment, and other investment. Direct investment occurs when the investor acquires a measure of control of the foreign business. In the U.S. balance of payments, acquisition of 10 percent or more of the voting shares of a business is considered giving a measure of control to the investor.

When Honda, a Japanese automobile manufacturer, built an assembly factory in Ohio, it was engaged in **foreign direct investment (FDI)**. Another example of direct investment was provided by Nestlé Corporation, a Swiss multinational firm, when it *acquired* Carnation, a U.S. firm. Of course, U.S. firms also are engaged in direct investments in foreign countries. For instance, Coca-Cola built bottling facilities all over the world. In recent years, many U.S. corporations moved their production facilities to Mexico and China, in part, to take advantage of lower costs of production. Generally speaking, foreign direct investments take place as firms attempt to take advantage of various market imperfections, such as underpriced labor services and protected markets. In 2006, U.S. direct investment overseas was $235.4 billion, whereas foreign direct investment in the United States was $180.6 billion.

Firms undertake foreign direct investments when the expected returns from foreign investments exceed the cost of capital, allowing for foreign exchange and political risks. The expected returns from foreign projects can be higher than those from domestic projects because of lower wage rates and material costs, subsidized financing, preferential tax treatment, exclusive access to local markets, and the like. The volume and direction of FDI can also be sensitive to exchange rate changes. For instance, Japanese FDI in the United States soared in the latter half of the 1980s, partly because of the sharp appreciation of the yen against the dollar. With a stronger yen, Japanese firms could better afford to acquire U.S. assets that became less expensive in terms of the yen. The same exchange rate movement discouraged U.S. firms from making FDI in Japan because Japanese assets became more expensive in terms of the dollar.

Portfolio investment, the second category of the capital account, mostly represents sales and purchases of foreign financial assets such as stocks and bonds that do not involve a transfer of control. International portfolio investments have boomed in recent years, partly due to the general relaxation of capital controls and regulations in many countries, and partly due to investors' desire to diversify risk globally. Portfolio investment comprises equity securities and debt securities. Equity securities include corporate shares, whereas debt securities include (1) bonds and notes, (2) money market instruments, and (3) financial derivatives like options. Exhibit 3.1 shows that in 2006, foreigners invested $1,017.4 billion in U.S. financial securities whereas Americans invested $426.1 billion in foreign securities, realizing a major surplus, $591.3 billion, for the United States. Much of the surplus represents foreigners' investment in U.S. debt securities. Exhibit 3.1 shows that foreigners invested $868.9 billion in U.S. debt securities in 2006, whereas U.S. investors invested $287.6 billion in foreign debt securities.

Investors typically diversify their investment portfolios to reduce risk. Since security returns tend to have low correlations among countries, investors can reduce risk more effectively if they diversify their portfolio holdings internationally rather than purely domestically. In addition, investors may be able to benefit from higher expected returns from some foreign markets.[3]

In recent years, government controlled investment funds, known as *sovereign wealth funds* (SWFs), are playing an increasingly visible role in international investments. SWFs are mostly domiciled in Asian and Middle Eastern countries and usually are responsible for recycling foreign exchange reserves of these countries swelled by trade surpluses and oil revenues. It is noted that SWFs invested large sums of money in many western banks that were severely affected by subprime mortgage-related losses (i.e., housing loans made to borrowers with marginal creditworthiness). For example, Abu Dhabi Investment Authority invested $7.5 billion in Citigroup, which needed to replenish its capital base in the wake of subprime losses, whereas Temasek Holdings,

---

[3]Refer to Chapter 15 for a detailed discussion of international portfolio investment.

Singapore's state-owned investment company, injected $5.0 billion into Merrill Lynch, one of the largest investment banks in the United States. Although SWFs play a positive role in stabilizing the global banking system and help the balance-of-payment situations of the host countries, they are increasingly under close scrutiny due to their sheer size and the lack of transparency about the way these funds are operating.

The third category of the capital account is **other investment**, which includes transactions in currency, bank deposits, trade credits, and so forth. These investments are quite sensitive to both changes in relative interest rates between countries and the anticipated change in the exchange rate. If the interest rate rises in the United States while other variables remain constant, the United States will experience capital inflows, as investors would like to deposit or invest in the United States to take advantage of the higher interest rate. On the other hand, if a higher U.S. interest rate is more or less offset by an expected depreciation of the U.S. dollar, capital inflows to the United States will not materialize.[4] Since both interest rates and exchange rate expectations are volatile, these capital flows are highly reversible. In 2006, the United States experienced a net inflow of $290.4 billion in this category.

Statistical Discrepancy

Exhibit 3.1 shows that there was a statistical discrepancy of −$18.0 billion in 2006, representing omitted and misrecorded transactions. Recordings of payments and receipts arising from international transactions are done at different times and places, possibly using different methods. As a result, these recordings, upon which the balance-of-payments statistics are constructed, are bound to be imperfect. While merchandise trade can be recorded with a certain degree of accuracy at the customs houses, provisions of invisible services like consulting can escape detection. Cross-border financial transactions, a bulk of which might have been conducted electronically, are far more difficult to keep track of. For this reason, the balance of payments always presents a "balancing" debit or credit as a statistical discrepancy.[5] It is interesting to note that the sum of the balance on capital account and the statistical discrepancy is very close to the balance of current account in magnitude, −$811.3 billion. This suggests that financial transactions may be mainly responsible for the discrepancy.

When we compute the *cumulative* balance of payments including the current account, capital account, and the statistical discrepancies, we obtain the so-called **overall balance** or **official settlement balance**. All the transactions comprising the overall balance take place *autonomously* for their own sake.[6] The overall balance is significant because it indicates a country's international payment gap that must be *accommodated* with the government's official reserve transactions.

It is also indicative of the pressure that a country's currency faces for depreciation or appreciation. If, for example, a country continuously realizes deficits on the overall balance, the country will eventually run out of reserve holdings and its currency may have to depreciate against foreign currencies. In 2006, the United States had a $2.4 billion deficit on the overall balance. This means that the U.S. had to make a net payment equal to that amount to the rest of the world. If the United States had realized a surplus on the overall balance, the U.S. would have received a net payment from the rest of the world.

---

[4]We will discuss the relationship between the relative interest rates and the expected exchange rate change in Chapter 6.

[5]Readers might wonder how to compute the statistical discrepancies in the balance of payments. Statistical discrepancies, which represent errors and omissions, by definition, cannot be known. Since, however, the balance of payments must balance to zero when every item is included, one can determine the statistical discrepancies in the "residual" manner.

[6]Autonomous transactions refer to those transactions that occur without regard to the goal of achieving the balance-of-payments equilibrium.

Official Reserve Account

When a country must make a net payment to foreigners because of a balance-of-payments deficit, the central bank of the country (the Federal Reserve System in the United States) should either run down its **official reserve assets**, such as gold, foreign exchanges, and SDRs, or borrow anew from foreign central banks. On the other hand, if a country has a balance-of-payments surplus, its central bank will either retire some of its foreign debts or acquire additional reserve assets from foreigners. Exhibit 3.1 shows that to take care of a $2.4 billion balance-of-payment deficit, the U.S. decreased its external reserve holdings by the same amount. When the U.S. decreases its reserve holdings by either liquidating its reserve holdings or borrowing anew, it will receive funds, which will be recorded under credits.

The official reserve account includes transactions undertaken by the authorities to finance the overall balance and intervene in foreign exchange markets. When the United States and foreign governments wish to support the value of the dollar in the foreign exchange markets, they sell foreign exchanges, SDRs, or gold to "buy" dollars. These transactions, which give rise to the demand for dollars, will be recorded as a positive entry under official reserves. On the other hand, if governments would like to see a weaker dollar, they "sell" dollars and buy gold, foreign exchanges, and so forth. These transactions, which give rise to the supply of dollars, will be recorded as a negative entry under official reserves. The more actively governments intervene in the foreign exchange markets, the greater the official reserve entry.

Until the advent of the Bretton Woods System in 1945, gold was the predominant international reserve asset. After 1945, however, international reserve assets comprise:

1. Gold.
2. Foreign exchanges.
3. Special drawing rights (SDRs).
4. Reserve positions in the International Monetary Fund (IMF).

As can be seen from Exhibit 3.3, the relative importance of gold as an international means of payment has steadily declined, whereas the importance of foreign exchanges has grown substantially. As of 2007, foreign exchanges account for about 96 percent of the total reserve assets held by IMF member countries, with gold accounting for less than 2 percent of the total reserves. Similar to gold, the relative importance of SDRs and reserve positions in the IMF have steadily declined.

As can be seen from Exhibit 3.4, the U.S. dollar's share in the world's foreign exchange reserves was 50.9 percent in 1991, followed by the German mark (15.7 percent), ECU (10.0 percent), Japanese yen (8.7 percent), British pound (3.4 percent), French franc (2.8 percent), Swiss franc (1.2 percent), and Dutch guilder (1.1 percent). The "predecessor" currencies of the euro, including the German mark, French franc, Dutch guilder, and ECU, collectively received a substantial weight, about 30 percent, in the world's foreign exchange reserves. For comparison, in 1997, the world's reserves comprised the U.S. dollar (59.1 percent), German mark (13.7 percent), Japanese yen (5.1 percent), British pound (3.3 percent), French franc (1.5 percent), ECU (5.0 percent), Swiss franc (0.5 percent), Dutch guilder (0.5 percent), and miscellaneous currencies (11.3 percent). In other words, the U.S. dollar's share has increased substantially throughout the 1990s at the expense of other currencies. This change can be attributed to a strong performance of the dollar in the 1990s and the uncertainty associated with the introduction of the new currency, that is, the euro. In 2006, the world reserves comprised the U.S. dollar (64.7 percent), euro (25.8 percent), Japanese yen (3.2 percent), British pound (4.4 percent), Swiss franc (0.2 percent), and miscellaneous currencies (1.7 percent). The dollar's dominant position in the world's reserve holdings may decline to a certain extent as the euro becomes a "known quantity" and its external value becomes more stable. In fact, the euro's share has increased from 13.5 percent in 1999 to 25.8 percent in 2006.

EXHIBIT 3.3

Composition of Total Official Reserves
(in Percent)

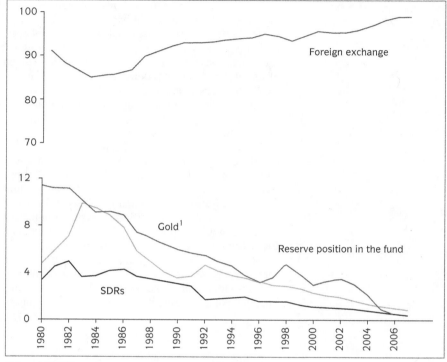

[1] Values at SDR 35 per ounce.

Source: IMF, *International Financial Statistics Yearbook,* 1995, 2007; *International Financial Statistics* November 2007.

In addition to the emergence of the euro as a credible reserve currency, continued U.S. trade deficits and foreigners' desire to diversify their currency holdings away from U.S. dollars could further diminish the position of the U.S. dollar as the dominant reserve currency. As pointed out by the International Finance in Practice box, "How One Word Haunts Dollar," the value of the U.S. dollar would also be very much affected by the currency diversification decisions of Asian central banks. These banks collectively hold an enormous amount of foreign currency reserves, mostly in dollars, arising from trade surpluses. Asian central banks also purchase U.S. dollars in foreign exchange markets in order to keep their local currencies from appreciating against the dollar.

EXHIBIT 3.4

Currency Composition of the World's Foreign Exchange Reserves
(Percent of Total)

Currency	1987	1989	1991	1993	1995	1997	1999	2001	2003	2006
U.S. dollar	56.0	51.9	50.9	56.2	53.4	59.1	64.9	66.9	63.8	64.7
Japanese yen	7.0	7.3	8.7	8.0	6.7	5.1	5.4	5.5	4.8	3.2
Pound sterling	2.2	2.6	3.4	3.1	2.8	3.3	3.6	4.0	4.4	4.4
Swiss franc	1.8	1.4	1.2	1.2	0.5	0.5	0.4	0.5	0.4	0.2
Euro	—	—	—	—	—	—	13.5	16.7	19.7	25.8
Deutsche mark	13.4	18.0	15.7	14.1	14.7	13.7	—	—	—	—
French franc	0.8	1.4	2.8	2.2	2.4	1.5	—	—	—	—
Netherlands guilder	1.2	1.1	1.1	0.6	0.5	0.5	—	—	—	—
ECU	14.2	10.5	10.0	8.3	6.8	5.0	—	—	—	—
Other currencies	3.4	5.7	6.2	6.2	12.1	11.3	12.1	6.4	6.8	1.7

Source: IMF, *Annual Report of the Executive Board,* 1996, 2007.

The Balance-of-Payments Identity

When the balance-of-payments accounts are recorded correctly, the combined balance of the current account, the capital account, and the reserves account must be zero, that is,

$$BCA + BKA + BRA = 0 \qquad (3.1)$$

where:

BCA = balance on the current account
BKA = balance on the capital account
BRA = balance on the reserves account

The balance on the reserves account, BRA, represents the change in the official reserves.

Equation 3.1 is the **balance-of-payments identity (BOPI)** that must necessarily hold. The BOPI equation indicates that a country can run a balance-of-payments surplus or deficit by increasing or decreasing its official reserves. Under the fixed exchange rate regime, countries maintain official reserves that allow them to have balance-of-payments disequilibrium, that is, BCA + BKA is nonzero, without adjusting the exchange rate. Under the fixed exchange rate regime, the combined balance on the current and capital accounts will be equal in size, but opposite in sign, to the change in the official reserves:

$$BCA + BKA = -BRA \qquad (3.2)$$

For example, if a country runs a deficit on the overall balance, that is, BCA + BKA is negative, the central bank of the country can supply foreign exchanges out of its reserve holdings. But if the deficit persists, the central bank will eventually run out of its reserves, and the country may be forced to devalue its currency. This is roughly what happened to the Mexican peso in December 1994.

Under the *pure* flexible exchange rate regime, central banks will not intervene in the foreign exchange markets. In fact, central banks do not need to maintain official reserves. Under this regime, the overall balance thus must necessarily balance, that is,

$$BCA = -BKA \qquad (3.3)$$

In other words, a current account surplus or deficit must be matched by a capital account deficit or surplus, and vice versa. In a *dirty* floating exchange rate system under which the central banks discreetly buy and sell foreign exchanges, Equation 3.3 will not hold tightly.

Being an identity, Equation 3.3 does not imply a causality by itself. A current account deficit (surplus) may cause a capital account surplus (deficit), or the opposite may hold. It has often been suggested that the persistent U.S. current account deficits made it necessary for the United States to run matching capital account surpluses, implying that the former *causes* the latter. One can argue, with equal justification, that the persistent U.S. capital account surpluses, which may have been caused by high U.S. interest rates, have caused the persistent current account deficits by strengthening the value of the dollar. The issue can be settled only by careful empirical studies.

Balance-of-Payments Trends in Major Countries

Considering the significant attention that balance-of-payments data receive in the news media, it is useful to closely examine balance-of-payments trends in some of the major countries. Exhibit 3.5 provides the balance on the current account (BCA) as well as the balance on the capital account (BKA) for each of the five key countries, China, Japan, Germany, the United Kingdom, and the United States, during the period 1982–2006.

Exhibit 3.5 shows first that the United States has experienced continuous deficits on the current account since 1982 and continuous surpluses on the capital account. Clearly, the magnitude of U.S. current account deficits is far greater than any that

INTERNATIONAL FINANCE IN PRACTICE

How One Word Haunts Dollar

A new bogeyman is haunting the dollar and U.S. fixed-income markets. It goes by the innocuous name of "central bank reserve diversification."

Three weeks ago, the South Korean central bank told the country's Parliament it intended to diversify its foreign-exchange reserves. Before Korea, it was Russia. Early last week, it was China, which said it always had a policy to diversify reserves. Last Thursday, it was the Japanese prime minister's turn, with Junichiro Koizumi telling a parliamentary committee that, in general, Japan needs to consider diversifying its foreign-exchange reserves. A day later, the governor of the Reserve Bank of India said diversification was being discussed within his central bank.

Given that the vast majority of these foreign-exchange reserves are held in dollars, that in effect is a slight on the dollar.

"Diversification is not a word you want to hear if you hold dollars," says Bob Prince, co-chief investment officer at Bridgewater Associates. "Since most central banks hold almost all of their reserves in U.S. dollars, diversification always means 'sell dollars and buy euros and yen.'"

Most central banks that talked of diversification also have said officially that they aren't selling dollars. Still, it is the possibility that the central banks might in the future that has spooked investors almost as much as if there were irrefutable evidence that they actually had. In the past month, the dollar has fallen nearly 3 percent against the euro and retreated 1.4 percent against the

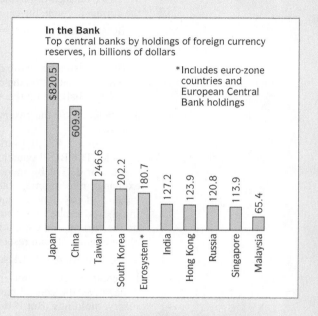

In the Bank
Top central banks by holdings of foreign currency reserves, in billions of dollars

*Includes euro-zone countries and European Central Bank holdings

Japan	$820.5
China	609.9
Taiwan	246.6
South Korea	202.2
Eurosystem*	180.7
India	127.2
Hong Kong	123.9
Russia	120.8
Singapore	113.9
Malaysia	65.4

yen. In New York yesterday afternoon, the euro stood at $1.3420, while the dollar was at 104.16 yen.

Note: Figures for China, Eurosystem, Russia and Malaysia are as of Dec. 31, 2004; other countries are as of Feb. 28, 2005.

Sources: The Bank of Tokyo—Mitsubishi, Bloomberg.

other countries ever experienced during the 25-year sample period. In 2006, the U.S. current account deficit reached $812 billion. The U.S. balance-of-payments trend is illustrated in Exhibit 3.6. The exhibit shows that the U.S. current account deficit has increased sharply since 1998. This situation has led some politicians and commentators to lament that Americans are living far beyond their means. As a matter of fact, the net international investment position of the United States turned negative in 1987 for the first time in decades and continued to deteriorate. The overseas debt burden of the United States—the difference between the value of foreign-owned assets in the United States and the value of U.S.-owned assets abroad—reached about $2,540 billion at the end of 2006, when valued by the replacement cost of the investments made abroad and at home. As recently as 1986, the United States was considered a net creditor nation, with about $35 billion more in assets overseas than foreigners owned in the United States. The International Finance in Practice box "The Dollar and the Deficit" addresses the issues associated with the U.S. trade deficit.

Second, Exhibit 3.5 reveals that Japan has had an unbroken string of current account surpluses since 1982 despite the fact that the value of the yen rose steadily until the mid-1990s. As can be expected, during this period Japan realized continuous capital account deficits; Japan invested heavily in foreign stocks and bonds, businesses, real estates, art objects, and the like to recycle its huge, persistent current account surpluses. Consequently, Japan emerged as the world's largest creditor nation, whereas the United States became the largest debtor nation. It is noted that Japan has a capital

Measured by reserves, the eight biggest Asian central banks—Japan, China, Taiwan, South Korea, India, Hong Kong, Singapore and Malaysia—combined hold roughly $2.3 trillion in foreign currency, the overwhelming amount in dollars. These reserves for the most part are the product of accumulated trade surpluses, foreign direct investment, funds held for emergency purposes and central-bank dollar purchases through market intervention.

Rather than just hoarding piles of cash, the central banks typically use their dollars to buy dollar-denominated short-term U.S. government debt, which has been a big factor in keeping Treasurys prices high and yields low.

Mr. Prince figures that if central banks stopped purchasing dollars "cold turkey," U.S. bond yields would have to rise about 1.5 percentage points from about 4.5 percent now and the dollar would have to decline roughly 30 percent to attract sufficient private-investor capital to offset lost central-bank purchases.

Despite the rhetoric from central bankers, there is much debate over whether and to what degree central banks really are diversifying away from the dollar. Most don't reveal the composition of their reserves, and data collected by the U.S. Treasury and most international organizations tend to be incomplete.

For instance, Japan's Treasury holdings declined in four out of five months through January, according to U.S. Treasury International Capital (TIC) data—a sign to some that Japan's central bank is starting to diversify its currency exposure. Yet some note that TIC data fail to capture money held by central banks in bank accounts and some purchases of U.S. securities, such as those bought from a foreign entity outside the U.S.

In fact, many currency strategists believe that, so far, diversification talk is more bark than bite. "There is little reliable evidence of any notable diversification out of the dollar by Asian central banks," says Derek Halpenny, a senior currency economist at Bank of Tokyo-Mitsubishi.

Even so, they acknowledge that the motives to diversify are growing. Even after Korean officials last month insisted they had no plans to sell dollars, they confirmed that the central bank intends to invest in "higher yielding" securities, including nongovernment debt.

There also are signs that central banks are looking at other investments, even dollar-denominated, other than Treasurys. Chinese official institutions were net buyers of $12 billion of corporate bonds last year, accounting for 26 percent of China's net purchases of U.S. securities, according to Treasury data. By contrast, corporate bonds in each of the previous three years amounted to only 7 percent to 13 percent of the country's new investments in the U.S. These purchases appear to have come at the expense of safer, but lower-yielding, U.S. Treasurys and federal-agency debt.

Others note, however, that big Asian central banks are unlikely to aggressively begin dumping their dollar holdings, if only because they would be shooting themselves in the foot. The value of their U.S. investments would plummet along with the dollar; they would risk damaging demand in their main export market, the U.S.; and they might prompt a political backlash, says Mark Cliffe, chief economist at ING Financial Markets.

Source: *The Wall Street Journal,* March 17, 2005, p. C16. Reprinted with permission.

account surplus in 2003 and 2004, reflecting increased foreign investments in Japanese securities and businesses. The persistent current account disequilibrium has been a major source of friction between Japan and its key trading partners, especially the United States. In fact, Japan has often been criticized for pursuing **mercantilism** to ensure continuous trade surpluses.[7]

Third, like the United States, the United Kingdom recently experienced continuous current account deficits, coupled with capital account surpluses. The magnitude, however, is far less than that of the United States. Germany, on the other hand, traditionally had current account surpluses. Since 1991, however, Germany has been experiencing current account deficits. This is largely due to German reunification and the resultant need to absorb more output domestically to rebuild the East German region. This has left less output available for exports. Since 2001, however, Germany starts to realize current account surpluses and capital account deficits, returning to the earlier pattern.

Fourth, like Japan, China tends to have a balance-of-payment surplus on the current account. Unlike Japan, however, China tends to realize a surplus on the capital account as

www.ecb.int/stats

This website provides balance-of-payment data on the euro-12 countries.

---

[7]Mercantilism, which originated in Europe during the period of absolute monarchies, holds that precious metals like gold and silver are the key components of national wealth, and that a continuing trade surplus should be a major policy goal as it ensures a continuing inflow of precious metals and thus continuous increases in national wealth. Mercantilists, therefore, abhor trade deficits and argue for imposing various restrictions on imports. Mercantilist ideas were criticized by such British thinkers as David Hume and Adam Smith. Both argued that the main source of wealth of a country is its productive capacity, not precious metals.

INTERNATIONAL FINANCE IN PRACTICE

The Dollar and the Deficit

The dollar is looking vulnerable. It is propped up not by the strength of America's exports, but by vast imports of capital. America, a country already rich in capital, has to borrow from abroad almost $2 billion net every working day to cover a current-account deficit forecast to reach almost $500 billion this year.

To most economists, this deficit represents an unsustainable drain on world savings. If the capital inflows were to dry up, some reckon that the dollar could lose a quarter of its value. Only Paul O'Neill, America's treasury secretary, appears unruffled. The current-account deficit, he declares, is a "meaningless concept," which he talks about only because others insist on doing so.

The dollar is not just a matter for America, because the dollar is not just America's currency. Over half of all dollar bills in circulation are held outside American's borders, and almost half of America's Treasury bonds are held as reserves by foreign central banks. The euro cannot yet rival this global reach. International financiers borrow and lend in dollars, and international traders use dollars, even if Americans are at neither end of the deal. No asset since gold has enjoyed such widespread acceptance as a medium of exchange and store of value. In fact, some economists, such as Paul Davidson of the University of Tennessee and Ronald McKinnon of Stanford University, take the argument

a step further (see references at end). They argue that the world is on a de facto dollar standard, akin to the 19th-century gold standard.

For roughly a century up to 1914, the world's main currencies were pegged to gold. You could buy an ounce for about four pounds or twenty dollars. The contemporary "dollar standard" is a looser affair. In principle, the world's currencies float in value against each other, but in reality few float freely. Countries fear losing competitiveness on world markets if their currency rises too much against the greenback; they fear inflation if it falls too far. As long as American prices remain stable, the dollar therefore provides an anchor for world currencies and prices, ensuring that they do not become completely unmoored.

In the days of the gold standard, the volume of money and credit in circulation was tied to the amount of gold in a country's vaults. Economies laboured under the "tyranny" of the gold regime, booming when gold was abundant, deflating when it was scarce. The dollar standard is a more liberal system. Central banks retain the right to expand the volume of domestic credit to keep pace with the growth of the home economy.

Eventually, however, growth in the world's economies translates into a growing demand for dollar assets. The more money central banks print, the more dollars they like to hold in reserve to underpin their currency. The more business is done across

EXHIBIT 3.5	Balances on the Current (BCA) and Capital (BKA) Accounts of Five Major Countries: 1982–2006 ($ billion)[a]								
	China		**Japan**		**Germany**		**United Kingdom**		**United States**	
Year	BCA	BKA	BCA	BKA	BCA	BKA	BCA	BKA	BCA	BKA
1982	5.7	0.6	6.9	−11.6	4.9	−2.0	8.0	−10.6	−11.6	16.6
1983	4.2	−0.1	20.8	−19.3	4.6	−6.6	5.3	−7.1	−44.2	45.4
1984	2.0	−1.9	35.0	−32.9	9.6	−9.9	1.8	−2.8	−99.0	102.1
1985	−11.4	9.0	51.1	−51.6	17.6	−15.4	3.3	−0.7	−124.5	128.3
1986	−7.0	5.0	85.9	−70.7	40.9	−35.5	−1.3	5.0	−150.5	150.2
1987	0.3	4.5	84.4	−46.3	46.4	−24.9	−8.1	28.2	−166.5	157.3
1988	−3.8	6.2	79.2	−61.7	50.4	−66.0	−29.3	33.9	−127.7	131.6
1989	−4.3	3.8	63.2	−76.3	57.0	−54.1	−36.7	28.6	−104.3	129.5
1990	12.0	0.1	44.1	−53.2	48.3	−41.1	−32.5	32.5	−94.3	96.5
1991	13.3	1.3	68.2	−76.6	−17.7	11.5	−14.3	19.0	−9.3	3.5
1992	6.4	−8.5	112.6	−112.0	−19.1	56.3	−18.4	11.7	−61.4	57.4
1993	−11.6	13.4	131.6	−104.2	−13.9	−0.3	−15.5	21.0	−90.6	91.9
1994	6.9	23.5	130.3	−105.0	−20.9	18.9	−2.3	3.8	−132.9	127.6
1995	1.6	20.9	111.0	−52.4	−22.6	29.8	−5.9	5.0	−129.2	138.9
1996	7.2	24.5	65.9	−30.7	−13.8	12.6	−3.7	3.2	−148.7	142.1
1997	29.7	6.1	94.4	−87.8	−1.2	2.6	6.8	−11.0	−166.8	167.8
1998	31.5	−6.3	120.7	−116.8	−6.4	17.6	−8.0	0.2	−217.4	151.6
1999	21.1	5.2	106.9	−31.1	−18.0	−40.5	−31.9	31.0	−324.4	367.9
2000	20.5	2.0	116.9	−75.5	−18.7	13.2	−28.8	26.2	−444.7	443.6
2001	17.4	34.8	87.8	−51.0	1.7	−24.1	−32.1	31.5	−385.7	419.9
2002	35.4	32.3	112.4	−66.7	43.4	−70.4	−26.2	17.3	−473.9	572.7
2003	45.9	52.7	136.2	67.9	54.9	−79.3	−30.5	24.8	−530.7	541.2
2004	68.7	110.7	172.1	22.5	120.3	−146.9	−35.2	10.4	−640.2	553.9
2005	160.8	58.9	165.8	−122.7	131.8	−151.2	−55.0	73.8	−754.9	763.3
2006	249.9	6.0	170.5	−102.3	150.8	−179.8	−77.6	49.0	−811.5	830.8

[a]The balance on the capital account (BKA) includes statistical discrepancies.

Source: IMF, *International Financial Statistics Yearbook,* various issues.

borders, the more dollars traders need to cover their transactions. If the greenback is the new gold, Alan Greenspan, the Federal Reserve chairman, is the world's alchemist, responsible for concocting enough liquidity to keep world trade bubbling along nicely.

But America can play this role only if it is happy to allow foreigners to build up a huge mass of claims on its assets—and if foreigners are happy to go along. Some economists watch with consternation as the rest of the world's claims on America outstrip America's claims on the rest of the world. As they point out, even a dollar bill is an American liability, a promise of ultimate payment by the US Treasury. Can America keep making these promises to foreigners, without eventually emptying them of value?

According to Mr. Davidson, the world cannot risk America stopping. America's external deficit means an extra $500 billion is going into circulation in the world economy each year. If America reined in its current account, international commerce would suffer a liquidity crunch, as it did periodically under the gold standard. Hence America's deficit is neither a "meaningless concept" nor a lamentable drain on world savings. It is an indispensable fount of liquidity for world trade.

Spigot by Nature

But is the deficit sustainable? Many of America's creditors, Mr. McKinnon argues, have a stake in preserving the dollar standard, whatever the euro's potential charms. In particular, a large share of America's more liquid assets are held by foreign central banks, particularly in Asia, which dare not offload them for fear of undermining the competitiveness of their own currencies. "Willy nilly," Mr. McKinnon says, "foreign governments cannot avoid being important creditors of the United States." China, for one, added $60 billion to its reserves in the year to June by ploughing most of its trade surplus with America back into American assets.

This is not the first time America's external deficits have raised alarm. In 1966, as America's post-war trade surpluses began to dwindle, *The Economist* ran an article entitled "The dollar and world liquidity: a minority view." According to this view, the build-up of dollar claims by foreigners was not a "deficit" in need of "correction." Rather, the American capital market was acting like a global financial intermediary, providing essential liquidity to foreign governments and enterprises. In their own ways, Mr. Davidson and Mr. McKinnon echo this minority view today. A "correction" of America's current deficit, they say, would create more problems than it would solve. Whether the world's holders of dollars will always agree remains to be seen.

"Financial Markets, Money and the Real World" by Paul Davidson. Edward Elgar 2002.

"The International Dollar Standard and Sustainability of the U.S. Current Account Deficit" by Ronald McKinnon 2001. Available on www.stanford.edu/~mckinnon/papers.htm

Source: *The Economist*, September 14, 2002, p. 74. Reprinted with permission.

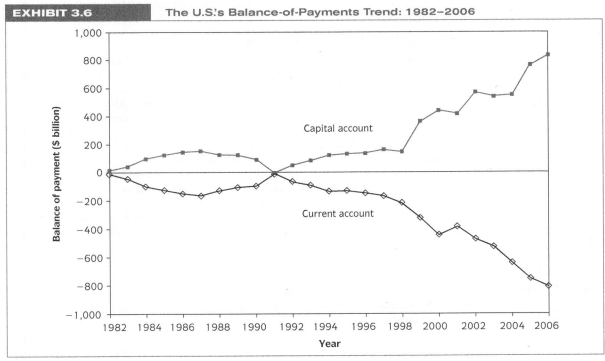

EXHIBIT 3.6   The U.S.'s Balance-of-Payments Trend: 1982–2006

Source: IMF, International Financial Statistics Yearbook, various issues.

EXHIBIT 3.7

Top U.S. Trading Partners, 2007 (in billions of dollars)

Rank	Country	Imports	Exports	Trade Balance	Total Trade
1	Canada	313.1	248.9	−64.2	562.0
2	China	321.5	65.2	−256.3	386.7
3	Mexico	210.8	136.5	−74.3	347.3
4	Japan	145.5	62.7	−82.8	208.1
5	Germany	94.4	49.7	−44.7	144.0
6	United Kingdom	56.9	50.3	−6.6	107.2
7	Korea	47.6	34.7	−12.9	82.3
8	France	41.6	27.4	−14.2	69.0
9	Taiwan	38.3	26.4	−11.9	64.7
10	Netherlands	18.4	33.0	14.6	51.4
11	Brazil	25.6	24.6	−1.0	50.3
12	Venezuela	39.9	10.2	−29.7	50.1
13	Italy	35.0	14.1	−20.9	49.2
14	Saudi Arabia	35.6	10.4	−25.2	46.0
15	Singapore	18.4	26.3	7.9	44.7

Source: Census Bureau.

well. In 2006, for instance, China had a $249.9 billion surplus on the current account and, at the same time, a $6.0 billion surplus on the capital account. This implies that China's official reserve holdings must have gone up for the year. In fact, China's official reserves have increased sharply in recent years, reaching about $1.5 trillion as of December 2007.

While perennial balance-of-payments deficits or surpluses can be a problem, each country need not achieve balance-of-payments equilibrium every year. Suppose a country is currently experiencing a trade deficit because of the import demand for capital goods that are necessary for economic development projects. In this case, the trade deficit can be self-correcting in the long run because once the projects are completed, the country may be able to export more or import less by substituting domestic products for foreign imports. In contrast, if the trade deficit is the result of importing consumption goods, the situation will not correct by itself. Thus, what matters is the nature and causes of the disequilibrium.

Lastly, let us briefly examine which countries the United States trades with most actively. Exhibit 3.7 provides the list of top 15 trading partners of the United States in terms of merchandise imports and exports. As can be expected, the United States trades most with Canada, its northern neighbor and a member of NAFTA, importing $313.1 billion and exporting $248.9 billion in 2007. China is the second most important trading partner for the United States, importing $321.5 billion and exporting $65.2 in 2007. Clearly, imports from China far exceed exports to the former, resulting in a bilateral trade deficit of $256.3 billion for the United States in 2007. This large trade surplus for China (and deficit for the United States) is a major factor driving a gradual appreciation of Chinese renminbi (RMB) against the United States dollar in recent years. Mexico, a southern neighbor of the United States and another member of NAFTA, is the third most important trading partner of the United States, followed by Japan and Germany. It is noted that the United States had trade deficits with most of its trading partners in 2007.

SUMMARY

1. The balance of payments can be defined as the statistical record of a country's international transactions over a certain period of time presented in the form of double-entry bookkeeping.

2. In the balance of payments, any transaction resulting in a receipt from foreigners is recorded as a credit, with a positive sign, whereas any transaction resulting in a payment to foreigners is recorded as a debit, with a minus sign.

3. A country's international transactions can be grouped into three main categories: the current account, the capital account, and the official reserve account. The current account includes exports and imports of goods and services, whereas the capital account includes all purchases and sales of assets such as stocks, bonds, bank accounts, real estate, and businesses. The official reserve account covers all purchases and sales of international reserve assets, such as dollars, foreign exchanges, gold, and SDRs.

4. The current account is divided into four subcategories: merchandise trade, services, factor income, and unilateral transfers. Merchandise trade represents exports and imports of tangible goods, whereas trade in services includes payments and receipts for legal, engineering, consulting, and other performed services and tourist expenditures. Factor income consists of payments and receipts of interest, dividends, and other income on previously made foreign investments. Lastly, unilateral transfer involves unrequited payments such as gifts, foreign aid, and reparations.

5. The capital account is divided into three subcategories: direct investment, portfolio investment, and other investment. Direct investment involves acquisitions of controlling interests in foreign businesses. Portfolio investment represents investments in foreign stocks and bonds that do not involve acquisitions of control. Other investment includes bank deposits, currency investment, trade credit, and the like.

6. When we compute the cumulative balance of payments including the current account, capital account, and the statistical discrepancies, we obtain the overall balance or official settlement balance. The overall balance is indicative of a country's balance-of-payments gap that must be accommodated by official reserve transactions. If a country must make a net payment to foreigners because of a balance-of-payments deficit, the country should either run down its official reserve assets, such as gold, foreign exchanges, and SDRs, or borrow anew from foreigners.

7. A country can run a balance-of-payments surplus or deficit by increasing or decreasing its official reserves. Under the fixed exchange rate regime, the combined balance on the current and capital accounts will be equal in size, but opposite in sign, to the change in the official reserves. Under the pure flexible exchange rate regime where the central bank does not maintain any official reserves, a current account surplus or deficit must be matched by a capital account deficit or surplus.

KEY WORDS

balance of payments, *60*	invisible trade, *63*	official settlement
balance-of-payments	J-curve effect, *63*	balance, *66*
identity (BOPI), *69*	mercantilism, *71*	other investment, *66*
capital account, *62*	merchandise trade, *63*	overall balance, *66*
current account, *62*	official reserve	portfolio investment, *65*
factor income, *63*	account, *62*	services, *63*
foreign direct investment	official reserve	trade balance, *63*
(FDI), *65*	assets, *67*	unilateral transfers, *63*

QUESTIONS

1. Define *balance of payments*.

2. Why would it be useful to examine a country's balance-of-payments data?

3. The United States has experienced continuous current account deficits since the early 1980s. What do you think are the main causes for the deficits? What would be the consequences of continuous U.S. current account deficits?

4. In contrast to the United States, Japan has realized continuous current account surpluses. What could be the main causes for these surpluses? Is it desirable to have continuous current account surpluses?

5. Comment on the following statement: "Since the United States imports more than it exports, it is necessary for the United States to import capital from foreign countries to finance its current account deficits."

www.mhhe.com/er5e

6. Explain how a country can run an overall balance-of-payments deficit or surplus.

7. Explain *official reserve assets* and its major components.

8. Explain how to compute the overall balance and discuss its significance.

9. Since the early 1980s, foreign portfolio investors have purchased a significant portion of U.S. Treasury bond issues. Discuss the short-term and long-term effects of foreigners' portfolio investment on the U.S. balance of payments.

10. Describe the *balance-of-payments identity* and discuss its implications under the fixed and flexible exchange rate regimes.

11. Exhibit 3.5 indicates that in 1999, Germany had a current account deficit and at the same time a capital account deficit. Explain how this can happen.

12. Explain how each of the following transactions will be classified and recorded in the debit and credit of the U.S. balance of payments:

   a. A Japanese insurance company purchases U.S. Treasury bonds and pays out of its bank account kept in New York City.

   b. A U.S. citizen consumes a meal at a restaurant in Paris and pays with her American Express card.

   c. An Indian immigrant living in Los Angeles sends a check drawn on his LA bank account as a gift to his parents living in Bombay.

   d. A U.S. computer programmer is hired by a British company for consulting and gets paid from the U.S. bank account maintained by the British company.

13. Construct the balance-of-payment table for Japan for the year of 2006 which is comparable in format to Exhibit 3.1, and interpret the numerical data. You may consult *International Financial Statistics* published by IMF or search for useful websites for the data yourself.

PROBLEMS

1. Examine the following summary of the U.S. balance of payments for 2000 (in $ billion) and fill in the blank entries.

	Credits	Debits
Current Account		
(1) Exports	1,418.64	
(1.1) Merchandise	774.86	
(1.2) Services	290.88	
(1.3) Factor income	352.90	
(2) Imports		−1,809.18
(2.1) Merchandise		☐
(2.2) Services		−217.07
(2.3) Factor income		−367.68
(3) Unilateral transfer	10.24	−64.39
Balance on current account		☐
Capital Account		
(4) Direct investment	287.68	−152.44
(5) Portfolio investment	474.59	−124.94
(5.1) Equity securities	193.85	−99.74
(5.2) Debt securities	280.74	−25.20
(6) Other investment	262.64	−303.27
Balance on capital account	☐	
(7) Statistical discrepancies	☐	
Overall balance	0.30	
Official Reserve Account		−0.30

Source: IMF, *International Financial Statistics Yearbook, 2001.*

INTERNET EXERCISES

1. Study the website of the International Monetary Fund (IMF), www.imf.org/external, and discuss the role of IMF in dealing with balance-of-payment and currency crises.

MINI CASE

Mexico's Balance-of-Payments Problem

Recently, Mexico experienced large-scale trade deficits, depletion of foreign reserve holdings, and a major currency devaluation in December 1994, followed by the decision to freely float the peso. These events also brought about a severe recession and higher unemployment in Mexico. Since the devaluation, however, the trade balance has improved.

Investigate the Mexican experiences in detail and write a report on the subject. In the report, you may:

1. Document the trend in Mexico's key economic indicators, such as the balance of payments, the exchange rate, and foreign reserve holdings, during the period 1994.1 through 1995.12.

2. Investigate the causes of Mexico's balance-of-payments difficulties prior to the peso devaluation.

3. Discuss what policy actions might have prevented or mitigated the balance-of-payments problem and the subsequent collapse of the peso.

4. Derive lessons from the Mexican experience that may be useful for other developing countries.

In your report, you may identify and address any other relevant issues concerning Mexico's balance-of-payments problem. *International Financial Statistics* published by IMF provides basic macroeconomic data on Mexico.

REFERENCES & SUGGESTED READINGS

Edwards, Sebastian. *Real Exchange Rates, Devaluation and Adjustment: Exchange Rate Policy in Developing Countries.* Cambridge, Mass.: MIT Press, 1989.

Grabbe, Orlin. *International Financial Markets.* New York: Elsevier, 1991.

Kemp, Donald. "Balance of Payments Concepts—What Do They Really Mean?" *Federal Reserve Bank of St. Louis Review*, July 1975, pp. 14–23.

Ohmae, Kenichi. "Lies, Damned Lies and Statistics: Why the Trade Deficit Doesn't Matter in a Borderless World." *Journal of Applied Corporate World*, Winter, 1991, pp. 98–106.

Salop, Joan, and Erich Spitaller. "Why Does the Current Account Matter?" International Monetary Fund, *Staff Papers*, March 1980, pp. 101–34.

U.S. Department of Commerce. "Report of the Advisory Committee on the Presentation of the Balance of Payments Statistics." *Survey of Current Business*, June, 1991, pp. 18–25.

Yeager, Leland. *International Monetary Relations.* New York: Harper & Row, 1965.

3A The Relationship Between Balance of Payments and National Income Accounting

This section is designed to explore the mathematical relationship between balance-of-payments accounting and national income accounting and to discuss the implications of this relationship. National income (Y), or gross domestic product (GDP), is identically equal to the sum of nominal consumption (C) of goods and services, private investment expenditures (I), government expenditures (G), and the difference between exports (X) and imports (M) of goods and services:

$$\text{GDP} \equiv Y \equiv C + I + G + X - M. \tag{3A.1}$$

Private savings (S) is defined as the amount left from national income after consumption and taxes (T) are paid:

$$S \equiv Y - C - T, \text{ or} \tag{3A.2}$$

$$S \equiv C + I + G + X - M - C - T. \tag{3A.3}$$

Noting that the BCA $\equiv X - M$, equation (3A.3) can be rearranged as:

$$(S - I) + (T - G) \equiv X - M \equiv \text{BCA}. \tag{3A.4}$$

Equation (3A.4) shows that there is an intimate relationship between a country's BCA and how the country finances its domestic investment and pays for government expenditures. In equation (3A.4), $(S - I)$ is the difference between a country's savings and investment. If $(S - I)$ is negative, it implies that a country's domestic savings is insufficient to finance domestic investment. Similarly, $(T - G)$ is the difference between tax revenue and government expenditures. If $(T - G)$ is negative, it implies that tax revenue is insufficient to cover government spending and a government budget deficit exists. This deficit must be financed by the government issuing debt securities.

Equation (3A.4) also shows that when a country imports more than it exports, its BCA will be negative because through trade foreigners obtain a larger claim to domestic assets than the claim the country's citizens obtain to foreign assets. Consequently, when BCA is negative, it implies that government budget deficits and/or part of domestic investment are being financed with foreign-controlled capital. In order for a country to reduce a BCA deficit, one of the following must occur:

1. For a given level of S and I, the government budget deficit $(T - G)$ must be reduced.
2. For a given level of I and $(T - G)$, S must be increased.
3. For a given level S and $(T - G)$, I must fall.

THUNDERBIRD
THE AMERICAN GRADUATE SCHOOL
OF INTERNATIONAL MANAGEMENT

A06-97-0002

CROSSWELL INTERNATIONAL

It is August 4, 1995, and the Mathieux brothers, Doug and Geoff, were concluding a summer-long effort of developing the Brazilian market for Crosswell International (U.S.). Crosswell's president and CEO, Hector Lans, is convinced that *Precious Ultra Thin Baby Diapers* will be a big seller in Brazil. In their role as brokers for Crosswell, the Mathieuxs have been exploring a number of different distribution channels in the Brazilian market. To date, the distributor response to *Precious* diapers has been enthusiastic, particularly in light of *Precious diapers'* superior quality compared to locally manufactured alternatives. The problem, however, is the price.

Brazilians base many purchasing decisions — at least in regard to disposable diapers — on cost, not on quality. The Mathieuxs find that distributors do not believe they can compete in the market with the relatively high prices offered by Crosswell, even with higher quality diapers. After much debate over how to improve the price competitiveness of *Precious* diapers, the Mathieuxs believe they may have found a solution. Their proposal is to combine extended credit terms to local distributors with Brazil's high domestic interest rates to effectively lower the diapers' price to Brazilian consumers.

The Brazilian Diaper Market

Until the latter part of the 1980s, most Brazilians had never heard of a disposable diaper, and not surprisingly, the disposable hygiene market in Brazil was virtually non-existent. By 1995, however, the personal care market was booming. This growth was largely a result of new-found economic stability and a growing middle class. As both the middle class and educational levels about hygiene expand, the personal care market should also expand.

Disposable diapers were first introduced in Brazil in the mid-1980s by U.S.-based multinational Johnson and Johnson (J&J). As J&J promoted its new diapers, Brazilians discovered the advantages of disposable diapers and sales grew steadily in the small upper-class market segment. The diapers were initially very expensive; retailers sold them at a Brazilian currency equivalent price of $1.50 - $2.00 per diaper (depending on size). J&J increased its diaper sales and in the mid-1980s set up manufacturing operations in São Paulo.

Eventually, J&J's large profit margins attracted competitors, so that by 1990 several other players had entered the game. Between 1990 and 1995 the market expanded dramatically, with U.S.-based Procter and Gamble (P&G) and several other major new entrants now manufacturing and distributing in Brazil. The good news for Crosswell is that these diapers are still largely inferior in quality to *Precious* due to technological and capital constraints on domestic producers.

By early 1995 the Brazilian disposable diaper market was growing rapidly as the Brazilian middle class expanded and its purchasing power increased. Competition, however, quickly reduced profit margins as competitors began cutting prices. J&J's leadership position eroded as it's market share dropped from 78% in 1990 to less than 15% in 1995. In an effort to keep its remaining market share, but maintain higher prices in an effort to recover its investment in local manufacturing facilities, J&J has spent freely to promote its premium product image. Exhibit 1 provides an overview of the major players, products, and prices in the Brazilian disposable diaper market in 1995.

EXHIBIT 1 Baby Diaper Prices and Qualities in the Brazilian Market, 1995

| Company (Country) | Brand | Quality | Prices per Diaper by Size | | | No. in Package |
			Small	Medium	Large	
Bebito (ARG)	Bebito	Low	R$0.198	R$0.232	R$0.302	24 / 20 / 16
Panales Duffy (ARG)	Duffy	Low	0.204	0.230	0.312	24 / 20 / 16
Cora Products (BRZ)	Pipita Anatomica	Low	0.248	0.290	0.380	24 / 20 / 16
Pom Pom (BRZ)	Pom Pom	Low	0.244	0.289	0.415	12 / 10 / 8
Chansommes (BRZ)	Puppet	Mid	0.279	0.332	0.463	12 / 10 / 8
Julie Joy (BRZ)	Julie Joy	Mid	0.265	0.301	0.437	24 / 20 / 16
Kenko (JAP)	Monica Plus	Mid	0.273	0.340	0.469	24 / 20 / 16
Kenko (JAP)	Tippy	Mid	0.363	0.425	0.544	24 / 20 / 16
Procter & Gamble (USA)	Pampers Uni	Mid	0.261	0.317	0.429	24 / 20 / 16
Johnson & Johnson (USA)	Sempre Seca Plus	Mid to High	0.396	0.451	0.594	24 / 20 / 16
French, Italian, Israeli, Japanese and U.S. firms	Various	High	Similar to Johnson & Johnson			Varies

Source: Authors, 1995. Average exchange rate of R$0.94/US$.

The Competitors

There were four main groups of competitors in the diaper market in Brazil. The first group, comprised of foreign multinational corporations producing in Brazil included J&J, P&G, and Kenko do Brasil. These companies commanded 40% of the market. J&J had the highest quality diaper produced in Brazil and commands the highest prices. P&G was viewed as the most efficient manufacturer, producing the mid-quality *Pampers*. Kenko do Brasil, a Japanese company, entered Brazil by acquiring several local Brazilian diaper producers. The company's brands, *Monica* and *Tippy*, were popular and held a substantial portion of the market. Kenko's quality and price were similar to P&G's *Pampers*.

The second group of competitors consisted of Brazilian companies that produced in-country. These companies generally used simpler manufacturing techniques due to limited financial backing and served the lower quality, lower-price market segment. Some brands, however, such as *Puppet* and *Julie Joy,* competed in the mid-price segment. These national brands had captured a 30% share of the market by 1995.

The third group of competitors consisted of Argentinian companies with brands such as *Duffy* and *Bebito.* These large diaper producers were taking advantage of the lower import tariffs resulting from the creation of *Mercosur* (as well as favorable exchange rates) by producing in Argentina and selling into Brazil.[1] The production costs of the Argentinians were low, and in the two years prior to 1995 they had captured a 20% market share in Brazil by offering low quality, low cost diapers.

The final group of competitors includes foreign companies from countries such as France, Italy, Israel, Japan and the United States. These companies are entering the market with imports of high quality diapers (at least higher in quality than the majority in the existing Brazilian market). However, they are priced at the high end of the market with prices close to those of J&J, and have garnered only a ten percent share to date. This is the market segment which Crosswell wanted.

Prices for large-size disposable baby diapers in Brazil range from R$0.30 to R$0.60 per diaper (R$ is the symbol for the Brazilian currency, the *Real*). Argentinian companies are at the low end of the range while J&J commands the highest prices.

In spite of the entry of more and more competitors and increasing production capacity, the Brazilian market was still seen as a high-growth market with excess demand. Brazilian President Fernando Henrique Cardoso's economic recovery plan, the *Real Plan*, is drastically restructuring the Brazilian economy and, in the opinion of most, for the better.[2] Consumers have gained confidence in the economy and consumer spending is rising. If the plan continues to be a success, the middle class will continue to grow in size and income, resulting in an expanding market for disposable diapers.

Hospital Specialty Company

Hospital Specialty Company (Hospeco) was the personal care products division of The Tranzonic Companies, a Cleveland, Ohio based manufacturer and distributor of a wide variety of paper, cloth and vinyl products. Tranzonic had sales of $131 million in 1994 and was listed on the New York Stock Exchange (symbol TRNZ). Appendix A provides a brief summary of Tranzonic's financial performance in the 1990s. Tranzonic was composed of four major operating divisions, the personal care division (Hospeco), the industrial textiles

---

[1] *Mercosur* is a regional common market including Argentina, Brazil, Paraguay, and Uruguay. It was implemented on January 1, 1995. This trading agreement set common external tariffs for the four members while reducing trade barriers and import tariffs for trade within the common market.

[2] The *Real Plan*, an economic program combining a new currency with new economic stabilization measures, is described in detail in a following section.

division, the housewares division, and the industrial packaging division. Hospeco was the largest operating unit within the company, manufacturing and distributing a full line of feminine hygiene products, infant's disposable diapers, adult incontinence products, obstetrical pads, toilet seat covers, and related disposable hygiene products. Hospeco brand names included SAFE & SOFT®, EVERYDAY®, SOFT & THIN®, MAXITHINS®, PRECIOUS®, HEALTH GARDS®, FRESH GARDS®, and AT EASE®. Production facilities were located in Cleveland, Ohio; Lexington, Kentucky; and Phoenix, Arizona.[3]

Although Hospeco faced margin pressures in 1994 (brand product manufacturers had been reducing prices to draw market share from the private label sector), the firm increased its sales and earnings over the 1995 fiscal year. In response to increased competition, the parent company made significant new investments to insure cost competitive manufacturing of high quality products. The goal of Tranzonic and Hospeco, was to develop and maintain the capacity to offer customers a broad line of products that were equivalent to international brands in terms of quality and performance. Hospeco proved itself adept at leveraging strong customer relationships and introducing new product lines. For example, its adult incontinence product lines and sales continued growing with the "graying of America" and the associated expansion of the elder-care market.

Hospeco and Crosswell International

Hospeco did not begin to explore market potential outside the United States until 1994. In 1993, Hospeco's president was approached by Hector Lans, a Cuban-born Miami-based businessman, who promised big results if he was allowed to direct a new international sales subsidiary, and given the resources to pursue large untapped international markets. Mr. Lans managed to convince Hospeco's directors of the international market potential — particularly in Latin America — for their line of personal care products, and Crosswell International was born. The subsidiary was placed in Miami, Florida to focus specifically on Latin America.

By May 1995, in a little over 18 months, Hector Lans had begun developing several Latin American markets, with the glaring omission of Brazil. The lack of any real activity in the Brazilian market was largely a result of the language barrier — Brazil is primarily Portuguese-speaking — and a general lack of familiarity with the market. But Brazil offered enormous potential. Lans sought out two brothers, Doug and Geoff Mathieux, who possessed not only business experience in the Brazilian market but, just as importantly, the language skills necessary to be penetrate it (both were fluent in Spanish, French, and most importantly for Brazil, Portuguese). The Mathieux brothers agreed to act as brokers on behalf of Crosswell International in Brazil and focus on the development of the *Precious Ultra Thin Baby Diaper* product line.

---

[3] *The Tranzonic Companies, Annual Report, 1994.*

Economic Situation in Brazil

The economic situation in Brazil improved dramatically after the implementation of President Cardoso's *Real Plan* on July 1, 1994. There were two key elements of the *Real Plan*: 1) the establishment of a new currency, the *Real (R$)*, and 2) a commitment to a tight monetary policy which would, once and for all, drive inflation from the Brazilian economic and social fabric. Success to date had been promising. Inflation dropped from a pre-plan level of 50% per month to 2% per month, and was expected to stay at that rate throughout 1995. The new currency, the *Real*, was stable against the dollar and the Brazilian government was committed to maintaining its value.

Interest rates were, however, still high at 3-4% per month (not per year) for corporate deposit rates, and 8% to 10% per month for loan rates, as a result of the tight monetary policy under the *Real Plan* (see Exhibit 2). These rates were expected to remain stable for the next several months, with hope that interest rates may slowly decline over the coming one to two years as inflationary pressures subsided. A continuing influx of foreign capital was also expected to aid in this process of stabilization as inflows would hopefully buoy the Real and prevent the currency itself from depreciating and adding to inflationary pressures.

EXHIBIT 2 Brazilian Exchange & Money Rates, August 4, 1995		
Real/US$ Exchange Rates	*Bid*	*Ask*
Commercial	0.9343	0.9357
Parallel	0.9070	0.9220
Tourist	0.9040	0.9270
Deposit Interest Rates	*Loan Interest Rates*	
3.69% per month	30 days: 8.25% per month	
	60 days: 8.75% per month	
	90 days: 9.25% per month	

Source: *Brasil FaxLetter,* Gilbert o L. DiPierro, August 4, 1995, Miami , Florida.

The Brazilian trade balance enjoyed a modest monthly surplus after several months of deficits during the beginning of 1995. Thanks to a large capital account surplus, Brazil was able to increase its volume of foreign reserves to over US$45 billion.[4] Foreign investment once again began flowing into Brazil, indicating that the *Tequila Effect* was wearing off.[5]

The stock market performed quite well during the last quarter, after several difficult months following Mexico's devaluation. These strong results were thought to be indicative of the new consumer and institutional confidence in the economy. After a year of strong growth, consumer spending and retail sales have leveled. Gross domestic product (GDP) growth was expected to reach 6.4% in 1995.

With the implementation of the Real Plan on June 30, 1994, the Brazilian *Cruzeiro (Crz)* was replaced with the *Real (R$)*, with the official exchange rate changing from ap-

---

[4] *Brazil Outlook*, Number 9, September 1995, Editora Tama, Ltda., Rio de Janeiro, Brazil.

[5] The Tequila Effect refers to the spreading of negative economic impacts to all of Latin America's markets following the devaluation of the Mexican peso in December 1994. Although the devaluation was confined to Mexico alone, international investors withdrew from many Latin American markets in fear that the devaluation might spread. It took over half a year to soothe the anxieties of international investors regarding the stability of the other countries in the region.

proximately Crz2750/US$ to R$1.00/US$. Given the relatively high inflation rates experienced by Brazil after that time, the Real should have depreciated against the dollar — but it didn't. The influx of foreign investment became substantial, with benefits to the Real itself. In fact, as illustrated in Exhibit 3, the Real appreciated slightly during the first year after the plan, and remained stable through most of 1995.[6] Simultaneously, monthly deposit interest rates dropped precipitously under the Plan, stabilizing at three to four percent per month.[7] Given the apparent health of the economy, the positive trade balance, and a central bank which was adding significantly to its foreign exchange reserves, the outlook for maintaining the Real's value looked promising.

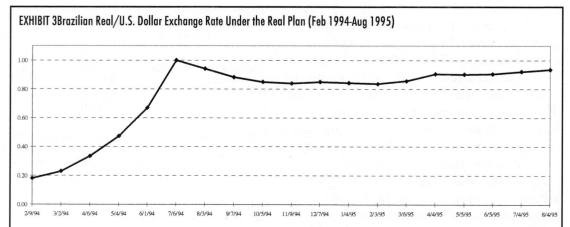

EXHIBIT 3 Brazilian Real/U.S. Dollar Exchange Rate Under the Real Plan (Feb 1994-Aug 1995)

Note: The Real replaced the Cruzeiro as the Brazilian currency on June 30, 1994. The exchange rate on that date, Crz2750/US$, is used to index the currency rate prior to June 30, resulting in the "falling value" of the Real from February to July 1994 illustrated here. For financial valuation purposes, the exchange rate prior to June 30, 1994 is not directly comparable to the rate in effect after revaluation.

Developing the Brazilian Market

When the Mathieux brothers arrived in Brazil in May 1995, they conducted an in-depth analysis of the disposable diaper market. Their primary interest was to isolate what price they believed the market could sustain for Crosswell's *Precious*. The Mathieuxs then completed a detailed import and distribution price analysis for *Precious*. Pricing was constructed in five stages (see Exhibit 4 for the detailed calculation), beginning with Crosswell's price to the Mathieuxs of $32.57 per case, and adding $1.50 per case commission for the Mathieuxs as brokers. The FOB price per case, Miami, was $34.07.[8]

---

[6] The Brazilian government had actually intervened in the currency markets to keep the Real from appreciating further and making Brazilian exports increasingly expensive and uncompetitive on world markets.

[7] Monthly deposit rates averaged between 40% and 47% for the first six months of 1994, the period just prior to the *Real Plan*.

[8] FOB, "free on board," is an international trade term in which the exporter's quoted price includes the cost of loading goods into transport vessels at a named point.

A06-97-0002

Local freight, loading, documentation and insurance expenses were incurred in the second stage, resulting in a CIF price to the distributor of $39.25 per case.[9] Although a number of larger firms were increasingly foregoing export insurance expenses — in this case 2.25% of CFR price — Doug and Geoff viewed the potential liabilities of a start-up business line such as this as too large, forcing them to incur the added expense. The price to the distributor was invoiced in U.S. dollars. Given the current spot rate of R$0.935/US$, this translated into a price of R$36.70 per case to the Brazilian distributor. The distributor would carry the currency risk, while the U.S. exporter (and broker in this case) were guaranteed their margins on the transfer price without risk of currency movements.

The third stage, the actual logistics of getting the diapers from Miami and through Brazilian customs to the local distributor, was not trivial in either cost or complexity. Given the various fees, tariffs, currency and brokerage fees, the price in Brazilian Real rose rapidly from a CIF price of R$36.70 to R$40.44 per case, an added 10%.

The Brazilian distributor's role, the fourth stage in the pricing saga, added storage costs, inventory financing expenses, and distributor's margin. The price to retailers was now R$52.27 per case. In the fifth and final stage, the retailer paid industrial and merchandise taxes (15% and 18%, respectively), and added a customary 30% markup, resulting in a final price to the consumer of R$92.21. This was a price roughly 2.5 times the price of the diaper prior to hitting the docks of the Brazilian port. Brazilian *Precious* consumers would pay R$0.480 per large, and R$0.524 per extra-large baby diaper. This placed *Precious* in the upper third of the baby diaper price range in Brazil.

The brothers then proceeded to meet with importers, distributors, local representatives of chambers of commerce, and even trade representatives of the American Embassy offices in Brazil. Several useful contacts were established in trade shows in both Rio de Janeiro and São Paulo. Initial discussions with a number of potential distributors were encouraging as a number of distributors displayed strong interest in the diaper product line. Distributors were impressed with the quality of the product, acknowledging the superiority to that of locally-manufactured brands.

The objection that the brothers ran into time and time again, however, was the price. Although all distributors were impressed by the quality, they insisted that *Precious* diapers could not effectively penetrate the Brazilian market at the proposed price (as developed in Exhibit 4). Although the Mathieuxs attempted to impress upon the distributors the changing structure of the Brazilian marketplace, and the opportunity they saw for a high-end high quality product at a premium price, distributors insisted that — at least at the time — success would only follow from a price which fell into the mid-priced segment of the diaper market. They also commented that "although the Americans saw the Real as stable, only time will convince us."

---

[9] CIF, cost, insurance, and freight, is the exporter's quoted price including the cost of packaging, freight or carriage, insurance premium, and other charges paid respecting the goods from the time of loading in the country of export to their arrival at the named port of destination or place of trans-shipment.

EXHIBIT 4 Precious Ultra-Thin Pricing

	Price / case	Rate	Applied
Cases per container		968	
Price/case to Mathieux bros (US$)	$32.57		
Commission (Mathieux)	1.50	1.50	US$ per case
FOB price per case (US$)	$34.07		
Freight, loading, & documentation	4.32	4180	$4180 per container
CFR price	$38.39		
Export insurance	0.86	2.250%	% of CFR
CIF/case to distributor (US$)	$39.25		
Exchange rate (R$/US$)	0.935	0.935	Average of bid/ask spread
CIF price/case to distributor (R$)	36.70		
Import duties (ID)	0.73	2.000%	% of CIF
Industrial product tax (IPI)	-	0.000%	% of CIF
Merchant marine renovation fee (MMRF)	1.01	25.00%	% of freight
Port storage	0.48	1.300%	% of CIF
Port handling fees	0.01	10.84	R$10.84 per container
Additional handling tax	0.10	20.000%	% of storage & handling
Indemnity for port employees	0.00	0.0407	R$0.0407 per container
Bank currency exchange fees	0.07	0.200%	% of CIF
Customs brokerage fees	0.73	2.000%	% of CIF
Tax on merc circulation services (ICMS)	-	0.000%	% of CIF+ ID+IPT+MMRF
Import license	0.05	50.00	R$50.0 per container
Local transportation	0.55	1.500%	% of CIF
Total cost to distributor (R$)	40.44		
Storage cost	0.55	1.500%	% of CIF * months
Cost of financing diaper inventory	2.57	7.000%	% of CIF * months
Distributor's margin	8.71	20.000%	% of Price + storage + cc
Price to retailer (R$)	52.27		
Industrial product tax (IPT-2)	7.84	15.000%	% of price to retailer
Tax on merc circulation services (ICMS-2)	10.82	18.000%	% of price + IPT2
Retailer costs and markup	21.28	30.000%	% of price + IPT2 + ICMS2
Price per case to consumer (R$)	92.21		

DIAPER PRICES	Bags of 8 per case	Diapers per case	Price to Consumer (R$/diaper)
Small	44	352	0.262
Medium	32	256	0.360
Large	24	192	0.480
Extra Large	22	176	0.524

Material Hospitalar, Ltd.

In June 1995 the Mathieux brothers were referred to Leonardo Sousa by the local American chamber of commerce. Leonardo Sousa was the president of Material Hospitalar, a distributor of health care products with contacts in the hospital and disposable hygiene markets, and one of the largest distributors of hospital supplies in Brazil. Mr. Sousa expressed a strong interest in distributing *Precious* after a demonstration of their superior absorbency, and wished to proceed with the development of a business plan in which he would work with the Mathieuxs in importing and distributing Hospeco's baby diaper products on behalf of Crosswell International.

Mr. Sousa believed that the time was right to enter the baby diaper market, even though competition was intense. The market was currently experiencing growth rates of 25% a year, and he was confident that *Precious* could capture one half percent of the potential baby diaper market in Brazil within a year. That represented imports of 15 containers a month with a value of almost $33,000 per container.[10] The Mathieux brothers provided Leonardo with a price list and outline of a potential representation agreement with payment and credit terms. Payment had to be made in cash in advance or with a confirmed, irrevocable documentary letter of credit with a sight draft. In return they requested financial statements, banking references, foreign commercial references, descriptions of regional sales forces, and sales forecasts. Mr. Sousa was interested in obtaining exclusive distributor rights to all of Brazil, and Crosswell was willing to grant it to the right distributor.

Negotiations between Leonardo Sousa and the Mathieux brothers progressed. Numerous meetings were held throughout the summer of 1995. The brothers visited Material Hospitalar's warehouse in Rio and met three of Leonardo's business associates. They were impressed. The only remaining issue was price. Sousa and his associates insisted that the FOB Miami price offered to Material Hospitalar was prohibitively high, and would prevent successful market penetration. Sousa was not willing to take the chance of entry failure due to the high price.

Like other distributors, Sousa explained that thrifty Brazilians would not purchase unknown, expensive diapers even if they were higher quality. He wanted Crosswell to cut its diaper prices and fund an advertising campaign to promote the *Precious* name. When the Mathieuxs approached Hector Lans about obtaining funding for promotional efforts, they were told that given Tranzonic/ Hospeco's recent financial performance, an ad campaign was out of the question. More specifically, Hector Lans had a limited budget and his superiors at Hospeco were pressuring him to show results for the expenditures related to the establishment of Crosswell. The Mathieuxs concluded that a lower price was the only way to reach an agreement with Sousa. "Once the *Precious* brand is known," he explained, "then you will be able to raise the price of the diaper. But remember, time is of the essence."

Sousa believed that Crosswell's price would have to drop by ten percent or more — the large size diaper needed to be priced at the consumer level at about R$0.43 to R$0.44 per diaper. This would place *Precious* in direct competition with the Brazilian-owned domestic producers, the *Chansommes* and *Julie Joy* brands. Sousa felt that the market shares held by these firms were particularly vulnerable given their inferior quality to that of *Precious*.

As a result, the brothers renewed negotiations with Hector Lans in Miami, explaining that a lower FOB price was necessary for successful market penetration. One suggestion made by the Mathieuxs was for Hospital Specialty to manufacture a cheaper, lower-quality

---

[10] Each container held 968 cases of diapers and each case cost $34.07 to Leonardo Sousa (968 * $34.07 = $32,980).

diaper which could more easily fit into the target price range. Although Hector agreed to a small discount — down to $32.07 per case (before commission) — he insisted that Hospeco would not change its manufacturing process for sales to Brazil. The Mathieuxs agreed to cut their commission to three percent ($1 per case). Unfortunately, these changes still only dropped the price to R$89.87 per case, when it needed — in the eyes of Leonardo Sousa — to reach R$83 per case. The Mathieuxs still needed to cut about R$7 out of the price.

Exploring Alternatives

The Mathieuxs were determined to find a solution to the impasse. They knew that they could not reduce their price further without shrinking their commission to unacceptable levels, and even that would not be enough. One potential solution for substantial gains was to find a way to reduce the financing costs of Material Hospitalar. This would enable Sousa to increase his margins and pass the savings on to the retailers.

They first looked into the Foreign Credit Insurance Association (FCIA) and the US Eximbank (Export-Import Bank). They knew that these organizations existed to encourage and facilitate exports from the United States by providing loan guarantees to help finance trade. But the brothers needed to start moving goods immediately. The conditions for entry into the personal care market in Brazil were excellent. Sales were growing and the brothers had identified an excellent potential distributor who was ready to attack the market with Hospeco's premium diapers. These organizations required time to evaluate the loan and verify the background of the companies involved. Obtaining loan guarantees from the FCIA or Eximbank would take too much time (a minimum of three months), and a mountain of paperwork. This was particularly true for a small Brazilian distributorship that had never imported from the United States. Moreover, Crosswell International was unfamiliar with the loan guarantee programs. The Mathieuxs decided that this option was only viable for the long run. Once Crosswell and Material Hospitalar had successfully established the business line, they could consider this as an option for import/export financing.

Another possibility that the Mathieux brothers considered was importing through Uruguay. The import tariffs there were about half as high as Brazilian tariffs. A distributor could import goods into Uruguay, pay the lower import tariffs, and truck the goods into Brazil. Additional tariffs at the Brazilian border would be minimal, thanks to the *Mercosur* regional trade agreement. This option offered the possibility of reduced prices in Brazil but would be very time-consuming, and would require the Mathieuxs to establish an intermediary distributor in Uruguay itself. This would involve either finding an importer or distributor in Uruguay or investing capital there to create an import/export corporation. The latter option did not fit Crosswell's strategy, while the former could take a few months of research and negotiation in Uruguay. Importing through Uruguay would also slow the flow of goods into Brazil, as trucking goods from Montevideo to Rio de Janeiro would add an additional two weeks to delivery time. To add to the list, Leonardo Sousa was adamantly against this option because he did not want to lose control of the flow of goods. In addition, some of the gains earned through lower import tariffs would be offset by the higher financing costs (due to the longer delivery time) and inland transportation costs. Finally, this option would be resented by the Brazilian government which would effectively lose tariff revenues due to the 'round-tripping' of Crosswell's goods. The proposal did not look promising.

A third alternative was suggested by Sousa himself. Brazilian regulations required all imports to be pre-approved via an import license. To obtain the license, importers had to present a pro forma invoice to the appropriate regulatory agency. It was common practice for exporters to under-invoice merchandise on pro forma invoices to Brazil, and therefore pay significantly lower import tariffs. An importer might typically pay for 50% of the purchase price in cash up front (the payment being made to a bank account somewhere outside of Brazil such as Miami). The remaining 50% would be paid with a letter of credit, upon which the tariff charges would be levied. And because the layers of tariffs in Brazil were compounded, under-invoicing resulted in substantial savings to the importer. The amount that was saved could then be passed on to the consumer in the form of lower prices. Tranzonic was a publicly traded firm, and under-invoicing for tax evasion purposes in Brazil would violate U.S.-SEC regulations. Under-invoicing was clearly not a justifiable option from either an ethical or legal standpoint.

Interest Rate Differentials

During a business lunch with the owner of an import-export firm in Rio de Janeiro, the Mathieuxs learned that foreign corporations (i.e., European automobile manufacturers and Chinese textile firms) were successfully undercutting national companies' prices by taking advantage of Brazil's high interest rates. Borrowing rates in the U.S. were substantially lower than deposit rates in Brazil, and given the stable exchange rate, this created an opportunity for uncovered interest rate arbitrage gains.

The basic strategy was premised on the ability to get extended terms from the seller (Crosswell International) and get paid for the goods quickly from the local Brazilian distributor (Leonardo Sousa). If Material Hospitalar could obtain 180-day credit terms, or a standard 180-day letter of credit from Crosswell, the firm could sell the goods into the local market for cash within 30 days of receiving the diapers at port. The cash proceeds from the resale could then be invested in the relatively "high-yielding" Real-denominated deposit rates. At the end of the following four to five months when the payment on the goods to Crosswell was due, the deposits could be closed and the profits taken to offset the cost of financing the purchase. This would reduce the R$2.57 per case financing cost of the distributor as described in the baseline analysis in Exhibit 4. Of course, this was only true if the Real/dollar exchange rate was stable over the period.

The Mathieux brothers were well aware that these interest rate differentials could not persist over the long-run. Eventually, interest rates in Brazil would fall (assuming inflation was not reignited). However, in the short run, many international firms were taking advantage of the situation to lower their effective prices and gain market share in Brazil. The Mathieux brothers returned to the U.S. intent on exploring payment methods and financing with Crosswell.

Methods of Payment

A contract between an importer and exporter specifies a number of critical transaction details, including the method of payment.[11] There are four methods by which an exporter can sell to a foreign buyer: 1) advanced payment or prepayment; 2) documentary collections; 3) letter of credit (L/C); and 4) open account. The critical differences in the methods primarily involved who assumes the commercial risk and who provides the financing, the importer or exporter.

1. **Advanced payment.** If the importer pays for the goods up front, *prepayment*, the importer assumes all of the risks of non-performance on the part of the seller. Because the buyer is paying for the goods prior to shipment, the buyer is financing the transaction. This is essentially a cash payment for goods like that of a retail sale.

2. **Documentary collection.** A documentary collection means that payment is due from the buyer upon presentation of certain documents (and explicitly not necessarily upon receipt of the actual goods). Also termed *collection of drafts*, the exporter issues an order to the importer for payment. This order, the *draft*, may require payment upon demand, a *sight draft*, or may require payment within a set number of days, a *time draft*.[12] A time draft therefore allows a delay in payment by the buyer, and is a form of financing provided by the exporter.[13]

   Another subcategory of documentary collection is whether the draft is *clean* or *documentary*. A *clean draft* is very simple and straightforward: the control of the merchandise is turned over to the buyer regardless of the importer's payment or acceptance, very similar to an open account transaction. Multinational firms shipping merchandise to their own foreign affiliates often use clean drafts to effect payment (they trust their own affiliates to make timely payment). A *documentary draft* requires that a number of other shipping documents be attached to the draft, and the buyer must either make payment (sight draft) or acceptance (time draft) in order to obtain possession of the documents needed to take possession of the goods. There is obviously a little less trust involved in a documentary draft transaction.

---

[11] The common items in a sales contract include: description of merchandise, specifying standards, grade or quality; exact quantity in units, specific weight, or volume; unit price expressed in a specified currency for payment; trade terms expressed as FOB or CIF, naming of specific ports of exit and entry, individual liabilities associated with individual costs and risks; packing; identifying markings; extent of insurance coverage and who is to provide it; shipping instructions including method of transportation and consignment, the documents required for shipping, and timing; type of payment method to be used (e.g., L/C).

[12] There are two major varieties of time drafts, the *bill of lading draft* and the *fixed maturity draft*. A *bill of lading draft* requires that payment be made a fixed number of days after the bill of lading date. The *fixed maturity draft* requires payment on a date specified in the draft.

[13] When a time draft is presented to the importer, the buyer stamps a notice of *acceptance* on its face. Once "accepted," it becomes a promise to pay a specified amount of money on a future date like a note or bond. If the draft is drawn upon and accepted by a bank, it becomes a "bankers acceptance."

3. Documentary letter of credit. A letter of credit (L/C) is a type of guarantee of payment provided by a bank upon the buyer's request. The issuing bank promises to pay the seller, the exporter, upon presentation of key documents specified in the terms of the credit. The promise to pay by the bank reduces the commercial risk to the exporter. The letter of credit may be confirmed or unconfirmed by the exporter's bank, depending on the contract between importer and exporter. A letter of credit is in many ways a documentary draft with the added safeguard of a bank's guarantee of payment. Although on the surface the cycle appears complex, the process simply involves the exchange of documents and money through intermediaries — normally commercial banks.

4. Open account. This is the form of most domestic business transactions where goods are shipped by the seller and a bill or invoice issued requesting payment within a set number of days. Credit terms associated with an open account method of payment may state a discount if paid within a set number of days and the final date on which payment is due (for example a 2% discount if paid within 10 days, with the payment due no later than 30 days, termed "2/10 net 30"). Credit terms internationally vary considerably across borders, and often reflect traditional business habits within a country-market.

The Proposal

The decision was made to use extended financing as the main selling point to bring Leonardo Sousa on board. The task facing the Mathieuxs was to be clear, yet convincing, when describing the potential benefits and associated risks of their proposed solution. Leonardo Sousa must understand that the success of the strategy was dependent on a stable Real/dollar exchange rate, and his ability to collect as quickly as possible for the diapers. Any significant depreciation of the Real against the dollar would increase the size of Material Hospitalar's obligations to Crosswell, as well as threaten the competitiveness of *Precious* diapers in the Brazilian market.

Doug and Geoff reviewed the financial cycle involved in exporting to Brazil with a 180-day letter of credit.[14] Crosswell would — at least for the first year — require a confirmed letter of credit from the Brazilian's bank in U.S. dollars. The cycle they were currently analyzing was for an order placed August 4, 1995, by Leonardo Sousa. Exhibit 5 details the steps involved if Leonardo Sousa placed the order. Unfortunately, there were no foreign currency futures or forwards available to hedge dollar-denominated accounts payable in the event that the Real did begin to depreciate.[15] The Mathieux brothers grew silent as they both wondered if their proposal would fly.

---

[14] Crosswell International could currently borrow short term in the U.S. dollar market at the following rates: 30 days - 8.40%, 60 days - 8.44%, 90 days - 8.50%, 120 days - 8.51%, 180 days - 8.60% (all rates per annum).

[15] The Chicago Mercantile Exchange was currently studying the possibility of trading a Brazilian Real/U.S. dollar futures contract, but it was as yet unavailable.

Case Questions

1. What actions would you recommend to Crosswell and to Leonardo Sousa that would enable them to hit the target of R$83.00 per case of diapers?

2. What are the benefits and risks to Mr. Sousa if he uses a U.S. dollar-denominated 180 day letter of credit to finance the import of 15 containers of *Precious Ultra Thin Baby Diapers*? What are the potential benefits and risks to Crosswell?

3. How much added profit can Mr. Sousa earn from taking advantage of the 180 day letter of credit? (Use the sequence of events and dates described in Exhibit 5. Assume the exchange rate and deposit rates of interest are stable.) Can this be used to reduce the price that Mr. Sousa charges the retailers? Would it be enough?

4. How important is the exchange rate and the exchange rate risk to this product's success in the Brazilian market? Would your answer change if the economy was experiencing hyperinflation as opposed to relative price stability? Would your answer differ if Crosswell had chosen to invoice in Brazilian Reals instead of U.S. dollars?

A06-97-0002

EXHIBIT 5   Proposed Process of Financing With the Letter of Credit

Aug 1   Importer requests a price from Crosswell

Aug 2   Crosswell responds, via fax, with an FOB price Miami of $34.07

Aug 5   Importer agrees to terms and faxes a purchase order to Crosswell

Aug 6   Crosswell faxes a *pro forma* invoice to the importer agreeing to price and terms

Aug 7   Importer makes an application to its bank for a letter of credit (L/C)

Aug 8   Importer's bank issues L/C and sends advice to Crosswell's bank in Miami that a L/C has been opened in its behalf, with instruction as to what documents are required for payment under the L/C. The L/C guarantees payment in U.S. dollars in 180 days upon presentation of specified documents. (The distributor could also request 30, 60, 90, or 120 day credit terms, depending on what is negotiated with Crosswell International at the time of the sale.)

Aug 9   Crosswell's bank confirms the L/C

Aug 12   Crosswell turns the goods over to a freight forwarder for shipment and consigns the goods to the order of the shipper. Crosswell keeps large stocks of diapers in its warehouse so that orders can be shipped immediately upon request.)

            Crosswell prefers to be paid up front rather than wait 180 days for the total amount. It is standard for the company to add any discount fee to the total amount appearing on the importer's invoice.

Aug 13   Shipping company issues the bill of lading. Crosswell issues a time draft in the name of its bank (since its bank confirmed the L/C) and presents documents to the bank. Crosswell's bank "accepts" the time draft creating a *bankers acceptance*.

            Crosswell can at this point choose to wait to be paid in 180 days, or present the 180-day letter of credit to its bank for payment now. If requesting payment now, the company receives the stated amount less a discount fee set by its bank. The discount rate is equal to the company's short-term borrowing rate in the U.S. on August 4, 1995. The rates vary according to the number of days in the terms of the letter of credit.

Aug 14   The documents are forwarded from the exporter's bank to the importer's bank

Sept 6   Importer receives the goods

Sept 10   Importer sells goods to retailer and is paid cash by the retailer. Importer deposits amount due to Crosswell in a savings account for five months.

Feb 10   Importer pays the Brazilian bank, which then pays Crosswell's bank (180 days after shipment of the goods).

Appendix A: Selected Financial Data for The Tranzonic Companies (years ended February 28/29)

	_1994_	_1993_	_1992_	_1991_	_1990_
Sales	131,182,128	119,951,373	110,717,585	107,333,543	96,705,806
Operating earnings	4,858,423	6,816,888	7,193,019	6,714,882	5,541,952
Earnings before income taxes and cum effect	4,599,265	6,785,982	7,411,281	6,953,690	5,914,428
Income taxes	1,800,000	2,572,000	2,835,000	2,635,000	1,746,000
Earnings before cumulative effect of change in acctg	2,799,265	4,213,982	4,576,281	4,318,690	4,168,428
Cum effect of change in acctg	—	—	—	—	701,500
Net earnings	2,799,265	4,213,982	4,576,281	4,318,690	4,869,928
Per share amounts:					
Earnings before cum effect	.80	1.19	1.29	1.23	1.15
Cum effect of chg in actg	—	—	—	—	.19
Net earnings per common share	.80	1.19	1.29	1.23	1.34
Cash dividends:					
Per Class A Common Share	.18	.165	.16	.16	.16
Per Class B Common Share	.34	.325	.32	.28	.28
Total assets	73,537,946	63,675,545	58,015,061	52,515,283	49,498,159
Long-term debt	9,000,000	2,900,000	195,000	195,000	1,022,770
Shareholders' equity	47,479,072	46,328,637	42,743,659	38,848,871	36,103,517
Shareholders equity per common share	13.75	13.21	12.32	11.24	10.31
Common shares outstanding	3,452,038	3,507,838	3,468,128	3,456,934	3,500,149

Fiscal year 1994 includes a $1,300,000 charge to operating earnings ($792,000 after-tax or 22 cents per share) for costs associated with restructuring the Housewares Division. Fiscal year 1990 includes the cumulative effect of a change in accounting for income taxes.

Appendix B: Consolidated Statement of Earnings (years ended February 28, 1994 and 1993, and February 29, 1992)

	1994	*1993*	*1992*
Sales	$131,182,128	119,951,373	110,717,585
Costs and expenses:			
Cost of goods sold	87,493,123	78,470,393	71,604,322
Selling, general and administrative expenses	37,530,582	34,664,092	31,920,244
Restructuring cost	1,300,000	—	—
	126,323,705	113,134,485	103,524,566
Operating earnings	4,858,423	6,816,888	7,193,019
Interest income	54,369	96,304	280,853
Interest expense	(313,527)	(127,210)	(62,591)
Earnings before income taxes	4,599,265	6,785,982	7,411,281
Income taxes	1,800,000	2,572,000	2,835,000
Net earnings	$ 2,799,265	4,213,982	4,576,281
Net earnings per common share	$ .80	1.19	1.29

THUNDERBIRD
THE AMERICAN GRADUATE SCHOOL
OF INTERNATIONAL MANAGEMENT

A06-99-0002

BRITISH COLUMBIA HYDRO

"Treasury cannot be seen as a passive activity," Bell says. "Once we isolated treasury as a separate subset of our business and set some goals for it, it helped our people view problems in a fresh way. If you think of it in terms of opportunities, it may be the biggest profit centre you have got in your company, particularly if you are capital intensive."

Larry Bell, CEO, British Columbia Hydro
Intermarket, September 1989.

British Columbia Hydroelectric and Power Authority (BC Hydro) is a Provincial Crown Corporation, a wholly owned subsidiary of the Province of British Columbia. BC Hydro is the fifth largest Canadian utility, generating, transmitting, and distributing electricity to more than one million customers in British Columbia. The fact that it is a government-owned utility does not change its need to manage treasury operations against financial risks.

BC Hydro has substantial exposure to financial risk. Larry Bell, as Chairman of BC Hydro, was determined to do something about the financial price risks—the movements of exchange rates, interest rates, and commodity prices—facing the firm. It was now March 1988, and the time for discussion had ended and the time for decisions had come.

Financial Exposures

Upon taking over as Chairman of BC Hydro in late 1987, Larry Bell started at the ground up in his analysis of the firm's financial exposures. Bell was formerly British Columbia's Deputy Minister of Finance, and therefore not a newcomer to issues in financial management. His first step was to isolate those major business and financial forces driving net income (revenues and operating costs) and the balance sheet (asset and liability component values).

BC Hydro was—at least by financial standards—relatively simple in financial structure. The firm's revenues came from power sales. Power sales were in turn divisible into residential and small business (60%), and transmission sales (40%). Residential power use was extremely stable, so that 60% of all revenues of BC Hydro were easily predictable. However, the same could not be said of transmission sales. This was power sold to large industrial users, user's who numbered only 80 at that time. The power use of these 80 industrial users was determined by their business needs, and needs were highly cyclical. BC

Hydro's sales were predominantly domestic, with only about 5% of all revenues generated from power sales to utilities across the border in the United States.

The cost structure of BC Hydro was also relatively simple—debt service. Debt service dominated operating expenses, averaging 55% of operating expenses over the mid-1980s. (Debt service rarely constitutes more than 15% of operating expenses in typical corporate financial structures.) Power generation, however, is extremely capital intensive. The requirements for capital are met primarily by debt.

In 1987 BC Hydro had approximately C\$8 billion in debt outstanding. Unfortunately, BC Hydro was a victim of its own attractiveness. It had been a direct beneficiary of the need for U.S.-based investors to diversity their exposures in the late 1970s and early 1980s. It had tapped the U.S. dollar debt markets at extremely attractive rates for the time. But now it was faced with the servicing of this U.S. dollar-denominated debt, a full-half of its total debt portfolio. Much of the U.S. dollar debt had been acquired when the U.S. dollar was weaker (approximately C\$1/US\$) and both U.S. and Canadian interest rates were higher. As shown in Exhibit 1, the appreciation of the U.S. dollar had resulted in an increase in the Canadian dollar debt equivalent of C\$750 million. Equity amounted to approximately C\$540 million. BC Hydro was highly leveraged to say the least.

Exhibit 1 Currency Composition and Exchange Rate Impacts on British Columbia Hydro's Liabilities and Net Worth		
	Initial Values	*March 1988*
Debt and Equity by Currency of Denomination	*(Canadian Dollars)*	*(Canadian Dollars)*
Debt Canadian dollar-denominated	4,000,000,000	4,000,000,000
U.S. dollar-denominated	3,250,000,000	4,000,000,000
Equity	540,000,000	540,000,000
Total liabilities and net worth	7,790,000,000	8,540,000,000
Exchange rate related gains (losses)		(750,000,000)

Source: BC Hydro and Moodys Canada. Initial values debt are Canadian dollar equivalents, regardless of original currency of denomination, on original date of issuance.

BC Hydro had followed the general principles of conservative capital structure management. It had financed long-term assets with long-term debt. The match of asset and liability maturities was quite good, but the currency of denomination was not. This currency mismatch constituted an enormous potential exposure to the financial viability of the firm.

Isolating the Issues

In early 1988 Chairman Larry Bell called in Bridgewater Associates, a Connecticut financial consulting firm, for help. Bob Prince and Ray Dalio (president) of Bridgewater, along with senior management of BC Hydro and representatives of the BC Ministry of Finance met at Whistler Mountain, British Columbia. The purpose of the retreat was to first identify the primary financial risk issues facing BC Hydro, and secondly purpose preliminary solutions. Chairman Bell encouraged an open exchange of ideas.[1]

---

[1] *Intermarket*, September 1989, p. 26.

We have to do what makes sense economically. We'll deal with the accounting and regulatory hurdles after they've been resolved. If someone wanted to point out that our legislation wouldn't allow us to trade in futures, that's fine. The legislature sits every year.

Bell felt that consideration of institutional or legal constraints would prevent the analysis from getting to the core issues. The group proceeded to isolate two basic questions that had to be addressed prior to moving forward:

1. Does BC Hydro want to eliminate all financial risk, or only manage it?

2. BC Hydro is in the business of providing power. Is it also in the business of trading or speculating in the financial markets?

Discussion was heated on these points and ended with no clear agreement initially. Ray Dalio of Bridgewater pushed the discussion by arguing that the interest rate and foreign exchange problems the firm was saddled with were the direct result of a simple basic problem: the lack of a plan.

BC Hydro hadn't thought through its financial activities strategically. They were thinking about running their business, not asset-liability management. You can't take that approach in a volatile economic environment.

The participants agreed to move on to a detailed discussion and analysis of the BC Hydro's financial exposures without resolving these first two issues.

Financial Price Risks

Financial risk management focuses on how the movement of financial prices (interest rates, exchange rates, and commodity prices) affect the value of the firm. Isolating these impacts on any individual firm requires the evaluation of how revenues and costs, both operational and financial, change with movements in these prices. Bridgewater Associates and BC Hydro's staff conducted a number of statistical studies to find what economic forces were at work in the costs and revenues of the firm.

Revenues. The results were quite clear. The 60% of power sales going to the 1.25 million small business and residential consumers was extremely stable, and was therefore insensitive to movements in interest rates, or other business cycle indicators such as unemployment or inflation. In fact residential power use was sensitive primarily to population size. The 40% of power sales to the large industrial users was, however, very cyclical. Closer analysis of the industrial users indicated that these users were sensitive to basic commodity prices (pulp, paper, chemicals mining, etc.). Statistically speaking, transmission sales were found to be heavily dependent on movements in commodity prices (positively related) and industrial production (positively related).

Costs. A closer look at the cost structure of BC Hydro also revealed a number of clear economic forces at work. Operating expenses were dominated by debt service, over 55% of the total. The remaining 45% of operating costs possessed little variable content. Although business conditions for industrial users could decline, the nature of the utility industry still required that operations continue with little change in operating expenses achievable.

Secondly, since 55% of operating expenses were debt service, costs could potentially move directly with interest rates. But BC Hydro's practice over the past decade had been to finance long-term assets with long-term debt, and long-term debt at fixed rates obviously did not move with shorter-cycle interest rate movements. Long-term interest rates were locked in. And interest rates (short-term and long-term rates) had in general been falling in both the United States and Canada since the early 1980s.

Short-term interest rates move with commodity prices. Because increases in commodity prices frequently lead to more inflation, and interest rates and bond yields must in turn move with changes in inflation, significant commodity price increases translated directly into rising interest rates.

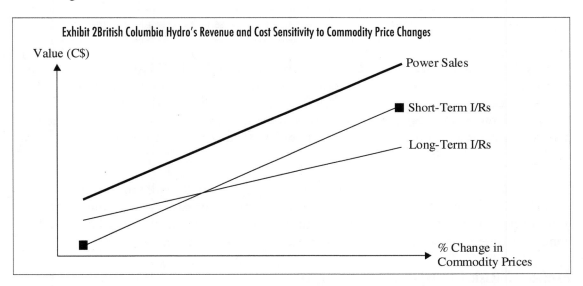

Exhibit 2 British Columbia Hydro's Revenue and Cost Sensitivity to Commodity Price Changes

It was now clear that if BC Hydro's revenues and cost structures were to be managed against underlying economic or financial forces, protection would be needed against commodity prices. Exhibit 2 illustrates how power sales moved positively with commodity price changes. At the same time, it also shows how short-term interest rates moved with commodity price changes, but long-term interest rates did not. Since BC Hydro was financed nearly exclusively with long-term debt, its present debt structure was not enjoying the fruits of these correlated movements (lower commodity prices and interest rates).

Currency Exposure. BC Hydro was facing an enormous foreign currency exposure. The fact that revenues were 95% Canadian dollar-denominated, while C$4 billion of total long-term debt was a U.S. dollar-denominated, meant that debt-service was completely exposed to currency risk. The firm earned only 5% of its revenues in U.S. dollars, and therefore had no "natural way" of obtaining the foreign currency it needed to service debt. As Exhibit 3 illustrates, although the U.S. dollar had risen versus the Canadian dollar steadily between 1980 and 1986, the Canadian dollar had regained some ground in the past two years.

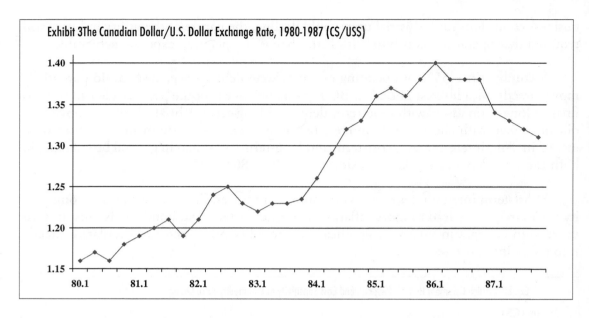

Exhibit 3 The Canadian Dollar/U.S. Dollar Exchange Rate, 1980-1987 (C$/US$)

By 1988 Larry Bell estimated that BC Hydro had realized C$350 million in foreign currency losses on its U.S. dollar debt, all of which passed through current income. The remaining exposure still approached C$400 million depending on the direction of the exchange rate movement. Something had to be done quickly. The urgency of the issue was particularly acute given that the total equity of BC Hydro amounted to only C$540 million!

The outstanding U.S. dollar debt was to be repaid in single "balloon" payments upon maturity. BC Hydro therefore had an enormous amount of cash flowing into a sinking fund for debt principal repayment. The funds were presently being reinvested in Canadian bonds, yielding short-term current rates on Canadian debt instruments.

Proposed Risk Management Strategies

Several alternative solutions were put forward for both the revenue-cost risks and the foreign currency risks. It seemed the solutions would have to be independently constructed.

The basic revenue-cost mismatch, the fact that BC Hydro held little short-term debt which would parallel the movement of revenues with commodity prices, was attacked first. The obvious solution was to increase the proportion of short-term debt. Although this approach would clearly increase the matching of commodity price cycles, it would do the opposite with regard to asset-liability maturity matching. It was argued that 60% of all power revenues were still very stable, and that the debt structure of the entire utility should not be reworked in order to pursue risk management goals. The critics of the short-term debt approach also emphasized that historical correlations might not hold up in the future. Movements of revenues and short-term interest rates correlated with commodity price movements may not hold true. The debate was heated.

The foreign currency exposure problem was at first glance, simple. The easiest and most risk-averse approach would simply be to buy U.S. dollars forward. There was little risk in that the debt-service schedule was known exactly in terms of amounts and timing, and the resulting forward cover would eliminate the currently risk.

Several senior finance ministry officials suggested a currency-interest rate swap instead. All agreed that both would work equally well. However, they were not certain that as a Crown Corporation they would be allowed to enter into a swap agreement. Late in the afternoon of the weekend retreat an additional detail was also recognized, that the signing of a forward contact (or series of forward contracts) to cover the U.S. dollar debt-service would require BC Hydro to recognize and realize (pass through the income statement) the total currency loss remaining, approximately C$500 million. This was obviously unacceptable.

A second alternative put forward by Ray Dalio of Bridgewater Associates was to move all sinking-fund capital out of Canadian dollar bonds into a similar risk category of U.S. dollar-denominated securities. This would result in the security values moving in the opposite direction of the U.S. dollar debt, thus offsetting adverse (or favorable) exchange rate changes; a natural hedge. But, this also meant that BC Hydro, a Crown Corporation, would be intentionally constructing an enormous uncovered foreign currency position. This met with considerable opposition by representatives of the British Columbia Ministry of Finance.

The participants returned from the quiet wilderness setting of Whistler Mountain to the hustle and bustle of Vancouver. It was now March 1988; Larry Bell needed a decision soon.

> *"When I came to BC Hydro, because half our costs are associated with debt servicing, there were significant opportunities that could be shaken loose in a proactive treasury operation,"* *he recalls. "As a manager, I shouldn't run this company unless I exploited all of those opportunities."*

CHAPTER

7 Futures and Options on Foreign Exchange

ON JANUARY 24, 2008 it was disclosed by Société Générale, France's second largest bank, that a 31-year-old rogue trader had taken unauthorized positions in European stock index futures contracts totaling $73 billion that resulted in trading losses of $7.2 billion when the stock market turned downward against the trader's positions. The trader was able to hide his positions for months by bypassing risk-management controls put in place by hacking into the bank's computer system designed to monitor trading. The loss forced Société Générale to raise $8 billion in emergency capital. Similarly, in 1995, another rogue trader brought down Barings PLC by losing $1.3 billion from an unhedged $27 billion position in various exchanged-traded futures and options contracts, primarily the Nikkei 225 stock index futures contract traded on the Singapore International Monetary Exchange. The losses occurred when the market moved unfavorably against the trader's speculative positions. Barings was taken over by ING Group, the Dutch banking and insurance conglomerate. The trader served three years in prison in Singapore for fraudulent trading.

As this story implies, futures and options contracts can be very risky investments, indeed, when used for speculative purposes. Nevertheless, they are also important risk-management tools. In this chapter, we introduce exchange-traded currency futures contracts, options contracts, and options on currency futures that are useful for both speculating on foreign exchange price movements and hedging exchange rate uncertainty. These contracts make up part of the foreign exchange market that was introduced in Chapter 5, where we discussed spot and forward exchange rates.

The discussion begins by comparing forward and futures contracts, noting similarities and differences between the two. We discuss the markets where futures are traded, the currencies on which contracts are written, and contract specifications for the various currency contracts. We also discuss Eurodollar interest rate futures contracts, which are useful for hedging short-term dollar interest rate risk.

Next, options contracts on foreign exchange are introduced, comparing and contrasting the options and the futures markets. The exchanges where options are traded are identified and contract terms are specified. The over-the-counter options market is also discussed. Basic option-pricing boundary relationships are illustrated using actual market prices. Additionally, illustrations of how a speculator might use currency options are also provided. The chapter closes with the development of a currency option-pricing model. This chapter and the knowledge gained about forward contracts in Chapters 5 and 6 set the stage for Chapters 8, 9, and 10, which explain how these vehicles can be used for hedging foreign exchange risk.

Futures Contracts: Some Preliminaries

In Chapter 5, a *forward contract* was defined as a vehicle for buying or selling a stated amount of foreign exchange at a stated price per unit at a specified time in the future. Both forward and futures contracts are classified as **derivative** or **contingent claim securities** because their values are derived from or contingent upon the value of the underlying security. But while a **futures** contract is similar to a forward contract, there are many distinctions between the two. A forward contract is tailor-made for a client by his international bank. In contrast, a futures contract has **standardized** features and is **exchange-traded,** that is, traded on organized exchanges rather than over the counter. A client desiring a position in futures contracts contacts his broker, who transmits the order to the exchange floor where it is transferred to the trading pit. In the trading pit, the price for the order is negotiated by open outcry between floor brokers or traders.

The main standardized features are the **contract size** specifying the amount of the underlying foreign currency for future purchase or sale and the **maturity date** of the contract. A futures contract is written for a specific amount of foreign currency rather than for a tailor-made sum. Hence, a position in multiple contracts may be necessary to establish a sizable hedge or speculative position. Futures contracts have specific **delivery months** during the year in which contracts mature on a specified day of the month.

An **initial performance bond** (formerly called *margin*) must be deposited into a collateral account to establish a futures position. The initial performance bond is generally equal to about 2 percent of the contract value. Either cash or Treasury bills may be used to meet the performance bond requirement. The account balance will fluctuate through daily settlement, as illustrated by the following discussion. The performance bond put up by the contract holder can be viewed as "good-faith" money that he will fulfill his side of the financial obligation.

The major difference between a forward contract and a futures contract is the way the underlying asset is priced for future purchase or sale. A forward contract states a price for the future transaction. By contrast, a futures contract is **settled-up,** or **marked-to-market**, daily at the settlement price. The **settlement price** is a price representative of futures transaction prices at the close of daily trading on the exchange. It is determined by a settlement committee for the commodity, and it may be somewhat arbitrary if trading volume for the contract has been light for the day. A buyer of a futures contract (one who holds a **long** position) in which the settlement price is higher (lower) than the previous day's settlement price has a positive (negative) settlement for the day. Since a long position entitles the owner to purchase the underlying asset, a higher (lower) settlement price means the futures price of the underlying asset has increased (decreased). Consequently, a long position in the contract is worth more (less). The change in settlement prices from one day to the next determines the settlement amount. That is, the change in settlement prices per unit of the underlying asset, multiplied by the size of the contract, equals the size of the daily settlement to be added to (or subtracted from) the long's performance bond account. Analogously, the seller of the futures contract (**short** position) will have his performance bond account increased (or decreased) by the amount the long's performance bond account is decreased (or increased). Thus, futures trading between the long and the short is a **zero-sum game**; that is, the sum of the long and short's daily settlement is zero. If the investor's performance bond account falls below a **maintenance performance bond** level (roughly equal to 75 percent of the initial performance bond), additional funds must be deposited into the account to bring it back to the initial performance bond level in order to keep the position open. An investor who suffers a liquidity crunch and cannot deposit additional funds will have his position liquidated by his broker.

The marking-to-market feature of futures markets means that market participants realize their profits or suffer their losses on a day-to-day basis rather than all at once at maturity as with a forward contract. At the end of daily trading, a futures contract

EXHIBIT 7.1

Differences between Futures and Forward Contracts

Trading Location
Futures: Traded competitively on organized exchanges.
Forward: Traded by bank dealers via a network of telephones and computerized dealing systems.

Contractual Size
Futures: Standardized amount of the underlying asset.
Forward: Tailor-made to the needs of the participant.

Settlement
Futures: Daily settlement, or marking-to-market, done by the futures clearinghouse through the participant's performance bond account.
Forward: Participant buys or sells the contractual amount of the underlying asset from the bank at maturity at the forward (contractual) price.

Expiration Date
Futures: Standardized delivery dates.
Forward: Tailor-made delivery date that meets the needs of the investor.

Delivery
Futures: Delivery of the underlying asset is seldom made. Usually a reversing trade is transacted to exit the market.
Forward: Delivery of the underlying asset is commonly made.

Trading Costs
Futures: Bid-ask spread plus broker's commission.
Forward: Bid-ask spread plus indirect bank charges via compensating balance requirements.

is analogous to a new forward contract on the underlying asset at the new settlement price with a one-day-shorter maturity. Because of the daily marking-to-market, the futures price will converge through time to the spot price on the last day of trading in the contract. That is, the final settlement price at which any transaction in the underlying asset will transpire is the spot price on the last day of trading. The effective price is, nevertheless, the original futures contract price, once the profit or loss in the performance bond account is included. Exhibit 7.1 summarizes the differences between forward and futures contracts.

Two types of market participants are necessary for a derivatives market to operate most efficiently: **speculators** and **hedgers**. A speculator attempts to profit from a change in the futures price. To do this, the speculator will take a long or short position in a futures contract depending upon his expectations of future price movement. A hedger, on the other hand, wants to avoid price variation by locking in a purchase price of the underlying asset through a long position in the futures contract or a sales price through a short position. In effect, the hedger passes off the risk of price variation to the speculator, who is better able, or at least more willing, to bear this risk.

Both forward and futures markets for foreign exchange are very liquid. A **reversing trade** can be made in either market that will close out, or neutralize, a position.[1] In forward markets, approximately 90 percent of all contracts result in the short making delivery of the underlying asset to the long. This is natural given the tailor-made terms of forward contracts. By contrast, only about 1 percent of currency futures contracts result in delivery. While futures contracts are useful for speculation and hedging, their standardized delivery dates are unlikely to correspond to the actual future dates when foreign exchange transactions will transpire. Thus, they are generally closed out in a reversing trade. The **commission** that buyers and sellers pay to transact in the futures

---

[1]In the forward market, the investor holds offsetting positions after a reversing trade; in the futures market the investor actually exits the marketplace.

market is a single amount paid up front that covers the *round-trip* transactions of initiating and closing out the position. These days, through a discount broker, the commission charge can be as little as $15 per currency futures contract.

In futures markets, a **clearinghouse** serves as the third party to all transactions. That is, the buyer of a futures contract effectively buys from the clearinghouse and the seller sells to the clearinghouse. This feature of futures markets facilitates active secondary market trading because the buyer and the seller do not have to evaluate one another's creditworthiness. The clearinghouse is made up of *clearing members*. Individual brokers who are not clearing members must deal through a clearing member to clear a customer's trade. In the event of default of one side of a futures trade, the clearing member stands in for the defaulting party, and then seeks restitution from that party. The clearinghouse's liability is limited because a contractholder's position is marked-to-market daily. Given the organizational structure, it is only logical that the clearinghouse maintains the futures performance bond accounts for the clearing members.

Frequently, a futures exchange may have a **daily price limit** on the futures price, that is, a limit as to how much the settlement price can increase or decrease from the previous day's settlement price. Forward markets do not have this. Obviously, when the price limit is hit, trading will halt as a new market-clearing equilibrium price cannot be obtained. Exchange rules exist for expanding the daily price limit in an orderly fashion until a market-clearing price can be established.

Currency Futures Markets

www.cme.com

This is the website of the Chicago Mercantile Exchange. It provides detailed information about the futures contracts and futures options contracts traded on it.

www.phlx.com

This is the website of the Philadelphia Stock Exchange and the Philadelphia Board of Trade. It provides detailed information about the stocks and derivative products that trade on the exchanges.

www.numa.com/ref/exchange.htm

This is the website of Numa Directory. It provides the website address of most of the stock and derivative exchanges in the world.

On May 16, 1972, trading in currency futures contracts began at the Chicago Mercantile Exchange (CME). Trading activity in currency futures has expanded rapidly at the CME. In 1978, only 2 million contracts were traded; this figure stood at over 139 million contracts in 2007. Most CME currency futures trade in a March, June, September, and December expiration cycle, with the delivery date being the third Wednesday of the expiration month. The last day of trading for most contracts is the second business day prior to the delivery date. Regular trading in CME currency futures contracts takes place each business day from 7:20 A.M. to 2:00 P.M. Chicago time. Additional CME currency futures trading takes place Monday through Thursday on the GLOBEX trading system from 5:00 P.M. to 4:00 P.M. Chicago time the next day. On Sundays trading begins at 3:00 P.M. GLOBEX is a worldwide automated order-entry and matching system for futures and options that facilitates nearly 24-hour trading after the close of regular exchange trading. Exhibit 7.2 summarizes the basic CME currency contract specifications. The International Finance in Practice box "CME Ramping Up FOREX Support, Targets OTC Business" provides a discussion of how CME currency futures will also be traded on the Reuters FX Dealing 3000 platform discussed in Chapter 5 on trading spot and forward foreign exchange.

The Philadelphia Board of Trade (PBOT), a subsidiary of the Philadelphia Stock Exchange, introduced currency futures trading in July 1986. Currently, the PBOT trades World Currency Futures for retail traders on the Australian dollar, British pound, Canadian dollar, euro, Japanese yen, and Swiss franc. These contracts are designed for retail market participants and cover a smaller amount of underlying currency than the corresponding CME contracts. Each PBOT contract covers 10,000 underlying currency units, except for the yen contract which covers JPY1,000,000. The PBOT currency futures contracts are cash settlement contracts in U.S. dollars. Contracts trade in the nearest three months in the March, June, September, and December expiration cycle. The last day of trading is the third Friday of the expiration month with settlement being the next business day. The trading hours of the PBOT contracts are 8:20 A.M. to 4:15 P.M. ET.

In addition to the CME and the PBOT, currency futures trading takes place on the New York Board of Trade, the Mexican Derivatives Exchange, the BM&F Exchange

CME Ramping Up FOREX Support, Targets OTC Business

The modern era of futures markets can be traced to 1972 when the Chicago Mercantile Exchange (CME) created the International Monetary Market (IMM) to begin trading foreign currency futures benchmarked against the U.S. dollar. Those first significant financial futures contracts set into motion a series of innovations that were the blueprint for today's markets that are dominated by contracts based on financial futures. Until recently, however, the granddaddy currency contracts had produced volume more reflective of their agricultural predecessors while trillion dollar volume days became standard place in the OTC interbank currency markets.

Currency futures began coming into their own, however, when the CME listed the currency complex virtually 24 hours on its electronic matching engine, GLOBEX. That move made currency futures more attractive to retail clientele. Now, an agreement with global information firm Reuters is literally making the currency futures available from thousands of institutional traders' desktops. Under the agreement, Reuters will offer the CME's electronic foreign exchange markets to its worldwide customers through the Reuters FX Dealing 3000 platform in a spot equivalent format. That means that the 3,500 institutions located in 123 countries—many large currency dealing banks—that trade cash and forward foreign exchange rates will be able to trade currency futures off of the same platform priced in the same format.

Leo Melamed, CME chairman emeritus and senior policy advisor, who shepherded the creation of the IMM while serving as exchange chairman, sees the move as completing his original vision.

"I would rate the agreement with Reuters as the culmination of 30 years worth of growth and proof that these future markets are intertwined with the cash markets of the world," Melamed says. "Right from the beginning, what I was trying to do was make sure that the Merc's currency markets were connected to the interbank markets."

CME Chairman Terry Duffy says the foreign exchange area has huge growth potential. "The FX market is a $1.2 trillion dollar a day market with about a $500 billion a day spot market. The notional value is staggering and while the CME having the lions share of the exchange-traded FX we think that our [market share]—we are 2% to 3% of the total [cash volume]—can grow. If we can increase that by a couple of percentage points it is big volume to the CME."

The move comes amid other efforts by the CME to make its currency complex more attractive, including adding additional crossrate products and reducing fees.

Despite these moves, some veteran FOREX market participants doubt whether large dealers will move to the listed market.

Osman Ghandour, who writes a FX newsletter and has traded the interbank market for years, says interbank trading offers unique benefits that will make it unlikely dealers would switch to an exchange-listed market.

"If I have 100 contracts to buy in the futures, there is no way they can guarantee [a fill]. . . . That quality is an advantage for the interbank market," Ghandour says. "If a hedge fund wants to buy or sell $1 billion worth of euros, I don't think he is going to go to the CME. He is going to pick up his phone and place an order with a bank and get one single unit price and be assured of that."

That said, there is little doubt the extra visibility does put the CME on more equal footing with the interbank market.

"The fact that the CME currency futures are now on the Reuters' platform is proof that the market truly is homogenous. Whether you are trading cash FX or futures, the exposures are identical," says CME President Phupinder Gill.

Source: Reprinted with permission of *Futures Magazine*, 833 W. Jackson Blvd., Chicago, IL 60607. Telephone 312-846-4600. All Rights Reserved.

in Brazil, the Budapest Commodity Exchange, and the Futures Market Division of the Korea Exchange.

Basic Currency Futures Relationships

Exhibit 7.3 shows quotations for CME futures contracts. For each delivery month for each currency, we see the opening price quotation, the high and the low quotes for the trading day (in this case January 4, 2008), and the settlement price. Each is presented in American terms, that is, $F(\$/i)$. (We use the same symbol F for futures prices as for forward prices, and explain why shortly.) For each contract, the **open interest** is also presented. This is the total number of short or long contracts

EXHIBIT 7.2

Chicago Mercantile Exchange Currency Futures Specifications

Currency	Contract Size
Price Quoted in U.S. Dollars	
Australian dollar	AUD100,000
Brazilian real	BRL100,000
British pound	GBP62,500
Canadian dollar	CAD100,000
Chinese renminbi	CNY1,000,000
Czech koruna	CZK4,000,000
Euro FX	EUR125,000
Hungarian forint	HUF30,000,000
Israeli shekel	ILS1,000,000
Japanese yen	JPY12,500,000
Korean won	KRW125,000,000
Mexican peso	MXN500,000
New Zealand dollar	NZD100,00
Norwegian krone	NOK2,000,000
Polish zloty	PLN500,000
Russian ruble	RUB2,500,000
South African rand	ZAR500,000
Swedish krona	SEK2,000,000
Swiss franc	CHF125,000
Cross-Rate Futures	
(Underlying Currency/Price Currency)	
Euro FX/British pound	EUR125,000
Euro FX/Japanese yen	EUR125,000
Euro FX/Swiss franc	EUR125,000

Source: Chicago Mercantile Exchange website, www.cme.com.

EXHIBIT 7.3 Chicago Mercantile Exchange Currency Futures Contract Quotations

	Open	High	Low	Settle	Chg	Open interest
Currency Futures						
Japanese Yen (CME)-¥12,500,000; $ per 100¥						
March	.9201	.9340	.9192	.9287	.0072	157,845
June	.9395	.9413	.9275	.9366	.0071	24,484
Canadian Dollar (CME)-CAD 100,000; $ per CAD						
March	1.0118	1.0167	.9961	.9988	−.0116	83,122
June	1.0104	1.0159	.9961	.9985	−.0116	3,758
British Pound (CME)-£62,500; $ per £						
March	1.9684	1.9815	1.9634	1.9686	−.0008	80,352
June	1.9625	1.9744	1.9579	1.9622	−.0010	309
Swiss Franc (CME)-CHF 125,000; $ per CHF						
March	.9029	.9109	.8993	.9081	.0050	66,265
June	.9042	.9136	.9028	.9112	.0048	57
Australian Dollar (CME)-AUD 100,000; $ per AUD						
March	.8761	.8800	.8659	.8689	−.0079	61,111
June	.8716	.8721	.8595	.8625	−.0079	436
Mexican Peso (CME)-MXN 500,000; $ per 10MXN						
March	.91625	.91625	.90900	.90975	−.00400	97,700
Euro/U.S. Dollar (CME)-125,000; $ per €						
March	1.4748	1.4830	1.4700	1.4777	.0028	172,396
June	1.4737	1.4818	1.4693	1.4763	.0025	2,266
Euro/British pound (CME)-€125,000; £ per €						
March	.7509	.7443	.7507	.0018	1,922	
Euro/Japanese yen (CME)-€125,000; ¥ per €						
March	160.37	158.64	159.11	−.94	8,487	
Euro/Swiss franc (CME)-€125,000; CHF per €						
March	1.6354	1.6270	1.6272	−.0060	1,352	

Sources: *The Wall Street Journal,* Saturday, January 5, 2008, p. B13. Reprinted by permission of *The Wall Street Journal,* © 2008 Dow Jones & Company, Inc. All Rights Reserved Worldwide. Euro/GBP, Euro/JPY, and Euro/CHF quotations are January 4, 2008 values from Bloomberg.

outstanding for the particular delivery month. Note that the open interest is greatest for each currency in the **nearby** contract, in this case the March 2008 contract. Since few of these contracts will actually result in delivery, if we were to follow the open interest in the March contracts through time, we would see the number for each different currency decrease as the last day of trading (March 17, 2008) approaches as a result of reversing trades. Additionally, we would note increased open interest in the June 2008 contract as trading interest in the soon-to-be nearby contract picks up. In general, open interest (loosely an indicator of demand) typically decreases with the term-to-maturity of most futures contracts.

EXAMPLE | 7.1: Reading Futures Quotations

As an example of reading futures quotations, let's use the June 2008 Canadian dollar contract. From Exhibit 7.3, we see that on Friday, January 4, 2008, the contract opened for trading at a price of $1.0104/CD, and traded in the range of $0.9961 CD/(low) to $1.0159/CD (high) throughout the day. The settlement ("closing") price was $0.9985/CD. The open interest, or the number of June 2008 contracts outstanding, was 3,758.

At the settlement price of $0.9985, the holder of a long position in one contract is committing himself to paying $99,850 for CD100,000 on the delivery day, June 18, 2008, if he actually takes delivery. Note that the settlement price decreased $0.0116 from the previous day. That is, it fell from $1.0101/CD to $0.9985/CD. Both the buyer and the seller of the contract would have their accounts marked-to-market by the change in the settlement prices. That is, one holding a long position from the previous day would have $1,160 (=$0.0116 × CD100,000) subtracted from his performance bond account and the short would have $1,160 added to his account.

Even though marking-to-market is an important economic difference between the operation of the futures market and the forward market, it has little effect on the pricing of futures contracts as opposed to the way forward contracts are priced. To see this, note the pattern of CD forward prices from the *Exchange Rates* presented in Exhibit 5.4 in Chapter 5. They go from a spot price of $0.9984/CD to $0.9986 (1-month) to $0.9988 (3-months) to $0.9979 (6-months). To the extent that forward prices are an unbiased predictor of future spot exchange rates, the market is anticipating the U.S. dollar first to depreciate and then to appreciate over the next six months relative to the Canadian dollar. Similarly, we see an appreciating pattern of the U.S. dollar from the pattern of settlement prices for the CD futures contracts: $0.9988 (March) to $0.9985 (June). It is also noteworthy that both the forward and the futures contracts together display a chronological pattern. For example, the 1-month forward price (with a value date of February 8) and the 3-month forward price (with a value date of April 8) surround the March futures contract price (with a delivery date of March 19); these coupled with the June futures contract price (with a delivery date of June 18) and the 6-month forward contract display a consistent pattern: $0.9984, $0.9986, $0.9988, $0.9988, $0.9985, and $0.9979, depreciating from January to March/April and then appreciating. Thus, both the forward market and the futures market are useful for **price discovery**, or obtaining the market's forecast of the spot exchange rate at different future dates.

Example 7.1 implies that futures are priced very similarly to forward contracts. In Chapter 6, we developed the Interest Rate Parity (IRP) model, which states that the forward price for delivery at time T is

$$F_T(\$/i) = S_0(\$/i) \frac{(1 + r_\$)^T}{(1 + r_i)^T}$$

(7.1)

We will use the same equation to define the futures price. This should work well since the similarities between the forward and the futures markets allow arbitrage opportunities if the prices between the markets are not roughly in accord.[2]

EXAMPLE | 7.2: Speculating and Hedging with Currency Futures

Suppose a trader takes a position on January 4, 2008 in one June 2008 CD futures contract at $0.9985/CD. The trader holds the position until the last day of trading when the spot price is $0.9830/CD. This will also be the final settlement price because of **price convergence**. The trader's profit or loss depends upon whether he had a long or short position in the June CD contract. If the trader had a long position, and he was a speculator with no underlying position in Canadian dollars, he would have a cumulative loss of −$1,550 [=($0.9830 − $0.9985) × CD100,000] from January 4 through June 18. This amount would be subtracted from his margin account as a result of daily marking-to-market. If he takes delivery, he will pay out-of-pocket $98,300 for the CD100,000 (which have a spot market value of $98,300). The effective cost, however, is $99,850 (= $98,300 + $1,550), including the amount subtracted from the margin money. Alternatively, as a hedger desiring to acquire CD100,000 on June 18 for $0.9985/CD, our trader has locked in a purchase price of $99,850 from a long position in the June CD futures contract.

If the trader had taken a short position, and he was a speculator with no underlying position in Canadian dollars, he would have a cumulative profit of $1,550 [= ($0.9985 − $0.9830) × CD100,000] from January 4 through June 18. This amount would be added to his margin account as a result of daily marking-to-market. If he makes delivery, he will receive $98,300 for the CD100,000 (which also cost $98,300 in the spot market). The effective amount he receives, however, is $99,850 (= $98,300 + $1,550), including the amount added to his margin account. Alternatively, as a hedger desiring to sell CD100,000 on June 18 for $0.9985/CD, our trader has locked in a sales price of $99,850 from a short position in the June CD futures contract. Exhibit 7.4 graphs these long and short futures positions.

Eurodollar Interest Rate Futures Contracts

www.ses.com.sg

This is the website of the Singapore Exchange. It provides detailed information about the derivative products traded on it.

To this point, we have considered only futures contracts written on foreign exchange. Nevertheless, future contracts are traded on many different underlying assets. One particularly important contract is the Eurodollar interest rate futures traded on the Chicago Mercantile Exchange and the Singapore Exchange. The Eurodollar contract has become the most widely used futures contract for hedging short-term U.S. dollar interest rate risk. Other Eurocurrency futures contracts that trade are the Euroyen, EuroSwiss, and the EURIBOR contract, which began trading after the introduction of the euro.

The CME Eurodollar futures contract is written on a hypothetical $1,000,000 ninety-day deposit of Eurodollars. The contract trades in the March, June, September, and December cycle and the four nearest noncycle months. The hypothetical delivery date is the third Wednesday of the delivery month. The last day of trading is two business days prior to the delivery date. The contract is a cash settlement contract. That is, the delivery of a $1,000,000 Eurodollar deposit is not actually made or received. Instead, final settlement is made through realizing profits or losses in the performance bond account on the delivery date based on the final settlement price on the last day of trading. Exhibit 7.5 presents an example of CME Eurodollar futures quotations. Note that contracts trade out many years into the future.

---

[2]As a theoretical proposition, Cox, Ingersoll, and Ross (1981) show that forward and futures prices should not be equal unless interest rates are constant or can be predicted with certainty. For our purposes, it is not necessary to be theoretically specific.

EXHIBIT 7.4

Graph of Long and Short Positions in the June 2008 Canadian Dollar Futures Contract

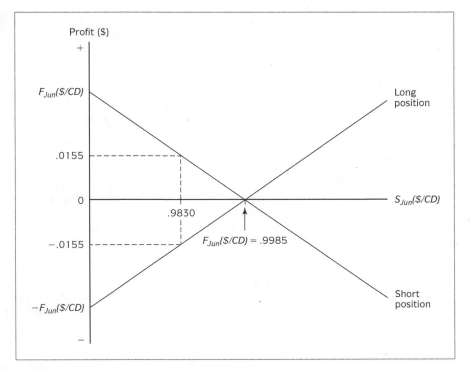

EXHIBIT 7.5

Chicago Mercantile Exchange Eurodollar Futures Contract Quotations

	High	Low	Settle	Change	Open Int	Vol
Eurodollar (CME)-$1,000,000; pts of 100%						
Mar08	96.035	95.880	96.025	+.115	1,462,993	421,218
Jun	96.530	96.365	96.520	+.095	1,477,703	403,784
Sep	96.805	96.625	96.790	+.100	1,339,213	524,168
Dec	96.940	96.760	96.920	+.105	1,499,832	557,348
Mar09	96.960	96.775	96.940	+.115	1,064,044	522,083
Jun	96.890	96.690	96.865	+.135	728,876	305,643
Sep	96.770	96.555	96.740	+.150	573,024	273,568
Dec	96.620	96.395	96.585	+.155	358,426	176,097
Mar10	96.460	96.235	96.420	+.155	240,482	67,508
Jun	96.275	96.055	96.235	+.150	253,186	45,202
Sep	96.125	95.905	96.075	+.140	159,878	35,029
Dec	95.995	95.780	95.935	+.125	120,956	21,411
Mar11	95.880	95.685	95.830	+.115	95,133	12,943
Jun	95.805	95.595	95.725	+.105	84,268	9,553
Sep	95.685	95.505	95.630	+.095	69,754	9,270
Dec	95.590	95.425	95.530	+.085	58,850	9,428
Mar12	95.500	95.435	95.450	+.075	48,209	5,708
Jun	95.390	95.360	95.360	+.065	46,160	4,290
Sep	95.340	95.280	95.275	+.055	29,592	4,484
Dec	95.225	95.160	95.180	+.045	20,508	4,037
Mar13	95.155	95.040	95.105	+.040	9,612	488
Jun	95.080	94.965	95.025	+.035	6,066	558
Sep	95.010	94.895	94.955	+.035	8,420	458
Dec	94.935	94.820	94.875	+.030	8,917	558
Mar14	94.850	94.765	94.815	+.025	14,980	631
Jun	94.795	94.710	94.760	+.025	6,718	81
Sep	94.745	94.660	94.710	+.025	3,987	111
Dec	94.680	94.595	94.645	+.025	3,690	141
Total open int 3,433,780; total vol 9,944,223.						

Source: Closing values on Friday, January 4, 2008, from Bloomberg.

EXAMPLE | 7.3: Reading Eurodollar Futures Quotations

Eurodollar futures prices are stated as an index number of three-month LIBOR, calculated as: $F = 100 - LIBOR$. For example, from Exhibit 7.5 we see that the June 2008 contract (with hypothetical delivery on June 18, 2008) had a settlement price of 96.52 on Friday, January 4, 2008. The implied three-month LIBOR yield is thus 3.48 percent. The minimum price change is one basis point (bp). On $1,000,000 of face value, a one-basis-point change represents $100 on an annual basis. Since the contract is for a 90-day deposit, one basis point corresponds to a $25 price change.

EXAMPLE | 7.4: Eurodollar Futures Hedge

As an example of how this contract can be used to hedge interest rate risk, consider the treasurer of a MNC, who on January 4, 2008 learns that his firm expects to receive $20,000,000 in cash from a large sale of merchandise on June 18, 2008. The money will not be needed for a period of 90 days. Thus, the treasurer should invest the excess funds for this period in a money market instrument such as a Eurodollar deposit.

The treasurer notes that three-month LIBOR is currently 4.62 percent. (See *Money Rates* in the inside back cover.) The implied three-month LIBOR rate in the June 2008 contract is considerably lower at 3.48 percent. Additionally, the treasurer notes that the pattern of future expected three-month LIBOR rates implied by the pattern of Eurodollar futures prices suggests that it is expected to decrease through March 2009. Nevertheless, the treasurer believes that a 90-day rate of return of 3.48 percent is a decent rate to "lock in," so he decides to hedge against lower three-month LIBOR in June 2008. By hedging, the treasurer is locking in a certain return of $174,000 (=$20,000,000 × .0348 × 90/360) for the 90-day period the MNC has $20,000,000 in excess funds.

To construct the hedge, the treasurer will need to buy, or take a long position, in Eurodollar futures contracts. At first it may seem counterintuitive that a long position is needed, but remember, a decrease in the implied three-month LIBOR yield causes the Eurodollar futures price to increase. To hedge the interest rate risk in a $20,000,000 deposit, the treasurer will need to buy 20 June 2008 contracts.

Assume that on the last day of trading in the June 2008 contract three-month LIBOR is 3.10 percent. The treasurer is indeed fortunate that he chose to hedge. At 3.10 percent, a 90-day Eurodollar deposit of $20,000,000 will generate only $155,000 of interest income, or $19,000 less than at a rate of 3.48 percent. In fact, the treasurer will have to deposit the excess funds at a rate of 3.10 percent. But the shortfall will be made up by profits from the long futures position. At a rate of 3.10 percent, the final settlement price on the June 2008 contract is 96.90 (=100 − 3.10). The profit earned on the futures position is calculated as: [96.90 − 96.52] × 100 bp × $25 × 20 contracts = 19,000. This is precisely the amount of the shortfall.

Options Contracts: Some Preliminaries

An **option** is a contract giving the owner the right, but not the obligation, to buy or sell a given quantity of an asset at a specified price at some time in the future. Like a futures or forward contract, an option is a derivative, or contingent claim, security. Its value is derived from its definable relationship with the underlying asset—in this chapter, foreign currency, or some claim on it. An option to buy the underlying asset is a **call**, and an option to sell the underlying asset is a **put**. Buying or selling the underlying asset via the option is known as exercising the option. The stated price paid (or received) is known as the **exercise** or **striking price**. In options terminology, the buyer of an option is frequently referred to as the long and the seller of an option is referred to as the **writer** of the option, or the short.

Because the option owner does not have to exercise the option if it is to his disadvantage, the option has a price, or **premium**. There are two types of options, American and European. The names do not refer to the continents where they are traded, but rather to their exercise characteristics. A **European option** can be exercised only at the maturity or expiration date of the contract, whereas an **American option** can be exercised at any time during the contract. Thus, the American option allows the owner to do everything he can do with a European option, and more.

Currency Options Markets

Prior to 1982, all currency option contracts were over-the-counter options written by international banks, investment banks, and brokerage houses. Over-the-counter options are tailor-made according to the specifications of the buyer in terms of maturity length, exercise price, and the amount of the underlying currency. Generally, these contracts are written for large amounts, at least $1,000,000 of the currency serving as the underlying asset. Frequently, they are written for U.S. dollars, with the euro, British pound, Japanese yen, Canadian dollar, and Swiss franc serving as the underlying currency, though options are also available on less actively traded currencies. Over-the-counter options are typically European style.

In December 1982, the Philadelphia Stock Exchange (PHLX) began trading options on foreign currency. Currently, the PHLX trades World Currency Options on the Australian dollar, British pound, Canadian dollar, euro, Japanese yen, and Swiss franc. Each PHLX contract covers 10,000 underlying currency units, except for the yen contract which covers JPY1,000,000. The PHLX currency futures contracts are cash settlement contracts in U.S. dollars. Contracts trade in the nearest two months in the March, June, September, and December expiration cycle plus two near-term months so that there are always options with one-, two-, and three-month expirations. These options are European style and are cash settled on the Saturday following the third Friday of the expiration month, which is the expiration date. The trading hours of these contracts are 9:30 A.M. to 4:00 P.M. Philadelphia time.

The volume of OTC currency options trading is much larger than that of organized-exchange option trading. According to the Bank for International Settlements, in 2007 the OTC volume was approximately $212 billion per day. By comparison exchange-traded currency option volume is negligible.

Currency Futures Options

The Chicago Mercantile Exchange trades American style options on most of the currency futures contracts it offers (refer to Exhibit 7.2.) With these options, the underlying asset is a futures contract on the foreign currency instead of the physical currency. One futures contract underlies one options contract. Additionally, European style options recently began trading on the key currency futures contracts.

Most CME futures options trade with expirations in the March, June, September, December expiration cycle of the underlying futures contract and two near-term non-cycle months plus four weekly expirations. For example, in January, options with expirations in January, February, March, June, September, and December would trade on futures with corresponding expirations. Monthly options expire on the second Friday prior to the third Wednesday of the options contract month. Weekly options expire on Friday. Regular trading takes place each business day from 7:20 A.M. to 2:00 P.M. Chicago time. For most contracts, extended-hour trading on the GLOBEX system begins at 2:00 P.M. and continues until 7:15 A.M. Chicago time. On Sundays, GLOBEX trading begins at 3:00 P.M.

Options on currency futures behave very similarly to options on the physical currency since the futures price converges to the spot price as the futures contract nears maturity. Exercise of a futures option results in a long futures position for the call buyer or the put writer and a short futures position for the put buyer or the call writer. If the futures position is not offset prior to the futures expiration date, receipt or delivery of the underlying currency will, respectively, result or be required. In addition to the PHLX and the CME, there is some limited exchange-traded currency options trading at the BM&F Exchange in Brazil, on Euronext, and at the Tel-Aviv Stock Exchange.

Basic Option-Pricing Relationships at Expiration

At expiration, a European option and an American option (which has not been previously exercised), both with the same exercise price, will have the same terminal value. For call options the time T expiration value per unit of foreign currency can be stated as:

$$C_{aT} = C_{eT} = Max\,[S_T - E, 0], \tag{7.2}$$

where C_{aT} denotes the value of the American call at expiration, C_{eT} is the value of the European call at expiration, E is the exercise price per unit of foreign currency, S_T is the expiration date spot price, and *Max* is an abbreviation for denoting the maximum of the arguments within the brackets. A call (put) option with $S_T > E$ ($E > S_T$) expires **in-the-money** and it will be exercised. If $S_T = E$ the option expires **at-the-money**. If $S_T < E$ ($E < S_T$) the call (put) option expires **out-of-the-money** and it will not be exercised.

> **EXAMPLE | 7.5:** Expiration Value of a European Call Option
>
> As an illustration of pricing Equation 7.2, consider the PHLX 147 Jun EUR European call option from Exhibit 7.6. This option has a current premium, C_e, of 3.73 cents per EUR. The exercise price is 147 cents per EUR and it expires on June 20, 2008. Suppose that at expiration the spot rate is $1.5125/EUR. In this event, the call option has an exercise value of $151.25 - 147 = 4.25$ cents per each of the EUR10,000 of the contract, or $425. That is, the call owner can buy EUR10,000, worth $15,125 (= EUR10,000 × $1.5125) in the spot market, for $14,700 (= EUR10,000 × $1.47). On the other hand, if the spot rate is $1.4507/EUR at expiration, the call option has a negative exercise value, $145.07 - 147 = -1.93$ cents per EUR. The call buyer is under no obligation to exercise the option if it is to his disadvantage, so he should not. He should let it expire worthless, or with zero value.
>
> Exhibit 7.7A graphs the 147 Jun EUR call option from the buyer's perspective and Exhibit 7.7B graphs it from the call writer's perspective at expiration. Note that the two graphs are mirror-images of one another. The call buyer can lose no more than the call premium but theoretically has an unlimited profit potential. The call writer can profit by no more than the call premium but theoretically can lose an unlimited amount. At an expiration spot price of $S_T = E + C_a = 147 + 3.73 = 150.73$ cents per EUR, both the call buyer and writer break even, that is, neither earns nor loses anything.
>
> The speculative possibilities of a long position in a call are clearly evident from Exhibit 7.7. Anytime the speculator believes that S_T will be in excess of the break-even point, he will establish a long position in the call. The speculator who is correct realizes a profit. If the speculator is incorrect in his forecast, the loss will be limited to the premium paid. Alternatively, if the speculator believes that S_T will be less than the breakeven point, a short position in the call will yield a profit, the largest amount being the call premium received from the buyer. If the speculator is incorrect, very large losses can result if S_T is much larger than the breakeven point.

Analogously, at expiration a European put and an American put will have the same value. Algebraically, the expiration value can be stated as:

$$P_{aT} = P_{eT} = Max\,[E - S_T, 0], \tag{7.3}$$

where P denotes the value of the put at expiration.

EXHIBIT 7.6

Philadelphia Stock Exchange European Currency Options Quotations

Options Philadelphia Exchange		Calls	Puts	
Euro				147.44
10,000 Euro-cents per unit.				
145	Mar	3.98	1.44	
146	Mar	3.33	1.78	
147	Mar	2.73	2.18	
148	Mar	2.22	2.66	
145	Jun	4.88	2.57	
146	Jun	4.28	2.90	
147	Jun	3.73	3.33	
148	Jun	3.23	3.83	
Japanese Yen				92.04
1,000,000 J.Yen-100ths of a cent per unit.				
91	Jan	1.76	.45	
92	Jan	1.21	.84	
93	Jan	.77	1.46	
91	Mar	3.00	1.10	
92	Mar	2.45	1.59	
93	Mar	2.09	2.16	
91	Jun	3.93	1.30	
92	Jun	3.48	1.73	
93	Jun	3.09	2.26	

Source: Mid-prices complied from bid and ask quotations obtained from Bloomberg on Friday, January 4, 2008.

EXHIBIT 7.7A

Graph of 147 June EUR Call Option: Buyer's Perspective

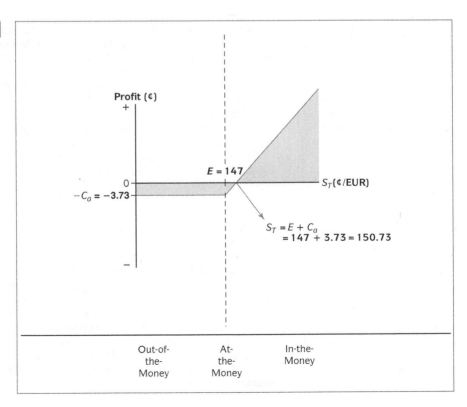

Global Finance: Investing and Managing Across Nations & Markets

EXHIBIT 7.7B

Graph of 147 June EUR
Call Option: Writer's
Perspective

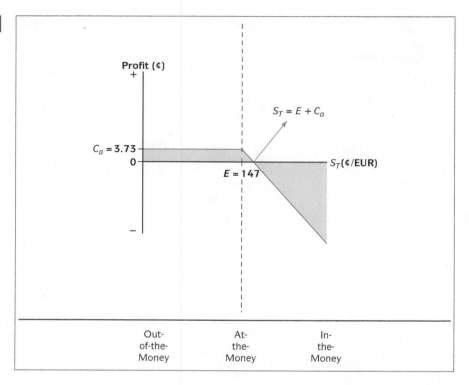

EXAMPLE | 7.6: Expiration Value of a European Put Option

As an example of pricing Equation 7.3, consider the 147 Jun EUR European put, which has a current premium, P_e, of 3.33 cents per EUR. If S_T is $1.4507/EUR, the put contract has an exercise value of $147 - 145.07 = 1.93$ cents per EUR for each of the EUR10,000 of the contract, or $193. That is, the put owner can sell EUR10,000, worth $14,507 (= EUR10,000 × $1.4507) in the spot market, for $14,700 (= EUR10,000 × $1.47). If $S_T = $1.5125/EUR$, the exercise value is $147 - 151.25 = -4.25$ cents per EUR. The put buyer would rationally not exercise the put; in other words, he should let it expire worthless with zero value.

Exhibit 7.8A graphs the 147 Jun EUR put from the buyer's perspective and Exhibit 7.8B graphs it from the put writer's perspective at expiration. The two graphs are mirror-images of one another. The put buyer can lose no more than the put premium and the put writer can profit by no more than the premium. The put buyer can earn a maximum profit of $E - P_a = 147 - 3.33 = 143.67$ cents per EUR if the terminal spot exchange rate is an unrealistic $0/EUR. The put writer's maximum loss is 143.67 cents per EUR. Additionally, at $S_T = E - P_a = 143.67$ cents per EUR, the put buyer and writer both break even; neither loses nor earns anything.

The speculative possibilities of a long position in a put are clearly evident from Exhibit 7.8. Anytime the speculator believes that S_T will be less than the breakeven point, he will establish a long position in the put. If the speculator is correct, he will realize a profit. If the speculator is incorrect in his forecast, the loss will be limited to the premium paid. Alternatively, if the speculator believes that S_T will be in excess of the breakeven point, a short position in the put will yield a profit, the largest amount being the put premium received from the buyer. If the speculator is incorrect, very large losses can result if S_T is much smaller than the breakeven point.

EXHIBIT 7.8A

Graph of 147 June EUR
Put Option: Buyer's
Perspective

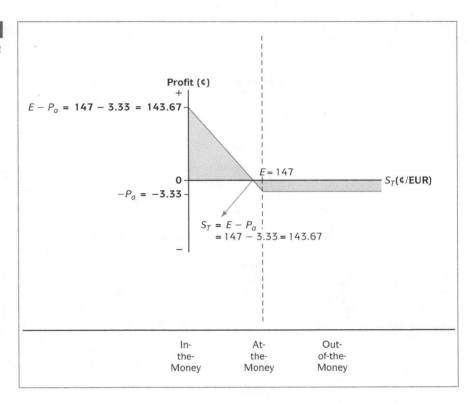

EXHIBIT 7.8B

Graph of 147 June EUR
Put Option: Writer's
Perspective

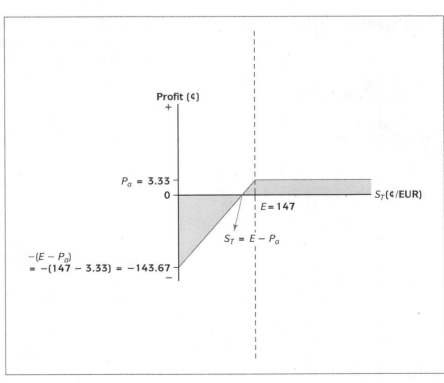

American Option-Pricing Relationships

An American call or put option can be exercised at any time prior to expiration. Consequently, in a rational marketplace, American options will satisfy the following basic pricing relationships at time t prior to expiration:

$$C_a \geq Max\,[S_t - E, 0] \tag{7.4}$$

and

$$P_a \geq Max\,[E - S_t, 0] \tag{7.5}$$

Verbally, these equations state that the American call and put premiums at time t will be at least as large as the immediate exercise value, or **intrinsic value**, of the call or put option. (The t subscripts are deleted from the call and put premiums to simplify the notation.) Since the owner of a long-maturity American option can exercise it on any date that he could exercise a shorter maturity option, or at some later date after the shorter maturity option expires, it follows that all else remaining the same, the longer-term American option will have a market price at least as large as the shorter-term option.

A call (put) option with $S_t > E$ ($E > S_t$) is referred to as trading in-the-money. If $S_t \cong E$ the option is trading at-the-money. If $S_t < E$ ($E < S_t$) the call (put) option is trading out-of-the-money. The difference between the option premium and the option's intrinsic value is nonnegative and sometimes referred to as the option's **time value**. For example, the time value for an American call is $C_a - Max\,[S_t - E, 0]$. The time value exists, meaning investors are willing to pay more than the immediate exercise value, because the option may move more in-the-money, and thus become more valuable, as time elapses. Exhibit 7.9 graphs the intrinsic value and time value for an American call option.

European Option-Pricing Relationships

The pricing boundaries for European put and call premiums are more complex because they can only be exercised at expiration. Hence, there is a time value element to the

---

EXHIBIT 7.9

Market Value, Time Value, and Intrinsic Value of an American Call Option

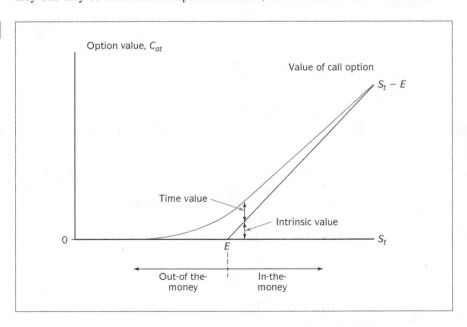

EXHIBIT 7.10

Equation for a
European Call Option
Lower Boundary

	Current Time	Expiration	
		$S_T \leq E$	$S_T > E$
Portfolio A:			
Buy Call	$-C_e$	0	$S_T - E$
Lend PV of E in U.S	$\dfrac{-E/(1 + r_\$)}{-C_e - E/(1 + r_\$)}$	$\dfrac{E}{E}$	$\dfrac{E}{S_T}$
Portfolio B:			
Lend PV of one unit of currency i at rate r_i	$-S_t/(1 + r_i)$	S_T	S_T

boundary expressions. Exhibit 7.10 develops the lower boundary expression for a European call.

Exhibit 7.10 compares the costs and payoffs of two portfolios a U.S. dollar investor could make. Portfolio A involves purchasing a European call option and lending (or investing) an amount equal to the present value of the exercise price, E, at the U.S. interest rate $r_\$$, which we assume corresponds to the length of the investment period. The cost of this investment is $C_e + E/(1 + r_\$)$. If at expiration, S_T is less than or equal to E, the call option will not have a positive exercise value and the call owner will let it expire worthless. If at expiration, S_T is greater than E, it will be to the call owner's advantage to exercise the call; the exercise value will be $S_T - E > 0$. The risk-free loan will pay off the amount E regardless of which state occurs at time T.

By comparison, the U.S. dollar investor could invest in portfolio B, which consists of lending the present value of one unit of foreign currency i at the foreign interest rate r_i, which we assume corresponds to the length of the investment period. In U.S. dollar terms, the cost of this investment is $S_t/(1 + r_i)$. Regardless of which state exists at time T, this investment will pay off one unit of foreign currency, which in U.S. dollar terms will have value S_T.

It is easily seen from Exhibit 7.10 that if $S_T > E$, portfolios A and B pay off the same amount, S_T. However, if $S_T \leq E$, portfolio A has a larger payoff than portfolio B. It follows that in a rational marketplace, portfolio A will be priced to sell for at least as much as portfolio B, that is, $C_e + E/(1 + r_\$) \geq S_t/(1 + r_i)$. This implies that

$$C_e \geq Max\left[\frac{S_t}{(1 + r_i)} - \frac{E}{(1 + r_\$)}, 0\right] \tag{7.6}$$

since the European call can never sell for a negative amount.

Similarly, it can be shown that the lower boundary pricing relationship for a European put is:

$$P_e \geq Max\left[\frac{E}{(1 + r_\$)} - \frac{S_t}{(1 + r_i)}, 0\right] \tag{7.7}$$

The derivation of this formula is left as an exercise for the reader. (Hint: Portfolio A involves buying a put and lending spot, portfolio B involves lending the present value of the exercise price.)

Note that both C_e and P_e are functions of only five variables: S_t, E, r_i, $r_\$$, and implicitly the term-to-maturity. From Equations 7.6 and 7.7, it can be determined that, when all else remains the same, the call premium C_e (put premium P_e) will increase:

1. The larger (smaller) is S_t,

2. The smaller (larger) is E,

3. The smaller (larger) is r_i,

4. The larger (smaller) is $r_\$$, and

5. The larger (smaller) $r_\$$ is relative to r_i.

Implicitly, both $r_\$$ and r_i will be larger the longer the length of the option period. When $r_\$$ and r_i are not too much different in size, a European FX call and put will increase in price when the option term-to-maturity increases. However, when $r_\$$ is very much larger than r_i, a European FX call will increase in price, but the put premium will decrease, when the option term-to-maturity increases. The opposite is true when r_i is very much greater than $r_\$$.

Recall that IRP implies $F_T = S_t[(1 + r_\$)/(1 + r_i)]$, which in turn implies that $F_T/(1 + r_\$) = S_t/(1 + r_i)$. Hence, European call and put prices on spot foreign exchange, Equations 7.6 and 7.7 can be, respectively, restated as:[3]

$$C_e \geq Max\left[\frac{(F_T - E)}{(1 + r_\$)}, 0\right] \tag{7.8}$$

and

$$P_e \geq Max\left[\frac{(E - F_T)}{(1 + r_\$)}, 0\right] \tag{7.9}$$

EXAMPLE | 7.7: European Option-Pricing Valuation

Let's see if Equations 7.8 and 7.9 actually hold for the 147 Jun EUR European call and the 147 Jun EUR European put options we considered. Both of these options expire on June 20, 2008, or in 168 days. The 6-month dollar LIBOR rate is 4.4675 percent. Thus, $(1 + r_\$)$ is [1 + .044675 (168/360)] = 1.02085. We will use the June futures price of \$1.4763 from Exhibit 7.3 for F_T. Thus, for the 147 June EUR call,

3.73 ≥ *Max* [(147.63 − 147)/(1.02085), 0] = *Max* [.62, 0] = .62.

Thus, the lower boundary relationship on the European call premium holds. For the 147 Jun EUR put,

3.33 ≥ *Max* [(147 − 147.63)/(1.02085), 0] = *Max* [−.62, 0] = 0.

Thus, the lower boundary relationship on the European put premium holds as well.

Binomial Option-Pricing Model

The option pricing relationships we have discussed to this point have been lower boundaries on the call and put premiums, instead of exact equality expressions for the premiums. The binomial option-pricing model provides an exact pricing formula for a European call or put.[4] We will examine only a simple one-step case of the binomial model to better understand the nature of option pricing.

We want to use the binomial model to value the PHLX 147 Jun EUR European call from Exhibit 7.6. We see from the exhibit that the option is quoted at a premium of 3.73 cents. The current spot price of the EUR in American terms is $S_0 = 147.44$ cents. Our estimate of the option's volatility (annualized standard deviation of the change

---

[3]An American option can be exercised at any time during its life. If it is not advantageous for the option owner to exercise it prior to maturity, the owner can let it behave as a European option, which can only be exercised at maturity. It follows from Equations 7.4 and 7.8 (for calls) and 7.5 and 7.9 (for puts) that a more restrictive lower boundary relationship for American call and put options are, respectively:

$$C_a \geq Max\ [S_t - E, (F - E)/(1 + r_\$), 0]\ \text{and}\ P_a \geq Max\ [E - S_t, (E - F)/(1 + r_\$), 0]$$

[4]The binomial option-pricing model was independently derived by Sharpe (1978), Rendleman and Bartter (1979), and Cox, Ross, and Rubinstein (1979).

in the spot rate) is $\sigma = 9.065$ percent, which was obtained from Bloomberg. This call option expires in 168 days on June 20, 2008, or in $T = 168/365 = .4603$ years. The one-step binomial model assumes that at the end of the option period the EUR will have appreciated to $S_{uT} = S_0 \cdot u$ or depreciated to $S_{dT} = S_0 \cdot d$, where $u = e^{\sigma \cdot \sqrt{T}}$ and $d = 1/u$. The spot rate at T will be either $156.79 = 147.44(1.06343)$ or $138.65 = 147.44(.94035)$ where $u = e^{.09065 \cdot \sqrt{.4603}} = 1.06343$ and $d = 1/u = .94035$. At the exercise price of $E = 147$, the option will only be exercised at time T if the EUR appreciates; its exercise value would be $C_{uT} = 9.79 = 156.79 - 147$. If the EUR depreciates it would not be rational to exercise the option; its value would be $C_{dT} = 0$.

The binominal option-pricing model only requires that $u > 1 + r_\$ > d$. From Example 7.7 we see that $1 + r_\$ = 1.02085$. Thus, we see that $1.06343 > 1.02085 > .94035$.

The binomial option-pricing model relies on the risk-neutral probabilities of the underlying asset increasing and decreasing in value. For our purposes, the risk-neutral probability of the EUR appreciating is calculated as:

$$q = (F_T - S_0 \cdot d)/S_0(u - d),$$

where F_T is the forward (or futures) price that spans the option period. We will use the June EUR futures price on January 4, 2008, as our estimate of $F_T(\$/EUR) = \$1.4763$. Therefore,

$$q = (147.63 - 138.65)/(156.79 - 138.65) = .4950.$$

It follows that the risk-neutral probability of the EUR depreciating is $1 - q = 1 - .4950 = .5050$.

Because the European call option can only be exercised at time T, the binomial call option premium is determined by:

$$C_0 = [qC_{uT} + (1 - q)C_{dT}]/(1 + r_\$)] \tag{7.10}$$
$$= [.4950(9.79) + .5050(0)]/(1.02085)]$$
$$= 4.75 \text{ cents per EUR.}$$

Alternatively, (if C_{uT} is positive) the binomial call price can be expressed as:

$$C_0 = [F_T \cdot h - E((S_0 \cdot u/E)(h - 1) + 1)]/(1 + r_\$)], \tag{7.11}$$

where $h = (C_{uT} - C_{dT})/S_0(u - d)$ is the risk-free hedge ratio. The *hedge ratio* is the size of the long (short) position the investor must have in the underlying asset per option the investor must write (buy) to have a risk-free offsetting investment that will result in the investor receiving the same terminal value at time T regardless of whether the underlying asset increases or decreases in value. For our example numbers, we see that

$$h = (9.79 - 0)/(156.79 - 138.65) = .5397$$

Thus, the call premium is:

$$C_0 = [147.63(.5397) - 147((156.79/147)(.5397 - 1) + 1)]/(1.02085)$$
$$= 4.75 \text{ cents per EUR.}$$

Equation 7.11 is more intuitive than Equation 7.10 because it is in the same general form as Equation 7.8. In an analogous manner, a binomial put option-pricing model can be developed. Nevertheless, for our example, the binomial call option-pricing model yielded a price that was too large compared to the actual market price of 3.73 cents. This is what we might expect with such a simple model, and when using such an arbitrary value for the option's volatility. In the next section, we consider a more refined option-pricing model.

European Option-Pricing Formula

In the last section, we examined a simple one-step version of binomial option-pricing model. Instead, we could have assumed the stock price followed a multiplicative binomial process by subdividing the option period into many subperiods. In this case, S_T and C_T could be many different values. When the number of subperiods into which the option period is subdivided goes to infinity, the European call and put pricing formulas presented in this section are obtained. Exact European call and put pricing formulas are:[5]

$$C_e = S_t e^{-r_i T} N(d_1) - E e^{-r_\$ T} N(d_2)$$ (7.12)

and

$$P_e = E e^{-r_\$ T} N(-d_2) - S_t e^{-r_i T} N(-d_1)$$ (7.13)

The interest rates r_i and $r_\$$ are assumed to be annualized and constant over the term-to-maturity T of the option contract, which is expressed as a fraction of a year.

Invoking IRP, where with continuous compounding $F_T = S_t e^{(r_\$ - r_i)T}$, C_e and P_e in Equations 7.12 and 7.13 can be, respectively, restated as:

$$C_e = [F_T N(d_1) - E N(d_2)] e^{-r_\$ T}$$ (7.14)

and

$$P_e = [E N(-d_2) - F_T N(-d_1)] e^{-r_\$ T}$$ (7.15)

where

$$d_1 = \frac{ln\,(F_T/E) + .5\sigma^2 T}{\sigma\sqrt{T}}$$

and

$$d_2 = d_1 - \sigma\sqrt{T}$$

$N(d)$ denotes the cumulative area under the standard normal density function from $-\infty$ to d_1 (or d_2). The variable σ is the annualized volatility of the change in exchange rate $ln(S_{t+1}/S_t)$. Equations 7.14 and 7.15 indicate that C_e and P_e are functions of only

---

EXAMPLE | 7.8: The European Option-Pricing Model

As an example of using the European options-pricing model, consider the PHLX 147 Jun EUR European call option from Exhibit 7.6. The option has a premium of 3.73 U.S. cents per EUR. The option will expire on June 20, 2008—168 days from the quotation date, or $T = 168/365 = .4603$. We will use the June futures price on January 4, 2008; as our estimate of $F_T(\$/EUR) = \$1.4763$. The rate $r_\$$ is estimated as the annualized six-month dollar LIBOR of 4.4675 percent on the same day. The estimated volatility is 9.065 percent and was obtained from Bloomberg.

The values d_1 and d_2 are:

$$d_1 = \frac{ln\,(147.63/147) + .5(.09065)^2\,(.4603)}{(.09065)\sqrt{.4603}} = .1003$$

and

$$d_2 = .1003 - (.09065)\sqrt{.4603} = .0388$$

Consequently, it can be determined that $N(.1003) = .5399$ and $N(.0388) = .5155$. We now have everything we need to compute the model price:

$$C_e = [147.63(.5399) - 147(.5155)]e^{-(.044675)\,(.4603)}$$
$$= [79.7054 - 75.7785]\,(.9796)$$
$$= 3.85 \text{ cents per EUR vs. the actual market mid-price of 3.73 cents.}$$

As we see, the model has done a good job of valuing the EUR call.

---

[5]The European option-pricing model was developed by Biger and Hull (1983), Garman and Kohlhagen (1983), and Grabbe (1983). The evolution of the model can be traced back to European option-pricing models developed by Merton (1973) and Black (1976).

five variables: F_T, E, $r_\$$, T, and σ. It can be shown that both C_e and P_e increase when σ becomes larger.

The value $N(d)$ can be calculated using the NORMSDIST function of Microsoft Excel. Equations 7.14 and 7.15 are widely used in practice, especially by international banks in trading OTC options.

Empirical Tests of Currency Options

Shastri and Tandon (1985) empirically test the American boundary relationships we developed in this chapter (Equations 7.4, 7.5, 7.6, 7.7, 7.8, and 7.9) using PHLX put and call data. They discover many violations of the boundary relationships, but conclude that nonsimultaneous data could account for most of the violations. Bodurtha and Courtadon (1986) test the immediate exercise boundary relationships (Equations 7.4 and 7.5) for PHLX American put and call options. They also find many violations when using last daily trade data. However, when they use simultaneous price data and incorporate transaction costs, they conclude that the PHLX American currency options are efficiently priced.

Shastri and Tandon (1986) also test the European option-pricing model using PHLX American put and call data. They determine that a nonmember of the PHLX could not earn abnormal profits from the hedging strategies they examine. This implies that the European option-pricing model works well in pricing American currency options. Barone-Adesi and Whaley (1987) also find that the European option-pricing model works well for pricing American currency options that are *at* or *out-of-the money,* but does not do well in pricing *in-the-money* calls and puts. For *in-the-money* options, their approximate American option-pricing model yields superior results.

SUMMARY

This chapter introduced currency futures and options on foreign exchange. These instruments are useful for speculating and hedging foreign exchange rate movements. In later chapters, it will be shown how to use these vehicles for hedging purposes.

1. Forward, futures, and options contracts are derivative, or contingent claim, securities. That is, their value is derived or contingent upon the value of the asset that underlies these securities.

2. Forward and futures contracts are similar instruments, but there are differences. Both are contracts to buy or sell a certain quantity of a specific underlying asset at some specific price in the future. Futures contracts, however, are exchange-traded, and there are standardized features that distinguish them from the tailor-made terms of forward contracts. The two main standardized features are contract size and maturity date.

3. Additionally, futures contracts are marked-to-market on a daily basis at the new settlement price. Hence, the performance bond account of an individual with a futures position is increased or decreased, reflecting daily realized profits or losses resulting from the change in the futures settlement price from the previous day's settlement price.

4. A futures market requires speculators and hedgers to effectively operate. Hedgers attempt to avoid the risk of price change of the underlying asset, and speculators attempt to profit from anticipating the direction of future price changes.

5. The Chicago Mercantile Exchange and the Philadelphia Board of Trade are the two largest currency futures exchanges.

6. The pricing equation typically used to price currency futures is the IRP relationship, which is also used to price currency forward contracts.

7. Eurodollar interest rate futures contracts were introduced as a vehicle for hedging short-term interest-rate risk.

8. An option is the right, but not the obligation, to buy or sell the underlying asset for a stated price over a stated time period. Call options give the owner the right to buy, put options the right to sell. American options can be exercised at any time during their life; European options can only be exercised at maturity.

9. Exchange-traded options with standardized features are traded on two exchanges. Options on spot foreign exchange are traded at the Philadelphia Stock Exchange, and options on currency futures are traded at the Chicago Mercantile Exchange.

10. Basic boundary expressions for put and call option prices were developed and examined using actual option-pricing data.

11. A European option-pricing model for put and call options was also presented and explained using actual market data.

KEY WORDS

American option, *175*	futures, *166*	premium, *175*
at-the-money, *176*	hedgers, *167*	price convergence, *172*
call, *174*	in-the-money, *176*	price discovery, *171*
clearinghouse, *168*	initial performance	put, *174*
commission, *167*	bond, *166*	reversing trade, *167*
contingent claim	intrinsic value, *180*	settled-up, *166*
security, *166*	long, *166*	settlement price, *166*
contract size, *166*	maintenance performance	short, *166*
daily price limit, *168*	bond, *166*	speculators, *167*
delivery months, *166*	marked-to-market, *166*	standardized, *166*
derivative	maturity date, *166*	striking price, *174*
security, *166*	nearby, *171*	time value, *180*
European option, *175*	open interest, *169*	writer, *174*
exchange-traded, *166*	option, *174*	zero-sum game, *166*
exercise price, *174*	out-of-the-money, *176*	

QUESTIONS

1. Explain the basic differences between the operation of a currency forward market and a futures market.

2. In order for a derivatives market to function most efficiently, two types of economic agents are needed: hedgers and speculators. Explain.

3. Why are most futures positions closed out through a reversing trade rather than held to delivery?

4. How can the FX futures market be used for price discovery?

5. What is the major difference in the obligation of one with a long position in a futures (or forward) contract in comparison to an options contract?

6. What is meant by the terminology that an option is in-, at-, or out-of-the-money?

7. List the arguments (variables) of which an FX call or put option model price is a function. How does the call and put premium change with respect to a change in the arguments?

PROBLEMS

1. Assume today's settlement price on a CME EUR futures contract is $1.3140/EUR. You have a short position in one contract. Your performance bond account currently has a balance of $1,700. The next three days' settlement prices are $1.3126, $1.3133, and $1.3049. Calculate the changes in the performance bond account

from daily marking-to-market and the balance of the performance bond account after the third day.

2. Do problem 1 again assuming you have a long position in the futures contract.

3. Using the quotations in Exhibit 7.3, calculate the face value of the open interest in the March 2008 Swiss franc futures contract.

4. Using the quotations in Exhibit 7.3, note that the March 2008 Mexican peso futures contract has a price of $0.90975 per 10MXN. You believe the spot price in March will be $0.97500 per 10MXN. What speculative position would you enter into to attempt to profit from your beliefs? Calculate your anticipated profits, assuming you take a position in three contracts. What is the size of your profit (loss) if the futures price is indeed an unbiased predictor of the future spot price and this price materializes?

5. Do problem 4 again assuming you believe the March 2008 spot price will be $0.77500 per 10MXN.

6. George Johnson is considering a possible six-month $100 million LIBOR-based, floating-rate bank loan to fund a project at terms shown in the table below. Johnson fears a possible rise in the LIBOR rate by December and wants to use the December Eurodollar futures contract to hedge this risk. The contract expires December 20, 1999, has a US$ 1 million contract size, and a discount yield of 7.3 percent. Johnson will ignore the cash flow implications of marking-to-market, initial performance bond requirements, and any timing mismatch between exchange-traded futures contract cash flows and the interest payments due in March.

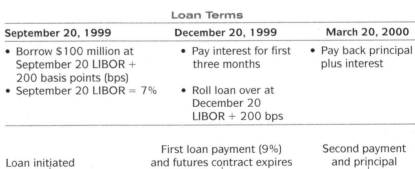

Loan Terms		
September 20, 1999	**December 20, 1999**	**March 20, 2000**
• Borrow $100 million at September 20 LIBOR + 200 basis points (bps) • September 20 LIBOR = 7%	• Pay interest for first three months • Roll loan over at December 20 LIBOR + 200 bps	• Pay back principal plus interest

Loan initiated — 9/20/99

First loan payment (9%) and futures contract expires — 12/20/99

Second payment and principal — 3/20/00

a. Formulate Johnson's September 20 floating-to-fixed-rate strategy using the Eurodollar future contracts discussed in the text above. Show that this strategy would result in a fixed-rate loan, assuming an increase in the LIBOR rate to 7.8 percent by December 20, which remains at 7.8 percent through March 20. Show all calculations.

Johnson is considering a 12-month loan as an alternative. This approach will result in two additional uncertain cash flows, as follows:

Loan initiated	First payment (9%)	Second payment	Third payment	Fourth payment and principal
9/20/99	12/20/99	3/20/00	6/20/00	9/20/00

CFA®
PROBLEMS

b. Describe the strip hedge that Johnson could use and explain how it hedges the 12-month loan (specify number of contracts.) No calculations are needed.

7. Jacob Bower has a liability that:
  • has a principal balance of $100 million on June 30, 1998,
  • accrues interest quarterly starting on June 30, 1998,
  • pays interest quarterly,
  • has a one-year term to maturity, and
  • calculates interest due based on 90-day LIBOR (the London Interbank Offered Rate).

   Bower wishes to hedge his remaining interest payments against changes in interest rates. Bower has correctly calculated that he needs to sell (short) 300 Eurodollar futures contracts to accomplish the hedge. He is considering the alternative hedging strategies outlined in the following table.

Initial Position (6/30/98) in 90-Day LIBOR Eurodollar Contracts		
Contract Month	Strategy A (contracts)	Strategy B (contracts)
September 1998	300	100
December 1998	0	100
March 1999	0	100

   a. Explain why strategy B is a more effective hedge than strategy A when the yield curve undergoes an instantaneous nonparallel shift.
   b. Discuss an interest rate scenario in which strategy A would be superior to strategy B.

8. Assume that the Japanese yen is trading at a spot price of 92.04 cents per 100 yen. Further assume that the premium of an American call (put) option with a striking price of 93 is 2.10 (2.20) cents. Calculate the intrinsic value and the time value of the call and put options.

9. Assume the spot Swiss franc is $0.7000 and the six-month forward rate is $0.6950. What is the minimum price that a six-month American call option with a striking price of $0.6800 should sell for in a rational market? Assume the annualized six-month Eurodollar rate is 3 1/2 percent.

10. Do problem 9 again assuming an American put option instead of a call option.

11. Use the European option-pricing models developed in the chapter to value the call of problem 9 and the put of problem 10. Assume the annualized volatility of the Swiss franc is 14.2 percent. This problem can be solved using the FXOPM.xls spreadsheet.

12. Use the binomial option-pricing model developed in the chapter to value the call of problem 9. The volatility of the Swiss franc is 14.2 percent.

INTERNET EXERCISES

1. Data on currency futures can be found at the Chicago Mercantile Exchange website, www.cme.com. Go to the "View All Delayed Quotes" section of this website and see which currency futures contracts have increasing and which have decreasing futures prices in current trading.

MINI CASE

The Options Speculator

A speculator is considering the purchase of five three-month Japanese yen call options with a striking price of 96 cents per 100 yen. The premium is 1.35 cents per 100 yen. The spot price is 95.28 cents per 100 yen and the 90-day forward rate is 95.71 cents. The speculator believes the yen will appreciate to $1.00 per 100 yen over the next three months. As the speculator's assistant, you have been asked to prepare the following:

1. Graph the call option cash flow schedule.
2. Determine the speculator's profit if the yen appreciates to $1.00/100 yen.
3. Determine the speculator's profit if the yen appreciates only to the forward rate.
4. Determine the future spot price at which the speculator will only break even.

REFERENCES & SUGGESTED READINGS

Barone-Adesi, Giovanni, and Robert Whaley. "Efficient Analytic Approximation of American Option Values." *Journal of Finance* 42 (1987), pp. 301–20.

Biger, Nahum, and John Hull. "The Valuation of Currency Options." *Financial Management* 12 (1983), pp. 24–28.

Black, Fischer. "The Pricing of Commodity Contracts." *Journal of Financial Economics* 3 (1976), pp. 167–79.

———— and Myron Scholes. "The Pricing of Options and Corporate Liabilities." *Journal of Political Economy* 81 (1973), pp. 637–54.

Bodurtha, James, Jr., and George Courtadon. "Efficiency Tests of the Foreign Currency Options Market." *Journal of Finance* 41 (1986), pp. 151–62.

Cox, John C., Jonathan E. Ingersoll, and Stephen A. Ross. "The Relation between Forward Prices and Futures Prices." *Journal of Financial Economics* 9 (1981), pp. 321–46.

Cox, John C., Stephen A. Ross, and Mark Rubinstein. "Option Pricing: A Simplified Approach." *Journal of Financial Economics* 7 (1979), pp. 229–63.

Garman, Mark, and Steven Kohlhagen. "Foreign Currency Option Values." *Journal of International Money and Finance* 2 (1983), pp. 231–38.

Grabbe, J. Orlin. "The Pricing of Call and Put Options on Foreign Exchange." *Journal of International Money and Finance* 2 (1983), pp. 239–54.

———— *International Financial Markets,* 3rd ed. Upper Saddle River, N.J.: Prentice Hall, 1996.

Merton, Robert. "Theory of Rational Option Pricing." *The Bell Journal of Economics and Management Science* 4 (1973), pp. 141–83.

Rendleman, Richard J., Jr., and Brit J. Bartter. "Two-State Option Pricing." *Journal of Finance* 34 (1979), pp. 1093–1110.

Sharpe, William F. "Chapter 14." *Investments.* Englewood Cliffs, N.J.: Prentice Hall, 1978.

Shastri, Kuldeep, and Kishore Tandon. "Arbitrage Tests of the Efficiency of the Foreign Currency Options Market." *Journal of International Money and Finance* 4 (1985), pp. 455–68.

———— "Valuation of Foreign Currency Options: Some Empirical Tests." *Journal of Financial and Quantitative Analysis* 21 (1986), pp. 145–60.

THUNDERBIRD
The American Graduate School
of International Management

A06-99-0028

LUFTHANSA

If Karl Marx could see what the foreign exchange market is doing to the world's captains of industry, he would surely be laughing. Not only do they put up with labor problems, competition, deregulation, and rapid changes in technology—no, that is not enough. Add currency volatility to that list in the last few years. And it's so bad that a successful corporate executive of one of the world's prestige airlines can put on a multimillion dollar currency speculation, and win—and still get lambasted by his critics. It's enough to make a capitalist cry.

- Intermarket, 1985

It was February 14, 1986, and Herr Heinz Ruhnau, Chairman of Lufthansa (Germany) was summoned to meet with Lufthansa's board. The board's task was to determine if Herr Ruhnau's term of office should be terminated. Herr Ruhnau had already been summoned by Germany's transportation minister to explain his supposed speculative management of Lufthansa's exposure in the purchase of Boeing aircraft.

In January 1985 Lufthansa, under the chairmanship of Herr Heinz Ruhnau, purchased twenty 737 jets from Boeing (U.S.). The agreed upon price was $500,000,000, payable in U.S. dollars on delivery of the aircraft in one year, in January 1986. The U.S. dollar had been rising steadily and rapidly since 1980, and was approximately DM3.2/$ in January 1985. If the dollar were to continue to rise, the cost of the jet aircraft to Lufthansa would rise substantially by the time payment was due.

Herr Ruhnau had his own *view* or expectations regarding the direction of the exchange rate. Like many others at the time, he believed the dollar had risen about as far as it was going to go, and would probably fall by the time January 1986 rolled around. But then again, it really wasn't his money to gamble with. He compromised. He sold half the exposure ($250,000,000) at a rate of DM3.2/$, and left the remaining half ($250,000,000) uncovered.

Evaluation of the Hedging Alternatives

Lufthansa and Herr Ruhnau had the same basic hedging alternatives available to all firms:

1. Remain uncovered,
2. Cover the entire exposure with forward contracts,
3. Cover some proportion of the exposure, leaving the balance uncovered,
4. Cover the exposure with foreign currency options,
5. Obtain U.S. dollars now and hold them until payment is due.

Although the final expense of each alternative could not be known beforehand, each alternative's outcome could be simulated over a range of potential ending exchange rates. Exhibit 1 illustrates the final net cost of the first four alternatives over a range of potential end-of-period spot exchange rates.

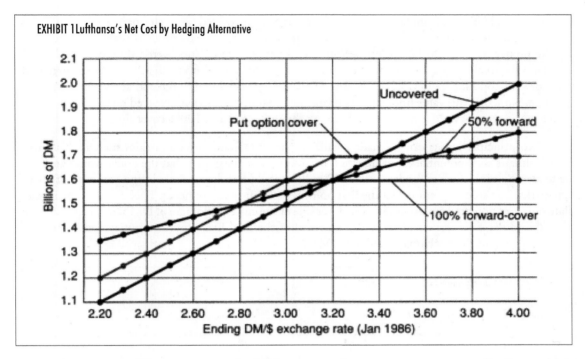

EXHIBIT 1 Lufthansa's Net Cost by Hedging Alternative

Of course one of the common methods of covering a foreign currency exposure for firms, which involves no use of financial contracts like forwards or options, is the matching of currency cash flows. Lufthansa did have inflows of U.S. dollars on a regular basis as a result of airline ticket purchases in the United States. Although Herr Ruhnau thought briefly about matching these U.S. dollar-denominated cash inflows against the dollar outflows to Boeing, the magnitude of the mismatch was obvious. Lufthansa simply did not receive anything close to $500 million a year in dollar-earnings, or even over several years for that matter.

1. Remain Uncovered. Remaining uncovered is the maximum risk approach. It therefore represents the greatest potential benefits (if the dollar weakens versus the Deutschemark), and the greatest potential cost (if the dollar continues to strengthen versus the Deutschemark). If the exchange rate were to drop to DM2.2/$ by January 1986, the purchase of the Boeing 737s would be only DM1.1 billion. Of course if the dollar continued to appreciate, rising to perhaps DM4.0/$ by 1986, the total cost would be DM2.0 billion. The uncovered position's risk is therefore shown as that value-line which has the steepest slope (covers the widest vertical distance) in Exhibit 1. This is obviously a sizeable level of risk for any firm to carry. Many firms believe the decision to leave a large exposure uncovered for a long period of time to be nothing other than currency speculation.

2. Full Forward Cover. If Lufthansa were very risk averse and wished to eliminate fully its currency exposure, it could buy forward contracts for the purchase of U.S. dollars for the entire amount. This would have locked-in an exchange rate of DM3.2/$, with a known final cost of DM1.6 billion. This alternative is represented by the horizontal value-line in Exhibit 1; the total cost of the Boeing 737s no longer has any risk or sensitivity to the ending spot exchange rate. Most firms believe they should accept or tolerate risk in their line of business, not in the process of payment. The 100% forward cover alternative is often used by firms as their benchmark, their comparison measure for actual currency costs when all is said and done.

3. Partial Forward Cover. This alternative would cover only part of the total exposure leaving the remaining exposure uncovered. Herr Ruhnau's expectations were for the dollar to fall, so he expected

Lufthansa would benefit from leaving more of the position uncovered (as in alternative #1 above). This strategy is somewhat arbitrary, however, in that there are few objective methods available for determining the proper balance (20/80, 40/60, 50/50, etc.) between covered/uncovered should be. Exhibit 1 illustrates the total ending cost of this alternative for a partial cover of 50/50; $250 million purchased with forward contracts of DM3.2/$, and the $250 million remaining purchased at the end-of-period spot rate. Note that this value line's slope is simply half that of the 100% uncovered position. Any other partial cover strategy would similarly fall between the unhedged and 100% cover lines.

Two principal points can be made regarding partial forward cover strategies such as this. First, Herr Ruhnau's total potential exposure is still unlimited. The possibility that the dollar would appreciate to astronomical levels still exists, and $250 million could translate into an infinite amount of Deutschemarks. The second point is that the first point is highly unlikely to occur. Therefore, for the immediate ranges of potential exchange rates on either side of the current spot rate of DM3.2/$, Herr Ruhnau has reduced the risk (vertical distance in Exhibit 1) of the final Deutschemark outlay over a range of ending values and the benchmark value of DM3.2/$.

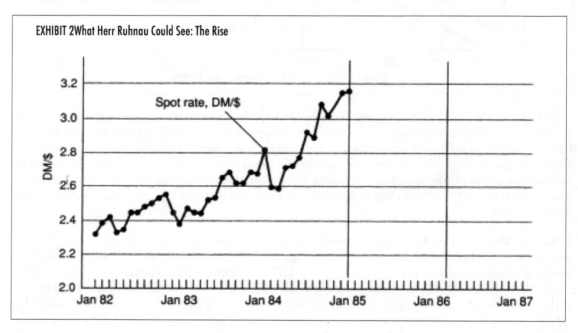

EXHIBIT 2 What Herr Ruhnau Could See: The Rise

4. Foreign Currency Options. The foreign currency option is unique among the hedging alternatives due to its kinked-shape value-line. If Herr Ruhnau had purchased a put option on marks at DM3.2/$, he could have obtained what many people believe is the best of both worlds. If the dollar had continued to strengthen above DM3.2/$, the total cost of obtaining $500 million could be locked-in at DM1.6 billion plus the cost of the option premium, as illustrated by the flat portion of the option alternative to the right of DM3.2/$. If, however, the dollar fell as Herr Ruhnau had expected, Lufthansa would be free to let the option expire and purchase the dollars at lower cost on the spot market. This alternative is shown by the falling value-line to the left of DM3.2/$. Note that the put option line falls at the same rate (same slope) as the uncovered position, but is higher by the cost of purchasing the option.

In this instance Herr Ruhnau would have had to buy put options for DM1.6 billion given an exercise price of DM3.2/$. In January 1985 when Herr Heinz Ruhnau was mulling over these alternatives, the option premium on Deutshemark put options was about 6%, equal to DM96,000,000 or $30,000,000. The total cost of the purchase in the event the put option was exercised would be DM1,696,000,000 (exercise plus premium).

It is important to understand what Herr Ruhnau would be hoping to happen if he had decided to purchase the put options. He would be expecting the dollar to weaken (ending up to the left of DM3.2/$ in Exhibit 1), therefore he would expect the option to expire without value. In the eyes of many corporate treasurers, DM96,000,000 is a lot of money for the purchase of an instrument which the hedger expects or hopes not to use!

5. Buy Dollars Now. The fifth alternative is a money-market hedge for an account payable: Obtain the $500 million now and hold those funds in an interest-bearing account or asset until payment was due. Although this would eliminate the currency exposure, it required that Lufthansa have all the capital in-hand now. The purchase of the Boeing jets had been made in conjunction with the on-going financing plans of Lufthansa, and these did not call for the capital to be available until January 1986. An added concern (and what ultimately eliminated this alternative from consideration) was that Lufthansa had several relatively strict covenants in place which limited the types, amounts, and currencies of denomination of the debt it could carry on its balance sheet.

Herr Ruhnau's Decision

Although Herr Ruhnau truly expected the dollar to weaken over the coming year, he believed remaining completely uncovered was too risky for Lufthansa. Few would argue this, particularly given the strong upward trend of the DM/$ exchange rate as seen in Exhibit 2. The dollar had shown a consistent three year trend of appreciation versus the Deutschemark, and that trend seemed to be accelerating over the most recent year.

Because he personally felt so strongly that the dollar would weaken, Herr Ruhnau chose to go with partial cover. He chose to cover 50% of the exposure ($250 million) with forward contracts (the one year forward rate was DM3.2/$) and to leave the remaining 50% ($250 million) uncovered. Because foreign currency options were as yet a relatively new tool for exposure management by many firms, and because of the sheer magnitude of the up-front premium required, the foreign currency option was not chosen. Time would tell if this was a wise decision.

How It Came Out

Herr Ruhnau was both right and wrong. He was definitely right in his expectations. The dollar appreciated for one more month, and then weakened over the coming year. In fact, it did not simply *weaken*, it plummeted. By January 1986 when payment was due to Boeing, the spot rate had fallen to DM2.3/$ from the previous year's DM3.2/$ as shown in Exhibit 3. This was a spot exchange rate movement in Lufthansa's favor.

The bad news was that the total Deutschemark cost with the partial forward cover was DM1.375 billion, a full DM225,000,000 more than if no hedging had been implemented at all! This was also DM129,000,000 more than what the foreign currency option hedge would have cost in total. The total cost of obtaining the needed $500 million for each alternative at the actual ending spot rate of DM2.3/$ would have been:

Alternative	Relevant Rate	Total DM Cost
1: Uncovered	DM 2.3/$	1,150,000,000
2: Full Forward Cover (100%)	DM 3.2/$	1,600,000,000
3: Partial Forward Cover	1/2(DM2.3) + 2(DM3.2)	1,375,000,000
4: DM Put Options	DM 3.2/$ strike	1,246,000,000

Herr Heinz's political rivals, both inside and outside of Lufthansa, were not so happy. Ruhnau was accused of recklessly speculating with Lufthansa's money, but the *speculation* was seen as the forward contract, not the amount of the dollar exposure left uncovered for the full year.

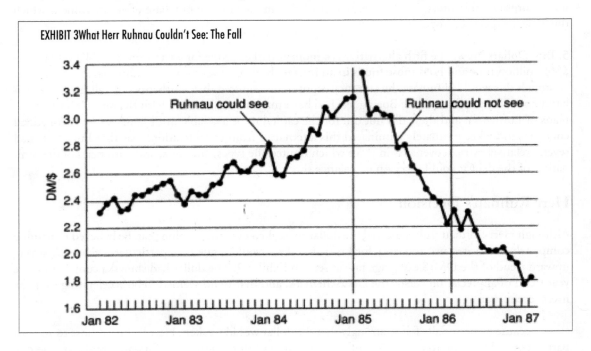

EXHIBIT 3 What Herr Ruhnau Couldn't See: The Fall

Case Questions

Herr Ruhnau was accused of making the following four mistakes:

1. Purchasing the Boeing aircraft at the wrong time. The U.S. dollar was at an all-time high at the time of the purchase, in January of 1985.

2. Choosing to hedge half the exposure when he expected the dollar to fall. If he had gone through with his instincts or expectations, he would have left the whole amount unhedged (which some critics have termed "whole hog").

3. Choosing to use forward contracts as his hedging tool instead of options. The purchase of put options would have allowed Herr Ruhnau to protect himself against adverse exchange rate movements while preserving the flexibility of exchanging DM for dollars spot if preferred.

4. Purchasing Boeing aircraft at all. Germany, as well as the other major European Economic Community countries, has a vested interest in the conglomerate Airbus. Airbus's chief rival was Boeing in the manufacture of large long-distance civil aircraft.

Given these criticisms, should the Board of Lufthansa retain Herr Heinz Ruhnau as Chairman? How should Ruhnau justify his actions and so justify his further employment?

THUNDERBIRD
THE AMERICAN GRADUATE SCHOOL
OF INTERNATIONAL MANAGEMENT

B03-03-0006

A GLOBAL MANAGER'S GUIDE TO CURRENCY RISK MANAGEMENT

Introduction

Since the advent of the floating exchange rates, any time that a transaction—whether that transaction is in goods, services, people, capital, or technology—has crossed borders, it has been subject to the influence of changes in exchange rates. The basic problem posed by exchange rates on the cross-border firm is that money across borders has no fixed value. Consequently, neither does a transaction undertaken across borders. In this Note, our purpose is to understand, categorize, and define the specific types of exchange rate risks that firms face across borders, and to address how managers can plan for, manage, and hedge these risks. Specifically, this Note provides an overview of the risks posed by exchange rates to the cross-border firm and the major strategies and solutions managers can employ to deal with them.

Why Should Companies Hedge?

Peter Drucker once noted that, "Not to hedge is to speculate. Exchange rates are a cost of production that financial executives must manage."[1] But what constitutes hedging and what constitutes speculation? What is the purpose of hedging? How, if at all, does hedging create value for shareholders?

An exchange rate hedge is an asset or position whose value changes (ΔH) in the opposite direction to that of an exposure (ΔX) as a result of a change in the exchange rate. A perfect hedge would be one whose value changes in an equal and opposite direction, resulting in a net change of zero in the value of the combined position:[2]

$$\Delta V = \Delta X + \Delta H$$

Hedging therefore protects the owner of the existing asset from loss. It is, however, important to note that while a hedge protects the firm against an exchange rate loss (relative to being unhedged), it can also eliminate any gains from an exchange rate change that is favorable.

But this does not really answer the question as to what is to be gained from hedging. The value of a firm is simply the net present value of all expected future cash flows discounted at an appropriate risk-adjusted discount rate. Hedging reduces the *variance* in expected cash flows, but does not necessarily affect the expected cash flows themselves. Reducing the variance—or what is referred to as "total risk" in the theory of finance—is not necessarily the same as reducing "risk," and therefore not necessarily the same as reducing the discount rate from the standpoint of the investor. From the investors' standpoint,

---

[1] *Keynote Address*, Peter Drucker, Business International's Chief Financial Officers Conference, San Francisco, 1990.

[2] Of course, as we will see, perfect hedges are nearly impossible to come by. To quote a professional colleague, Gunter Dufey (Professor Emeritus at the University of Michigan Business School), "A perfect hedge is only found in a Japanese garden."

the risk that matters is that portion of the total risk that cannot be diversified away, often called the "systematic risk." If currency risk is defined as "unsystematic risk" or "noise" in expected future cash flows arising from exchange rate changes, it has no impact on firm value. According to this argument, all that a manager does is waste the shareholder's money by such hedging.

That said, proponents cite a number of reasons for why hedging can be valuable to the firm. The argument most often made is that reduction of variance in future cash flows improves the planning capability of the firm. If the firm can more accurately predict future cash flows, it may have a greater incentive to undertake specific investments or activities which it might otherwise not consider. In a related (and somewhat more subtle) vein, hedging can put a floor on the internally generated cash flows of the firm, and, by doing so, can obviate the need to source externally generated capital in meeting its investment and growth needs. This can be valuable if external capital is more expensive than internally generated capital—and, for a number of reasons such as transactions costs and signaling costs, it turns out that external capital is, indeed, more expensive than internal capital.[3]

Reduction of risk in future cash flows reduces the likelihood that the firm's cash flows will fall below the minimum required to make debt-service payments. Hedging can therefore reduce the likelihood of financial distress. Yet another reason that is advocated is that management has a comparative advantage over the investor in knowing the actual currency risk of the firm.[4] Regardless of the level of disclosure provided by the firm to the public, management may possess an advantage in knowing the depth and breadth of the real risks and returns inherent in the firm's business. Thus, they may be aware of the benefits to a hedge that an investor does not see. Markets can be in disequilibrium because of structural and institutional imperfections, as well as external shocks (such as an oil crisis or war). Management is in a better position than stockholders to recognize disequilibrium conditions and to take advantage of one-time opportunities to enhance firm value through selective hedging.[5] Finally, there are those who argue that by reducing the variance in cash flows, hedging can smooth the reported net income, and this may be valuable in a financial market that pays undue attention to quarterly earnings fluctuations rather than focus of the long-term free cash flows.

Opponents of currency hedging make a number of equally persuasive arguments:[6] Stockholders are much more capable of diversifying currency risk than management of the firm. If stockholders do not wish to accept the currency risk of any specific firm, they can diversify their own portfolios or directly hedge against such risks. As noted above, reducing currency risk is not necessarily the same as adding value to the firm. In fact, since they are not free, hedging instruments use up precious resources of the firm which can lead to a net reduction in value. It is also possible that management conducts hedging activity because it benefits them, even if it is at the expense of the stockholder. Deriving from the idea of separation of control and ownership, agency theory argues that management (control) is generally more risk-averse than stockholders (ownership) because their undiversifiable human capital is tied up in the firm. If they bear firm-specific risks that are nondiversifiable, they will have the incentive to worry about, i.e., want to lower, total risk rather than just systematic risk.

Similarly, many argue that managers cannot outguess the market. If foreign exchange markets are in equilibrium with respect to parity conditions, the expected net present value of hedging is zero—in other words, all hedges will be fairly priced by the market. How would managers know when the market

---

[3] See K. Froot, D. Scharfstein, and J. Stein, "A Framework for Risk Management." *Harvard Business Review,* 72, September-October 1994, 59-71. The set of ideas surrounding the costs of externally generated versus internally generated capital and its implications for financial decisions is sometimes referred to as the "pecking order theory of capital structure."

[4] See Rene M. Stulz, "Optimal Hedging Policies," *Journal of Financial and Quantitative Analysis*, Vol. 19, No. 2, June 1984, p. 127.

[5] *Selective hedging* usually refers to the hedging of large, one-time, exceptional exposures, or the occasional use of hedging when management has a definitive expectation on the direction of exchange rates.

[6] Good overviews of the "why hedge?" debate include Stulz (1984), Smith and Stulz (1985), Levi and Sercu (1991), Froot, Scharfstein, and Stein (1992), Smith (1998), and Muelbroek (2002).

is not in equilibrium? Indeed, if they did have such special skills and know that, would they not be able to create more value for both themselves and their stockholders by speculating in currencies, rather than producing and selling goods and services? It is also possible that management's motivation to reduce variance is sometimes driven by accounting reasons, rather than market value reasons. Management may believe it will be criticized more severely for incurring foreign exchange losses in its financial statements than for incurring similar or even higher cash costs in avoiding the foreign exchange loss by undertaking hedging. However, efficient market theorists believe that investors can see through the "accounting veil" and therefore have already factored the foreign exchange effect into a firm's market valuation.

As is the case with any such debate, the conclusion will vary with the individuals—both stockholders and managements—involved. If there is any indication of who is winning the "why hedge?" debate, the reality is that more and more firms globally are practicing currency risk management every day. Hence what follows.

Management of Foreign Exchange Risk

The Management Process

Successful management of foreign exchange risk requires a well-designed and well-implemented risk management program. This requires a five-step process of understanding the motivation, the perception, the identification, the construction, and the implementation of a comprehensive risk management program.

[a] Motivation. Management strives to combine maximum sustainable growth in earnings with adequate yet prudently minimized commitments of capital. Some combination of these financial dimensions—the income statement and the balance sheet—give rise to the cash flows which are the true sources of value. And value is found by growth of stockholder wealth. If the assumption is then made that value arises from the business line(s) of the firm, i.e., the real activities that it undertakes, financial risks such as those posed by exchange rates, interest rates, and commodity prices can be seen for what they are—risks to the successful pursuit of the business's value. It is therefore management's responsibility to organize, structure, and operate the business and its variety of financial functions to capture as many of the positive characteristics of exchange rate changes as possible, while minimizing the downsides associated with them. The premise is that stockholders invest in a firm's ability to profit from its line of business, not from its ability to speculate or maneuver in the world's currency markets.

[b] Perception. Risks are managed on the basis of how they are perceived. For example, risks may be interpreted as continuous or discrete. A risk which is continuous can be accepted as inevitable, and gains and losses to the business arising from this risk can be accepted passively. A risk which is perceived as discrete, as foreign exchange risk often is, may be considered as one which occurs only periodically and will perhaps be more actively managed.

[c] Identification. If a risk cannot be measured accurately, it cannot be managed. The most common error made by managers with regard to currency risks is to rush into the selection of a financial fix or a derivative which will eliminate a risk which has been only barely identified. Mistakes are commonly made because inadequate time and effort have been spent in trying to understand the complexity of the problem. A comprehensive exposure analysis must include all traditional functional dimensions of the business including pricing, marketing, operations, accounting, finance and even compensation.

[d] Construction. Although the subject of most of the literature (particularly sales literature by financial services providers), this is in many respects the easiest part of the problem. Once an exposure has been properly identified and the firm's risk management motivations and needs acknowledged,

the construction of the hedge can be undertaken. This is in many ways one of the simpler aspects of the entire decision process.

[e] <u>Implementation</u>. The highly publicized derivative debacles of the 1990s have raised the consciousness that risk management programs may *themselves* constitute a risk to the firm when not identified, constructed, or implemented properly. Lack of front office/back office separation (the organizational separation of the traders or dealers taking the positions and the legal and documentary staff recording and monitoring the positions taken) led to many of the major fiascos, including the currency losses of Allied Lyons of the United Kingdom, Procter & Gamble in the United States, and Shell Showa in Japan. Questions such as the following need to be thought through. Who should manage and oversee the risk management process? Should it be centralized or decentralized? What are the performance evaluation issues raised by the risk management process for divisions and subsidiaries? What are the information technology and reporting needs to manage such values at risk in real time?

Types of Exchange Rate Exposure

The cross-border firm is affected by exchange rate changes three different ways. These three types of exposure (see Figure 1) are: transaction exposure, translation exposure, and economic exposure.

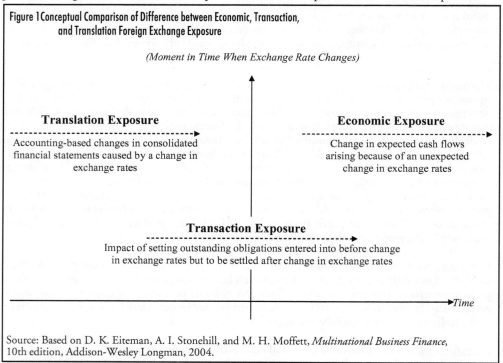

Figure 1 Conceptual Comparison of Difference between Economic, Transaction, and Translation Foreign Exchange Exposure

(Moment in Time When Exchange Rate Changes)

Translation Exposure
Accounting-based changes in consolidated financial statements caused by a change in exchange rates

Economic Exposure
Change in expected cash flows arising because of an unexpected change in exchange rates

Transaction Exposure
Impact of setting outstanding obligations entered into before change in exchange rates but to be settled after change in exchange rates

Time

Source: Based on D. K. Eiteman, A. I. Stonehill, and M. H. Moffett, *Multinational Business Finance*, 10th edition, Addison-Wesley Longman, 2004.

[a] <u>Transaction exposure</u>. A transaction exposure arises whenever the firm commits (or is contractually obligated) to make or receive a payment at a future date denominated in a foreign currency. Transaction exposures can therefore arise from operating and free cash flows, e.g., accounts receivable and payable arising from the conduct of business; commitments to buy or lease capital equipment or financing cash flows, e.g., debt or equity service obligations arising from the funding of the firm's business.

[b] <u>Translation exposure</u>. A cross-border firm must periodically remeasure all of its global operations into a single currency for reporting purposes. This requires that the balance sheets and income

statements of all affiliate operations worldwide be translated and consolidated into the currency of the parent company. Imbalances resulting from translation represent a potential change in the firm's reported consolidated income, reported capital base, or both.

[c] Economic exposure. Aside from existing obligations of the firm which will be settled in foreign currencies at future dates (transaction exposure) and the imbalances resulting from consolidation practices (translation exposure), the firm's present value—firm value—will change as the value of expected future cash flows (and costs of capital) change as a result of unexpected exchange rate changes. More precisely, a firm is said to have economic exposure to exchange rates when unanticipated *real* (as opposed to nominal, a distinction we will clarify later in the Note) exchange rate changes have a non-zero effect on its expected future cash flows. People also sometimes use the terms operating exposure, real exposure, and competitive exposure as synonyms for such economic exposure.

Transaction Exposure Management

A transaction exposure of the firm is a singular event, an individual foreign currency-denominated cash flow commitment which exposes the firm to a loss or gain upon settlement of the outstanding obligation. The individual transaction exposure can be measured in a number of different ways. Consider, for example, a U.S.-based manufacturer of heavy machine tools who accepts an order from a British buyer and agrees to invoice the sale in British pounds. He is exposed to the movement of the U.S. dollar/ British pound exchange rate. If the sale is made for £100,000, payment due in 90 days from receipt of invoice, the U.S. firm will not know the exact amount in U.S. dollars until actual cash settlement.

When the British buyer first asked for a price quote from the American firm, a transaction exposure was implicitly created. Although far from certain at this point—many price quotes are made by sellers without receiving orders—the American firm has committed itself for some specified period of time to making the sale at the stated foreign currency price. The price is quoted as £100,000, and suppose the spot exchange rate on that date is $1.6000/£. Seven days later, when the spot rate is $1.6300/ £, the order is made. Now this quotation becomes a contractual obligation of the firm, a true transaction exposure. But even at this stage, it is an obligation which is largely invisible. This is because although the firm has committed itself to the production and shipment of the machine tool, the contract itself is essentially work-in-process and not individually identified among the assets of the firm as a foreign currency-denominated asset. For this reason many firms do not identify the transaction as a transaction exposure at this point in time. It may take an additional few weeks to fill the order and ready for shipment.

Upon shipment, however, things change. When the firm ships the product, losing physical control over the goods, an accounts receivable is issued and the sale is now entered into the books of the firm as a foreign currency denominated receivable. Settlement is due in 90 days. The value of the receivable is then booked in current sales at the spot exchange rate in effect on the posting date. If the spot rate was $1.6200/£ on the shipping date, the sale would be booked as £100,000 x $1.6200/£, or $162,000. At the end of the 90-day period upon settlement of the receivable, the final settlement is recorded at the spot rate of exchange on that date, $1.6100/£, and any difference between booking and settlement is categorized as a currency gain or loss.

How are these gains and losses accounted for? In this case, a foreign currency loss of $1,000 is recorded on the American firm's books, settlement of $161,000 less a booked amount of $162,000. The somewhat counter-intuitive result of accounting practices is seen here, as a loss is recognized on the company's income statement although the transaction's value is higher at all dates, including settlement, than it was upon the initial quotation! As illustrated it is obvious that although generally accepted accounting practices record the transaction and exchange rate at the booking date, internally, the firm itself should be expecting a home currency value at settlement closer to that at which it initially quoted the potential sale.

Management Alternatives in Transaction Exposure

Transaction exposures can be managed, or hedged, using either contractual solutions or operational solutions. Contractual solutions include forward contracts, foreign currency options, and foreign currency futures. These are financial derivatives, with their values changing over time as the asset underlying their value—in this case, a currency—changes. Contractual solutions enter the firm into derivative-based positions which manage the individual transaction exposure, at the end of which they are either liquidated or simply expire. Their cost ranges from zero out-of-pocket expense (forward contracts, although the bid-ask spreads represent an implicit transaction cost) to up-front payment (currency options).

Operational solutions include risk-sharing agreements and currency matching. Risk-sharing agreements are pricing agreements whereby the buyer and seller of goods or services agree on a formula-based "sharing" of exchange rate changes. Currency matching is the ongoing process of matching cash inflows and outflows by currency per period of time. Although operational solutions are inherently multi-period, many firms will, as a result of the structure of their continuing business, incur the same basic transaction exposure over and over again. Although many firms do not view operational solutions as relevant to the individual transaction exposure, they are as relevant a choice for transaction exposure management as are forwards, futures, and options.

Directional Views, Forwards and Options. The selection of the proper hedge is as much about the firm's philosophy towards exchange rate risks as it is about the financial theories underlying derivative instruments. There are two determinants in the hedge instrument selection process: (1) the willingness of the firm to take a directional view on the movement of exchange rates over the period of the exposure and (2) the willingness to accept downside risk upon getting the directional view wrong.

A firm which wishes to hedge an individual transaction exposure, such as the £100,000 receivable described previously, could enter into a forward contract with one of its banks to sell pounds at a specific exchange rate upon receipt in 90 days. This forward contract eliminates the currency risk and the firm gains the knowledge now of what the foreign currency denominated cash flow's value will be in domestic currency terms upon settlement. Risk—both downside and upside—has been eliminated. The firm will now know with certainty the dollar revenues to be received and the currency gain or loss to be incurred.[7] While the use of the forward contract does not require management to explicitly predict the movement of exchange rates, it is important to recognize that the firm incurs an opportunity loss associated with the gain foregone if the foreign currency had moved in the firm's favor by the end of the life of the exposure. (In our example, this would be the case if the British pound appreciated instead of depreciating.)

The use of currency options, however, requires the firm to form a directional view on the movement of the exchange rate over the period in question. If management predicts that the exchange rate will move against it—in the case of the British pound denominated receivable, this would be for the pound to depreciate from $1.6000/£ toward, say, $1.5500/£—the firm could purchase a put option on British pounds. The put option will give it the right, not the obligation, to sell the British pounds at a future date (maturity) for an agreed-upon exchange rate (the exercise price). The option would be purchased as insurance against a depreciation of the British pound relative to the exercise price.[8] If the

---

[7] Because the forward rate is calculated from the current spot rate and the differential in the two currency's euro-currency deposit interest rates using a model known as the Covered Interest Parity model, the forward rate will normally differ from the spot rate. This will result in the firm realizing a currency gain or loss on settlement; the gain or loss will, however, be known on the date on which the position is taken. For more details on Covered Interest Parity and the basics of how currency markets work, see the Thunderbird Case Series Note "Currency Markets and Parity Conditions."

[8] The option would require an up-front payment for purchase, the premium, which may vary between 1% and 8%, depending on market conditions.

British pound appreciates, i.e., ends up greater than $1.6000/£, the put option would be allowed to expire worthless, since the firm can now bring back home more dollars than initially anticipated. If, however, the British pound depreciates to below $1.6000/£, the put option would be exercised to guarantee that the firm receives an exchange rate that is the originally agreed upon exercise price at settlement. In other words *by using a put option to protect its U.S. dollar receivable against the depreciation of the foreign currency, the firm has put a <u>floor</u> on the home currency value of its expected receipts.*

In a similar vein, when the firm wishes to hedge a foreign currency payable—or more generally expected future payments in the foreign currency—and it has formed the directional view that the foreign currency would appreciate, it will buy a call option on the foreign currency. The call option will give it the right, not the obligation, to buy the foreign currency at maturity for a certain exercise price. If the foreign currency depreciates, the call option would be allowed to expire worthless, since the firm can now put out fewer dollars than initially anticipated to meet its foreign currency payment obligation. If, however, the foreign currency appreciates, the call would be exercised to guarantee that the firm pays no more than the exercise price for the exchange rate originally agreed upon. In other words, *by using a call option to protect its U.S. dollar payable against the appreciation of the foreign currency, the firm has put a <u>ceiling</u> on the home currency value of its expected payments.*

There are, however, complexities. Given the increasing sophistication of derivative securities like currency options, it is easy for management to lose sight of the significance of the individual transaction within the context of management's general financial responsibilities. A firm which only occasionally incurs foreign currency denominated transactions may be comfortable using only the simplest in financial derivatives, for example, forward contracts, whereas firms which denominate large proportions of their cash flows in foreign currencies may develop a more aggressive approach. Often the resources employed by firms to monitor markets and form directional views do not justify the resulting occasional gains and losses arising from a directional view-based hedging program. In most firms, currency gains above some benchmark such as the forward rate do not justify the losses incurred when directional viewpoints prove off the mark.

A second complexity is that of derivative accounting and hedge accounting. Hedge accounting practices, as outlined by the Financial Accounting Standards Board (FASB),[9] allows that gains and losses on hedging instruments be recognized in earnings at the same time as the effects of changes in the value of the items being hedged are recognized, assuming certain criteria are met. If a forward contract was purchased as a hedge of the British pound receivable noted previously, changes in the value of the forward contract would only be recognized in firm income when the changes in the value of the receivable were recognized, typically on settlement.

This would seem obvious except for the possibility that the 90-day receivable was created during one year, but would be settled in the following year, e.g., after December 31, the firm's end-of-year balance sheet date. Under traditional accounting practices, the firm would have to value the forward contract and the receivable on December 31 at the spot exchange rate on that date, and recognize those valuation impacts in current income.[10] This alters reported current income even though no cash flows have occurred. Many firms legitimately feel that such a practice defeats the purpose of hedging. The criteria set forth by FASB for hedge accounting sometimes create a difficulty. According to FAS 52, paragraph 21:

---

[9] The Financial Accounting Standards Board (FASB) is the authority in the U.S. that determines accounting policy for U.S. firms and certified public accountants. FAS Statement No. 52, applying to fiscal years beginning on or after December 15, 1982, contains the primary provisions and practices to be used in the financial reporting related to foreign currency. FAS Statement No. 133, applying to fiscal years beginning on or after June 15, 2000, altered some of the primary terminology related to the use of financial derivatives used in foreign currency accounting and reporting, but largely left the reporting treatments for foreign currency established under Statement No. 52 unchanged (and as amended by FAS No. 138).

[10] Accounting practices would simply require the firm to value the forward contract and the receivable independently and at current market value (marked-to-market). This is the procedure followed for all financial contracts or speculative instruments which any or all firms may enter into.

> *A foreign currency transaction shall be considered a hedge of an identifiable foreign currency commitment provided both of the following are met:*
>
> *1.the foreign currency transaction is designated as, and is effective as, a hedge of a foreign currency commitment.*
> *2.the foreign currency commitment is firm.*

The first condition focuses on the ability of the forward contract to act effectively as a hedge, its value moving in the opposite direction to that of the exposure given a spot exchange rate change. This condition is typically met. The second condition is controversial. For a commitment to be considered "firm," the exposure must have some type of financial certainty of occurring. For example, if a company has sold merchandise to a foreign buyer, a contract exists and the buyer can be expected to actually pay as agreed. If, however, the receivable resulted from the sale of merchandise to an affiliate of the same firm, there must be some basis for expecting the payment to occur in the amount and on the date designated. This is a difficult requirement for most multinational firms to meet since most intra-firm sales and transactions do not have explicit contracts or penalties for nonperformance.

Translation Exposure Management

Translation exposure arises because financial statements of foreign affiliates must be restated in the parent's currency in order to consolidate financial statements. Foreign affiliates of U.S. companies must restate local currency statements into U.S. dollars so the foreign values can be added to the parent's balance sheet and income statement. Although the main purpose of translation is to prepare consolidated statements, they are also often used by management to assess the performance of foreign affiliates. Such restatement of all affiliate statements into the single common denominator of one currency facilitates management comparison. Translation or accounting exposure results from change in the parent's net worth, assets, liabilities, and reported net income caused by a change in exchange rates since the last translation.

According to FAS Statement No. 52, the motivation for consolidation procedures is the following:

> *Financial statements are intended to present information in financial terms about the performance, financial position, and cash flows of an enterprise. For this purpose, the financial statements of separate entities within an enterprise, which may exist and operate in different economic and currency environments, are consolidated and presented as though they were the financial statements of a single enterprise. Because it is not possible to combine, add, or subtract measurements expressed in different currencies, it is necessary to translate into a single reporting currency those assets, liabilities, revenues, expenses, gains and losses that are measured or denominated in a foreign currency.*[11]

The objectives of translation according to FAS No. 52 are: (1) to provide information that is generally compatible with the expected economic effects of a rate change on an enterprise's cash flows and equity and (2) to reflect in consolidated statements the financial results and relationships of the individual consolidated entities as measured in their functional currencies in conformity with U.S. generally accepted accounting principles.

<u>Functional Versus Reporting Currency</u>. FAS Statement #52 uses what is termed the "functional" currency approach. According to the FASB: "An entity's functional currency is the currency of the primary economic environment in which the entity operates; normally, that is the currency of the environment in which an entity primarily generates and expends cash."[12] The selection of the functional currency for the remeasurement of the financial statements of a foreign operation has two primary

---

[11] FAS No. 52, paragraph 4.
[12] Statement of FAS No. 52, Foreign Currency Translation, FASB, December 1981, paragraph 5.

effects: (1) it determines the procedures to be used in the measurement—in home currency terms—of its financial position and operational results and (2) whether the exchange gains and losses resulting from remeasurement are to be included in the consolidated net income of the firm or reported as a separate component of the consolidated stockholders' equity.

The problem is that a foreign affiliate's functional currency can differ from its reporting currency. A reporting currency is the currency used by the parent to present its own financial statements and thus normally its home currency. The determination of functional currency is left up to management. Management must evaluate the nature and purpose of its foreign operations to decide on the appropriate functional currency for each. The core principle behind functional currency determination is the identification of which currency cash flow is the driving force of the affiliate's business. The choice of functional currency, in turn, determines the method—the "current rate" method or the "temporal" method—that is used to restate the financial statements of the foreign affiliate. A proper understanding of the differences between these restatement procedures depends on a number of very specific definitions of how certain assets, liabilities, and cash flows do or do not change with exchange rate movements.

<u>Methods Used To Restate Financial Statements.</u> When the foreign affiliate's functional currency is the same as the currency of its books, the appropriate procedure is referred to as "translation" by FAS No. 52. Translation requires that all elements of the affiliate's balance sheet be restated into U.S. dollars using the exchange rate that prevails on the translation date and income statement items be translated at the actual exchange rate at which transactions occurred, or some weighted average exchange rate. Any resulting gains or losses resulting from the translation of the foreign affiliate's financial statements are reported as adjustments to stockholder's equity and are termed translation adjustments or cumulative translation adjustments (CTAs). Income statement items are translated as the actual exchange rates prevailing on the date of transaction (or some weighted average). This method is often referred to as the "current rate" method.

When the foreign affiliate's functional currency is the U.S. dollar then the appropriate procedure is referred to as "remeasurement." Remeasurement, as described by FAS No. 52, requires that both historical and current exchange rates be used in the restatement of the foreign affiliate's financial statements into U.S. dollars. All monetary assets and liabilities are restated at current exchange rates, while all non-monetary assets and liabilities are restated at the historical exchange rates. Monetary assets and liabilities are those balance sheet items whose amounts are fixed in currency units. For example, the accounts receivable of the German subsidiary which are denominated in euro are fixed in the quantity of euro which are to be received on a specific future date. Because the exchange rate on that future date is not now known, the receivable is valued at the spot exchange rate on the date of restatement. Non-monetary assets and liabilities are those balance sheet items whose amounts change with market prices. Any gains or losses resulting from the remeasurement of the foreign affiliate's financial statements are included in consolidated income. This method is often referred to as the "temporal" method.

Figure 2 demonstrates the current rate method and the temporal method for the translation of the balance sheet of a Mexican subsidiary of a U.S.-based company. Note that the current rate method results in translation adjustment loss (which would go to consolidated equity), whereas the temporal method results in a translation gain (which would go to consolidated income). The primary issue from management's viewpoint is where the translation gains (losses) are reflected. Since the temporal method views the currency of economic consequence of the subsidiary to be the same as the parent's, any gains (losses) arising from remeasurement are reflected in consolidated income. For a subsidiary whose functional currency is that of the local market, however, gains (losses) resulting from its translation will be reflected in consolidated equity, not in current income.

Management of translation exposure continues to be a topic of substantial debate. On the one hand, the accounting method itself produces no underlying cash flow changes. On the other hand, under the "remeasurement" procedures of the temporal method, consolidated income could be affected dramatically.

Figure 2 Balance Sheet Translation of a Mexican Subsidiary of a U.S.-Based Company: A Comparison of the Current Rate Method and Temporal Method

Panel A: Current Rate Method (Mexican peso is functional currency)

Assets	Mexican pesos	Ps/$	U.S. dollars	Ps/$	U.S. dollars
Cash	1,000,000	3.20	312,500	5.50	181,818
Accounts receivable	7,500,000	3.20	2,343,750	5.50	1,363,636
Inventory	13,000,000	3.20	4,062,500	5.50	2,363,636
Net plant and equipment	18,500,000	3.20	5,781,250	5.50	3,363,636
Total assets	40,000,000		12,500,000		7,272,727

Liabilities & Net Worth					
Accounts payable	2,500,000	3.20	781,250	5.50	454,545
Short-term bank debt	3,000,000	3.20	937,500	5.50	545,455
Long-term debt	15,000,000	3.20	4,687,500	5.50	2,727,273
Equity capital[a]	15,000,000	3.00	5,000,000	3.00	5,000,000
Retained earnings	4,500,000	3.10	1,451,613	3.10	1,451,613
Total liabilities & net worth	40,000,000		12,857,863		10,178,886
Cumulative Translation Adjustment (CTA)[b]			(357,863)		(2,906,158)

Panel B: Temporal Method (U.S. dollar is functional currency)

Assets	Mexican pesos	Ps/$	U.S. dollars	Ps/$	U.S. dollars
Cash	1,000,000	3.20	312,500	5.50	181,818
Accounts receivable	7,500,000	3.20	2,343,750	5.50	1,363,636
Inventory	13,000,000	3.10	4,193,548	3.10	4,193,548
Net plant and equipment	18,500,000	3.00	6,166,667	3.00	6,166,667
Total assets	40,000,000		13,016,465		11,905,670

Liabilities & Net Worth					
Accounts payable	2,500,000	3.20	781,250	5.50	454,545
Short-term bank debt	3,000,000	3.20	937,500	5.50	545,455
Long-term debt	15,000,000	3.20	4,687,500	5.50	2,727,273
Equity capital[a]	15,000,000	3.00	5,000,000	3.00	5,000,000
Retained earnings	4,500,000	3.10	1,451,613	3.10	1,451,613
Total liabilities & net worth	40,000,000		12,857,863		10,178,886
Translation gain (loss)[b]			158,602		1,726,784

[a] Equity capital was injected when the exchange rate was Ps3.00/$, and retained earnings reflect a vintage of exchange rates and earnings as retained.
[b] Translation adjustments and gains (losses) are in essence a plug value which maintains the balance of the entire translated balance sheet.

Management Alternatives in Translation Exposure

There are a number of motivations for active management of translation exposure and not all of them are justifiable. The first is in the event of subsidiary liquidation. If a subsidiary has created CTAs, these gains and losses will be realized in current income upon liquidation. A firm planning such a liquidation could hedge against those in the period prior to liquidation.

A second motivation is to preserve the integrity of balance sheet ratios, particularly in light of covenants or other restrictions by creditors. A firm experiencing continual translation losses which are accumulating in its equity accounts may see deteriorating ratios. To the extent that this leads to an increase in the firm's cost of debt financing and, hence, its cost of capital, it could have an impact on the value of the firm.

A third motivation for the management of translation is managerial compensation. Management compensation is frequently based on post-translation financials. During periods of appreciation of the consolidation currency, management of subsidiary operations may feel that they are being unfairly held to account for the movement of currencies, rather than for their ability to manage and grow the subsidiary.

The fourth situation in which translation exposure may deserve active management is when a subsidiary is operating in an economic environment in which the currency is rapidly depreciating. Although accounting standards refer to this as "hyper-inflation," the problem is currency depreciation, not necessarily inflation. (The linkage between prices and exchange rates is explored in the following section in detail.) For example, according to FAS No. 52, a subsidiary operating in an economic environment with a cumulative inflation rate of 100% or more over a three-year period must use the temporal method and pass all remeasurement losses through current income. This could obviously result in a substantial impact on consolidated income, something that the parent may wish to manage.

The final instance in which management or hedging of translation exposure has become significant is in the protection of consolidated reporting earnings. In recent years a number of major multinational firms have discovered that they can protect the reported U.S. dollar value of foreign earnings by hedging them. For example, in the third and fourth quarters of 2000, a number of major U.S. multinationals grew increasingly concerned over the depreciation of the euro (see Figure 3). Given the significant contribution of profits earned in euros to total profits, the depreciation of the euro resulted in deterioration of reported earnings per share. Some, like the Coca Cola Company which hedged the dollar value of its projected euro earnings, showed little material declines in consolidated earnings. Others, like Goodyear and Caterpillar, saw double-digit percentage reductions in consolidated earnings as a result of their unhedged euro earnings.

Figure 3 The Impact of the Depreciating Euro on Selected U.S. Multinationals

	3Q/2000 Operating Income($ m)	Reduction because of Euro Depreciation
Goodyear	$ 683	0.0%
Caterpillar	$2941	2.0%
McDonald's	$ 910	5.0%
Kimberly-Clark	$ 667	2.5%

Source: "Business Won't Hedge the Euro Away," *Business Week*, December 4, 2000.

Actual management of translation exposure is difficult and potentially costly. Currency gains (losses) associated with liquidation may be covered with something as simple as a forward contract. CTA losses which are accumulating over time in the parent's consolidated equity, however, are much more difficult to deal with. The basic balance sheet of the subsidiary must be altered by currency of denomination in order to reduce "exposed assets" without simultaneously reducing "exposed liabilities." For example, if the Mexican subsidiary were to acquire additional debt and hold the proceeds in non-peso denominated assets of some kind—say, U.S. dollars—it could effectively reduce its exposure to losses arising from translation. This can, however, have a real cash flow impact in terms of differences in interest rates either paid or received when altering assets and liabilities purely for translation purposes.

Management of Economic Exposure

On June 21, 1994, John F. Welch, then-Chairman and CEO of General Electric, wrote an op-ed article in the *Wall Street Journal* arguing that "Global competitors [of U.S. firms] are taking actions that could push U.S. manufacturers from the deceptive tranquility of the eye back into the turbulence of a hurricane, a hurricane that this time will come with a ferocity that could be intensified should the currency go the wrong way." He went on to say, "If the Japanese are preparing to compete at 90 yen [to the U.S. dollar], the U.S. must be ready to compete at 130. Until we are, we delude ourselves if we think we are in control of our own fate."

What was Mr. Welch talking about?

As it turns out, he was addressing an important issue concerning the impact of exchange rates on the competitive position of U.S. multinationals, or a type of exchange rate exposure referred to as "economic exposure to exchange rates." It is an issue that many CFOs—let alone General Managers and CEOs—do not actively think about for a number of reasons. One, it deals with the effects of exchange rates that have not happened yet, but could happen. Unfortunately it is inherent in the nature of many incentive systems that managers get rewarded for their ability to deal with problems that have arisen in the past rather than their ability to avoid problems of the future by careful anticipation. Two, it deals with the effects of exchange rates that are sometimes difficult to pin down and measure; since information systems have a bias toward focusing attention on those things that can be measured, this issue often gets overlooked. Three, understanding economic exposures requires us to understand a subtle distinction between *nominal* and *real* exchange rates, a distinction that managers often do not worry about.

Economic exposure to exchange rate says that the only exchange rate change that matters for the value of cross-border cash flows is an *unexpected real change* in the value of a firm's home currency against the currencies in which a firm is conducting its business; a purely nominal change in the exchange rate does not matter. Unlike the cases of translation and transaction exposures which can be managed using appropriate tools of risk management, economic exposure often requires resolution through longer-term operational and strategic decisions made by the firm. Financial risk management tools may not only be ineffective in managing economic exposure to exchange rates, but they may actually be counterproductive.

The Intuition Behind Real and Nominal Changes in Currency Values

Analogous to concerns with the effects of inflation in the domestic setting on nominal versus real price levels, the effects of relative inflation rates between the home economy and the foreign economy matter for the exchange rate between the two countries.

Taking the purely domestic case, when inflation rates are higher, goods and services cost more in an economy. But does that mean that purchasing power has eroded in that economy? Not necessarily. Whether or not purchasing power has eroded depends on what happens to incomes in the domestic economy. If incomes go up by exactly the same percentage as the rate of inflation in prices, nothing happens to the real value of purchasing power in the economy. More precisely, there has been a nominal increase in price levels, but real purchasing power has remained the same.

An analogous idea holds in the international setting. When the foreign inflation rate is higher—and the domestic inflation rate does not change—the foreign country currency would be expected to depreciate against the domestic currency. In other words, the foreign currency costs less to buy using domestic currency. But that does not necessarily mean that the real value of our purchases of goods and services across borders has become cheaper. Why? Since inflation rates are higher abroad than at home, if the increase in foreign prices for goods and services has exactly offset the decline in the value of the foreign currency, then purchasing power would remain the same. Just as in the domestic case, while the foreign currency has undergone a nominal depreciation, it has not undergone a real depreciation.[13]

Thus, what matters for purchasing power across any two countries is the change in the nominal value of a currency after adjustment for the changes in the relative inflation rates between the two countries. This change, i.e., the change in nominal currency value between two countries over and above that which would be predicted by the relative inflation rates between the two countries, is called the real exchange rate change. When a currency appreciates in real terms, its purchasing power abroad has increased; when it depreciates in real terms, its purchasing power abroad has eroded.

Currencies and Purchasing Power Parity

Assume the United States (U.S.) is the home country and the dollar ($) the home currency, and the European Union (EU), with its currency the euro (€), is the foreign country. Define the $/€ exchange rate—that is, the number of U.S. dollars it takes to buy each euro—as e.[14] Suppose the $/€ exchange rate one month ago was $0.80/€, but the exchange rate is now $0.90/€—in other words, e has gone up by 10¢. But since it costs ¢10 more to buy the euro than it did one month ago, the dollar has depreciated by ¢10 against the euro (or equivalently, the euro has appreciated by ¢10 against the dollar). Suppose we denote the percentage change in the value of the dollar against the euro as Δe. Then during the past month, $\Delta e = (0.90 - 0.80)/(0.80) = 12.50\%$ or, the euro has appreciated by 12.50% against the U.S. dollar. Note that this is a positive number, that is, $\Delta e > 0$. What if e had moved down to $0.70/€? In this case, the euro has become ¢10 cheaper during the past month, and $\Delta e = (0.70 - 0.80)/(0.80) = -12.50\%$ or the euro has depreciated nominally by 12.50% against the U.S. dollar. Note that this is a negative number, that is, $\Delta e < 0$.

The theory of PPP, perhaps one of the most influential ideas in all of economics, establishes a link between prices in any two countries and their exchange rate. Suppose the domestic price level is P, the foreign price level is P*, and the exchange rate (direct quote from the standpoint of the domestic country) is e. Then a version of PPP theory called Absolute PPP (APPP for short) would argue that the domestic price level must equal the exchange rate-adjusted foreign price level, or:

$$(1) \quad P = eP^*$$

Consider a simple example. Suppose a BMW automobile costs €60,000 in France and the $/€ exchange rate is $1/€. Then APPP (using the formula above) says that a similar BMW should cost $60,000 in the U.S. If not, the argument goes, there would be an arbitrage opportunity to buy in the country where the exchange rate-adjusted price is cheaper and sell in the country where it is more expensive. The very process of a free goods market undertaking such transactions would eliminate such an arbitrage opportunity, with the result that APPP will become true in equilibrium.

---

[13] The idea that currencies will be expected to depreciate in nominal terms when their inflation rates are expected to be relatively higher is one of the most basic ideas in the theory of international finance, and is called the *theory of purchasing power parity (PPP)*. The theory is developed more precisely in the next section. For a more substantial development of the ideas in this section, see the Thunderbird Case Series Note, "Currency Markets and Parity Conditions."

[14] Such a definition of exchange rates—the number of units of domestic currency it takes to buy each unit of the foreign currency—is called the *direct* (or American) quote. The reverse quotation—the number of units of the foreign currency its takes to buy one unit of the domestic currency—is called the *indirect* (or European) quote. All of the following discussion will use direct quotes.

Suppose, for instance, the BMW costs only $50,000 in the U.S. At the current $/€ exchange rate, this works out to €50,000. French traders would have the incentive to start buying their BMWs in the U.S. by paying $50,000 and selling in France for €60,000, thereby making an arbitrage profit of €10,000. However, this happy situation will not last long. The demand for BMWs in the U.S. would go up, and thereby start to increase the U.S. price; likewise, the excess supply of BMWs in France would start to lower the euro price. Moreover, in the process of paying for their BMWs in the U.S., the French traders would be supplying euros and demanding dollars in the foreign exchange markets; this would, in turn, depreciate the value of the euro and appreciate the value of the dollar (in other words e, defined from the dollar viewpoint, will start to decrease). More generally, going back to our APPP definition, P would start to rise and both e and P* would start to fall, until such time that the prices for BMWs would be the same in the two countries. In other words P (the U.S. dollar price) would be equal to eP* (the euro price adjusted for the exchange rate).

This insight can then be used across a wide range of traded goods and services between any two countries (or even a country and all of its trading partners). The result is the idea of PPP holding at the national level (with respect to some aggregate measure of prices such as the producer or consumer price index) and with respect to the exchange rate between the two countries.

But note something important from the example above. Since prices were higher in France, the ultimate result of this disequilibrium was to depreciate the euro against the U.S. dollar, so as to bring things back into equilibrium. More generally, we might say that when inflation rates are higher in France relative to the U.S., we would expect the euro to undergo a nominal depreciation against the U.S. dollar. This idea can be made more precise, and it provides us with the most commonly used and understood version of PPP (it is, sometimes, also called Relative PPP). If we call ΔP the expected domestic inflation rate, ΔP^* the expected foreign inflation rate, and Δe is the expected change in the value of the U.S. dollar against the €, then the precise definition of relative PPP, or RPPP, says that:

$$1 + \Delta P = (1 + \Delta e)(1 + \Delta P^*)$$

This can be rearranged to form a simple expression for predicting the expected exchange rate change given expected inflation rates between the two countries:

$$\Delta e = \frac{(1 + \Delta P)}{(1 + \Delta P^*)} - 1$$

Note that when the domestic inflation rate is higher than the foreign inflation rate (that is, ΔP is greater than ΔP^*), Δe will be a positive number, and hence, the foreign currency would be expected to appreciate. When the reverse it true, Δe would be a negative number and the foreign currency would be expected to depreciate.

For example, if the expected inflation rate in France is 10% and the expected inflation rate in the U.S. is 5%, then PPP would predict that $\Delta e = [(1.05)/(1.10)] - 1 = -4.55\%$ meaning the euro would be expected to depreciate by 4.55% against the U.S. dollar. Given the initial exchange rate of $1/€, the new predicted exchange rate (e_{New}) would be:

$$e_{New} = 1 \times (1 - .0455) = \$0.9545/€$$

Now we are ready to tackle the idea of changes in the real exchange rate. Once we have done so, it becomes possible to precisely define economic exposure to exchange rates and to explore the managerial implications. In the example above, we saw that if PPP held, then given our inflation assumptions, we would expect the euro to depreciate by 4.55% against the U.S. dollar. Suppose, however, that the actual depreciation—or the *nominal* depreciation—turned out to be, say, only 2.5%. In other words, as events actually turned out, the euro depreciated by less than was predicted by PPP (by 2.05% less).

This difference of 2.05% is the real exchange rate change. In this particular case, although the euro has undergone a nominal depreciation of 2.5%, the French franc has undergone a *real appreciation* of 2.05%! Why? Inflation differentials, i.e., RPPP, would have predicted a 4.55% depreciation; instead, the actual (or nominal) depreciation was only 2.5%. The euro ended up depreciating by less than predicted, and hence in real terms, this is tantamount to an appreciation.

More generally, if we define the real exchange rate as s, and the change in the real exchange rate as Δs, then the real exchange rate change is defined as:

(4) Δs = {Actual exchange rate change} *minus* {PPP-predicted exchange rate change}

$$= \{\Delta e_{Actual}\} - \left\{ \frac{(1+\Delta P)}{(1+\Delta P^*)} - 1 \right\}$$

In the example above, the PPP-predicted change was –4.55%, and the actual (or nominal) change was –2.5% (recalling that appreciation will have a negative sign when using direct quotes). The value of the actual minus the PPP-predicted change is –2.5% – (–4.55%) = +2.05%, and since we are using direct quotes and the change is a positive number, it is a real appreciation of the euro.

Definition and Sources of Economic Exposure

A firm is said to have economic exposure to exchange rates when unanticipated changes in real exchange rates have a non-zero effect on its expected future cash flows.[15] (People also sometimes use the terms operating exposure, real exposure, and competitive exposure as rough synonyms for such economic exposure.) In the previous section we argued that what matters for economic exposure is real, and not nominal, exchange rate changes.

Let us now see why through a simple example. Suppose a U.S. firm is competing against a Japanese firm (in Japan) by exporting its products from the U.S. Its products are priced in yen (¥), but its costs are incurred in the US$. Assume that the initial exchange rate is ¥100/US$ (the direct quote from the Japanese standpoint). Assume further that: (1) Initially, price per unit and average costs are the same for the U.S. and the Japanese firm (they both are equally competitive); (2) They both sell the same number of units, in fact, just one each of the product; and (3) The price per unit is, say ¥100 (= $1 at the current exchange rate) and cost per unit is, say, ¥80 (= $0.80 at the current exchange rate). All of these are simplifying assumptions. The initial profit margin for both firms is, therefore, 20%.

Panel A of Figure 4 summarizes the initial competitive situation for the two firms.

Suppose the U.S. inflation rate goes up to 10%, while there is no price inflation in Japan (that is, the Japanese inflation rate is 0%). Using the RPPP formula (and treating Japan as the home country), we can calculate what would be expected to happen to the ¥/$ exchange rate:

$$\Delta e = \frac{(1+\Delta P)}{(1+\Delta P^*)} - 1 = (1/1.1) - 1 = -9.1\%$$

---

[15] As an aside, economists would define it as follows: A firms is said to have economic exposure to exchange rates when $\partial\pi\partial s$ is greater than or less than zero (where π is the firm's cash flows, s is the real exchange rate, ∂ can be interpreted as the "change in." Thus, "$\partial\pi\partial s$" captures the idea of the "change in the firm's cash flows with respect to a change in the real exchange rate."

Figure 4 Real Currency Changes and Economic Exposure:
Initial Situation (Panel A) and PPP Holds (Panel B)

Panel A: Initial Situation

<u>Exchange rate = ¥100/$</u>   <u>U.S. Exporter</u>   <u>Japanese Competitor</u>
Revenue $1.00 ¥100
Costs $0.80 ¥ 80
Profits $0.20 ¥ 20
            Profit Margin 20% 20%

Panel B: PPP Holds (10% U.S. inflation; 0% Japanese inflation)

<u>Exchange rate = ¥90.9/$*</u>   <u>U.S. Exporter</u>   <u>Japanese Competitor</u>
Revenue $1.10 ¥100
Costs $0.88 ¥ 80
Profits $0.22 ¥ 20
            Profit Margin 20% 20%

* The new exchange rate is derived by applying PPP formula to obtain Δe,
and then multiplying (1 + Δe) by the initial exchange rate of ¥100/$.

Thus, RPPP would predict that, given the 10% higher inflation rate in the U.S. compared to Japan, the U.S. dollar will depreciate by 9.1% against the Japanese yen. Therefore the new predicted exchange rate would be:

$$e_{New} = (¥100/\$) \times (1 - 0.091) = ¥90.9/\$.$$

Suppose the exchange rate moves exactly as predicted by PPP—in other words, all of the exchange rate change is purely nominal. What would happen to the competitive position of the U.S. firm against the Japanese firm? Panel B of Figure 4 examines this. First, note that nothing happens to the Japanese firm (since there is no inflation in Japan): its still sells its product for ¥100, incurs a cost per unit of ¥80, and makes a profit of ¥20 for a profit margin of 20%. What about the U.S. firm? Given the 10% inflation in the U.S., its costs have gone up by 10%, to 88 cents for each unit produced and sold. However, its revenues have also gone up by 10%. This is because, at the new exchange rate of ¥90.9/$, its Japanese sales of ¥100 are translated to $1.10 back in the U.S. Its profit is now 22 cents and its profit margin is the same 20% as before. In other words, because PPP held, all the change in the exchange rate was purely nominal, and nothing happens to the competitive position of either firm.[16]

Figure 5 Real Currency Changes and Economic Exposure: PPP Does   <u>Not Hold</u>

<u>Exchange rate = ¥100/$*</u>   <u>U.S. Exporter</u>   <u>Japanese Competitor</u>
Revenue $1.00 ¥100
Costs $0.88 ¥ 80
Profits $0.12 ¥ 20
        Profit Margin 12% 20%

* Assumes 10% U.S. inflation rate, 0% Japanese inflation rate, but exchange rate does not change from the initial level of ¥100/$ as shown in Panel A of Figure 4.

---

[16] But you may be asking, "Isn't the U.S. firm making 22 cents now compared to 20 cents before?" The answer is, "Of course!" but the 22 cents today is worth only yesterday's 20 cents in terms of purchasing power, since there is a 10% inflation rate in the U.S.!

Now let us see what happens if PPP fails to hold. Despite the 10% inflation rate in the U.S., suppose the ¥/$ exchange rate stayed the same as before, at ¥100/$. This would imply that, instead of depreciating by the expected 9.1% as predicted by PPP, the US$ stayed put, and therefore, it actually appreciated in real terms by 9.1%. Figure 5 addresses what happens to the competitive positions of the two firms:

Again, we see that nothing happens to the Japanese firm: its domestic revenues stay at ¥100, its cost at ¥80, profit at ¥20, and its profit margin is the same 20% as before. But the U.S. firm is now in trouble—since there is 10% inflation in the U.S., its costs have still gone up, 88 cents. However, its yen revenue of ¥100, when translated into US$, brings in only $1.00 at the still prevailing exchange rate of ¥100/$. The U.S. firm's profit shrinks to 12 cents, and its profit margin to 12%. (And the manager of this firm might be asking, "What is going on here?" given that the exchange rate hasn't even changed.)

In fact, this is a relatively benign scenario. A worse competitive situation would be one where the Japanese competitor, knowing this, was to start lowering his yen prices and thereby start to take away market share. This would put pressure on the U.S. firm to either reduce its profit margins further (by matching the competitor's pricing move in order to keep market share) or lose share and lower total profits.

We can take away a number of important insights from this seemingly simple example:

- Purely nominal changes in currency values are irrelevant for economic exposure to exchange rates. What matters is a real appreciation or a real depreciation.

- A real appreciation of the home currency is bad news for those whose costs are incurred in the home currency and revenues are incurred in the foreign currency. This is typically the case with export-intensive firms, or firms that have sales subsidiaries abroad that are financed in the home currency, or firms that rely on income sources such as royalty payments from abroad. A real depreciation, on the other hand, is good news for such firms.

- A real depreciation of the home currency is bad news for those whose revenues are incurred in the home currency and costs are incurred in the foreign currency. This is typically the case with import-intensive firms, or firms that have subsidiaries abroad that supply to the parent company, or firms that have to make royalty payments in the foreign currency. A real appreciation, on the other hand, is good news for such firms.

- If your costs are denominated in the home currency and your competitor's costs in the foreign currency, then a real appreciation will make you less competitive. The reverse is true with a real depreciation.

Management Alternatives for Economic Exposure

The simple example above suggests that there are three categories of exchange rates that matter in order to figure out whether (and how much) a firm or division has economic exposure: (1) The currency of denomination of the firm's revenues; (2) The currency of denomination of the firm's costs; and (3) The currency of denomination of the firm's competitors' revenues and costs. A firm is likely to have economic exposure to exchange rates whenever the currency of denomination of its revenues is different from the currency of denomination of its costs, i.e., when (1) and (2) are in different currencies, or when the currency of denomination of its revenues and costs are different from that of its competitors, i.e., even if (1) and (2) are in the same currency, when they are different from (3).

Thus, the first set of questions that a manager needs to ask concerning the possible existence of economic exposure are the following:

- What is the currency of denomination of my costs versus that of my revenues? Are they different?

•What is the currency of denomination of my costs and revenues versus those of my competitor? Are they different?

If the answer to either question is "yes," then a firm (or a division) is likely to have economic exposure to exchange rates.

An Example: The Case of Jaguar plc. Towards the end of 1984, Jaguar plc, a U.K.-based manufacturer of luxury high-priced automobiles, was assessing its economic exposure to exchange rates. In their London offices, CFO John Edwards was getting advice from his economic advisors and he himself was convinced that the sustained real appreciation of the U.S. dollar had begun to run out of steam, and the currency value was about to reverse course. To the extent that price changes took place in this market, one firm usually played the role of price leader—in the U.S. market, Daimler Benz plays this role.

Jaguar sold over 50% of its cars in the U.S., and its production costs and factories are U.K.-based; further, labor accounts for a significant portion of the cost base for luxury cars. In the recent past, Jaguar has performed extremely well in the U.S. market, thanks in large part to the substantial real appreciation of the U.S. dollar against all European currencies. While the strong dollar gave Jaguar the opportunity to cut its prices, it had not done so (nor had its competition). Mr. Edwards knew that the projected depreciation of the U.S. dollar would seriously cut into his profitability, and some upward revision of prices would be required if the depreciation did happen. For starters he had to make a broad assessment of the nature of Jaguar's economic exposure to exchange rates.

The first question confronting Mr. Edwards was, which are the main currencies that he should worry about vis-à-vis his economic exposure to exchange rates? The U.S. dollar only, the U.K. pound only, or the Deutsche mark only, or all three? The answer is, all three.

His exposure to the US$ and UK£ is fairly obvious. First, since a substantial part of his revenues are denominated in the US$, he should worry about the US$ as the currency of denomination of his revenues. Second, since most of his costs are U.K.-based, the currency of denomination of costs is the UK£. Given the mismatch between the two, the $/£ exchange rate is a crucial (and direct) determinant of his economic exposure. Any real appreciation of the UK£ (and thus a real depreciation of the US$) will have the immediate effect of lowering his revenues in UK£ terms (or increasing his costs in US$ terms). If he were to increase his US$ prices of cars to keep his profit margins constant at the pre-U.S. dollar depreciation level, demand would drop and he would sell fewer cars. If he kept his US$ price the same, his profit margins would be squeezed, and hence possibly the company's share price as well.

On top of these considerations, he also must worry about the indirect, competitive exposure to the DM, since that is the currency of denomination of the costs of his major competitor, Daimler Benz. Daimler Benz's ability to price its products in the U.S. (and hence create competitive pressure for Jaguar sales in the U.S.) will depend on what happens to the $/DM exchange rate, and since that, in turn, will automatically imply an exchange rate between the UK£ and the DM, Mr. Edwards must closely monitor developments in the UK£/DM exchange rate as well.

Assuming that a real depreciation of the U.S. dollar is a very strong likelihood, what would be the ideal scenario of exchange rate changes that Jaguar could hope for, in order to at least mitigate the impact of the dollar depreciation? His only hope from a competitive standpoint is that the US$ depreciates by a greater percentage against the DM than it does against the UK£. That would squeeze his competitor's margins worse than his own, and perhaps force Daimler Benz to raise its US$ prices, thereby providing Jaguar the cover for a price increase of its own.

Sources of Economic Exposure: Any time that a firm undertakes a transaction across borders— whether that transaction is in goods, services, capital, people, or technology—it puts itself into a situation where there is the likelihood of direct economic exposure to exchange rates. In addition, as we have seen, even a firm (or division) that considers itself purely domestic (in other words it both sources and sells locally) is not necessarily immune to economic exposure: If the source of its competition is from abroad, it faces competitive exposure to exchange rates. Thus, economic exposures arise from the operational and strategic decisions that a firm makes. Any time that a market is chosen, a sale is made, a product or raw material is purchased, financing is taken on, royalty payments received, or a new plant is located in a foreign country, the firm faces the likelihood of economic exposure to exchange rates. In addition, any time that a foreign competitor enters the competitive picture, there is possibly competitive exposure as well.

Thus, it is important to recognize that exposures are created continuously, at the frontlines of corporate activity. More often than not, economic exposures are actually created by the marketing manager, the production manager, and the purchasing manager. While this may seem obvious after the fact, it is nonetheless an important point to make—non-financial managers often simply assume that exchange rates are something to "just let the Treasury worry about." Indeed, the office of the CFO has a relatively limited role in creating economic exposure. It does so only if it makes financing decisions in currencies that are different from the currency of denomination of its assets. Given the fact that the source of economic exposure is the operational and strategic decisions made by a firm, the solutions also largely lie in the operational and strategic arena. Unlike the case of the other two types of exposure, the CFO's role is more limited (although, as we will see, the CFO's office can also perform a role in limiting economic exposures)—management of economic exposures is the task of a General Manager more than it is a task of the CFO.

<u>Managing Economic Exposure on the Revenues' Side</u>. In managing economic exposure on the revenues' side, the fundamental issue comes down to that of finding the appropriate mix between the price at which the product is sold abroad and the volume sold. In turn, there are at least eight factors to consider:

(i) the demand elasticity;
(ii) the nature of returns to scale;
(iii) whether the currency change is expected to be temporary or permanent;
(iv) whether the firm can create entry barriers;
(v) whether the product is differentiated;
(vi) how distribution channels and consumers will react to price cuts;
(vii) the currency invoicing strategies used;
(viii) and finally, whether competitors will react passively or aggressively to any pricing moves.

Suppose, for specificity, that we are considering a U.S. exporter selling a product in Japan, incurring most of its costs in the U.S., competing against Japanese firms. Also, suppose the Japanese yen has undergone a real appreciation against the dollar. The firm is now faced with an interesting choice: (1) maintain the yen price at the pre-depreciation level, let the dollar price rise thereby yielding extra dollar profits on each unit sold and maintain market share; or (2) lower the yen price, maintain the dollar price at the previous level, maintain per-unit profitability at least at previous levels, thereby gaining extra market share from the increased Japanese demand resulting from lowered yen prices. How should the exporter respond to this situation?

The price elasticity of demand for its product would determine the extent of increase in demand—the higher the elasticity, the better off the firm in terms of increasing its market share in Japan from a price cut. It is possible that the firm may have scale economies resulting from the increased volume, e.g., because it may have excess capacity, or it might be able to take advantage of the learning curve by producing extra units, or there may be cost savings through access to fixed distribution and transportation costs, etc. Such scale economies would actually increase the dollar per-unit profit margin (compared to previous levels).

Next, the firm has to form a judgment on whether the depreciation is expected to be a temporary phenomenon. For example, what if, a few months later, the yen depreciated back to its original level? If this happened the exporter might have to raise its yen prices in order to return to its original level of profitability. Whether or not it can do so will depend on a number of factors, including its ability to create entry barriers (e.g., is the product differentiated and does the firm have blocking access to distribution channels?); whether and how consumers will react to price fluctuations (e.g., are consumers likely to be alienated by the uncertainty at the point of purchase resulting from price changes that occur every time exchange rates fluctuate?); the competitive structure of the product-market (e.g., does the firm compete in a market with "aggressive" competitors or "passive" competitors?).

Moreover, the firm has to consider whether the distribution channels in Japan would simply soak up the yen price cut, so that the consumer does not see any significant price reduction at the point of purchase. If this happened, then the firm would see no benefits from cutting yen prices. Invoicing strategies also matter. If the exporting firm invoices in its home country currency (in this case, the dollar), then the appreciation automatically translates, by default, to the market share-increasing decision, i.e., maintain the dollar price, thereby lower the yen price by the full extent of the depreciation. If, on the other hand, the exporting firm invoices in the foreign currency (in this case, the yen), its decision, by default, is to maintain the yen price, thereby automatically increasing the dollar price and maintaining market share.

The main thing to note from the discussion above—we are in the realm of operational and strategic decisions that would have to be made by a marketing manager or a general manager, rather than financial risk management decisions by a CFO!

Managing Economic Exposure on the Cost Side. Most import-based firms, particularly those that rely on natural resources such as petroleum and minerals (e.g., firms in oil, steel, and commodities) and firms in food processing and textiles as well as firms that tend to outsource their component and parts supplies from abroad (e.g., firms in computers, commercial aircraft, and automobiles), are often equally affected by real currency movements on the cost side as they are on the revenues side.

In many ways, cost management strategies in the face of a real currency movement are the reverse of those related to revenue strategies, in that a similar underlying set of variables affect strategic choices. First, note that currency movements matter for the firm's costs only in situations where the firm sources some or all of its inputs, e.g., raw material, intermediate products, labor, technology, from abroad. If the firm buys its inputs solely in the domestic markets, any direct currency effects are unlikely. If the firm's home currency appreciates against the supplier's currency, cost management is less of a problem, and indeed, becomes more of an opportunity for managing additional profits arising from cost reduction. The reason is that, under an appreciation, the firm has to pay fewer units of its home currency to buy the same amount of inputs in the foreign currency. There is, however, the issue of whether the firm should pass on any of the currency-related savings to its input suppliers.

The difficult cost management issue arises from a depreciation of the home currency against supplier currencies and is as follows: given that most firms have input sourced from abroad, how much of the home currency depreciation can be (i) passed-through to the suppliers of these inputs; (ii) in the event that pass-through of costs to suppliers is difficult, how much can be passed-through to consumers through price increases; (iii) in the event that both (i) and (ii) are difficult to accomplish, what are the options available to diversify into new sourcing alternatives from more favorable currency areas? The answers to these questions depend on (a) the buyer power that the firm exercises over its suppliers; (b) the nature of the contracting relationship between the supplier and the firm; (c) the currency invoicing strategies used; (d) the availability of alternate suppliers of inputs and (e) the permanence of currency movements.

Clearly, the firm's ability to pass-through the impact of a depreciation to suppliers will depend on the power it has over its suppliers, as well as the nature of contracting with its suppliers. The higher the buyer power of the firm, the greater its ability to insulate its costs from the impact of currency movements. However, the more formal and long-term the contracting between the firm and its suppliers, the lower its ability to insulate its costs from the impact of currency movements. Similarly, if the firm invoices its supplies in its home currency, it obviates the problem and lowers the impact of currency movements. On the other hand, if it invoices its supplies in the seller's currency, any currency movement impacts are passed-through directly to the firm's costs.

What if a firm has little power over its suppliers, or is unable to undertake spot contracting with its suppliers, or operates in a supplier market in which the invoicing is done in the seller's currency? The first option is to examine whether the impact of the cost increase resulting from the currency depreciation can be passed-through to customers. Decision variables in this case revert to those we discussed under pricing and revenue strategies in the previous section. A more stable—and longer term—option is for the firm to diversify its supplier base across at least two or three major currency areas, e.g., the U.S. dollar, euro, and Japanese yen currency blocs. This sourcing flexibility is particularly crucial if the currency movement can be expected to be more than temporary—say, expected to last two or three years, not an unusual scenario if the events of the past decade are any guide. Again note, the appropriate responses to economic exposure requires operational and strategic, rather than financial decisions. That said, it turns out that the CFO's office can help.

Managing Economic Exposure Through Financial Decisions. Financing decisions can play a role, too, in hedging economic exposures. However, these opportunities present themselves primarily in the management of revenue-based economic exposure rather than cost-based or competition-based economic exposure. When the firm has revenues denominated in a currency other than its home currency, what it has, in essence, is an asset denominated in the foreign currency. This can be managed by creating an appropriate liability (that is, financing) in the foreign currency. If the foreign asset is long-lived, that is, the firm foresees the possibility that such foreign currency revenues will be an integral part of its long-term global strategy, then it would be appropriate to take on long-term financing in that currency.

There are two broad choices: issue foreign currency debt, or issue equity by listing its stock in the foreign country. It is beyond the scope of this Note to go into the ramifications of the debt versus equity decision, except to point out that if debt is chosen as the source of long-term foreign currency financing, the firm may wish to consider whether there are opportunities to undertake foreign currency swaps. In many instances, the market for foreign currency swaps are more liquid (and go out to longer maturities) than the markets for straight debt issues. Moreover, it may be possible for the firm to profitably swap some of its existing home currency long-term liabilities rather than issue new debt.

Consider the case of Walt Disney Company in the 1980s. In the mid-1980s, Disney set up Tokyo Disneyland as a franchise from which it was expecting substantial (and fast-growing) yen revenues well into the foreseeable future—thus it had a substantial yen asset on its books. Soon thereafter Disney undertook a number of foreign currency swaps worldwide. It issued debt in many different currencies, e.g., Swiss francs, French francs, and so forth, and swapped them back to yen to create a yen liability, with a counterparty that was interested in getting rid of its yen liability and taking on the liability in the currency in which Disney was issuing its debt. Disney, however, refrained from issuing equity in Japan, perhaps because a royalty stream is a relatively steady, senior, and nonresidual cash flow to Disney, and hence there was no need to back it with an equity-type financial instrument. As a result of such financing decisions, by the early 1990s, Disney was able to hedge away a major portion of its economic exposure to yen.

An Example of Economic Exposure Management by Japanese Firms. The period 1994 to early 1995 was a rough one for many Japanese exporters. During this period the yen appreciated by 33% in real terms against the dollar (from about ¥120/$ to ¥80/$). The earnings of many well-known firms in Japan were quite substantially hurt and many of them reported record losses because of this sudden and severe appreciation of the yen against the dollar. How did Japanese firms cope with this appreciation?

Japanese firms undertook aggressive cost-cutting. Specifically: (1) they focused on continuous cost improvement, by cutting production costs and by laying off later entrants into the workforce; (2) they altered sourcing strategies, by moving production abroad, especially to low-to-middle income

Asian countries such as the Philippines and Thailand and by aggressively squeezing their second-tier and third-tier suppliers; (3) they altered their pricing strategies, by cutting profit margins rather than increasing the dollar price of their exports.

As a result, by mid-1995, many Japanese firms were leaner and more cost-competitive (measured purely in the domestic currency) than they were prior to the yen appreciation. The results of this cost-cutting were strikingly evident in an annual survey conducted by the Economic Planning Agency of Japan on the breakeven yen per dollar exchange rate at which major Japanese exporters would cease to be profitable. The survey results, for the years 1994-96 are shown in Figure 6:

Figure 6 Breakeven Exchange Rates: Percentage of Japanese Firms Placing Own Breakeven Rates in the Range Indicated		
	1994	**1995**	**1996**
Less than ¥100/$	Neg	13.7%	22.9%
¥100/$ to ¥110/$	14.1%	37.3%	41.4%
¥110/$ to ¥120/$	36.9%	30.1%	25.4%
¥120/$ to ¥130/$	37.7%	14.2%	8.5%
More than ¥130/$	10.8%	4.7%	1.8%
Source: Economic Planning Agency of Japan.			

In 1994 about 50% of Japanese firms said that they would remain profitable if the yen appreciated to less than ¥120/$—in other words, it would require a yen-dollar exchange rate of ¥120/$ and above for nearly half the Japanese firms to continue to make a profit. Indeed, fewer than 1% of firms surveyed indicated that they would be profitable if the yen were to appreciate to less than ¥100/$.

By 1996, after two years of cost-cutting, things had changed quite a bit. Over 90% of Japanese firms indicated that they would be profitable if the yen were to stay at a level of ¥120/$ or above. Most striking of all, compared to less than 1% of all firms in 1994, nearly one-quarter of the surveyed Japanese firms indicated that they would remain profitable even if the yen were to appreciate to less than ¥100/$. No wonder Mr. Welch was worried![7]

Overall Guidelines on Currency Exposure Management

It should be obvious by now that active management of economic exposure requires a firm-wide response and one that should be the concern of a General Manager rather than just the CFO. One, the first step is to ask the two key questions raised earlier regarding the currency of denomination of a firm's revenues and costs and the currency of its competitors' revenues and costs. In making this assessment, it is not necessary for the firm to expend its resources to track every exposure by every single currency; rather, it makes sense to use an 80/20 approach, i.e., 80% of what is relevant is often to be found in just 20% of the detail. Usually, two or three currencies tend to account for a large portion of direct economic exposures, just as competitors from just one or two major currency areas often account for a major portion of competitive exposures. It is imperative that General Managers of multinational firms know what these currencies are.

Two, the firm must set up a currency reporting system to track exposures as they develop. Such a system should encompass exposures by currency, by maturity, and by operating unit. It is necessary to make operating divisions responsible for reporting their exposures at least monthly, so that the firm can keep track of developments before real currency values stray too far.

---

[7] The survey also found that if the exchange rate stabilized to around ¥110/$, Japanese car manufacturers would, on average, more than double their profits (relative to ¥80/$). As of the time of writing, the exchange rate had stabilized around ¥118/$.

Three, it is necessary to involve Treasury at early stages of major sales or purchase decisions that involve a currency other than the firm's home currency. This does not mean that the Treasury must have a say in the choice of currency (let alone the structure of the deal), but it does mean that line managers must take on the responsibility of alerting Treasurers at an early enough stage so that any potential problems that might arise further down the road can be anticipated and managed better. Moreover Treasury is often the source of information concerning natural currency offsets or operational hedges that may be available elsewhere in the firm and may also be able to mitigate exposures by making smarter financing choices early on.

Four—and perhaps most important—it is necessary to inculcate a clear sense among line managers that they are the ones that actually create the exposures and they are also the ones that can be most effective in managing the risks. Too many line managers in too many organizations have the tendency to dismiss currency-related issues with the view that "it's Treasury's problem."

Finally, all of these suggestions presume that incentive systems in organizations are, at least to some reasonable degree, geared toward rewarding managers for their skills of anticipation (i.e., dealing before-the-fact with major problems that could have arisen, but didn't), rather than solving problems (i.e., dealing after-the-fact with problems that do arise).

Setting Up a Risk Management Program

Evidence of foreign exchange risk management provides some insight into how firms today are addressing and managing their currency exposures.

Figure 7 provides some results from a recent survey conducted by Bank of America. Whereas only 54% of surveyed firms actually identify their economic exposures, 70% identified transaction exposure and a full 80% identified translation exposure. As might be predicted, firms continue to be quite active in the hedging of transaction exposures (80% hedge them), but few are hedging their translation exposure at this time (30% hedge translation). Due to the inherent complexity of identification and management, only 5% of the firms surveyed are actively hedging their economic exposure.

Figure 7 Bank of America Corporate FX Risk Management Survey Results, 1996

Percentage of Firms Surveyed Who:

Currency Exposure	Identify	Hedge	Do Not Hedge	Fully Hedge	Partially Hedge
Translation	80%	30%	70%	15%	15%
Transaction	60%	80%	20%	30%	55%
Anticipated	70%	57%	43%	2%	55%
Contingent	52%	15%	85%	4%	11%
Economic	54%	5%	95%	5%	Neg
Balance Sheet	30%	22%	78%	6%	15%
Income Statement	44%	39%	61%	6%	33%

Source: "Corporate America: FX Risk Management 1996," Global Capital Markets Group, Bank of America, Monograph 78, Winter 1996/97, pp. 1-3.

The continuing challenges lie within the realm of economic exposure management.

There are a number of additional practical concerns which will need to be addressed before the firm can operationalize a truly effective risk management program and although they are beyond the scope of this Note, they are worth mentioning:

a. Should risk management be centralized or decentralized?

b. What are the managerial compensation issues, and multinational control issues raised by the firm's risk management policies?

c. Are there operational and control issues related to conflicts between currency exposures and interest rate exposures?

d. What is the process of confirmation and settlement of contractual commitments involving financial derivatives?

e. What are the information technology needs for real-time value-at-risk analysis of the multitude of exposures and positions which the firm deals with in a cross-border setting?

Many of the well-known currency-related losses suffered by non-financial firms in the past decade have arisen either from lack of exposure planning and identification, or from inadequate controls imposed over commitments of the firm, or from inadequate real-time monitoring of derivative values associated with positions outstanding. These losses are the failures of management, not failures inherent to the financial derivatives utilized. A risk management program is no better or worse than the skills of those who construct, operate, and monitor it. Perhaps most importantly, unless the motivations behind such risk management are clearly thought out and well-articulated, the risk management tools themselves can take the firm only so far.

Suggested Readings

Bodnar, G. M., S. H. Gregory, and R. C. Marston, "1998 Wharton Survey of Financial Risk Management by U.S. Non-financial Firms," *Financial Management*, Vol. 27, No. 4, 1998.

Dornbusch, R., "Exchange Rates and Prices," *American Economic Review*, 77, 1987.

Dufey, G., "Corporate Finance and Exchange Rate Variations," *Financial Management*, Summer 1972, pp. 51-57.

Eiteman, D. K., A. I. Stonehill, and M. H. Moffett, *Multinational Business Finance*, 9th edition, Addison-Wesley Longman, 2001.

Fisher, E., "A Model of Exchange Rate Pass-Through," *Journal of International Economics*, 26, 1989.

Froot, K., and P. D. Klemperer, "Exchange Rate Pass Through When Market Share Matters," *American Economic Review*, 80, 1990.

Froot, K., D. Scharfstein, and J. Stein, "A Framework for Risk Management." *Harvard Business Review*, 72, September-October 1994, 59-71.

Froot, K., J. Stein, and D. Scharfstein, "Risk Management: Coordinating Corporate Investment and Financing Policies," *NBER Working Paper No. 4084*, 1992.

Jorion, P., "The Exchange Rate Exposure of U.S. Multinationals," *The Journal of Business*, 63, 1990.

Knetter, M, "Goods Prices and Exchange Rates: What Have We Learned?" *Journal of Economic Literature*, September 1997.

Krugman, P., "Pricing to Market When the Exchange Rate Changes," *NBER Working Paper No. 1926*, 1986.

Lessard, D., and E. Flood, "On the Measurement of Operating Exposure to Exchange Rates: A Conceptual Approach," *Financial Management*, Spring 1986.

Lessard, D., and J. B. Lightstone, "Volatile Exchange Rates Can Put International Operations at Risk," *Harvard Business Review*, July-August, 1986.

Levi, M. D., and P. Sercu, "Erroneous and Valid Reasons for Hedging Foreign Exchange Rate Exposure," *Journal of Multinational Financial Management*, Vol. 1, No. 2, 1991, pp. 19-28.

Luehrman, T., "The Exchange Rate Exposure of a Global Competitor," *Journal of International Business Studies*, 21, 1990.

Meulbroek, L., "Integrated Risk Management for the Firm: A Senior Manager's Guide," *Harvard Business School Working Paper No. 02-046* 2002.

Moffett, M. H., and D. J. Skinner, "Issues in Foreign Exchange Hedge Accounting," *Journal of Applied Corporate Finance*, 8, No. 3, Fall 1995.

Moffett, M. H., and J. K. Karlsen, "Managing Foreign Exchange Rate Economic Exposure," *Journal of International Financial Management and Accounting*, 5, No. 2, June 1994.

Smith, C. W., and R. M. Stulz, "The Determinants of Firms' Hedging Policies," *Journal of Financial and Quantitative Analysis*, Vol. 20, No. 4, December 1985, pp. 390-405.

Smith C. W., C. W. Smithson, and D. S. Wilford, "Why Hedge?" *Intermarket*, July 1989, pp. 12-16.

Smith, C. W., "Corporate Risk Management: Theory and Practice," *Journal of Derivatives*, Vol. 2, No. 4, 1998

Stulz, R. M., "Optimal Hedging Policies," *Journal of Financial and Quantitative Analysis*, Vol. 19, No. 2, June 1984, pp. 127-140.

Stulz, R. M., "Rethinking Risk Management," *Journal of Applied Corporate Finance*, 9, Fall 1996.

Sundaram, A., and J. S. Black, "The Environment and Internal Organization of Multinational Enterprises," *Academy of Management Review*, October 1992.

Sundaram, A., and J. S. Black, *The International Business Environment: Text and Cases* Prentice-Hall: NJ, 1995 (see Chapters 3 to 5).

Sundaram, A., and V. Mishra, "Currency Movements and Corporate Pricing Strategies," *Recent Developments in International Banking and Finance*, S. Khoury (ed.), Volume IV-V, Elsevier, 1991.

Sundaram, A., and V. Mishra, "Economic Exposure to Exchange Rates: A Review," *Tuck School Working Paper*, March 1990.

III. Emerging Markets

The Emerging Markets Phenomenon

Questions:

What has been the history of developing countries' engagement with global financial markets?

What happened in the debt crisis of the 1980s?

Why did capital flows resume so quickly after the losses of the debt crisis?

What have been the investment characteristics and performance of EFM securities?

In what ways is the risk of investing in EFMs unique?

Introduction

Developing countries have existed for a long time, and for much of their history they have attempted two related tasks: to build their local financial institutions and markets, and to attract international investment. Some have succeeded quite admirably while others have a great deal of work left to do. As time has gone by, the words we use to describe these countries and their markets have undergone considerable change. In the 1950s and 1960s it was common to speak of an "underdeveloped country." This soon gave way to the more polite "less developed country" (LDC) that was prevalent in the 1970s and 1980s. Then the phrase "emerging financial market" (EFM) caught on in the 1990s, as a worldwide change of ideas away from state-sponsored development and toward the opening of free markets brought a burst of progress and performance.

The International Finance Corporation (IFC), the private sector arm of the World Bank Group, began using the phrase "emerging financial markets" to describe a set of countries for which they kept and published standardized stock indexes starting in 1981. Their original list contained only nine countries whose stock markets looked particularly promising. This list was later expanded to 25 countries, for which the informal criterion was 30 to 50 listed companies with a market capitalization of $1 billion or more and annual trading volume of $100 million or more. The phrase "emerging financial markets" is now widely used to describe all developing countries.

The year 1993 will be long remembered as the year of miracles in emerging financial markets. Portfolio investors from developed countries, who in 1992 had supplied $10 billion of new debt capital and $11 billion of new equity capital to EFMs, raised those amounts almost fourfold to $36 billion and $45 billion, respectively, in 1993. The IFC reported that stock price indexes, measured in U.S. dollars, rose dramatically in almost all developing countries, led by the Philippines (+133 percent), Turkey (+214 percent), and Poland (+718 percent). The total market capitalization of all EFMs nearly doubled from $884 billion to $1,591 billion.

It was a year of boundless optimism. The recession in the United States had come to an end and U.S. stock markets were rising. Communism had been swept almost totally from the world stage during 1989–1991. Democracy had spread so widely that for the first time every government in Latin America except Cuba's was democratically elected. Privatization was being aggressively pursued in every region of the world. The energy unleashed in world financial markets by these events caught the attention of portfolio managers everywhere. Academics began to publish studies of the astonishing behavior of EFMs.

This heady pace of financial expansion did not last. Important setbacks lay just a few years ahead for many countries in every major region. The Mexican currency and capital market collapsed abruptly at the end of 1994, sending the economy into a tail-spin, with important spillover effects in Argentina and Brazil. This propelled average emerging market bond yields from a range of 400 to 800 basis points above U.S. Trea-sury bonds (from 1991 to mid-1994) to the range of 800 to 1,800 basis points (from mid-1994 through 1995). During 1996 and early 1997 yield spreads fell back to about 400 basis points, but then rose dramatically to 1995 levels again in the wake of the 1997–1998 East Asian crises, when Thailand, Malaysia, Indonesia, the Philippines, and Korea experienced collapses much like Mexico's.[1] The East Asian economies, cel-ebrated as "miracles" in the early 1990s, saw large output losses during 1997 and 1998 in the aftermath of these events. The Russian default of August 1998 seemed to finish off any remaining investor enthusiasm for EFMs.

Many people assume that capital flows into EFMs dried up as a result of these crises, but the reality is somewhat more complex, as shown in Table 1.1. Foreign direct investment continued a path of almost uninterrupted growth during the 1990s, and accelerated rather than slowed down during the crisis years of 1995–1998. Portfolio investment has been more variable, but has been *net positive* in each year of the 1990s; that is, portfolio investors reduced their new commitments in the crisis years of 1995–1998 back to the level of 1991–1992 but continued to invest. It is the banks that have withdrawn capital as quickly and on as large a scale as they put it in. Further-more, as we shall see in more detail in Chapter 2, the pace of privatization and finan-cial liberalization did not slow but actually accelerated in 1998.

In the late 1980s and early 1990s, the financial world changed fundamentally in a way that is not likely to be reversed. For the first time, many countries in the develop-ing world have adopted a strategy of international openness and private domestic own-ership, a strategy embodied in newly liberalized trade relations and privatized corpora-tions. International commodity and capital markets have demonstrated how quickly import demands and capital inflows from the developed nations could respond to new opportunities in developing countries, and have proved how quickly impressive eco-nomic results could be obtained for newly liberalizing economies. The financial crises of the late 1990s pose a new challenge to successful openness and liberalization—one that we will examine in detail in this book—but they have not undermined the core faith in these mechanisms as the necessary path to overcoming poverty.

A Brief Look at History

Cycles of Enthusiasm and Despair

The 1990s cycle of boundless enthusiasm followed by collapse and dismay in EFMs is, in many ways, not new. Because developing countries have attracted capital for a great many years, it is useful to look at the nature of capital flows and the experience of investors in the past. It is natural to assume that developing countries have long afforded interesting opportunities to obtain above-average returns although at the cost

---

[1]IMF (1998), p. 3.

4   *Chapter 1   The Emerging Markets Phenomenon*

TABLE 1.1   Net Private Flows of Capital to Developing Countries (in billions of U.S. dollars)

	1990	1991	1992	1993	1994	1995	1996	1997	1998
Foreign direct investment	18.4	31.3	35.5	56.8	82.6	96.7	115.0	140.0	131.0
Portfolio investment	17.4	36.9	51.1	113.6	105.6	41.2	80.8	66.8	36.7
Bank loans and other	11.9	55.6	32.7	11.5	−35.5	55.4	16.3	−57.6	−103.5
Total net private flows	47.7	123.8	119.3	181.9	152.8	193.3	212.1	149.2	64.3

Source: International Monetary Fund, 1999, Table 1.3.1.

of above-average risk. Certainly many private fortunes have been made in the developing world, though this has involved private equity or foreign direct investment (FDI) more often than investments in publicly held EFM stocks.

Equity markets in EFMs typically have a long history. For example, a stock market was organized in Turkey in 1866, in Brazil in 1877, and in Indonesia in 1912. Yet that history has been discontinuous; public securities markets frequently have not provided effective means for raising capital over long periods of time. The records of prices in these markets are often incomplete, and the markets themselves were often interrupted by war, revolution, or economic collapse.

A recent study pieced together a composite record of long-term stock market returns in many countries, which is summarized in Figure 1.1.[2] This figure shows real annual rates of return (nominal returns less actual inflation) in these stock markets against the number of years since 1921 the market has existed without interruption. Notice that in nearly half of the countries the returns were actually negative; that is, nominal returns did not keep up with inflation. The only countries that have sustained high real returns for many years are those considered as developed (see the upper right-hand corner). Figure 1.1 therefore offers a basic piece of wisdom about EFMs: They have often provided negative returns to arm's-length equity investors, frequently because of a major national or institutional collapse.

Debt investors have fared somewhat better, though they have suffered repeated periods of default and rescheduling. One study, for example, followed 10 developing countries from 1850 to 1970, comparing the returns promised and realized, expressed as a premium above the benchmark alternative of home-country government bonds.[3] The average promised return was 1.81 percent above the benchmark and the average realized return was 0.42 percent above the benchmark; that is, lenders not only did not lose their principal, but actually did better on average than they would have done on home-country bonds, though only by a small margin.

The Appendix to this chapter gives a listing of the many episodes of default and rescheduling of private loans to sovereign borrowers from 1800 to 1992. As can be seen, the list is very long and includes most countries of the world, some as many as six times. Interestingly, however, Asian countries, along with the independent Arab states, have rarely defaulted. The Appendix reminds us of another fundamental truth: that periodic default and rescheduling have been the norm of international lending in most regions since international lending began.

[2]Jorion and Goetzmann (1999).
[3]Lindert and Morton (1989).

A Brief Look at History   **5**

FIGURE 1.1

Real returns on global stock markets sorted by years of existence

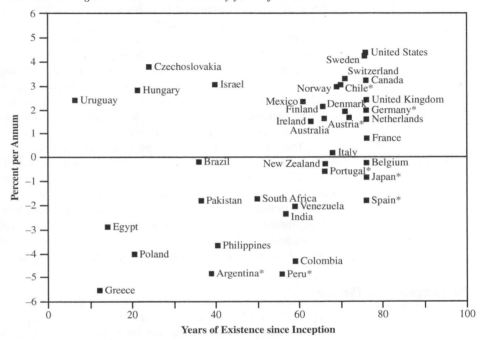

Note: An asterisk indicates that the market suffered a long-term break during its years of existence, the effect of which on returns cannot be measured but is almost surely negative.
Source: Jorion and Goetzmann (1999).

What explains these recurring cycles of high returns on equity and debt followed by stock market collapses and debt defaults? One point of view is that investors are only partially rational, and that they are prone to extremes of enthusiasm and despair. Some economic historians refer to historical cycles of "euphoria" and "revulsion" in international capital investment.[4] In this view of the world, people keep making the same mistakes because they have not learned from the past and let their temporary emotions shape their longer-term investment decisions.

Our view is rather different.[5] We believe that investors are rational for the most part, but that risks in emerging markets are inherently different. Investments in emerging markets are best viewed as complex institutional experiments with highly uncertain long-run outcomes. Unlike the returns histories of developed economies, which aggregate roughly into bell-shaped distributions of outcomes, emerging market countries tend to follow more discontinuous short-run paths and more "bimodal" long-run paths, oscillating between states with very high returns (when institutional experiments seem to be going well) and states with very low returns (when those experiments seem to be failing).

---

[4]Kindleberger (1989) is particularly associated with this view and expounds it with clarity and enthusiasm.

[5]For an introduction to the view of financial fragility that emphasizes the role of information problems and institutional constraints in capital markets rather than irrationality of investors see Hubbard (1990, 1991) and Calomiris (1995).

6   *Chapter 1   The Emerging Markets Phenomenon*

Adding to, and magnifying, the political uncertainties of EFM experiments in some countries are their undiversified export sectors. Particular commodities often dominate export earnings. Chile, for example, is heavily dependent on copper earnings, Brazil on coffee, and Mexico and Venezuela on oil. The lack of export diversity can produce extreme variations in the terms of trade for EFM countries (the prices of their exports relative to their imports) as international commodity prices fluctuate. Those fluctuations can undermine the more fragile EFM experiments and lead to collapses of equity and debt values. As shown in Figure 1.2, the terms of trade for countries with a lower gross domestic product (GDP) per capita tend to have substantially higher standard deviations than those of richer countries. As can be seen, oil producers have particularly volatile terms of trade.

Thus, EFMs pose new challenges for international investors. It will take time and experience for international investors, EFM governments, and EFM corporations to learn how to measure and manage the risks of economic liberalization. In particular, investors are learning about the importance of fundamental differences in legal and political institutions in determining long-run financial risk, and about how to measure the quality of those institutions. The measurement and management of risk are not static: countries evolve and investors learn. Market collapses are painful for all sides, and learning from them often guides important reforms in the next phase of capital market development.

The Longer-Term Picture

Figure 1.3 illustrates the longer-term history of capital flows to developing countries. This displays the annual real net investment by foreign creditors in the government debt of 10 countries during 1850–1982. The spike in 1894 is probably spurious, as it

FIGURE 1.2

Volatility of terms of trade

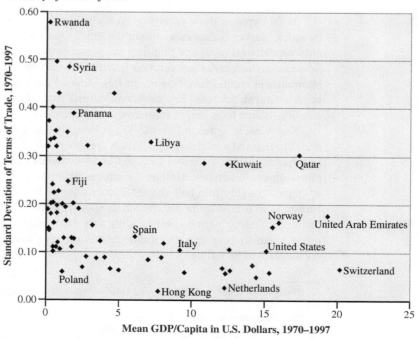

Source: International Financial Statistics (1999) and authors' calculations.

comes primarily from one large loan to the Russian government that was called external borrowing but that may well have come from internal sources. Note that the investment flows were relatively strong in the late 19th and early 20th centuries. This was a period of considerable stability and prosperity. It was the time of the gold standard, which effectively provided fixed exchange rates among currencies, and also a time of very free trade. Capital flows followed the trade flows, and Great Britain was the dominant country mediating both. In the decades prior to World War I, capital flows to developing economies were a larger fraction of world GDP than they are today, and the elasticity of those flows (the extent to which capital moved quickly in search of new opportunities) seems to have been greater as well.[6]

The era of enormous capital flows was brought to an end by World War I, but resumed in the 1920s as the United States became the world's principal source of international capital. The late 1920s witnessed a new period of euphoria, in which U.S. bond investors eagerly took up issues for Latin American and other sovereign governments in greater absolute value than any previous wave. Unfortunately, almost all of these bonds defaulted during the worldwide Great Depression of the 1930s. These defaults were not fully resolved until the 1950s or, in some cases, the 1960s. Although investors often eventually got their money back, even with a small positive return, the length of the workout period substantially interrupted the process of transferring capital to high-productivity uses in developing countries. Protracted default meant that developing economies could not sell bonds in the developed world again until the workout process was complete and international investors had regained confidence in the capacity and ability of developing economies to repay new debt.

FIGURE 1.3

Real net investment by foreign creditors in the government debt of 10 countries

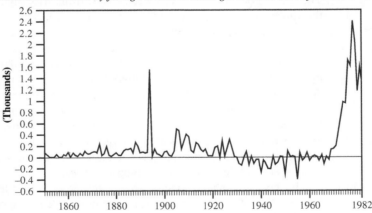

Notes: The vertical axis measures the real value of fresh lending to 10 governments—Argentina, Australia, Brazil, Canada, Chile, Egypt, Japan, Mexico, Russia, and Turkey—by foreign creditors, predominantly private, less retirements on the same external debt in the same year. The figures are in millions of dollars at 1913 prices, with flows in other currencies converted at the 1913 exchange rates. Payments of interest are not included, nor are changes in the real value of outstanding debt due to movements in the consumer-price deflator. The large "spike" of 1894 was a loan package of $1,489.5 million to the Russian government, much of which may have been purchased by Russian creditors. . . . The genuine rise after 1973 is slightly exaggerated in relative terms by a change in series. For developing countries the post-1970 data cover not only bonds but the other types of lending captured in the World Bank's loan disbursements data.

Source: Lindert and Morton (1989).

---

[6]Obstfeld and Taylor (1999).

Note in Figure 1.3 that net investment turns negative in the period 1930 to 1955. This reflects, of course, the devastation of the Great Depression and World War II. The gold standard had collapsed, foreign trade had contracted, and countries everywhere tried to protect their currencies with exchange controls and tariff walls. Bonds were in default and new investment was not replacing the workout payments on the defaulted bonds.

After World War II developing countries had few available sources of capital. Their first relief came from the World Bank, one of the multilateral "Bretton Woods" institutions set up to create a new international financial order after the war. The World Bank, whose official name is the International Bank for Reconstruction and Development, attended first to the need for the reconstruction of Europe and only later to the needs of developing nations. Toward the end of the 1950s, however, it began to make development a top priority. At the same time, the United States, and eventually other developed countries, began to experiment with foreign aid. But World Bank loans and foreign aid were strictly for governments.[7] Private companies in developing countries generally had to rely on local banks heavily controlled by local governments.

For most of modern history up to the 1960s, the large banks in developed countries were not important sources of capital for the developing world. The traditional view of bankers was that cross-border lending, particularly to developing areas, was simply too risky for the commitment of depositors' funds. But this began to change in the 1960s, primarily because the U.S. banking industry began to change.

During this period U.S. banks lost a major portion of their domestic corporate loan market to an efficient securities market alternative, namely commercial paper (i.e., short-term IOUs of corporations, sold either directly to investors or through the services of a securities firm).[8] It is invariably cheaper for a corporation with access to the commercial paper market to borrow short-term funds this way than through banks. The use of commercial paper by large U.S. firms with high credit quality exploded in the 1960s and deprived the banks of many of their best borrowers.

Furthermore, banks lost most of their low-cost sources of money (demand deposit accounts and low-interest savings accounts). They were able to raise large quantities of deposits in the international markets, but for this they had to pay the full market rate of interest. The London Interbank Offered Rate (LIBOR) is the benchmark short-term dollar interest rate announced daily by the British Bankers Association based on the offer side of the market for Eurodollar bank deposits with a 1 to 12 months' term, and is the international standard for bank loan pricing. What banks needed was a new category of borrower that could absorb large quantities of capital and pay LIBOR plus a reasonable *spread* (profit margin) for the banks. To meet this need, banks began to experiment with lending to developing countries.

In the 1970s another factor accelerated cross-border lending. The newly formed Organization of Petroleum Exporting Countries (OPEC) approximately tripled international oil prices in 1973 and again in 1979. The members of OPEC suddenly had billions of dollars in new cash. They deposited the bulk of those funds in the large banks

---

[7]Today the "World Bank Group" of institutions includes the International Finance Corporation (IFC), dedicated to financing the private sector in developing countries; the Multilateral Investment Guarantee Agency (MIGA), offering insurance to foreign direct investors against political risks; and the International Center for Settlement of Investment Disputes (ICSID) as well as the International Development Association (IDA), offering low-interest loans to governments of the poorest countries.

[8]See the discussion of loss of bank franchise value in Chapter 7. For a review of the growth of commercial paper, see Calomiris, Himmelberg, and Wachtel (1995).

of Europe and the United States. The banks in turn were then in a position to lend vast new amounts, but domestic markets for bank credit in industrial countries were insufficient to consume this new supply of funds.

Thus began the wave of syndicated loans to sovereign governments that dominated the international banking scene in the 1970s. Mexico and Brazil were the two largest borrowers, but many other governments joined the game. The early view was that banks were merely "recycling" oil money: Developing countries purchased oil from OPEC, OPEC redeposited the funds in banks, and banks re-lent the money to developing countries. That view, however, failed to note that the countries borrowing heavily had to repay the debt from their export earnings, and in most cases the increase in the relative price of oil had actually worsened their terms of trade. Furthermore, borrowing countries were borrowing far more than their oil import needs, and were using the new funds to promote large-scale, risky, government investments in transportation, power, and new import-competing industries.

Sovereign loans were syndicated to many small banks who had no knowledge whatsoever of the borrowing countries or the uses to which the funds were put. The period 1979–1982 became something of a feeding frenzy as banks lent and syndicated and countries borrowed ever-greater sums. In retrospect, LDC debt was growing much faster than LDC capacity to pay. This wave is represented by the large spike on the right-hand side of Figure 1.3. As can be seen, its volume was unprecedented, much larger than previous flows of capital to developing countries.

On the developing countries' side, foreign borrowing was fueled by the absence of domestic sources of funding. Banking systems were small and securities markets were virtually nonexistent in most developing economies.[9] The extremely low real rates of interest on offer from foreign banks during the 1970s were hard to resist. Most of the LDC lending was in U.S. dollars. A typical loan by banks to an LDC would be priced at LIBOR plus a spread of perhaps 0.5 percent to 3.0 percent.

LIBOR was unusually low in real terms (i.e., after adjusting for inflation) during the 1970s. Figure 1.4 shows a graph of three-month LIBOR and the inflation rate during the 1970s and 1980s. The LIBOR line was 2 to 3 percent above the inflation line in 1972 and 1973. But after 1973 real rates declined because dollar inflation was accelerating. Figure 1.4 shows a line for the typical interest rate at which an LDC might borrow (LIBOR + 1 percent) minus the actual realized rate of inflation. As can be seen, the realized real rate was close to zero. It is no wonder that borrowers were enthusiastic.

Because LDC borrowing cost was indexed to LIBOR, the low real rates of interest of the 1970s were not guaranteed to persist. LIBOR maintained a very different relation to inflation in the 1980s. Paul Volcker became chairman of the Federal Reserve Board in the autumn of 1979 with a mandate to squeeze inflation out of the dollar. Thus began the most massive monetary squeeze in modern times. Interest rates on the dollar, including LIBOR, were propelled into the mid-teens and stayed there even as inflation declined. The result was that real interest rates rose substantially. As can be seen in Figure 1.4, the real rate paid by a typical LDC went from near zero to approximately 10 percent by 1982.

Furthermore, the monetary squeeze induced a major recession in the United States, and by extension in other countries, during 1980–1984. This meant that the United States and other developed countries wanted fewer of the items that LDCs

---

[9]For an excellent review of emerging capital markets circa 1970, see Wai and Patrick (1973).

FIGURE 1.4

Real borrowing rates (%)

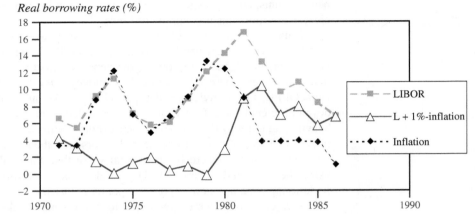

Note: The line designated "L + 1%-inflation" represents the *ex post* real borrowing rate for a typical country that borrows at LIBOR + 1% and experiences actual inflation.
Source: Citibase and authors' calculations.

exported. Lower exports combined with very high real interest rates to make LDC debt unmanageable. In August 1982 Mexico announced that it was unable to maintain interest payments on its foreign debt. This was followed in rapid succession by default announcements of governments throughout Latin America. Numerous other LDCs joined the wave of defaults, including the Philippines, Yugoslavia, and Nigeria. The great global debt crisis of the 1980s had begun.

The Debt Crisis of the 1980s and Its Aftermath

It is difficult to appreciate the magnitude of this crisis. Figure 1.3 suggested how very large the capital flows of the 1970s had been in comparison with earlier periods. Figure 1.5 gives a closer look at the debt and Figure 1.6 the debt service requirements of all LDCs. Official debt—that is, loans from governments and quasi-governmental entities such as the World Bank—rose by a factor of four, but private (i.e., bank) debt rose by a factor of 10 from 1972 to 1982. By the end of 1982, when the crisis began, total private debt stood at $255 billion.

At first the banks denied that the loan defaults implied losses. It was argued that LDCs had a temporary liquidity problem, not a fundamental problem of insolvency. It was widely believed that economic conditions were highly unusual and bound to improve soon. And there were some reasons to believe this: The world economy was deep in recession, interest rates were at all-time highs, and commodity prices (on which LDC export earnings often depended) were very low in comparison to the 1970s. An economic turnaround might restore the LDCs to health and allow them to service their debts.

In 1982 Walter Wriston, the chairman of Citibank, famously remarked that "a country does not go bankrupt." The remark was not as fatuous as it sounds in retrospect. Wriston was expressing confidence in the power of taxation. Government debt is supposed to be safer than corporate debt because governments, unlike corporations,

The Debt Crisis of the 1980s and Its Aftermath **11**

FIGURE 1.5

Long-term debt of all LDCs (in billions of $ U.S.)

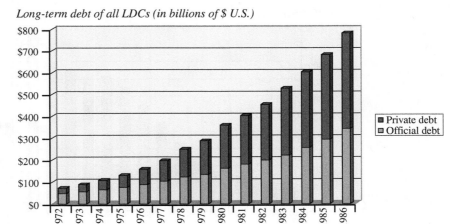

Source: World Bank, *World Debt Tables.*

can set their own revenues through taxation. As we shall see later in this book, that power is freely and ingeniously used to avoid default in EFMs on domestic debt. Local taxation does not, however, produce the foreign exchange needed to repay dollar-denominated international debt; for that, dollars must be earned through exports, and dollar debt must be written down if exports are insufficient to carry the debt.

Banks at first negotiated with the defaulting countries year after year, with the encouragement and support of the IMF, to lend new amounts that could pay the interest on the old amounts. This capitalization of interest would have been a sensible approach if the problem were indeed a temporary one. But insofar as the problem was fundamental and permanent, rolling up interest into more principal only made the debt overhang worse and the probability of full repayment lower.

That is why, despite the defaults in 1982, the total volume of debt kept growing without interruption through 1986, as is clear from Figure 1.5. The annual debt service requirements had actually grown faster than the debt principal during 1972–1982 because of rising interest rates. The rescheduling starting in 1983 slowed the growth of debt service only briefly; by 1986 it too had climbed to new heights, as can be seen in Figure 1.6.

Unfortunately, the LDCs did not recover their equilibrium as the banks had hoped they would. Table 1.2 tells the story clearly. The per capita growth in real GDP dropped from 3.6 percent into negative territory, and negative growth (i.e., a contraction of living standards) persisted for four years. Even after that time, per capita GDP remained essentially stagnant. Inflation, which had averaged less than 30 percent before the crisis, grew persistently into triple digits. Gross capital formation (i.e., new physical investment in capital goods) dropped from 25 percent to as low as 16 percent of GDP. And the ratio of debt to exports seemed to climb inexorably as each year's interest was capitalized. The overhang of excessive debt seemed to suppress the ability of developing countries to join the economic recovery taking place in the developed world by 1985.

By 1986 the LDC debt to private banks had grown to $437 billion, and still no major international bank had taken significant reserves against the likely losses.

12   *Chapter 1   The Emerging Markets Phenomenon*

FIGURE 1.6

LDC annual debt service requirements (in billions of $ U.S.)

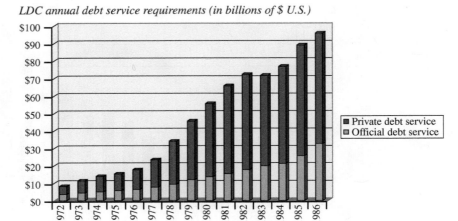

Source: World Bank, *World Debt Tables*.

Traders had begun to trade the defaulted loans. The prices depended on the country but in early 1986 ranged from about 5 percent of par for Bolivia to about 80 percent of par for Venezuela; of the biggest debtors Mexico was priced at 60 percent and Brazil at 75 percent.[10] By mid-1988, however, all such prices had fallen substantially (except for Bolivia, which rose from 5 percent to 11 percent because of a special buyback of half of its debt financed by donor nations). Mexico and Brazil were now both at 52 percent, and the highest value for any defaulted loan was Uruguay at 60 percent. It seemed that banks were facing losses of about 50 percent of the LDC loan exposure (i.e., at least $200 billion in the aggregate), which was especially painful for the U.S. banks that had led the lending binge. The situation seemed to get worse with each passing year.

This was quite different from earlier episodes in which countries defaulted on and rescheduled their bonds. First, the quantities were orders of magnitude larger: The lending and the defaults were of unprecedented size. Second, the lenders were banks rather than bondholders; banks are everywhere regulated by government and can be pressured by governments in a way that private bondholders cannot. Third, this time losses averaging about 50 percent began to appear inevitable. These losses greatly outweighed the interest spreads of 0.5 percent to 3 percent that banks had earned annually on these loans in the good years. Fourth, governments and the IMF encouraged banks and borrowers to postpone workouts by rescheduling debts. That policy error produced the ballooning debt problem—the size of debts grew while the capacity to pay debts shrank.[11] These four factors made the 1980s crisis unlike any the world had experienced before.

The crisis deeply depressed the stock prices of the banks with heavy LDC loan exposures. Indeed, the discounts implicit in the prices of LDC loans and the discounts implicit in the stock prices of heavily exposed banks moved together fairly closely throughout the period 1982–1987.[12] In mid-1987 the banks began to take loss provi-

---

[10]Huizinga (1989) lists prices for March 11, 1986, and June 9, 1988.

[11]For a review of the public policy debate surrounding the debt crisis, see Sachs (1989).

[12]Sachs and Huizinga (1987).

TABLE 1.2 The Economic Crisis in Heavily Indebted Countries

	Per Capita GDP (Annual Change)	Inflation (Annual Rate)	Gross Capital Formation/GDP	Debt/Export Ratio
Average 1969–1978	3.6%	28.5%	N/A	N/A
1979	3.6	40.8	24.9%	182.3%
1980	2.6	47.4	24.7	167.1
1981	−1.6	53.2	24.5	201.4
1982	−2.7	57.7	22.3	269.8
1983	−5.5	90.8	18.2	289.7
1984	−0.1	116.4	17.4	272.1
1985	0.9	126.9	16.5	284.2
1986	1.4	76.2	16.8	337.9

Source: International Monetary Fund, *World Economic Outlook*, April 1987.
Adapted from Lindert and Morton (1989).

sions (deductions from net income reflecting likely losses) of 20 to 25 percent of their LDC loans. By the end of 1987, developing country exposure as a percent of primary capital (equity plus reserves for losses) stood at 79 percent for Citibank, 80 percent for Bankers Trust, 97 percent for Chemical Bank, 112 percent for Chase Manhattan, 124 percent for Bank of America, and 145 percent for Manufacturers Hanover.[13] If half the exposures were lost, no bank would be wiped out but many would suffer severe reductions in their net worth.

Governments of developed countries had generally urged the banks to lend to the LDCs back in the mid-1970s, when the biggest problem the banks faced was how to "recycle" the incoming petrodollars. Furthermore, when the debt crisis first began, the same governments were very permissive in not forcing banks to take loss provisions against their LDC exposures, which would have severely depleted the book value of capital of many large banks. But that was then. Now (in the late 1980s) governments were alarmed at the deepening recession in the developing countries and began to fear political unrest and upheavals. So they began to pressure the banks to recognize their losses in order to bring the crisis to an end.

Numerous proposals were advanced to resolve the debt crisis. Many observers believed that the deeply discounted market prices of the loans held a key to resolution: By getting banks to accept these as losses already incurred, countries might be offered a reduction in the principal value of their debts. Several dozen proposals were advanced to establish a new international agency that would somehow buy up the discounted loans and exchange them for bonds or loans of lower principal amount but higher likelihood of payment.

No such proposals ever got close to realization, because each was fraught with incentive and resource problems. For example, what would prevent countries from acting uncooperatively with banks, breaking agreements and postponing reforms, to drive the price of their loans even lower and make resolution more favorable to themselves? Or what would prevent a bank from *free riding* on other creditors by refusing to make the exchange, knowing that if others made it, then the value of the bank's existing loans would surely rise toward face value? Furthermore, assuring the credit quality of any new instruments appeared to require commitment of government support in massive quantities, which was difficult to envisage politically. Alternatively, credit quality

---
[13]Huizinga (1989).

could be assured if all the old loans were subordinated to the new instruments, but then how much confidence could the agency holding the old loans have of ever being repaid?

Academics began to argue that voluntary debt reduction was in the banks' own interest, and some banks began experiments of swapping defaulted loans for new bonds, real assets, or corporate equity within the borrowing countries. Then in January 1989, Treasury Secretary Nicholas Brady called upon banks to negotiate voluntary debt reductions with the LDCs. His speech hinted that government resources could be marshaled to assist this process if the banks were willing to go along. Negotiations soon began with the government of Mexico to see if this formulation could work.

The promise of government support proved difficult to pin down and in the end scarcely materialized. Mexico offered to exchange new bonds for the defaulted Mexican loans held by the banks. The bonds, whose terms are summarized in Table 1.3, came to be known as *Brady bonds*. They had a 30-year term, with all principal repaid on the final day of the term.

The U.S. government did agree to sell to Mexico some 30-year zero-coupon bonds (ZCBs) at about 11 percent of face value. Since this was the fair market price for zero-coupon Treasuries, there was no government subsidy, just a market transaction. Mexico then pledged these bonds to a trustee to secure the principal payment of new 30-year bonds, whose annual interest would be paid by Mexico. Brady bonds were, in essence, a form of collateralized debt with the collateral held in escrow. This arrangement limited the potential magnitude of sovereign default in the future.

Brady bonds became the pivotal instrument for resolving the debt crisis and are still widely traded in the market. As shown in Table 1.3, there were two types of Mexican Brady bonds: one with a floating rate of interest and one with a low fixed rate. The combination of Mexican coupons and U.S. government-secured principal created an interesting valuation problem, and Table 1.3 shows the estimated values at the time the bonds were issued.

In the end, banks with loans to Mexico were offered three choices: (1) to swap their loans for 65 percent face value of Brady bonds with a floating interest rate; (2) to swap their loans for 100 percent face value of Brady bonds with a low fixed interest rate; or (3) to keep the loans and lend new money equal to 25 percent of their exposure. The fair market value of the first two options was 33 percent and 37 percent or par respectively—that is, somewhat less than the market price of Mexican loans, which by that time had fallen to about 40 percent. Banks would be taking an effective loss of nearly two-thirds of their loans whichever option they chose.

TABLE 1.3   The Mexican Brady Bonds

	Option (1)	*Option (2)*
Term	30 years	30 years
Principal paid	All at end of term	All at end of term
Security	U.S. 30-year ZCB	U.S. 30-year ZCB
Interest rate	LIBOR plus $\frac{13}{16}$ %	6.25% fixed
Market value of bond (M)	51% of face value	37% of face value
Face value of bond offered per dollar of defaulted loans (Q)	65% of loans	100% of loans
Value offered (MxQ)	33% of loans	37% of loans

Source: Authors' calculations.

Governments of all the major developed countries encouraged all banks with Mexican exposure in their jurisdiction to accept one of the three options, so as to minimize free riding. While banks could, in principle, have rejected the Brady approach, government encouragement was a powerful force for change. In the United States, government influence may have been enhanced by the increased dependence of weakened U.S. banks on the government safety net (the discount window and deposit insurance) and on continuing government tolerance of the high asset risk and low capital ratios of U.S. banks.

Mexico succeeded in reducing the economic worth of its bank debt by about two-thirds. This markdown was not necessarily reflected on the books of the banks, nor of Mexico, mainly because of the popularity of option (2) above. Under most bank regulatory and accounting regimes, provision for loss is taken if the principal value (not the economic value) is impaired. Because option (2) involved a low fixed interest rate but no reduction in principal value, and the full principal value was secured even though distant in time, the nominal amount of the banks' loans was not reduced by this choice. Nevertheless, it was an extraordinarily painful moment for the banks.

Seven more heavily indebted countries went through "Brady Plan" negotiations between 1990 and 1992: Argentina, Brazil, Costa Rica, Nigeria, Philippines (twice), Uruguay, and Venezuela. The menus of choices became somewhat longer and more refined, but all were variations on the pattern that Mexico had set. The value of the securities offered in exchange for the loans of these countries were closely calibrated to the trading price of the loans, and ranged from about 18 percent in Costa Rica to 52 percent in Uruguay.

By the end of 1992 the great debt crisis was over, having lasted an entire decade. Banks had taken an enormous loss. The developing countries had freed themselves from the largest of the debt overhangs that had dragged them down for a decade, but were not yet looking strong. The United States had again slipped into a recession in 1990, though it was not as severe as the recession of the early 1980s. It was a sober moment. But the seeds of a remarkable revitalization had been planted.

The Resumption of Capital Flows

Resurgence of the Private Sector

Even as the debt crisis was ending, private capital again began to flow into the developing countries. Figure 1.7 shows the aggregate net private capital flows by year and by region. East Asia, except for the Philippines, had not been part of the debt crisis, and that region benefited most from these new flows. The early 1990s were a high point of East Asian economic performance and prestige. The "Four Tigers" of Korea, Taiwan, Hong Kong, and Singapore had lifted themselves out of the developing category and were generally referred to as "newly industrialized nations." The "Tiger Cubs" of Southeast Asia were growing at a pace that was the envy of the world. And China had finally awoken from its long stagnation; although the government still called itself communist it seemed to be embracing private markets with exceptional enthusiasm. The growth rate of China's real GDP hit 14 percent in 1992 and continued in double digits through 1995. It is no wonder that East Asia attracted capital.

More remarkable, perhaps, was the resurgence of Latin America. The debt crisis, which had affected almost the entire region, might have left a stigma to frighten investors for some time. But the speed with which Latin America recovered was impressive, and a few countries (such as Chile and later Argentina) were setting

16   *Chapter 1   The Emerging Markets Phenomenon*

FIGURE 1.7

Net private capital flows to EFMs

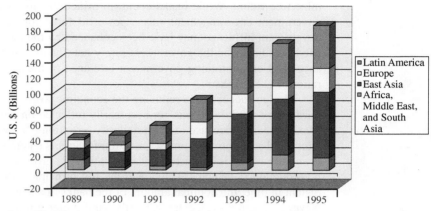

Source: World Bank, *World Debt Tables*.

standards of economic performance comparable to those of East Asia; Chile even harbored a frequently stated ambition to be "the Japan of South America."

As that phrase suggests, Asia imparted an important "demonstration effect" to many countries of Latin America. The export-led growth that had powered so many Asian economies led many Latin Americans to question their closed, inward-oriented systems. One result was a major round of trade liberalization, of which NAFTA (the North American Free Trade Agreement between Mexico, the United States, and Canada) is one expression. As we shall explore in more depth later in this book, several Latin American countries—including Brazil, Chile, Mexico, and Argentina—embarked on a remarkable series of innovations in exchange rate policies, pension reforms, financial market deregulation, and corporate privatization. For the first time, globalization and liberalization had reached Latin America, and with it came a new flow of capital.

The transition countries of Central and Eastern Europe and Central Asia were only modest beneficiaries of the capital boom. Having just shed communism, they had to make transformations of their economies and societies far more drastic than countries in other regions. The process of transformation to a market economy had serious ups and downs, periods of success and then periods of setback, as we will examine in detail in Chapter 3. Global investors were far more cautious about committing capital to this region than to Latin America and East Asia.

Finally, the group of other regions including Sub-Saharan Africa, North Africa and the Middle East, and South Asia attracted the least capital. Though there were individual success stories, these regions taken as a whole seemed to have much more difficulty in transforming themselves into vibrant economies. The process of political and social change seemed slower in these regions, and statism generally maintained a stronger grip here than anywhere else in the world.

Figure 1.8 divides these capital flows between public sector and private sector issuers. The most salient feature of this new rush of investment into emerging markets is how concentrated it was on the private sector. Financing of the public sector was small and static by comparison. Only in Central and Eastern Europe did the public sector rival the private sector in raising capital from private markets, primarily because

The Resumption of Capital Flows **17**

FIGURE 1.8

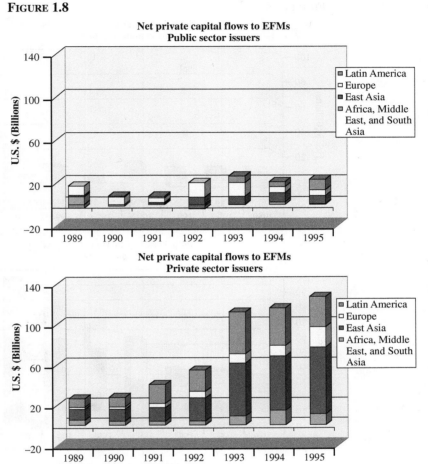

Source: World Bank, *World Debt Tables.*

the public sector was still very large and the private sector so new. Yet even in that region the public sector was declining and the private sector was growing by 1993 to 1995. This shift to the private sector is significant when contrasted with the public sector's previous dominance in raising capital.

Who Were the Investors?

When we break the flows down by type of investor, as in Figure 1.9, further interesting patterns emerge. First, it is obvious from this figure that banks were not important players in these markets through the first half of the 1990s. Having been badly burned by the debt crisis, they made only modest new commitments to the EFMs. They actually withdrew net capital from Latin America in 1989 and from Central and Eastern Europe in 1990 and 1991. The only region that drew significant commitments from banks was East Asia, and even here, despite the impressive economic performance, the banks were much more reticent than other investors. Finally, in 1994 and 1995 the banks began carefully to resume lending in Latin America.

18 *Chapter 1   The Emerging Markets Phenomenon*

FIGURE 1.9

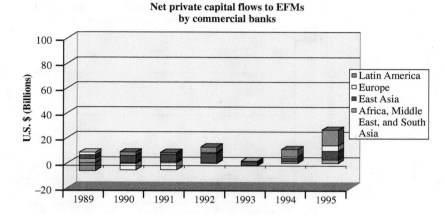

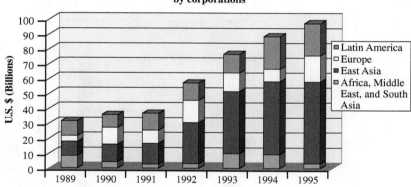

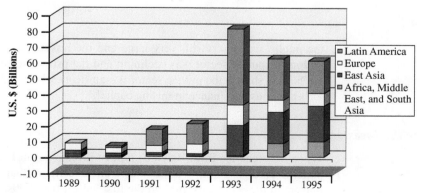

Source: World Bank, *World Debt Tables*.

Portfolio investors were similarly cautious during 1989 and 1990, but began buying Latin American bonds and stocks in serious quantities in 1991 and 1992. They got
over any remaining inhibitions in 1993, with major plunges into Latin America and
East Asia from 1993 to 1995. But why should bonds, which are debt instruments, have

been so attractive so soon after the debt crisis of the 1980s? The answer may be that bonds did not default during the debt crisis. Very few Latin American bonds were outstanding in the 1980s, but those that existed paid off promptly even as banks were being forced into massive losses.

There was no legal or economic basis requiring debtors to pay on bonds but not loans; the sovereign countries simply chose to handle their debts that way. But the consequence was a marketplace impression that bonds were somehow safer than loans. This facilitated the use of Brady bonds in the debt crisis resolution, and it also facilitated the sale of new-money bonds in the 1990s. It also explains why Brady bonds, which were issued to and generally held by banks, required somewhat higher spreads (after adjusting for the presence of U.S. zero-coupon bonds) than new money bonds. Yields on Brady bond "strips" (the part of Brady bonds' future cash flows unrelated to U.S. zero-coupon bonds) have remained higher than yields on other bonds, suggesting that markets still treat Brady bonds differently than other bonds. Indeed, in August 1999, when Ecuador suffered a political and financial crisis, it defaulted selectively on its Brady bonds. This strongly reinforced the perception that Brady bonds are riskier than other bonds and further increased the market yield spreads between Brady strips and other bonds.[14]

It is interesting to note how often the relative preference for bank loans and bonds has been reversed. In the 1940s and 1950s, many foreign bonds were in default, while the small amount of bank credit that existed paid currently. In the 1980s many countries defaulted on bank loans but continued to pay the small amount of bonds outstanding. Then in the Mexican crisis of 1994–1995 and the Asian crisis of 1997–1998, bondholders suffered market losses (though few defaults) while both local and international banks were bailed out with public money. It must be remembered that debt is always at risk and that the relative safety of bonds compared to bank loans is a moving target.

The main message of Figure 1.9 is that corporations have been not only the largest but also the most consistent suppliers of capital to EFMs during 1989–1995. Portfolio investors rushed in during 1993 but then began to pull back, while corporations necessarily take a longer view because their investments are direct and illiquid rather than in the form of tradable securities. It is also clear from Figure 1.9 that the corporations heavily favored East Asia as the developing region of choice. While some commitments were made to Latin America and Central and Eastern Europe, the real growth in corporate commitments came from East Asia.

Some of the portfolio investment shown in Figure 1.9 may actually be disguised bank investment. The presence of banks in the market for EFM bonds may be inferred from the high percentage (35–50 percent) of such bonds with floating rates of interest. Floating rates appeal primarily to commercial banks because bank funding comes mainly from deposits whose cost varies from month to month. A bank protects itself from major interest rate fluctuations by letting the interest rate on its loans fluctuate with the interest rate on its deposits. Since its deposits are typically priced at or close to LIBOR, it prefers to earn LIBOR plus a spread on its assets. Therefore, when we see international bonds whose interest rate floats at LIBOR plus a spread, as we see

---

[14]There is a long history of government discrimination in the treatment of default on creditors. Governments may benefit from such discrimination, for a variety of reasons. For a discussion of these reasons, and the early U.S. experience with sovereign defaults and discrimination, see Calomiris (1991). For a discussion of the recent experience with Ecuadoran Bradys, see Vogel and Druckerman (1999) and *The Wall Street Journal* (1999).

for about half of the EFM bonds in the 1990s, we may reasonably infer that many of the buyers of these instruments are banks.

Furthermore, a bond-by-bond review of the issues in the World Bank's *World Debt Tables*[15] reveals that a disproportionate number of floating-rate issues come from a few major countries in East Asia: Indonesia, Thailand, and especially Korea. This may also explain the apparent bias of banks toward Latin America in Figure 1.9. In reality, banks were probably supplying more capital to East Asia than the figure suggests, through the mechanism of floating-rate bonds.

Debt versus Equity

The same data are cut between debt and equity in Figure 1.10. This shows another surprising pattern: Equity investments far outweighed debt investments. One might have imagined that debt, being generally safer than equity, would be favored in a risky region. On the contrary, investors seemed determined to participate in the much higher

FIGURE 1.10

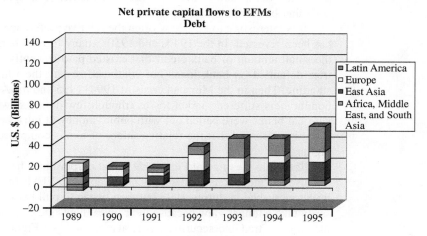

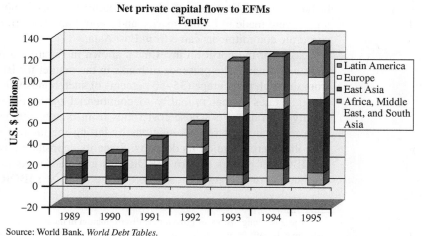

Source: World Bank, *World Debt Tables.*

---

[15]*World Debt Tables* changed its name to *Global Development Finance* in 1997, reflecting the new importance of equity flows.

The Resumption of Capital Flows   **21**

returns of equity. This was again particularly true of Asia: Debt investments in Latin America actually exceeded those in East Asia in 1993 and 1995, while equity flowed more to East Asia than to Latin America throughout the 1990s.

We gain a somewhat different impression by looking just at portfolio debt (bonds) and portfolio equity (stocks) as in Figure 1.11. Here the division is more nearly equal, and the relative popularity of Latin America for equity investing is much higher. Thus, both the bias toward equity investment and the preference for East Asian equity came from the corporations; portfolio investors showed greater caution (greater relative preference for debt instruments). When they invested in East Asia, portfolio investors showed a slight preference for equity and in Central and Eastern Europe a distinct preference for debt. Indeed, very little equity from Central and Eastern Europe was sold to portfolio investors during this period.

These patterns are not difficult to understand. Since debt is safer than equity, those investors who are worried about the downside will prefer it. Portfolio investors make their capital commitments at arm's length, with much less information than corporations, who make direct investments in firms they are typically involved in managing. So it is natural that portfolio investors should tilt relatively more toward debt. This is doubly true in Central and Eastern Europe, where the problems of transition made

FIGURE 1.11

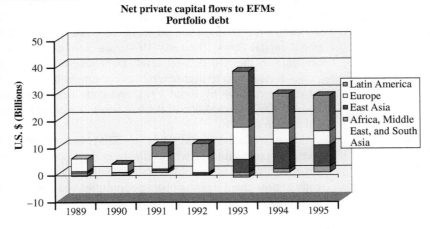

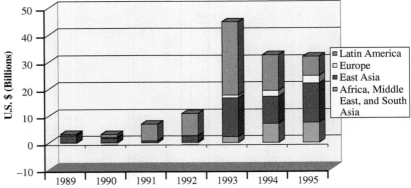

Source: World Bank, *World Debt Tables.*

22   *Chapter 1   The Emerging Markets Phenomenon*

portfolio investment particularly difficult. Only East Asia and Latin America were perceived as having the combination of opportunities and institutions to make the promised upside rewards of equity dominate the downside protection of debt for portfolio investors.

The net capital flows to EFMs that we have been examining need to be understood in a broader context. Not only was capital flowing to EFMs but across borders everywhere, particularly among the developed countries, and this was true for banks, corporations, and portfolio investors. Figure 1.12 shows in dramatic fashion how both banks and portfolio investors had increased their appetites for international investment over at least a decade before the EFM boom began.

Panel (a) shows how banks in member countries of the Organization for Economic Cooperation and Development (OECD), despite the debt crisis, had greatly expanded cross-border lending between 1980 and 1991. Since the OECD is essentially the set of developed countries, this shows the internationalization of bank lending among developed countries. Panel (b) shows the explosion of volume in international bonds again within the OECD, and panel (c) shows the astonishing increase in the appetite of portfolio investors in three developed countries for cross-border trades.

The forces underlying these changes included the expansion of international trade, which created a new demand for international finance; technological changes in communications, computing, and risk measurement, which facilitated the global reach of competing financial institutions and markets; and the deregulation of institutions and markets throughout the world, which was largely driven by the first two influences.

As in the 1970s, changes in interest rates also contributed to the attraction of global capital flows. The early 1990s saw nominal interest rates denominated in dollars drop to the 5–6 percent level. Debt investors in the developed world who had grown accustomed to higher returns first sought high-yield bonds, for which the market recovered fully by about 1993, and then increasingly debt from EFMs, which by the mid-1990s offered one of the few ways in which large amounts of capital could be lent at high spreads.

Thus, while the capital flows into EFMs in the 1990s reflected growing enthusiasm over the opportunities newly available in developing countries, it is also true that the attractive changes in the EFMs occurred at a very opportune time, when investors were ready to hear about international opportunities and equipped to take advantage of them.

FIGURE 1.12

Globalization of investors

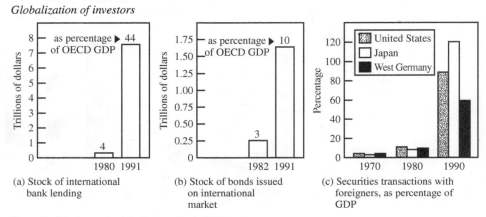

(a) Stock of international
    bank lending

(b) Stock of bonds issued
    on international
    market

(c) Securities transactions with
    foreigners, as percentage of
    GDP

Source: Bank for International Settlements; Crook (1992).

EFM Securities, Performance, and Risk

It is now time to take a closer look at the instruments behind these EFM capital flows and their risks.

International Bonds

Banks, of course, make loans with their own resources and corporations do much the same with their direct investment. But bonds come from a variety of markets. In a few cases, local bonds are available to foreign investors, but the majority of bonds sold by developing country issuers to portfolio investors are *international bonds*; that is, bonds designed for cross-border investors and not registered under the national rules of any country. These bonds are not denominated in local currency but in one of the developed country currencies such as U.S. dollars, Japanese yen, or German marks. Their interest is paid free of any withholding taxes.

International bonds were developed in the 1960s as a kind of freewheeling, unregulated securities market in which issuers from various countries could raise capital away from the internal markets of the developed countries. In the early days of the market, international bonds could only be sold if the issuer was of the highest credit with strong name recognition. Gradually, the international bond market has become more tolerant of lower credits and developing countries.

By 1994 the international bond market was offering a broad list of mainly private sector bonds from many countries and denominated in all major currencies. The largest issuers were from major countries such as Argentina, Brazil, Indonesia, Korea, Mexico, and Thailand, but a great many other countries also had access to this market, including in 1995 Estonia, Ghana, Jordan, Lebanon, Lithuania, Malta, Mauritius, Panama, Slovakia, and Sri Lanka.

International bond maturities in the mid-1990s were most often medium term (two to five years) for EFM issuers, but some bonds ranged out as far as 17 years. About half were at fixed rates of interest and about half at floating rates of interest tied, like a bank loan, to three-month or six-month LIBOR. The fixed interest rates can be best understood as a spread above U.S. Treasuries of comparable maturity. These spreads range from about 100 basis points (1 percent) to 500 basis points (5 percent). As can be seen in Figure 1.13, maturities and spreads are negatively correlated, with both dependent on the market's perception of the country's creditworthiness.

Creditworthiness is most commonly measured by bond ratings. Moody's Investor Services and Standard and Poor's Corporation (S&P), the two most widely followed rating agencies, were rating most EFM international bond issues by the mid-1990s. In 1995, for example, Korea was rated A1 by S&P and was upgraded from A+ to AA− by Moody's; Thailand was rated A2 by Moody's and A by S&P; the Czech Republic was rated Baa2 by Moody's and BBB+ by S&P. All of these were "investment grade" ratings; that is, they were not "junk bonds."

A study of bond ratings for sovereign risks[16] showed that a few factors affecting the capacity and willingness to repay debt (GDP per capita, growth of GDP, the historical record of default, inflation, and the amount of existing sovereign debt) explain more than 90 percent of the cross-country variation in bond ratings. Yet identifying the turning points in country risk assessment is notoriously difficult to do. Despite their high ratings in 1995, two years later Korea, Thailand, and the Czech Republic would

---

[16]Cantor and Packer (1997).

24   *Chapter 1   The Emerging Markets Phenomenon*

FIGURE 1.13

Terms of fixed-rate international bond issues, 1994–1995

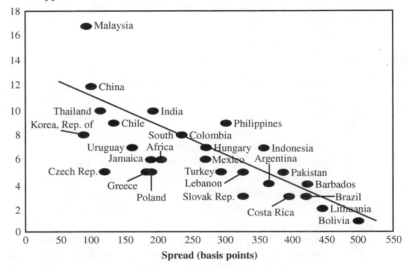

Note: Maturities and spreads are based on U.S. dollar–denominated fixed rate issues. Spreads are over the benchmark U.S. Treasury securities, except for Hungary, for which Deutschmark issues were used as a proxy.

Source: World Bank, *World Debt Tables* 1996.

all be on the brink of default. It is a sobering comment on EFM risk that the best financial professionals, including the bond rating agencies and the institutional investors pricing bonds in Figure 1.13, were unable to foresee (even months in advance) the kind of major setbacks that became realities in 1997. Despite an enormous amount of progress in quantifying risk throughout the world, EFM crises are very difficult to forecast.[17]

Equities

The riskiest of the EFM investments are publicly traded equities. The number and volume of traded EFM equities is far fewer than the number of traded bonds for three reasons. First, traded debt includes sovereign as well as private debt. Second, problems of information limit the number of firms that can qualify in equity markets since investors are relatively unprotected against downside losses on equity instruments. Third, a given company may have dozens of different bonds outstanding but it usually has only one stock, or at most two when voting rights are concentrated in a control stock kept in a few hands.

Most stocks, unlike bonds, are traded locally in stock exchanges. Thus, when international portfolio investors want to buy a local stock, it might seem natural for them to go directly to the local exchange. However, the complexities of multiple currencies, languages, taxes, and laws related to equity investments make it desirable to "translate" local stocks into a global format. Thus, for many years stocks with an international following have been offered as American Depository Receipts (ADRs) or Global Depository Receipts (GDRs). In this structure, a trustee holds a block of an EFM stock and issues "receipts" to investors for as many shares as it holds. The

---

[17]For a survey of approaches to forecasting crises, see Hunter et al. (1999).

receipts transmit the benefits of ownership to their holders, but they pay in a global currency and meet standards for listing on developed country exchanges. This arrangement avoids many problems that might arise if investors attempted to own EFM stocks directly, and the listing on developed country exchanges adds greatly to the investment's liquidity.

The need to diversify the risk of EFM stocks has led to the creation of hundreds of mutual funds, both redeemable (open-end) and nonredeemable (closed-end) that invest in the stocks of a particular country or region or EFM stocks generally. *Diversification* is one of the great lessons of modern finance theory: By investing in diversified portfolios, investors smooth out the idiosyncratic ups and downs of particular companies or countries. This reduces the overall risk of the investment without reducing the expected return, and should therefore be sought by all rational investors. Funds are the institutional expression of the need for diversification, and also allow investors to subcontract the job of particular stock selection to a professional engaged full-time in this difficult task. From the end of 1992 to the end of 1994, the total assets of EFM equity funds rose about tenfold from $2 billion to $23 billion.

The Unique Risk of EFMs

The rush of interest in EFM stock investments caused a number of academic researchers to take a longer look at performance in these markets compared with the risk, and the initial impression was quite favorable. Table 1.4 shows the average one-year returns on IFC global stock indexes for 20 EFMs from 1976 until 1992 (unless the market in question did not "emerge" until after 1976), omitting the extraordinary performance of 1993, and compares it with the performance of the Morgan Stanley Capital International (MSCI) index, a broadly based index of international equity investment.

As can be seen, the EFMs show a significantly higher mean return over this 16-year period; indeed, a mean 20 percent annual return over a long term is about as good as equity investments get even for the most aggressive investments, such as venture capital. Of course, the standard deviations are very high, and one cannot reject the possibility that the high mean return was merely random. Assuming, however, that the results are meaningful, it is important to compare them to risk. The sample standard deviation of returns is higher for EFMs than for the MSCI, but the standard deviation is a misleading measure of risk.

According to standard finance theory (the *Capital Asset Pricing Model*, or CAPM), if investors can diversify the idiosyncratic risks of particular countries by buying broadly based stock funds that invest worldwide, what should matter most for measuring and pricing risk is the correlation of EFMs with a broader portfolio index

TABLE 1.4   Average One-Year Returns from 1976 through 1992

	20 EFMs (%)	*MSCI (%)*
Mean return	20.4	13.9
Standard deviation	24.9	14.4
Correlation with MSCI	0.16	1.00
Auto-correlation	0.15	0.01

MSCI = Morgan Stanley Capital International index (value-weighted)
Source: Harvey (1995).

such as MSCI. From that point of view, EFM investments appear almost too good to be true, for they combine very high mean returns with very low correlation. This suggests that all rational investors should add large amounts of EFM stocks to their portfolios, and that doing so would raise the expected portfolio return while actually lowering portfolio risk.

Furthermore, the autocorrelation of EFM returns suggests elements of predictability: One good (or bad) year is more likely than not to be followed by another, which is also of considerable interest to investors. Although such patterns may be explicable by autocorrelation in risk, high autocorrelation of returns is sometimes viewed as an investing opportunity—a way for savvy investors to take advantage of stock market "momentum" by buying shares when returns rise and selling them when returns fall. The autocorrelation of EFM stocks may indicate special momentum opportunities in these shares.

When something appears too good to be true, it usually is. On closer examination of these results some problems emerge, and alternative interpretations of the data seem more reasonable. One problem with using the data in Table 1.4 to forecast future returns and risk is *survival bias*. This refers to the distortion of analysis that happens when we look back in time at a sample that disproportionately represents investments that have survived over time, and filters out many that have disappeared from the market. The easiest way to understand survival bias is to think about mutual fund performance, since poorly performing mutual funds are frequently shut down or merged out of existence. When we look at the historical average of the returns for funds that exist today, we form an overly optimistic view of expected future returns because the backward-looking data do not include the funds that have failed and disappeared.

An ingenious academic study[18] applied this concept to EFM stocks. It created a computer-based simulation in which a number of synthetic markets with the statistical characteristics of EFMs start their lives at a point in time and then evolve, subject to "submerging" whenever their level falls below a certain boundary. The study showed that the simple omission of "submerged" markets (i.e., those which had collapsed or which were not yet fully visible) could produce a pattern remarkably like that of Table 1.4—abnormally high returns right after "emergence," low correlation with world risk factors and autocorrelation—even if the actual expected returns of EFMs were no higher than those of the U.S. equity market.

But aside from survival bias there is a deeper problem with the logic that would use the data in Table 1.4 to suggest the availability of high risk-adjusted profits from EFM equity investments: Equity risk in EFMs is fundamentally different from that of equity markets in developed countries. In particular, a low country *beta* (the CAPM risk measure) provides a false signal of low risk in EFM equities.

Why are low country betas not indicative of low risk in EFM stocks? There are two reasons: First, the assumption that there are enough EFM countries in the world to diversify away idiosyncratic risk is highly questionable. Only a handful of countries in Latin America and Asia produce enough shares to offer international investors the chance to diversify their portfolios. Furthermore, EFM countries have interdependent risks in some states of the world, particularly during bad times. When one EFM country suffers an adverse shock (e.g., Russia in 1998), losses to international investors may lead them to shed other risky EFM assets, leading to a transmission of loss from one EFM equity market to another. Data on EFM equity returns show substantially

---

[18]Goetzmann and Jorion (1997).

larger correlation of returns across countries during the Mexican, Asian, and Russian financial crises.[19]

Second, the value of EFM stocks is highly dependent on the success of their countries' liberalization experiments. Thus their long-run returns—during the early phases of economic development—have a certain *bimodal* (win or lose) character. In other words, investors in EFM stocks are learning over time and updating the probability of a successful economywide experiment in institution building. These experiments typically involve interrelated and risky changes in fiscal policy, bank regulation, foreign exchange and central bank policies, pension restructuring, and electoral reform. Economies that successfully graduate from this stage will enjoy highly positive long-run stock returns; those that do not will see their stock markets collapse alongside their exchange rates, banking systems, and, often, their governments. The opportunities available in Russian equities in mid-1999 discussed in the box below give an example of how potential stock returns are often perceived to be dramatically bimodal.

Russia's Shaky Options

The Russian stock market has become flavour of the year with emerging market investors once more in spite of the country's shattering financial crash, which occurred a year ago tomorrow, and continuing political turmoil. Since the start of 1999, the Russian stock market has surged more than 100 percent in local currency terms on the back of higher oil prices and a stronger than anticipated industrial recovery, making it one of the best performing markets in the world.

But the scarcely apprehended truth about Russia is that it still does not have a stock market. Rather, it boasts a highly volatile options market. Buying a Russian equity does not give investors enforceable ownership rights over a company's assets nor guarantee a slice of future cash flows. A Russian share is perhaps more accurately viewed as an exotic type of option, which may be converted into real equity one bright, shining morning in the future, when the country has built the infrastructure of an effective market economy and an independent judicial regime.

As Bill Browder, director of Hermitage Capital Management, says: "The Russian market is not really valuing anything on a fundamental economic basis. The market is more a perception of whether Russia will become a proper member of democratic, capitalist society. If Russia breeds an environment where equities really are equities, then everything is ridiculously undervalued. If they do not, then all of this speculation up and down is essentially a worthless exercise."

Of course, much the same could have been said of many other emerging markets at different points in the past. Brazil, for example, remained in the investment doldrums for decades as the country battled to get public sector deficits and inflation under control. But when Brazil introduced sounder monetary policies and more responsible government, the value of its corporate assets soared. The hope is that Russia's Gazprom—which trades at about a 95 percent discount to Exxon of the U.S.—could one day be revalued in a similarly striking way to Telebras in Brazil.

Reprinted from the *Financial Times*, August 16, 1999.

---

[19]Also, if there is a stable linear relationship between returns in one market and returns in another, reflecting economic interdependence, then the correlation of returns in the two markets will automatically increase when volatility of returns increases. See Forbes and Rigobon (1999).

The bimodal character of long-run outcomes for EFM stocks violates a basic assumption of the CAPM, on which the usefulness of beta as a risk measure depends: namely the normality of long-run stock returns. The violations of normality are also visible in short-run returns. It has been shown that short-run EFM returns are not normally distributed; instead the EFM return-generating process contains jumps or discontinuities (and these discontinuities are often correlated across countries, as during financial crises).[20]

The effects of these two problems—small numbers of significant stock issuing EFMs and nonnormal returns distributions—on risk are also interrelated. Bimodal long-run returns and discontinuities in short-run returns worsen the problem of diversification because the more extreme any one country's outcomes, the harder it is to diversify idiosyncratic risk by pooling stocks from different countries.

The autocorrelation of returns for EFMs is also explicable as a consequence of long-run bimodal outcomes of EFM experiments. Serial correlation could reflect the fact that, as the results of the EFM experiments unfold over time, investors update their beliefs about the relative probabilities of long-run success or failure—probabilities that evolve slowly over time, generating a degree of autocorrelation in returns.

Financial economists have sometimes considered the possible effect on asset prices of drastic events, which have low probability but large potential impact. This implies a major departure from normally distributed returns and is called, appropriately, the *peso problem*. It has been invoked to explain what seem to be unreasonably large forward discounts in inflationary currencies,[21] unreasonably large risk premiums in equity returns,[22] and apparent distortions in the term structure of interest rates.[23] Peso problems have not yet found their way into the mainstream theories that explain asset pricing, yet we need to keep them at the front of our minds as we consider market risk in countries where the peso lives.

A unique feature of EFM securities is the apparent pattern of *contagion*. On a day-to-day basis EFM stocks are not highly correlated across countries; but when a financial crisis (collapse of both stock and currency values) develops in one country, it sometimes seems to leap from that country to others like a contagious disease so that cross-country correlation is suddenly high. There are at least four reasons for this pattern, two related to trade and two to capital markets.

First, if the currency of country B collapses, its imports from country A may become prohibitively expensive, damaging A's real economy. For example, Argentina sells a substantial portion of its exports to Brazil; when the Brazilian *real* collapsed in early 1999, Argentina's exports contracted. Second, if the currency of country B collapses, it may become a far more attractive export competitor to country A. The collapse of the Thai baht, for example, which fell by about 25 percent in July 1997, put competitive pressure on Indonesia, Malaysia, and the Philippines, triggering collapses of their currencies. Then when the Indonesian rupiah lost 80 percent of its value during 1997–1998, it gained a competitive advantage over Thailand and the Philippines, complicating their recoveries.

Third, investors are often poorly informed and may imagine the worst. When one country suffers a financial collapse, it is natural to worry about which other countries might have a similar problem, without understanding the precise details. This may cause other countries' securities to be sold although if later information proves no real effects, they should soon recover. For example, Taiwan's currency and security values

---

[20]Harvey (1995).
[21]Krasker (1980).
[22]Rietz (1988)
[23]Lewis (1991).

fell during the early days of the Asia crisis in 1997, but soon recovered. Fourth, certain investors in EFM securities are leveraged (i.e., hedge funds and banks). When such investors suffer a serious loss in one part of their portfolio, they may need to protect the quality of their own debt issues by selling other risky assets to pay down debt. Thus, the losses created in Russia's 1998 collapse caused declines in other EFM securities.

In summary, the capital asset pricing model and its risk measure beta, while standard (if controversial) tools of analysis in developed markets, seem to be particularly ill suited to measuring EFM equity risk. CAPM is based on an assumption that pooling of idiosyncratic risks is feasible, that asset prices evolve continuously over time, and that the distribution of returns is stable and normally distributed.[24] The evolution of stock prices in EFMs is different, so the meaning of risk is also somewhat different, and the CAPM is not a sufficient tool for coming to grips with that risk.[25] In EFMs, the dominant concern is not the beta of a firm, an industry, or even a country, but the probability of failure of the liberalization experiment in which the country is engaged or the probability of a disruption to global capital markets coming from a similar failure in another EFM.

Consistent with that view, sovereign debt ratings are the most successful predictor of the cross-section of expected returns for different countries' EFM stock market indexes. Sovereign ratings themselves are largely governed by the risk of the institutional experiments in economic liberalization.[26]

Variation in the risk premium of EFM stocks and debts is often guided by sudden changes in perceptions about the long-term viability of the core institutions within EFM countries, since capital market risk is closely related to the health of the financial system and the government's fiscal balance. For example, as described in the nearby box, the Persian Gulf crisis had significant and sudden effects on various EFM securities through its effects on international trade and financial flows. Thus, one cannot fully understand EFM risk by extrapolating from day-to-day fluctuations of stock returns and their covariances under the standard assumptions used for developed markets. A standard analysis of those covariances would lead one to commit large amounts of resources to EFM stocks. Yet anyone who did so in 1993 based on these measures suffered a severe setback as the result of the discontinuities and correlations among EFM returns during the various crises of 1994–1998.

Perhaps when all countries are further up the financial learning curve, when EFM legal foundations are strengthened, information flows institutionalized and currencies stabilized, when banks and other financial intermediaries have learned what can go wrong and how to manage risk, when investors have learned better how to understand market anomalies and arbitrage them away, then perhaps large shocks will be fewer and securities returns may become more normally distributed.

EFM liberalization experiments are complex and multidimensional, involving at once financing market opening (discussed in Chapters 2 and 3), the privatization of state-owned enterprises (the subject of Chapter 3), legal system reforms (analyzed in Chapter 4), the development of new information, accounting, and corporate governance systems (the subject of Chapter 5), the restructuring of government finances and exchange rate policy (reviewed in Chapter 6), and the prudential regulation of the

[24]Alternatively, CAPM can be based on an assumption that investors have quadratic utility functions, which seems even less realistic.

[25]Interestingly, despite differences in the time series properties of returns for EFMs and developed equity markets, the factors that explain the cross-section of equity returns for individual firms within EFMs seem to be quite similar to the factors that work well in developed markets, as discussed in Rouwenhorst (1999).

[26]Erb, Harvey, and Viskanta (1997).

Shifting Sands of Risk: The Persian Gulf War

The standard determinants of sovereign risk change slowly: Long-run growth prospects, the volume of outstanding sovereign debt, a country's fiscal balance, and its history of default or repayment may remain unchanged for years or decades. But sovereign risk sometimes can shift suddenly in the face of important changes in import or export prices, or political events that otherwise influence the trade balance or the fiscal balance. After all, anything that interrupts the expected future flow of exports (which generate hard currency earnings), the cost of imports, or the government's tax receipts (the means for the sovereign to capture its share of export earnings) can threaten the government's ability to repay.

A particularly telling example of a sudden change of fortunes—with consequences that differed markedly across EFMs—was the Persian Gulf crisis of 1990–1991. Using the standard finance tool of *event study analysis,* Suk Hum Lee, Hyun Mo Sung, and Jorge L. Urrutia (1996) studied the effects of the crisis on the returns to holders of EFM syndicated bank loans. They found that the value of these debt offerings from oil exporting countries rose in response to the crisis, while the value of oil importing countries' debts fell. The size of the effect on bank loan values depended on the extent of a country's indebtedness. The debts of highly indebted oil importers were severely affected, while oil importers with little debt saw no significant change in their debt values.

The Middle East was also a destination for many foreign workers who remitted their earnings to their home countries, which sometimes provided those home countries with a significant share of their foreign currency receipts. The interruption of these remittances also had an adverse effect on the values of debt offerings by the remittance-dependent countries.

The consequences of the Persian Gulf War for the syndicated bank loans of EFM countries illustrate three points. First, sudden changes in the values of exports, import costs, and flows of remittances can have important effects on the sovereign risks of EFMs. Second, changes in sovereign risk are reflected in private debt claims as well as public debt claims; when an EFM's sovereign rating deteriorates, its private debt and equity issuers also suffer higher costs of funding. Third, the same event can have dramatically different consequences for EFMs depending on their risk exposures.

banking system (the subject of Chapter 7). The shape of EFM liberalization along each of these dimensions affects the risk of the securities issued by EFM governments and corporations. For example, one study found that successful privatizations of state-owned enterprises contribute to the reduction in "political risk" (the risk of a collapse of market-friendly government policies), and that this risk reduction is reflected in substantial reductions in EFM equity risk premiums.[27] That finding illustrates how market participants in emerging markets must be able to judge whether the sudden, dramatic, multifaceted changes accompanying liberalization are likely to succeed or fail, and price EFM securities accordingly. To make those judgments they must understand the determinants of success and failure along each of the crucial dimensions of reform, and how best to manage the risks of "experiment failure" to protect themselves from the costs of failure.

The issues of jump risk, financial crisis, and stock market survival make it clear that EFM securities not only involve more risk than those of developed countries, but

---

[27]Perotti (2000).

they involve a different kind of risk. On the surface, EFM stocks and bonds appear similar to the stocks and bonds of developed markets. But we need to understand what is happening beneath the surface. We will never understand EFM securities based on statistical behavior alone and developed-market models such as the CAPM. At a deeper level, the markets are based on quite different legal foundations, information flows, and currency considerations, and these factors in turn are connected with deep differences in culture, politics, and financial institutions. Penetrating to these levels is the primary task of this book.

32   *Chapter 1   The Emerging Markets Phenomenon*

APPENDIX

PRIVATE LENDING TO SOVEREIGNS: DEFAULTS AND RESCHEDULINGS, 1800–1992[a]

Country	Beginning of Period	End of Period	Form[b]	Notes
Albania	1990	1992	L	Soviet collapse
Angola	1988	1992	S, L	Civil unrest
Argentina	1890	1893	B	Refinancing problem (Baring crisis)
	1956	1965	S	Post-Peron budget crisis, beet export drops
	1982	1992	L	Oil and interest rate shocks, budget crisis
Austria	1802	1816	B	Napoleonic wars
	1868	1870	B	Coupon tax after Hapsburg dual monarchy
	1914	1915	B	World War I
	1932	1952	B	Depression, German occupation, and World War II
Bolivia	1875	1879	B	
	1931	1957	B	Depression
	1980	1992	L	Oil and interest rate shocks
Brazil	1826	1829	B	War with Portugal and United Provinces
	1898	1910	B	Coffee prices collapse
	1914	1919	B	End of rubber boom and coffee price drop
	1931	1943	B	Depression
	1961	1964	S	Budget crisis
	1983	1992	L	Oil and interest rate shocks and budget crisis
Bulgaria	1915	1920	B	World War I and civil unrest
	1932	1992	B	Depression, World War II, and Communist takeover
	1990	1992	L	Soviet collapse
Cameroon	1989	1992	L	
Chile	1826	1842	B	Independence war and civil unrest
	1880	1883	B	War of the Pacific
	1931	1948	B	Nitrate market collapse and Depression
	1965		S	Copper price drop
	1972	1975	S	Budget crisis and coup
	1983	1990	L	Oil and interest rate shocks
China	1921	1949	B	Civil war, World War II, and Communist repudiation
Colombia	1826	1861	B	Independence war and civil unrest
	1873		B	
	1880	1904	B	Trade depression, then civil war
	1932	1944	B	Depression
Congo	1986	1992	L	Oil and interest rate shocks
Costa Rica	1828	1840	B	Independence war and split from Central American Federation
	1874	1885	B	Central American chaos
	1895	1911	B	
	1932	1953	B	Depression
	1981	1990	L	Oil and interest rate shocks
Côte d'Ivoire	1984	1992	L	Oil and interest rate shocks
Cuba	1933	1934	B	Depression
	1960	1963	B	Communist revolution and repudiation
	1982	1992	L	Oil and interest rate shocks; Soviet collapse
Czechoslovakia	1938	1946	B	Nazi occupation, World War II
	1952	1959	B	Communist takeover and repudiation
Dominican Republic	1872	1907	B	Civil unrest and war, repudiations
	1931	1934	B	Hurricane and Depression
	1982	1992	L	Oil and interest rate shocks

Appendix   **33**

Country	*Beginning of Period*	*End of Period*	*Form^b*	*Notes*
Ecuador	1832	1855	B	Independence war and split from Colombia
	1868	1898	B	
	1906	1955	B	Civil unrest, then Depression
	1982	1992	L	Oil and interest rate shocks
Egypt	1816	1880	B	Budget crisis; British and French intervention
	1984	1992	L	Oil and interest rate shocks
El Salvador	1828	1860	B	Independence war and split from Central American Federation
	1921	1922	B	
	1932	1946	B	Depression
Germany	1932	1953	B	Nazi policy and World War II
	1949	1992	B	Communist takeover (East Germany only)
Gabon	1978		S	Interest rate shocks
	1986	1992	L	Oil price swings
Gambia	1986	1988	L	
Ghana	1969	1974	S	
Greece	1826	1878	B	Independence war and turmoil
	1894	1897	B	Budget crisis and political instability
	1932	1964	B	Depression and World War II
Guatemala	1828	1856	B	Independence war and split from Central American Federation
	1876	1888	B	Central American chaos
	1894	1917	B	
	1933	1936	B	Depression
Guinea	1985	1992	S, L	Oil and interest rate shocks
Guyana	1982	1992	L	Oil and interest rate shocks
Honduras	1828	1867	B	Independence war and split from Central American Federation
	1873	1925	B	Central American chaos
	1981	1992	L	Oil and interest rate shocks
Hungary	1932	1967	B	Depression, World War II, and Communist takeover
Iran	1992		L	
Iraq	1990	1992	L	Gulf War
Italy	1940	1946	B	World War II
Jamaica	1978	1990	L	Oil and interest rate shocks, budget crisis
Japan	1942	1952	B	World War II
Jordan	1989	1992	L	
Liberia	1875	1898	B	
	1912	1923	B	Budget crisis
	1932	1935	B	Depression
	1980	1992	S, L	Oil and interest rate shocks, civil unrest
Madagascar	1981	1992	S, L	Oil and interest rate shocks
Malawi	1982	1988	L	Oil and interest rate shocks
Mexico	1828	1850	B	Post- independence chaos and war with United States
	1859	1885	B	Civil war, French intervention, then repudiation
	1914	1922	B	Revolutionary period and partial repudiation
	1928	1942	B	
	1982	1990	L	Interest rate shocks
Morocco	1903	1904	B	
	1983	1990	L	Oil and interest rate shocks
Mozambique	1984	1992	L	Oil and interest rate shocks
Netherlands	1802	1814	B	Napoleonic wars
Nicaragua	1828	1874	B	Independence war and split from Central American Federation

Country	Beginning of Period	End of Period	Form[b]	Notes
	1894	1895	B	
	1911	1917	B	
	1932	1937	B	Depression
	1980	1992	L	Oil and interest rate shocks
Niger	1983	1991	L	Oil and interest rate shocks
Nigeria	1983	1991	L	Interest rate shocks and civil unrest
Panama	1932	1946	B	Depression
	1983	1992	L	Oil and interest rate shocks
Paraguay	1874	1885	B	Following war with Argentina, Brazil, and Uruguay
	1892	1895	B	
	1920	1924	B	
	1932	1944	B	Depression and war with Bolivia
	1986	1992	L	Oil and interest rate shocks
Peru	1826	1848	B	Independence war and civil unrest
	1876	1889	B	Guano price collapse and War of the Pacific
	1931	1951	B	Civil unrest, conflict with Chile, and Depression
	1968	1969	S, L	Fishmeal price drop and budget crisis
	1978	1992	S, L	Sharp exports contraction, oil and interest rate shocks
Philippines	1983	1992	L	Oil and interest rate shocks, natural disasters
Poland	1936	1952	B	Depression and World War II
	1981	1992	L	Soviet collapse, oil and interest rate shocks
Portugal	1834	1841	B	Repudiation of usurper's loan
	1850	1856	B	
	1892	1901	B	Budget crisis
Romania	1933	1958	B	Depression and World War II
	1982	1987	L	Soviet collapse, oil and interest rate shocks
Russia	1839		B	
	1885		B	Small coupon tax
	1917	1918	B	Revolution and repudiation
	1991	1992	L	Soviet collapse
Senegal	1981	1992	S, L	Oil and interest rate shocks
Sierra Leone	1977	1992	S, L	Oil and interest rate shocks
South Africa	1985	1992	L	Sanctions-induced capital outflows
Spain	1820		B	Troops mutiny against king
	1831	1834	B	Carlist wars
	1851		B	Civil unrest
	1867	1872	B	Civil unrest prior to Liberal uprising
	1882		B	
Sudan	1979	1992	S, L	Drop in cotton exports, interest rate shocks
Tanzania	1984	1992	S, L	Oil and interest rate shocks
Togo	1979	1992	S, L	Oil and interest rate shocks
Trinidad and Tobago	1989	1989	L	
Tunisia	1867	1870	B	
Turkey	1876	1881	B	Russo-Turkish War, budget crisis
	1915	1932	B	World War I, European occupation, Depression
	1940	1943	B	World War II
	1959		L	
	1965		L	
	1978	1982	S, L	Oil and interest rate shocks
Uganda	1981	1992	S	Oil and interest rate shocks
Uruguay	1876	1878	B	
	1891		B	
	1915	1921	B	
	1933	1938	B	Depression
	1983	1991	L	Oil and interest rate shocks
Venezuela	1832	1840	B	Independence war and split with Colombia

Appendix 35

Country	Beginning of Period	End of Period	Form[b]	Notes
	1848	1881	B	Revolutions and civil unrest
	1892		B	Civil unrest
	1898	1905	B	Revolutions and European blockades
	1982	1990	L	Interest rate shocks and budget crisis
Vietnam	1985	1992	L	Oil and interest rate shocks
Yugoslavia	1895		B	Serbian default
	1933	1960	B	Depression and World War II
	1983	1992	L	Oil and interest rate shocks and civil war
Zaire	1961		B	Default following independence
	1976	1992	S, L	Budget crisis, and copper, oil, and interest rate shocks
Zambia	1983	1992	L	Oil and interest rate shocks
Zimbabwe	1965	1980	B	Repudiation following independence

[a]See below for methodology and sources.

[b]B = bonds, S = suppliers' credits, L = bank loans.

Source: This entire table and its accompanying notes are taken from Purcell and Kaufman (1993).

Methodology and Sources

This Appendix lists all the major periods of sovereign debt servicing incapacity from 1800 through 1992. There are, however, several important issues involved in compiling such a list:

Lender Only private lending through bonds, suppliers' credits, or bank loans is considered. Intergovernmental loans, such as World War I debts, are excluded because of the heavily political nature of such lending, and because private sector investors are not directly affected.

Borrower Only lending to sovereign nations is included. The volume of loans to states, provinces, cities, and private corporations generally has been much smaller than that to sovereign governments. Furthermore, data and commentary on subsovereign and corporate defaults are scarce.

Extent of Default or Rescheduling Not every instance of technical default on bond or loan covenants is listed; to list them all would be virtually impossible. Instead, we identified extended periods (six months or more) where all or part of interest and/or principal payments due were reduced or rescheduled. Some of the defaults and reschedulings involved outright repudiation (a legislative or executive act of government denying liability), while others were minor and announced ahead of time in a conciliatory fashion by debtor nations. The end of each period of default or rescheduling was recorded when full payments resumed or a restructuring was agreed upon. Periods of default or rescheduling within five years of each other were combined. Where a formal repudiation was identified, its date served as the end of the period of default and the repudiation is noted in the notes (e.g., Cuba in 1963); where no clear repudiation was announced, the default was listed as persisting through 1992 (Bulgaria). Voluntary refinancings (Colombia in 1985 and Algeria in 1992) were not included.

Period Covered The beginning of the 19th century was chosen as a starting point because of two important developments. First, the proliferation of constitutional forms of government led to more stable nation-states that recognized their continuing liability to lenders (in earlier periods, most loans were made to individual rulers). Second, financial relations were becoming more institutionalized as witnessed by the growth of incorporated banks and stock exchanges.

Unit of Analysis National names and borders change. Where a national name is changed but the borders and population stay roughly the same, then defaults are listed under the nation's most recent name: New Granada is subsumed under Colombia, Santo Domingo under the Dominican Republic, and Rhodesia under Zimbabwe. Where a sovereign nation split into more than one country, defaults prior to the separation are listed only for the apparent successor country (e.g.,

Colombia, after Ecuador and Venezuela became independent; Turkey, when Bulgaria, Romania, and Montenegro left the Ottoman Empire; Russia, after the Soviet disintegration; and Austria, after the collapse of the Austro-Hungarian Empire). Defaults are not listed for six countries that no longer exist (Prussia, Westphalia, Hesse, Schleswig-Holstein, the Transvaal, and the Orange Free State). The East German default is listed under Germany. For an overview of the subject of state succession and public indebtedness, see Hoeflict (1982).

Sources   The primary sources were the annual reports of the Corporation of Foreign Bondholders and the Foreign Bondholders Protective Council, Borchard (1951), Hardy (1982), International Monetary Fund (1992), Suter (1992), Winkler (1933) and data provided by the Institute of International Finance. . . . When the sources differed as to the date or duration of a default or rescheduling (as they often did), we determined a consensus. Our list may not include small loans to minor debtors that were not publicly disclosed.

References

Borchard, Edwin. 1951. *State Insolvency and Foreign Bondholders: General Principles*. Vol. 1. New Haven: Yale University Press.

Calomiris, Charles W. 1991. The motives of U.S. debt-management policy, 1790–1880: Efficient discrimination and time consistency. *Research in Economic History* 13: 67–105.

———. 1995. Financial fragility: Issues and policy implications. *Journal of Financial Services Research* 9: 241–57.

Calomiris, Charles W., Charles P. Himmelberg, and Paul Wachtel. 1995. Commercial paper, corporate finance, and the business cycle: A microeconomic Perspective. *Carnegie-Rochester Conference Series on Public Policy* 42: 203–50.

Cantor, Richard, and Frank Packer. 1997. Determinants and impact of sovereign credit ratings. *Quarterly Review*, Federal Reserve Bank of New York 2, no. 2. pp. 37–53.

Corporation of Foreign Bondholders. Various years. *Annual Report of the Council of the Corporation of Foreign Bondholders*. London: Corporation of Foreign Bondholders.

Crook, Clive. 1992. Fear of finance. *The Economist,* September 19, 1992: 5–18.

Eichengreen, Barry, and Peter H. Lindert, eds. 1989. *The International Debt Crisis in Historical Perspective*. Cambridge: MIT Press.

Erb, Claude B., Campbell R. Harvey, and Tadas E. Viskanta. 1997. Country risk in global financial management. CIBER Working Paper 97–001, Fuqua School of Business, Duke University.

Forbes, Kristin, and Roberto Rigobon. 1999. No contagion, only interdependence; measuring stock market co-movements. Working Paper no. 7267, National Bureau of Economic Research.

Foreign Bondholders Protective Council. Various years. *Annual Report*. New York: Foreign Bondholders Protective Council.

Goetzmann, William N., and Philippe Jorion. 1997. Re-emerging markets. Working Paper no. 5906, National Bureau of Economic Research.

Hardy, Chandra S. 1982. *Rescheduling Developing Country Debts, 1956–1981: Lessons and Recommendations*. Washington, DC: Overseas Development Council.

Harvey, Campbell R. 1995. Predictable risk and returns in emerging markets. *Journal of Financial Studies* 8, no. 3: 773–816.

Hoeflict, M. E. 1982. Through a glass darkly: Reflections upon the history of the international law of public debt in connection with state succession. *University of Illinois Law Review* 1982, no. 1: 39–70.

Hubbard, R. Glenn, ed. 1990. *Asymmetric Information, Corporate Finance, and Investment*. Chicago: University of Chicago Press.

———. 1991. *Financial Markets and Financial Crises*. Chicago: University of Chicago Press.

Huizinga, Harry. 1989. The commercial bank claims on developing countries: How have banks been affected? In *Dealing with the Debt Crisis*. Washington, DC: World Bank.

Hunter, William C., George G. Kaufman, and Thomas H. Krueger, eds. 1999. *The Asian Financial Crisis: Origins, Implications, and Solutions*. Boston: Kluwer Academic Publishers.

International Monetary Fund. 1992. *Private Market Financing for Developing Countries*. Washington, DC: IMF.

———. 1998. *World Economic Outlook and International Capital Markets: Interim Assessment*. Washington, DC: IMF.

———. 1999. *International Capital Markets*. Washington, DC: IMF.

Jorion, Philippe, and William N. Goetzmann. 1999. Global stock markets in the twentieth century. *Journal of Finance* 54: 953–80.

Kindleberger, Charles P. 1989. *Manias, Panics and Crashes*. New York: Wiley Investment Classics.

King, Robert G., and Ross Levine. 1993a. Financial intermediation and economic development. In *Financial Intermediation in the Construction of Europe*. Ed. by Colin Mayer and Xavier Vives. London: Centre for Economic Policy Research: 156–89.

———. 1993b. Finance and growth: Schumpeter might be right. *Quarterly Journal of Economics* 108: 717–38.

———. 1993c. Finance, entrepreneurship and growth: Theory and evidence. *Journal of Monetary Economics* 32: 512–42.

Krasker, William S. 1980. The "peso problem" in testing the efficiency of forward exchange markets. *Journal of Monetary Economics* 6: 269–76.

Lee, Suk Hun, Hyun Mo Sung, and Jorge L. Urrutia. 1996. The impact of the Persian Gulf crisis on the prices of LDCs' loans. *Journal of Financial Services Research* 10: 143–62.

Levine, Ross. 1997. Financial development and economic growth: Views and agenda. *Journal of Economic Literature* 35, no. 2: 688–726.

Levine, Ross, and Sara Zervos. 1995. Stock markets, banks and economic growth. Working paper, World Bank.

Lewis, Karen K. 1991. Was there a "peso problem" in the U.S. term structure of interest rates: 1979–1982? *International Economic Review* 32: 159–73.

Lindert, Peter, and Peter Morton. 1989. How sovereign debt has worked. In *The International Financial System, 1: Developing Country Debt and Economic Performance*. Ed. by Jeffrey Sachs. Chicago: University of Chicago Press.

Obstfeld, Maurice, and Alan Taylor. 1999. *Global Capital Markets: Integration, Crisis, and Growth*. Cambridge: Cambridge University Press.

Perotti, Enrico. 2000. Privatization, political risk and stock market development in emerging markets. Working paper, University of Amsterdam.

Purcell, John F. H., and Jeffrey A. Kaufman. 1993. *The Risks of Sovereign Lending: Lessons from History*. New York: Salomon Brothers.

Rich, Jennifer L. 1999. The incredible shrinking markets. *Latin Finance* 109 (August): 17–24.

Rietz, Thomas A. 1988. The equity risk premium: a solution, *Journal of Monetary Economics* 22: 117–31.

Romer, Paul. 1998. Idea gaps and object gaps in economic development. *Journal of Monetary Economics* 32, no. 3: 543–74.

Rouwenhorst, K. Geert. 1999 Local return factors and turnover in emerging stock markets. *Journal of Finance* 54: 1439–64.

Sachs, Jeffrey D., ed. 1989. *Developing Country Debt and the World Economy*. Chicago: University of Chicago Press.

Sachs, Jeffrey D., and Harry Huizinga. 1987. U.S. commercial banks and the developing-country debt crisis. *Brookings Papers on Economic Activity* no. 2: 555–601.

Suter, Christian. 1992. *Debt Cycles in the World-Economy: Foreign Loans, Financial Crises, and Debt Settlements, 1820–1990*. Boulder, CO: Westview Press.

Vogel, Thomas T., Jr., and Pamela Druckerman. 1999. Ecuador buys time, but task remains tough. *The Wall Street Journal,* August 26, p. A13.

Wai, U Tun, and Hugh T. Patrick. 1973. Stock and bond issues and capital markets in less developed economies. *IMF Staff Papers,* July: 253–317.

The Wall Street Journal. 1999. Ecuador's bond deadline stirs wider tremors, August 23.

Winkler, Max. 1933. *Foreign Bonds, an Autopsy: A Study of Defaults and Repudiations of Government Obligations*. Philadelphia: Roland Swain.

THUNDERBIRD
THE AMERICAN GRADUATE SCHOOL
OF INTERNATIONAL MANAGEMENT

A06-00-0001

AVICULAR CONTROLS &
PAKISTAN INTERNATIONAL AIRLINES

Gabriel Benguela had just walked into his office from attending an operations review when the telephone rang. Gabriel guessed that this late in the day, the call must be from one of his Marketing Managers based in the Far East. It was indeed; Peter Mai was calling from Avicular's Singapore office. Peter was the lead negotiator on a deal under negotiation with Pakistan International Airlines (PIA). It was July 6, 1997.

Peter: "Gabriel, we have a problem with the PIA proposal. Although our local agent keeps assuring me that we have won this competition and we will get the deal, I'm not so sure. Pakistan's negotiations with the International Monetary Fund (IMF) to secure yet another loan to finance their current account deficit is causing more problems for this deal. Recent economic data for the country is also not very good, with low economic growth and continuing employment problems. There have been more demonstrations in Lahore because of the European Union's recent anti-dumping ruling imposing high tariffs against several cotton exporting countries including Pakistan. The export of cotton is not only a major source of employment, but also a source of badly needed hard currency. All this on the heels of the IMF's austerity program."

Gabriel: "What does PIA want now? How long have we been trying to finalize this deal?"

Peter: "Seven months. PIA has asked that we accept local currency."

Gabriel: "That's just great! Peter, you know our division never accepts payment in local currency. Although nearly 50% of our business is international, we are just not set up to accept the risk that denominating sales in other currencies would bring. In fact, the whole aerospace business is conducted in U.S. dollars."

Peter: "Hey, blame the IMF. They should be charged for inciting riots and billed for our expenses."

Gabriel: "We need this program badly. These large cockpit retrofit opportunities are hard to find and it seems that our division's management has already committed this $23.7 million sale to Corporate on our latest stretch goal."

Peter: "There is an alternative. Our agent, Makran, advised me that they can buy the receivable from us at a 5% discount and take all of the currency risk. Their Los Angeles subsidiary would pay us 30 days after our invoice."

Gabriel: "But we can't take another hit to the return on sales on this deal. As the deal stands, we had to go to Group Level for approval on this one. This isn't good. I'll speak with the finance people and call you back within 24 hours."

Avicular Controls

Avicular Controls, Inc. (ACI), based in Chicago, had dominated the field of automatic controls since its founding in 1903. Beginning with furnace controls for the steel and power industries in 1903, it continued to grow for over 90 years. By 1996, Avicular employed 13,000 people and conducted business in 52 countries. ACI was composed of two major business units: Industrial Process Controls (AvIPC, 1996 sales of $1.75 billion), and Aviation Control (AvAC, 1996 sales of $1.21 billion). In the summer of 1997 ACI was positioned to achieve its sales growth goal of $4 billion by the year 2000.

AvAC was once again on a growth path after several tough years. Avicular was recognized as the dominant force in the avionics market; market share had grown to a hefty 53% by 1996. But the industry had suffered a severe downturn beginning in 1992, and was only now reaching the sales levels achieved last in 1991. In fact, AvAC sales had been $1.6 billion in 1991, and would hopefully once again break the $1.5 billion line in 1997. The commercial aircraft industry returned to a healthy growth path in 1996 and early 1997, and growth was expected to stay robust through the year 2000.

ACI, specifically the Air Transport Systems division of the Space and Aviation Control business unit had recorded a number of major wins in 1996. These wins included the contract for the cockpit retrofits for a major overnight package delivery firm's fleet of DC-10s, and numerous orders for the firm's new enhanced airborne collision avoidance system. Although U.S. government spending for electronic components was leveling off, international opportunities for military avionics retrofits and space systems were on the rise. Commercial space programs were also projected to grow rapidly, and ACI had landed key initial contracts with NASA and Lockheed Martin.

ACI was not new to international business, establishing its first foreign subsidiaries in 1936. Global treasury was headquartered (along with corporate) near O'Hare International Airport outside Chicago. Corporate treasury was a profit center, and charged 1% commission on all sales. Treasury, however, passed on the currency risk to the business unit. If a local affiliate, joint venture, or subsidiary required local currency, then Treasury would try and match those requirements by accepting the A/R in the local currency. For many developing countries where ACI had little or no activities (such as Pakistan), this was only done on an exception basis. Treasury did agree that Aviation Controls could use their local affiliates to manage the sale of aviation products, but would have to pay between 3% and 8% for currency cover (the final fee would have to be negotiated between Treasury and Aviation Controls). This was something that the division had an unwritten policy of *not* doing; the standard transfer charge imposed by Treasury cut into sales margins.

Pakistan International Airlines (PIA)

Pakistan International Airlines Corporation (PIA) was the national flag carrier of the Islamic Republic of Pakistan. Founded in 1954, PIA operated both scheduled passenger and cargo services. The firm was 57% state-owned, with the remaining 43% held by private investors internal to Pakistan. PIA had been Pakistan's only airline for over 40 years, but in 1993 Aero Asia International Ltd. was born. By 1996, however, it had captured little of the domestic or Pakistan international market (only 5% of Aero Asia's sales were international). Two other recent entrants into the domestic market, Bhoja Airlines Pvt. LTD and Shaheen Air, had captured little of the market.

The International Air Transport Association's (IATA) latest projections indicated that passenger and cargo traffic would double in Asia by the year 2010. Asia was expected to surpass Europe and North America in both size of fleets and passenger/cargo hauled. PIA was experiencing some of this growth, but its aging fleet was resulting in losses. Increasing numbers of flights were either delayed or canceled as a result of maintenance problems. Although a larger and larger proportion of the population was traveling by air, given the choice of taking a PIA or foreign carrier, passenger traffic was opting for the latter. It was imperative that PIA modernize its fleet.

In addition to PIA's traditional passenger and cargo services, a growing proportion of sales was arising from the yearly Islamic Haj (pilgrimage) traffic to Mecca and Medina in Saudia Arabia. Demand had always been strong, but increasing numbers of Pakistani citizens were obtaining visas for the pilgrimage, as Saudi Arabia had recently shuffled the allocation of Haj visas among nations and Pakistan had benefited. PIA was a direct beneficiary of the increased visa allocation.

PIA had originally planned to purchase new commercial aircraft to replace and add to their existing fleet. The fleet modernization program, however, was put on hold due to higher priorities within the Pakistan government in Islamabad. These priorities were established after a review by the IMF of the government's spending plan. Much to PIA's discomfort, the austerity plan proposed by the IMF did not include funds for modernization. PIA had been counting on this fleet modernization and had postponed the incorporation of some Federal Aviation Administration (FAA) safety directives. With the cancellation of the fleet modernization program, PIA now had to move fast to ensure compliance with FAA safety mandates, or face being locked out of some of its most profitable gates. If PIA did not have some of these safety systems and quieter engines installed on their aircraft by June 30, 1998, they would be barred from U.S. airspace.

PIA was in a predicament. It knew exactly what should be done, but government control—especially in these times of crisis—left it no choice. Once PIA agreed to putting the fleet *modernization program* on hold, the managing board decided to pursue a fleet *renovation program* which would require much less hard currency. This plan called for extensively refurbishing PIA's existing aircraft at their new heavy maintenance facility in Karachi. For example, instead of the new quieter engines which new aircraft possessed, PIA would have to make do with the use of *hush kits* for the older engines. It would also require completely new cockpit avionics to take advantage of not only FAA mandates, but recent improvements in the Air Traffic Network (ATN) infrastructure. The first aircraft to be modified would be those utilized on their long-haul flights to the United States, primarily the *B747 classics* (Boeing). Aircraft engine suppliers were approached first and negotiations concluded.

What remained on the table was the cockpit avionics integration supplier. A cockpit retrofit program would require contracts both with the appropriate original equipment manufacturer (OEM), in this case Boeing, and a systems integrator, such as Avicular. Prior to the adoption of the economic austerity plan, Karachi had been the sight of an intense competition between the largest OEMs, Boeing, McDonnell Douglas, and Airbus, for new aircraft sales. It was only after the adoption of the austerity plan that Boeing was willing to discuss cockpit retrofits instead. Due to ACI's extensive experience with a variety of control systems for Boeing, its history with PIA, and its recent work on cockpit retrofit for McDonnell Douglas aircraft, ACI felt it was truly the preferred supplier for PIA. ACI believed that if any other vendor were selected, the added regulatory certification costs and delays would be prohibitively expensive. However, ACI had not undertaken Boeing cockpit retrofits to date (no one had), and looked to the PIA deal as an opportunity to build a new competitive base. But ACI's best and final bid had been too high. PIA's insistence on payment in local currency terms was now thought to be a tactic to extract better concessions from ACI and their agent, Makran.

The Pakistani Economy

Pakistan was divided from India in 1947 as a homeland for Muslims. Pakistan's relationship with India had, however, been under continuous strain since that time for a variety of reasons. The sources of friction included overlapping claims to Kashmir, India's involvement in the demise of East Pakistan, and the birth of Bangladesh in 1971, to name but a few. Because of these conflicts the military had always loomed large over politics in Pakistan. The country's persistence in continuing a nuclear rivalry with India, when neither nation was thought to be able to afford such a *luxury*, was one indication of this. The United States is frequently at odds with Pakistan regarding its nuclear weapons program. The U.S. has suspended military aid on several occasions, including a large F16 purchase in the early 1990s. However, Pakistan's proximity to Afghanistan and India make it strategically important to U.S. interests.

Pakistan practices Islamic Banking, which is based on the *shariah*. This code prohibits the payment of interest, and the suppliers of funds find themselves becoming *investors,* rather than *creditors.* Although financial profit in most forms was looked down upon under Islamic rule, there were 28 publicly traded equities in Pakistan in 1996. The trading of equity shares for profit was also somewhat inconsistent with the *shariah.*

Pakistan has relied upon the World Bank (WB), the IMF, and other multinational lenders (in addition to specific national foreign aid and investment providers) for much of its capital. The country's deteriorating trade gap in the mid-1990s had caused a sudden and significant drop in foreign currency reserves, from US$3 billion to less than US$1.5 billion in September of 1996. The IMF immediately interceded in the economy, imposing an austerity program in October. The government submitted to this austerity plan as a precondition of receiving a $600 million standby loan extended to cover balance of payments shortfalls. The political repercussions were swift and severe: the fall of the Benazir Bhutto administration.[1]

A central part of the IMF's austerity program was a devaluation of the Pakistan rupee by 7.86% against the U.S. dollar on October 22, 1996. Roughly six months later, there was renewed speculation that another devaluation was imminent in order to limit imports and help the export sector earn badly needed hard currency. Another recent economic setback had been the ruling by the European Union that Pakistan was guilty of dumping cotton, and had imposed anti-dumping fines of between 13.0% and 22.9% on Pakistani cotton. It was a painful blow to the export sector. The current exchange rate of 40.4795 Pakistan rupee (Rp) per dollar was maintained by the Pakistani Central Bank; all currency transactions were controlled by the Pakistani government, and were conducted at the official rate. The *black market rate* was approaching Rp50/US$, and as the spread between the black market rate and official rate increased, the probability of devaluation increased. There was no forward market for the Pakistani rupee.[2] Exhibit 1 illustrates the recent travails of the rupee.

The Avicular/PIA Relationship

ACI had been the preferred avionics supplier to PIA for many years, and the retrofit segment of the business was thought to fit well with the overall strategy of the division. The group president was personally involved with the PIA proposal since this new retrofit market niche was central to the division's growth plan.

---

[1] Benazir Bhutto is the daughter of the assassinated former Prime Minster Ali Bhutto and the first woman elected to lead a Muslim nation.

[2] Forward markets for currencies are contracts offered by financial institutions for exchanges of currency at future dates at predetermined exchange rates. These forward contracts are an extremely common and efficient method of managing currency risk on short-to-medium-term transactions. Unfortunately, forward contracts have in the past been typically limited in availability to the 10 or 15 most widely traded world currencies.

 A06-00-0001

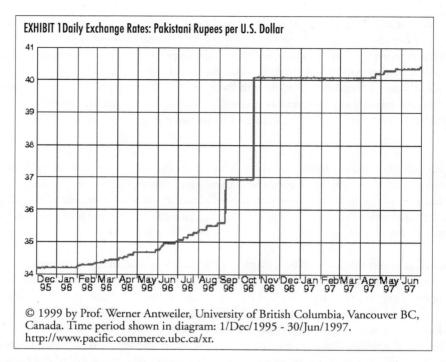

EXHIBIT 1 Daily Exchange Rates: Pakistani Rupees per U.S. Dollar

© 1999 by Prof. Werner Antweiler, University of British Columbia, Vancouver BC, Canada. Time period shown in diagram: 1/Dec/1995 - 30/Jun/1997. http://www.pacific.commerce.ubc.ca/xr.

The avionics business was divided into two segments: Standard Furnished Equipment (SFE) and Buyer Furnished Equipment (BFE). OEMs such as Boeing, McDonnell Douglas, and Airbus purchased avionics equipment to be installed on new aircraft as SFE. The margins in selling to this segment were traditionally very low due to the competitive necessity of keeping competitors "off the aircraft." The low margins on OEM sales, however, were made up by higher margins in the sales of spare avionics packages to the same airlines. The purchase of BFE (also called *freedom of choice*) by the airlines is optional, and usually bid among three suppliers. BFE was purchased directly by the airline and installed by either the airline itself or the OEM. Each time an airline made a new aircraft purchase, a BFE proposal would be presented to the airline. The PIA B747 classic fleet retrofit fell into this category.

The major players in the global avionics business in 1996, in addition to Avicular (US), were Honeywell Incorporated (US), Rockwell Collins (US), Allied-Signal (US), and Sextant Avionique (France). To a lesser extent, Litton Industries (US) and Smiths Industries (UK) competed in small specialized segments. Of this competition, however, only Rockwell Collins and Honeywell had the capability to take on such a large cockpit retrofit job. Rockwell Collins was considered very competitive, and had extensive experience in dealing with the Pakistani government on several large military contracts completed under the U.S. Foreign Military Assistance program.

The global aerospace industry was historically a U.S. dollar business; a dollar-denominated industry. The large airframe manufacturers like Boeing had long taken the lead with the sheer size of their purchase deals. Recently, however, cracks were appearing in this business practice. Competition now focused on more than price. Other competitive elements included credit terms, credit risk, as well as currency of contract denomination.

Ibrahim Makran Pvt. LTD

In countries like Pakistan, the use of an agent is often considered a necessary evil. The agent can oftentimes help to bridge the two business cultures and provide invaluable information—at a cost. ACI's agent,

Ibrahim Makran Pvt. LTD., based in Hyderabad, was considered one of the most reliable and well connected in Pakistan. Makran was also one of the largest import/export trading houses in Pakistan, giving it access to hard currency. It was 100% family-owned and managed.

Standard practice in the avionics business was to provide the agent with a 10% commission (10% of the total final sales price paid after payment is received). Typically, it was the agent who identified the business opportunity and submitted a Business Opportunity Request (BOR) to ACI Marketing. Sometimes this commission was negotiated, but due to the size and importance of this proposal, the commission was accepted without debate.

After PIA contacted ACI and Makran with their latest demand, Makran knew that ACI would want to maintain the deal in U.S. dollars. Makran had immediately inquired as to the availability of dollar funds from its own finance department for a deal of this size. The finance department confirmed that they had the necessary U.S. dollar funds to pay ACI, but noted that the standard fee was 5% of the invoiced amount.

Makran then advised ACI that it would be willing to purchase the receivable for the additional 5% (in addition to the 10% commission). The company's U.S. subsidiary based in Los Angeles would credit ACI within 30 days of ACI invoicing Makran. PIA advised Makran that if ACI accepted payment in Pakistan rupees, then local (Pakistan) payment terms would apply. This meant 180 days in principle, but often was much longer in practice. The agent also advised ACI that the Pakistan rupee was due for another devaluation soon. When pressed for more information, Makran simply replied that the company president, the elder Ibrahim Makran, had "good connections."

The ATS Finance Department

Philip Costa, the finance director for AvAC, had always wanted to be an engineer. His passion for exactness and numbers had, however, included the dollar sign, and he had moved up through the ranks at ACI quickly. The finance department he led was now in the midst of redesigning most of their processes and systems to reduce net working capital (NWC). One of these initiatives included a thorough review of existing payment terms and worldwide days sales receivable (DSR) rates. The department had a goal of reducing the worldwide DSR rate from 55 to 45 days in the current fiscal year. The *Pay for Performance* target for the current year (the annual performance bonus system at ACI) included NWC goals, and there was concern in the organization that the NWC goal might prove the obstacle to achieving a payout bonus despite excellent sales growth. And all cash flows, in and out, were to be evaluated in present value terms using a 12% discount rate. Philip started his assessment by reviewing the latest DSR report shown in Exhibit 2.

ACI payment terms were net 30 from date of invoice. However, payment terms and practices varied dramatically across country and region. ACI had not in the past enforced stringent credit terms on many customers; for example, neither contracts nor invoices stated any penalties for late payment. Many airlines did pay on time, but others availed themselves of ACI's low-cost financing.

A review of PIA's accounts receivable history indicated they consistently paid their invoices late. The current average DSR was 264 days. PIA had been repeatedly put on hold by the collections department, forcing marketing staff representatives to press the agent who in turn pressed PIA for payment. Philip's concern over the collection had driven him to search for guarantees of prompt payment. In the end, he had required the inclusion of a 20% advance payment clause in the contract as a means of self-insuring. Although marketing took the high DSR rate up with PIA and the agent, this deal was expected to be the same if not worse. One positive attribute of the contract was the fact that deliveries would not

EXHIBIT 2 Average Days Sales Receivables by Region and OEM, Aviation Systems Division

Region	Actual	Target	Amount
North America	44	40	$31 million
South America	129	70	$2.1 million
Europe	55	45	$5.7 million
Middle East	93	60	$3.2 million
Asia	75	55	$11 million
PIA	264	180	$0.7 million
Boeing		3930	$41 million
McDonnell Douglas	35	30	$18 million
Airbus Industrie	70	45	$13 million
Worldwide	55	45	

1. Many foreign carriers make purchases through U.S.-based trading companies, distorting the actual DSR practices by country.
2. The spread between individual customers within regions can be extremely large.
3. Disputed invoices are included. Amount is for all products, services, and exchanges.
4. Firms consistently meeting ACI's net 30-day terms were eligible for participation in ACI's preferred supplier program which entitled them to a 10% discount on future purchases. Only the largest customers had, to date, taken advantage of this discount.

commence until one year after project start. If the expected improvements to the DSR were made in the meantime, maybe the high DSR rate on the PIA deal could be averaged with the rest of Asia. The 20% advance payment would be used to fund the front-end engineering work. Philip also insisted that it was the responsibility of his department to assess *credit risk* for the project. This typically required a detailed review of the buyer's financials. Unfortunately, the most recent published financial data for PIA was extremely sparse, and out of date (1990).

Meeting with Finance

Gabriel: "Good morning, Philip. I am sorry to trouble you yet again with this PIA deal, but we have a problem. Peter called me last night and advised me that PIA wanted to pay in local currency. If we don't agree, we risk losing the deal. I think it's fallout from the 20% advance payment clause. Our agent, Makran, said they could accept the risk and net 30 payment terms for 5% of the sales price. Although we're confident that we are the only competing company that can meet PIA's requirements, should this requirement be real and we refuse, it could derail the whole PIA project."

Philip: "Five percent is too steep! We simply cannot accept that. This is already one of the riskiest projects we have undertaken. The 20% advance payment is to help with the DSR since it is one of our primary goals. The DSR is being watched on a daily basis by division management. We already had to secure Group Level approval for this deal because it fell below our minimum 20% ROS [return on sales] target. Whose side is this agent on?"

Gabriel: "Why don't we accept the forex risk? After all, the rupee is fixed by the government."

Philip: "Gabriel, fixed exchanged rates are actually less stable than floating rates. If you consider the IMF and World Bank part of the Pakistani government, then you are right. However, the IMF and World Bank have far more influence over Pakistan's exchange rate than the Pakistani government. The recent currency devaluations in many emerging markets could keep spreading. In the last few days the Thai baht and Philippine peso were devalued, and this is likely to spill over to other Asian export-based countries. The Pakistan rupee was devalued late last year, and I would expect another late this year or early next year."

Gabriel: "I agree we would prefer not to accept this risk, but we need to make the sale so we don't create a hole in our strategic plan. If PIA certifies our latest B777 cockpit technology in their B747 classics, we have a tremendous opportunity worldwide with that workhorse jumbo. What about our other unit, the local Industrial Process Controls (AvIPC) unit in Pakistan? Didn't they recently score a big contract with the national Pakistani petrochemical company? Don't they need rupees?"

Philip: "True, they must. Unfortunately, the CMS system charges 1% transaction cost but still passes on the currency risk to us. Unless we pay substantially more. If we were to receive the rupee receivable in the next few weeks, I might be willing to pay the 1% and take the risk, but that's not the case here. The dollar is continuing to climb, and it looks like a lot of Asia is starting to fall."

Gabriel: "I need to get back to Peter. What should we do?"

A06-00-0001

THE AMERICAN GRADUATE SCHOOL
OF INTERNATIONAL MANAGEMENT

A05-00-0012

PRAGUE VENTURE GROUP

As the summer of 1998 waned, Thomas Renton, the Prague-based managing partner of Prague Venture Group (PVG), confided to his family and closest friends that he faced the specter of failure. Renton had devoted nearly five years to establishing a venture capital investment company in Eastern Europe. To demonstrate the feasibility of investing American private capital in formerly state-owned companies, Renton had focused his efforts on a proposed refinancing deal with Vertikon, a recently privatized Czech optical manufacturing firm. Negotiations with Vertikon's owners had turned out to be unexpectedly time-consuming and treacherous, however, and in the end had led Renton to fundamentally revise his investment strategy in favor of a green field investment, called Prague Custom Optics. With Renton just short of raising $1.5 million in start-up capital for Prague Custom Optics, Renton's financial backers in America had grown frustratingly cautious, and a strategic investor had apparently defected. Renton realized that an upcoming conference call with PVG's principals would likely provide a last opportunity to salvage his dream of creating a capitalist success story out of the ruins of communism. He also had doubts whether that dream was still attainable.

The Czech Republic: Economic and Political Context

The End of Communist Rule

In November 1989, Czechoslovakia commenced an era of profound social and political change, ignited by a Velvet Revolution which peacefully brought forty years of communist rule to an end and reoriented the country towards the West. A product of the dissolution of the Austro-Hungarian Empire in 1918, Czechoslovakia enjoyed independent status and industrial affluence as a republic, until occupied by Nazi Germany in 1938-1939. In 1946, a year after Germany's defeat in the Second World War, the first Czechoslovak elections were held. These elections resulted in a victory for the Communist Party, which subsequently seized absolute control of the country in 1948. For the next forty years, Czechoslovakia was politically subordinate to the Soviet Union, and economically linked to other centrally planned Warsaw Pact nations via the Soviet-managed Council for Mutual Economic Cooperation (COMECON). In 1968 a brief period of national liberalization was crushed by the August invasion of the country by Russian-led Warsaw Pact armies. This crisis resulted in Czechoslovakia's becoming perhaps the most tightly ruled nation in the Soviet bloc, with severe limitations on private ownership and an ensuing neglect of the economy's service sector. Despite these handicaps, Czechoslovakia enjoyed the highest standard of living in the Soviet bloc, and a respectable level of productivity was achieved in a variety of industries and technologies. Czechoslovak armaments and electronics products were an important strategic resource in the Soviet system. Illustratively, Czechoslovak-built fighter aircraft were judged by pilots to be far superior to identical designs produced in Russia.

Privatization

The fall of its communist government and the free elections, which followed shortly in 1990, put Czechoslovakia on the road to resurrecting the parliamentary democracy and capitalist economy it had enjoyed between the world wars. By autumn, Parliament approved an ambitious "Scenario of Economic Reform" entailing rapid privatization of the economy and the liberalization of trade and prices. Among the first measures undertaken by the new parliament were acts to restore to citizens and descendants private property (mainly real estate) confiscated after 1948.

Since most Czechoslovak enterprises were creations of the state and state-owned, a mass voucher program was settled upon as a means of privatizing industry. Under this program, begun in 1992, some 5.5 million citizens were provided vouchers, nominally worth about $30 each, with which they could bid for the newly created shares of nearly 1,000 state-owned enterprises. In 1994 a second wave of voucher privatization saw a further 861 enterprises privatized, with 6.2 million citizens bidding individually or through investment funds for the shares. In both instances, investment funds, set up by private entrepreneurs and by state-owned banks, accumulated approximately two thirds of the purchasing power created by the voucher system. This level of investment fund control was achieved through exchanging shares in investment funds or making cash payments for the vouchers held by individual citizens. Many citizens, believing their vouchers to be nearly worthless, had been only too eager to sell them to investment funds.

The voucher system ultimately proved controversial, as privatization left the state in direct or indirect control of about 40% of the firms affected. The state retained ownership of key sectors of the economy including banking, and the banking sector in turn controlled a large portion of the shares purchased with vouchers. Additionally, voucher privatization was not universal, and hundreds of enterprises were transferred to private hands via auction, often at bargain-basement terms. Hundreds of former state enterprises were sold to individuals, particularly to plant managers, with credit available freely from local banks during the early years of the transition.

A popular perception arose, never convincingly refuted, that the most advantageous transfers of ownership accrued to members of the former Czechoslovak secret police and similarly well-placed Communist Party members. In addition, the dismantling of the state-owned economy resulted in numerous abuses by both Czech and foreign participants, who frequently had no intention of running the enterprises they acquired. A new word—tunneling—entered the Czech vocabulary to broadly catalog the dozens of methods used by new owners to loot enterprise assets and leave only a shell behind.

Political Development and Government Policy Towards Economic Reform

The 1992 elections saw a fragmentation of the political consensus that had ushered in the Velvet Revolution. Conflicts arose, which led to the dissolution of the Czech and Slovak Federative Republic and its transformation into two separate states, the Czech Republic and the Slovak Republic. Former imprisoned dissident and playwright Vaclav Havel, the last President of the Federative Republic, was elected to the Presidency of the Czech Republic in January 1993 by the Czech Parliament.

Under the center-right leadership of the new Prime Minister, Vaclav Klaus, the Czechs proceeded with rapid, albeit partial, privatization via transfer of ownership to individuals from the state. However, the hallmark of the Klaus government's vision of creating capitalism was its disdain for a significant state role in providing an institutional infrastructure conducive to business. In particular, Klaus's strongly professed neo-liberal stance—that markets can by themselves sort out most problems—placed legal reform at the bottom of the country's legislative priorities. As a result, for several years the initial wave of foreign investment flowing into the Republic masked fundamental flaws in the new economy. These flaws included a lack of basic protections, such as enforceability of business contracts and of the ability of creditors to foreclose on collateral.

Despite its anti-interventionist public posture, Klaus's government acquiesced in evergreen loans to large, non-competitive firms, loading up the portfolios of state-owned banks with valueless paper. Simultaneously, the laissez-faire attitude of the Czech government under Klaus militated against programs aimed at encouraging new enterprises. From the mid-1990s on, large Czech banks restricted new credit in response to their losses on large firm loans. New smaller Czech enterprises had very limited access to equity capital and few could afford the steep interest rates charged them by banks heavily burdened with non-performing assets.

In 1998, new parliamentary elections saw the replacement in power of Vaclav Klaus's Civic Democratic Party (ODS) by the center-left Social Democratic Party (CSSD) of Milos Zeman. Under the Zeman government the problems confronting the Czech economy became more obvious, to both domestic and foreign observers. The new government moved with little apparent enthusiasm to implement changes, including the myriad of new laws and reforms required if the Czech Republic was to accede to the European Union. In the early 1990s the Czech Republic was the darling of the international business press, which had proclaimed it "an investor's paradise." By the close of the decade, however, it was unmistakable that the country lacked the institutional framework which promotes an efficient economy. A 1998 report by the European Union summarized, with cautious optimism, Czech progress toward implementing improvements:

> *Overall, recent developments have shown that progress in the area of structural reform has been insufficient. The current programme of reform measures designed to improve corporate governance and reduce the links between the financial and the enterprise sector, once fully implemented, will go a long way towards strengthening financial discipline and deepening enterprise restructuring. This will result in more efficient enterprise and banking sectors and will clear the way for sustained increases in productivity and greater competitiveness. The country can continue to be regarded as able to cope with competitive pressures and market forces within the Union in the medium term, provided that it vigorously implements its programme of reforms.[1]*

History of Prague Venture Group

Thomas Renton had nineteen years of commercial banking experience in the United States, rising to the senior vice presidency of an independent Florida bank. In 1990 the bank's chairman, Harrison Schmidt, sent him to London to establish and operate a bank consultancy. Schmidt also wanted Renton to scout possible investment opportunities in Europe for the bank's five main shareholders. Renton had already been traveling to Europe for three years as a board member of a foundation devoted to fostering democracy and free enterprise behind the Iron Curtain. He had earned a reputation among Soviet reformers as an idealistic and reliable proponent of socially responsible capitalism. Soon after his arrival in London, Renton was offered profitable consulting contracts to advise Russian banks on Western banking practices. These activities more than paid for the Florida bank's maintenance of an office in London, and the bank's directors enjoyed the monthly faxes which Renton sent them, describing the breathtaking transformation taking place behind the Iron Curtain.

In 1993, after two years of commuting to Moscow from London, Renton was retained by the founders of Bank Boleslav, a new Czech commercial bank, to serve as their strategic advisor. At this point Renton also learned from the chairman of its board that his Florida employer was up for sale.

---

[1] *Regular Report from the Commission on Czech Republic's Progress Towards Accession*, Brussels, 1998, page 19.

Shortly thereafter, when he was offered a five-year position on Bank Boleslav's Board of Directors, with a generous pay offer, Renton resigned from the Florida bank, which was indeed acquired by an East Coast bank just six weeks later. Renton realized it might be a tough challenge to transplant American-style internal procedures and lending practices to the Czech environment. Nevertheless, he quickly found that he liked Prague at least as much as London, and took up his new job with enthusiasm.

After several months at Bank Boleslav, Renton concluded that most Czech business owners did not understand that, to succeed in the transition from communism to capitalism, their firms needed equity capital, not additional debt. Since no real capital market existed, most Czech companies had been capitalized completely with borrowed funds. A typical bank loan to privatize a company carried an interest rate of 17% to 22%, fully amortized over four years. Once privatized, many former state enterprises discovered they could afford neither to upgrade their equipment nor develop new markets to offset the sales lost with the disbanding of the former state-owned trading companies. Their high financial leverage left no room for new financing for survival or expansion.

Renton also noted that primarily investment bankers funded foreign investment in the Czech Republic. Many of them created offshore investment funds for this purpose. However, rather than providing new capital for Czech firms, much of the new money went to purchase shares of companies traded on the Prague Stock Exchange. In general, foreign portfolio investors aimed at short-term gains in stock trading, or takeovers of larger state-owned companies. Czech banks were accumulating their own investments in local companies, through investment funds that they controlled. As a rule, the Western investors Renton met wanted quick profits while their Czech counterparts wanted control over company assets.

With these factors in mind, Renton surmised that there was room for a new kind of entity devoted to placing offshore capital into smaller Czech firms with competitive products. The Czech Republic's inexpensive, well-trained work force, combined with the country's engineering and technical prowess, provided fundamental competitive strengths which ensured that well-managed Czech firms could thrive in the capitalist global market. Renton felt that by providing funding, plus marketing and management skills, Western investors could make a satisfactory return, create value, and be a catalyst for helping Czechs succeed in the transition from state to private ownership. He was excited by the prospects.

Renton had many wealthy contacts in the U.S. and had already met many Czech businessmen through his banking activities. In early 1994 he sent letters to the former main shareholders of his former Florida employer, describing the possibilities of raising a $30 million venture capital fund to invest in the Czech Republic. By October he had commitments from five of the latter to join him in investing start-up capital in Prague Venture Group (PVG). Per Renton's strategy, the basic concept was that PVG would raise and operate venture capital funds throughout Central and Eastern Europe. The initial fund would focus on investing in promising enterprises in the Czech Republic.

By March 1995, PVG was incorporated in Delaware, and had filed the necessary registration documents to operate in the Czech Republic. The company's initial equity capitalization was $180,000, with equal contributions from Renton and his five American partners (Exhibit 1). While awaiting PVG's incorporation, Renton retained a British accounting firm to draw up a preliminary prospectus for raising the capital which PVG would invest in small and medium-sized Czech enterprises on behalf of Western investors.

During the summer and autumn of 1995 Renton made visits to major financial houses in London, New York and Boston. To his surprise he encountered little interest in partaking in $500,000 shares of the $30 million limited partnership ("Czech Emerging Markets Fund") advertised in PVG's preliminary prospectus. Although institutional investors agreed with Renton that there might be lucrative venture investment opportunities in Central Europe's newly private economy, they were typically seeking individual deals of over $100 million and did not have time for monitoring a comparatively small investment in Renton's proposed venture fund. Some investors to whom Renton was introduced, including several high-net-worth individuals, were willing to participate in smaller deals, but most of these prospects expressed hesitation to invest in a venture fund whose manager, Renton, lacked U.S. venture capital experience. Renton could persuade few listeners that U.S. venture capital experience would be largely irrelevant, given how the post-Soviet business environment was not comparable to what professional venture capital managers in the West are accustomed to.

At the end of the year, Renton conferred with his partners in Florida. Renton felt embarrassed by having depleted $55,000 of PVG's start-up capital on his failed attempt to raise a $30 million venture fund. With his partners' encouragement, however, Renton agreed to press ahead, by identifying promising Czech acquisition prospects. PVG's individual partners would then have first rights to participate in deals pre-screened by Renton on a case-by-case basis. Despite his original setback, Renton hoped that with the deep pockets of PVG's principals—who had cash to invest after the lucrative sale of their bank—PVG could create an investment track record which would give him credibility in future attempts to raise funds from Western institutional sources. In the long term, Thomas Renton felt PVG was well situated to become a leading provider of venture capital to small and medium enterprises in the heart of Europe.

Vertikon

Vertikon was established in 1923 by an entrepreneur of Czech-German descent and two Czech engineering students, who had fought in the same unit on the Italian front during World War I. High quality glass making had a long tradition in the Czech lands. Many industrialists, including Vertikon's founders, recognized that this expertise could be profitably applied to the mass production of lenses. The first product of the company was range-finding periscopes, which were successfully sold to the French and Belgian armies. During the German occupation of 1939-1945, Vertikon made binoculars and field telescopes for the army (Wehrmacht), and also produced lenses used in the Luftwaffe's high-altitude reconnaissance cameras. From 1946 to 1950 the company survived by manufacturing cheaply made hobby telescopes, but eventually, under state ownership, returned to the manufacture of high-quality military optics. Vertikon's exceptionally durable binoculars were in use by four Warsaw Pact armies, and the firm also participated in the manufacture of the complex gun sights for the high-altitude, supersonic MIG 25 interceptor. The company also had a small side-business manufacturing surveying instruments, which were exported as far away as India and Viet Nam.

Following the end of the Cold War, in late 1989 Vertikon's orders from the State of Czechoslovakia and other COMECON customers slumped. In 1993, as part of the Czech Republic's privatization program, the Ministry of Industry put the company up for sale at auction. Four former senior employees of Vertikon purchased the company, paying the Czech government $1,000,000 which the group borrowed from state-owned Slavia Bank. The new co-owners let go several clerical employees, thereby reducing staff to 28, and set about trying to find new customers in Western Europe. With employee salaries and benefits averaging about $400 per month, Vertikon had a decisive price advantage which partly offset the firm's lack of reputation in the West. All in all, the new marketing effort was modestly successful, with Vertikon landing a small contract to supply binoculars to the Dutch armed forces. The company also found a military surplus dealer, based in Chicago, who pasted Red Army insignia over the Vertikon logo and sold the firm's binoculars to collectors. More promising for the firm's future were

[2] All amounts in the case are expressed in U.S. dollars.

seven successive orders from a British firm for custom lenses used in cinematography. Vertikon's management was learning that custom lenses could be a very profitable business segment. The firm also had preliminary discussions with a Swedish company, which Vertikon approached in regard to supplying lenses for use in optometric equipment.

Prague Venture Group and Vertikon

In November 1995, Renton received a fax from Peter Schwarz, one of PVG's shareholders. Schwarz, who had emigrated to the United States from Czechoslovakia in 1969, had read about Vertikon's privatization in a Czech newspaper and suggested that Renton call on the company. Following up on this tip from Schwarz, Renton made an appointment to meet with Vertikon's co-owners. Renton's initial contact with Vertikon revealed it to be a prime candidate for investment. In a nutshell, Vertikon appeared to be a financially strapped producer of excellent products, which needed only a reasonable capital injection and some good marketing advice to begin realizing its potential.

Renton was particularly encouraged by Vertikon's co-owners' strong optics backgrounds. Three of the four were seasoned experts in optics manufacturing, while the fourth had twenty years of experience handling the optical sales of a large state trading company. Renton was also heartened to learn that Vertikon's co-owners were paying themselves the same salaries they had made under communism—between $500 and $1,000 per month. Though the co-owners were clearly novices at running an enterprise under capitalist rules, they were a mature and well-trained group who seemed to work together well. Additionally, they seemed receptive to hearing what Renton had to say about how Prague Venture Group could help Vertikon survive and prosper.

At the same time, Renton could see that Vertikon's problems were serious. Despite efforts to carve out new markets for Vertikon's products, sales did not cover expenses, and the firm was losing the equivalent of $200,000 annually. After paying merely one $3,000 installment, Vertikon's management had defaulted on their four-year, 17% loan from Slavia Bank. A secondary shadow over Vertikon's future was that the firm had not been able to make any expenditures for much-needed computerized production equipment. Renton was amazed to see that a substantial part of Vertikon's lenses were being laboriously produced by hand, and—adding to Renton's worries—by workers who seemed to be approaching retirement age.

Within a month of meeting Vertikon's owners, Renton had sketched out a preliminary plan for refinancing the optics firm. The two pillars of Renton's plan were to retire Vertikon's swollen debt, and to link Vertikon with a strategic partner in the optics industry, which could distribute Vertikon's products in North America. This strategic partner could also provide technical assistance to help Vertikon modernize.

Under Czech commercial law Slavia Bank would find it difficult to foreclose on Vertikon's assets. Therefore, Renton was confident that the bank would happily accept an offer to repay the original loan amount, forgiving accumulated interest and penalties. Renton envisaged Prague Venture Group acquiring a 67% stake in Vertikon for an investment totaling $2 million. The 67% ownership target would give PVG a super majority interest under Czech law, ensuring Renton the total management control which potential American investors in the deal would require. The four Czechs would retain 33% of the company and also obtain long-term management contracts. Half of PVG's planned contribution was earmarked for retiring Vertikon's bank debt, leaving some $800,000 for acquisition of high-tech German production equipment and $200,000 for working capital.

During the remainder of 1996, in addition to his duties as a director at Bank Boleslav, Renton continued his negotiations with Vertikon's owners. Discussions hit an early snag over the future direction of Vertikon. It took Renton several months to persuade Vertikon's management that their best bet was not binocular production—where the firm enjoyed no international brand identity—but on sales of lenses and lens assemblies to better-established manufacturers of branded optics. Renton's idea of focusing on making components rather than finished products became more persuasive to Vertikon's co-owners after Renton made several trip to the U.S. to call on major optics firms on Vertikon's behalf.

The growing trust between Renton and Vertikon management was also jeopardized by an appraisal of the company by the Czech Ministry of Industry. Based on no apparent logic, the Ministry valued Vertikon at $3.8 million for tax purposes. This valuation was much higher than what Renton felt could be obtained in an arms-length sale. On several occasions afterwards, Vertikon's partners asked Renton to explain why PVG should be entitled to two-thirds ownership of their company, if PVG's investment represented only about half of the Ministry's valuation. It was not clear to Renton whether the partners completely understood that until their loan to Slavia Bank was paid off, the bank owned Vertikon's assets. Despite these seeming misunderstandings, Vertikon's management seemed receptive to Renton's ideas about recapitalizing the company.

By November 1996, a year after they had begun, Renton's discussions with Vertikon seemed to have sufficiently progressed for him to draft a formal letter to the company's principals (Exhibit 3). Renton considered the deal outlined in his letter a generous offer, considering the liquidity position of the optics company and that the co-owners had invested none of their own money in acquiring it.

Since Renton had first entered into negotiations with Vertikon, Slavia Bank had started court proceedings to seize the optics firm's fixed assets, which were pledged as collateral. Even though the Czech legal system was so sluggish that this action posed no immediate threat to Vertikon, Renton believed it was strongly in management's interest to eliminate this bank debt. Evidently realizing this also, Vertikon's owners had invited Renton to attend several crisis meetings with Slavia Bank, whose forbearance was sought while Vertikon completed its restructuring with Prague Venture Group. Renton also knew that Vertikon was having trouble meeting its payroll. Thus, in Renton's eyes, the proposal outlined in his letter was a win-win scenario for all parties. He was pleased with his apparently successful negotiations with both the owners of the company and its creditor bank.

Shortly after putting his proposal in writing to Vertikon, Renton and an accountant he had retained began the task of completing a 77-page Private Placement Memorandum (PPM) to be submitted to potential investors in the $2 million deal. In the spring of 1997 Renton began circulating the PPM along with a supplement which estimated an eventual Return on Investment of nearly 55%—an extremely attractive yield (Exhibit 4). By early autumn Renton had obtained commitments from each of PVG's Florida-based backers, totaling $1,750,000 (Exhibit 2). In late October Renton wrote Vertikon that he expected to be able to raise the balance of $250,000 by the end of the year. He also advised Vertikon that he'd had promising discussions with a well-known U.S. optics firm, which had expressed keen interest in participating in the deal as a strategic investor.

Renton's Meeting with Drosc

On November 3, 1997 Renton returned to his downtown Prague residence to find a phone message awaiting him. Ivan Drosc, one of the four Czech co-owners of Vertikon, wanted to speak to Renton immediately. When Renton reached Drosc, the optics engineer was reluctant to talk on the phone. He simply said, "Can we meet sometime later today or tonight?" Two hours later, Drosc met Renton in a

Prague hotel lobby. There, Drosc explained that the three other principals in Vertikon were not dealing in good faith with Renton. "They have been using your prospectus to solicit optics customers in the United States on their own, and they have also shown it to Slavia Bank to renegotiate our loan terms. The fact is, they will never give PVG management control." Drosc even went so far as to speculate that his three partners were giving payoffs to a loan officer at Slavia Bank to permanently forestall a bankruptcy petition against the company. Finally, he warned Renton that two of Vertikon's co-owners had had secret police connections before the Velvet Revolution, and still had friends in powerful places. When Renton quizzed him why he was finally coming forward with this information, Drosc replied that he believed that the PVG financing represented Vertikon's last real hope, and therefore his own future depended on Renton's outmaneuvering Drosc's untrustworthy partners.

Based on Drosc's disclosures, Renton decided that the acquisition of Vertikon could not be allowed to go ahead as planned. However, Renton felt the situation could be salvaged. Within a few days he had contacted his PVG partners, advising them apologetically that he was withdrawing the proposed deal, but would be back to them promptly with what should be a more promising investment opportunity. During the next two months Renton feverishly drafted a second PPM, based on a new scenario which excluded Vertikon and ensured greater management control by PVG. Because of the intensive demands of writing a new business plan, Renton also resigned his position with Bank Boleslav.

Prague Custom Optics

Fortuitously, several days before he met with Renton, Drosc had sealed a promising sales deal for Vertikon with a major American distributor of lenses, owned by Tomas Zubar, a Czech emigrant living in New Hampshire. The New Hampshire firm was able to sell almost any amount of Czech product it could obtain, and Zubar, when subsequently approached by Renton, proved keen to invest up to $400,000 to guarantee himself a supply of high quality lenses. Zubar also knew about the availability of three barely used, state-of-the-art production machines, the envisaged purchase of which became the cornerstone of a planned green field firm which Renton dubbed Prague Custom Optics. In March 1998 Renton began circulating the new prospectus, titled PVG-PCO Fund, LLC. This prospectus sought to raise only $1.5 million, as compared to the $2 million Renton originally had tried to raise for Vertikon. Because Prague Custom Optics did not have bank debt to repay, the new business plan, despite its smaller capitalization, gave Prague Custom Optics more working capital than a refinanced Vertikon. With only Drosc on the payroll via a key man contract and a planned staff totaling less than half that of Vertikon's, the green field route boded high profit.

Renton was therefore chagrined when he got a cautious response to the new prospectus from his PVG associates. One PVG partner declined to invest whatsoever, while three PVG principals pledged smaller amounts than they had agreed to invest earlier in the Vertikon deal. The reason they gave—never expressed previously—was that they would feel more comfortable if Renton could interest a Czech investor to underwrite a portion of the financing. In response to this, Renton met with dozens of prospects. The Czechs he spoke to did not, as a rule, want minority ownership positions, while Czech banks, including Bank Boleslav, were at that moment under instructions from the central bank to cut back on commercial lending. Renton arranged several dozen meetings in Prague during July 1998, but he failed to obtain immediate commitments to participate in the Prague Custom Optics financing. By this point Renton had nearly exhausted PVG's original working capital, and he was subsidizing his fund-raising efforts with fast-depleting personal funds. For all his efforts, he was still short $125,000 to close the deal. Adding to his frustration, Renton had begun to receive regular phone calls from New Hampshire, where Tomas Zubar was anxiously awaiting shipments from Prague Custom Optics to begin. In late July, Renton flew to Florida and pleaded with his partners to ante up the negligible sum needed to complete the transaction. They urged him to redouble his efforts to find a Czech co-investor, or, failing that, a Western European, to make up the shortfall.

Conclusion

On August 11, 1998 Renton, back in Prague, received an e-mail from Alan Binder, a PVG shareholder, requesting that Renton telephone Binder's Miami law offices at 10 A.M. the following day, for a conference call with four of PVG's principals. On the agenda was a phone call which Peter Schwarz, PVG's wealthiest participant, had received from Tomas Zubar. That the New Hampshire optics distributor had gone around Renton and communicated directly with Schwarz was hardly a good omen. But Renton was completely unprepared for the e-mail's next disclosure: Zubar was seeking investors to finance a deal of his own, conceivably involving the New Hampshire firm's acquisition of Vertikon. Binder's e-mail concluded on an uncomfortably sharp note: *We here feel entitled to an explanation of why you apparently have lost control of the situation, and we are anxious to learn what you are going to do about it.* Renton knew the conference call could decide his and PVG's fate. As he looked out his apartment window towards Prague Castle, he began to rehearse what he might tell his American associates the next day. Another, greater worry entered his mind: even if he weathered tomorrow's storm and bought additional time for PVG, it might only be a temporary reprieve. He wondered whether the time had come to pull the plug on PVG.

EXHIBIT 1 Principals of Prague Venture Group (PVG)

Alan Binder
Age: 60[1]
Residence: Florida
Occupation: Attorney

Thane Leggett
Age: 56
Residence: Florida
Occupation: Engineer/Entrepreneur

Thomas Renton
Age: 55
Residence: Czech Republic
Occupation: Former Commercial Banker; Managing Partner of PVG

Harrison Schmidt
Age: 66
Residence: Florida
Occupation: Retired Bank Chairman

Peter Schwarz
Age: 54
Residence: Florida
Occupation: Real Estate Developer

Claudio Tempest
Age: 65
Residence: Florida
Occupation: Entrepreneur/Real Estate Investor

EXHIBIT 2 Personal Investment Pledges by PVG Principals

	PVG-Vertikon Fund[2]	**PVG-Prague Custom Optics Fund**[3]
Alan Binder	$ 300,000	$ 250,000
Thane Leggett	250,000	100,000
Thomas Renton	-0-	-0-
Harrison Schmidt	375,000	225,000
Peter Schwarz	725,000	400,000
Claudio Tempest	100,00	-0-
	$1,750,000	$ 975,000

---

[1] As of January 1998.
[2] As of November 1, 1997. Funding needed to close the PPM was $2,000,000. Offer was withdrawn in mid-November 1997 following Renton's meeting with Drosc.
[3] As of August 1, 1998. Funding needed to close the PPM was $1,500,000. A $400,000 pledge from New Hampshire optics firm owner Tomas Zubar brought the total pledged subscriptions to the deal to $1,375,000.

EXHIBIT 3

Prague Venture Group

A Delaware Corporation

1338 Sebastian Way, Suite 88Narodni 7
Hallandale, FL 33009110 01 Prague 1
(305) 456-7000(42) 2-259-7831
United States of AmericaCzech Republic

November 4, 1996

Mr. Jaroslav Bynchl
Mr. Ivan Drosc
Mr. Petr Hajler
Mr. Miroslav Jindrich
Vertikon, S.R.O.
Ceskobrodska 177
200 22 Praha 9

Dear Jaroslav, Ivan, Petr, and Miroslav:

I am writing, first, to express my appreciation for the time you have given me during the past year, and your willingness to engage in frank discussions with Prague Venture Group. We have made substantial progress toward creating an outcome that will ensure the success of both our firms. In addition, I want you to know that I have come to admire your entrepreneurial spirit in purchasing Vertikon. Moving to a market economy is a serious challenge, but once started it cannot be reversed. You are pioneers in this process of change, and your dedication to your company is an inspiration.

Vertikon's situation is similar to that of other Czech firms: lack of working capital and new markets. My view is that you have superior products and good management; Prague Venture Group, I believe, can supply the critical ingredients missing.

My understanding of the current situation is as follows:

• In regards to creating new markets for Vertikon, my trips to the U.S. have identified several potential strategic partners, who not only have expressed willingness to purchase your products, but also invest in your firm through Prague Venture Group.

• Prague Venture Group has also had a series of discussions with Slavia Bank. The bank has stated its unwillingness to renegotiate the interest rate and terms of the 33 million Czech Crown loan used to purchase Vertikon from the Czech Government. Nor will the Bank provide you with new funding.

• Prague Venture Group believes it has been successful during the past several months in persuading Slavia Bank to delay recovery of its loan through legal action. At the last meeting, the bank gave Vertikon until January 28 to provide an acceptable repayment plan.

• Prague Venture Group believes that it can satisfy Slavia Bank, bring needed working capital to the company and, with the involvement of a strategic partner, significantly increase sales.

• Vertikon is continuing to lose money. There are no funds to purchase new equipment, increase salaries to prevent the departure of essential staff, continue running the marketing plan drawn up a year ago, or meet other capital needs.

• It is only a matter of time before the bank takes over the company, or forces its sale. The future of the existing owners is clearly in jeopardy.

Messrs. Bynchl, Drosc, Hajler and Jindrich
November 4, 1996
Page 2

In view of the above, I am providing you with our preliminary proposal:

1. Vertikon makes "Sale and Lease Back" arrangement with Prague Venture Group (PVG), whereby PVG takes title to the primary fixed assets and leases them back to the company at a favorable rate. Vertikon would have the right to buy back the same fixed assets from PVG on an equitable basis.

2. Simultaneously with Step 1 above, Prague Venture Group will be responsible for retiring the bank debt, with Prague Venture Group responsible for all negotiations with the bank.

3. Prague Venture Group will also make a significant equity investment into a newly established joint-stock company. This joint investment will be large enough to justify an ownership position on the part of Prague Venture Group on a super majority (>67%) basis.

4. Prague Venture Group will, on a best-efforts basis, endeavor to involve a strategic investment partner in PVG's ownership stake in Vertikon. As of this date, PVG has had discussions with five leading optics firms in the USA, and we believe we can ensure the involvement of one of them in this investment, pending your final agreement to the terms outlined. The role of the strategic investment partner will be to act as a distributor of Vertikon products worldwide and to provide management support, while Vertikon's role will be to improve production quality and efficiency.

5. Appropriate salary increases for management and staff will be implemented, along with employment contracts for managers.

6. An employee stock ownership program will be introduced, allowing employees to purchase shares in the company.

7. The equity investment by Prague Venture Group will be used to make necessary repairs and improvements to the building, upgrade equipment, produce high-quality sales brochures, cover travel costs for re-establishing old markets, and install state-of-the-art management systems.

8. Finally, it is the intent of Prague Venture Group to liquidate its ownership of Vertikon in three to five years. Exit possibilities include: (a) taking the company public through a share offering on the Prague Stock Exchange; (b) management buy-out; (c) purchase by a strategic partner; (d) refinancing through bank term debt; (e) a combination thereof.

I believe we first need to agree in principle as to the basic plan and majority ownership structure, and then negotiate percentages, roles, and financial details. This proposal is intended to fully disclose how your company can be adequately recapitalized with partners who can bring added value, and position itself on a sound business-like basis for long-term growth. By working together I believe we can bring to Vertikon great financial rewards and recapture pride and prestige in the international market.

After you have read and discussed this proposal, I would like to meet and elaborate on any items and answer any questions you may have.

Sincerely,

Thomas Renton
Managing Partner

EXHIBIT 4

Prague Venture Group
A Delaware Corporation

1338 Sebastian Way, Suite 88Narodni 7
Hallandale, FL 33009110 01 Prague 1
(305) 456-7000(42) 2-259-7831
United States of AmericaCzech Republic

Appendix to Private Placement Memorandum,
Prague Venture Group-Vertikon Fund, LLC

PERFORMANCE AND PROJECTIONS FOR THE COMPANY

DISCLAIMER:

PROJECTIONS ARE INHERENTLY SUBJECT TO VARYING DEGREES OF UNCERTAINTY AND THEIR ACHIEVABILITY DEPENDS UPON THE TIMING AND PROBABILITY OF OCCURRENCE OF A COMPLEX SERIES OF FUTURE EVENTS, BOTH INTERNAL AND EXTERNAL. ACTUAL OPERATING RESULTS COULD VARY MATERIALLY FROM THOSE PROJECTED. WHILE THE MANAGER BELIEVES THAT THE ASSUMPTIONS USED IN PREPARATION OF THE PROJECTIONS ARE REASONABLE, THERE CAN BE NO ASSURANCE THAT SUCH ASSUMPTIONS ARE ACCURATE OR, IF ACCURATE, THAT THE ASSUMPTIONS OR THE RESULTS DEPICTED WILL BE ATTAINABLE BY THE COMPANY. A POTENTIAL INVESTOR SHOULD EVALUATE ON HIS OWN BEHALF THE REASONABLENESS OF THE ASSUMPTIONS AND THE LIKELIHOOD OF ATTAINMENT OF THE RESULTS DEPICTED.

Assumptions to Financial Projections—1998 through 2002

1. Total sales in 1996 were $426 thousand, of which binoculars represented $114 thousand and precision lenses for various purposes represented $263 thousand. The remainder was assembly of specialized optical equipment. 1997 sales are expected to be about $475 thousand, and with the implementation of this plan are projected to rise to $585 thousand in 1998.

2. The increase in sale of optical components is based on the following:

  a. The Company is currently operating at 50% of production capacity.
  b. The Company's inventory of tooling will be properly catalogued and organized for faster access.
  c. The Company presently has on site an inactive optics-centering machine owned by the Czech Army, which can be purchased for $182 thousand. The activation of this piece of equipment will allow for significant increases in production of optical components.
  d. The acquisition cost includes the purchase of almost $900 thousand in new or replacement equipment and technology, which will increase capacity further and allow the production of other products attractive in Western Europe and North America.

3. Approximately ten metric tons of raw glass inventoried for binocular and custom instrument lens production.

4. Cost of goods sold represents the direct and indirect costs of production, excluding depreciation and amortization. Marketing expenses are shown separately. The management fee charged includes some personal marketing by the manager.

5. Salaries and benefits increase by 15% on an annualized basis through 2002. The Company has a total of 25 employees, with average monthly wages and benefits of $401 per month, including management. Existing administrative staff and indirect labor can adequately meet planned increases in production. However, direct labor is expected to rise in proportion to the increase in output.

6. Other operating expenses increase by annual rates reflecting the requirement to import some items with a potentially depreciating currency, and the higher costs anticipated by the government program of deregulation of utilities.

7. Depreciation/amortization applies to the building (45 years) and the current and new equipment (8 years). Although the equipment transaction may be structured as a sale and leaseback to provide investors with direct control of this asset, the accounting presentation for a capital lease and related lease liability is essentially the same as for purchase of the asset and the related long-term loan.

8. The management fee is to be paid to TR Inc. for my management services. It will be $15,000 for 1998 and $25,000 plus 1% of total sales thereafter. This fee structure is not burdensome to Vertikon, and will maintain my strong incentive to ensure Vertikon's continuing prosperity.

9. The tax rate is assumed to be 35% of accounting income, which is the same as taxable income under Czech rules with the given depreciation rates. It is possible that the effective rate may decrease to 31% in the future, under proposed government legislation. Such a change would benefit both majority and minority shareholders of Vertikon.

10. In order to ensure adequate cash flow for continuing operations, dividends will not be paid until both profit and cash position can sustain them. This plan proposes cash dividends of $50 thousand beginning in 2001, assuming satisfaction of these criteria. The actual timing of dividend payments could be accelerated or delayed, depending on the financial condition of the company.

Detailed assumptions for each revenue and expense category are included with the pro forma (projected) financial statements.

Financial Analysis—Highlights

- Earnings before tax and depreciation of $683.9 thousand in year five with a market multiple of seven equals an estimated market value of $4.787 million. With annual net income after tax included, this represents an average annual ROI on the original investment of $2.0 million of 54.8%. Alternatively, considering just this market value plus dividends paid, the average annual ROI is 48.8%.

- Using a price-earnings multiple of ten on the after-tax net income at year five of $328.5 thousand gives an estimated market value of $3.285 million. By itself, this would give an annual ROI of 32.8% on a $2.0 million investment. Including annual net income after tax gives an annual ROI of 39.1%.

- For its investment of $2.0 million, PVG will receive after-tax interest, return of principal, and its share of dividends and the net cash position of Vertikon. Based on a projected loan of ten years at an interest rate of 12%, the debt interest and principal can be projected. The present value of these repayments, at a market rate of 17% and a tax rate of 31% is $841 thousand.[1]

Equity cash flows have grown from $(23.3) in 1999 to $235.6 in 2002. (1998 is excluded for growth purposes, due to the initial set-up). Including the dividends paid, cash flows approximately doubled each of the last two years. Under a conservative assumption, cash flows before dividends will continue to increase at 50% per year for another five years, then grow at about 15% per year thereafter. Including the dividends paid in years 2001 and 2002, the value of the equity position would then be as follows:

Discount Rate 25% 30% 35%
Present Value of Vertikon $3.540 $1.970 $1.248
Equity Cash Flows ($millions)

Prague Venture Group's Share (67%) $2.372 $1.320 $0.836
Value of Loan Repayments 0.841 0.841 0.841
Total Value to PVG[2] $3.213 $2.161 $1.677

---

[1] The loan is subsidized at a rate of 12% per year, compounded monthly. Using the monthly effective rate of 1%, the monthly payments of principal and interest for 10 years can be found. The market rate of 17% is an effective rate of .65*17 = 11.05% after tax of 35%. Using compounding, this is an effective monthly rate of 0.877245%. The interest payments received by PVG are taxable, so must be decreased by 35%. The principal repayments are not taxable, and so are not decreased. Using these revised cash flows to PVG and the calculated monthly rate gives the present value of these loans of $841 thousand at the market interest rate of 17%.
[2] The net present value has a range of -$0.323 million to $1.215 million for equity discount rates of 25% and 35%, respectively, and a debt discount rate of 17%.

Vertikon - Prague Venture Group
Projected Income Statements
(Thousands of U.S. Dollars)

	1998	1999	2000	2001	2002
Sales:					
Binoculars	135.0	178.5	236.1	312.3	413.0
Print System Optics	85.0	107.5	136.0	172.1	217.7
Cinematic Lenses	155.0	206.3	280.0	376.3	505.7
Other Export Optics	133.5	168.2	211.9	267.1	336.5
Research and Development	21.2	32.6	50.3	77.4	119.2
Czech Domestic Sales	55.3	63.2	72.2	82.4	94.2
Total Sales	585.0	758.4	986.5	1,287.5	1,686.3
Cost of Goods Sold:					
Direct Labor	76.1	98.6	128.2	167.4	219.2
Materials	99.5	128.9	167.7	218.9	286.7
Total Variable COGS	175.5	227.5	296.0	386.3	505.9
Indirect Labor	15.0	18.8	23.4	29.3	36.6
Supplies	12.8	16.6	21.6	28.1	36.6
Total Fixed COGS	27.8	35.4	45.1	57.4	73.2
Total Cost of Goods Sold	203.3	262.9	341.0	443.7	579.1
Gross Profit	381.7	495.5	645.5	843.9	1,107.2
Selling Expenses:					
Advertising and Promotions	8.8	11.4	14.8	19.3	25.3
Incentives and Bonuses	4.7	6.1	7.9	10.3	13.5
Sales Commissions	5.9	7.6	9.9	12.9	16.9
Trade Shows and Travel	14.6	19.0	24.7	32.2	42.2
Total Selling Expenses	33.9	44.0	57.2	74.7	97.8
Administrative and General Expenses:					
Salaries	32.3	37.1	42.7	49.1	56.5
Research and Development	12.3	14.1	16.3	18.7	21.5
Equipment Rental	15.8	16.6	17.4	18.3	19.2
Office Rental	31.2	31.8	32.5	33.1	33.8
Office Expenses	4.8	5.0	5.3	5.6	5.8
Depreciation/Amortization	75.0	158.0	164.5	171.4	178.5
Telephone and Utilities	7.0	8.1	9.3	10.6	12.2
Insurance	8.0	9.0	10.0	11.2	12.6
Accounting	8.0	8.6	9.3	10.1	10.9
Bad Debts	5.9	7.6	9.9	12.9	16.9
Management Fee	15.0	32.6	34.9	37.9	41.9
Non-Income Taxes	2.0	2.6	3.4	4.4	5.7
Interest Expense	79.2	128.8	113.4	98.3	88.6
Total Administrative Expenses	296.5	459.9	468.8	481.5	504.0

Vertikon - Prague Venture Group
Projected Balance Sheets
(Thousands of U.S. Dollars)

	1998	1999	2000	2001	2002
Current Assets:					
Cash and Bank Account	111.0	-	-	103.9	339.6
Accounts Receivable	55.0	113.8	148.0	193.1	252.9
Inventory	45.5	91.0	118.4	154.5	202.4
Total Current Assets	211.5	204.8	266.4	451.5	794.9
Fixed Assets					
Land	176.0	176.0	176.0	176.0	176.0
Leashold Improvements	242.0	261.4	282.3	304.9	329.2
Equipment	1,221.0	1,269.8	1,320.6	1,373.5	1,428.4
Less Accum. Depreciation	(75.0)	(233.0)	(397.5)	(568.9)	(747.3)
Net Fixed Assets	1,564.0	1,474.2	1,381.4	1,285.4	1,186.3
Total Assets	1,775.5	1,679.0	1,647.7	1,736.9	1,981.1
Current Liabilities:					
Short Term Bank Loan	176.0	88.3	12.0	-	-
Accounts Payable	22.9	37.9	49.3	64.4	84.3
Accrued Liabilities	5.6	37.9	49.3	64.4	84.3
Total Current Liabilities	204.5	164.1	110.7	128.8	168.6
Long Term Liabilities					
Equipment Loan (PVG)	950.0	902.2	843.8	778.0	703.8
Total Liabilities	1,154.5	1,066.4	954.5	906.7	872.4
Capital:					
Common Shares (PVG)	393.7	393.7	393.7	393.7	393.7
Common Shares (Minority)	193.9	193.9	193.9	193.9	193.9
Retained Earnings	33.4	25.0	105.6	242.6	521.1

Vertikon - Prague Venture Group
Projected Annual Cash Flows
(Thousands of U.S. Dollars)

	1998*	1999	2000	2001	2002
Operating Cash Flows:					
Net Income after Tax	33.4	(8.4)	80.6	187.0	328.5
Add Non-Cash Expense Items					
Depreciation / Amortization	75.0	158.0	164.5	171.4	178.5
Sub-total	108.4	149.6	245.1	358.3	506.9
Adj. for Change in Working Capital					
Accounts Receivable	(55.0)	(58.8)	(34.2)	(45.2)	(59.8)
Inventory	(45.5)	(45.5)	(27.4)	(36.1)	(47.8)
Accounts Payable	22.9	15.0	11.4	15.1	19.9
Accruals	5.6	32.3	11.4	15.1	19.9
Net Cash Flows from Operations	36.4	92.6	206.4	307.2	439.2
Investment Cash Flows:					
Land	(176.0)	-	-	-	-
Leasehold Improvements	(242.0)	(19.4)	(20.9)	(22.6)	(24.4)
Equipment	(1,221.0)	(48.8)	(50.8)	(52.8)	(54.9)
Net Cash Flows to Investments	(1,639.0)	(68.2)	(71.7)	(75.4)	(79.3)
Financing Cash Flows:					
Net New Long Term Debt	950.0	(47.8)	(58.4)	(65.8)	(74.2)
Net New Common Equity (PVG)	393.7	-	-	-	-
Net New Common Equity (Minority)	193.9	-	-	-	-
Less Proposed Dividends	-	-	-	(50.0)	(50.0)
Net Cash Flows from Financing	1,537.6	(47.8)	(58.4)	(115.8)	(124.2)
Net Change in Cash Position	(65.0)	(23.3)	76.2	115.9	235.6
Opening Net Cash / (Short Term Loan)	-	(65.0)	(88.3)	(12.1)	103.8
Closing Cash / (Short Term Loan)	(65.0)	(88.3)	(12.1)	103.8	339.5

Vertikon - Prague Venture Group
Input Assumptions

Percentage of Vertikon purchased by Prague Venture Group		67.0%
Income Tax Rate		35.0%

Growth in Annual Sales after 1998	Real	Inflation
Binoculars	15.0%	15.0%
Print System Optics	15.0%	10.0%
Cinematic Lenses	20.0%	12.0%
Other Export Optics	20.0%	5.0%
Research and Development	40.0%	10.0%
Czech Domestic Sales	12.0%	2.0%

Variable Costs as a Percentage of Sales:
Direct Labor	13.0%
Materials	17.0%
Advertising and Promotions	1.5%
Incentives and Bonuses	0.8%
Sales Commissions	1.0%
Trade Shows and Travel	2.5%
Bad Debts	1.0%

Fixed Cost Rates of Inflation:
Indirect Labor	25.0%
Supplies	30.0%
Salaries	15.0%
Research and Development	15.0%
Equipment Rental	5.0%
Office Rental	2.0%
Office Expenses	5.0%
Telephone and Utilities	15.0%
Insurance	12.0%
Accounting	8.0%
Non-Income Taxes	30.0%

Capital Expenditures:
After initial expenditure, building leasehold improvements growth.	8.0%
After initial expenditure, equipment expenditures growth.	4.0%

Depreciation/Amortization Rate:
Building and Improvements	2.2%
Equipment	12.5%

Management Fee: $15 k. first year, then $25 k. + % of net sales.	1.0%

THUNDERBIRD
THE AMERICAN GRADUATE SCHOOL
OF INTERNATIONAL MANAGEMENT

A06-99-0003

THE FAR EAST TRADING COMPANY

"We have worked 30 to 40 years to develop our countries to this level, but along comes a man with a few billion dollars, and who in a period of just two weeks, has undone most of the work we have done. As a result, the people of our countries suffer. You talk about human rights and protecting people. But they must be protected from people like Soros who has so much money and so much power and totally thoughtless because he is not only hurting the people of Myanmar, but the poor people in Indonesia, Malaysia, the Philippines and Thailand."

Prime Minister Datuk Seri Dr. Mahathir Mohamad of Malaysia
New Straits Times, Kuala Lumpur, July 27, 1997

For Thailand to blame Mr. Soros for its plight is rather like condemning an undertaker for burying a suicide.

The Economist, August 2, 1997, p. 57.

Jan Karl Karlsen, CFO of The Far East Trading Company A/B, hurried down the Kuala Lumpur hotel corridor to his meeting with the financial controllers of many of the company's regional operating units. His task this morning was to explain personally the profit warning reported by the company in a press release the previous Friday, November 21, 1997, in Stockholm. This had been the second official profit warning of the year, and FETC's shares on the Stockholm Stock Exchange had once again fallen. The questions from shareholders, creditors, and analysts were increasingly numerous and pointed.

Karlsen's thoughts on the flight from Stockholm to Kuala Lumpur had been dominated by what he considered the three critical factors facing FETC's management: *cash flow, confidence,* and *control.* FETC was expected to suffer significant losses from the current Asian currency crisis. Operating units throughout East Asia were already reeling from currency exposures, working capital financing shortfalls, and the general economic slowdown spreading out from the currency crisis which had begun in July in Thailand. These growing losses were now causing downward revisions in forecasted cash flows for the second half of 1997 and would most certainly continue into 1998. This in turn caused declining confidence in management as FETC was once again in the headlines of the business press in Sweden, FETC's home country. With losses came increasing criticism of management and increasing influence of the company's creditors. Ultimately, control of the company could be at stake if management did not take action.

The Company

The Far East Trading Company A/B was incorporated in Stockholm, Sweden, on March 27, 1897, by H.N. Johansson. Johansson, an experienced sea captain, had established a trading house in Bangkok, Thailand, in 1884 and wished to establish a trading company in Sweden which could serve as a financial base for continuous trade between the Far East and Europe. In the early years, the Far East Company made markets in rice, oilseed, spice, and timber. As the company expanded with the turn of the century, FETC opened trade routes to Africa, the Indies, North America, and Australia, eventually making shipping itself a major part of its business.

What differentiated the Far East Trading Company in 1897 was still significant in 1997. FETC was a global trading company which had no real domestic business base but, instead, served to provide a cultural and corporate center for the conduct of global trade. For the next century, no matter what market or business it was involved in, the continuity of Swedish management was the only constant. Throughout the Twentieth Century, the company prospered and faltered, like so many others, but persevered and maintained its corporate charter in Stockholm. Due to the immense distances in time and space for the conduct of trade, the firm was a loosely knit collection of independent country units from its very beginnings. The individual business lines conducted by FETC were under the direct and active management of the country manager assigned from the Swedish home office, and the decentralized organizational structure produced what many came to call *country kingdoms*. The individual country-based operating units were inherently entrepreneurial, entering into any area of trading or distribution which offered profit potential. The result was an amazingly diverse set of global businesses.

The recent history of FETC had been dominated by a major reorganization and management change in 1992. After sustaining growing losses throughout its European and Asian country businesses, a new management group took control in 1992 headed by the new Managing Director, Jesper Erickson, and the new CFO, Jan Karl Karlsen. Although FETC was a Swedish corporation, Erickson focused on the fact that nearly 75% of its earnings were in the Far East. Erickson immediately moved to assert central control over the loosely linked worldwide operations, sell off much of the Group's remaining European business units, and reorganize the FETC Group along two different lines, *FETC Core Businesses* and *FETC Businesses* (Exhibit 1). Erickson's long-term strategy was to concentrate FETC's activities in fewer business areas in order to pursue growth prospects in line with FETC's expertise.

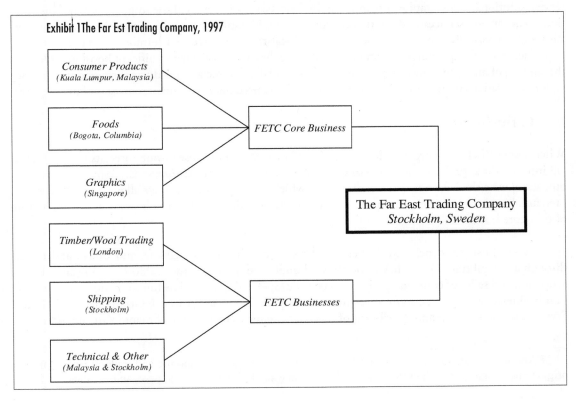

Exhibit 1 The Far Est Trading Company, 1997

FETC Core Businesses

FETC's strength—and future prospects in the eyes of management—was in three core areas of identified competence: *Consumer Products*, *Foods*, and *Graphics*. These three areas were expected to make up over 70% of FETC's turnover in the coming decade. The company's plan was to organize activities around these business areas across countries, rather than by country as under the historical organizational structure. Each of the core businesses would be managed independently from an identified business center of its activities: *Consumer Products*—Kuala Lumpur, Malaysia; *Graphics*—Singapore; *Foods*—Bogota, Colombia.

The *Consumer Products* segment was made up of two major sub-segments: marketing services and nutritional products. The Marketing Services Group provided marketing, sales, distribution, and merchandising services to consumer product firms without significant in-country operations in the ASEAN[1] countries and Greater China. Name-brand clients utilizing the marketing services segment included Philip Morris, Lego, and Sara Lee. The *Nutritions Group* was largely composed of a newly operational state-of-the-art dairy plant in Shanghai, China. The Shanghai plant produced dry and liquid infant and baby nutritional products, but was not yet operating at full capacity.

The second core business, the *Foods* segment, was the newest of the three core business segments. Unique for FETC, Foods was purely South American in composition, and headquartered in Bogotá, Columbia. Serving the Andean Region, the Foods Group focused on meats and meat products, including manufacture of concentrated animal feed, pig farming, slaughterhouses, meat-processing plants, and their associated distribution networks. It had been quite successful to date. Foods made up only 9% of FETC Core Business sales in 1996, but created over 30% of operating profits.

The *Graphics* business segment, the third of the FETC core businesses, provided material and service solutions to the graphic arts industry in East Asia. This included the importation and distribution of equipment, services, and solution consumables to this rapidly growing sector of the Asian economy. Although historically the unit had served as the local representative of a number of major European manufacturers of graphic arts equipment, the product line had received a significant boost in 1996 with the signing of an agreement to represent Eastman Kodak's graphic arts products throughout its service region. Operations in the region had been recently reorganized under one management roof in Singapore.

FETC Businesses

When Jesper Erickson reorganized much of FETC in 1992, all of those Group interests which did not fall into the three *FETC Core Businesses* were collected under *FETC Businesses*. Erickson believed these businesses were the leftovers of the earlier era in which country managers were allowed to follow entrepreneurial instincts, not the proven competency of the organization. The result was a steady liquidation of non-core businesses.

FETC Businesses included timber (procured in Southeast Asia, Ghana, and Brazil, and traded through a central trading unit in London); wool under the trading name Stanford & Wilson (a buyer, processor, and seller of combed-wool products in Europe); shipping and technical services. All shipping unit businesses were scheduled for divestment and liquidation. The Chemicals Group, part of Technical Services, was a marketer and distributor of specialty chemicals to a variety of manufacturing industries.

---

[1] ASEAN, the Association of Southeast Asian Nations, is a regional economic and trade organization with original membership including Brunei, Indonesia, Malaysia, Philippines, Singapore, and Thailand.

In addition to distributing third-party products, Chemicals produced and distributed via a number of joint ventures in Thailand. The long-standing success of Chemicals in Thailand had built a base for expansion of the segment to a number of other Asian country markets, with entries into Vietnam, Myanmar, and most recently, Indonesia.

Other activities included in FETC Businesses' results included plantations in Malaysia which were recently liquidated, and unallocated expenses related to the Corporate Center in Stockholm and other regional centers in Asia.

Exhibit 2 FETC Turnover & Operating Profit Margins, 1995-1996 (millions of Swedish krona)							
	1996	1996	1995	1995			
FETC Core Businesses	**Sales**	**%**	**Profits**	**%**	**Sales**	**%**	**Profits**	**%**
Consumer Products	6,809	60%	7	3%	5,113	45%	65	20%
Marketing Services	6,085		(26)		4,504		24	
Nutrition	724		33		609		41	
Logistics	—				—			
Foods	966	9%	84	30%	1,217	11%	116	35%
Graphics	3,574	31%	187	67%	3,085	27%	151	45%
Total Core	11,349	100%	278	100%	9,415	100%	332	100%
FETC Businesses								
Timber	979	19%	26	8%	900	18%	16	5%
Wool	803	16%	19	6%	816	17%	(27)	-9%
Shipping	737	14%	(8)	-3%	778	16%	12	4%
Technical	825	16%	71	23%	702	14%	85	28%
Other activities	1,761	34%	202	65%	1,744	35%	217	72%
Total Businesses	5,105	100%	310	100%	4,940	100%	303	100%
Core Businesses	11,349	69%	278	47%	9,415	66%	332	52%
Businesses	5,105	31%	310	53%	4,940	34%	303	48%
Total FETC Group	16,454	100%	588	100%	14,355	100%	635	100%

1997 Half-Year Results

With FETC's half-year report (for the January-June period) published in August (Exhibit 3), problems were apparent. Although sales were up by 12% in Swedish krona terms, operating income was down by a full 26%. Sales were up in all three Core Businesses and four of the seven FETC Businesses, but the operating results of Consumer Products (-144%), Foods (-77%), Wool (-82%), and Other Activities (-30%) were down. The causes, as best as Jan Karlsen could determine, combined both operating and financing cost problems.

Operations. The report noted specifically that cost control and utilization issues in Asian market segments were largely to blame. The core business units in Thailand had experienced significant inventory pilferage and accounting fraud (postponed orders had continued to be booked as current sales) since the first of the year. Unit management had been quickly replaced, but the declining Thai market continued to put pressure on management performance. Days sales outstanding on receivables were stretching out, and many suppliers had simultaneously begun drawing in their credit terms. Both sales and costs had grown.

Exhibit 3FETC Net Sales and Operating Results, Half-Year Report, 1997
(millions of Swedish krona)

	Net Sales			Operating Result		
	Actual	Actual	Chg	Actual	Actual	Chg
Segment	**1997**	**1996**	**in %**	**1997**	**1996**	**in %**
Graphics	1,747	1,618	8%	78	67	16%
Consumer Products	3,949	3,169	25%	-15	34	-144%
Foods	554	464	19%	9	39	-77%
Total Core Business	6,250	5,251	19%	72	140	-49%
Chemicals	342	323	6%	52	54	-4%
Technical Business	509	349	46%	34	34	0%
Timber	592	471	26%	20	9	122%
Wool	277	428	-35%	3	17	-82%
Shipping	121	402	-70%	17	-19	189%
Foods/Germany	325	—	—%	-6	—	—%
Other Activities	270	529	-49%	28	40	-30%
Total FETC Businesses	2,436	2,502	3%	148	135	10%
Total FETC	8,686	7,753	12%	220	275	-20%
Administrative Expenses*	—	—	—	-85	-93	-9%
Total	8,686	7,753	12%	135	182	-26%

*Administrative expenses are predominantly composed of unallocated overheads of corporate centers.

The Chinese powdered milk plant, a major capital project, was still operating at less than 70% capacity, adding to the continuing operating burden on the Chinese subsidiary. This state-of-the-art factory, recently brought online in Shanghai for the production of infant nutritional products, was continuing to suffer high per-unit costs. A recent stockholder briefing had summarized management's outlook on the Chinese investment:

> *It is our strong belief that these commitments to and investments in China, despite the difficulties and risks in the near term, will provide attractive future profits and worthwhile long term returns. It must be underlined, however, that China will require prolonged nurturing, and that substantial expenses and investments will be required in 1997 and 1998.*

Financing. Financing expenses were significantly higher than in the previous year. The individual subsidiaries were largely responsible for their own funding. The parent company had provided minimal equity investment in the beginning, and additional funding needs were supplied over time through retained earnings and debt. The majority of the debt acquired by individual units was from outside the organization, typically from local and regional banks, not from the parent company. As opposed to many multinational firms which had only recently entered Asia, FETC's long history in the region had allowed it to build bank relations over time. The reliance on debt had risen throughout the 1990s as profits had declined.

In 1995 and 1996 many of the Asian units had moved to reduce financing expenses by financing both long-term debt and short-term working capital financing needs offshore in U.S. dollars. The stable currencies of the region allowed the firm to borrow dollars offshore at an average interest rate of 9% in 1996, as opposed to 14% for Malaysian ringgit or 18% for Thai baht. The parent company had also encouraged the individual units to decrease capital needs through improved inventory turns and reduced cycle times, as well as capital costs through more aggressive financial management. But in June 1997 the dollar had strengthened, leading to rising debt service expenses and foreign exchange losses.

FETC had concluded its half-year report to stockholders in August with a profit warning that "... it is expected that 1997 full-year operating profits will be lower than in 1996." FETC's share price suffered another setback, and Jan Karlsen was spending more and more of his time meeting with both institutional investors and the major creditors of the company.

The Asian Currency Crisis

The roots of the Asian currency crisis extended from a fundamental change in the economics of the region, the transition of many Asian nations from net exporters to net importers. Starting as early as 1990 in Thailand, the rapidly expanding economies of the Far East began importing more than they exported, requiring major net capital inflows to support their currencies. As long as the capital continued to flow in—capital for manufacturing plants, dam projects, infrastructure development, and even real estate speculation—the pegged exchange rates of the region could be maintained. When the investment capital inflows stopped, however, crisis was inevitable.

The most visible roots of the crisis were in the excesses in capital flows into Thailand in 1996 and early 1997. With rapid economic growth and rising profits forming the backdrop, Thai firms, banks, and finance companies found they had ready access to capital on the international markets, finding U.S. dollar debt cheap offshore. Thai banks continued to raise capital internationally, extending credits to a variety of domestic investments and enterprises beyond that which the Thai economy could support. As capital flows into the Thai market hit record rates, financial flows poured into investments of all kinds, including manufacturing, real estate, and even equity market margin-lending. As the investment *bubble* expanded, some participants raised questions about the economy's ability to repay the rising debt. The baht came under sudden and severe pressure.

As the Thai government and central bank intervened in the foreign exchange markets directly (using up precious hard currency reserves) and indirectly (by raising interest rates to attempt to stop the continual outflow), the Thai investment markets ground to a halt. This caused massive currency losses and bank failures. On July 2, 1997, the Thai central bank, which had been expending massive amounts of its limited foreign exchange reserves to defend the baht's value, finally allowed the baht to float (or sink in this case). The baht fell 17% against the U.S. dollar and over 12% against the Japanese yen in a matter of hours. By November, the baht had fallen from Baht25/US$ to Baht40/US$, a fall of about 38%. In the aftermath, the international speculator and philanthropist George Soros was the object of much criticism, primarily by the Prime Minister of Malaysia, Dr Mahathir Mohamad, for being the cause of the crisis. Soros, however, was likely only the messenger.

Within days, in Asia's own version of the *tequila effect*, a number of neighboring Asian nations, some with and some without similar characteristics to Thailand, came under speculative attack by currency traders and capital markets.[2] The Philippine peso, the Malaysian ringgit, and the Indonesian rupiah all fell within months (see Exhibit 4). In late October, Taiwan caught the markets off-balance with a surprise competitive devaluation of 15%. The Taiwanese devaluation only seemed to renew the momentum of the crisis. Although the Hong Kong dollar survived (at great expense to the central bank's foreign exchange reserves), the Korean won was not so lucky. In November the historically stable Korean

---

[2] The *tequila effect* is the term used to describe how the Mexican peso crisis of December 1994 quickly spread to other Latin American currency and equity markets, a form of financial panic termed *contagion*.

won also fell victim, falling from Won900/US$ to more than Won1100/US$. By the end of November the Korean government was in the process of negotiating a US$50 billion bailout of its financial sector with the International Monetary Fund (IMF). The only currency which had not fallen besides the Hong Kong dollar was the Chinese renminbi (Rmb), which was not freely convertible. Although the renminbi had not been devalued, there was rising speculation that the Chinese government would devalue soon for competitiven reasons.

Exhibit 4 The Economies and Currencies of Asia, July-November 1997

	1996 Current Acct (bil US$)	Liabilities to Foreign Banks (bil US$)	Exchange Rate July (per US$)	November (per US$)	% Change
Weaker Econmies					
Indonesia (rupiah)	-9.0	29.7	2400	3600	- 33.3 %
Korea (won)	-23.1	36.5	900	1100	- 18.2 %
Malaysia (ringgit)	-8.0	27.0	2.5	3.5	- 28.6 %
Philippines (peso)	-3.0	2.8	27	34	- 20.6 %
Thailand (baht)	-14.7	48.0	25	40	- 37.5 %
Stronger Economies					
China (renminbi)	47.2	56.0	8.4	8.4	+ 0.0 %
Hong Kong (dollar)	0.0	28.8	7.75	7.73	+ 0.0 %
Singapore (dollar)	14.3	55.3	1.43	1.60	- 10.6 %
Taiwan (dollar)	11.0	17.6	27.8	32.7	- 15.0 %

Source: International Monetary Fund, *International Financial Statistics*, October-November, 1997.

Asian Crisis Impact

The falling value of Asian currencies was reflected in a series of impacts on the FETC Group's financial results. First, business units across Asia individually suffered currency *transaction losses* associated with exposures to non-domestic currencies (most frequently, either accounts payable or debt obligations in U.S. dollars). Local management in these business units, however, argued that although their Swedish krona value was diminished, these units were in many instances continuing to make significant progress and take growing market shares in local currency terms—which was what mattered.

Secondly, the FETC Group would suffer currency *translation losses* in both earnings and asset values on a consolidated basis. These translation losses would include not only the reduced Swedish krona value of Asian currency financial results, but also the reduced equity value of the Asian businesses themselves. This was the reduced Swedish krona value of the firm's original equity investments in its Asian businesses as recorded in consolidated equity. (In anticipation of the potential fall of the Thai baht, FETC had declared dividends from Thai units in 1996 which surpassed their total income for the period.)

FETC had pursued a relatively common practice of hedging its (corporate) net equity investment in its subsidiaries (an asset) by borrowing in the currency of the subsidiary (a liability). But FETC had borrowed U.S. dollars, not Thai baht or Malaysian ringgit, in the belief that these currencies would maintain their pegs to the U.S. dollar. However, with the devaluations of the Asian currencies, FETC was now realizing substantial equity losses with no corresponding fall in the value of the dollar liabilities.

Third, the *operating exposure* of the firm, the firm's changing long-term competitiveness as a result of the currency changes, was yet to be determined. The currency crisis had already caused the World Bank and IMF to intervene in the region in the hopes of preventing a general recession as a result of failing financial institutions and general economic collapse. Regardless, it appeared East Asia was headed for an extended recession. The consumer product and graphics units were already finding themselves squeezed as a result of importing increasingly expensive dollar-denominated merchandise requiring higher retail prices than the market would support. And local competitors were gaining lost market share.

Of immediate need in the eyes of Karlsen was the firming-up of the Group's many working capital lines with banks. The banks were repeatedly denying expanded working capital lines, even for units with growing sales. The Kuala Lumpur and Singapore units had both recently begun lagging intra-firm payments, including debt service, due to capital shortfalls. Currency charges were also rising as all intra-firm payments were required to be in U.S. dollars. More and more scheduled payments were not occurring as promised.

FETC's Second Profit Warning: November 21, 1997

Jan Karlsen concluded that with the continually declining earnings in the Core Business segments, there was little choice but to go public with a second profit warning.

> *FETC's Management and Supervisory Board have evaluated the consequences of the crisis in a number of Asian financial markets, and the impact the recession in several Asian countries has on FETC's businesses and earnings. On the assumption that conditions in our main markets are unchanged for the balance of the year, FETC expects a loss after tax of about SKK 300 million in 1997 after a number of non-recurring costs and provisions ...*

It now appeared that management had no choice but to take rather drastic measures if FETC was to have hopes of returning to profitability within the near term. Erickson and Karlsen returned to a topic of constant debate between them: the potential liquidation of FETC's non-core businesses. Erickson wanted to liquidate them immediately, at any price. This would generate additional capital for the reduction of corporate debt loads and signal shareholders that management was taking positive actions in the crisis. Karlsen was more reluctant to sell off these other units quite yet, arguing that if they waited they would be able to find buyers who would pay at least 20% more. In the meantime, the businesses would continue to generate cash flows which were critically needed.

An emergency meeting between the senior management team and institutional investors had concluded with the agreed expectation that the Group would return positive results by the second half of 1998. The first profit warning of the year had left the share price at about SKK80. It was still unclear what this second profit warning would do to it.

As Jan Karl Karlsen entered the Kuala Lumpur hotel meeting room, still focusing on the three C's of *cash flow, confidence,* and *control,* he consciously changed his thoughts from Swedish to English. He knew there were two sets of questions he had to answer: (1) what FETC's corporate outlook was from the Stockholm perspective; and (2) what actions were needed immediately in the regional business units.

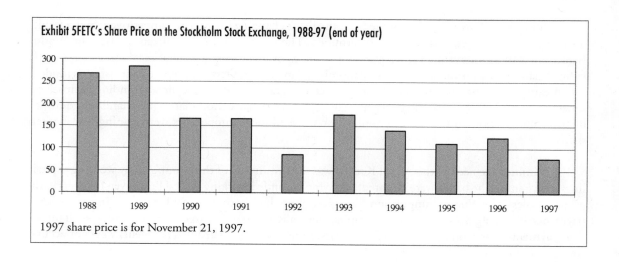

Exhibit 5 FETC's Share Price on the Stockholm Stock Exchange, 1988-97 (end of year)

1997 share price is for November 21, 1997.

CHAPTER
7

The Trouble with Banks

Questions:
Why have banks failed in record numbers and at record cost in the 1980s and 1990s?
Is it all right for banks to lend to their owners, directors, and their companies?
Why do insolvent or nearly insolvent banks sometimes take extreme risks?
Why aren't failed banks liquidated like failed industrial firms?
What are the best approaches for government policy toward weak or failed banks?

Introduction

The Epidemic of Systemic Failures

Banks are the dominant financial institution in virtually all emerging financial markets. This is the direct consequence of legal frameworks and information institutions insufficient to support strong public capital markets. Banks, of course, benefit as well from a strong legal framework, but they are better able than public markets to survive in environments where legal foundations are insufficient. They are also very well adapted to private screening and monitoring in environments of imperfect information.

A central feature of banks is that they are relational: They invest in relationships with their customers and gain access to private information through these relationships. This investment is costly, but once made can give the bank that made it an informational advantage with the customer in question. Banks have more muscle than market investors in enforcing their rights when borrowers are recalcitrant. Banks can even profit from inflation and currency instability. Thus, it is no surprise that banks dominate EFMs.

Furthermore, EFM governments tend to favor banks in a number of ways. For example, if interest rates are regulated, government often lets banks collect a subsidy by limiting legally permissible interest payments from banks to savers. In some EFMs the banks are owned directly by the government, but even where this is not true, governments often lean on banks informally to direct and manage the flows of capital within their countries. Banks are the perfect instrument for this purpose. Whereas markets are diffuse and difficult to control, banks can be influenced quietly and privately to favor certain industries, firms, projects, or regions.

Nevertheless, during the 1980s and 1990s, banks in virtually all EFMs have been privatized and the links between them and their governments have weakened. Reserve requirements have been lowered and interest rate controls loosened or abandoned. Many banking markets have been opened to foreign competition. All of this gained general support by the early 1990s among economists and others concerned with the pace of economic development.

But something is going wrong. As countries develop and financial markets liberalize and grow increasingly intertwined, as banks are privatized, and as information technology expands, banks throughout the world are often in trouble in industrialized countries as well as developing ones. The United States experienced a collapse of its thrift institutions—savings banks and savings and loan associations—in the 1980s. Even before that was resolved, U.S. banks located in the southwestern states and in New England began to fail in large numbers; almost all banks and bank holding companies of significant size in Texas and Oklahoma failed between 1986 and 1990. The total number of U.S. (nonthrift) bank failures in this period exceeded 1,000.

During the same period, almost every large bank in Norway, Sweden, and Finland either failed or was bailed out by its government for fear of failure. The governments also intervened in several notable European banks such as Crédit Lyonnais in France and Banesto in Spain. Nonperforming loans in Japan's banks were rumored to be as much as $500 billion by 1990; though these estimates were initially denied by the government, it became apparent by 1997 that such estimates were actually low. In 1998 two Japanese banks, Long Term Credit Bank and Nippon Credit Bank, were taken over by the Japanese government. At this point the official estimate of total nonperforming loans rose to $400 billion; private estimates were as high as $1 trillion.[1] The Obuchi Plan of 1998 provided about $500 billion of public funds for resolution. That sum, however, will likely be insufficient to cover the large losses in banks, local cooperative banks, and credit unions.

In the developing world, it is difficult to identify a country that did *not* experience a banking crisis in the late 20th century. Celebrated cases include the "southern cone" collapse in Chile, Argentina, and Uruguay during the early 1980s, the Mexican collapse of 1994–1995, and the Asian financial crisis of 1997–1998. These three events had a particularly virulent quality because they affected countries that were highly admired and undergoing rapid liberalization. They involved the intersection of a banking crisis with the collapse of a pegged exchange rate regime and a rapid reversal of previous capital inflows. This now familiar and distinctively modern type of EFM crisis is studied in detail in Chapter 8.

It is important to see, however, that these well-known collapses are only a small subset of the much broader set of banking crises that seem to affect the great majority of the countries in both the industrialized and developing world. The immense global wave of bank failures has attracted a great deal of attention from the academic community, governments, and international organizations. An important starting point is simply to list all the banking crises that have happened and to agree on their magnitude. Gerald Caprio Jr. and Daniela Klingebiel, two World Bank researchers, have published the most comprehensive database of bank failures to date, and have analyzed it in detail.[2] The Appendix reproduces an updated summary of their database,

---

[1] *The Economist*, January 23, 1999.
[2] Caprio and Klingebiel (1996a and 1996b).

258   *Chapter 7   The Trouble with Banks*

showing the countries, dates, and extent of each crisis during the period 1977–1979, and where possible an estimate of the cost of resolution.

This Appendix list is long and astonishing, and it warrants careful attention. Caprio and Klingebiel have divided bank crises into two categories: systemic and lesser cases. A *systemic* case is one in which *most or all bank capital is exhausted.* Note that the Appendix lists 112 systemic crises in the last 25 years of the 20th century, involving 94 countries! These are not minor events, but collapses of most or all banks within a country's banking system. Some countries suffered repeat systemic crises, and two countries (Kenya and Argentina) went through this experience three times in the 25-year time frame.

Many of these crises proved extremely expensive to resolve. Table 7.1 shows some of the higher resolution costs, those of 10 percent of GDP or more, as shown in the Appendix. Note that Caprio and Klingebiel were unable to estimate resolution costs in a substantial number of cases; had they been able to report resolution costs for all their cases, Table 7.1 might have been considerably longer.

Banking crises have occurred throughout history, as long as there have been banks, but the magnitude of losses recently has been a departure from the past. The United States suffered one of the most unstable banking systems of the 19th and early 20th centuries, and experienced 11 severe banking panics between 1800 and the beginning of World War I. In that era, when the losses of failed banks were borne by depositors rather than governments, the fraction of the banking system that failed during crises and the related losses were rather small. For example, the worst banking crisis of the so-called

TABLE 7.1   Resolution Cost of Selected Bank Crises

Country	Years	Cost as Percent of GDP
Argentina	1980–1982	55%
Benin	1988–1990	17
Bulgaria	1990s	13
Chile	1981–1983	41
China	1990s	47
Côte d'Ivoire	1988–1991	25
Czech Republic	1991–1994	12
Finland	1991–1994	11
Hungary	1991–1995	10
Indonesia	1997–1999	50
Israel	1977–1983	30
Japan	1990s	12
Korea	1997–1999	20
Macedonia	1993–1994	32
Malaysia	1997–1999	20
Mauritania	1984–1993	15
Mexico	1995	15
Philippines	1981–1987	19
Senegal	1988–1991	17
Spain	1977–1985	17
Taiwan	1997	11
Tanzania	1987	10
Thailand	1997–1999	42
Uruguay	1981–1984	24
Venezuela	1994–1995	18

Source: Appendix, page 279–87.

national banking era (1863–1913) occurred in 1893. The negative net worth of the banks that failed during that crisis was less than 0.10 percent of GDP.[3] The banking crises of the Great Depression of the 1930s reflected unprecedented strains on U.S. banks, resulting from deflationary monetary policy and the collapsing fortunes of bank borrowers. Yet during the Great Depression, when roughly a quarter of America's banks closed, the negative net worth of failed banks was only about 3 percent of GDP.[4]

Other countries historically had similar, or even better, records of infrequent banking system collapses and low banking system losses. Many emerging market countries of the pre–World War I era never experienced a banking crisis in which depositors or taxpayers suffered significant losses from failed banks. This was a period when most emerging market countries rigidly adhered to the gold standard, established competitive banking systems, and relied on large international flows of capital to finance their growth—capital flows that reached much higher levels relative to GDP than those of today. So in many respects the pre–World War I period was a precursor of the post-1980 period of EFM liberalization. Yet during that era, Canada, Germany, Japan, Mexico, Russia, and Sweden all avoided significant banking crises. Only Argentina (in 1890), Australia (in 1893), Brazil (in 1892 and 1901), Italy (in 1893), and Norway (in 1901) experienced banking crises in which the negative net worth of failed banks reached or exceeded 1 percent of GDP, and none of these six banking crises resulted in costs in excess of 10 percent of GDP.[5]

Why Are Losses So Large?

The magnitudes of banking crises in the 1980s and 1990s, in terms of number of countries, percentage of banks involved, and cost of resolution, were strikingly greater: The world had not seen anything like the epidemic of bank losses of the late 20th century. Furthermore, this was a period of substantial prosperity—nothing like the Great Depression of the 1930s was occurring, nor the economic volatility of the pre–World War I period, when shifts in the terms of trade often produced deep recessions in the real economy of many countries. What in the world was going on? Had there been a global outbreak of stupidity among bankers and bank regulators? How could it be stopped? This had become the most pressing question in the entire study of emerging financial markets by the turn of the century.

Economists have focused their attention primarily on the highly visible financial crises that are associated with massive external capital flows and collapses of currency value. The interaction of these elements is a particularly dangerous and complex phenomenon, associated with a general collapse of the real economy, and is studied in detail in Chapter 8. Such crises invite explanations in terms of international illiquidity and fixed, overvalued exchange rates, and we shall look at these interacting elements particularly in connection with the Mexican collapse of 1994–1995 and the East Asian crisis of 1997–1998.

For the moment, we simply note that banking crises before the 1980s have usually occurred independently of currency crises. Furthermore the pre–World War I period, as noted, was one in which exchange rates were fixed and in which very large capital flows took place into and out of developing countries; yet in that era we did not witness the powerful interaction of these elements with banking crises that we observe in the late 20th cen-

---

[3]Calomiris (2000).
[4]Calomiris (1998).
[5]Calomiris (2000).

tury. The magnitude and frequency of modern currency collapses is also impressive relative to past experience. Indeed, one study found that in recent years virtually no EFM fixed exchange rate survives for more than a few years without collapsing.[6] Yet not all currency collapses are associated with systemic banking failures and collapse of the real economy.

So we find it useful to study banking crises separately, and return to the interaction with currency collapse in the next chapter. How can it happen that in so many countries the capital of entire banking systems has been wiped out? Where did the capital go? When banks repeatedly make loans that are not repaid, one must conclude that their borrowers are destroying value. The existence of large bank loan losses, often preceding a collapse of the banking system by months or years, is *prima facie* evidence that poor lending decisions were made. If the job of financial markets is to allocate funds to their most profitable uses, then EFM banks taken as a whole have failed to perform acceptably. They have repeatedly directed resources to low-value uses that have not even been able to pay interest, let alone repay principal.

Of course, this merely refocuses the question. Why have banks been such poor fund allocators? Is it that they are unskilled and would do better with more training and experience? Or are there structural problems in EFM banking that have led repeatedly to these outcomes? If something is deeply wrong, then the problems, costs, and crises will continue until the underlying issues are addressed.

We suggest three factors that can explain bad banking decisions. Taken together they may account for much of the unprecedented size and scope of losses that we now observe in banks: connected lending, moral hazard, and overcapacity.

Connected Lending

Connected lending occurs when a bank directs loans to parties who are somehow connected with the bank: its owners, its board of directors, their families and friends, and companies with which the bank has special ties, either because the bank owns equity in them or because it maintains some important governance relationship with the recipient. The opposite of connected lending is arm's-length lending.

At first glance, connected lending seems entirely normal, harmless, and inherent to banking. After all, banking is supposed to be about relationships and private information. This seems to lead quite naturally to firms with which the owners and boards of banks have personal connections.

But connected lending is a complex issue, which we might better understand through an extreme example. Suppose a bank has assets of 1,000, deposit liabilities of 900, and equity of 100. The owner of the equity now takes out 600 of loans, steals the proceeds, and flees to some tropical island. The bank fails, its equity is lost, and the government closes it down. The owner nevertheless has a net gain of $600 - 100 = 500$, not a bad return on an investment of 100. In short, an unscrupulous bank owner can profitably loot his or her own bank. This is by no means unrealistic. Willie Sutton said he robbed banks because "that's where the money is," and there are modern equivalents. If this sounds fanciful, consider the story of BCCI.

The Bank of Credit and Commerce International (BCCI) was formed in 1972 by Agha Hasan Abedi, a Pakistani banker with a taste for rich and powerful friends. BCCI expanded rapidly throughout the Muslim world, with deposits from rich and poor alike. It practiced a special form of Islamic banking that in many cases replaced inter-

---

[6]Obstfeld and Rogoff (1995).

est income with lavish gifts and personal favors.[7] Loans were made to Abedi's friends without interest, without collateral, and in some cases without documentation. BCCI was closed in July 1991 after a meeting of regulators from several countries convened by the Bank of England. Its ultimate losses totaled between $12 and $14 billion, which were paid for primarily by depositors who did not benefit from deposit insurance, and who received 30 to 40 percent of their deposits in partial settlement.[8] This was a spectacular case of connected lending at a level that amounted to looting.

One recent study constructed a formal economic model of looting. Its key ingredient is a creditor that behaves inefficiently; that is, that supplies financing or guarantees it without monitoring adequately or protecting itself against self-dealing by the owners in the way that private lenders do through their contracts and their behavior. The creditor (or guarantor of the bank) is most often the government, but could also be a particularly naïve and uninformed set of depositors, like those of BCCI. When owners discover they can extract value through self-dealing, they sometimes do so to the maximum extent, driving the net worth deeply negative. The authors show how their theory might explain some cases during the thrift debacle in the United States and the Chilean collapse of 1982.[9]

Suppose bank owners use the bank's lending capacity almost exclusively to assist themselves and their associates to buy industrial companies. This would be particularly likely during a period of privatization in which financial liberalization preceded privatization of industrial enterprises. This is just what happened in Chile during 1977–1980 and in Russia during 1991–1994: In both cases depositors were trusting and no regulator existed to monitor bank behavior.

Banks that are used in this way become the centers of industrial empires. They enable entrepreneurs to leverage their own resources and acquire many more firms than they would otherwise be able to obtain. In some sense these are not true banks at all, for they do relatively little arm's-length lending. Furthermore, the criteria on which they lend are not likely to match the arm's-length criteria of profitability and economic value. In many developing economies plagued by connected lending, banks do not diversify their portfolios to reduce their risk-adjusted profits.[10] Instead of being purely for-profit enterprises, banks become instruments for channeling subsidized credit and control to favored entrepreneurs; their willingness to lend becomes a tool in the exercise of power.

Banks of this description usually fail, as happened in Chile in 1982 and in Russia in 1998. This fits the description of looting if the owners had no intention of continuing the banks in business, but were simply taking a short-term gain. Perhaps a less harsh description would say that the owners did not plan on failure, but neither would they be greatly harmed if failure occurred. Their goal was not the well-being of a bank but the aggrandizement of an industrial empire, which they acquired through the bank and would continue to own even if the bank failed.

A more respectable version of connected lending is found in Japan and Korea, where many of the largest enterprises are organized into large industrial groups, *keiretsu* in Japan and *chaebols* in Korea. The *keiretsu* have been studied extensively, and for a number of years were thought to represent an interesting model of governance

---

[7]Islamic law forbids charging interest, which is viewed as usury. Profit sharing is the typical form of compensation received for lending.

[8]Numerous books have been written about BCCI's failure. See, for example, Truell and Gurwin (1992).

[9]Akerlof and Romer (1993). See also Calomiris and Kahn (1991).

[10]Caprio and Wilson (1997) show that EFM banking systems often forgo important opportunities for diversification.

Banco Latino and the Venezuelan Banking Collapse

Venezuela's banking collapse of 1992–1994 gets less public attention than the events in Mexico and Argentina that soon followed. It had little to do with international capital flows or currency markets. But it did have a great deal to do with "crony capitalism." It resulted in estimated government losses of nearly $11 billion, approximately 13.5 percent of GDP. This figure is particularly striking in comparison with total Venezuelan bank deposits of $11.2 billion.

Venezuelan President Carlos Andrés Perez maintained an inner circle of the business elite widely referred to as the "twelve apostles," all of whom became very wealthy during his administration. Policies were enacted and enforced by the same few who stood to benefit most from them. These businessmen and their families controlled industrial empires with family-owned banks at their center.

The most influential of these banks was Banco Latino. In 1989 Perez appointed Banco Latino's president and major shareholder, Pedro Tinoco, as head of the bank regulatory commission under the central bank. Even while serving at the central bank, Tinoco remained very involved with Banco Latino. Four other "apostles" were represented on Banco Latino's board of directors, and Perez's brother was also a board member. At the same time FOGADE, the deposit insurance fund, decided to hold more than half of its assets on deposit at Banco Latino and a closely related bank, thereby putting the fund at the same risk as the deposits they were insuring.

Also in 1989, President Perez issued a presidential decree authorizing "debt reconversion." Designed to subsidize Venezuelan companies during a period of economic stringency, this decree enabled firms to buy Venezuelan public debt at low global prices and resell it to the government at full face value. Approximately half of all such transactions were passed through Banco Latino, and companies controlled by the "apostles" were the principal beneficiaries.

Banco Latino operated a "money desk" to lend money under favorable terms to companies controlled by the bank's directors and their friends. In some cases these companies were shells that simply siphoned cash to the personal offshore accounts of the directors. The bank also gave complimentary jet aircraft to many of the directors. These aircraft were either purchased by the bank or leased at inflated rates from companies controlled by directors. The bank also purchased real estate at up to three times market prices from companies controlled by its directors. By 1993, approximately 70 percent of Banco Latino's loans were to shareholders, directors, and other insiders. Nonperforming loans were officially stated at 7.2 percent.

Bank regulation was lax and ineffective. Neither the central bank nor the bank superintendency had any political autonomy or adequate regulatory staff. Yet the pattern of abuse was so obvious that the bank was forced to pay a premium in deposit markets. Toward the end of 1993 Banco Latino offered interest rates up to 105 percent, about twice the market rate, to keep depositors from withdrawing funds. A deposit insurance scheme was in effect, but in principle it covered only Bs 250,000 (about $1,000) per person. In the event, government insurance implicitly covered all bank liabilities, but the risk premium on bank debt reflected the fact that *ex ante* there was some risk that the government would be unwilling or unable to bail out *de jure* uninsured claimants.

Pedro Tinoco died in March 1993 and Perez was impeached on corruption charges in May. Rafael Caldera's election and inauguration as president in December provoked a run on the bank. The bank was closed in January 1994. Soon after, the government faced the additional bailout of nine of Banco Latino's affiliates. By the end of 1994 sixteen banks, representing nearly two-thirds of Venezuela's bank assets, had been taken over by the government.

Source: Numerous accounts from newspapers and magazines, including *The Wall Street Journal, The Washington Post, Financial Times, The Economist, Global Finance,* and *Euromoney.*

that appeared to have important advantages over the Western model of shareholder governance.

As the extent of bank losses in Japan have become known, however, fewer observers have been willing to defend this system as an attractive form of corporate control. While the Japanese banks have been reasonably professional and open to non-family business, they have also suffered from massive *nonperforming loans*, suggesting capital allocation decisions that were less than optimal. We may learn more in the future about why so many poor decisions were made, but some at least may be related to the political nature of the banks' role at the center of the *keiretsu*.

How can connected lending be controlled? It is difficult to think how a rule can be written to prevent the abuses of connected lending without somehow banning close banking relationships. Probably the best answer is disclosure and monitoring. Banks should be required to declare and list in detail all loans to parties connected with the bank. Government regulators should examine these declarations and review a selection of them to see if they conform to good lending practice. Finally, there needs to be a limit on the total percentage of assets that any bank can dedicate to each set of enterprises, to ensure diversification of risk.

Effective regulations limiting connected lending can be tricky to enforce. As part of the Mexican bank liberalization of the early 1990s, Mexican law forbade industrial firms from owning banks. But the concentration of wealth is so great in Mexico that a few families, who owned the large industrial conglomerates (*grupos*), were also able to acquire control of the banks and use them as tools for their own financing needs and as instruments of political patronage. The experience of Mexico, Chile, and Venezuela with connected lending led Argentina to develop strict rules in the mid-1990s to limit cross-holdings of ownership interests by individuals or firms in banks and their client firms. Enforcing these rules requires a detailed monitoring of the composition of stockholders of firms throughout the economy.

Moral Hazard

Definition of Moral Hazard

In a normal risk decision, the agent making the decision bears the full weight of its consequences: If the decision is a good one, the agent benefits proportionately, but if the decision is a bad one, the agent pays an equivalent price. Most bank lending decisions are normal in this sense: If the loan pays off, the bank's equity gains value and if it defaults the equity loses value. Similarly, the bank officer making the loan in a well-run bank will gain in reputation and compensation if his or her portfolio is sound, but will suffer personal penalties including dismissal if his or her portfolio is filled with losses. The owners' equity and the officer's personal risk aversion protect the bank from excessive risk taking.

Moral hazard is a problem of skewed incentives. It occurs when a risk decision is asymmetric: The agent making the decision stands to benefit if the decision is a good one, but for one reason or another does not pay a commensurate price if the decision is bad. It is a case of "heads I win, tails someone else loses." For example, when banks lack net worth, they have little to lose from bad outcomes (the bank is already insolvent) but much to gain from good outcomes (the possibility of financial resurrection). Agents faced with this kind of incentive structure will rationally want to massively increase the amount of risk taken. This can lead to exceptionally large losses. This simple concept can help to explain the magnitude of many banking losses observed around the world.

Moral hazard can also arise from conflicts of goals and incentives between bank stockholders and their employees as the result of faulty compensation systems. For this reason, traditionally, banks have not paid large cash bonuses to their loan officers. Bank managers have long understood that this could distort the loan officers' incentives and lead to large volumes of apparently profitable loans whose poor quality would only be clear after the passage of time. Among traders, however, the tradition of cash bonuses is strong, because the profitability of most trading positions is marked to market daily, and losing positions are quickly closed out. One need not wait several years to discover whether a trader made good decisions, so traders may be safely compensated in cash. However, traders understand how to game the system.[11] Moral hazard can pose a deadly risk for trading banks. (See the box on the fall of Barings.)

In a well-run bank in a healthy economy, moral hazard is not usually a problem. Bank owners and managers have a good deal to lose—their equity stake in the bank and their jobs, respectively—if the bank should fail, and so they will not want to take unreasonable risks. But the moral hazard problem becomes particularly pronounced when a bank's net worth is low or negative. Consider what happens when the bank's capital erodes and falls below regulatory benchmarks. If the regulators are alert, they should pressure the bank to increase its capital at once or shrink its assets. But regulators often do not perform this function appropriately.

For example, the entire thrift industry (savings banks and savings and loan associations) in the United States lived for many decades on taking short-term deposits and investing them in long-term, fixed-rate home mortgages. Because the value of fixed-rate mortgages declines when interest rates rise, the primary risk of this business was that some day interest rates would rise substantially; if that happened, the thrifts would face income losses if they carried the mortgages (because they would have to pay more interest on deposits than the mortgages earned) and record even larger capital losses if they tried to sell the mortgages at their reduced prices.

These events finally occurred in the period from 1979 to 1982, and the thrift industry suffered serious immediate losses. While some thrifts were in better shape than others, the losses were highly correlated across all thrifts—just the kind of event risk that could bankrupt the deposit insurance fund. The thrift regulators, with the aggressive encouragement of the U.S. Congress, pampered the industry rather than force it to deal with its weakened condition.

In 1982 Congress broadened the business definition of thrifts beyond home mortgages, so that they could move their business definition toward something more like a commercial bank. While in principle this was a good idea, most thrifts did not have the net worth, skills, and credit culture of a healthy bank, so that trouble might have been expected. The same law sanctioned "regulatory accounting," which created the illusion of capital when generally accepted accounting principles would have found little or none. When even this facade crumbled, the regulators engaged in "forbearance," meaning that they decided not to enforce their own rules.

The result was a disquieting number of what Edward Kane has termed "zombie thrifts"—the living dead—firms that had lost all their capital but still continued in business. In a normal industry, no one would fund such companies. But banks and thrifts are different because they benefit from deposit insurance. Some zombie thrifts began to grow at a phenomenal rate, taking a wild level of risk that led to some of

---

[11]For example, when trading in thin markets a trader can execute a small transaction, as a buyer, at an inflated price and thereby record a large capital gain on a preexisting position, entitling him to a large bonus.

Moral Hazard and the Fall of Barings

Barings PLC, one of the most venerable of British merchant banks with 233 years of history, failed on February 26, 1995. Its downfall was due to the activities of a single trader in its Singapore office, Nicholas Leeson. His portfolio of futures and options lost $1.3 billion, which exceeded the capital of the bank. The story is a lesson in moral hazard.[12]

Leeson's job was to trade futures on the Nikkei 225 index of Japanese stocks. He was in fact not a very good trader, but he had learned to conceal his losing trades in a secret "error account" and to show only the profitable ones, so that he enjoyed an undeservedly good reputation.

The Nikkei index had fallen from about 40,000 to 19,000 in the course of three years. But by 1994 the index seemed to have stabilized, and Leeson's bottom line in that year was less than he would have hoped. So he decided to sell options on the index. In particular, he sold 35,000 each of both puts and calls, a position known as a short straddle. This is essentially a bet against volatility; he showed immediate income because the options were sold for a significant premium, and he would only give that profit back if the index went quite far either above or below 19,000. Note how easy it is to show a short-term profit in a financial institution: You have only to take on risk.

All went well until the Kobe earthquake struck on January 17, 1995, when the Nikkei fell to below 18,000, then recovered to nearly 19,000 again, and then began a six-week slide down to about 17,000. At this level, Leeson's straddle would show a loss of about $150 million. A loss this large could not be concealed. Leeson knew he would lose his job and his reputation, the maximum sanction the bank had against him.

With his back to the wall and nothing left to lose personally, Leeson gambled on a comeback. He began to buy the Nikkei futures in unprecedented quantities, trying single-handedly to drive the price back up. He also sold futures on the Japanese government's 10-year bond, possibly in the mistaken belief that the government would have to borrow massively to repair the earthquake damage. He accumulated an astonishing total of $7 billion face amount of futures, and still was unable to get the index back up. He wrote fraudulent orders for customers to buy the futures as well.

What is interesting from a moral hazard point of view is that the total loss expanded to $1.3 billion. If only he had folded his position instead of defending it, his losses would have been less than $150 million. In other words, the losses expanded almost tenfold in a six-week period. But this additional loss was for Barings' account, not Leeson's. Had the strategy worked, his cash bonus might have been huge. The asymmetrical incentives created a situation in which risk massively expanded, turning a bad loss into a catastrophic loss and bankrupting the firm.

Sources: Fay (1997), Hunt and Heinrich (1996), and Jorion (1997).

---

the largest losses of the thrift crisis. It has been clearly documented that this risk taking occurred *after* the institutions had become insolvent.[13] The losses reached $180 billion by the time the government finally faced the consequences in 1989. This is far more than it would have cost the government to simply shut down the failed thrifts as they lost their capital. Moral hazard had turned a serious loss into a catastrophic one.

---

[12]Jorion (1997) provides a numerical analysis of Leeson's position.
[13]Barth and Batholomew (1992).

Government Safety Nets

An extreme kind of moral hazard can occur in a setting where the government not only guarantees bank deposits but also pampers the banks' owners and managers—and even the owners and managers of the firms unable to pay their debts to the banks. Such a regulator shows no sign of ever closing the banks in question.

The problem may begin with a government that wishes to promote certain favored industries and projects. It uses its persuasive powers to encourage banks to lend and companies to borrow in order to build these industries and projects. The result is an implied assurance that the government will take care of any problems. This is not a contract or a formal guarantee, but it affects bank and borrower behavior all the same.

Companies might not make such investments on their own because they appear too risky. But the government seems to say: Do this for us, and if the investment goes well we will all prosper; if it goes badly we will work with you to resolve any problems. Firms now face asymmetrical incentives—heads I win, tails the government loses— and so take greater risks than they otherwise would, including borrowing heavily to finance risky projects, thus compounding operating risk with increased financial risk.

The banks are in a similar position, since the government urges them to make loans to the companies with much the same kind of assurances. In the case of the banks, the assurances might imply that (1) the government will not close banks that get into trouble and/or (2) the government may simply provide cash infusions to banks that get into trouble. Indeed, one of the striking problems in Japan throughout the 1990s was the incapacity of the political system to resolve the increasingly obvious problems of banks with huge nonperforming loans. The dominant Liberal Democratic Party showed an astonishing preference for simply handing out cash to all banks, regardless of condition, rather than confronting those in the most serious trouble. Only in 1998, after the onset of the financial crisis throughout East Asia and increasing pressure from the opposition parties, did the government actually take over two important banks.

Some observers believe that this kind of diffuse, implicit, economywide moral hazard stimulated excessive risk taking throughout East Asia during the 1990s and lies at the root of Asia's financial collapse.[14] At the very least, say others, the message from the government was ambiguous and some agents might have felt they had protection against bad outcomes. If so, the result would be a general sense of overconfidence and overinvestment, both of which can be observed in Asia during this era.

Whether one accepts this interpretation of the Asian events or not, moral hazard clearly does encourage excessive risk taking by banks in cases where a bank is permitted to operate despite having exhausted or nearly exhausted its capital. The phenomenon is not a mere abstraction, but seems responsible for a significant part of the bank losses observed throughout the world.

Overcapacity, Franchise Value, and Liberalization

Securities Markets and Bank Disintermediation

There is another reason why banks so often find themselves in trouble in the modern era—namely, the evolution of all countries, over time, toward more efficient and

---

[14]See Corsetti, Pesenti, and Roubini (1998), Krugman (1998), and Pomerleano (1998).

competitive financial markets, and a related decline in the profitability of traditional bank lending. The consequence is typically overcapacity and loss of bank franchise value. In simplest terms, when banks' screening and monitoring services become less necessary, banks become less profitable, and we need fewer banks. The logical consequence should be the shrinkage, failure, or voluntary closure of at least some banks, yet governments and banks alike often resist this. From this point of view, the closure of many banks can be a natural process that governments should allow to proceed, rather than fight through repeated and increasingly expensive *bailouts*. But because banks are political as well as economic institutions—that is, institutions that broker political power as well as financial transactions—bankers and politicians will resist market solutions that eliminate the "intermediation" of political influence. We will start by describing the decline of traditional banking in developed countries and then return to the problem of banks in emerging financial markets.

As securities markets grow and communications technology improves, information about companies becomes widely available at low cost. Today, for example, anyone in the world can obtain detailed financial and other information about all public companies in the United States simply by downloading their required filings at the Securities and Exchange Commission from that agency's website. It takes no more than a minute and its marginal cost is zero.

When their financial information is widely disseminated, firms rely increasingly on securities markets to handle financial intermediation because these markets do not suffer the high operating costs of banks, and hence can deliver more attractive rates to savers and borrowers alike, so long as information production (i.e., screening and monitoring of borrowers by the lender) is not necessary. Consider, for example, the dilemma for banks shown in Figure 7.1.

The agents in this diagram are all institutions. The investors want short-term (one to six months) liquid investments of high quality. Such investors include money market mutual funds and corporate treasuries. They face a choice between two alternatives: They can deposit their money in a bank or they can buy *commercial paper*, which is a short-term promissory note of a borrowing corporation. From the investors' point of view, these are very similar. The commercial paper is a short-term I.O.U. of a company, and the deposit (e.g., a certificate of deposit, or CD) is a short-term I.O.U. of a bank. Provided the company and the bank are both strong credits, the investors are relatively indifferent between them. For this reason, the interest rates on bank CDs and commercial paper are very similar.

The bank now attempts to lend the money to a borrower. The interest rate it charges will equal its cost of funds (i.e., the deposit interest rate) plus a *spread*. For a high-quality borrower, the spread might be as low as 0.25 to 0.50 percent, but it cannot be zero because the bank needs to cover the cost of maintaining its staff, buildings, and

FIGURE 7.1

Disintermediation of banks

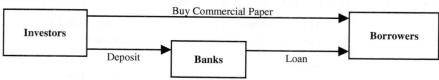

so forth. But now the borrower faces a choice: The commercial paper financing route will be cheaper if market purchasers of commercial paper have sufficient information about the borrower's high quality. In that case, by borrowing directly from the investors, the borrower saves on interest cost.

This phenomenon is called *disintermediation,* and it swept the U.S. financial system in the 1960s, 1970s, and 1980s.[15] During that period, banks lost a large portion of their highest-quality borrowers to less expensive securities markets. This included not only commercial paper, but also, in the 1980s, expanding bond markets for lower-quality credit. Banks are middlemen in the flow of funds, and as financial markets become ever more efficient, there is increasingly less room for middlemen to make money. If all investors and borrowers could find each other with little cost or effort, there would be little role for bank lending.

Of course, banks might be protected from this outcome if their cost of funds were lower than commercial paper rates. That is why some governments have continued controls on deposit interest rates, in an effort to provide a funding advantage to banks, even as markets liberalize. But in a sophisticated, modern financial system, depositors can avoid earning artificially low rates by putting their savings into a money market fund, which in turn buys commercial paper, an alternative form of disintermediation. This is precisely what happened in the United States from the late 1960s onward, forcing the United States government to abandon its own interest rate controls.

We have seen that a legitimate need for bank lending comes from information and control problems, which banks are well equipped to solve. But as financial information becomes more widely and easily available, banks tend to lose their informational monopolies. Alternatively, they can build informational monopolies only for small firms that are not publicly owned and widely followed.

This explains why, in developed economies, traditional deposit-and-loan business tends to shrink over time. In the United States, for example, banks provided 35 percent of funds to nonfinancial borrowers in 1974 and 22 percent in 1994; the banking industry's share of total financial intermediary assets fell from about 40 percent in the 1960–1980 period to less than 30 percent at the end of 1993.[16]

Strategic Response of Banks to Franchise Loss

What can a bank do in the face of declining value in its traditional business and franchise? One option is simply to shrink, though most institutions resist shrinking. Another option is to enter the securities business; if this form of financial intermediation is best for the clients, perhaps the banks can offer it as well, and build a new franchise in these services. Associated with securities is the derivatives business, which many large banks have entered in a major way.

But a third option is to replace the missing high-end business with larger quantities of low-end business—that is, the banks take more risk, pushing down into lower categories of creditworthiness where their predecessors would not have ventured in earlier times. Many U.S. banks that felt they had neither the resources nor the business culture to enter the securities and derivatives business chose this option during the 1970–1990 period.

In a purely market-driven system, banks that take more risk would face higher costs and declining availability of funds. But government protection of banks by

---

[15]Calomiris, Himmelberg, and Wachtel (1995).
[16]Edwards and Mishkin (1995).

means of deposit insurance and discount window lending (which lower banks' cost of funds) increases the banking system's ability to maintain market share and resist disintermediation. Government protection helps banks avoid the discipline of the marketplace that otherwise would have forced their shrinkage. But it does so at the cost of subsidizing increased risk taking as banks move into lower-quality credits without having to pay the penalty that this would normally entail.

That protection explains a large number of risk-seeking decisions by U.S. banks in the 1970–1990 period. For example, most banks did not lend across national borders until the late 1960s; for centuries, international lending typically was conducted by wealthy individuals or through bond markets, but was thought too risky a use for depositor funds. Then, in the late 1960s and 1970s, banks began a wave of lending to developing countries on an unprecedented scale, as shown in Chapter 1, Figure 1.3. Why? In large part, because they needed borrowers to replace those lost to disintermediation. Not wanting to shrink, banks pressed into higher-risk lending where most of them had little private information or insight. Not surprisingly, this ended in major losses during the 1980s. Such losses can properly be attributed to prior losses of franchise value in home markets.

Another example is real estate. Before the late 20th century, real estate lending was also thought a dubious activity for banks. The main exception was home mortgages, in which thrift institutions specialized. But from the 1960s onward, just as commercial paper usage was rapidly expanding, U.S. banks began to increase their commercial real estate lending. Real estate loans rose from 11 percent of total commercial bank assets in 1960 to 25 percent of assets in 1990.[17]

The first wave of this lending was through real estate investment trusts (REITs), a vehicle favored by U.S. tax law. But the bank-owned REITs collapsed in the 1970s, severely damaging a number of the largest banks. The second wave occurred in the 1980s, when commercial real estate lending by U.S. banks returned on such a scale that almost all U.S. cities were 20 to 30 percent overbuilt in commercial space by the end of the decade. This also ended in debacle during the late 1980s.

Increased risk taking might be a successful strategy if the risks are attractively priced. But U.S. banks do not seem to charge high spreads for these increasingly risky loans. Whether the borrower is a developing country, a real estate project, or a small company, U.S. banks in the 1980s and 1990s rarely charged a spread of more than 3 percent above their cost of funds.[18] These low spreads reflected overcapacity: Too many banks were competing for the risky loans. The failure of about 1,300 U.S. banks in the regional economic downturns of 1985–1989 and the general recession of 1989–1992 confirmed the high cost of the risks that banks had assumed so willingly. It was as if the market's "invisible hand" were trying to sweep away the excess capacity.[19]

The Japanese banking crisis also seems rooted to some degree in overcapacity and a decline in bank franchise value. Throughout the second half of the 20th century, Japan's Ministry of Finance (MOF) built and supported an exceptionally strong set of bank franchises. Banks were privileged, but the trade-off was strong direction from MOF on where capital should flow. Although the stock market flourished, no corporate bond market and no commercial paper market was permitted in Japan until the 1980s, and even then they were only allowed to grow slowly. By the end of the 1980s,

---

[17]Gorton and Rosen (1995), Figure 7.7.

[18]Loan Pricing Corporation database.

[19]Gorton and Rosen (1995) argued that the tolerance of low spreads and suboptimal profitability reflected managerial entrenchment, which was a consequence of regulatory limitations on bank acquisitions.

Japan's banks had become the largest in the world and provided more than 80 percent of all funding needs of Japanese firms.

But as the large Japanese firms grew more internationalized, they gained access to international capital markets. MOF's control was weakened because Japanese firms could not be restricted to Japan's borders. Over the long term, financial liberalization is hard to resist because firms will finally demand and get the efficiencies that modern financial markets can provide. As liberalization finally reached Japan, the country's oversized banking system began to develop problems.

Many of the banks' lending decisions turned out to be poorly conceived and/or poorly priced. As noted earlier, the nonperforming loans in Japanese banks reached more than $500 billion by the early 1990s, a level that threatened the survival of many large and small banks. The government did not force a cleanup, and the banks responded by taking new risks, notably in East Asia. It is an extreme example of banking overcapacity.

Effects of Financial Liberalization

In developing countries, the value of bank franchises can be adversely affected by financial liberalization. Governments control interest rates and limit entry into banking, particularly foreign entry. Rules of this sort substantially increase the profitability of banks, whether well or poorly managed. This creates franchise value, even though it is franchise based on government-protected rents rather than on the creation of economic value. When governments liberalize, they take away some of these privileges, which lowers the value of the bank franchise. This is an appropriate step, over time even a necessary step, that forces banks to create value in new ways. But during the transition period, liberalization can reduce the value of many bank franchises. When inefficient, protected banks lose franchise value, they are further tempted to take on lower value, riskier business. This adds to the systemic vulnerability of liberalizing banking systems.[20]

Furthermore, countries that liberalize rapidly without providing strong foundations for a private financial system can get into serious trouble. In Russia, for example, thousands of banks formed quickly in the early 1990s without the appropriate legal structure or control systems. In the infamous "loans-for-shares" program, the government financed its deficits by borrowing from these banks, offering shares of state-owned enterprises as security. When the loans defaulted, banks and their owners acquired empires at very low prices and became centers of connected lending. The entire system collapsed, leading to a sovereign Russian default in August 1998.

Two things seem quite clear. The first is that financial liberalization is important for the long-run health of the economy. We have seen its connection to economic growth in Chapters 2 and 3. The other is that *quasi*-liberalization—where banks' profits are privatized, but banks are protected from competition and subsidized by taxpayer bailouts of their losses—can be riskier than no liberalization. If privatization of banks creates a new set of banking institutions that act as the political and economic tools of oligarchs and their protected industrial firms, then those banks are liable to engage in excessive insider lending, take risky market positions, hold little capital, and undertake negative NPV investments. This is a recipe for disastrous banking collapses.

The task is to liberalize in a way that avoids the incentive distortions that produce banking collapses. Very few governments have gotten the pace and sequence of bank-

---

[20]Keeley (1990), and Hellman, Murdock, and Stiglitz (1998a, 1998b).

ing liberalization and regulation exactly right. And academics have devoted considerable effort to studying exactly what the optimal pace and sequence might be. This will depend in part on conditions unique to each country.[21] As bank competition increases and bank profitability declines, each bank must develop a plan for a new strategy in the changing environment. It should not be surprising that at least some banks cannot find a sensible way of doing business in the more demanding market environment and thus fail during the liberalization process.

The challenge for EFM governments is to manage the process of financial liberalization carefully and deliberately, allowing banks to come down from their protected positions and enter a more difficult but normal market world without collapsing. This typically requires some orderly bank capacity reductions, often through mergers, sometimes through failure of weaker banks. This does not happen easily, and getting it wrong undoubtedly accounts for some of the large banking losses seen at the end of the 20th century.

Government and Banks

Liquidity and Bank Runs

The three kinds of problems that plague banks around the world—connected lending, moral hazard, and excess capacity—are greatly magnified by the central problem of government protection of banks. Bank depositors and other debt holders historically were a powerful force for ensuring conservative behavior and value creation by banks. They limited insider lending, excessive risk taking, and wasteful lending of excess deposits by withdrawing their funds as soon as they sensed trouble.

Government protection insulates banks from such pressures. When the government guarantees deposits and other bank liabilities, bank depositors and other debt holders need not concern themselves with how well the bank is run. Instead, government agents must perform the monitoring. Banking risk becomes socialized and can grow very large because government discipline is much more permissive than market discipline.

Governments everywhere tend to embrace banks, protect them, regulate them, and use them as instruments of policy. Sometimes the government embrace smothers market efficiency. Part of successful financial liberalization involves changing the nature of this relationship from one in which governments treat banks as their instruments of policy to one in which governments accept banks as fully independent institutions but regulate them in ways that create appropriate incentives for good behavior.

To understand the complexity of the modern and evolving relationship between government and banks, it is useful to see why and how government involvement in banking evolved, and how that protection has become a political tool that is often abused.

The primary economic justification for government involvement in protecting banks is that banks are not only very important to the economy, but also they are uniquely vulnerable to economic disturbances because their most fundamental role is to provide *liquidity* to the real economy.[22] Firms are liquid when they have on hand or can readily obtain all the cash they need to meet their obligations and exploit their

---

[21]See McKinnon (1993) for a detailed discussion.
[22]Rajan (1996).

opportunities. Liquidity is the lubricant of business: When firms are liquid, bills are paid on time and investments move forward on schedule. When firms are illiquid, the economy slows down—firms feel short of cash, so they delay their projects, reduce credit extended to their customers, and minimize their obligations.

Firms are liquid when they have sufficient short-dated assets; that is, a net surplus of assets that will convert into cash within a short period of time. Assets that will convert into cash in less than one year are called current assets, and liabilities that must be settled in cash in less than one year are called current liabilities. An accounting measure of liquidity is working capital, the excess of current assets over current liabilities. Anyone attempting to set up a business needs ample working capital as well as fixed assets such as plant, property, and equipment. Firms can also enhance their liquidity by long-dated liabilities; that is, obligations that will not fall due in cash for many years. For liquidity reasons, most industrial firms borrow significant amounts of long-term debt.

So firms ensure sufficient liquidity by having substantial net quantities of short-dated assets and long-dated liabilities. Banks meet this need by putting themselves into the reverse position: They have long-dated assets and short-dated liabilities. A bank's long-dated assets are its loans of more than one year. Its short-dated liabilities are its deposits, almost all of which are repayable in less than one year and some of which are repayable at any time on demand. A bank's liquidity position is the mirror image of that of its customers. By accommodating its customers' needs for liquidity, a bank puts itself in constant risk of illiquidity.

In particular, a bank gets into trouble if too many customers want to withdraw their deposits at one time. This is particularly true since the bank's loan portfolio is inherently illiquid in the sense of being nonmarketable. In the prototypical case, the loans are based on private information about the borrowers, and thus cannot readily be sold to others who, because of asymmetric information, do not know the borrowers and would not trust a bank that wanted to sell loans about which it was better informed than any buyer could be.

Some depositors may learn that a particular bank has problems in its loan portfolio, or hear rumors to that effect, leading them to withdraw their deposits. Other, uninformed observers who notice this now begin to worry that the bank may not be able to meet all its obligations. So they decide to withdraw as well, and the result is a cascading demand for deposit withdrawal. This phenomenon is known as a *bank run*. Runs have occurred throughout banking history and have been extensively studied by theorists and empiricists. The ability of depositors to demand their money back is a form of monitoring system, encouraging banks to behave conservatively, thus counteracting the incentives banks might otherwise face to abscond with depositors' funds or to channel those funds into excessively risky ventures.[23]

Bank Failures in Earlier Eras

Bank runs can lead quickly to bank failures. The most frightening aspect of a bank run is the possibility that it would destroy healthy, solvent banks as well as those that, in retrospect, truly deserve to be shut down. To protect themselves against this risk, banks long ago learned to join together in associations for mutual support. A common institution was the *central bank,* which in some countries in earlier centuries was a private organization rather than a government agency. Commercial banks would leave a por-

---

[23]Calomiris and Kahn (1991).

tion of their deposits on reserve at the central bank, in a pool that could be drawn upon at a time of need. Countries without central banks formed similar pools (e.g., the New York Clearing House).[24]

A fundamental question is whether bank runs turn out to be well founded or flights of fancy—that is, were depositors aware of problems that in retrospect were real and serious threats to their bank's solvency, or did their actions arbitrarily destroy a sound and solvent bank based on whim, rumor, and emotion? One way to answer this is to see whether, once the crisis was resolved, many banks had actually failed, and if so why. In particular, how often did a solvent bank fail simply because it was subjected to a run?

Evidence from 19th-century U.S. history, when the United States was an emerging market, is particularly telling. From 1863 to 1913 (the national banking era) six major nationwide panics occurred. In all six cases, the panics were preceded by several months of unusually large declines in stock prices and unusual increases in business failures. Indeed, using dual threshold criteria—a minimum percentage decline in stock prices and a minimum percentage increase in business failures—one can predict the incidence of banking panics.[25] Table 7.2 reviews the history of national bank failures in each of these panics. It shows the number of bank failures that occurred during each crisis, and the reasons bank examiners gave for those failures.

It is clear from Table 7.2 that the number of failures was small, compared to the thousands of banks in the United States in the late 19th century, and the reasons for the failures apparently traceable to fundamentals. Another interesting fact about these panics was that they tended to occur either in the spring or the fall. The asset risk of banks increases with the loan-to-asset ratio, which tends to hit seasonal highs in the spring and autumn, and this may explain the seasonality in the pattern of banking panics. Similar studies of bank failures during the Great Depression have also traced the causes of failures to fundamental insolvency problems of banks. Market discipline over banks seems not to have been capricious.

Nevertheless, over time, the protection of banks and their insulation from market discipline became a governmental function in almost all countries. This did not eliminate banking panics, but it did change the way their costs were allocated. The total losses in historical banking panics were relatively small, rarely more than 1

TABLE 7.2   Causes of U.S. National Bank Failures during Panics

	Panic of:					
	1873	*1884*	*1890*	*1893*	*1896*	*1907*
Total number of failures	9	6	10	49	34	6
Attributed to asset depreciation alone	4	2	5	31	26	3
Attributed to fraud alone	0	2	0	7	3	2
Attributed to both asset depreciation and fraud	5	4	5	11	5	0
Asset depreciation attributed to monetary stringency	0	0	0	17	8	0
Asset depreciation only; attributed to real estate	0	1	2	0	4	0
Attributed to real estate depreciation and fraud	0	1	2	0	1	0
Attributed to run on bank	0	0	0	0	0	1

Source: Calomiris and Gorton (1991)

---

[24]Calomiris and Gorton (1991).
[25]Ibid.

percent of GDP. However, the losses fell primarily on individual depositors, which became a political problem, especially in more recent times, as the level of losses increased. Historically, bank borrowers also suffered during times of banking system stress. As banks scrambled to reassure depositors that bank loan losses would not result in losses to depositors, they cut back on lending and accumulated cash reserves (to reduce bank asset risk and enhance bank liquidity).[26] In those circumstances, borrowers found themselves in an illiquid position, facing higher interest costs.

Government Protection of Depositors

In the United States, small bankers and their depositors and dependent borrowers—all of whom were most vulnerable to banking crises and therefore stood to gain the most from government protection of banks—became vocal proponents of protection. That protection took the form of state-level bank insurance systems (some of which were founded as early as the 1820s), subsidized loans from the central bank (after the founding of the Federal Reserve System in 1914), and, later, federal deposit insurance and government injections of capital into banks in the 1930s.

The United States initiated the first national program of deposit insurance by government in 1933, primarily as an accommodation to small banks during the Great Depression. At first this was a modest program designed to protect only the smallest depositors; each depositor was insured only up to $5,000. Over time, however, the insured amount expanded in stages to $100,000, and in 1984 the United States extended *de facto* government protection to uninsured depositors, not by statute but by the actions of the Federal Deposit Insurance Corporation (FDIC) in bailing out the Continental Illinois National Bank.[27]

The same outcome has been reached along various paths in virtually all countries. Many countries had no formal depositor protection, but found themselves under political pressure to make depositors whole when crises erupted. As noted in Chapter 3, Chile tried to renounce depositor protection in the late 1970s, but was unable to resist the pressures created by multiple bank failures in 1982. Venezuela had a similar experience in the early 1990s, trying unsuccessfully to limit government losses to the low level of formal deposit insurance. Today many countries offer virtually complete governmental insurance to depositors, even if their laws do not explicitly say so.

This comprehensive *safety net* has indeed stopped bank runs from occurring, but it has done so at a significant price. Protected depositors have no incentive whatever to monitor the risk of their banks or to withdraw funds from banks that are clearly losing money. Indeed, the safety net enables banks that are certifiably insolvent to go on attracting deposits and making loans. This shifts the burden of monitoring and control from the bank debt market to the government regulatory agencies, which must act decisively to shut down insolvent banks or risk an explosion of bad loans caused by the moral hazard of low or negative capital.

---

[26]Calomiris and Wilson (1998).

[27]That bailout was justified by appeal to the "too-big-to-fail" doctrine—the view that the failure of a large bank would be too disruptive to the financial system. In response to growing criticism of that doctrine and concerns about its moral hazard consequences, the ability of the FDIC to bail out uninsured depositors was restricted in 1991.

This sea change alters the very nature of what constitutes a banking crisis. Bank runs are replaced by

> a more silent form of financial distress . . . when a significant portion of the system is insolvent but remains open, perhaps the most pernicious type of insolvency . . . Financial distress can persist for years, overlooked by weak supervisory and regulatory systems and obscured by bankers' ability to make bad loans look good by granting new loans.[28]

The critical variable at this point becomes the behavior of the bank regulators. Their optimal behavior is careful monitoring and decisive action to close insolvent banks. Such action is necessary for two reasons. First, insolvent banks have clearly destroyed value for the economy and are likely to go on destroying value unless they are stopped. Second, as we have seen, banks whose capital is zero or negative undergo a powerful change of incentives as equity and management are tempted to take massive new risks to resurrect their fortunes.

Bank Capital and Loan Losses

Standards for appropriate behavior by government regulators are widely recognized as crucial. In the 1980s an international agreement establishing minimal standards for the prudential regulation of international banks was adopted, and the Basel Committee (which set those guidelines) continues to offer its opinions on appropriate supervisory and regulatory standards.[29] One of its key tenets is that banking supervisors must set prudent and appropriate minimum capital adequacy requirements for all banks. Bank capital is the protective cushion, the "deductible" in deposit insurance. Any asset losses should first run down the capital and only second endanger the ability to repay deposits.

Optimal regulatory behavior also means that banks with low but still positive capital are not permitted to go on lending until their capital ratios are brought back to acceptable levels. If capital levels are kept sufficiently high, then deposit insurance alone may not cause major incentive problems. Managers and bank owners still have a good deal to lose and so are not subject to moral hazard. In this circumstance, the depositors are protected against all downside risk but the owners and managers are not, and it is owners and managers who make risk decisions.

Unfortunately, bank capital is a more elusive matter than it first appears. One would like to think of it as the bedrock on which the bank's balance sheet is built, but in reality it depends heavily on the policies of management and regulators toward nonperforming loans (i.e., loans on which scheduled payments of principal and interest are past due).

Under internationally accepted accounting standards, banks should take a *loss provision* for loans as soon as they suspect that a loan is in trouble, and certainly by the time it is nonperforming. Such a provision is deducted from income, and so reduces capital, but it is a noncash charge made wholly at the judgment of management. Such a loss can be avoided by extending a new loan to the troubled borrower so that the old loan will not default, or simply by ignoring the default and pretending it has no consequence.

The judgmental element in loss provisions means that actual bank behavior with respect to loan losses varies widely; some banks act conservatively by providing for losses and others cover up their problems. The conservative banks then show relatively less capital. A bank with massive loan losses may appear to have relatively more capital simply because it has not taken appropriate provisions for loss.

---

[28]Caprio and Klingebiel (1996b), p. 84.
[29]Basel Committee (1997).

For example, a bank may report capital equal to 8 percent of risk-weighted assets, the Basel Committee minimum standard. But if 16 percent of the loans are nonperforming and few provisions have been taken, the bank is likely to be insolvent because bank recoveries on nonperforming loans are substantially less than 50 percent in most EFMs. The bank should have taken a provision of at least 8 percent, wiping out capital. But this, of course, is tantamount to declaring bankruptcy, something few owners or managers will voluntarily do. If regulators are not sufficiently vigilant about the bank's practices and procedures for evaluating the quality of assets and taking provisions, they will not even know how much real capital the bank has. Regulators understand this arithmetic, but often they are very permissive with troubled banks. They may not press for larger loan provisions or they may indulge in "forbearance" of capital requirements—that is, not enforce the rules.

Resolving Insolvent Banks

The old-fashioned discipline of bank runs had the disadvantage of forcing individual depositors to bear the risk of loss, but like all market-based control systems, its action was swift and sure to stop value destruction. Unfortunately, few bank regulators act in this decisive way. One reason they do not is that most human beings find it hard to be as unfeeling as markets. But there are additional factors as well. Banks and their dependent borrowers are powerful political entities; government supervisors can find it politically difficult to discipline them. Furthermore, unlike private depositors, supervisors suffer little personal harm from turning a blind eye to bank weakness.

A key factor aggravating the political opposition to disciplining banks is that serious bank insolvency almost always occurs at a time of economic downturn. Closing a bank during an economic downturn or forcing it to reduce its lending so as to limit its risk, while essential to effective bank regulation, can be politically difficult when politicians look to banks to provide loans to stimulate a recovery. For this reason, bank regulators typically allow undercapitalized and even insolvent banks to continue in operation. Japan, for example, became mired in a recession during the 1990s that seemed never to end. The many weak banks were not purged by regulators for fear of aggravating the recession in the short term through the act of closure. Yet in the longer term, the most important step the government could have taken in Japan, and in many other cases, would have been to cleanse the banking system of bad loans at an early date, so that strengthened banks could begin lending on a sound basis once again.

Another factor is that closing insolvent banks requires substantial amounts of cash. Optimal economic behavior would be to close the bank, pay off all the deposits, take over the loan portfolio, and then realize the portfolio's value over time. But paying off the depositors in even a small bank requires billions of dollars of cash; in a very large bank it requires hundreds of billions. Governments have difficulty in mobilizing this amount of cash, and therefore often choose a nonoptimal course of resolution.

A favorite technique of embattled bank regulators is to promote a merger of the insolvent bank into a stronger bank. This avoids the need for cash and also avoids the possible criticism of closing a bank during a time of economic stress. It passes the entire resolution problem to a management that appears competent. The difficulty is that the strong bank is then saddled with all the problems of the failed bank, which may even drive the strong bank toward insolvency.

An even worse solution, though it was the one selected by the Japanese government in the mid-1990s and is often chosen by EFM regulators, is simply to give cash to the banks, either as a grant or as a purchase of a junior security such as preferred stock. This temporizes, providing an "instant recapitalization" of the weak banks. But its incentive effects are the worst possible: Nothing could be better designed to tell bank managements that taking excessive risk is an outstanding strategy, since the government will explicitly subsidize all the negative outcomes while the bank's owners and managements will benefit from all the positive outcomes. This is moral hazard at its most obvious and most destructive.

Finally, the strategy of simply doing nothing is also a terrible choice. Banks can go on functioning even if totally insolvent so long as the government is willing to guarantee all deposits. But, as noted before, the behavior of bank management changes when equity is low or negative. The pursuit of high-risk strategies by insolvent banks can be extremely dangerous, converting a modest bank crisis into a catastrophic loss.

In June 2000, the World Bank held a conference on the design and implementation of deposit insurance in developing countries, with a focus on the role of safety nets in promoting moral hazard in banking systems. This conference brought together some of the first careful academic studies that make use of new World Bank data sets that track the specific design features of deposit insurance systems and the extent to which governments go beyond deposit insurance with special bailouts of insolvent banks. The findings of these studies were remarkably consistent and uniform, despite the diversity of methodologies and backgrounds of the participants.[30]

One study by Edward Kane constructed measures of the quality of different countries' legal, informational, and regulatory environments and found that generous government protection of banks without effective regulation and supervision was highest in countries with weak "informational, ethical, and corporate-governance environment[s]." A second study, by Asli Demirgüç-Kunt of the World Bank and Enrica Detragiache of the IMF, found that the more extensive and credible the protection offered by government deposit insurance, the greater the likelihood of banking crises. A third paper, by Demirgüç-Kunt and Harry Huizinga, investigated the mechanism through which deposit insurance systems with relatively generous protection were able to create moral hazard. The authors found that generous protection made bank debt holders complacent and thus eroded market discipline, which freed banks to pursue excessive risk taking. The absence of market discipline is reflected in the absence of the risk pricing of bank debt (that is, interest rate charges that are relatively insensitive to the true risk of bank failure).

Three other papers, by Patrick Honohan and Daniela Klingebiel of the World Bank, by John Boyd and others, and by Robert Cull of the World Bank and others, examined the link between government bailout policies and the size of bailout costs (measured both in terms of the budgetary costs of paying insolvent banks' debts and the forgone GDP that results in the wake of bank credit collapses during and after banking crises). Honohan and Klingebiel found that "unlimited deposit guarantees, open-ended liquidity support [for banks], repeated recapitalizations [of banks], debtor bailouts and regulatory forbearance add significantly and sizably to [the fiscal] costs of resolving banking crises." Boyd et al. also found the size of post-crisis economic decline was larger when bailouts were more generous. Finally, the paper by Cull et al. found that relatively generous bank safety net policies tended to be associated with low long-run growth in output, and smaller and more volatile financial systems. Taken together, these six papers offer

---

[30]These papers include, among others, Boyd, Gomis, Kwak, and Smith (2000), Cull, Senbet, and Sorge (2000), Demirgüç-Kunt and Detragiache (2000), Demirgüç-Kunt and Huizinga (2000), Honohan and Klingebiel (2000), and Kane (2000). These and other papers presented at the conference are available at the World Bank's website, **www.worldbank.org/finance/html**.

strong and consistent evidence that government safety net policies have been a major contributor to banking crises and underdevelopment in emerging market countries.

The particular initiating causes for banking crises have not changed much through time: macroeconomic shocks, bank fraud and mismanagement, falling asset values. What has changed a great deal is the size of banking system losses and the allocation of responsibility for bearing losses and disciplining the banking system. Private markets used to assume both roles, but now government has assumed them. Government regulators in EFMs have in many cases only begun to realize what a difficult challenge this is. How can government regulators be smart enough, diligent enough, and imaginative enough to ferret out problems before they become crises? Once problems are uncovered, how can government be tough enough and fast enough to impose real costs on those bank owners and managements who destroy value? In particular, in settings where bank owners and managers have substantial political power, what will prevent the pernicious pattern of governments simply passing money to misbehaving bank owners and managers?

Within the framework of government protection of depositors, there may be room to restore at least some element of market discipline. For example, if governments require all banks to issue a layer of subordinated, uninsured debt to a class of arm's-length investors, then those investors may become effective monitors of the banks.[31] Argentina has implemented a version of this system and other countries are currently considering this approach. Time will tell its effectiveness.

In summary, the nature of government's relationship to banks may have more to do with bank losses than any other variable. If the government owns the banks and uses them as a conduit for capital flows to favored projects, as in China today, the result is almost sure to be large numbers of nonperforming loans. If the government quasi-liberalizes—privatizing profits within a protected, risk-subsidized banking system, without preparing a careful monitoring and control system—the result is likely to be even worse.

The only path to safety and lasting growth is a program of credible financial liberalization that is carefully designed and implemented to promote competition and discourage abuse of government protection. Government must subject the private banks to a well-crafted system of incentives, monitoring, and control. It must require a sufficient quantity of capital, honestly measured, to be maintained at all times. When banks develop problems, government must act decisively to bring the bank into compliance or close it. Finally, government must be prepared to act forcefully against owners and managers who destroy value, closing the banks where this occurs.

The world is still learning how to find the right relationship between banks and governments, and the job is not an easy one. Some EFMs have come a long way and seem closer to achieving the best practices than many industrialized countries. Argentina, Chile, and Singapore, for example, seem to be on a promising track. Argentina has allowed foreign banks to enter, buy local banks, and compete; foreign banks now control about half of bank assets. It also has one of the highest capital requirements in the world. Argentina's many banking reforms are described in detail in the box on page 339.

We are all learning. There is no single universal explanation for the cascade of bank loan losses, but there clearly are common themes, including those highlighted in this chapter. Countries that manage their banking systems inappropriately are now paying high prices for these mistakes. Still, there is room for optimism: No country can afford to do this for long.

---

[31]Calomiris (1997).

APPENDIX

The following appendix material is an updated summary of the data provided in Gerard Caprio and Daniela Klingebiel (1996a). We are grateful to the authors for supplying it to us. The data are divided into two sections: Systemic banking crises in which most or all of banking system capital is exhausted, and borderline or smaller cases. Each of these tables is grouped by region and shows the country, the origins and causes of each crisis, and its cost of resolution where possible.

TABLE 7.A1   Systemic Banking Crises:
Cases in which Most or All of Banking System Capital Is Eroded

Country	Scope of Crisis	Estimate of Total Costs
Africa		
Algeria		
1990–1992	Banking system nonperforming loan ratio (NPLs) reached 50%	
Benin		
1988–1990	All three commercial banks collapsed; 80% of banks' loan portfolio nonperforming	CFA95 billion, equivalent to 17% of GDP
Burkina Faso		
1988–1994	Banking system NPLs estimated at 34%	
Burundi		
1994–ongoing	Banking system NPLs estimated at 25% of total loans in 1995; one bank liquidated	
Cameroon		
1987–1993	In 1989, banking sector NPLs ratio reached 60–70%; five commercial banks closed, three banks restructured	
1995–1998	At year-end 1996, NPLs accounted for 30% of total loans; three banks restructured and two closed	
Cape Verde		
1993–ongoing	At year-end 1995, commercial banks' NPL ratio 30%	
Central African Republic		
1976–1992	Four banks liquidated	
1988–1999	Two largest banks, accounting for 90% of total assets, restructured; banking sector NPL ratio 40%	
Congo (Brazzaville)		
1992–ongoing	Two large banks placed in liquidation; the remaining three banks insolvent; situation aggravated by civil war	
Congo, Democratic Republic of (former Zaire)		
1980s		
1991–1992	Four state-owned banks insolvent; fifth bank to be recapitalized with private participation	
1994–ongoing	NPLs to the private sector 75%; two state-owned banks liquidated and two others privatized; in 1997, 12 banks in serious financial difficulties	
Chad		
1980s	Private sector NPL ratio 35%	
1992		
Côte d'Ivoire		
1988–1991	Four large banks affected, accounting for 90% of banking system loans; three definitely insolvent and one perhaps so; six government banks closed	Government costs estimated at CFA677 billion equivalent to 25% of GDP

Country	*Scope of Crisis*	*Estimate of Total Costs*
Djibouti 1991–1993	Two of six commercial banks ceased operations in 1991 and 1992; other banks experienced difficulties	
Equatorial Guinea 1983–1985	Two of country's largest banks liquidated	
Eritrea 1993	Most of banking system insolvent	
Ghana 1982–1989	Seven audited banks (of 11) insolvent; rural banking sector affected	Restructuring costs estimated at 6% of GNP
Guinea 1985	Six banks accounting for 99% of total system deposits deemed insolvent	Repayment of deposits amounted to 3% of 1986 GDP
1993–1994	Two banks insolvent accounting for 22.4% of financial system assets; one other bank in serious financial difficulties; these three banks accounted for 45% of the market	
Guinea–Bissau 1995–?	At year-end 1995, NPLs accounted for 45% of commercial banks' total loan portfolio	
Kenya 1985–1989	Four banks and 24 nonbank financial institutions faced liquidity and solvency problems; together accounted for 15% of total liabilities of financial system	
1992	Intervention in two local banks	
1993–1995	Serious systemic problems with banks accounting for more than 30% of assets of financial system facing solvency problems	
Liberia 1991-1995	Seven of 11 banks nonoperational; assets equivalent to 60% of total bank assets at mid-1995	
Madagascar 1988	25% of banking sector loans deemed irrecoverable	
Mali 1987–1989	NPLs of largest bank 75%	
Mauritania 1984–1993	In 1984, five major banks had nonperforming assets ranging from 45% to 70% of their portfolio	Cost of rehabilitation estimated at 15% of GDP in 1988
Mozambique 1987–1995?	BCM, main commercial bank, experienced solvency problems apparent after 1992	
Niger 1983–?	In the mid-1980s, banking system NPLs reached 50%; four banks liquidated and three restructured in the late 1980s	
Nigeria 1990s	1993: insolvent banks account for 20% of total assets and 22% of banking system deposits; 1995: almost half of banks reported in financial distress	
São Tomé and Príncipe 1980s, 1990s	At year-end 1992, 90% of Monobank's loans nonperforming; in 1993, commercial and development departments of former Monobank liquidated, as was the only financial institution; two new banks licensed, which took over many assets of their predecessors; credit operations of one newly created bank suspended since year-end 1994	
Senegal 1988–1991	In 1988, 50% of banking system loans nonperforming; six commercial banks and one development bank closed accounting for 20–30% of financial system assets	US$830 million, equivalent to 17% of GDP

Country	*Scope of Crisis*	*Estimate of Total Costs*
Sierra Leone 1990–ongoing	In 1995, 40–50% of banking system loans nonperforming; license of one bank suspended in 1994; recapitalization and restructuring of the banks ongoing	
Swaziland 1995	Central Bank also took over Meridien BIAO Swaziland and Swaziland Development and Savings Bank (SDSB), which faced severe portfolio problems	
Tanzania Late 1980s, 1990s	1987: main financial institutions had arrears amounting to half of their portfolio; 1995: National Bank of Commerce, accounting for 95% of banking system assets, insolvent since 1990–1992	1987: implied losses amount to nearly 10% of GNP
Togo 1993–1995		
Uganda 1994–ongoing	50% of banking system facing solvency problems	
Zambia 1995	Meridian Bank insolvent, accounting for 13% of commercial bank assets	Rough estimate of US$50 million (1.4% of GDP)
Zimbabwe 1995–ongoing	Two of five commercial banks recorded high NPL ratio	
<u>**Asia**</u> **Bangladesh** late 1980s–1996	In 1987, four banks accounting for 70% of total credit had estimated NPL ratio of 20%; since late 1980s, entire private/public banking system technically insolvent	
China 1990s	At year-end 1998, China's four large state-owned commercial banks, accounting for 68.3% of total banking system assets, deemed insolvent; total banking system NPLs estimated at 50%	Net losses estimated to reach US$427.6 billion, or 47.4% of GDP in 1999
Indonesia 1997–ongoing	By March 1999, Bank of Indonesia had closed down 61 banks and nationalized 54 banks, of a total of 240; NPL estimates for total banking system at 65–75% of total loans	Fiscal costs estimated at 50–55% of GDP
Malaysia 1997–ongoing	Finance company sector being restructured and number of finance companies to be reduced from 39 to 16 through mergers; two finance companies taken over by Central Bank, including MBF Finance, the largest independent finance company; two banks, deemed insolvent, accounting for 14.2% of financial system assets, to be merged with other banks; at year-end 1998, NPLs estimated at 25–35% of total banking system assets	Net loss estimated at US$14.9 billion, or 20.5% of GDP by 1999
Nepal 1988	In early 1988, reported arrears of three banks accounting for 95% of financial system, averaged 29% of all assets	
Philippines 1981–1987	Two public banks accounting for 50% of banking system assets, six private banks accounting for 12%, 32 thrifts accounting for 53.2% of thrift banking assets, and 128 rural banks	At its peak, central bank assistance to financial institutions amounted to 19.1 billion pesos (3% of GDP)
1998–ongoing	Since January 1998, one commercial bank, seven of 88 thrifts, and 40 of 750 rural banks placed under receivership; banking system NPLs reached 10.8% by August 1998 and 12.4% by November 1998; expected to reach 20% in 1999	Net loss estimated at US$4.0 billion, or 6.7% of GDP by 1999

282   *Chapter 7   The Trouble with Banks*

Country	*Scope of Crisis*	*Estimate of Total Costs*
South Korea 1997–ongoing	By March 1999, 2 of 26 commercial banks accounting for 11.8% of total banking system assets nationalized; 5 banks, accounting for 7.8% of total banking system assets, closed; seven banks, accounting for 38% of banking system assets, placed under special supervision; overall, banking system NPLs expected to peak at 30–40%	Net losses estimated at US$68.3 billion, or 20.3% of GDP in 1999
Sri Lanka 1989–1993	State-owned banks, comprising 70% of banking system, estimated to have nonperforming loan ratio of about 35%	Restructuring cost amounted to 25 billion rupees (5% of GDP)
Taiwan 1997	Banking system NPLs estimated at 15%, at year-end 1998	In 1999 net losses estimated at US$26.7 billion, or 11.5% of GDP
Thailand 1983–1987	Authorities intervened in 50 finance and security firms and 5 commercial banks or about 25% of total financial system assets; 3 commercial banks judged insolvent (14.1% of commercial banking assets)	Government cost for 50 finance companies estimated at 0.5% of GNP; government cost for subsidized loans amounted to about 0.2% of GDP annually
1997–ongoing	To March 1999, Bank of Thailand intervened in 70 finance companies (of 91), which together accounted for 12.8% of financial system assets or 72% of finance company assets. Also intervened in six banks that together had a market share of 12.3%; at year-end 1998 banking system NPLs reached 46% of total loans	Net losses estimated at US$59.7 billion, or 42.3% of GDP in 1999
Vietnam 1997–ongoing	Two of four large state-owned commercial banks, accounting for 50.7% of banking system loans, deemed insolvent; other two experiencing significant solvency problems; several joint stocks banks in severe financial distress; total banking system NPLs reached 18.2% of total loans in late 1998	
<u>Central America and the Caribbean</u>		
Costa Rica Several instances	In 1987, public banks, accounting for 90% of total banking system loans, in financial distress; 32% of their loans considered uncollectible	Implied losses of at least twice the capital plus reserves
El Salvador 1989	Nine state-owned commercial banks recorded NPL ratios of 37% on average in 1989	
Jamaica 1994–ongoing	In 1994, a merchant banking group closed; in 1995, a medium-sized bank received financial support; in 1997, the Financial Credit Adjustment Company intervened in and effectively nationalized five of six commercial banks as a result of sharp deterioration of their asset quality and virtual erosion of their capital base	
Panama 1988–1989	In 1988, Panama's banking system underwent a nine-week banking holiday; financial position of most state-owned and private commercial banks weak; as a result, 15 banks ceased operations	
Mexico 1981–1982 1995–ongoing	Government took over troubled banking system Of 34 commercial banks in 1994, nine were intervened in and 11 more participated in the loan/purchase recapitalization program; these intervened banks accounted for 18.9% of total financial system assets and were deemed insolvent	Total estimated cost of bank rescue US$65 billion by February 1998, or nearly 15% of GDP
Nicaragua Late 1980s–1996	Banking system NPLs reached 50% in 1996	

Country	Scope of Crisis	Estimate of Total Costs
South America		
Argentina		
1980–1982	More than 70 institutions liquidated or subject to central bank intervention, accounting for 16% of assets of commercial banks and 35% of total assets of finance companies	55.3% of GDP
1989–1990	Nonperforming assets constituted 27% of the aggregate portfolio and 37% of the portfolios of state-owned banks; failed banks held 40% of financial system assets	
1995	Suspension of eight banks and collapse of three banks; overall through year-end 1997, 63 of 205 banking institutions either closed or merged	Direct and indirect cost to public estimated at 1.6% of GDP
Bolivia		
1986–1987	Five banks liquidated; total NPLs of banking system reached 29.8% in 1987; in mid-1988 reported arrears stood at 92% of commercial banks' net worth	
1994–ongoing	Two banks with 11% of banking system assets closed in November 1994; in 1995, 4 of 15 domestic banks, accounting for 30% of banking system assets, experienced liquidity problems and suffered from high levels of NPLs	
Brazil		
1990	Deposit to bond conversion	
1994–ongoing	By year-end 1997, Central Bank had intervened in or put under the Temporary Special Administration Regime (RAET) system, 43 financial institutions; nonperforming loans of entire banking system reached 15%	In 1996, negative net worth of selected state and federal banks estimated at 5–10% of GDP; costs of individual bank recapitalization, by year-end 1997: Banco Econômico, US$2.9 billion Bamerindus: US$3 billion Banco do Brazil, US$8 billion Unibanco, US$4.9 billion In 1998, cost of public support to private banking sector estimated at 1–2% of GDP
Chile		
1976	Entire mortgage system insolvent	
1981–1983	Authorities intervened in four banks and four nonbank financial institutions (with 33% of outstanding loans) in 1981; in 1983, seven banks and one *financiera* accounted for 45% of total assets; by year-end 1983, 19% of loans were nonperforming	1982–1985: government spent 41.2% of GDP
Colombia		
1982–1987	Central Bank intervened in six banks accounting for 25% of banking system assets	Costs of restructuring estimated at 5% of GDP
Ecuador		
Early 1980s	Implementation of exchange program (domestic for foreign debt) to bail out banking system	
1996–ongoing	Authorities intervened in several smaller financial institutions in late 1995 to early 1996 and in the fifth largest commercial bank in 1996; seven financial institutions, accounting for 25–30% of commercial banking assets, closed in 1998–1999; in March 1999, authorities declared one-week bank holiday	
Paraguay		
1995–ongoing	Government Superintendency intervened in two interconnected commercial banks, two other banks, and six related finance houses, accounting for 10% of financial system deposits; by July 1998 government had intervened in six other financial institutions, including the country's largest public bank and the largest savings and loans; by year-end 1998 government intervened in most of remaining domestic private and public banks and a number of finance companies	By end of May 1998, government had spent US$500 million, equivalent to 5.1% of GDP

284   *Chapter 7   The Trouble with Banks*

Country	Scope of Crisis	Estimate of Total Costs
Peru 1983–1990	Two large banks failed; rest of system suffered from high levels of nonperforming loans and financial disintermediation following the nationalization of the banking system in 1987	
Uruguay 1981–1984	Affected institutions accounted for 30% of financial system assets; insolvent banks accounted for 20% of financial system deposits	Costs of recapitalizing banks estimated at US$350 million (7% of GNP); Central Bank's quasi-fiscal losses associated with subsidized credit operations and purchase of loan portfolios amounted to 24.2% of GDP during 1982–1985
Venezuela 1994–ongoing	Insolvent banks accounted for 30% of financial system deposits; authorities intervened in 13 of 47 banks, which held 50% of deposits in 1994, and in five additional banks in 1995	Estimated losses at more than 18% of GDP
Middle East & North Africa		
Egypt Early 1980s	Several large investment companies closed	
Israel 1977–1983	Virtually entire banking sector affected, representing 60% of stock market capitalization; stock exchange closed for 18 days; bank share prices fell over 40%	About 30% of GDP in 1983
Kuwait 1980s	An estimated 40% of loans nonperforming by 1986	
Lebanon 1988–1990	Four banks insolvent; 11 banks resorted to Central Bank lending	
Morocco Early 1980s		
Turkey 1982–1985	Three banks merged with the state-owned Agriculture Bank and then liquidated; two large banks restructured	1982–1985: rescue cost equivalent to 2.5% of GNP
Yemen 1996–ongoing	Banks suffered from extensive nonperforming loans and heavy foreign currency exposure	
Transitional Socialist Economies		
Albania 1992–ongoing	31% of "new" (post-July 1992 cleanup) banking system loans nonperforming; some banks faced liquidity problems owing to logjam of interbank liabilities	
Armenia 1994–1996	Since August 1994, Central Bank closed half of active banks; large banks continued to suffer from high NPL ratios; savings bank financially weak	
Azerbaijan 1995–ongoing	12 private banks closed; 3 large state-owned banks deemed insolvent; 1 large state-owned bank faced serious liquidity problems	
Bosnia-Herzegovina 1992–present	Banking system suffers from high ratios of NPLs due to the breakup of former Yugoslavia and civil war	
Bulgaria 1990s	In 1995 an estimated 75% of all loans in banking system substandard; banking system experienced a run in early 1996; government then ceased carrying out bailouts, prompting the closure of 19 banks accounting for one-third of assets of the sector. Surviving banks recapitalized by 1997	By early 1996, the sector had a negative net worth estimated at 13% of GDP

Country	Scope of Crisis	Estimate of Total Costs
Croatia 1996	Five banks accounting for about 50% of banking system loans deemed insolvent and taken over by the Bank Rehabilitation Agency during 1996	
Czech Republic 1991–ongoing	Several banks closed since 1993; during 1994–1995, 38% of banking system loans were nonperforming	12% of GDP spent on bank support through 1994
Estonia 1992–1995	Insolvent banks accounted for 41% of financial system assets; licenses of five banks revoked; two major banks merged and nationalized; two large banks merged and converted to loan-recovery agency	Recapitalization outlays for new entity 300 million EEK (1.4% of 1993 GDP)
1994	Social Bank, which controlled 10% of financial system assets, failed	
Georgia 1991–?	Most large banks virtually insolvent; about one-third of total banking system loans nonperforming	
Hungary 1991–1995	Second half of 1993: eight banks, accounting for 25% of financial system assets, insolvent	Overall resolution cost estimated at 10% of GDP
Kyrgyzstan 1990s	80–90% of total banking system loans doubtful; four small commercial banks closed in 1995	
Latvia 1994–ongoing	Between 1994 and 1999, 35 banks either saw their license revoked, were closed, or ceased operations	In 1995, negative net worth of banking system estimated at US$320 million or 7% of 1995 GDP; aggregate loss of the Latvian banking system in 1998 expected to reach US$172 million, about 2.9% of GDP
Lithuania 1995–1996	In 1995, 12 small banks of 25 liquidated, 3 private banks accounting for 29% of banking system deposits failed, and three state-owned banks deemed insolvent	
Macedonia 1993–1994	70% of total banking system loans nonperforming; government took over banks' foreign debts and closed second largest bank	Costs of banking system rehabilitation, obligations from assumption of external debt, liabilities of frozen foreign exchange and contingent liabilities in banks estimated at 32% of GDP
Poland 1990s	Seven of nine treasury-owned banks with 90% share of total credit market, the Bank for Food Economy, and the cooperative banking sector experienced solvency problems in 1991	1993: recapitalization costs of US$750 million for seven commercial banks; recapitalization costs for Bank for Food Economy and cooperative banking sector amounted to US$900 million, together equivalent to 1.9% of GDP
Romania 1990–ongoing	In 1998, nonperforming loans estimated at 25–30% of the total loans of the six major state-owned banks	Agricultural Bank recapitalized on a flow basis; Central Bank injected $210 million into Bancorex, the largest state bank, about 0.6% of 1998 GDP; another $60 million to be injected in 1999

Country	*Scope of Crisis*	*Estimate of Total Costs*
Russia 1995	On August 24, 1995, interbank loan market stopped working due to concern about connected lending in many new banks	
1998	Nearly 720 banks, one-half of all those operating, deemed insolvent; these banks account for 4% of the sector's assets and 32% of retail deposits; Central Bank of Russia estimates 18 banks, holding 40% of the sector's assets and 41% of household deposits, to be in serious difficulties, requiring rescue by the state	In 1999, cost of full bailout estimated at about US$15 billion, or 5–7% of GDP
Slovakia 1991–ongoing	In 1997, total amount of unrecoverable loans was estimated at 101 billion crowns, equal to approximately 31.4% of total loans and 15.3% of GDP	
Slovenia 1992–1994	Three banks, accounting for two-thirds of banking system assets, restructured	Recapitalization costs of US$1.3 billion
Ukraine 1997	By 1997, 32 of 195 banks being liquidated; a further 25 undergoing financial rehabilitation; bad loans constitute 50 to 65% of assets of country's leading banks; in 1998, Ukraine banks further hit by government's decision to restructure government debt	
Industrialized Countries **Finland** 1991–1994	Savings banking sector badly affected; government took control of three banks that together accounted for 31% of total system deposits	Recapitalization costs amounted to 11% of GDP
Japan 1990s	Banks suffering from sharp decline in stock market and real estate prices; official estimate of NPLs: ¥40 trillion (US$469 billion) in 1995 (10% of GDP); unofficial estimates put NPLs at ¥1 trillion or 25% of GDP; banks have already made provisions for some bad loans. At year-end 1998, total banking system NPLs estimated at ¥87.5 trillion (US$725 billion), about 17.9% of GDP; in March 1999, Hokkaido Takushodu bank closed, Long Term Credit Bank nationalized, Yatsuda Trust merged with Fuji Bank, and Mitsui Trust merged with Chuo Trust	In 1996, rescue costs estimated at over US$100 billion In 1998, government announced Obuchi Plan, which provides ¥60 trillion (US$500 billion), about 12.3% of GDP, in public funds for loan losses, recapitalization of banks, and depositor protection
Norway 1987–1993	Central Bank provided special loans to six banks, suffering from post-oil recession of 1985–1986 and from problem real estate loans; state took control of three largest banks (equivalent to 85% of banking system assets, whose loan losses had wiped out capital), partly through a Government Bank Investment Fund (Nkr 5 billion) and the state-backed Bank Insurance Fund had to increase capital to Nkr 11 billion.	Recapitalization costs amounted to 8% of GDP
Spain 1977–1985	1978–1983: 24 institutions rescued; four liquidated, four merged, and 20 small/medium-sized banks (Rumasa Group) nationalized. In total, 52 of 110 banks experiencing solvency problems, representing 20% of total banking system deposits	Estimated losses of banks were equivalent to approximately 16.8% of GNP
Sweden 1991	Nordbanken and Gota Bank insolvent, accounting for 21.6% of total banking system assets; Sparbanken Foresta intervened, accounting for 24% of total banking system assets; overall, five of six largest banks, accounting for over 70% of banking system assets, experienced difficulties	Cost of recapitalization amounted to 4% of GDP

TABLE 7.A2 Borderline or Smaller Banking Crises

Country	Scope of Crisis	Estimate of Total Costs
Africa		
Angola		
1991–ongoing	Two state-owned commercial banks experienced solvency problems	
Botswana		
1994–1995	One problem bank merged in 1994, a small bank liquidated in 1995, and state-owned National Development Bank recapitalized	Recapitalization cost of National Development Bank amounted to 0.6% of GDP
Ethiopia		
1994–1995	A government-owned bank was restructured and its nonperforming loans taken over by the government	
Gabon		
1995–ongoing	One bank temporarily closed in 1995	
Gambia		
1985–1992	In 1992, a government bank restructured and privatized	
Ghana		
1997–ongoing	NPL levels increased sharply during 1997 from 15.5% of loans outstanding to 26.5%; two state-owned commercial banks, accounting for 33.9% of market share, in bad shape; three banks, accounting for 3.6% of market share in terms of deposits, insolvent	
Kenya		
1996–ongoing	At end of 1996, NPLs reached 18.6% of total banking system loans	
Lesotho		
1988–ongoing	One small bank of four commercial banks suffered from large portfolio of nonperforming loans	
Mauritius		
1996	Central Bank closed 2 of 12 commercial banks for fraud and other irregularities	
Nigeria		
1997	Distressed banks accounted for 3.9% of banking system assets	
Rwanda		
1991–?	One bank, with well-established network, closed	
South Africa		
1977	Trust Bank	
1989–?		
Tunisia		
1991–1995	In 1991, most commercial banks undercapitalized	1991–1994, banking system raised equity equivalent to 1.5% of GDP and made provisions equivalent to another 1.5%; recapitalization through 1994 required at least 3% of GDP
Asia		
Brunei Darussalam		
Mid–1980s	Several financial firms failed in mid-1980s; second largest bank failed in 1986; in 1991, 9% of loans past due	
Hong Kong		
1982–1983	Nine deposit-taking companies failed	
1983–1986	Seven banks or deposit-taking institutions liquidated or taken over	
1998	One large investment bank fails	

288   *Chapter 7   The Trouble with Banks*

Country	*Scope of Crisis*	*Estimate of Total Costs*
India 1993–ongoing	Nonperforming assets of the 27 public sector banks estimated at 19.5% of total loans and advances as of end of March 1995; nonperforming assets to total assets reached 10.8% in 1993–1994; at year end 1998, NPLs estimated at 16% of total loans	
Indonesia 1994	Classified assets equal to over 14% of banking system assets with over 70% in state banks	Recapitalization cost for five state banks expected to amount to 1.8% of GDP
Laos Early 1990s		Recapitalization of state-owned commercial banks amounted to 1.5% of GDP
Malaysia 1985–1988	Insolvent institutions account for 3.4% of financial system deposits; marginally capitalized and perhaps insolvent institutions account for another 4.4% of financial system deposits	Reported losses equivalent to 4.7% of GNP
Myanmar 1996–?	Largest state-owned commercial bank reported with large ratio of NPLs	
Papua New Guinea 1989–?	85% of savings and loan associations ceased operations	
Singapore 1982	Domestic commercial banks' nonperforming loans rose to about $200 million or 0.63% of GDP	
Taiwan 1983–1984	Four trust companies and 11 cooperatives failed	
1995	Failure of credit cooperative Changua Fourth in late July sparked runs on other credit unions in central and southern Taiwan	

Central America and the Caribbean

Costa Rica 1994–ongoing	One large state-owned commercial bank closed in December 1994; ratio of overdue loans (net of provisions) to net worth in state commercial banks exceeded 100% in June 1995	
Guatemala 1990s	Two small state-owned banks had high nonperforming assets; these banks discontinued operations in early 1990s	
Trinidad and Tobago 1982–1993	In early 1980s, several financial institutions experienced solvency problems, resulting in merger of three government-owned banks in 1993	

South America

Venezuela Late 1970s and 1980s	Notable bank failures: Banco Nacional de Descuento (1978); BANDAGRO (1981); Banco de los Trabajadores de Venezuela (1982); Banco de Comercio (1985); BHCU (1985); BHCO (1985); Banco Lara (1986)	

Transitional Socialist Economies

Belarus 1995–ongoing	Many banks undercapitalized; forced mergers burdened some banks with poor loan portfolios	
Estonia 1998	Three banks failed in 1998: Maapank (Agricultural Bank), which accounted for 3% of banking system assets, and two smaller banks, EVEA and ERA	Maapank's total losses reached US$500 million
Tajikistan 1996–ongoing	One of largest banks insolvent; one small bank closed, and another (of 17) in process of liquidation	

Country	Scope of Crisis	Estimate of Total Costs
Middle East and North Africa		
Egypt		
1991–1995	Four public sector banks given capital assistance	
Jordan		
1989–1990	Third largest bank failed in August 1989	Central bank provided overdrafts equivalent to 10% of GDP to meet a run on deposits and allowed banks to settle foreign obligations
Turkey		Up to June 1994, authorities spent
1994	Three banks failed in April 1994	1.1% of GDP
Industrialized Countries		
Australia		
1989–1992	Two large banks received capital from government to cover losses; nonperforming loans rose to 6% of total assets in 1991–1992	Rescue cost of state-owned banks estimated to be 1.9% of GDP
Canada		
1983–1985	15 members of Canadian Deposit Insurance Corporation, including two banks, failed	
Denmark		
1987–1992	Cumulative loan losses 1990–1992 were 9% of loans; 40 of 60 problem banks merged	
France		
1994–1995	Crédit Lyonnais	Unofficial estimates put losses at US$10 billion, making it the largest single bank failure up to that time
Germany		
Late 1970s	So-called Giroinstitutions faced problems	
Great Britain		
1974–1976	"Secondary Banking Crisis"	
1980s and 1990s	Notable bank failures: Johnson Matthey (1984), Bank of Credit and Commerce International (1991), Barings (1995)	
Greece		
1991–1995	Localized problems required significant injections of public funds into specialized lending institutions	
Iceland		
1985–1986	One of three state-owned banks became insolvent; eventually privatized in a merger with three private banks	
1993	Government forced to inject capital into one of the largest state-owned commercial banks after it suffered serious loan losses	
Italy		
1990–1995	58 banks, accounting for 11% of total lending, merged with other institutions	
New Zealand		
1987–1990	One large state-owned bank, accounting for one-fourth of banking assets, experienced serious solvency problems due to high NPLs	Bank required a capital injection amounting to 1% of GDP
United States		
1984–1991	More than 1,400 savings & loans and 1,300 banks failed	Cost of savings & loan cleanup estimated at US$180 billion, equivalent to 3.2% of GDP

References

Akerlof, George A., and Paul Romer. 1993. Looting: The economic underworld of bankruptcy for profit. *Brookings Papers on Economic Activity* 2: 1–73.

Barth, James R., and Philip F. Batholomew. 1992. The thrift industry crisis: Revealed weaknesses in the Federal deposit insurance system. In *The Reform of Federal Deposit Insurance*. Ed. by James R. Barth and R. Dan Brumbaugh, Jr. New York: Harper Business.

Basel Committee on Banking Supervision. 1997. *Core Principles for Effective Banking Supervision*. Basel, Switzerland: Bank for International Settlements.

Boyd, John, Pedro Gomis, Sungkyu Kwak, and Bruce Smith. 2000. A user's guide to banking crises. Conference paper, World Bank.

Calomiris, Charles W. 1997. *The Postmodern Bank Safety Net: Lessons from Developed and Developing Economies*. Washington, DC: American Enterprise Institute.

———. 1998. The IMF's imprudent role as lender of last resort. *Cato Journal* 17: 275–94.

———. 2000. *Victorian Perspectives on the Banking Collapses of the 1980s and 1990s*. Manuscript.

Calomiris, Charles W., and Gary Gorton. 1991. The origin of banking panics: Models, facts and bank regulation. In *Financial Markets and Financial Crises*. Ed. by R. Glenn Hubbard. Chicago: University of Chicago Press.

Calomiris, Charles W., Charles Himmelberg, and Paul Wachtel. 1995. Commercial paper, corporate finance, and the business cycle: A microeconomic perspective. *Carnegie-Rochester Conference Series on Public Policy* 42: 203–50.

Calomiris, Charles W., and Charles M. Kahn. 1991. The role of demandable debt in structuring optimal banking arrangements. *American Economic Review* 81: 497–513.

Calomiris, Charles W., and Eugene N. White. 1994. The origins of federal deposit insurance. In *The Regulated Economy*. Ed. by Claudia Goldin and Gary Libecap. Chicago: University of Chicago Press.

Calomiris, Charles W., and Berry Wilson. 1998. Bank capital and portfolio management: The 1930s capital crunch and scramble to shed risk. Working Paper no. 6649, National Bureau of Economic Research.

Caprio, Gerard, and Daniela Klingebiel. 1996a. Bank insolvencies: Cross-country experience. Working Paper no. 1620, World Bank.

———. 1996b. Bank insolvency: Bad luck, bad policy or bad banking? In *Annual Bank Conference on Development Economics 1996*. Washington, DC: World Bank.

Caprio, Gerard, and Berry Wilson. 1997. On not putting all the eggs in one basket: The role of diversification in banking. Paper presented at the 1997 World Bank annual meeting, Hong Kong.

Cole, R., J. McKenzie, and L. White. 1995. Deregulation gone awry: Moral hazard in the savings and loan industry. In *The Causes and Consequences of Depository Institution Failures*. Ed. by A. Cottrell, M. Lawlor, and J. Wood. Boston: Kluwer Academic Publishers.

Corsetti, Giancarlo, Paolo Pesenti, and Nouriel Roubini. 1998. What caused the Asian currency and financial crisis? Part I: A macroeconomic overview. Working Paper no. 6833, National Bureau of Economic Research.

Cull, Robert, Lemma W. Senbet, and Marco Sorge. 2000. Deposit insurance and financial development, Conference paper, World Bank.

Demirgüç-Kunt, Asli, and Enrica Detragiache. 2000. Does deposit insurance increase banking system stability? Conference paper, World Bank.

Demirgüç-Kunt, Asli, and Harry Huizinga. Marker discipline and financial safety net design. Conference paper, World Bank.

Edwards, Franklin R., and Frederic S. Mishkin. 1995. The decline of traditional banking: Implications for financial stability and regulatory policy. Federal Reserve Bank of New York. *Economic Policy Review* 2: 27–45.

Fay, Stephen. 1997. *The Collapse of Barings*. New York: W.W. Norton.

Friedman, Milton, and Anna Schwartz. 1963. *A Monetary History of the United States, 1867–1960*. Princeton, NJ: Princeton University Press.

References **291**

Gorton, Gary, and Rosen. 1995. Corporate control, portfolio choice, and the decline of banking. *Journal of Finance* 50: 1377–1420.

Hellman, Thomas, Kevin Murdock, and Joseph Stiglitz. 1998a. Liberalization, moral hazard in banking, and prudential regulation: Are capital requirements enough? Working paper, Stanford University.

———. 1998b. Financial restraint: Towards a new paradigm. Working paper, Stanford University.

Honohan, Patrick, and Daniela Klingebiel. 2000. Controlling fiscal costs of banking crises. Conference paper, World Bank.

Hunt, Luke, and Karen Heinrich. 1996. *Barings Lost*. Oxford: Butterworth-Heinemann.

Jorion, Philippe. 1997. *Value at Risk*. Burr Ridge, IL: Richard D. Irwin.

Kane, Edward. 2000. Designing financial safety nets to fit country circumstances. Conference paper, World Bank.

Keeley, Michael. 1990. Deposit insurance, risk and market power in banking. *American Economic Review* 80: 1183–1200.

Krugman, Paul. 1998. What caused Asia's crisis? Working paper, Massachusetts Institute of Technology.

McKinnon, Ronald I. 1993. *The Order of Economic Liberalization*. 2nd ed. Baltimore: Johns Hopkins University Press.

Obstfeld, Maurice, and Kenneth Rogoff. 1995. The mirage of fixed exchange rates. *Journal of Economic Perspectives* 9, no. 4: 73–96.

Pomerleano, Michael. 1998. The East Asia crisis and corporate finances: The untold micro story. Policy Research Working Paper no. 1990, World Bank.

Rajan, Raghuram. 1996. Why banks have a future: Toward a new theory of commercial banking. *Journal of Applied Corporate Finance* 9, no. 2: 114–28.

Truell, Peter, and Larry Gurwin. 1992. *False Profits: The Inside Story of BCCI, the World's Most Corrupt Financial Empire*. New York: Houghton Mifflin.

A06-99-0021

BARING BROTHERS & CO.
TECHNICAL NOTE ON ROGUE TRADER NICHOLAS LEESON

Introduction

Nicholas Leeson was a rogue trader who reduced the value of the venerable Baring Brothers & Co (BB&Co) Bank from roughly $500 million dollars to $1.60. Leeson traded futures contracts on the Nikkei 225 and on Japanese Government Bonds without authorization while management at Barings, the Singapore International Monetary Exchange, the Osaka Stock Exchange, and other governing bodies in Britain and Singapore disregarded or failed to recognize the potential for financial disaster. The failure of Barings Bank provides a lesson in the risks and responsibilities involved in organizing and monitoring derivatives trading.

Baring Brothers History

Baring Brothers had a long history in the London financial district with the distinction of having gone global with its operations in the Eighteenth Century. Founded in the late 1700s, the bank was turned into a general-banking and mercantile operation by Sir Francis Baring. During his tenure, the bank developed several lines of business: underwriting bonds, accepting deposits, and trading commodities.

Baring Brothers reached the height of its reputation after the Napoleonic Wars in Europe. The bank led the funding of the French reparations to the victors and was lauded, in 1817, by the French Duc de Richelieu, as the "*sixth power in Europe*," after Great Britain, France, Russia, Austria, and Prussia. Baring Brothers helped finance the Louisiana Purchase for the United States, underwrote railroad construction in Canada, and financed other projects throughout the Americas. One of those other projects was underwriting a £2 million share issue for the Buenos Aires Water Supply and Drainage Co. in 1890. The issue did not sell but Baring Brothers had already sent the money and was on the brink of failure when the Bank of England organized a consortium to bail it out.[1] Thereafter, it was known as Baring Brothers & Co.

For all its long history in cross-border transactions, the bank never grew along with the size of the markets it served. In 1995, Baring Brothers & Co. remained a small, family-controlled bank ranked 474th in the world banking market.

---

[1] Stephen Fay, *The Collapse of Barings* (New York: W.W. Norton Co. Inc., 1997), p. 10.

Barings entered the securities market in 1984 when it acquired the Far East department of Henderson Crothwaite (British stockbrokers). This new entity at Barings, was called Baring Securities Ltd. (BSL). Christopher Heath, a specialist in Japanese instruments, managed to maintain independent control of Baring Securities until 1993.

During eight consecutive profitable years, everyone at Barings became accustomed to large bonuses, largely funded by profits in Baring Securities. In 1989, BSL provided £50 million of £65 million total profit for Barings.[2] Unfortunately, the losses incurred in 1992 lead to Heath being asked to resign in March 1993.

Nicholas Leeson

Nicholas Leeson was two days shy of his twenty-eighth birthday when his trading activities forced Baring Brothers into bankruptcy. Leeson left a note on his desk saying "I'm sorry"[3] and bolted to Kuala Lumpur with his wife following shortly thereafter.

Nick Leeson was born in Watford, England, just outside of London. His father was a plasterer and his mother was a nurse. He was the oldest of four children. Leeson did not attend university; instead, he went directly to work in London upon completion of high school. He worked with a British bank, Coutts & Co., and then Morgan Stanley, before moving to Barings Securities London in 1989.

Nick Leeson was twenty-two years old when he was hired for the position at Baring Securities London (BSLL). BSLL was looking to fill a position settling trades completed in Japan. Leeson, who had experience at Morgan Stanley settling futures and options in Japan, was a good replacement. He worked hard, kept to himself and was known as someone anxious to learn and eager to please. He was subsequently selected as a member of a team of four people assigned to straighten out back office problems in Jakarta.

In 1992, he was selected to run the back office for the new Baring Futures Singapore (BFS), a subsidiary that would trade futures and options. His exact responsibilities were somewhat unclear, although they did include responsibility for both the back office accounting and control functions as well as for executing clients' orders. This was when Leeson's unauthorized trading activities began. On his initiative, Leeson sat for and passed the futures-trading exam to become registered as an associated person with the Singapore International Monetary Exchange (SIMEX). He did not need the license to fulfill his responsibilities, but he did need it to execute trades. To meet his Baring's responsibilities, he only needed to take orders from clients, and pass them to a trader for execution.

In 1992, Leeson established the error account 88888;[4] which, according to SIMEX investigators, he immediately began using to conceal unauthorized trading activities.[5] While a legitimate error account numbered 99002, was known to BSLL, the 88888 account did not show on files or statements transmitted from Singapore to London. Account 88888 was known to SIMEX, but as a customer account, not as an error account. Leeson had to represent it differently to each group because he could not hide the existence of 88888 from SIMEX, and he could not explain its volume and balance to BSLL (but he could hide it from them).

---

[2] Ibid., p. 56.
[3] "Billion-Dollar Man," *Asiaweek*, December 29, 1995, p. 40.
[4] Eight is considered a lucky number by the Chinese.
[5] Fay, *Collapse*, p. 94.

Derivatives

Since the early 1970s, derivatives have increasingly been used by firms to manage their exposure to risks. When purchasing a derivative, only part of the value of the underlying asset is at risk, while the opportunity to benefit from favorable price fluctuations is retained. Derivatives can offer potentially enormous gains, which can lead to their use as speculative instruments. They also offer potentially debilitating losses depending on the positions taken.

Nick Leeson was trading futures and options on the Nikkei 225, an index of Japanese securities. Leeson was long Nikkei 225 futures, short Japanese government bond futures, and short both put and call options on the Nikkei index. He was betting that the Nikkei index would rise. He was wrong and ended up losing $1.39 billion. For Leeson to suffer losses of this magnitude in futures positions during January and February of 1995, he had to have held approximately one quarter of the entire open interest on the Osaka and Singapore stock exchanges. Unfortunately, since management had given such free rein to Leeson by allowing him to control both front and back office operations, this level of investment went undetected by the firm.[6]

Leeson offset any losses incurred on his long positions in Nikkei futures by writing Nikkei options. That is, when Leeson purchased futures contracts, he was required to pay cash, a margin of 15% of the contract's value to SIMEX, and when the losses on the contracts accumulated, additional margin was required because futures contracts are marked-to-market on a daily basis. However, when he wrote the options, he received cash, in the form of premiums. The premiums from the Nikkei options served two purposes: 1) they were used to hide losses created by the futures, which would otherwise have shown in BFS' financial statements, and 2) the premiums served to cover the margin calls on the futures. Leeson was able to do this due to the nature of the Japanese futures market at this time. In Japan, margin is posted on a net basis for all customers. Therefore, if many customers were short index futures, the firm can take long positions without having to post cash margin. In addition, daily settlement was one-sided. That is, losers must cover their losses daily, but winners were not permitted to withdraw gains. Therefore, it was possible to cover the firm's losses with customer gains. Another aspect of the Japanese futures market, which enabled Leeson to do this, was that the exchange did not require a separation between customer and proprietary funds. Therefore, it was impossible to distinguish between the firm's and the customers' positions.

The Nikkei 225 experienced an extended bull run throughout the late 1980s, reaching a height of close to 40,000 in 1989. By mid-1994, Leeson was convinced that since the Nikkei had fallen to half of its 1989 high, and interest rates were low, it would likely recover in the near future. He was convinced it would not fall below 19,000 and he was willing to put a lot of Baring's money at risk based on that belief. However, a rise in interest rates would hurt him and, accordingly, he took short positions in Japanese Government Bonds futures contracts that would pay off if interest rates rose.

Leeson's options positions were founded on his belief that volatility would be low. In fact, he had traded enough contracts by the time of the collapse that he was causing volatility to remain low. Increasingly, he had to write a larger volume of options in order to get the same amount of premiums. When it became increasingly difficult for the options' premiums to cover the margin calls on the futures, Leeson requested money from London. By February 23, 1995, BSLL had sent approximately $600 million to BFS. BSLL funded his request with little information, and with the understanding that a portion of the money was 'loans to clients', as portrayed on the BFS balance sheet.

---

[6] Hans R. Stoll, "Lost Barings: A Tale in Three Parts Concluding with a Lesson," *The Journal of Derivatives,* Fall 1995, Vol.3, No.1.

The Losses

Leeson began trading futures in July 1992 and by the end of the month, he had bought and sold 2,051 Nikkei futures, suffering a loss of approximately $64,000 immediately.[7] By the end of the year, his losses in account 88888 were more than $3.2 million. The numbers turned somewhat in his favor by mid-1993 when the losses amounted to only $40,000. Unfortunately, Leeson intended to keep trading until his numbers were positive. By the end of 1993, the losses were approximately $30 million. At this point, Leeson wrote options for approximately $35 million to offset the futures losses and to avoid suspicion from London and the auditors. Throughout this time period, Leeson was reporting record profits, and was being heralded as a superstar.

By the end of 1994, the Nikkei had fallen to just under 20,000 and Leeson's losses approached $330 million. Meanwhile, Barings executives were expecting an estimated $20 million in profits from BFS for 1994.

Leeson's activities in the first few months of 1995 were like those of any self-respecting speculator. On January 13, 1995, the Nikkei reached 19,331 and Barings was long 3,024 Nikkei futures contracts. But, on January 17, 1995, an earthquake measuring 7.2 devastated the Japanese city of Kobe. The Nikkei plummeted below 18,840 by January 20, at which point Leeson doubled his contracts to 7,135.[8] This process continued as the Nikkei fell to 18,000 on February 23, 1995, and Leeson's exposure grew to more than 55,399 unhedged Nikkei futures.[9] Compounding the problem, interest rates did not rise as Leeson had expected and he was losing on the Japanese Government Bond futures as well.

By Friday, February 24, 1995, Barings and the world discovered that Leeson had incurred losses approaching $1.1 billion,[10] more than double the capitalization of the bank. The bank was headed toward bankruptcy. When the markets opened in Singapore and Osaka on Monday, the exchanges would declare Barings in default on its margins.

Throughout that weekend, the Bank of England hosted meetings in London to try to form a consortium to bail out Barings. Barclays Bank assumed the leadership role and was able to attain commitments for $900 million for three months. Unfortunately for Barings, no one would assume the contingent risk of additional, but as yet undiscovered losses, and the efforts failed. At the time, it was already known that on Monday, February 27, 1995 there would be an additional $370 million in losses from Barings positions, bringing the total loss to $1.39 billion.[11] Barings was bankrupt. A detailed time-line is presented in Exhibit 1.

Controls & Responsibility

Internal

Leeson engaged in unauthorized trading, as well as fraud. However, it is clear that he was hidden in the organized chaos that characterized Barings. "There were no clearly laid down reporting lines with regard to Leeson, through the management chain to Ron Baker [Head of Financial Products Group for Barings]"[12] In fact, it seems there were several people responsible for monitoring Leeson's performance, each of whom assumed the other was watching more closely than he.

---

[7] Fay, *Collapse*, p. 97.
[8] Time, *"On Going Broke,"* p. 44.
[9] Fay, *Collapse*, p. 275.
[10] "Report of the Board of Banking Supervision Inquiry into the Circumstances of the Collapse of Barings," Bank of England, July 18, 1995 p. 2 (hereafter referred to as Bank of England).
[11] Martin Mayer, *The Bankers: The Next Generation* (New York: Truman Talley Books/Plume, 1997), p. 335.
[12] Bank of England, p. 235.

In August 1994, James Baker completed an internal audit of the Singapore office. He made several recommendations that should have alerted Barings executives to the potential for unauthorized trading: 1) segregation of front and back office activities—a fundamental principle in the industry, 2) a comprehensive review of Leeson's funding requirements, and 3) position limits on Leeson's activities. None of these had been acted upon by the time of the bank's collapse.

With regard to the first concern, Simon Jones, Director of BFS and Finance Director of BSS, in Singapore, offered assurances that he would address the segregation issue. However, he never took action to segregate Leeson's front and back office activities. Tony Hawes, Barings Treasurer in London agreed to complete a review of the funding requirements within the coming year. Ian Hopkins, Director and Head of Treasury and Risk in London, placed the issue of position limits on the risk committee's agenda, but it had not been decided when the collapse occurred.

According to the Bank of England report, senior management in London considered Jones a poor communicator and were concerned that he was not as involved as he should have been in the affairs of BFS. In fact, Peter Norris, the chief executive officer for Baring Securities Limited wanted to replace Jones. Jones, however, was protected by James Bax, Managing Director of Baring Securities Singapore, who was well liked in London. [13]

The Bank of England also found fault with the process of funding Leeson's activities from London. First, there was no clear understanding of whether the funds were needed for clients or for Baring's own accounts, making reconciliation impossible. Second, given the large amounts, credit checks should have been completed as well. The report places the responsibility for the lack of due diligence with Tony Hawes, Ian Hopkins, and the Chairman of the Barings Credit Committee.

The issue of proper reconciliation arose as early as April 1992 when Gordon Bowser, the risk manager in London, recommended that a reconciliation process be developed. Unfortunately, Bowser left Simon Jones and Tony Dickel, who had sent Leeson to Singapore, to agree on a procedure. With internal conflict over who was responsible for Leeson's activities, no agreement was reached between those two, and Leeson was left to establish reconciliation procedures for himself. [14]

There are numerous similar examples of internal conflict benefiting Leeson's covert trading throughout the three years. But one of the late failures occurred in January 1995 when SIMEX raised concern over Barings' ability to meet its large margins. In a letter dated January 11, 1995, and addressed to Simon Jones, SIMEX officials noted that there should have been an additional $100 million in the margin account for 88888. Jones passed the letter to Leeson to draft a response.

External

In January 1995, SIMEX was getting close to Leeson's activities, but had not yet managed to determine what was happening. In response to a second letter dated January 27, 1995 and sent to James Bax in Singapore, SIMEX expressed concerns regarding Barings' ability to fund its margin calls. Bax referred the letter to London, and SIMEX received reassurance that opposite positions were held in Japan. Unfortunately, SIMEX officials did not follow up with the Osaka Stock Exchange to verify the existence of those positions. [15]

SIMEX assumed that Barings was hedging and not speculating when it granted an exemption on the number of contracts that Barings could hold. Due to Barings' reputation for being a conservative

---

[13] Bank of England, p. 235.
[14] Fay, *Collapse,* p. 86-90.
[15] Mayer, *The Bankers,* p. 357.

firm, the exchange and clearing houses were operating under a false sense of security. In addition, the speculative position of Barings was hidden due to use of an omnibus account to clear trades. With an omnibus account, the identity of the broker's customers is hidden from the exchange and the clearinghouse.

Several incidents in London also made Leeson's activities easier to manage and hide. The Bank of England had a Large Exposure rule where a bank could not lend more than 25% of its capital to any one entity. However, Barings had requested that an exception be made, arguing that an exchange should not be treated as one entity. Christopher Thompson, the supervisor in charge of Barings activities, acknowledged receipt of the request and said he would review it. In the meantime, he offered an informal concession for Japan, which Barings took the liberty of also applying to Singapore and Hong Kong. Thompson did not respond for a year, and when he did on February 1, 1995, the answer was that an exception could not be made for exchanges and that the positions taken under the informal concession should be unwound.

The second incident was the solo-consolidation of Baring Securities Ltd and Baring Brothers & Co. This allowed them to be treated as one entity for capital adequacy and large exposure purposes. This meant Leeson had access to a larger amount of capital. The Bank of England found the process of solo-consolidation to have been too informal and the results to have facilitated Leeson's fraudulent activities.[16]

Recommended Reforms

Due to incidents of staggering losses to corporate and banking entities as early as 1993, calls for financial reforms, particularly in relation to derivatives, had been ongoing for quite some time. However, it took the Baring Brothers bankruptcy to finally bring about action. The Bank of England, SIMEX and the Group of Thirty all created reports on how regulators, administrators, legislators, international firms and associations could address the issues of regulating financial activities.

The Bank of England wrote a report describing how the losses occurred, why they went unnoticed within and outside Barings, and lessons learned. How the losses occurred and why they went unnoticed has already been explained. The Bank produced five lessons from the bankruptcy. They are:[17]

1) Management teams have a duty to understand fully the businesses they manage;
2) Responsibility for each business activity has to be clearly established and communicated;
3) Clear segregation of duties is fundamental to any effective control system;
4) Relevant internal controls, including independent risk management, have to be established for all business activities;
5) Top management and the Audit Committee have to ensure that significant weaknesses, identified to them by internal audit or otherwise, are resolved quickly.

Despite these simplistic recommendations, at least one and usually several, of the points was the reason why firms lost large sums of money within the derivatives market.

SIMEX, like the other exchanges in the world, implemented changes to decrease default and counterparty risk as well as systemic risks. These changes were made as a direct result of the Barings collapse. SIMEX joined with other exchanges to share information about similar positions participants held on different exchanges. To reduce the risk of non-payment of contracts, SIMEX and other exchanges placed the resources of their entire membership behind the settlements.

---

[16] Bank of England, p. 246-247.
[17] Bank of England Report.

The Group of Thirty based out of Washington, DC, has become particularly concerned with the risks derivatives pose. Since 1995, it has issued several publications to address these problems. The first of these was published in August 1996, and is titled "International Insolvencies in the Financial Sector, Discussion Draft." This document advances fourteen ideas to reduce the risk in the financial sector particularly with regard to derivatives (see Exhibit 2 for the complete list). The second publication printed in April of 1997 is titled "International Insolvencies in the Financial Sector, Summary of Comments from Respondent Countries on Discussion Draft." This publication gives the responses and opinions of those member countries to the proposed reforms. The support for these reforms was generally very strong among all the countries that responded. Germany and other countries did mention several drawbacks to some of the reforms, but they, too, were generally supportive. Ironically, Singapore expressed reservations or outright opposition to five of the reforms (#1, 2, 4, 6 and 9).[18]

A third publication dealing with the aftermath of Barings, is titled "Global Institutions, National Supervision and Systemic Risk" (1997). This discusses reforms that have already been put in place. These reforms include "expanded use of netting and collateral; improvements in measuring risk; greater disclosure of off-balance-sheet risk; substantial increases in equity capital of major financial institutions; financial sector consolidation; and the growth of securitization."[19]

Postscript

ING, a Dutch insurance company, was looking to enter the banking business, especially in Asia. It paid one pound sterling for Baring Brothers and added an additional $1 billion to pay off the debts Baring Brothers had accumulated and restore the bank's capital position. In addition, ING also had to pay $677 million to the holders of subordinated debt that was issued by Barings plc, the holding company, just before the bankruptcy.[20] Legally, ING was not liable for the bonds, but since the bondholders were Barings best customers, ING had to make good on the notes in order to save the customer relationships.[21]

On February 23, 1995, Nick Leeson fled in his Mercedes across the bridge from Singapore to Malaysia. He hid out in Thailand for the next week with his wife and was caught flying into Germany one week later. He was extradited back to Singapore, stood trial and was subsequently sentenced to 6.5 years in a Singapore prison for fraud. In August 1998, Leeson underwent surgery for colon cancer and began receiving chemotherapy. Despite his condition, authorities in Singapore did not release Leeson until June 1999.

Christopher Thompson was the Bank of England supervisor in charge of Baring Brothers at the time of the bankruptcy. He was responsible for allowing Baring Brothers to invest over the legal limit of 25% of its capital in the SIMEX and OSE. The day before the Bank of England report was to be published about the Baring Brothers collapse, Thompson resigned.[22]

---

[18] Group of Thirty, "International Insolvencies in the Financial Sector," *Summary of Comments from Respondent Countries on Discussion Draft*, April 1997, pp. i–iii.
[19] Group of Thirty, *Global Institutions, National Supervision and Systemic Risk*, 1997, p. v.
[20] Hans R. Stoll, "Lost Barings: A Tale in Three Parts Concluding with a Lesson," *The Journal of Derivatives*, Fall 1995, Vol. 3, No.1.
[21] Mayer, *The Bankers*.
[22] Fay, *Collapse*.

Exhibit 1 KEY EVENTS

1989: Nick Leeson is hired as a trade office clerk who settles accounts.

1992: Leeson moves to Singapore where he is responsible for the back office of Baring Futures Singapore (BFS) and the execution of clients' trades.

June 1992: Leeson obtains a license to trade for BFS in the Singapore International Monetary Exchange. He is not authorized by Barings to trade beyond execution of clients' requests.

July 1992: Leeson sets up the error account 88888, used to conduct unauthorized trading.

October 1992: Losses in 88888 reach £4.5 million.

June 1993: Losses in 88888 reach a low point of £34,000.

October 1993: Leeson is given discretion by Barings to decide when and at what price to trade on behalf of Barings. Losses in 88888 are at £24.39 million

1993: Baring Brothers & Co becomes one of the first banks to complete a solo-consolidation (merging its banking business with its securities business) under new regulations.

March 1994: $40 million is lost by CS First Boston in a scheme that had the bank reimbursing a client for unauthorized money-losing derivative trades within its account.

April 1994: Joseph Jett is exposed by his employer, Kidder Peabody, for $350 million of false profit.

Procter & Gamble [P&G] joins the ranks of derivative losers. It loses $157 million in interest rate swaps. Bankers Trust is at the heart of the controversy. P&G refuses to pay arguing misrepresentation on the part of Banker's Trust.

October 1994: Eastman Kodak loses $220 million in swaps and options.

August 1994: Internal audit is conducted at BFS. It criticizes Leeson's control of back and front office activities and expresses concern over reconciliation of funds received from London.

December 1994: Orange County loses $1.7 billion and goes bankrupt on inverse floaters. Merrill Lynch is sued and pays roughly $480 million to Orange County and fines to the SEC.

Dec. 31, 1994: Losses in account 88888 exceed £208 million. Baring executives expected an estimated $20-36 million in profits for the bank from BFS.

Jan 11, 1995: SIMEX sends a letter to BFS explaining that the margin for account 88888 is short $100 million. It is referred to Leeson for a response.

Jan. 13, 1995: The Nikkei is at 19,331 and Barings has 3,024 Nikkei futures contracts.

Jan. 17, 1995: Kobe, Japan suffers a disastrous earthquake. The damage is estimated at over $100 billion. This drives down the Nikkei, causing the value of Barings' futures positions to drop precipitously.

Jan. 20, 1995: Leeson doubles down to 7,135 contracts in the Nikkei, hoping for a reversal of fortune.

Jan. 25, 1995: The Nikkei drops below 18,000. Leeson doubles again to 17,000 (est.) contracts on Jan. 27.

Feb. 17, 1995: Leeson increases the number of contracts to 20,076.

Feb. 23, 1995: Losses approach $1.1 billion, more than twice Baring Bank's capitalization. The bank goes bankrupt and Leeson flees Singapore, two days before his twenty-eighth birthday.

Exhibit 2GROUP OF THIRTY RECOMMENDATIONS FOR REFORM

The following are the Group's recommendations:[23]

1) Insolvency practitioners and governments should ensure that measure taken to improve cooperation, recognition and access will also provide for speed and certainty in international financial insolvencies.

2) Legislators should enact laws to provide for speed and certainty on the issues of judicial cooperation, access and recognition in international financial insolvencies, preferably supporting the norms of universality.

3) Financial regulators should pursue international contact among regulators of different types and with insolvency practitioners.

4) National regulators should work through the international regulatory groups to develop a protocol on the organization, timing and type of assistance they should extend to foreign administrators.

5) National regulators should take the insolvency regime in the home country into account when licensing the operations of foreign financial firms.

6) International financial firms should aim to have up-to-date information on all significant exposures by transaction, agreement, legal entity and jurisdiction, held centrally and in a readily available, standard form.

7) As part of sound credit-risk management, international firms should monitor, measure and manage all sizable exposures by legal entity, form of documentation and law of jurisdiction.

8) National regulators, sometimes working through international regulatory groups, should encourage the speedy adoption of measures to reduce the risks in clearance and settlement.

9) In jurisdictions where there is still doubt about the enforceability of closeout netting, legislators should clarify the position as quickly as possible.

10) In countries that draw no clear distinction between house and client assets, the law should be amended.

11) Laws are needed to make it possible for administrators of financial firms to continue operating in the interests of managing market risk.

12) Just as widespread use of master agreements for over-the-counter transactions has standardized contract terms and enforceability of netting, netting should be extended across agreements, ultimately through development of a single master agreement covering many different products.

13) The international regulatory groups should help establish standards on the handover of proprietary models by insolvent firms.

14) Regulators should consider sponsoring a forum to explore ways to speed up the process of assigning a portfolio of over-the-counter instruments in case of insolvency.

---

[23] Group of Thirty, "International Insolvencies in the Financial Sector," August 1996, pp. 5-14.

III. Managing Multinational Companies and Direct Foreign Investment

CHAPTER
6

Inflation and Currency Stability

Questions:
How serious is the inflation problem in emerging financial markets?
What is the relationship between fiscal deficits, money supply growth, and inflation?
In what sense is inflation a form of taxation?
Can inflation be controlled by pegging the currency value?
What effects does inflation have on debt markets?
What effects does inflation have on foreign exchange markets?
What effects does inflation have on banks?

Introduction

We have so far discussed two basic foundations of all financial markets: law and information. We have seen that financial markets cannot flourish and perform their critical capital allocation function without explicit legal protection of investors and effective institutions of information. We now come to the third foundation, currency stability.

Inflation and Devaluation

When people save and invest, they put aside a certain amount of money with the hope of earning a profit. Eventually they liquidate their investment and receive some amount of money back. Their *nominal* return can be measured by comparing what they received with what they invested, using units of the currency in question. But the currency itself may have lost value.

Loss of currency value has two meanings, one internal and one external. Internal deterioration of currency value, of interest to domestic investors, takes the form of *inflation*: Does the money investors receive have as much power to purchase domestic real goods and services as the money they invested? Inflation measures the extent to which prices have risen, and therefore the extent to which money buys fewer goods and services. External deterioration, of interest to foreign investors, means exchange rate *devaluation*: Does the money investors receive translate into as many dollars, euros, or other strong currency as the money they invested? The exchange rate is the

Introduction **229**

price of local currency as measured in units of dollars, euros, or other strong currency, and devaluation means that this price has fallen.

In characterizing the currencies of industrialized countries as strong, we imply that they are not themselves subject to much deterioration. We must not overlook, however, the bouts of inflation and exchange rate devaluation that the dollar and many of the European currencies have suffered, notably during the 1970s. Since that time, the industrialized countries have adopted numerous agreements to avoid currency deterioration; indeed the launching of the euro in 1999 is the most important such agreement and would not have been possible unless all member countries of the European Union had faith in each other's long-term commitment to currency stability.[1]

Inflation and exchange rate devaluation, the two types of currency deterioration, are closely related. If the condition known as relative *purchasing power parity* (PPP) holds, then inflation and devaluation are highly correlated. This condition is described in the accompanying box, but essentially means that the pace of exchange rate devaluation on average matches the pace of relative inflation, so that the relative ability of a currency to purchase real goods and services at home or abroad is unchanged. Relative PPP typically does not hold in the short term, but it holds better over the longer term, so that the two types of currency deterioration tend to coincide over long horizons.

Inflation and exchange rate devaluation would be perfectly correlated if both were caused by the same single factor: growth of the country's money supply at a rate faster than growth of the real economy. The actual long-term correspondence between inflation and depreciation suggests that just such a common causal influence is at work. This is illustrated in Figure 6.1, which gives a 25-year look at average annual inflation relative to the U.S. dollar[2] and average annual currency devaluation against the dollar of countries for which a 25-year record is available in International Financial Statistics

FIGURE 6.1

Annual inflation versus devaluation of local currency in various countries, 1972–1996

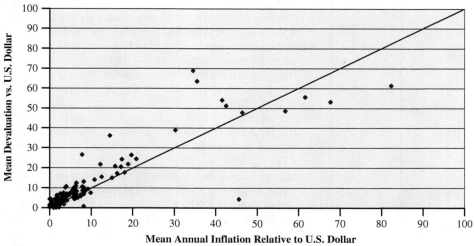

[1]Some authors have argued that this faith is misplaced, that a lack of long-term credibility in fiscal policy will undermine the stable value of the euro. For discussions of this problem and potential remedies, see Calomiris (1999) and Casella (1999).

[2]Relative inflation is calculated as $(1 + \pi_i)/(1 + \pi_S) - 1$, where π_i is the annual realized inflation of country i and π_S is the annual realized inflation of the dollar.

Purchasing Power Parity

Suppose that all tradable goods could be transported across countries with no costs, delays, or impediments. For example, if melons sold for $1 in New York and the equivalent of $5 in Tokyo, melon traders would buy them up in New York and send them instantly to Tokyo where they could be sold for a profit. In such a world the Law of One Price would prevail: Every traded good in the world would sell for the same currency-adjusted price. If prices deviated from this equality, goods *arbitrage* such as that described for melons would drive the prices together. In this perfect world, you could find the exchange rate between any two currencies by simply comparing the price of melons or any other tradable single good.

A related but different "law" is *absolute purchasing power parity (PPP)*. Suppose some typical basket of consumer goods costs P dollars in New York and P^* yen in Tokyo. Then absolute PPP says that the currency exchange rate will be $E = P^*/P$ yen per dollar. The idea is straightforward: Exchange rates are determined by the ratio of the average prices of a sufficiently broad set of goods. The basket of consumer goods is of course the concept on which consumer price indexes are based.

However, absolute PPP does not generally hold, for two reasons. First, consumers do not consume the same bundles of goods across countries or over time, so there is no "universal" basket of goods on which to base all price indexes. Second, any country's consumer price index contains nontraded goods such as housing, which can differ dramatically in cost across countries and whose prices are not driven together by goods arbitrage.

But even if absolute PPP does not hold, a weaker condition may prevail. Whatever the present exchange rate level, it may be that annual *changes* in exchange rates reflect primarily changes in the average price levels of the two countries. Suppose that E does not equal P^*/P but is related to it, and that we can approximate the relationship by $E = kP^*/P$, where k is a scalar that is slow to change and reflects differences such as the relative levels of industrialization or productivity. Then if inflation proceeds at an annual rate π in the first country and π^* in the second, the price levels after one year will be $P(1 + \pi)$ in the first country and $P^*(1 + \pi^*)$ in the second. We might reasonably expect that the exchange rate should move to $kP^*(1 + \pi^*)/P(1 + \pi)$, that is, last year's exchange rate times the relative inflation $(1 + \pi^*)/(1 + \pi)$.

The claim that the equilibrium exchange rate evolves according to relative inflation is known as *relative PPP*. Figure 6.1 can be interpreted as a simple examination of this claim. In that figure, the 25-year average annual relative inflation $(1 + \pi^*)/(1 + \pi) - 1$ is plotted against the 25-year average devaluation of the local currency against the dollar.

This long-term relationship is quite close on average. When mean annual devaluation is regressed on mean relative inflation for this set of countries, forcing the intercept to zero, the regression coefficient is 0.98 with a standard error of 0.04. Statistically, the average relationship is not distinguishable from a one-to-one equivalence. Furthermore, $R^2 = 0.76$, suggesting a high level of explanatory power for this relationship. The regression line is shown in Figure 6.1.

The number $k = EP/P^*$ used above has a name. It is called the *real exchange rate*; that is, the exchange rate adjusted by the ratio of the consumer price indexes in the two countries. PPP is equivalent to the claim that the real exchange rate is constant. When the real exchange rate is not constant, it implies that a country's exports are gaining or losing competitiveness. We will use this concept in Chapter 8 to examine the role of exchange rate competitiveness in financial crises.

(excluding a few outliers for which either mean was greater than 100 percent per annum). As can be seen, the relationship is strong, confirming that relative PPP tends to work reasonably well over long time horizons.

One reason why inflation and devaluation are not as well correlated in the short term is that the spot exchange rate, like all financial prices, reflects not only current and recent events but also expected future events. If investors believe that inflation is going to be much worse in the future than it has been recently, they will not wait for inflation to rise but will mark down the value of the currency immediately.

Thus, large currency moves sometimes occur in sudden jumps, when a new event or a new piece of information suddenly changes investors' opinions about future inflation. Like all financial markets, foreign exchange markets are subject to sudden changes of sentiment and unpredictable shifts in perceptions of the future. The abruptness of adjustment in foreign exchange markets compared with the more gradual realization of changes in inflation is a primary reason why inflation and devaluation do not match as closely in the short term.

Inflation Uncertainty

The most damaging effects of inflation come from its uncertainty. If it were known for certain that a particular currency would experience inflation at a rate exactly 10 percent higher than that of the dollar over the next 20 years, then the exchange rate might devalue quite smoothly at a rate of 10 percent a year against the dollar. All investors and other parties could plan on this and reflect it in their contracts. The interest rate on the local currency would be set at 10 percent above dollar interest rates so that both internal and external lenders would be exactly compensated for the currency value lost.

But life is not that simple. Investors must take a guess at future inflation and set today's interest rates and exchange rates accordingly. This is not too difficult if inflation is low, because low inflation tends to be stable and hence fairly predictable. But the higher the rate of inflation, the more variable it becomes.

Figure 6.2 shows the average annual inflation of many countries over 25 years, plotted against the standard deviation of annual inflation over the same period,

FIGURE 6.2

Mean versus standard deviation of annual inflation in various countries, 1972–1996

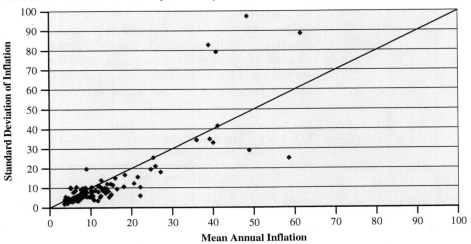

calculated for those countries for which a 25-year record is available in International Financial Statistics and excluding a few outliers for which either the mean or standard deviation exceeds 100 percent. The regression in this case shows a coefficient of 1.01 with a standard error of 0.05, so that again the relationship is not distinguishable from a one-to-one relationship in which the standard deviation simply equals the mean. The R^2 is 0.66. The regression line is shown in Figure 6.2. This illustrates quite clearly that high inflation tends to be variable inflation.

Extent of Inflation in Emerging Financial Markets

How serious is the inflation problem in EFMs generally? Are there patterns that we can study and learn from? It is useful to describe the overall magnitudes involved. The IFS database goes back to 1970, so that we can take a long view, but in many cases part of the data is missing, which complicates analysis. However, for 98 countries we have uninterrupted data from 1970 through 1995, and the comments in this section are based on these. The descriptive statistics for inflation in these 98 countries for 1970 to 1995 are summarized in Table 6.1 below.

A first observation from Table 6.1 is a further confirmation that the standard deviation of inflation (13.3 percent) is approximately equal to the mean level of inflation (14.7 percent). But it is also instructive to note that the median inflation over all countries (11.0 percent) is less than the mean (14.7 percent). This suggests that the inflation rate is not normally distributed among countries, but is skewed to the left, so that there are more low-inflation countries than high-inflation ones. This is confirmed by the positive skewness statistic in Table 6.1. Also, there is excess kurtosis, meaning that there are more extreme observations than a normal distribution would imply. This is caused by a number of unusually large observations, as is clear from the raw data.

Table 6.1 also shows descriptive statistics for the natural logarithm of 1 + inflation. For a small level of inflation, $\pi \approx \log(1 + \pi)$, so that the two numbers are close. But taking the logarithm moderates the swings out to large values. We see from the table that the median is somewhat closer to the mean in the logarithmic column, and that skewness and excess kurtosis are both reduced.

Table 6.2 shows the primary descriptive statistics for overlapping 10-year periods. We note that the means are surprisingly similar from one period to the next. Taken by itself, this would suggest that the distribution of inflation is quite stationary. However, we see in the next column that median inflation has been falling somewhat. This suggests that the median country is making progress in controlling inflation, but that this effect on the mean is offset by a smaller number of countries for which inflation is more of a problem recently than it was before. That interpretation is confirmed by the standard deviation, which rises slightly over time.

TABLE 6.1   Mean Inflation Statistics, 1970–1995
                 (*Means of 98 Countries*)

	Annual Inflation (%)	Log(1 + inflation)
Mean	14.7%	0.121
Median	11.0	0.100
Standard Deviation	13.3	0.091
Skewness	1.1	0.879
Excess Kurtosis	2.1	1.417

This review of the data confirms our intuition that inflation was particularly troublesome in the 1970s for the EFMs as it was for the industrialized world; that the 1980s continued to be inflationary for the developing world although inflation came more under control in industrialized countries; and that the 1990s have seen a reduction in inflation for most but not all EFMs, as many countries privatized and pursued fiscal reforms and thereby reduced their budget deficits and inflationary pressures.

The Appendix lists the country-by-country data that are summarized in the first column of Table 6.2 (i.e., the mean rate of inflation for each country in the four overlapping decades shown). This enables us to see which countries have become significantly more inflationary in recent years, contrary to the general trend. Such countries include Venezuela, Ecuador, Suriname, and Uruguay as well as Sudan, Sierra Leone, Turkey, and Lebanon. The table also shows some countries that have made particularly impressive progress in controlling inflation, including Saudi Arabia, Bahrain, Burkina Faso, Niger, Barbados, Dominica, and Korea.

Economists have studied at some length why inflation and inflation volatility should damage economic growth and capital allocation. While there is no unanimity in the profession, the following connections summarize the most widely held views. First, perhaps the most important connection is that uncertainty about the prices of goods and services makes it substantially more difficult for markets to do their job of optimally allocating resources. Uncertainty about price signals interferes with Adam Smith's invisible hand in the market for goods and services.

The same is true in the market for money and capital. If inflation is uncertain, real interest rates are uncertain and capital allocations are similarly suboptimal, but in the case of interest rates another factor is at work. Uncertainty about real interest rates will make investors nervous, which will be expressed as a risk premium in all rates of return, raising investors' required returns above where they would normally be. We will look at this phenomenon in more detail later in this chapter, but for now it should be clear that any such risk premium will make capital needlessly expensive and will depress and distort investment.

Second, inflation distorts capital gains taxation. If all prices trend upward, then the selling of a capital asset that had little or no real gain in value will nevertheless generate a taxable capital gain. This will make investors reluctant to sell capital assets at all, which impedes the work of capital markets.

Third, as discussed more fully in the following section, inflation imposes a tax on everyone who holds noninterest-bearing money, so people will wish to hold as little such money as possible. Too much cost and effort will be devoted to moving money rapidly before it loses further value.

To understand the magnitude of the above effects, empirical studies have tried to examine the effect of inflation and inflation volatility on economic growth. This is a

TABLE 6.2   **Mean Inflation Statistics in Overlapping 10-Year Periods**
(Means of 98 Countries)

	Mean of 10-Year Means	*Median of 10-Year Medians*	*Mean of 10-Year Standard Deviations*
1970–1979	13.3%	9.4%	9.4%
1976–1985	15.3	10.4	8.9
1980–1989	15.7	8.3	10.7
1986–1995	15.4	7.2	10.6

difficult job because economic growth is affected by many different variables. Furthermore, inflation and its volatility are highly correlated, as we have seen, so it is difficult to disentangle which has the actual impact on growth.

Despite these difficulties, many recent studies have found a significant negative correlation between inflation and growth.[3] Separating the effect of average inflation level from inflation volatility was accomplished in a further study, which used quarterly data.[4] This more frequent sampling shows volatility to be on average higher than the mean level of inflation and less highly correlated with it. This study found that both higher inflation and greater inflation volatility slow economic growth, though the impact of volatility was greater and the effect of the inflation level could only be detected if the level exceeded 10 percent.

The connection between high inflation and low output growth for EFMs is also apparent in simple comparisons of recent GDP growth rates across countries. *The Economist* reported in its August 21, 1999, issue that a sample of 25 EFMs posted an average GDP growth rate for the most recent year of 0.58 percent. Only three countries within this group (Russia, Turkey, and Venezuela) had CPI inflation rates in excess of 20 percent (the rates were 126.3 percent, 65.0 percent, and 23.0 percent, respectively), and these three countries all experienced substantially negative GDP growth rates (−3.9 percent, −8.5 percent, and −8.2 percent, respectively).

Thus, currency stability matters. Financial markets in high-inflation countries become restricted in ways that we will study later in this chapter, with serious consequences for capital allocation and economic growth. Investors value credible assurances that the currency in which they are repaid is not going to be worth a significant and indeterminate amount less than the value of the currency they invested.

Causes and Cures

What Causes Inflation?

If high and variable inflation is costly, why does it occur in the first place? The literature on the causes of inflation, like other literatures in economics, is populated by various schools of thought. Despite the many areas of disagreement within the inflation literature, there is substantial agreement on the narrowly focused question of what causes the high inflation that has plagued EFMs: excessive growth of the supply of money.

Milton Friedman famously remarked that inflation is "always and everywhere a monetary phenomenon." This statement can be viewed in two ways: as a definitional statement and as a causal theory. By definition, inflation (which measures the value of money) is a "monetary" phenomenon. But that does not necessarily mean that growth in the supply of money (controlled by the central bank) *causes* countries "always and everywhere" to experience inflation.

Many economists argue, for example, that real money demand (the ratio of desired money relative to the price level) relative to real income varies over time (the reciprocal of that ratio is defined as *velocity*). That variation implies that the money supply and the price level need not move together in lockstep. Other influences on the price level, therefore, can cause inflation to occur, even when money balances are not changing. For example, if fiscal policy causes output to expand, prices would tend to rise even if money balances are held constant. Or, if the world were physically to run

---

[3]For example see Fischer (1993), Motley (1994), and Barro (1995).
[4]Judson and Orphanides (1996).

short on basic inputs such as petroleum and minerals, the costs of those inputs would increase and this would be reflected in a rise of prices generally, alongside a decline in output because these inputs affect the great majority of physical goods produced. (This phenomenon, which gripped the world in the 1970s, became known as stagflation.) Similarly, if goods become more abundant and accessible because of a rise in productivity, then holding constant the level of money supplied in the economy, prices will tend to fall as output rises. So the connection between money supply changes and price changes is far from perfect.

These qualifications to Friedman's view of the causal role of money growth for inflation, however, are mainly relevant for explaining relatively small (single-digit) variations in inflation around its trend, associated with differences in money supply growth and inflation.[5] The significant differences in the *trends* of inflation across countries are "always and everywhere" traceable to different *growth rates* of the supplies of money. In particular, when one looks at the experiences of EFMs—where inflation rates can vary from zero percent per year to thousands of percent per year—there is a very clear and close connection between differences in money growth and differences in inflation.

It is important to recognize, however, that money growth itself has a deeper cause. High-inflation EFMs do not increase their money supplies unwittingly. They use high money growth as a fiscal device—a means of paying for expenditures when direct taxation is not sufficient. Thus, fiscal deficits are the ultimate driver of monetary expansion and hence inflation in EFMs. We note that at an early stage of his career Milton Friedman advocated a government debt rule as a means of controlling inflation, in recognition of the threat that rising government deficits pose to stable monetary policy.

Monetary Growth and Fiscal Deficits

In the modern world, as throughout much of history, money is a creation of government, so government is responsible for its quantity and quality. Governments do not usually set out to generate ballooning deficits, with their inflationary consequences, out of malice or stupidity; rather, deficits result from the political dilemma of managing government finances. Governments have legitimate goals that propel expenditures. They also face purely political constraints as constituents often demand pecuniary rewards for supporting a group of politicians. Most governments try to benefit as many groups, projects, and regions as possible so they can enjoy greater political support, while taxing as little as possible (since taxation is politically unpopular). This combination of large expenditures and small tax receipts produces deficits in the government budget. It is an ancient problem. The Roman Empire, as it tried to unify Europe during the first three centuries A.D., spent more than it could collect in taxes; it solved the shortfall by minting coins with less and less gold content. This degradation provides us with a physical record of currency devaluation during the period, which was mirrored over the long term by inflation of prices measured in such coins.[6]

Modern countries in Western Europe have had similar problems. They have a strong political commitment to state-sponsored social programs that have proven increasingly expensive. They have varied substantially in their willingness to raise taxes sufficiently to pay for such programs, and the resulting policy differences have

---

[5]The literature on the patterns and causes of cyclical variation in inflation around its trend is large. Important contributions include Phillips (1958), Phelps (1967), Friedman (1968), and Lucas (1972). The recent literature emphasizes that the cyclical pattern of inflation around its trend, particularly the correlation between inflation and economic activity over the cycle, and the extent to which money supply growth affects short-term inflation and output change are influenced by expectations of inflation.

[6]See DeCecco (1985).

236

led to differing rates of inflation that in turn caused their currencies' values to move away from each other during the 1970s and 1980s. Only in the 1990s have they sworn to stabilize their currencies by agreeing to common targets for inflation and budget deficits as part of their historic *Economic and Monetary Union* (EMU).

The United States experienced high inflation during the surge in spending on the Civil War; but this was followed by very low inflation, and sometimes even deflation, from the end of the Civil War (1865) until the beginning of World War I (1914). America experienced inflation in both world wars, but its worst bout of inflation in the 20th century came at the crest of enthusiasm for state intervention in the economy, during the 1960–1980 period. The cost of the war in Vietnam along with a domestic "Great Society" war on poverty in the 1960s caused serious budget deficits, and these spurred inflation through their direct effects on the demand for output and through the pressures they placed on the central bank to expand the money supply. But by the end of the 1990s, the United States had moved into a budget surplus and its rate of inflation had fallen to less than 2 percent per year. The long-term credibility of a low-inflation monetary policy stance on the part of the Federal Reserve has been buttressed by the government's strong fiscal position.

Developing countries, with less-developed tax bases but social problems and economic needs more urgent than those of the developed world, have particular difficulty in balancing their budgets. Furthermore, as noted in Chapter 3, developing countries became even more committed to statism than developed countries in the post–World War II era. Only by drastic privatization programs have some of them been able to bring their budget deficits under control. Thus, the problem of government budget deficits has been more intractable in EFMs than elsewhere.

In an open market economy a government facing a budget deficit has only three options: It can spend its international reserves, it can borrow, or it can *monetize* the deficit. Monetizing the deficit usually means that the government sells bonds to its own central bank. The central bank pays for the bonds by crediting the government's deposit account at the central bank. The government then writes checks against this account to pay for its purchases; the checks are deposited in commercial banks. The commercial banks redeposit a fraction of these as reserves at the central bank. The net effect is that the money supply is expanded, as both commercial banks and central bank expand their balance sheets. It is the modern equivalent of printing money to pay government expenses. Monetizing the deficit leads directly to inflation, as the larger money supply is spread over the same quantity of real goods.

Drawing down foreign exchange reserves or borrowing from bond investors other than the central bank to finance the deficit avoids the immediate inflationary impact of monetizing it, but neither action can be continued indefinitely. Reserves disappear when drawn down repeatedly. Borrowing abroad can only be done up to a certain limit, beyond which arm's-length lenders first raise the risk premium and finally refuse to lend more at any rate. Borrowing domestically has more scope, particularly when the government can sell its bonds to banks, but even this can be done only up to a certain limit. The real value of government debt outstanding cannot continue to increase unless the public expects future taxes to be levied to service that debt.

Therefore, drawing down reserves or borrowing can only be used as a temporary expedient unless the deficit is so small that sustainability ceases to be an issue. Sooner or later, a government with large deficits must turn to monetization, and the markets will see this coming. The currency value may fall when reserves fall even though inflation has not yet been realized. Most developing countries have already borrowed up to prudent limits (given their capacity to tax in the future to repay that debt) and do not have excess reserves, so monetization and consequent inflation are often the only option.

The relationship between deficits and monetary growth is much closer for EFMs than for developed economies. In developed economies, independent central banks typically maintain a low long-run target for the inflation rate and vary monetary policy over the business cycle in an effort to smooth economic fluctuations. The central bankers of developed countries can act independently of deficits because their governments' deficits are not a binding constraint on the long-run growth of the supply of money. In contrast, in many EFMs the need to spend without any politically viable prospect of paying for those expenditures with current or future taxes makes monetary policy subordinate to fiscal expediency. Many EFM central banks have little discretion over monetary policy, since there is a direct link between the amount the government spends and the amount of currency the central bank must print.

In What Sense Is Inflation a Tax?

Inflation takes value away from those who hold unprotected financial assets including money. For example, if you have a checking account containing 50,000 pesos and the peso loses 10 percent of its value while you hold the account, you have less ability to purchase real goods and services than you had at the beginning of the period. The value loss is 5,000 pesos. Where did this value go?

In the first instance, the bank in which you hold the account captures the value. This is why banks often prosper in times of high inflation, an idea to which we return in detail at the end of this chapter. On the other hand, the bank is required to redeposit a fraction of its deposits as noninterest-bearing reserves at the central bank. To the extent it holds such reserves, the central bank (government) collects the missing value. This makes inflation a kind of tax.

To be more precise, the quantity of money on which the government captures inflation tax is the sum of currency plus bank reserves deposited at the central bank—that is, all liabilities of the central bank that do not pay interest. This is known as the *monetary base* (*M*). Suppose the government decides to create some additional quantity of money (ΔM) to pay for its budget deficit. Then

$$\text{Deficit} = \Delta M = (\Delta M/M) \times M = \pi M$$

where we have associated the growth rate of the monetary base ($\Delta M/M$) with the rate of inflation (π). The monetary base M is the quantity being taxed and the inflation rate π is the tax rate. The inflation tax is precisely what pays for the deficit. We can also put the equation shown into *real* terms by dividing through by the price level P:

$$\text{Deficit}/P = \Delta M/P = (\Delta M/M) \times (M/P) = \pi(M/P)$$

Thus, inflation is not just the by-product of budget deficits; it is a solution to budget deficits. Inflation is a very expedient form of taxation: It is almost costless to collect and its effects are widely spread through the economy. It causes less political protest than the explicit effort to extract taxes from some target group. Indeed, it has such agreeable political qualities that governments can become quite addicted to financing their expenditures in this way. This is why inflation becomes endemic in most EFMs.

We have so far considered only noninterest-bearing claims because holders of interest-bearing claims can be compensated for inflation through the interest rate. As we shall examine later in this chapter, interest rates normally include both a real component and a component to compensate for expected inflation. For example, if the investor requires a real return of 4 percent and inflation is expected to equal 6 percent during the coming year, then one-year interest rates should be at least

10 percent. Provided actual inflation turns out to be 6 percent, such an investor is not taxed by inflation.[7]

But suppose there is a surprise burst of inflation. Perhaps actual inflation turns out to be 15 percent. Then the investor suffers a negative real return of 5 percent—a real value loss. If the government issued the debt instrument, then the government captures the missing value since it repays its obligations in a currency with much less real value than expected. Such a surprise burst of inflation could be described as a partial government default: Because of the surprise inflation, the government simply does not give back to the investor the full value that the investor had expected. Alternatively, we could call this the *unanticipated inflation tax,* whose base is *M* plus the total amount of interest-bearing government debt.

The real revenues that can be earned from the unanticipated inflation tax on domestic money and bonds can be large. For example, Robert Eisner argued that the inflationary burst in the United States in the 1960s and 1970s created one-time capital gains for the U.S. government that turned apparent deficits into surpluses, after properly accounting for the capital gains.[8] But large capital gains from surprise inflation are not a continuing source of revenue. Bondholders will raise yields in anticipation of higher inflation, and—following Abraham Lincoln's maxim about the difficulty of "fooling all of the people all of the time"—those yields will compensate bondholders for any inflation-induced capital losses on principal. And money holdings will decline in real terms from their pre-surprise levels, leaving the government with a smaller future steady stream of revenue from the anticipated inflation tax on money balances.

It is sometimes said that government debt is free of default risk because governments have unlimited power to tax and unlimited power to print money. But consider the sequence of sources to which a government may turn when it needs to make payments, particularly payments on its debt. The first recourse is taxation. But explicit taxation has a definite limit, beyond which political protest and noncompliance will frustrate even an authoritarian government. When this point is reached, the government can print money and collect the inflation tax.

However, the inflation tax cannot generate an infinite amount of real resources for the government. People will defend themselves against it by trying to reduce the amount of real currency and checking balances that they hold. The quantity M/P will shrink as they do this. At a sufficiently high rate of inflation, further increases in π may be more than offset by reductions in M/P. When the government cannot extract more real resources to cover its real deficit, what happens? At such a point the government is likely to save real resources by defaulting on its external debt. Thus, there is a subtle connection between inflation and default. Up to a point, inflation is a default substitute, but this cannot continue indefinitely.

Government debt denominated in local currency rarely suffers default because the government can always pay it by printing more local currency.[9] But foreign currency debt must be paid with real resources. Empirical studies of sovereign default risk on international debt find that domestic inflation is a powerful predictor of sovereign yield spreads: Countries that are fiscally weak display high rates of inflation.[10] A high-inflation country has likely come near the end of its fiscal rope; having exhausted its

---

[7]Except, of course, to the extent that the investor must pay income taxes on the entire 10 percent.

[8]Eisner (1986).

[9]In August 1998 the Russian government defaulted on its ruble-denominated treasury bills (GKOs) and then offered to settle them for a tiny fraction of face value.

[10]Cantor and Packer (1996).

capacity to tax directly or through inflation, any further fiscal deficit increase may have to be financed with outright default.

Coping with Inflation through Indexing

Some governments have attempted to deal with price instability by inflation *indexing*. That is, contracts of many kinds (including bank accounts and government debts) can come with built-in adjustment clauses keyed to the rate of inflation, so that wages, interest rates, and other cash payments rise to compensate for the currency's loss of purchasing power. Such indexing is always imperfect and generally favors the rich and sophisticated over the poor and uneducated. But even more important, it raises the government's cost of wages, interest, and the like, so that the nominal deficit in the next period is even greater and requires yet more printing of money. In these conditions inflation can soon escalate into hyperinflation.

The fundamental problem with indexing is that it attempts to protect people from the inflation tax while still collecting the tax. Viewed from this perspective, inflation must rise to ever-higher levels to succeed in solving the fiscal problem it is supposed to solve. The better people's protection against the tax, the more the inflation tax base will decline as inflation rises, and the higher the inflation tax rate must go to have the desired effect. That is why indexing often leads to acceleration of inflation.

Countries that suffer hyperinflation typically try to cure it with radical new plans. Such plans may include a variety of elements such as price freezes, business–union pacts, currency pegging, and extensive rhetoric. But the only countries that have succeeded in taming inflation have been those that committed themselves to the elimination of the fiscal deficits, primarily through privatization. This characterizes Bolivia (1985), Mexico (1989), and Argentina (1991). Brazil tried numerous stabilization plans in the 1970s and 1980s, but continued to suffer significant inflation primarily because it had not yet been sufficiently resolute about privatization and fiscal reform (including at the state level, since it has a federal political system); and Brazil continued to be addicted to inflation indexing.

Monetization of Brazilian deficits became so predictable during the 1970s that the exchange rate depreciated and the price level inflated in reaction to government debt growth even before it was monetized.[11] The extent of the inflation acceleration produced a substantial decline in the inflation tax base. Monetary velocity nearly doubled during the 1970s, as the real demand for currency and zero-interest reserves fell. Depositors with sufficient wealth were able to substitute away from zero-interest or low-interest cash and deposits, and into indexed bonds or bank repurchase agreements backed by treasury bills, which earned market returns that compensated for expected inflation. These opportunities, especially in the repurchase market, accounted for the remarkable increase in money velocity that occurred in the 1970s.

Even when indexing does not lead to hyperinflation, it can have the perverse effect of institutionalizing inflation, making it far more difficult to eradicate. Indexing creates a momentum effect whereby inflation can persist long after the underlying fiscal imbalances have been corrected.

An example may help to clarify this point. As illustrated in Figure 6.3, the Chilean government of Salvador Allende increased the fiscal deficit from 2.8 percent of GDP in 1970 to a peak of 12.8 percent of GDP in 1972. The inflationary impact followed

---

[11]Calomiris and Domowitz (1989)

240   *Chapter 6   Inflation and Currency Stability*

FIGURE 6.3

Deficits and inflation in Chile

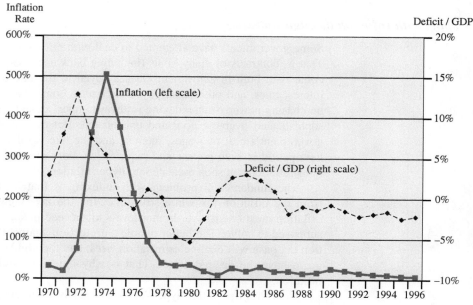

with a one- to two-year lag and was very largely due to indexing: Inflation rose from 20 percent in 1971 to 505 percent in 1974. The deficit fell to zero or even a slight surplus by 1975 and was in the 4 to 5 percent surplus range by 1979–1980. This should have brought inflation down more promptly, but indexing had created considerable momentum. Inflation fell steadily from 1974 to 1982, but did not fall to 10 percent until 1982. By that time the deficit was rising moderately but then subsided into balance by 1986 and was in surplus for every year thereafter through 1996. Inflation, however, remained stubbornly in double digits, although it finally reached single digits by 1995.

Having identified fiscal deficits as the ultimate cause of high, persisting inflation, we must add that the connection is often not immediate or direct, at least in the short term. Not only are there momentum effects, but in an open economy such as Chile's the time path of local inflation is affected by variables such as international oil prices, export prices, dollar inflation, and the currency exchange regime selected by the government.[12] Since the latter issue is particularly important to EFMs, we shall now examine it in some detail.

Currency Exchange Regimes

Fixed Exchange Rates as Inflation Control

We have seen that inflation and currency devaluation are intimately connected in the sense that expected future inflation will depress today's value of the currency. But it turns out that causality can work both ways. Not only can inflation cause devaluation,

---

[12]For a careful analysis of all such factors in the case of Chile, see Budnevich and Godoy (1995).

but devaluation can also cause inflation. A simple way to visualize this reverse connection is as follows: Imagine a small, open economy where *all* goods are traded on international markets. In such an economy, local prices would be set outside the country and simply reflect a translation of world prices into local currency. In this setting, any devaluation of the currency would immediately cause local prices to adjust upward. While this is an extreme example, it does show why devaluation causes inflation, especially in small, open economies.

Partly in recognition of this, many EFM governments seek to control inflation by anchoring the value of their currencies. The most radical and effective way to do this is simply to use another country's currency. Panama, for example, uses the U.S. dollar as its currency and hence follows roughly the U.S. level of inflation. With this type of currency regime, monetizing a fiscal deficit is not possible: There is no local currency to print. This means that any fiscal deficit must be paid out of foreign exchange reserves or borrowed in dollars. Panama was able to run budget deficits equal to 5 to 10 percent of GDP in the 1970s when banks were lending freely to developing countries; indeed the deficit reached 13.3 percent of GDP in 1979. But after the debt crisis of the 1980s such deficits could no longer be financed. Panama put its fiscal house in order because it had no choice—there was no way a deficit could be financed by printing money. Indeed, Panama was obliged to run a fiscal surplus in the first half of the 1990s, enabling some government debt to be repaid.

In countries suffering serious currency weakness, a strong currency such as the dollar may come into general use informally as a medium of exchange. In Russia, for example, dollars have circulated throughout the 1990s, particularly $100 bills, which became in many ways the safest way to store wealth—much safer than deposits in Russian banks, which collapsed in 1998. Similarly Argentina experienced significant "dollarization" during its hyperinflation of the late 1980s. The widespread acceptance of the dollar prepared the way for Argentina to adopt a currency board in the 1990s.

A *currency board* is a legal framework that enables local currency to be issued only under strictly limited circumstances. The goal is to ensure that local currency is at all times fully or almost fully backed by reserves of a strong currency such as the dollar, so that the two become nearly perfect substitutes. It involves a legislative commitment to exchange the two currencies at a fixed rate, usually one-for-one, combined with restrictions on the issuing authority (the currency board) such that new local currency is issued only in the presence of sufficient reserves of external currency, so that the exchange commitment is always credible.

Currency boards are sometimes adopted by small countries that want a local currency for reasons of symbolism and pride, but which in substance are willing to use the strong currency of another country. Thus, Bermuda, Brunei Darussalam, Cayman Islands, Djibouti, the Eastern Caribbean Central Bank, Estonia, the Falkland Islands, Gibraltar, Hong Kong, and Lithuania have adopted currency boards. The related external currencies have included the dollar, the German mark, and the pound sterling.[13]

These arrangements come closer in spirit to the classic gold standard than any others in the modern era. Like the gold standard under the classic "rules of the game" of the pre–World War I era, currency boards exert a harsh discipline by forestalling the option to monetize fiscal deficits. Deficits can only be paid for by borrowing or by drawing down the government's accumulated reserves. Insofar as government reserve holdings are drawn down to pay foreign debt (a form of capital outflow), domestic currency must be retired, so that the money supply actually shrinks.

---

[13]See Baliño and Enoch (1997) for a detailed analysis of currency boards.

The contractionary effect of this discipline means that countries that adopt this system (e.g., Argentina) must be prepared to suffer severe recession in times of stress, which tests the will of the government to maintain the currency board system. For this to work, there must be a strong anti-inflationary popular will. That was certainly present in Argentina in the 1990s given the suffering from inflation during the previous decades, but this will was severely tested by the speculative attack on the Argentine peso during the "tequila crisis" of 1995. By the end of the century, currency boards in Argentina, Estonia, Hong Kong, and Lithuania had all successfully withstood speculative attack, although Argentina remained in recession and continued to build its debt to cover deficits.

Since a currency board immediately translates deficits into debt or contraction of the money supply, it can hardly be recommended to a country whose fiscal deficits are quite large; this would quickly create unmanageable stresses. When President Suharto of Indonesia proposed to adopt a currency board arrangement after the collapse of the Indonesian currency and financial institutions in 1997, the IMF and most economists opposed this on the grounds that the country did not have sufficient reforms in place to create the stability that a currency board can reinforce but not single-handedly create.

While currency boards are still somewhat rare, a majority of EFM governments in the 1990s adopted some form of "peg" to the dollar or other strong currency that permitted some of the benefits of a currency board without the same rigidities. This usually amounted to little more than an announcement that the government would manage its foreign exchange market in such a way that currency would be bought or sold by the government in an effort to keep its price at or close to some stated value. The credibility of this promise is a function of the country's international reserves and its fiscal policies. Countries with large international reserves and good fundamentals that are determined to defend their currencies' values may be able to withstand major assaults on the pegged value, but no country has unlimited reserves nor unlimited will to spend reserves in this way.

When a country with a pegged currency spends reserves to defend the currency's value, this intervention is usually *sterilized*. This means that the central bank buys local currency bonds from local banks in quantities about equal to the foreign reserves it has drawn down, so that the overall monetary base (central bank liability structure) remains unchanged. Both foreign reserves and domestic bonds are assets of the central bank; sterilization is the replacement of a disappearing asset over which the central bank has little control (reserves) with an asset that the central bank can increase at will (government bonds purchased through open market operations). This action prevents conversions of domestic currency into foreign currency from having the contractionary effect on the money supply just described for a country with a currency board. But sterilization violates the classic gold standard "rules of the game," under which the deflationary action of reserve outflows is not offset. In other words, sterilization makes currency stabilization less painful, but it is very much akin to monetization of deficits. Sterilization can undermine the long-run credibility of the exchange peg by sending a bad signal about long-run monetary policy, and by increasing the ratio of domestic money to foreign reserves, which can encourage further reserve outflows. Sterilization cannot be pursued for very long without causing a collapse of the exchange rate peg.

If a country adopts another country's currency or establishes a currency board, it has literally surrendered the right to an independent monetary policy. Currency pegs other than currency boards formally permit the government to have a monetary policy separate from that of the external currency; that is, to print money through sterilization or otherwise to prevent an economic contraction. But unless the monetary policy adopted is very similar to that of the strong-currency country it will sooner or later

become impossible to maintain the peg. The underlying idea is that differential inflation rates will sooner or later pull currencies apart (i.e., that relative PPP holds).

Crawling Pegs and Trading Bands

Crawling Pegs. A variant on the currency peg that tries to accommodate differences
in inflation is the *crawling peg*. This is an arrangement in which the pegged exchange
rate is moved slowly but frequently in response to actual realized inflation, or to a
longer-term inflation target, relative to inflation in the strong-currency country,
following the relative PPP formula discussed earlier. The idea is to keep the peg at the
relative PPP equilibrium point. This can work effectively if local inflation is not too
severe and if the equilibrium real exchange rate remains relatively constant (i.e., if k—
as defined on page 230—does not vary much over time). Otherwise, however, it will be
hard to maintain and likely will be undone by uncertainty. High, uncertain, and variable
inflation is likely eventually to overwhelm any peg system, even a crawling peg. If we
cannot be sure where inflation is headed and what the real purchasing power of the
currency should be in the future, then we cannot have confidence in the crawling peg.

The main argument in favor of a currency peg, fixed or crawling, is that it provides an anchor, enabling the local currency to capture at least some of the credibility
of the stronger currency. Conceivably, this can control both actual inflation and inflationary expectations, which explains the great popularity of pegs. However, the arguments against pegging are also strong.[14] First, pegging severely limits the scope of
monetary policy, as noted above. Second, it makes a country vulnerable to economic
shocks taking place in the strong-currency country that need not otherwise have
affected it. Third, and most importantly, it offers a tempting target for speculative
attack: When a currency weakens against its peg, speculators pile on, selling the currency spot and forward with very little risk of its strengthening and with the possibility
of huge gains if the peg breaks.

Indeed, the speculators involved in currency crises usually include and sometimes
consist primarily of local individuals, companies, and banks, many of whom are intimately involved with the government. These insiders are often among the first to see a
crisis coming because of a growing perception that the peg is holding the currency at
too high a level, and they rush to sell their local currency and hedge their hard-
currency borrowing before it is too late. This phenomenon, known as *capital flight,* is
made possible by the obliging central bank, which continues to buy local currency at a
price increasingly deemed too high by the market. This portrayal of capital flight by
insiders explains why some observers described Indonesia's proposal to establish a
currency board at the peak of the Asian crisis in 1997 as an "exit strategy for wealthy
Indonesians."

Finally, when a currency peg does break, the consequences can be very severe. We
will look at EFM financial crises in detail in Chapter 8, but there is no doubt that some
of them were made much worse by first holding a peg in place and then releasing it.
The resulting cascade can swamp even the best-run governments and result in
extended periods of high interest rates and economic contraction much more severe
than would have occurred if the currency had not been pegged in the first place.

In short, successful pegs are excellent and broken pegs can be catastrophic. The
moral would seem to be that a country should not adopt a peg unless (1) its fundamentals

---

[14]See Mishkin (1998) for an excellent statement of the case against pegging.

are in very good shape, in particular with little or no fiscal deficit, and (2) the country is prepared to suffer periods of stress when the peg is attacked, including high interest rates and economic contraction. If these conditions are met, as they have been so far in Hong Kong and Argentina, then the country can and perhaps should adopt the strongest form of peg (currency board) to give it as much credibility as possible.

Trading Bands.   When these conditions are not met, countries sometimes opt for a soft form of pegging, a *trading band.* This means that the country declares a fundamental exchange rate that it believes to be sustainable and then promises to defend a band of, say, plus or munus 10 percent around it. If the currency falls to the bottom of the band, the government promises to intervene by buying currency; if it rises to the top, then the government will intervene by selling currency. The central rate and hence the entire band then may or may not crawl through frequent small adjustments in inflation according to relative PPP.

The best example of a noncrawling band is the experience of the European Community (EC) during 1975–1995, prior to the Maastricht Treaty, which committed the EC to EMU. For several decades, the countries of the EC tried to stabilize their currencies against each other through the *Exchange Rate Mechanism* (ERM), a system of pegging EC currencies to the dollar through a trading band. The results were less than satisfactory. The bands were frequently adjusted, generally to widen them and accommodate market movements. Finally, in 1992 the United Kingdom and Italy fell out of even the wide bands after fears about inflation (future more than present inflation) drove speculative attacks on their currencies.

Rather than abandon the goal of currency stability, the member countries of the EC resolved to coordinate their economic policies ever more closely together, and this led to the Maastricht Treaty and EMU. Since a common currency requires common policies, especially common monetary policies, policy conditions were agreed upon. The three key conditions were (1) a public sector deficit/GDP ratio less than 3 percent, (2) a national debt/GDP ratio less than 60 percent, and (3) inflation less than 3 percent. All of these were designed to keep inflation low enough in all member countries so that the various currencies could be combined. Despite widespread skepticism in other regions, the euro was launched on January 1, 1999. This nearly unprecedented event represented a significant surrender of monetary policy independence by sovereign countries, illustrating how far one must go to control inflation and make currency stability work.

Russia and Indonesia adopted crawling bands in 1996 and 1997, respectively, but quickly abandoned them in the collapse of 1998. Four other countries—Chile, Colombia, Ecuador, and Israel—were able to maintain their crawling bands. A commission in India recommended in 1997 an even weaker concept that it called a "monitoring band," which involves no commitment to intervene at the edges of a band, but reserves the right to do so when the currency is outside the band.[15] As bands become weaker and commitments to them less clear, the exchange regime becomes what has been termed a "dirty float," where intervention is decided upon on a case-by-case basis.

Finally, countries may simply let their currencies float freely. This is the default solution when no other system is in place, or a peg has been broken by an attack. Floating is simple and does not risk a sudden collapse. But its disadvantage is that volatility in the foreign exchange markets continues to be very high, so that not only a country's imports and exports, but also its own inflation rate, are likely to be blown around by erratic market events over which the government has no control.

---

[15]See Williamson (1998) for a defense of crawling and monitoring bands.

To summarize, there are two simple, polar choices of exchange rate regime: purely fixed and purely floating, with a variety of often unsuccessful efforts to construct alternative arrangements in between. Purely floating is low cost and easy to implement, but does not bring stability. Therefore, many EFM governments attempt to anchor their currency as firmly as possible to a strong external currency in the hope that this will help to control inflation. The system can work, but only under special conditions: Fiscal deficits must be small enough not to pose a threat to monetary discipline and the peg must be made as strong and credible as possible, backed by substantial international reserves that the government is prepared to pledge to support the currency. If these preconditions are not met, then currency pegs are most likely to lead to currency overvaluation, resulting capital flight, and eventual financial crisis. Following the Asian crisis, many countries shifted to floating exchange rates, though most were soon operating with trading bands, and one country (Malaysia) adopted a new peg to the dollar.

The Impact of Inflation on Debt Markets

Effect on Interest Rates

Inflation has a serious and negative effect on debt markets. Those who contemplate lending money must be concerned about the value of the money they later receive in repayment. In general, expected inflation raises interest rates, shortens the available lending maturities, and reduces the availability of loans.

The first-order effect on interest rates is to raise them by approximately the amount of the expected inflation. Consider inflation's effect on interest rates with a simple model in which a lender who will lend for a single period contracts to earn a nominal interest rate i. At the end of the period he or she finds that prices have risen by π percent, and thus real wealth has increased only by a smaller *real rate r*:

$$1 + r \equiv (1 + i) / (1 + \pi)$$

This is the definition of the *ex post* real rate r. We turn this relationship around and imagine that all lenders have in mind their target *ex ante* real rate r and combine it with their expected rate of future inflation π^e to produce a nominal interest rate i in the following way:

$$1 + i = (1 + r)(1 + \pi^e) \approx 1 + r + \pi^e$$

That is,

$$i \approx r + \pi^e.$$

This is, of course, quite an abstraction since neither the real rate r nor the expected inflation π^e can be observed directly in most cases.

Whenever interest rates are indexed to inflation, we have an opportunity to observe the real rate directly. For example, inflation-indexed Treasury bonds were introduced into the United States capital markets in January 1997 with a 10-year issue bearing a (real) rate of 3.375 percent plus an ongoing adjustment of principal to reflect changes in the consumer price index. One subsequent five-year issue was sold in 1997 with a 3.625 percent interest rate, and in 1998 10-year and 30-year issues were sold, both with coupons of 3.625 percent. By year-end 1998 all four issues were trading to yield between 3.8 percent and 4.0 percent, while the longer maturities among regular (nonindexed) Treasury bonds were trading to yield 5.2 percent to 5.4 percent. We may conclude that the market's expectation of inflation was about 1.4 percent, which seems consistent with 1998 inflation and with what most economists were saying about future inflation in the United States.

The above model must be considered only a first approximation, however, as it takes no account of inflation *risk*. Since future inflation is an unknown quantity, we must take into account the possibility that it will be higher than the value we reasonably expect; that is, our expectations may turn out to be wrong. Lenders at fixed interest rates are damaged by inflation, so unexpected inflation (i.e., the chance that inflation may be worse than its expected future value) must enter into their calculations. If lenders are risk averse, as they almost surely are, then they will require extra compensation for this risk: We can reasonably assume that lenders require some *inflation risk premium m*:

$$1 + i = (1 + r)(1 + \pi^e)(1 + m) \approx 1 + r + \pi^e + m$$

That is,

$$i \approx r + \pi^e + m.$$

The magnitude of the risk premium m depends on the variability of inflation, and we have seen that inflation variability is highly correlated with the level of inflation. In the case of the United States, m was essentially zero by the late 1990s because almost no one was seriously concerned about inflation risk. The greater the inflation risk, the higher the risk premium. A study of inflation-indexed and nonindexed bonds in the United Kingdom concluded that the risk premium in sterling was about 0.70 percent on average from October 1992 to July 1997, when the Bank of England adopted an inflation-targeting regime, and about 1.00 percent over a longer horizon reaching back to July 1982 when inflation risk was greater.[16]

When we look at EFMs, however, the inflation risk premiums become dramatically higher than in developed economies. Israel is another country with inflation-indexed bonds, which provide the basis for measuring real interest rates and hence inflation risk premiums. Furthermore, as is clear from the Appendix to this chapter, Israel is one of the most inflationary of all EFMs over a long period of time. Israel's rate of inflation averaged 3.179 percent per month or 45.6 percent a year during the period from September 1984 to March 1992. One study[17] estimated the inflation risk premium during this period to be 0.34 percent a month or 4.16 percent a year.[18] Furthermore, if one looks just at a period of runaway inflation from September 1984 to July 1985, prior to the adoption of a strict austerity program, average inflation was 15.2 percent a month or 443 percent a year, and the inflation risk premium rose to 2.36 percent a month or 32.3 percent on an annual basis! This level of risk premium, which appears to the borrower as additional real interest to be paid, makes borrowing prohibitively expensive.

The tendency for EFM currencies to command significantly higher interest rates than currencies of industrialized countries—because of expected and unexpected inflation—continues to be evident even in most cases where the EFM government has pegged its currency to an external anchor such as the dollar. If the peg were perfectly credible, external investors would have an easy, risk-free arbitrage opportunity: Borrow dollars, sell them for local currency, and lend the local currency at a much higher rate. Suppose, for example, that a bank pays 5 percent for dollar deposits and that local currency deposits pay 12 percent. The simple arbitrage described would yield 7 percent,

---

[16]Remolona, Wickens, and Gong (1998).
[17]Kandel, Ofer, and Sarig (1996).
[18]If r, π, and m are monthly, annual $1 + i = (1 + r)^{12}(1 + \pi)^{12}(1 + m)^{12}$. Then, $(1 + .0034)^{12} = 1.0416$.

an enormous spread. If this operation were conducted on $1 billion, for example, a perfectly feasible number given the size of international banks, it would pay $70 million a year provided the currency price did not change.

One of the most fundamental tenets of finance theory is that risk-free arbitrage opportunities cannot exist more than fleetingly, and that financial returns rise as risk increases. That makes it clear that the opportunity described, apparently so very profitable, is far from risk-free; its very magnitude suggests that the risk is also very high. The risk in question is that the peg will break and the EFM currency will devalue. The very existence of an interest rate differential indicates doubt that the currency peg is firm. Indeed, the magnitude of the interest rate differential is a reasonably good measure of the risk of the peg breaking.

A bank that acquired the asset-liability pair described would own an explosive package of risk and reward. The same package could be acquired off balance sheet through a forward purchase of local currency, if a forward market exists, since by interest parity (reviewed in the box in the next section) the asset–liability pair is exactly equivalent to a forward purchase. Similarly, many derivatives such as swaps, which amount to multiperiod forward purchases of currency, offer another off-balance-sheet method of taking the risk and attempting to earn the reward.

This is not just an abstraction; it is known throughout EFMs as the "short dollar position." Banks all over Asia were taking this bet prior to the Asia crisis, creating a kind of powder keg that would explode when the currencies collapsed. Mexican banks were not permitted to take such unmatched exchange risks in 1994 (except to the extent of 15 percent of their capital), but managed to do so anyway through derivatives, which greatly increased the damage from Mexico's currency collapse. We will look at these situations in detail in Chapter 8.

Lending Terms and Volumes

There is also a level of risk beyond which neither external nor internal investors will invest at all, and when this happens, markets simply shut down. For example, in the autumn of 1989 it became clear that the United States was entering a significant recession and that the future outlook was bleak and uncertain. This followed several years in which high-yield debt ("junk bonds") had been sold with interest coverage levels lower than at any other time in recent memory. When the change in circumstances happened, the market for these bonds temporarily dried up and the firm of Drexel Burnham Lambert, the most important underwriter and trader of junk bonds, failed.

Similarly, in 1998 currency instability that began in East Asia in 1997 spread to Latin America and Central and Eastern Europe. In late summer of that year, a currency collapse and debt default in Russia caused a major sell-off in stock markets around the world and virtually shut down the market for new issues of EFM stocks and bonds. Not since the great debt crisis of the 1980s had capital flows to EFMs come so close to a near standstill. Uncertainty and illiquidity had reached the point at which investors no longer tried to price risk but simply avoided some kinds of risks altogether.

This shutdown is not a discontinuity so much as the extreme end of a spectrum of risk. In almost all debt markets, strong borrowers can borrow more than weak ones. That is, the volume of new risky lending and the ability to sell risky assets at their previous peak prices will tend to diminish as investors' credit standings decline and/or the riskiness of investments increase. Firms that have experienced losses dump risky assets and try to lower their leverage to put themselves in a stronger position for the future. Those willing to lend become fewer in number as risk increases and liquidity declines, until a finite risk point is reached at which few will lend at any interest rate.

The phenomenon of market shutdown above a certain level of risk also explains why in every debt market there is a maximum term, the longest time period for which any investor will lend at a fixed rate of interest. This is a function of the level and volatility of inflation. When inflation becomes high, this maximum term may shrink to months or weeks. Indeed, during Brazil's hyperinflation of the late 1980s, the maximum term shrank to one or two days. In such an economy, there is no longer a yield curve but just a "yield point."

To summarize, inflation damages debt markets by increasing interest rates not only by the amount of expected inflation but also by a premium for unexpected inflation. In addition, inflation shortens the maximum term for which any investor will lend at a fixed rate of interest, sometimes quite dramatically, and reduces the volume of fixed-rate bonds that investors are willing to hold.

The Impact of Inflation on Foreign Exchange Markets

Volatility of Exchange Rates

The most important effect of inflation on exchange rates is to make them substantially more volatile. This happens because foreign exchange markets are dominated not by agents who trade goods, but by agents who invest and lend. Investors incorporate into foreign exchange rates their estimates of all future inflation, and opinions about the future can change suddenly and dramatically.

We have seen that much of the damage from inflation arises from its volatility, which increases with its level, and that foreign exchange rate determination has a great deal to do with expected inflation. The inescapable conclusion is that countries that tolerate even moderate levels of inflation are likely to suffer from periods in which their foreign exchange rates fluctuate in unexpected and sometimes extreme ways. As we have also seen, this cannot easily be fixed by just pegging the exchange rate.

In this section we will focus on a second impact of inflation on foreign exchange markets, namely its effect on the forward rate. This is a direct consequence of its impact on interest rates, as should be clear from the nearby box on *interest parity*.

Forward Exchange Rates

Covered interest parity makes it clear that forward exchange rates are not anyone's prediction of what later spot exchange rates will be; rather, they are a simple, mechanical consequence of interest rate differentials in the two countries. Nevertheless, we can gain some additional insight into forward rates by replacing the interest rates with their decomposition into required real rates, expected inflation, and risk premium. We will assume that the weaker currency ("pesos") has an inflation risk premium and that the dollar has none. Then:

$$F_{P/\$} = E_{P/\$}(1 + i_p)/(1 + i_\$) = E_{P/\$}(1 + r_p)(1 + \pi_p^e)(1 + m_p)/(1 + r_\$)(1 + \pi_\$^e)$$

Now we make a strong assumption: Suppose that the required real rate of interest (abstracting from inflation risk) is the same in both countries, so that $1 + r_p = 1 + r_\$$. This implies that capital earns the same real return in both countries, so that capital does not persistently flow from one to the other. The capital flows in the 1990s show how unrealistic this assumption is: Most of the time, capital is rapidly flowing either into or out of EFMs, reflecting changes in perceived real rates of return. But if we reached a state of equilibrium in which capital remained voluntar-

Covered Interest Parity

Covered interest parity is a relationship between the interest rates in two countries, the spot exchange rate of their currencies, and the forward exchange rate of their currencies. An easy way to understand it is with the diagram below. In this diagram, the top horizontal line represents dollars and the bottom horizontal line represents pesos. The left vertical line represents time today ($t = 0$) and the right vertical line represents a future point in time $t = T$.

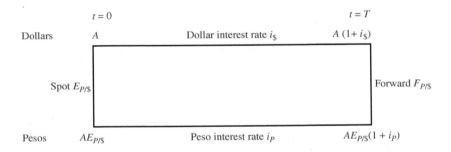

The upper left-hand corner therefore represents dollars today. The lower left-hand corner represents pesos today. The upper right-hand corner represents dollars at time T. The lower right-hand corner represents pesos at time T.

The upper edge of the box connects dollars today with dollars at time T and so is the dollar interest rate for term T. The lower edge of the box connects pesos today with pesos at time T and so is the peso interest rate for term T. The left-hand edge of the box connects dollars today with pesos today and so is the spot (current) exchange rate $E_{P/\$}$ expressed in pesos per dollar. The right-hand edge of the box represents the forward exchange rate $F_{P/\$}$ also expressed in pesos per dollar.

The point of covered interest parity is that these four quantities are not independent of each other: Given any three of them, one can compute what the fourth must be. In particular, if we know the spot exchange rate and the two interest rates, we already know what the forward exchange rate must be.

We reason as follows. Start with A dollars today in the upper left-hand corner. These dollars can be invested at the dollar interest rate and become $A(1 + i_\$)$ dollars by time T. Alternatively, the A dollars can be converted to pesos at the spot exchange rate, yielding $AE_{P/\$}$. This amount of pesos can then be invested at the peso interest rate and become $AE_{P/\$}(1 + i_p)$ by time T.

In all major currency markets and some smaller ones, traders are willing to trade forward exchange rates—that is, to agree today that come time T they will exchange dollars for pesos at a rate $F_{P/\$}$ that is agreed upon today. If there is a forward market for pesos, the peso investment in the lower right-hand corner can be today sold forward, guaranteeing that at time T we will have $AE_{P/\$}(1 + i_p)/F_{P/\$}$ dollars.

So we have two different ways to change our A dollars today into dollars at time T. One way is to go across the top of the box, investing them directly as dollars. The other way around the box is to convert them to pesos, earn the peso rate, and today sell the resulting pesos forward, guaranteeing our outcome. The financial principle of no risk-free

continued

concluded

arbitrage says that if two strategies are fully equivalent, they must have the same return; hence:

$$A(1 + i_\$) = AE_{P/\$}(1 + i_P)/F_{P/\$}$$

The *A* on each side cancels, since the amount for which we transact has no importance, and the result is the formula for the forward exchange rate:

$$F_{P/\$} = E_{P/\$}(1 + i_P)/(1 + i_\$)$$

This tells us that if the forward exchange rate is traded, its price is equal to the spot exchange rate times a fraction whose numerator is one plus the peso interest rate and whose denominator is one plus the dollar interest rate. This is called the *covered interest parity* relationship. The word "covered" means that the foreign exchange risk of moving into pesos has been hedged by also selling the pesos forward. The word "parity" means equality or equivalence. The formula tells us that it will do us no good to chase a high peso interest rate: If we hedge, the consequence is exactly the same as investing in dollars in the first place.

ily at rest, the real interest rates would cancel each other out in the above expression, leaving:

$$F_{P/\$} = E_{P/\$}(1 + \pi_P^e)(1 + m_P)/(1 + \pi_\$^e)$$

This is close to the statement of relative PPP, in which the future exchange rate will move to reflect the ratio of expected inflation. Indeed, it is exactly equivalent except for the presence of the risk premium term $1 + m_P$. What the risk premium does is to bias the forward rate away from the expected future exchange rate predicted by relative PPP. In particular, $F_{P/\$}$ will be higher, and hence $F_{\$/P}$ will be lower, than the expected future exchange rate predicted by relative PPP. The latter is the price of the peso measured in dollars, so we may say that the forward value of the peso will be depressed below its equilibrium level by the risk premium.

If there were no inflation risk premium in pesos (i.e., if $m_P = 0$), then the forward exchange rate $F_{\$/P}$ would be an unbiased estimate of the future value of the peso, according to relative PPP. When $m_P > 0$, though, $F_{\$/P}$ is biased low. This means that hedging peso holdings by selling pesos forward becomes very expensive. The inflation risk premium m_P discourages hedging currency risk, just as it discourages borrowing in pesos.

In summary, inflation distorts foreign exchange markets in two ways. The most important effect is that even moderate inflation will lead to significant exchange rate volatility, and that high inflation will lead to extreme exchange rate volatility. The only way to finally tame the volatility is to tame the fiscal deficits that are the ultimate drivers of high inflation risk. A secondary effect of inflation is to depress the forward foreign exchange rate below its equilibrium level because of the presence of inflation risk premiums in interest rates. This substantially raises the cost of hedging out of local currency.

Inflation and Banks

Banks and Float

While inflation has serious and negative effects on both debt markets and foreign exchange markets, raising risk premiums and creating troubling instabilities, the story is quite different when we come to banks.

EFM banks often benefit from inflation, primarily because inflation increases the velocity of money and the number of monetary transactions. When the currency is deteriorating by the day, no one wants to hold it any longer than necessary, and so it tends to be spent more quickly.[19] In periods of hyperinflation, people may run to stores rather than walk, to spend currency quickly on real goods before it loses more value.

Similarly, people will write checks rapidly, drawing down their checking balances to the lowest possible level. The money is not lost to the banking system as a whole, but merely passes from one account to another. What does grow is the *float,* the quantity of money in transition from one account to another. The float typically is "owned" by the banks for a day or two while it is in transit.

Banks do not pay interest on the float, so it becomes an interest-free source of funding. Furthermore, the balances in checking accounts pay little or no interest. The sum of checking account balances and checks in the process of collection represent a most attractive source of funding for the banks. A significant fraction of this free funding must be shared with the central bank (where banks hold zero-interest reserves), and to this extent the government also profits from inflation, but the rest greatly increases the profitability of the banks.

Thus, it often happens that the banking sector appears quite robust in inflationary economies. The fraction of the GDP represented by banking services can expand to as much as 15 percent of GDP (as in Brazil during the late 1980s and early 1990s) from the more normal level of 3 to 5 percent. Banks may be the most profitable of all business sectors in such economies.

One might imagine that prosperous banks would stimulate the entire business sector because a banking system flush with funds should want to lend those funds out to businesses. However, other factors intrude. First, inflation is often associated with reduced *real* money holdings (M/P) and hence a reduced supply of real loanable funds in the banking system. Second, the inflation risk premium appears to borrowers as a higher real rate, discouraging them from borrowing. Finally, banks do not need to take the default risks associated with lending in a highly inflationary environment; they can earn high returns on capital simply by putting most of their funds into government bonds.

Banks and Government Bonds

High deficits generate a growing supply of government bonds for the local market. The usual problem is to find sufficient local savings to support the purchase of these bonds. Banks that profit from float are natural purchasers of the liquid bonds. The liquidity of the bonds is attractive because in a rapidly changing market it is desirable to be able to change the composition of assets quickly. Volatility can be especially problematic when the source of financing bank assets is float.

In all countries, even the most developed, banks hold a certain fraction of their assets as government bonds. This has long been deemed essential for liquidity. But in inflationary economies, the proportion of bank assets held as government bonds is likely to be especially high. The government is issuing large quantities of bonds, and the banks need an asset liquid enough to be financed by float, so banks find it beneficial to hold large quantities of government bonds. Such holdings are typically quite profitable for the banks because the government bonds pay a high and often inflation-adjusted rate of interest.

[19]Widespread inflation indexing makes it unnecessary to quickly spend bank balances on which indexed interest is earned, but the above remarks hold for cash and checking deposits.

The consequence is that government funding often crowds out the private sector in inflationary economies. What the government is doing, first by its reserve requirements and second by its massive sale of bonds to the banks, is preempting the national savings for itself to pay for its deficits. Banks in inflationary economies can be "hollowed out" by their governments, so that skills in private sector lending actually decline and banking becomes a business of manipulating bonds, interest rate futures, inflation indexes, and other instruments unrelated to the private sector's need for loans. In an extreme case, such as Mexico in the 1980s, the government drops all pretense and simply nationalizes the banks, taking all the national savings for its own purposes.

In summary, inflation can make banks prosper, but beneath that prosperity often lies a deep distortion of capital allocation whose net result is to crowd out the private sector, preempt the national savings to pay for the government's deficits, and undermine the private intermediation function of banks.

Appendix **253**

APPENDIX: MEAN ANNUAL INFLATION, 1970–1995

The following table is based on the IMF's *International Financial Statistics* (1999).

Country	Mean 1970–1995	Means 1970–1979	1976–1985	1980–1989	1986–1995
Panama	3.78	6.01	5.08	3.15	0.80
Germany	3.78	4.89	3.97	2.90	2.46
Singapore	3.97	5.91	3.52	2.79	1.93
Switzerland	3.99	4.98	3.32	3.27	2.85
Malta	4.26	5.56	5.40	3.58	2.37
Netherlands	4.44	7.06	5.13	2.87	1.73
Malaysia	4.46	5.50	4.61	3.65	3.07
Austria	4.57	6.10	5.08	3.84	2.71
Japan	4.85	9.09	4.71	2.53	1.36
Luxembourg	4.99	6.50	6.63	4.72	2.27
Belgium	5.23	7.13	6.71	4.90	2.28
Saudi Arabia	5.33	12.47	4.64	0.04	1.06
United States	5.67	7.10	7.22	5.55	3.55
Netherlands Antilles	5.72	8.31	6.86	4.98	2.73
Cyprus	5.93	6.79	7.49	5.80	3.94
Canada	5.96	7.38	8.11	6.51	3.36
Bahrain	5.99	12.56	8.30	2.25	0.54
Bahamas	5.99	6.92	6.44	6.28	4.47
Burkina Faso	6.31	8.08	9.68	5.04	3.13
Thailand	6.47	8.00	7.42	5.82	4.35
Niger	6.60	10.35	11.40	3.57	1.82
Denmark	6.71	9.29	9.18	6.91	2.95
France	6.82	8.90	10.08	7.38	2.65
Norway	7.04	8.37	8.74	8.34	4.32
Morocco	7.34	7.79	9.80	7.58	5.40
Finland	7.47	10.41	9.67	7.32	3.57
Sweden	7.56	8.57	9.76	7.94	5.22
Togo	7.67	9.52	8.92	5.04	5.70
Australia	7.78	9.83	9.46	8.41	5.22
Senegal	7.88	9.79	9.39	6.91	3.87
Fiji	8.01	10.62	8.15	7.45	5.30
Jordan	8.30	10.81	8.53	7.02	6.97
St. Lucia	8.32	13.39	8.21	5.77	3.92
Gabon	8.50	11.06	11.44	6.49	4.87
Ethiopia	8.57	10.42	11.89	4.60	7.52
Barbados	8.69	13.87	8.92	6.89	3.42
United Kingdom	8.74	12.63	10.82	7.43	4.68
India	8.77	7.54	6.76	9.12	9.45
Côte d'Ivoire	8.93	11.71	11.20	6.75	7.23
Ireland	9.11	12.75	13.27	9.34	2.91
Congo, Rep.	9.12	8.15	10.34	7.60	9.20
Cameroon	9.26	10.28	11.37	9.10	6.79
Dominica	9.31	16.30	12.62	6.89	3.31
New Zealand	9.61	11.46	13.45	11.86	5.76
Nepal	9.65	7.81	7.85	10.84	11.20
Burundi	9.71	11.90	12.09	7.17	8.66
Pakistan	9.82	11.76	7.95	7.27	8.99
Italy	10.27	12.33	15.09	11.20	5.35
Honduras	10.32	6.63	8.40	7.40	14.92
Rwanda	10.33	12.45	8.98	4.70	10.42
Mauritius	10.39	10.97	13.27	11.15	7.30
Sri Lanka	10.39	6.89	11.25	12.83	11.42

continued

254

Chapter 6   Inflation and Currency Stability

Country	Mean 1970–1995	Means			
		1970–1979	1976–1985	1980–1989	1986–1995
Western Samoa	10.44	9.32	14.20	13.45	6.88
Korea	10.61	15.22	12.36	8.41	5.82
Spain	10.73	14.39	15.44	10.25	5.82
Trinidad and Tobago	10.77	11.66	12.70	11.72	8.38
Haiti	11.98	9.26	8.72	6.62	15.56
South Africa	12.07	9.67	12.95	14.61	13.31
Gambia	12.17	9.63	11.91	17.47	14.55
Indonesia	12.23	16.92	12.20	9.63	8.20
Swaziland	12.31	10.17	14.68	14.23	12.38
Guatemala	12.49	8.86	9.19	12.07	18.70
Algeria	12.64	8.23	10.56	9.03	19.10
Guyana	12.78	9.24	16.26	19.30	12.73
Bangladesh	12.98	19.60	9.98	11.26	6.89
Egypt	12.98	7.78	13.51	17.35	16.86
Zimbabwe	13.69	7.27	12.60	12.81	20.23
Myanmar (Burma)	13.94	10.86	4.44	10.09	23.03
Philippines	13.98	14.64	16.89	15.05	9.20
Kenya	14.12	10.92	13.20	11.74	17.71
El Salvador	14.15	9.39	13.78	18.52	18.29
Syria	15.17	9.25	11.74	22.61	21.74
Portugal	15.28	17.14	22.48	17.64	9.28
Madagascar	15.29	7.90	14.90	18.56	19.83
Greece	15.69	12.31	18.53	19.49	15.67
Dominican Republic	16.49	9.20	13.63	20.87	23.36
Paraguay	17.13	11.08	15.48	20.47	23.24
Iran	17.73	11.00	16.10	19.82	25.08
Costa Rica	18.65	9.79	22.78	27.09	18.21
Jamaica	21.39	17.27	19.66	15.60	27.17
Venezuela	21.59	6.61	11.14	23.02	41.88
Colombia	22.37	19.31	23.43	23.46	25.01
Tanzania	22.51	10.99	21.93	30.07	29.39
Nigeria	24.59	15.67	18.03	23.07	37.40
Ecuador	27.13	11.87	19.89	33.97	43.34
Iceland	27.72	29.55	45.84	39.16	11.97
Mexico	36.69	14.68	41.87	69.05	46.88
Sudan	39.25	15.34	25.49	37.96	80.52
Suriname	40.62	8.78	9.26	12.93	91.91
Ghana	40.79	38.84	66.18	48.27	31.05
Sierra Leone	41.90	10.83	33.25	62.95	70.62
Turkey	46.26	23.32	45.07	51.27	66.72
Lebanon	48.44	12.13	20.82	87.54	108.12
Uruguay	61.25	59.26	51.34	57.58	70.66
Israel	65.50	32.49	138.71	129.67	18.59
Chile	79.03	174.56	51.98	21.37	16.67

References

Baliño, Tomás J. T., and Charles Enoch. 1997. *Currency Board Arrangements: Issues and Experiences.* Washington, DC: International Monetary Fund.

Barro, Robert J. 1995. Inflation and economic growth. *Bank of England Quarterly Bulletin* 35: 166–76.

Budnevich, Carlos L., and Sergio Godoy. 1995. Un análisis empírico y de política económica de la inflación en Chile: 1984–1992. In *Análisis Empírico de la Inflación en Chile.* Ed. by Felipe Morande and Francisco Rosende. Santiago: Instituto de Economía, Pontificia Universidad Católica de Chile.

Calomiris, Charles W. 1999. The impending collapse of the European Monetary Union. *Cato Journal* 18: 445–52.

Calomiris, Charles W., and Ian Domowitz. 1989. Asset substitution, money demand, and the inflation process in Brazil. *Journal of Money Credit and Banking* 21: 78–89.

Cantor, Richard, and Frank Packer. 1996. Determinants and impacts of sovereign credit ratings. Research Paper no. 9608, Federal Reserve Bank of New York.

Casella, Alessandra. 1999. Tradable deficit permits: Efficient implementation of the stability pact in the European Monetary Union. Working Paper no. 7278, National Bureau of Economic Research.

DeCecco, Marcello. 1985. Monetary theory and Roman history. *Journal of Economic History* 45: 809–22.

Eichenbaum, Martin, and Charles Evans. 1993. Some empirical evidence on the effects of monetary policy shocks on exchange rates. Working Paper no. 4271, National Bureau of Economic Research.

Eisner, Robert. 1986. *How Real Is the Federal Deficit?* New York: Free Press.

Fischer, Stanley. 1993. The role of macroeconomic factors in growth. *Journal of Monetary Economics* 32: 485–512.

Friedman, Milton. 1968. Inflation: Causes and consequences. In *Dollars and Deficits.* Englewood Cliffs, NJ: Prentice Hall.

Judson, Ruth, and Athanasios Orphanides. 1996. Inflation, volatility and growth. Working paper, Board of Governors of the Federal Reserve System.

Kandel, Shmuel, Aharon R. Ofer, and Oded Sarig. 1996. Real interest rates and inflation: An ex-ante empirical analysis. *Journal of Finance* 51, no. 1: 205–25.

Lucas, Robert E., Jr. 1972. Expectations and the neutrality of money. *Journal of Economic Theory* 4: 103–24.

Marrinan, Jane. 1989. Exchange rate determination: Sorting out theory and evidence. Federal Reserve Bank of Boston, *New England Economic Review,* November–December: 38–51.

Mishkin, Frederic S. 1998. The dangers of exchange-rate pegging in emerging-market countries. *International Finance* 1: 81–101.

Motley, Brian. 1994. Growth and inflation: A cross-country study. Working Paper no. 94-08, Federal Reserve Bank of San Francisco.

Phelps, A. W. 1967. Phillips curve, expectations of inflation and optimal unemployment over time. *Economica* 34: 254–81.

Phillips, A. W. 1958. The relationship between unemployment and the rate of change of money wage rates in the United Kingdom, 1861–1959. *Economica* 25: 283–99.

Remolona, Eli M., Michael R. Wickens, and Frank F. Gong. 1998. What was the market's view of UK monetary policy? Estimating inflation risk and expected inflation with indexed bonds. Staff Report no. 57, Federal Reserve Bank of New York.

Williamson, John. 1998. Crawling bands or monitoring bands: How to manage exchange rates in a world of capital mobility. *International Finance* 1: 59–79.

THUNDERBIRD
THE AMERICAN GRADUATE SCHOOL
OF INTERNATIONAL MANAGEMENT

A06-99-0026

MULTIQUIMICA DO BRASIL 1999

"I'm really concerned about our position in Brazil. Our pharmaceutical products are being hurt by both local and foreign producers and our foreign exchange policies may well be to blame." So said Don Howard, controller of the foreign operations of the pharmaceutical group of Multichemical Industries, Inc. "Look at Levadol, for example; our sales are falling while those of Hoffman are up."

This conversation took place in January 1999 as Don was reviewing the preliminary 1998 results of the foreign operations of the pharmaceutical group with the group's general manager, Paul McConnell. The men were in the company's corporate offices in Houston, Texas.

Background

Multichemcial Industries, Inc. sold 75 different products in over 50 countries during 1998. Sales for the year were $3.1 billion (see Appendix 1 for financial data). The company's principal product groups were: pharmaceuticals, industrial chemicals, agricultural chemicals, and petrochemicals. Multichemical's overseas subsidiaries accounted for 35% of sales in 1998, with the majority of the activity taking place in Europe.

Multiquimica do Brasil (MB) was responsible for all sales and manufacturing which took place in Brazil. Thus, its managers had responsibility for products in several of the firm's product groups. Sales during the year were $65 million, 6% of foreign sales. This wholly owned subsidiary was formed in 1993 with the initial purpose of establishing manufacturing facilities for agricultural chemical, industrial chemical, and pharmaceutical products in Brazil. Prior to that, Multichemcial had been active in Brazil through export sales. In other words, products that were manufactured in the United States had been sold in Brazil through local, independent importers. Multichemical did not operate either manufacturing facilities or a division office in the country until 1993.

The new subsidiary began manufacturing and selling herbicides in 1993. MB did not show a profit until 1996. The losses that were incurred were primarily attributable to two factors: the larger startup costs associated with a new business and a weak economic period in Brazil. As a result of the losses sustained during the 1993 to 1996 period, MB was entitled to a substantial amount in tax loss carryforwards on its Brazilian Tax return. (The term "tax loss carryforward" refers to the fact that net operating losses, to the extent that they exceed taxable income of the preceding three years, can be carried forward, thus reducing future taxable income.)

In late 1995, the company installed a manufacturing plant to process Levadol, an aspirin-free pain reliever. Such facilities were included in the original operating plans for MB. They were scheduled, however, for the late 1990s. They went on stream sooner than originally planned due to an increase in the amount of duty on imports.

The manufacture of this product involved shipping the raw materials in bulk form from the United States. The raw materials were formulated, converted into tablet form, and packaged in the Brazilian plant, and then sold to distributors. MB sales of Levadol in 1998 were $6.8 million.

Product and Pricing Flow for Levadol

The raw materials for Levadol were shipped from a domestic subsidiary of Multichemical to MB. The invoiced price for the transferred goods during 1998 averaged $60/case equivalent (invoiced in U.S. dollars). The cost of goods sold on MB's books for Levadol averaged $131/case. This figure included the $60/case raw material cost, plus $31/case for import duty and $40/case to formulate, convert, and package.

The product was sold to wholesalers serving both drugstores and chain stores, usually on 90-day payment terms, for a price of approximately $218/case. The $87/case difference between the sales price and the cost of goods sold consisted of marketing costs (roughly 20% of sales), administration, distribution, and interest expenses, and approximately a 5% profit margin before taxes. The distributors, in turn, usually added a 10-20% margin. This was designed to both cover their costs and provide a profit margin.

Dollar Linkage Billing

Multichemical had recently instituted a management accounting system which worked to the benefit of the Brazilian subsidiary—a system known as *dollar linkage billing*. A statement on the invoice which was sent from the domestic (U.S.) subsidiary to MB said, "payable at the exchange rate in effect on the date of the receipt of goods." The exact amount of *real* payable to the parent was therefore set on the date on which the goods were received in Brazil, and not on the date of shipment by the U.S. business unit. (It typically took 30 days for goods to pass from the U.S. subsidiary to the Brazilian subsidiary.) The books used for management and control internal to the firm therefore recorded the intra-firm sales as if invoiced in local currency (Brazilian *real* in this case).

Customary Brazilian credit terms on imports were 180 days. Since the Brazilian *real* (R$) lost value in relation to the dollar on a more or less continuous basis, a foreign exchange loss would normally show up on a Brazilian firm's *real* denominated books. Given the above-mentioned system, however, the foreign exchange loss showed up on the U.S. tax books.

Even within the context of the Brazilian domestic market, MB's reported profit in dollar terms was affected by the more or less continuous change in the value of the *real*.[1] The major problem here was tied to the fact that competition had forced MB to offer 90-day payment terms to their customers. Given the fact that the *real* was formally devalued by a small amount on a continuous basis, any domestic subsidiary with terms of 90 days was faced with a currency loss—*translation loss*—whenever its books were translated back into dollar terms. This translation loss resulted from the *dollar value* of the original *real*

---

[1] The *real* was introduced as Brazil's official currency on July 1, 1994, under then President Cardoso's *Real Plan*. The *Plan* combined the introduction of a new currency with renewed commitment to a tight monetary policy to drive inflation once and for all from the Brazilian economy. As illustrated in Appendix 2, inflation fell dramatically in 1995 and 1996, while the real was devalued only marginally from its initial value.

A06-99-0026

denominated sale exceeding the *dollar value* of the actual *real denominated* settlement of the account receivable some 90 days later.

In an attempt to deal with the situation, MB put into place a method known as "forward pricing." Under the assumptions of this method, MB's management predicted the amount of *real* devaluation which would occur during the forthcoming 90 days. This estimate then served as the basis for raising the then-current sales price. In other words, they passed along the expected loss due to the devaluation of the *real* to the customers. As a result of this policy, product prices were revised monthly.

Hedging Policies

Although the Brazilian inflation rate had fallen from over 2700% in 1993 to 16% in 1996 and 7% in 1997, the exchange rate had not moved proportionally to the change in purchasing power.[2] The *real* had been regularly devalued by the government, but had clearly not changed completely in line with the rate of inflation. A future devaluation seemed inevitable. Many had expected a major devaluation in the fall of 1998 following the Russian economic crisis, but it had not happened. MB reacted by pushing up its prices, a policy which it continued to adhere to throughout 1998. Exhibit 1 illustrates the gradual devaluation policy implemented by the Brazilian government.

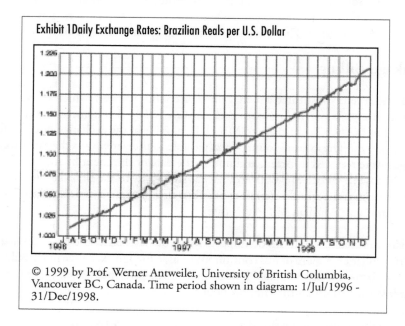

Exhibit 1 Daily Exchange Rates: Brazilian Reals per U.S. Dollar

© 1999 by Prof. Werner Antweiler, University of British Columbia, Vancouver BC, Canada. Time period shown in diagram: 1/Jul/1996 - 31/Dec/1998.

Beginning in late 1995, the corporate treasurer's office of Multichemical began to encourage MB to borrow locally. Such a policy was designed to match assets and liabilities in *real* terms and thus offset the translation loss on assets with a translation gain on liabilities. By having the subsidiaries borrow locally, the corporate treasurer was hoping to eliminate the risk of having to report large translation losses

---

[2] For example, the *real* should have fallen much faster than it had according to the *theory of purchasing power parity* (PPP). PPP states that the exchange rate should change in proportion to relative inflation rates between the two currencies. With a 1994 end-of-year rate of R$0.846/$, and Brazilian and U.S. inflation rates of 66% and 3% for 1995, respectively, the *real* should have fallen to R$1.364/$ at end-of-year 1995, not R$0.972/$:

$$\text{Exchange Rate}_{1995} = \text{R\$0.846/\$} \times \frac{1 + .66}{1 + .03} = \text{R\$1.364/\$}$$

on the corporate income statement.[3] Local borrowing, in essence, helped to smooth the corporation's reported income stream by substituting a periodic interest expense for less frequent, but presumably larger, losses due to translation. There was a cost, however. Interest rates in Brazil in 1998 averaged 28%. (See Appendix 2 for exchange rate, interest rate, and inflation rate data.)

Performance Measurement Policies

Multichemical had recently changed its internal reporting system. Previous to the change, operating managers had been held responsible for the performance of their units as measured by the *operating income* figures. This meant that items such as other income, other expenses, interest expenses, and foreign exchange gains and losses were not focused upon in the quarterly business results review meetings. Over time, the senior management at the corporate level had come to feel that this system of performance measurement ignored the impact of some business decisions which could (or should) be taken by some of the operating managers in question.

After a thorough study of both the existing internal reporting system and a set of alternative systems, a new system was designed and introduced. *Full Responsibility Accounting,* as the new system was called, was made effective with the 1998 data. Under the terms of this new system, both individual product managers and product group managers were to be held responsible for the relationship between their profit-after-tax figures and the net assets under their control on both a worldwide and *major country* basis. The term *net assets* for a particular sub-unit of the overall corporate was defined as net property (gross property less accumulated depreciation) plus net working capital. Thus, both individual product managers and product group managers subsequently bore some of the responsibility for such items as interest expense and foreign exchange gains and losses.

The new system was designed with the intention that it would, among other things, force top management to delegate expansion and curtailment decisions to lower levels. The individual product managers and their superiors (the product group managers), sometimes in conjunction with an (geographic) area manager, were to have total responsibility for the assets which they employed in the process of producing, distributing, and selling their particular product. The firm's capital budgeting and operational budgeting systems were to be altered such that the full year's capital expenditures would be approved at once, and there would be agreement reached during the operational budgeting cycle as to the appropriate levels for inventories and receivables for the budget year in questions.

While the new system was very focused upon a return-on-assets figure, two other measures were to receive emphasis under the terms of the new program. Both net income and cash flow were to be measured and monitored. The former would be measured against a budgeted target and the latter would be assessed in respect to an understanding of the underlying strategy for the sub-unit. Thus, a sub-unit with a growth strategy might be expected to generate little or no cash (or indeed, even use cash) over a short- to medium-term time period. Of particular concern to product group managers, such as Paul McConnell, was the fact that they were now responsible for currency gains and losses and interest expense, the latter of which could be very high in the case of local borrowing.

---

[3] Consolidation practices for foreign subsidiaries of U.S.-based companies are governed by Financial Accounting Standard 52. According to this standard, any foreign currency related gains and losses arising from the translation and consolidation of foreign affiliates would have to be passed through consolidated income for countries like Brazil which were experiencing hyper-inflationary conditions. Hyperinflation was defined as a cumulative inflation rate of 100% over a three-year period.

A06-99-0026

Competition

MB had been able to successfully position Levadol such that a significant number of the population asked for Levadol when they wanted an aspirin-free pain reliever. This had become an important issue as the product became more widely stocked by the various grocery chains and cooperatives (with their open, freestanding shelves). Every year, MB sold a greater amount of Levadol through grocery stores than it had the year before. During 1998, it was estimated that 60% of the retail sales of all aspirin-free pain relievers in Brazil took place in grocery stores, while the remaining 40% were sold through some type of drug-related outlet.

During 1998, MB lost both volume and market share on Levadol. Over 36,000 cases of Levadol were sold in 1996. Less than 32,000 were sold in 1998 (see Exhibit 2 for volume and market share data). Although it was considered a premium product, an increasing number of distributors were reacting to the recession by substituting lower cost products.

Exhibit 2 Aspirin-Free Pain Relievers
(percentage of market share by major competitors)

Year	*MB*	*Hoffman*	*Generic*	*All Other*	*Total Volume (000s cases)*
1993	3%	7%	31%	59%	125
1994	8	12	25	55	152
1995	9	17	21	53	202
1996	15	25	17	43	240
1997	13	32	13	42	287
1998	10	32	15	43	320

MB's primary competition during 1998 was the Swiss firm Hoffman et Cie which sold a similar, but not identical, product. Hoffman's product was priced slightly lower than Levadol. The Swiss franc had depreciated versus the dollar in 1996 and 1997, and therefore had not appreciated against the *real* to the same degree as the dollar (see Appendix 2). Thus, the apparent incentive for Hoffman to raise its price to cover a translation loss was not as great as MB's. Also, Hoffman had been known to be somewhat more concerned with market share than with short-term reported profits.

Other reasons for Hoffman's strength had to do with the company's size in Brazil. In addition to having a large percentage of the pharmaceutical market, it also had a very large share of the market in agricultural chemicals. Its field sales force was about three to four times the size of MB's. Also, Hoffman gave somewhat longer payment terms. Hoffman's management apparently felt that they could squeeze the profit margin in pharmaceuticals a bit because of their strong position and high profits with agricultural chemicals.

In addition to Hoffman and other foreign-based firms, two local producers sold a generic substitute. The raw materials for the generic product were sourced in Brazil. The local patent covering this product had already expired. One result of this was that the industry was currently afflicted with an overcapacity of manufacturing facilities for product such as generic brand pain relievers. The price of the generic aspirin-free pain reliever had risen 16% in the preceding two years while the price of Levadol had risen 20%, making the price difference $18/case (see Exhibit 3).

Exhibit 3	Average Wholesale Price of Aspirin-Free Pain Relievers (U.S. dollars per case)		
Year	*MB*	*Hoffman*	*Generic*
1996	$182	$180	$172
1997	201	218	187
1998	218	212	200

"My greatest fear about Brazil is that we're being finessed by firms with a better knowledge of international business. Levadol should not be losing market share to Hoffman," said Paul McConnell. "I could understand some loss of market to the locals, but even there we should be able to sell the customer on our product superiority. Hoffman has a premium product. But it's not as good as ours."

A06-99-0026

Appendix 1
Multiquimica do Brasil
Financial Data: Consolidated Corporate Results
(millions of U.S. dollars)

Income Statement	1998	1997
Sales		
Agricultural chemicals	$ 658	$ 600
Industrial chemicals	583	513
Petrochemicals	652	585
Pharmaceutical products	1,210	1,086
Subtotal	$3,103	$2,784
Cost of goods sold	$1,300	$1,169
Selling and administrative expenses	884	793
Depreciation	296	262
Research expense	292	250
Subtotal	$2,772	$2,474
Operating Income	$ 331	$ 310
Interest expense	45	42
Other income, net	41	30
Subtotal	$ 4	$ 12
Income before taxes	$ 327	$ 298
Income taxes	126	110
Net income	$ 201	$ 188

Balance Sheet	1998	1997
Current assets	$1,016	$1,001
Net property, plant and equipment	1,536	1,338
Other assets	241	139
Total Assets	$2,793	$2,478
Current liabilities	$ 363	$ 297
Long-term debt	394	309
Deferred income taxes	140	124
Stockholders' equity	1,896	1,748
Total Liabilities and Stockholders' Equity	$2,793	$2,478

Source: Multichemical Industries Inc., 1998 Annual Report (preliminary).

Appendix 2
Multiquimica do Brasil

Foreign Exchange Rates and Interest Rates (end of year)

Year	Brazilian *real* (R$/$)	Brazilian Interest Rates (% per annum)	Swiss francs (SF/$)	Swiss Interest Rates (% per annum)	U.S. dollar Interest Rates (% per annum)
1992	——	nm	1.4560	7.80	6.25
1993	0.119	nm	1.4795	6.40	6.00
1994	0.846	nm	1.3115	5.51	7.14
1995	0.972	52.25	1.1505	5.48	8.83
1996	1.039	26.45	1.3464	4.97	8.27
1997	1.117	24.35	1.4553	4.47	8.44
1998	1.210	28.00	1.3765	4.07	8.35

nm = not meaningful. With inflation rates of over 2000% in the 1992-1994 period, nominal interest rates were artificially set by government at rates frequently below the rate of inflation. Officially, interest rates in Brazil in 1993 and 1994 were 3,293.5% and 5,175.24%, respectively. All interest rates are lending rates (prime rates).

Note on Brazilian exchange rate: On March 16, 1990, the *cruzeiro* replaced the *new cruzado* as the official currency at a 1 to 1 basis. On August 1, 1993, the *cruzeiro real* replaced the *cruzeiro* as the official exchange rate, with 1,000 *cruzeiros* equaling 1 *cruzeiro real*. On July 1, 1994, the *real* replaced the *cruzeiro real* as the official currency at a rate of 2,750 *cruzeiro real* per *real*.

Consumer Price Index Numbers and Yearly Percentage Changes

Year	Brazil Index	Brazil % Chg	Switzerland Index	Switzerland % Chg	United States Index	United States % Chg
1992	0.1	94.3	92.1			
1993	2.8	2700%	97.4	3%	94.8	3%
1994	60.2	2050%	98.2	1%	97.3	3%
1995	100.0	66%	100.0	2%	100.0	3%
1996	115.8	16%	100.8	1%	102.9	3%
1997	123.8	7%	101.3	0%	105.3	2%
1998	127.7	3%	101.3	0%	107.0	2%

Source: *International Financial Statistics*, International Monetary Fund, monthly.

HARVARD | BUSINESS | SCHOOL

9-707-512
DECEMBER 12, 2006

PANKAJ GHEMAWAT
RAYMOND HILL
L. G. THOMAS

Southern Company's Investment in CEMIG

In the spring of 1997, the U.S. electric utility industry was beginning its fifth year of expansion into overseas markets. Prior to 1992, the investing activities of U.S. electric utilities had been closely restricted since the passage of the 1935 Electric Holding Company Act, adopted in response to perceived manipulation of utility stocks in the 1920s. As the 1990s began, however, a worldwide movement was beginning to privatize and deregulate utilities of all types: telecommunications, airlines, water and natural gas, as well as electricity. Chile had been the earliest country to privatize its electric utilities, but the real momentum came when Margaret Thatcher's government in the United Kingdom not only privatized its government-owned electric system, but also established a competitive market structure for most of the industry.

Southern Company, a holding company for five utilities in the southeastern United States, was an early participant in the wave of overseas investment. Southern was one of the largest utility companies in the United States—the cover of its 1996 annual report featured a picture of a gorilla to illustrate its claim that it was the "900 pound gorilla" of the industry. Southern had begun with investments in Argentina, Chile, and the Bahamas in 1993. In 1994, Bill Dahlberg, a charismatic leader who had worked his way up from a job washing electric meters, had become the company's President and CEO. Dahlberg had increased the speed and scale of Southern's overseas investments with expansions into Europe and Asia. The company was now focused on Brazil, the major attraction in Latin America. With an economy almost three times the size of Argentina's and ten times the size of Chile's, Brazil offered growth opportunities on a scale that could make a significant contribution to a $30 billion (in assets) company like Southern. Brazil's privatization had started slowly in 1995 with the sale of a single utility without any participation from foreign investors. In 1996, however, consortia led by U.S. and European companies had bought two large utilities serving the area around Rio de Janeiro, and the government expected a full calendar of further asset sales in 1997—and active competition for those assets.

In addition to Brazil's attractions as a new electricity market, Southern's team in Brazil had developed a unique opportunity for its initial investment there, in Companhia Energetica do Minas Gerais (CEMIG). CEMIG was one of the largest electric utilities in Latin America, distributing electricity to almost 17 million people in an area accounting for around 12% of Brazil's GDP. Unlike most other Brazilian distribution companies, CEMIG also owned a significant amount (roughly 5000 MW) of its own generating capacity, allowing it to generate about 85% of the electricity it sold.

Professor Pankaj Ghemawat and Professors Raymond Hill and L. G. Thomas of Emory Univesity prepared this case. This case was developed from published sources. HBS cases are developed solely as the basis for class discussion. Cases are not intended to serve as endorsements, sources of primary data, or illustrations of effective or ineffective management.

Although CEMIG was a publicly traded company, the state government of Minas Gerais was the controlling shareholder, with 84% ownership, and would continue to be the majority owner after selling off a 33% interest. The 33% block would be sold to the highest bidder under a sealed bid process, but Southern thought that it had created a privileged position for itself. Knowing that the state government would be concerned about the identity of the company's new co-owner, Southern's team had been working with Minas Gerais officials for months on a shareholders' agreement that would go into effect if Southern were the winning bidder. The shareholder agreement would provide Southern with specific representation on the board of directors, as well as the right to fill some key operational and management positions. Southern's management thought that the shareholders' agreement significantly enhanced the value of the minority stake in CEMIG.

In April 1997, about a month before the expected share sale, Bill Dalhberg was preparing to discuss the CEMIG investment proposal with his board of directors. He was pleased with the work his team had done, but he knew that the board would be concerned about the risk of investing in a country with Brazil's volatile economic history. The state government had set a minimal acceptable bid of R$60 per 1000 shares, or just over US $1 billion for the shares the state was selling. Before he took this investment to his board, Dahlberg needed to convince himself that it was worth that price.

The Electricity Supply Industry

At the birth of the industry in the 1880s, each user generated his own electricity and consumed it on site. These "isolated plant" electrical systems were the most common supplier of electricity to customers in most countries until 1915. Gradually, new technologies for generation permitted construction of large, efficient plants far from final consumers. The electricity these large plants generated had to be transmitted long distances over high-voltage lines and then distributed to retail customers over low-voltage local lines. In the United States, the number of large-scale generating stations grew from fewer than 24 in 1882, to 500 in 1885, to 2000 by 1891.[1]

The 20ᵗʰ-Century Industry

By the 1920s, centralized supply had largely replaced isolated plants, and the electricity industry had assumed the structure that it would retain through most of the 20th century. Three distinct vertical stages were distinguishable—generation, transmission, and distribution—each potentially a "natural monopoly." An industry was considered a natural monopoly when production exhibited unlimited economies of scale—unit costs continuously fell as the size of operations increased. A single large supplier would, in such situations, always have lower unit costs than smaller suppliers that collectively produced the same output. The historical drivers of economies of scale differed by vertical stage. Economies of scale in generation were concentrated at the plant level (due to spreading of fixed costs) and at the firm level (due to use of a portfolio of multiple plants to meet variable demand). Economies of scale in transmission and distribution occurred because the carrying capacity of cables rose geometrically with their size (a single larger cable is always more efficient than multiple smaller cables) and because of the huge fixed costs of constructing a cable grid. As a result, a single grid for transmission or distribution should have been cheaper than a combination of multiple, competing grids.

The cost structure for electricity supply required a long-term perspective by investors, as the majority of costs represented recovery of investment in fixed assets with very long lives. Coal or oil generation plants were typically treated as 40- to 50-year investments. Indeed, a recent study found the majority of generation capacity in California to be over 35-years-old.[2] Transmission and distribution grids had even longer lives. McKinsey estimated that "it takes 20 to 30 years to create value on a net present value basis" for typical electricity investments.[3]

Not only was the 20th-century electricity supply industry consolidated into monopolies at each vertical stage, but it was also usually vertically integrated. A single firm typically owned all three industry segments, generating electricity in its own plants, transmitting it over its own power lines, and distributing it over its own local grids. The rationale for this arrangement was that if the chain of monopoly were split vertically into separate firms, monopoly suppliers of power would have confronted monopsony purchasers, creating all kinds of contracting problems.

The localization of competition implied by strong segmentation of electricity demand, both geographically and over time, exacerbated concerns about monopoly power. In many geographies, the potential markets linking generation, transmission, and distribution remained thin, only a handful of suppliers or buyers faced each other. The time dimension magnified this small-numbers problem. Almost uniquely among commodities, electricity could not be practically stored, but had to be consumed as produced. Unfortunately, final demand for it was highly volatile. Thus, final demand was greater in the day than at night, and was usually greater on hot summer days than in winter ones. The combination of non-storable supply with volatile demand required significant capacity to be built in the industry to serve only peak loads. Indeed, some generation and transmission capacity was used only for a few hours on a few hot summer afternoons. The costs of serving peak demand were, therefore, much higher than those for off-peak demand. In a sense, electricity supply at each instant in time was a separate commodity with its own distinct costs. This "intertemporal segmentation" made markets that were thin to begin with vulnerable to manipulation.

A New Era

The electricity supply industry had great importance for a nation's economy. Electricity was usually the largest single industry in any economy, making up some ten percent of a nation's GDP.[4] Further, the price other companies paid for electricity affected their own performance and competitiveness. While vertical integration removed risks of market manipulation within links of the electricity supply chain, final consumers were exposed to an enormous monopoly supplier. To protect consumers from monopoly, the 20th-century electricity industry was subjected to government control.

State control solved the problem of monopoly, but created different problems in its place. State-owned firms and, to a lesser extent, state-regulated firms often lacked incentives for efficiency and innovation. Managers had little incentive to fire excess workers as long as revenues generated covered operating costs. In some countries, electricity firms were run as a jobs program for the politically well connected, creating significant overstaffing. For example, employment in the generation sector of the British industry went from 48,000 to 24,000 after privatization.[5] Worse, in several less-developed countries, governments failed to make necessary investments in expansion, or even maintenance of electricity fixed assets. Some generation plants in developing countries operated at 20 percent of name-plate capacity. Blackouts and other supply problems were frequent. The resulting productivity of national electricity firms differed dramatically across countries (see **Exhibit 1**).

Additionally, regulated or state-controlled electricity firms had disincentives to adopt new technologies that eroded (or "stranded") the value of their existing capital assets. Yet, beginning in the 1980s, new technologies for generation of electricity emerged that challenged the established firms' large, centralized plants. Some of these new technologies were not competitive on financial grounds, but had strong environmental benefits (solar, wind, geothermal). In order to hasten adoption of these nascent technologies, governments in several nations allowed new firms, called independent power producers (IPPs), to enter the generation sector. Several governments permitted the IPPs to connect directly to the transmission grid and forced established electricity monopolies to carry IPP power to final consumers. Interconnection charges had to be tightly regulated to prevent established firms from pricing the IPPs out of the market.

As the 1980s unfolded, IPPs indeed proliferated in the electricity supply industry. However, the key technology they used was not one that environmentalists anticipated. Military research for advanced aircraft jet engines, the deregulation of the U.S. natural gas market in the1980s, and forced access for IPP firms all came together in the form of a new technology: combined-cycle gas turbine (CCGT) technology. CCGT recycled the hot exhaust gas from gas turbines to generate additional electricity and increase output efficiency, and was developed and championed by turbine manufacturers, led by General Electric. Prices for natural gas fell with deregulation, making CCGT plants significantly more efficient and less expensive than older coal-fired plants (see **Exhibit 2**). CCGT capital costs ran to half those for coal plants, with lower maintenance costs, as well. CCGT plants also had significant environmental advantages over coal or oil-fired power plants.

The entry of IPP firms was expected to reduce wholesale prices for electricity by ten to 20 percent,[6] and permit the deregulation of generation. The typical deregulatory process vertically separated generation from transmission and distribution, and then opened generation sectors to competitive entry. Both the high-voltage transmission grid and the low-voltage distribution grid typically continued to be treated as natural monopolies that were required to carry or "wheel" power between IPPs and final consumers at tariffs that were regulated. Often, the owner of transmission and distribution grids was required to divest any generation assets, to forestall access problems for new entrants in generation. This reconfiguration fundamentally altered the supply chain for electric power. It also blurred the boundaries between the natural gas and electricity industries and their formerly separate supply chains.

Proponents of deregulation thought that the new supply chain for electric power also allowed significant profit opportunities for innovative merchant firms (see **Exhibit 3**). Upstream, deregulated generation firms should be able to bid for more peak-load demand, with associated higher prices. And restructuring of generation would allow better cost control, particularly through elimination of excess staff and excess reserve capacity, both of which had burgeoned under state control. Midstream, the still-regulated transmission business was expected to offer surprising possibilities for profit through consolidation to achieve economies of scale and scope and operational improvements: thus, the equity value of the regulated British transmission businesses had tripled after their privatization in 1990.[7] Downstream, the competitive power-services market was anticipated to offer opportunities for value-added services. Management of energy infrastructure for large customers provided one promising path, particularly with integration of formerly separate markets for natural gas and electricity. Merchant trading of electricity, as well as associated risk-management products with features of insurance or derivatives, were seen as an even more promising new source of profit. Derivatives were traded for many commodities (oil, wheat, currency). The complexity of electricity markets, with their geographic and intertemporal segmentation, greatly increased the possibilities for financial arbitrage. This complexity was generally seen as providing an initial advantage in merchant trading to firms with actual operations in the electricity industry (or, in the case of the leading trader, Enron, in natural gas) over the financial institutions that dominated other derivative markets.

The Emerging Global Industry

The demand for electricity was growing worldwide, with the fastest growth expected in the developing countries. The OECD predicted that through 2020, nearly 3000 GW of new generating capacity would be installed throughout the globe, or roughly the equivalent of four and a half times current U.S. market size (see **Exhibit 4**). About one fifth of this construction was expected to replace existing generation plants, and the remainder to meet new demand. And more than half of this new capacity was expected to be added in developing countries. Total global investments in new power plants were estimated to reach $3 trillion, with $1.7 trillion in developing countries. The need to refurbish existing plants due to age and inadequate maintenance added to these investment needs. Investments in transmission lines and distribution systems could be as large again, especially in developing countries that needed significant network expansion.

These massive investments loomed large in relation to the financial resources of most of the developing world. Globalization of the electricity industry was widely seen as the best answer to this financing problem. Advocates of globalization, ranging from universities, consulting firms (notably McKinsey and Cambridge Energy Research Associates), governments of the developed nations, and multilateral institutions (including the World Bank and regional development banks), all provided prestigious support for foreign direct investment. The established electricity supply firms from the developed countries of North American and Western Europe were widely seen as the most likely providers of such investment. In the immediate aftermath of World War II, electricity generation in Latin America in general and Brazil in particular had been dominated by private utilities (see **Exhibit 5**). Rapid growth over the next several decades was largely accounted for, however, by state-owned utilities, to the point where private utilities' share of the total shrank to about 10% by 1975. A variety of problems with this state-owned model (limited supply, inefficient management, and lack of investment) subsequently led to reforms in this industry.[8] Reforms involving privatization and restructuring began with Chile in the 1980s, spread in 1992 to Argentina and then to Peru, Bolivia, Panama, El Salvador, Guatemala, Nicaragua, Costa Rica, Honduras, and Brazil, with Venezuela, Mexico and Ecuador also taking some steps in this direction. This first generation of deregulation was thought to have had generally positive effects in terms of reducing shortages and theft and increasing labor productivity and electrification, with the major complaints being sounded around higher prices for what was widely perceived to be an essential service.

The opening up of the electricity sector in Latin America and around the world had induced an extremely broad array of firms to undertake foreign direct investment (FDI) in electricity supply. These multinational investors included established utilities from America, Europe, Hong Kong, and Chile; petroleum firms such as Exxon and Shell; equipment firms such as General Electric and ABB; and American IPP energy firms such as Enron and AES. Market shares were quite fragmented across these international electricity suppliers (see **Exhibit 6**), and the targets of their investment were quite diffuse (see **Exhibit 7**). But such aggregate data masked the passage of control of entire national electricity industries (such as those in Argentina and Peru) into foreign hands. The cycle completed in the United Kingdom—of reforms, entry by foreign firms, increased competition and, finally, the emergence of merchant trading—was seen by many as a model for how competition in many other deregulating electricity markets would evolve.

Southern Company

In the United States, electricity was provided by a patchwork of many companies. In addition to dozens of municipal and cooperative electric companies, there were over 100 investor-owned electric utilities in the U.S. serving customers within a regulated franchise area. Most of these utilities operated in only part of the geographic area of a single state. In contrast, Southern Company was a holding company that owned five utilities operating in four different states: Georgia, Alabama, Mississippi, and Florida. Two of these utilities, Georgia Power and Alabama Power, were, individually, among the fifteen largest electric utilities in the United States.

Southern was first organized as a holding company for four southeastern utilities in 1924. In 1930, it merged into an even bigger holding company, Commonwealth and Southern, which controlled an even larger number of utilities extending from Florida to Michigan. In the aftermath of the stock market crash of 1929, utility holding companies were seen as an instrument for stock manipulation. The 1935 Public Utility Holding Company Act created a special SEC oversight for utility holding companies and imposed on them a number of restrictions and special reporting requirements. Among the new restrictions was the requirement that all utilities under common ownership be geographically contiguous, thus reducing Southern to its present area of operation.

Over time, Southern developed a reputation as a reliable provider of relatively low-cost power (due, in part, to a fleet of large, efficient, coal-fired power plants). The company benefited from and contributed to the rapid economic growth experienced by the post-WWII South. Southern also enjoyed the reputation of astutely managing its relationships with regulators. Like a number of other utilities, in the early 1980s, Southern had suffered from the combination of regulated tariffs lagging the high inflation of the period, slow economic growth producing slower than expected growth in demand, and significant cost over-runs in the construction of nuclear plants begun as a response to the earlier oil crises. By the early 1990s, Southern had re-established its financial strength and enjoyed a return on equity significantly above the industry average. In most years, Southern was named the country's "Most Admired Utility" in *Fortune* magazine's annual ranking. Its stock market capitalization was typically the highest of all U.S. utilities.

During the 1980s, several utilities had established subsidiaries to participate in the independent power business, which Congress had created with its enactment of the Public Utility Regulatory Policy Act (PURPA). PURPA required utilities to buy power from independent producers at their "avoided cost" under long-term contracts and represented a first step in bringing competition to electricity generation. Southern had entered the independent power business in a peripheral way through one of its subsidiaries, Southern Electric International (SEI). SEI had been formed in the early 1980s primarily to provide consulting services to other utilities, using personnel who had become redundant with the virtual cessation of new plant construction by Southern's regulated operating companies. Under several different management teams, SEI had attempted the development of several independent power projects, but, aside from some small investments in projects developed by others, had accomplished little by 1992.

The Energy Policy Act of 1992 provided a legal basis for holding companies like Southern to invest overseas and also expanded their ability to invest in independent power projects. In response, Southern's management and board engaged outside consultants to review the potential scope of the new business opportunities now open to them. Southern became convinced that the next decade would see a wave of privatizations and repeated opportunities to build plants in countries where the demand for electricity was growing much more rapidly than in Southern's home territory. Tom Boren, a career Southern employee who had developed a reputation as a strong and ambitious manager, was named as SEI's new president, with a mandate to design and implement a business plan that would accelerate Southern's growth. A year later, SEI made its first overseas investment, buying a controlling interest in a utility in the Bahamas. In 1993, SEI also won the bidding for a 1000 MW hydro station in Argentina and a majority interest in a generating and transmission utility in northern Chile.

In 1994, SEI led a partnership as the winning bidder when Trinidad and Tobago privatized a controlling interest in its national generating company. Later that year, A.W. "Bill" Dahlberg became Southern's chairman and CEO. Dahlberg was enthusiastic about the company's international expansion; and, in 1995, the scale of SEI's foreign activity rose considerably when it completed a $1.6 billion hostile takeover of SWEB, one of the recently privatized British distribution companies—the first hostile cross-border acquisition in the industry's history. Following the U.K. acquisition, Dahlberg set a specific and aggressive goal for SEI: by 2003, the subsidiary should contribute 30% of Southern's total net income. Since Southern's 1996 net income was approximately $1 billion, SEI's annual earnings target was several hundred million dollars, or several times its 1996 contribution. To publicize this growth strategy, Southern launched the electric utility industry's first-ever national advertising campaign in January 1997, highlighting, in particular, the company's "experience in more than 30 countries on four continents."[9]

Dahlberg's push for Southern Company to grow faster reflected a general trend in the industry, as utilities sought to capitalize on a stock market that seemed to place particular weight on earnings growth. From the beginning of 1996 through the first quarter of 1997, the Dow Jones Industrial Index had risen by 35%, but the utility index had actually declined slightly. Southern's stock price was down more than 6% in the middle of this stock market boom! Since the utility industry as a whole was limited by the slow growth off aggregate domestic demand for its principal product, electric companies focused on two avenues for growth: through acquisition at home or expansion abroad. Duke, Southern's primary rival, in terms of size and prestige, as the industry's pre-eminent firm, was following both paths. In addition to expansion in Latin America, Duke announced in November 1996 that it would acquire Pan Energy, a natural gas pipeline company in the U.S., for $7.7 billion.

Other utilities had rushed to make acquisitions in the United Kingdom, following Southern's example. Within 18 months of Southern's takeover of SWEB, nine additional U.S. utilities had jumped on the bandwagon to acquire all or part of a British utility (not including those who tried and failed).

The pressure to consolidate or go overseas was reinforced by the expectation that further de-regulation in the U.S. would shrink the size of utilities that did not adapt. Barry Abramson, a leading utility stock analyst with Prudential, noted that, "The business environment for electric utilities in the U.S. is only going to get tougher due to the likely implementation of retail electric competition."[10] Many analysts and industry executives agreed with this perspective, believing that the utilities that did not change their business models would not only shrink, but would also likely disappear through acquisition by the companies following a growth strategy.

Dahlberg's plans to expand Southern internationally appeared to be roughly on track. In the fall of 1996, SEI had reached an agreement to buy CEPA, the largest independent power company in Asia. CEPA had plants in operation and under development in China, the Philippines, Pakistan, and Indonesia, and was a vehicle that would let Southern capitalize on the rapidly growing demand for electricity in Asian markets. By January 1997, SEI had also begun negotiations with the city of Berlin, which wanted to divest its shares in the local utility, BEWAG. These negotiations looked as though they would be successful, giving Southern a major position on the European continent later in the year. With SWEB and BEWAG in Europe and CEPA in Asia, Latin America now became the smallest part of Southern's overseas business. The chance to acquire a significant foothold in Brazil through CEMIG was being presented as an attractive complement to these other businesses. (See **Exhibit 8** for an overview of Southern's international businesses).

The capital markets were generally bullish about Southern's strategy. A report by analysts at Morgan Stanley Dean Witter was not atypical:

We are resuming coverage of Southern Company with an Outperform rating. Along with Duke Energy and the two largest California companies, we believe SO represents the highest ranks of the Hyper-Electric thesis—a play on the successful exploiting of the opportunities in unregulated gas and electricity that can, we believe, produce stable growth rates at least in the high single digits.

Among SO's advantages for investors, we believe, is the fact that it already has critical mass and first-mover advantages in its extensive scope—its market cap is second only to Duke's, allowing flexibility in growth.[11]

The CEMIG Transaction

Under its distribution concession, CEMIG supplied approximately 97% of the electricity consumed in the state of Minas Gerais. Minas Gerais, the second largest (by population) state in Brazil, was home to a number of energy-intensive industries, such as aluminum, cement, steel, and mining. Minas Gerais accounted for approximately 12.5% of Brazil's GDP.

Historically, CEMIG's retail tariffs had been set to allow it to earn a target rate of return on capital. However, Brazil was now in the middle of a transition to the type of rate-setting model used in the United Kingdom and Argentina. Under this new model, companies had a tariff schedule fixed for, say, seven or eight years. During that period, the company passed along to its customers annual inflation adjustments and retained the benefits of any cost reductions that it achieved. A new regulatory agency had been established in December 1996 and was in the process of writing the rules for the new system.

A regulatory regime in which it kept the benefit of efficiency gains was important to CEMIG and any future investor in its privatization. CEMIG was already relatively efficient by the standards of the average Brazilian or Latin American utility, but there was still significant room for improvement. In 1996, with 15,100 employees, CEMIG had distributed about 2,000 MWH of electricity per employee, and its annual personnel costs topped R$500 million. Southern's largest subsidiary, Georgia Power, distributed about three times that amount of electricity per employee, and even the Chilean utilities, which had been privatized a decade earlier, were twice as efficient as CEMIG in this respect. A new investor could take comfort in the fact that CEMIG had already shown some success in reducing its workforce through a reduction of about 1,400 personnel over the preceding year.

In 1996, CEMIG sold approximately 32,000 GWH of electricity. Most industry analysts expected CEMIG's sales volume to grow by about 3% over the foreseeable future. Unlike most of the Brazilian distribution companies, CEMIG owned a substantial amount of generation capacity—5000 MW—and produced 27,500 GHW of the power that it distributed. Almost all of CEMIG's generating capacity was in hydroelectric plants. CEMIG might be able to roughly double its generating capacity over time, given the state's hydro resources. This would allow CEMIG to become a major player as a competitive wholesale market developed in Brazil.

CEMIG had a strong financial position and its long-term debt was less than Reais 1.0 billion, or less than 10% of total capital. (See **Exhibit 9** for summary financial statements.) About 75% of this debt was denominated in foreign currencies. The company's cash flow easily covered capital expenditures while allowing dividends to be increased. The Brazilian government used discounted cash flow (DCF) analysis to set minimum prices for privatizations, and most security analysts who followed the industry used DCF to value utility shares, as well. Mario Epelbaum, Morgan Stanley's analyst, used a projection of the company's EBITDA (see **Exhibit 10**) as the basis for his cash flow forecast. Embedded in his EBITDA forecast were assumptions that CEMIG would be able to reduce employment costs by 17%, would receive an 8%-9% tariff increase when the new regulatory regime was implemented later in the year, and would be able to make additional tariff increases reflecting Brazilian inflation. Epelbaum subtracted an estimated US$340m of annual capital expenditure requirements to arrive at a forecast of net cash flow. He concluded that discounting at a 13% weighted average cost of capital would produce a valuation approximately equal to the minimum price of R$60 per 1,000 shares set by the state of Minas Gerais for the CEMIG share sale. A significant component of his valuation was a terminal value multiple of 14 times cash flow, which assumed continuing good management and a reasonable regulatory environment over the long run.

Prior to the privatization wave of the 1990s, most electricity assets in Brazil had come to be either owned by state governments or controlled by Electrobras, which was, in turn, owned by the Federal government. When the Real currency stabilization plan was implemented, the Brazilian government began a large-scale program of privatization partly as a way of backing it up. The first three distribution companies to be sold, Escelsa, Light, and CERJ, were all under federal control. As was common, the privatization was executed in two steps. In the first step, bidders were qualified by demonstrating that they had the technical and financial capacity to complete the purchase and supervise the operations of the company being sold. In the second step, the government set a minimum price and there was an auction of the government-owned shares. This process insured that the government's shares went to the highest bidder who was qualified and who met the minimum price.

The national government influenced the privatization of the state-owned electric companies only indirectly. In the case of CEMIG, the national government's primary lever for promoting privatization was the indebtedness of the state of Minais Gerais to the national development bank, BNDES. The state government had defaulted on a loan from BNDES secured by shares in CEMIG equal to 33% of the voting stock. BNDES was now forcing the sale of the share bloc in order to repay the debt. Since the state government owned 84% of CEMIG's voting shares, it would still retain a majority control. CEMIG also had non-voting preferred shares outstanding whose financial claims (including the right to receive dividends) on the company were identical to the voting shares. Because of these additional non-voting shares, the 33% bloc of voting shares represented only 14.4% of the approximately 130 billion total shares outstanding—or one-seventh of the financial value of CEMIG.

SEI's business development team had been on the ground in Brazil since early 1995. SEI had originally considered bidding on Escelsa, but had dropped the idea because, at the time of the auction, the government was just beginning to define the institutional and legal framework that would regulate the sector. SEI's team turned its attention to CEMIG after months of discussion with BNDES and state government as well as federal officials.

Having identified CEMIG as a target, the SEI team focused on ways to reduce the risk of a potential investment. There were at least two dimensions of risk to be addressed. The first level was macroeconomic. Southern's investment would be in dollars, but CEMIG's revenues and dividends, the source of Southern's investment return, would be in Brazilian Reais. While the Real Plan appeared to have achieved relative stability in the exchange rate, an investor could hardly ignore Brazil's historical volatility. The SEI team saw no effective way of hedging this currency risk and therefore concentrated on designing a financial structure that would minimize the amount of equity Southern had at risk. Southern's prior use of non-recourse debt to fund a portion of an overseas investment provided a helpful model. Since BNDES was eager to facilitate the transaction, it agreed to facilitate such a financing for the CEMIG privatization. At the minimum price of R$60 per 1000 shares, the bloc of shares would cost nearly US$1.1 billion at the prevailing exchange rate. To help with the financing, BNDES committed to providing letters of credit to support a 12-year loan of US$550 million at an interest rate of 9.8%. With the BNDES credit support, the loan would be non-recourse to Southern. As a result, if the dividend stream from CEMIG were insufficient to service this debt, Southern would have the option of walking away and leaving BNDES on the hook for slightly over one-half the total investment.

The second dimension of risk related to CEMIG's future financial performance. In order for Southern to earn an acceptable return and still pay a price acceptable to the state government, CEMIG's financial performance needed to improve. Southern felt confident that it could bring about such an improvement by cutting costs and growing CEMIG's generating capacity to supply electricity to distribution companies in other states. Under the state's privatization plan, though, it would still retain a majority interest, rendering a new investor incapable of forcing through changes over the opposition of the state government. The SEI team sought to address this risk by negotiating a shareholders' agreement with the state government. Under the agreement, Southern would be entitled to appoint four members to the eleven-person CEMIG board and control the appointments to some key financial and operating positions in management. The agreement also gave Southern control over certain operating decisions, such as significant deviations from the budget. It did not, however, provide Southern with absolute protection. As long as the state continued to own a majority of the voting shares, it could find a way to implement unilateral decisions if it chose to do so potentially frustrating Southern's plans for the company. The SEI team did believe, though, that the agreement laid a solid foundation for a relationship between Southern and the state government, allowing them to work toward common goals.

It was public knowledge that Southern was discussing these arrangements with the state government and Southern had specifically informed BNDES about them. Nonetheless, while the BNDES funding was likely to be available to any qualifying bidder, the shareholders' agreement was only between Southern and the state of Minas Gerais. It appeared that, from the state government's perspective, the shareholder agreement represented a way of asserting control: it might be forced by a federal entity to sell a bloc of shares, but it would retain the right to select its partner. After months of work by the SEI team, state officials had become convinced that Southern—because of its size, financial strength, and experience in managing regulated, integrated utilities—was an acceptable partner in this privatization that was being imposed on them. Investors other than Southern could certainly bid for and win the share auction, but they would be minority owners if they did win, without the protective mantle of the shareholder agreement.

Exhibit 1   Industry Productivity Comparisons, Selected Nations

World power industry productivity comparisons

Sales per employee in gigawatt hours, 1990

United States	5.9
Japan	5.6
Canada	4.8
Belgium	4.0
New Zealand	3.2
France	3.1
Spain	3.0
Netherlands	2.6
United Kingdom	2.3
Australia	2.2
Germany	2.1
Mexico	1.2
Portugal	1.1
Greece	1.0
China	0.6
India	0.2

Source: Silverman, L.P. "Electric Power—The Next Generation" *McKinsey Quarterly* (1994, 3).

Exhibit 2   Innovation in Generation: CCGT versus Established Technology

	Combined Cycle Gas Turbine	Traditional Coal Generator
Average time to be fully operational (years)	1.5–2.0	3.0–3.5
Capital investment ($ per kilowatt)	525	1,500
Minimum scale (megawatts)	150	300–500
Efficiency (percentage)	55–60	35–40
Operations Costs (¢ per kilowatt-hour)	1.7–2.4	2.3

Source: Leslie, K., K. Kausman, and G. Bard "European Power: Managing Through Deregulation" McKinsey Quarterly (1999, 1).

Exhibit 3   Supply Chains, Vertically Integrated Monopolies vs. Energy Merchants

Electricity sector vision

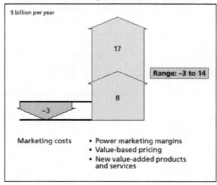

Value at stake in generation

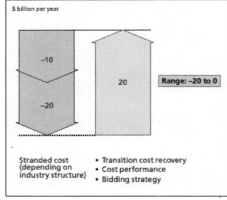

Value at stake in the wires business

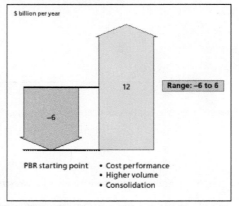

Value at stake in the power services business

Source: Heller, W.J., P.J. Jansen, and L.P. Silverman "The New Electric Industry: What's At Stake?" *McKinsey Quarterly* (1996, 3).

Southern Company's Investment in CEMIG   707-512

Exhibit 4   Forecast World Electricity Consumption (Billion Kilowatt-Hours)

	1990	1993	1995	2000	2005	2010	2015	2020
OECD								
North America	3,362.7	3,562.9	3,771.6	4,304.4	4,585	5,093	5,605	6,100
United States	2,816.7	2,988.4	3,162.4	3,621.0	3,793	4,170	4,556	4,916
Canada	438.3	454.7	474.8	499.8	558	612	661	711
Mexico	107.1	119.2	133.7	182.8	235	311	388	473
Europe	2,372.3	2,536.4	2,654.3	2,942.7	3185	3457	3744	4078
Pacific (NZ and Australia)	165.8	177.3	187.4	221.8	255	278	299	322
Japan	764.6	806.4	881.4	943.7	1,036	1,117	1,194	1,275
Other OECD (South Korea)	93.4	125.4	176.3	254.1	309	348	392	429
TOTAL OECD	**6747.9**	**7108.6**	**7565.0**	**8586.9**	**9371**	**10,293**	**11,234**	**12,204**
non-OECD								
EE/FSU	1,597.8	1,374.1	1,227.2	1,201.9	1,331	1,452	1,611	1,740
Former Soviet Union	1,488.4	1,286.4	1,133.5	1,116.4	1,218	1,331	1,479	1,600
Eastern Europe (less OECD)	109.4	87.7	93.7	85.5	112	121	131	140
Western Europe non-OECD	74.0	66.8	63.2	65.1				
Asia	1,165.9	1,467.2	1,725.5	2,340.7	2,784	3,552	4,427	5,429
China	550.9	744.1	883.4	1,206.3	1,523	2,031	2,631	3,349
India	257.1	316.9	369.7	509.9	537	649	784	923
Other Asia	358.0	406.2	472.4	624.5	724	872	1,012	1,157
Middle East	212.8	259.5	302.5	412.8	449	546	642	742
Africa	286.9	305.6	327.8	386.6	460	550	671	776
Central and South America	462.4	529.8	591.9	724.3	788	988	1,249	1,517
Total non-OECD	**3,800.6**	**3,936.1**	**4,175.0**	**5,066.2**	**5,811.6**	**7,088.1**	**8,599.8**	**10,204.4**
World Total	**10,548.6**	**11,044.8**	**11,740.0**	**13,653.1**	**15,183.0**	**17,381.0**	**19,834.0**	**22,408.0**

Source: Cumulative FDI, 1992-1996.

Exhibit 5   Electricity Generation in Latin America, 1950–1975

Year	Brazil				Rest of Latin America			
	Electricity Generated (Gwh)	Private Utilities	Government Utilities	Self-Generated	Electricity Generated (Gwh)	Private Utilities	Government Utilities	Self-Generated
1950	8.2	91%	0%	9%	19.4	57%	14%	29%
1960	22.9	65%	16%	19%	44.8	22%	49%	29%
1975	80.4	11%	83%	6%	149.1	9%	76%	15%

Source: Joseph W. Mullen, *Energy in Latin America: The Historical Record* (Santiago, Chile: United Nations, CEPAL, 1978), p. 65.

Southern Company's Investment in CEMIG

Exhibit 6   The 20 Largest Investors in Electricity FDI (Cumulative FDI, 1992-1996)

RANK	FIRM	HQ COUNTRY	US$ MILLION
1.	Electricité de France	France	1,464
2.	International Power	Britain	1,263
3.	Tractabel	Belgium	1,242
4.	Southern	USA, Georgia	1,130
5.	Edison International	USA, California	1,124
6.	Endesa	Spain	1,112
7.	TXU	USA, Texas	917
8.	AEP	USA, Ohio	869
9.	Enron	USA, IPP	815
10.	Gener	Chile	808
11.	Entergy	USA, Louisiana	692
12.	GPU	USA, New Jersey	692
13.	AES	USA, IPP	690
14.	CalEnergy	USA, IPP	679
15.	RWE	Germany	665
16.	Cinergy	USA, Ohio	586
17.	Endesa de Chile	Chile	518
18.	Reliant	USA, Texas	490
19.	Dominion	USA, Virginia	479
20.	E.On Energie	Germany	469

Source: Casewriters.

Exhibit 7   The 20 Largest Recipients of Electricity FDI, (Cumulative FDI, 1992-1996)

Rank	Recipient County	# of Projects	US$ Million
1.	Britain	19	4,321
2.	Australia	10	2,462
3.	Argentina	35	2,167
4.	China	23	1,717
5.	Hungary	9	1,250
6.	Brazil	5	1,131
7.	Colombia	5	1,076
8.	Peru	9	765
9.	USA	14	709
10.	Philippines	10	701
11.	Pakistan	8	605
12.	Indonesia	6	588
13.	Chile	5	430
14.	Germany	7	422
15.	Switzerland	2	400
16.	India	8	343
17.	Bolivia	8	271
18.	Sweden	2	267
19.	Thailand	5	257
20.	Portugal	3	231

Source: Casewriters.

Southern Company's Investment in CEMIG

707-512

Exhibit 8a Southern's International Operations

		1993	1994	1995	1996
	Latin America	54	181	189	197
Operating Revenues	International	54	181	561	1506
	Southern	8489	8297	9180	10358
	Latin America	11	36	35	0
Operating Income	International	11	36	73	141
	Southern	1765	1715	1886	1854
	Latin America	733	1167	1141	1457
Assets	International	733	1167	4505	4423
	Southern	25911	27042	30522	30292
Equity Invested	Latin America	304	406	406	406
	International	304	406	1124	944
Book equity	Southern	7684	8186	8772	9216

Notes: 1) "Latin America" includes the Caribbean

2) "Equity Investment" is amount invested less non-recourse debt and proceeds from asset sales. It does not include any dividends received.

Source: Compiled by case writers from Southern Company 10-k filings with the SEC.

Exhibit 8b Distribution of Southern's Foreign Direct Investment by Region, May 1997*

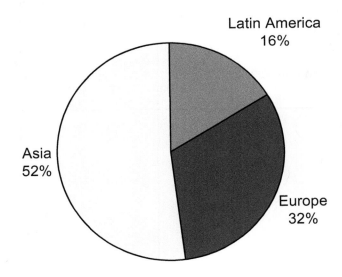

* Pro-forma for BEWAG = $2.4 bn

Source: Compiled by case writers from Southern Company 10-k filings with the SEC.

Exhibit 9   CEMIG Financial Statements (millions of reais)

	1995	1996		1995	1996
Net operating revenues	1,726	1,956	Assets		
			Current assets	640	750
Operating expense			Property, plant, equipment	10,981	11,273
Personnel	(510)	(553)	Other long term assets	974	1,180
Electricity purchases	(462)	(435)	Total assets	12,595	13,203
Dep. and Amort.	(467)	(441)			
Other	(272)	(292)	Liabilities		
Total	(1,711)	(1,721)	Current liabilities	857	993
Other income	100	98	Long term debt	747	880
			Deferred income tax	492	524
Taxes and social contribution	(68)	(78)	Other long term payables	1,106	1,237
Deferred income tax	190	8	Total liabilities	3,202	3,634
Profit sharing	-	(21)			
			Stockholders equity	9,393	9,569
Net income	237	242			

Source: Donaldson, Lufkin & Jenrette, May 29 1997.

Exhibit 10   Forecasts of CEMIG Cashflows

	1996	1997	1998	1999	2000	2001
Bear Stearns 1/10/97						
EBITDA US$ millions	791	948	1,138	1,304	1,462	na
Morgan Stanley 6/21/97						
EBITDA Reais millions	722	931	1,210	1,446	1,775	1,881
Exchange rate	1.04	1.14	1.25	1.38	1.49	1.61
Donaldson, Lufkin & Jenrette 5/29/97						
EBITDA Reais millions	774	907	1,117	1,352	1,611	na
Exchange rate	1.04	1.14	1.21	1.28	1.30	

Source: Compiled by case writers.

End Notes

[1] Granovetter, M. and P. McGuire "The Making of an Industry: Electricity in the United States" in M. Callon ed. *The Laws of Markets* Oxford: Blackwell, 1998.

[2] CERTS (Consortium for Electric Reliability Technology Solutions) *California's Electricity Generation and Transmission Interconnection Needs Under Alternative Scenarios* (California Energy Commission, November 2003).

[3] Galonski, B. S. Gorner, and V.H. Hoffmann, "When Payback Can Take Decades" *McKinsey Quarterly* (2004, 3).

[4] Dobbs, R. and M. Elson "Regulating Utilities: Have We Got the Formula Right?" *McKinsey Quarterly* (1999, 1).

[5] Brower, M.C., S.D. Thomas, and C. Mitchell *The British Electric Utility Restructuring Experience: History and Lessons for the United States* National Conference of State Legislatures, www.ncsl.org, 1996.

[6] Heller, W.J., P.J. Jansen, and L.P. Silverman "The New Electric Industry: What's At Stake?" *McKinsey Quarterly* (1996, 3).

[7] Heller, et al., 1996.

[8] Rudnick, H. and J. Zolezzi "Electric Sector Deregulation and Restructuring in Latin America: Lessons to Be Learnt and Possible Ways Forward" *IEEE Proceeding Generation, Transmission and Distribution* 148, 2001: 180-184.

[9] *Power Engineering* "The Southern Company Launches National TV Ad Campaign" (March 1, 1997; 11).

[10] Abramson. B.M. "International Investing by U.S. Utilities: We've Only Seen the Tip of the Iceberg" *Institutional Investor* (October 1, 1996; E3).

[11] Morgan Stanley Dean Witter (Kit Konolige) *Electric Utilities Resuming Coverage: Southern Company (SO): A Strong Hyper-Electric* New York: US Investment Research, October 28, 1998.

IV. Project Finance

USING PROJECT FINANCE TO FUND INFRASTRUCTURE INVESTMENTS

by Richard A. Brealey,
Ian A. Cooper, and
Michel A. Habib,
London Business School*

T hroughout most of the history of the industrialized world, much of the funding for large-scale public works such as the building of roads and canals has come from private sources of capital. It was only toward the end of the 19th century that public financing of large "infrastructure" projects began to dominate private finance, and this trend continued throughout most of the 20th century.

Since the early 1980s, however, private-sector financing of large infrastructure investments has experienced a dramatic revival. And, in recent years, such private funding has increasingly taken the form of project finance. The principal features of such project financings have been the following:

■ A project is established as a separate company, which operates under a concession obtained from the host government.

■ A major proportion of the equity of the project company is provided by the project manager or sponsor, thereby tying the provision of finance to the management of the project.

■ The project company enters into comprehensive contractual arrangements with suppliers and customers.

■ The project company operates with a high ratio of debt to equity, with lenders having only limited recourse to the government or to the equity-holders in the event of default.

The above characteristics clearly distinguish project finance from traditional lending. In conventional financing arrangements, projects are generally not incorporated as separate companies; the contractual arrangements are not as comprehensive, nor are the debt-equity ratios as high, as those observed in the case of project finance; and the vast majority of loans offer lenders recourse to the assets of borrowers in case of default.

Our purpose in this paper is to explore some possible rationales for the distinctive characteristics of project finance, from the viewpoint of both the project sponsor and the host government. We do so in the specific context of infrastructure investments. After providing some information about the growth of project finance in funding such investments, we note that project finance is but one of several mechanisms for involving the private sector in funding and managing infrastructure projects. We show how project finance, and the complex web of contractual arrangements that such funding entails, can be used to address "agency problems" that reduce efficiency in large organizations, private as well as public. We also view the contracts among the multiple parties to project financings as risk management devices designed to shift a variety of project risks to those parties best able to appraise and control them. In closing, we discuss what we believe are some common misconceptions about the benefits and costs of project finance—particularly, the notion that project finance represents "expensive finance" for governments—and we contrast project finance with other private-sector options such as privatization and the use of service contracts with private-sector companies.

*We would like to thank Joseph Blum, Carlo Bongianni, Don Lessard, Gill Raine, Mary Wan and Adam Wilson for helpful discussions. The third author would like to acknowledge the financial support of the International Programme on the Management of Engineering and Construction.

THE GROWTH IN PROJECT FINANCE: SOME EVIDENCE

Comprehensive data on the financing of infrastructure projects do not appear to be available. Table 1 does, however, provide information about the growth in the value of those projects in developing countries that have been partially financed by the International Finance Corporation (the World Bank's private sector affiliate).

TABLE 1
VALUE OF PROJECTS INVOLVING IFC PARTICIPATION IN DEVELOPING COUNTRIES

Year of approval	No. of projects	Value of projects $ million
1966-1987	7	517
1988	2	409
1989	6	704
1990	4	1279
1991	6	1103
1992	8	1384
1993	15	3699
1994(1st 6 months)	30	5512

Source: G. Bond and L. Carter, "Financing Private Infrastructure Projects; Emerging Trends from IFC's Experience," International Finance Corporation, Discussion Paper 23, 1994.

Over 80 percent (by value) of the projects involving the IFC have been in the power and telecommunication industries, with the remainder in transportation (roads, railroads, and ports), water, and pipelines. About 50% of the projects have been in Latin America, with the bulk of the remainder in Asia.

The use of project finance has not been restricted to infrastructure investments in developing countries. Indeed, over 40 percent of the project finance loans reported in the 1995 survey conducted by *IFR Project Finance International* were for projects in the United States, Australia, or the United Kingdom. In the United States, the passage of the Public Utility Regulatory Power Act (PURPA) in 1978 provided a major stimulus to the use of project finance by requiring that electric utilities purchase power from independent power produc-

ers. This encouraged the formation of stand-alone power producers able to borrow large sums on the basis of the long-term power purchase agreements they had entered into with electric utilities. Since these projects do not directly involve a government or a government agency, they are somewhat beyond the scope of this article. So are projects in Australia, which have primarily been in extractive industries rather than in infrastructure.

In the U.K. by contrast, the government has been directly involved in a growing number of infrastructure projects since it announced in 1992 the establishment of the Private Finance Initiative (PFI). The PFI is designed to involve the private sector in the financing and the management of infrastructure and other projects. Private finance has so far been used principally for transportation projects such as the £320 million rail link to Heathrow Airport, the £2.7 billion Channel Tunnel Rail Link, a £250 million scheme to build and maintain a new air traffic control center in Scotland, and projects worth more than £500 million to design, build, finance, and operate (DBFO) trunk roads. But the potential scope of the PFI is wide. Over 1,000 potential PFI projects have been identified, and the government has signed contracts to build and maintain such diverse assets as prisons, hospitals, subway cars, and the National Insurance computer system.[1]

SOME ALTERNATIVES TO PROJECT FINANCE

A government need not involve the private sector in either the financing or the management of projects, and may choose to undertake both itself. As we will argue below, the desirability of private-sector involvement in infrastructure projects depends in large part on the extent to which (1) the provision of high-powered incentives is necessary to the success of the project and (2) such incentives can be specified in a verifiable contract.

It is important to note that high-powered incentives need not always be beneficial. For example, consider the hypothetical case of privatized parking enforcement agencies. Such organizations would probably be subject to severe moral hazard problems if provided with high-powered incentives, for they may then have an incentive to claim an offence has been committed even where none has.

1. See Standard & Poor's, *Global Project Finance*, July 1996, pages 24-28, and OXERA, *Infrastructure in the UK.*

The desirability of private sector involvement in infrastructure projects depends in large part on the extent to which the provision of high-powered incentives is necessary to the success of the project. The dominant reason for the growing importance of project finance in funding infrastructure investment is that it addresses agency problems in a way that other forms of financing do not.

It should further be noted that public-sector organizations are not entirely devoid of incentives, and that these are often of the same nature as the incentives found in private-sector companies. Both voters and shareholders have an interest in efficient management, the former as taxpayers and the latter as owners. Both use their votes to discipline inefficient management, the former by voting for a new government, and the latter by voting for a new management. Nonetheless, the greater power and prevalence of incentives in private-sector organizations suggests an important role for these organizations when high-powered incentives are desired.

A government that uses project finance to fund a project obtains both private-sector funding and private-sector management. Project finance therefore reduces the need for government borrowing, shifts part of the risks presented by the project to the private sector, and aims to achieve more effective management of the project. But, as we indicate in Table 2, there are a number of other means of involving the private sector in infrastructure investment. The government can do so through privatization, for example, in which case the private sector provides capital and management services to an entire industry rather than to individual projects. Thus, the government can privatize a public utility that generates and distributes electric power, rather than grant a concession to a private company to generate power that is then sold to the public utility.

If the government simply wishes to benefit from private-sector management expertise, it can contract with the private sector for the provision of management services while continuing to finance the project and retaining ownership of the project's assets. Conversely, the government can simply secure finance by leasing the project's assets from the private sector, while continuing to be responsible for the management of the project.

TABLE 2
WAYS THAT INFRASTRUCTURE PROJECTS CAN BE FUNDED AND MANAGED

Arrangement	Finance	Management
Project finance	Private	Private
Privatization	Private	Private
Service contracts	Government	Private
Leases	Private	Government
Nationalization	Government	Government

In view of these alternatives to project finance, it is natural to ask why it has developed into such an important mechanism for funding infrastructure investments. We argue that the dominant reason for the growing importance of project finance in funding infrastructure investment is that it addresses agency problems in a way that other forms of financing do not.

PROJECT FINANCE AS A RESPONSE TO AGENCY PROBLEMS

Agency problems arise from the differing, and sometimes conflicting, interests of the various parties involved in any large enterprise. Success of the enterprise therefore requires that these parties be provided with incentives to work together for the common good. This can be achieved, to some extent at least, by the appropriate choice of a company's financial structure.

Consider, for example, the problem faced by shareholders in a public corporation who wish to motivate the CEO to work hard to increase firm value. Shareholders would like the CEO to do her utmost to increase shareholder wealth, and they may wish to write a contract that specifies what she should do in all the various circumstances that she may encounter. But such a contract would be impossible to write, if only because of the difficulty of envisaging and describing these various circumstances. Any contract between shareholders and corporate managers will therefore inevitably be incomplete. Furthermore, even if it were possible to write a complete contract that specified exactly what the CEO were to do in every circumstance, it would be very costly for shareholders to monitor the manager to ensure that she was keeping to the contract.

One solution to these problems of incomplete contracting and costly monitoring is to arrange for the manager to take an equity stake in the business. Such a stake ties the manager's wealth to her actions, thus rewarding her for hard work and penalizing her for sloth. The "residual claimancy" associated with the ownership of equity therefore serves to motivate the manager, to some extent at least, in the cases where contracts fail to do so.

The above example illustrates the role of financial structure in solving agency problems. Notice that the CEO's equity stake in the business provides her with the incentive to act in the shareholders'

FIGURE 1
PARTIES TO PROJECT
FINANCING

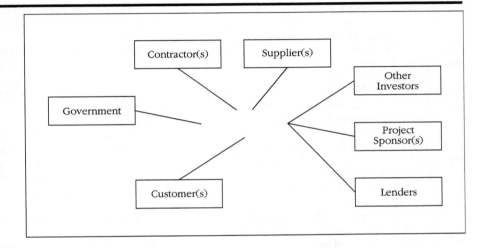

interest by exposing her to part of the risk of the business. The creation of incentives and the transfer of risk from the shareholders to the manager are therefore two sides of the same coin. This transfer of risk is not beneficial in itself; for the manager, unlike the shareholders, does not hold a diversified portfolio. She therefore requires a higher return than do the shareholders for bearing this risk. The transfer of risk is beneficial *only* to the extent that it improves efficiency.

In the case of project finance, a complex series of contracts and financing arrangements distributes the different risks presented by a project among the various parties involved in the project. As in the case of our simple example of the management compensation contract, these transfers of risk are rarely advantageous in themselves, but have important incentive effects. To see how this occurs, we need to look at the structure of a typical project financing.

THE MAIN PARTIES

There are numerous parties involved in the structuring of a typical project financing. As shown in Figure 1, besides the lenders and the project company, these parties typically include one or more project sponsors, contractors, suppliers, major customers, and a host government.

Sponsors and Investors. A separate company is established for the purpose of undertaking the project. A controlling stake in the equity of that company will typically be owned by a single project sponsor, or by a group of sponsors, who will generally be involved in the construction and the management of the project. Other equity-holders may be companies with commercial ties to the project, such as customers and suppliers, or they may be financial investors. For example, the shareholders of the PT. Paiton Energy Co. (PEC), which is building the Paiton 7 and 8 power stations in Indonesia, are Edison Mission Energy (40%), General Electric Capital Corp. (12.5%), Mitsui & Co. Ltd. (32.5%), and PT. Batu Hitam Perkasa (15%). As is typical of such projects, the main shareholders of the project company are the main contractor of the plant, Mitsui, and its operator, Edison Mission Energy, which will operate and maintain the plant through PT. MOMI Indonesia, the local affiliate of Mission Operation & Maintenance Inc. General Electric Co., of which General Electric Capital Corp. is the finance affiliate, will supply the steam turbine generators. The Indonesian company PT. Batu Hitam Perkasa appears to have no operational involvement in the project, but may carry political clout.

Lenders. Infrastructure projects involve substantial investments. A large fraction of the needed finance is generally raised in the form of debt from a syndicate of lenders such as banks and specialized lending institutions and, less frequently, from the bond markets. In the case of PEC, for example, equity-holders provided $680 million in equity and subordinated debt. $1.8 billion was provided in the form of senior debt, of which 90 percent was bank debt and 10 percent was senior secured bonds.

Most infrastructure projects are financed by bank loans. The concentrated ownership of bank debt encourages lenders to devote considerable resources to evaluating the project, and to monitoring its progress on a continuing basis. It also facilitates the renegotiation of the debt should the project company experience difficulties in servicing it.

Project companies will sometimes enter into production payment arrangements instead of issuing ordinary debt. These arrangements are functionally equivalent to borrowing: a bank provides cash up-front as advance payment for a project's output, and the project company undertakes to deliver the output to the bank and arranges for the output to be repurchased at a guaranteed price.

Most infrastructure facilities have very long lives. This suggests that they should be financed with long-term debt. Yet, most infrastructure projects are financed by bank loans, which have maturities that rarely exceed 10 to 12 years, rather than by long-term bonds.

Some observers have suggested that the difficulty in arranging long-term bond financing is due to the fact that bondholders are particularly risk-averse. But, since most bondholders also hold substantial portfolios of equities, this seems improbable. Our explanation for the widespread use of bank finance, and the correspondingly limited role of bond finance, focuses instead on the ownership structures of these two forms of financing. The concentrated ownership of bank debt encourages lending banks to devote considerable resources to evaluating the project, and to monitoring its progress on a continuing basis. It also facilitates the renegotiation of the debt should the project company experience difficulties in servicing it. By contrast, the more diffuse nature of bond ownership reduces the incentives of bondholders to evaluate and monitor the progress of the project, and makes it difficult to take concerted action if covenants are breached or require modification. Thus, it does not seem surprising that many bond issues, such as the $180 million issue made by PEC, have been privately placed under rule 144a. This ensures that ownership remains in the hands of a limited number of qualified institutional buyers (or QIBs).

A bond issue to fund a green-field project is likely only in the case of a low-risk project. Even then, it is commonly enhanced by a credit guarantee from an insurance company, or a political risk guarantee from a national or supranational agency. For example, a project company established to upgrade two major roads in England was able to raise the majority of its debt by an issue of bonds that were enhanced by a Aaa/AAA guarantee from AMBAC Indemnity Corporation.

Bonds are also commonly used in project finance in one other set of circumstances. Once construction is completed and project facilities become operational, bond financing is often used to replace existing bank debt. This can be explained by the fact that the need for monitoring falls upon completion of the construction phase.

Government. The project company will in most cases need to obtain a concession from the host government to build a road or a railway, for example, or to operate a telecommunication service. The government may also need to establish a new regulatory framework, guarantee currency convertibility, and provide environmental permits.

In many cases, the project company retains ownership of the project's assets. Such arrangements are known as "build-own-operate" projects (BOOs). In other cases, ownership of the project's assets is transferred to the government at the end of the concession period. These arrangements are known as "build-operate-transfer" projects (BOTs).[2]

Contractors. As noted above, the main contractor of the plant will often hold a stake in the equity of the project company. Other contractors may also do so, although generally to a lesser extent.

Suppliers and Customers. Once the project facility has been built and has become operational, the project company will need to purchase the supplies it requires, and to sell the products it produces or the services it provides. Sometimes, as in the case of a pipeline, there will be in effect only one customer. Often in this case the customer will be a government-owned utility, or the government itself. For example, the sole customer for the electricity produced by the Paiton 7 and 8 power stations will be the Indonesian state-owned electric utility. In other cases, as in that of a toll road, there may be many possible customers.

CONTRACTUAL ARRANGEMENTS

Although a project company is unusual in that it is established to undertake a single project, there is nothing unusual about the identity of the parties involved in the project. All companies have owners, lenders, suppliers, and customers, and all have dealings with the government. The difference in the case of project finance lies in the overriding impor-

---

2. It should however be noted that the terms BOO and BOT are sometimes used interchangeably.

tance of the contractual and financing arrangements that exist between these various parties. These are more than a series of independent bilateral arrangements. In particular, the complete package of contracts needs to be put in place before debt finance can be secured.

We discuss the contractual arrangements first. These are designed to allocate every major risk presented by a project to the party that is best able to appraise and control that risk. Because a party to a project will agree to bear a given risk at a non-prohibitive price only if it has a clear understanding of that risk, most projects involve established technologies, as is the case for power stations, roads, and airports. Project finance is less appropriate for projects that involve complex or untried technologies, as evidenced by the failure of the U.K. government to secure project financing for research and development projects.

Let us look briefly at the various ways in which contractual arrangements distribute risk among the various parties to a project:

■ The project sponsors bear the risks of project completion, operation, and maintenance. This is achieved through a facility management contract that includes guarantees that the project facility will be completed on time, and that it will be built and operated to the desired specifications. The project sponsor may also enter into a "working capital maintenance" agreement or a "cash deficiency" agreement with the lending banks. Such agreements ensure adequate funding for the project in its early years.

■ The lenders to the project will require the usual assurances from the project company, including security for their loans. But, especially in the early stages of the project, lenders will also have recourse to the project sponsors in the event of specific problems such as cost overruns. Lenders will particularly want to ensure that cash that can be used to service the debt is not paid out to equity-holders. The amount of debt service may therefore be linked to the project's output, and any earnings in excess of debt service requirements may be placed in a "reclaim" account and drawn on if subsequent earnings do not suffice to service the debt.

■ The main contractor is obviously best able to ensure that construction is completed within cost and on schedule. He will therefore often enter into a turnkey contract that specifies a fixed price and

penalties for delays, and he will usually be required to post a performance bond.

■ When there is a major supplier to the project, there will be a contract with that supplier to ensure that (1) he does not abuse his possible monopoly power and (2) he produces efficiently. For example, if the project company is a major purchaser of energy from a monopolistic state-owned enterprise (SOE), the project company will enter into a long-term supply contract with the SOE. The contract purchase price will often be fixed, or indexed to inflation or some other variable that affects project revenues; and the contract may require the SOE to compensate the project company if the SOE fails to supply the contracted energy.

■ When there are only a few potential customers for the project's output, revenue risk is likely to be transferred to those customers by means of long-term sales contracts. These will often include a take-or-pay clause or, as in the case of a pipeline, a throughput agreement that obliges the customer to make some minimum use of the pipeline. Another arrangement for transferring revenue risk to a customer is a tolling contract, whereby the customer agrees to deliver to the project company materials that it is to process and return to the customer. Some power projects, such as Navotas in the Philippines, have been structured in a similar way: the purchasing utility provides the fuel and the project company is simply paid for converting it to electricity. The purpose of transferring revenue risk to customers is to provide them with the incentive to estimate their demand for the project's output as carefully and honestly as possible.

The contract between project company and customers will as much as possible seek to ensure that the prices of the product are indexed to its costs; and, where there is considerable currency uncertainty, prices may also be indexed to exchange rates as in the case of the Paiton power project.

■ When there are many customers, as in the case of a toll road, long-term purchase contracts with these customers may be impossible. Indeed, if alternative routes are not subject to a toll, it may be infeasible to set a price that provides the project company with a satisfactory return. For example, one of the problems in attracting private finance to the funding of rail projects within central London has been that the revenues from such projects are likely to be highly dependent on transport policy towards *other* means of transportation in the capital. In such cases, it may

> In project finance, the complete package of contracts needs to be put in place before debt finance can be secured. This web of contractual arrangements is designed to allocate the various risks presented by the project to those parties that can best appraise and control those risks.

be possible to attract project finance only if the government guarantees some minimum payment to investors.

■ When the government grants a concession to a project company, there will need to be a concession agreement that gives the company the right to build and operate the project facility. The concession agreement may also require the government to construct supporting facilities such as access roads. Failure to do so may lead to the failure of the project, or may decrease the return on the project. For example, the profitability of Eurostar, the company that operates rail services through the Channel Tunnel, has suffered from the delays in the construction of a promised high-speed rail link in England and a new railway station south of London. The government may also need to guarantee the performance of state-owned companies. For example, if a project sells electricity to a state-owned power utility, the government may need to guarantee the contractual obligations of that utility.

The project company will also be concerned about currency convertibility, in particular its ability to service its foreign currency debt and pay dividends to its equity-holders. The government may therefore be asked to provide guarantees or comfort letters; and, if the project has hard currency revenues, it may have to consent to having these revenues paid into an offshore escrow account.

As we have already observed, this web of contractual arrangements, which may vary over time in line with the progress of a project, is designed to allocate the various risks presented by the project to those parties that can best appraise and control those risks. An attempt to allocate a given risk to a party that is not best able to control that risk will generally fail. For example, the private financing of prisons in the U.K. ran into difficulties when the government sought to link its payments to private prisons to the number of prisoners that were sent to these prisons. The problem, of course, was that the number of prisoners was outside the control of the project companies, but at least partially within that of the government. Conversely, failure to allocate a given risk to the party that is best able to control that risk will lead to a loss in efficiency. As one example, government guarantees of fair rates of return to utilities or project companies remove any incentive for these organizations to reduce their costs.

OWNERSHIP, CAPITAL STRUCTURE, AND INCENTIVES

We now turn to the financing arrangements observed in the case of project finance. Among the questions we address are the following:

■ Why are projects incorporated in separate companies?
■ Why are the operators and the main contractors of the project typically the main equity-holders in that company?
■ Why are project companies highly leveraged?
■ Why does this leverage take the form of non-recourse financing?

The object of the contractual arrangements that we have described above is to ensure that a project company is not exposed to an abuse of monopoly power, and to provide all parties to the project with the incentives to act efficiently by transferring the risk of poor performance to those best able to manage it. Construction risk is thus borne by the contractor, the risk of insufficient demand by the purchaser, and similarly for the other risks presented by the project.

But this does not explain the widespread practice of incorporating the project in a separate company, and tying the management of a project to its financing. Indeed, a government could easily raise money directly for infrastructure investment and contract with each party to provide the required services. But, as we pointed out earlier, there is a limit to how much can be written into a contract and how efficiently that contract can be monitored. Contractual arrangements therefore need to be complemented by financing arrangements.

Think, for example, why the operator and the main contractor of a project should be made to be equity-holders in the project. These equity holdings would not be needed if it were possible to write and monitor complete contracts with the contractor and the operator. The operation of the project could then be separated from its financing. This sometimes happens—most recently, in the case of a South African road project. But it is usually not possible to write and monitor sufficiently comprehensive contracts. In such cases, the equity holdings that the contractor and the operator have in the project company provide them with an incentive to be efficient by making them residual claimants whose profits depend on how well the project facility is built and operated.

Project companies are highly levered: the average debt ratio for IFC-financed projects, for example, is around 60 percent. Such leverage is used despite the fact that there is reputed to be a shortage of potential lenders for project finance, and that it is costly to structure the project to make these high debt levels possible. Furthermore, lenders lend directly to the project company rather than to the sponsors, and they have only limited recourse to the sponsors in case of default by the project company. This last observation suggests that the motive for the high leverage observed cannot be that debt is a "cheap" source of finance. If that were the case, the loans could equally well be made to the sponsors.

In their classic paper on capital structure, Miller and Modigliani showed that, in perfectly competitive capital markets, company value would be independent of the degree of leverage. Similar arguments can be used to show that, under the same restrictive set of conditions, value cannot be enhanced simply by concentrating debt in a subsidiary or an associated company. As illustrated in Exhibit 1 below, the total cash flow to all security holders is independent of whether debt is located in a project company or in its parent company.

Why, then, do we observe a high concentration of debt in the project company? As happens so often in discussions of capital structure, there is an abundance of possible explanations, none of which appears to be capable of explaining all the facts.

EXHIBIT 1 ■ THE IMPACT OF PROJECT FINANCE IN AN M&M WORLD

The example below illustrates (a) that, in a Miller-Modigliani world, project finance does not affect the total value of the firm and (b) that project finance can potentially affect value when debt default is costly.

Panel 1 shows a firm with existing assets and debt undertaking a large project. Both the assets and the project give a single cash flow and have pure discount debt. Panel 2 shows the payoffs in different states of the world to debt and equity if the project is undertaken as part of the general activities of the firm. Panel 3 shows the payoffs to project debt, existing debt, and parent equity if the project is undertaken as a separate entity (project finance).

In a Miller-Modigliani world without taxes, project finance has no impact on the total value of the firm. This can be seen by comparing the final columns of Panel 2 and Panel 3, where the total cash flows accruing to all security holders are identical in all states. In a complete securities market, this guarantees that the total value of the firm is independent of the way that financial claims on the firm are structured.

The impact of project finance on default risk can be seen by comparing Panel 3 (project finance) with Panel 2. The net impact of project finance on default is to:

A. Prevent the existing assets bringing down the project in state 2.

B. Prevent the project bringing down the existing assets in state 3.

C. Make the project default in state 5 because the coinsurance of the existing assets is lost.

By thus rearranging the states of the world in which default occurs, project finance can change the associated costs of default.

	CHARACTERISTICS OF EXISTING ASSETS AND PROJECT					SECURITY PAYOFFS IN THE CASE OF TRADITIONAL FINANCE				SECURITY PAYOFFS IN THE CASE OF PROJECT FINANCE						
State	PANEL 1	Debt Face Value: Existing Assets	Debt Face Value: Project	Cash Flow: Existing Assets	Cash Flow: Project	PANEL 2	Debt	Equity	Total Cash Flow	PANEL 3	Project Debt	Project Equity	Total Cash Flow to Sponsor	Parent Debt	Parent Equity	Total Cash Flow: Project Debt + Existing Debt + Parent Equity
1		100	100	50	50		100*	0	100		50*	0	50	50*	0	100
2		100	100	50	130		180*	0	180		100	30	80	80*	0	180
3		100	100	130	50		180*	0	180		50*	0	130	100	30	180
4		100	100	130	130		200	60	260		100	30	160	100	60	260
5		100	100	300	50		200	150	350		50*	0	300	100	200	350
6		100	100	300	130		200	230	430		100	30	330	100	230	430

*Indicates default.

> **If the bankruptcy costs of the sponsor are higher than those of the project company, it could be more efficient to isolate the debt in the project company to ensure that the sponsor's business is not damaged by a possible bankruptcy of the project.**

Many of these explanations are related to the incompleteness of contracts. We discuss below some of the more common explanations (and summarize in Exhibit 2 four of the principal theoretical models of project finance).

Bankruptcy Costs. The example in Exhibit 1 shows that the total cash flows to investors are independent of whether the firm employs project financing when bankruptcy costs are assumed to be zero, as in an M & M world. The example also shows, however, that project finance changes the states of the world in which the debt is in default. In so doing, project finance changes the expected costs of default.

The projects undertaken by project companies typically have low bankruptcy costs. This is because their assets are largely tangible assets, which are likely to go through a bankruptcy process largely unscathed. For example, a change in ownership is unlikely to affect the efficiency with which a power station or a toll road is operated. In addition, if the bankruptcy costs of the sponsor are higher than those of the project company, it could be more efficient to isolate the debt in the project company to ensure that the sponsor's business is not damaged by a possible bankruptcy of the project.[3] A trading and construction company such as Mitsui, for example, is likely to lose much more of its operating value than the project company building the Paiton power stations, and it should therefore attempt to contain the effects of a possible project failure through the use of project finance. The low cost of bankruptcy for project companies may therefore help to explain why project companies carry heavy, non-recourse debt loads, but it does not explain why these companies enter into a variety of credit-enhancing contracts, such as insurance and hedging contracts (we return to this issue later).

Taxes. When a project is located in a high-tax country, and the project company in a lower-tax country, it may be beneficial for the sponsor to locate the debt in the high-tax country. The company maximizes its interest tax shields in so doing. But the difference in tax rates does not explain why the debt has limited recourse, nor does it explain the

concentration of debt in the project company when both the sponsor and the project company are located in the same jurisdiction.

Myopia. Some of the arguments for placing the debt in the project company assume that the lenders are blinkered. For example, it is sometimes suggested that the limited recourse of the debt holders to the project sponsors provides the sponsors with a free lunch, and that project finance allows the debt to be "off-balance-sheet" to the sponsors (for example, by structuring the contractual obligation as a production payment rather than as a loan). However, it is very doubtful that lenders are misled by such stratagems.

Political Risk. We have argued that the difficulty of writing complete contracts with operators and contractors provides the motive for tying project financing and management. Similarly, the difficulty of writing a comprehensive and binding concession agreement with a host government provides the need for financing arrangements that make it difficult for the government to take actions that may render the project unprofitable.

One such arrangement is for the host government to take equity in the project company. Another is an extensive reliance on limited recourse financing. By arranging for the project company to issue such debt, the sponsors ensure that the cost of adverse government action falls directly on the lending banks and agencies. These generally consist of a syndicate of major banks from a wide range of countries, together with national or supranational bodies such as the export-import banks of the main industrial countries, the World Bank, the International Finance Corporation, the Asian Development Bank, and the Inter-American Development Bank. All have considerable political clout, and can bring pressure to bear upon the host government if necessary. Moreover, the national and supranational agencies commonly hold subordinated debt that further exposes them to the consequences of adverse government actions. In contrast, the commercial banks tend to hold senior debt in the project.

In addition, the national and supranational agencies also provide loan guarantees, which are

---

3. See Michel Habib and D. Bruce Johnsen, "User Specialisation and Asset Financing," working paper, London Business School, 1996. It may not simply be the sponsor's business that is damaged by bankruptcy. The management of the sponsoring company may have valuable control rights such as perquisites and an enhanced reputation, and the project may have synergies with other projects run by the same management. Management may therefore wish to isolate the project to protect its control rights. See T. Chemmanur and K. John, "Optimal Incorporation, Structure of Debt Contracts, and Limited-Recourse Project Financing," working paper, New York University, 1992.

generally intended to protect lenders against political risk, but rarely provide protection against commercial risk, again illustrating the principle that risk should be allocated to those that can best manage it. For example, the World Bank may assist the project company in raising debt by offering a partial risk guarantee that covers the host government's contractual obligations and political *force majeure* risks, as in the case of the Hub power project in Pakistan. Similarly, one level of government may guarantee the performance of another. For example, the Indian central government was contractually liable for any loss to the sponsor of the Dabhol power project that was a consequence of government action. This encouraged the Indian central government to put pressure on the state government of Maharashtra to resume construction of the plant,

in spite of the electoral promises of the new state government to cancel the project.

Protection against political risk may go far towards explaining the debt structure of project companies in developing countries. It does not explain why projects in politically stable countries are also heavily levered. Of course, such countries are not free from political risk. Environmental legislation or court awards in liability suits may sometimes pose serious threats to business. However, these risks generally threaten the sponsors of the project as much as the project company, and are therefore unlikely to explain the concentration of debt in the project company.

Information Costs. The granting of a loan clearly requires that the lenders evaluate the creditworthiness of the borrower, and monitor his use of the assets financed by the loan. A possible benefit

---

EXHIBIT 2 ■ THEORETICAL MODELS OF PROJECT FINANCE

Model	Benefit of Debt	Cost of Debt	Benefit of Project Finance	Cost of Project Finance
Habib and Johnsen (1996)[a]: Asset specific investment by the initial user and the alternative user of an asset.	Induces both users to make the first-best investment in case the asset is to be transferred over some range of states.	May distort the asset-specific investment made by the initial user in case the asset is not to be transferred.	Avoids the distortion of asset-specific investment in the case of many assets and many alternative users.	
Chemmanur and John (1992)[b]: Private benefits of control	Avoids selling outside equity, thus lowering the probability of losing control to outsiders	Increases the probability of bankruptcy and the monitoring of management by debt-holders.	Avoids having a high-risk project bankrupt a low-risk project.	Loses the coinsurance property of debt.
John and John (1991)[c]: Tax benefits and agency costs of debt.	Tax savings.	Foregone growth opportunities (Myers underinvestment).	Enables trade-offs between the costs and the benefits of debt that are specific to the project and to existing assets.	
Shah and Thakor (1987)[d]: Signalling with debt.	Tax savings.	Signals high risk.	Lowers the cost of information gathering by creditors. Avoids the joint credit evaluation of the projects and existing assets.	Precludes optimal leverage for the entire firm.

a. M. Habib and D.B. Johnsen, "User Specialisation and Asset Financing," Working Paper, London Business School, 1996.
b. T. Chemmanur and K. John, "Optimal Incorporation, Structure of Debt Contracts, and Limited-Recourse Project Financing," Working Paper, New York University, 1992.
c. T. John and K. John, "Optimality of Project Financing: Theory and Empirical Implications in Finance and Accounting," *Review of Quantitative Finance and Accounting* 1 (1991), 51-74.
d. S. Shah and A. Thakor, "Optimal Capital Structure and Project Financing," *Journal of Economic Theory* 42 (1987), 209-243.

> **By arranging for the project company to [fund itself heavily with debt], the sponsors ensure that the cost of adverse government action falls directly on the lending banks and agencies. These generally consist of a syndicate of major banks from a wide range of countries, together with national or supranational bodies such as the World Bank... All have considerable political clout.**

of project finance, and of the associated lack of recourse, is that it allows lenders to the project to confine their evaluation and monitoring to the project only, and saves them from having to evaluate and monitor the sponsors as well.

Free Cash Flow. Michael Jensen has argued that companies with a surplus of cash and a lack of worthwhile projects have a tendency to invest this cash in negative NPV projects rather than return it to shareholders. Leverage ensures that cash is needed to service debt, and is not frittered away. That is, heavy debt financing can provide stronger incentives both to generate more cash, and to pay out what cash cannot be profitably reinvested in the company.

The above argument leaves open the question as to why the debt is located in the project company rather than in the parent companies. After all, if the parent companies assumed the debt, they would have an equally great incentive for ensuring that cash was distributed to them rather than reinvested unproductively.

There are two possible reasons why the location of the debt could matter. One is that the parent companies may find it difficult or costly to monitor the efficiency with which cash is used within the project company, and therefore cannot prevent the waste of free cash flow. The other is that, when there is more than one parent company, the owners may have different views about how to use cash. For example, if one parent is a potential supplier to the project company while another has a purely financial interest in it, the two parents may disagree about the desirability of having the company reinvest its free cash flow. By ensuring that cash flows are used to service debt, such disagreements are avoided.

INSURANCE AND HEDGING

The risk transfer contracts that we described earlier have the effect of transferring many of the project risks from the project sponsor to the other parties to the project. Further risks are transferred by a variety of insurance contracts, such as completion insurance, insurance against *force majeure*, and insurance against political risks.

Although an insurance company may have particular expertise at pricing these risks and may possibly be skillful at monitoring them, it has no control over them. An insurer cannot control whether there will be a flood, a hurricane, or other natural catastrophes. Insurance contracts therefore should have no beneficial effect, and may well have detrimental effects, on incentives, as they reduce the incentives of the project company to exert effort that would minimize the effects of such disasters. Therefore, the probable purpose of such risk transfers is simply to enable the project company to operate at higher debt ratios than it otherwise could.

In addition to the protection against firm-specific risks they purchase from insurance companies, project companies may also undertake to hedge themselves against market risks, such as any remaining currency risk, interest rate risk, and commodity price risk. These contracts too enable the project company to operate at high debt ratios.

BIDDING

Project finance is expensive to arrange. It involves establishing the project company, forming a consortium of equity-holders and lenders, gaining agreement to a complex set of contractual arrangements between the parties involved, and arranging costly documentation.

Governments commonly advertise for competing bids. Of course, in preparing their bid, companies recognize both the cost of doing so and the probability that they will not be awarded the contract. For this reason, an open auction will not necessarily result in the optimal number of bidders, or the lowest cost to the government. For example, a common complaint by contractors in the U.K. has been that they have incurred large bidding costs under the Private Finance Initiative, with a low probability of success. Bidding costs are reputed to have been up to five times higher than for private sector projects.[4]

Where each potential bidder has access to the same technology and is equally well-equipped to undertake the project, there is no gain in social welfare from inviting a large number of bids. The government needs to invite only a sufficient number of bids to avoid collusion or the exercise of monopoly power.

---

4. *The Financial Times*, 10 November 1995.

BUILD-OPERATE-TRANSFER

In the case of BOT (build-operate-transfer) as opposed to BOO (build-own-operate) projects, ownership of a project's assets is transferred to the government at the end of the concession period. For example, ownership of privately financed toll roads and bridges is often eventually transferred to the government.

Of course this is not a free lunch: sponsors will recognize the limited nature of the concession in their bidding. Since project sponsors need to recover their investment within the limited period of the concession, it may not be possible to arrange BOT finance even for projects that provide a satisfactory return over their complete life. An often-cited example is the early Mexican toll road program, where a 10-year concession period obliged sponsors to charge such high tolls that motorists avoided using the roads. The other danger with BOT contracts is that, as the end of the concession period approaches, there is little incentive for the sponsor to invest more in the project, and every incentive for him to take as much cash out as he can. For example, oil rights with a limited life encourage the franchisee to extract oil earlier than may be desirable.

Why, then, are some projects organized as BOT contracts? We suggest that such an arrangement makes sense where there is a need for the government to support the project by continuing infrastructure investments that cannot easily be specified by contract. Knowing that the project will eventually revert to government ownership provides an incentive for the government to invest in the supporting infrastructure.

The government sometimes has an option to terminate the concession before the end of the concession period. This may be particularly important when the original concession agreement may prevent government policy changes in (say) the regulatory framework.

CONCLUDING REMARKS

We conclude this paper by discussing what we believe are some common misconceptions about project finance, and by briefly contrasting project finance with the alternatives of privatization and service contracts.

It is sometimes argued that project finance is attractive simply because "the mobilisation of private capital is the only way in which public service is likely to be maintained,"[5] or because it saves the government money by transferring the investment expenditure from the public to the private sector. For example, the British government recently agreed to sell homes occupied by military personnel to private firms which would manage those homes and lease them back to the government. This, it was asserted, would reduce government spending by £500 million, thus cutting the government's borrowing requirements. While this is literally correct, the sale of the homes also makes the government liable for a series of future rental payments. Unless the private sector is more efficient at managing these homes, the cash flows paid out by the government in the sale-and-leaseback arrangement can be exactly replicated by government borrowing. Of course, by using project finance rather than direct government borrowing, a government may reduce its apparent deficit and avoid contravening IMF requirements on borrowing, or rules for admission to European Monetary Union. But it is difficult to believe that such transparent dodges provide a reliable long-term basis for the use of project finance.[6]

Some *critics* of the use of project finance for infrastructure investment argue that the cheaper financing available to the government could well outweigh the gains in efficiency made possible by private-sector management. The government is said to have a lower cost of capital than do private-sector companies because it is able to borrow at blue-chip rates, whereas a project company is likely to pay a higher rate of interest on its debt and may need to offer the project sponsors a prospective return of 20 or 30 percent on their equity investment in the company. For example, *The Economist* quotes a report on a Scottish water project by Chemical Bank, which estimates that "if the works were privately built, owned and operated, interest rates and the need to achieve a return on equity investment would make the finance costs 50% more expensive than the

---

5. As Ross Goobey argued in *The Times* (22 June 1996).
6. It may however be the case that project finance, by allocating the revenues from a project to the project company, serves to remove these revenues from the reach of the government, which may otherwise divert them to uses other than the repayment of the debt. This may justify the view of project finance as "off-balance-sheet" finance in the case of governments, but it does not explain why such projects should be highly leveraged.

> **While governments can borrow more cheaply than corporations and do not have to provide a return to shareholders, this does not imply that the total cost of capital is lower to governments than it is to the private sector. Indeed, because the capital markets share risk better than does the tax system, the cost of capital for the government could well be *higher* than for corporations.**

£201 million costs that would be incurred under the normal public-borrowing rules. There would be no chance... to recoup the higher financing costs through the greater efficiency of a private operator, because the costs of running a £100m sewage work is only about £5m a year."[7] The World Bank, too, appears to subscribe to the view that governments have a lower cost of capital than private sector companies, commenting that "[i]n infrastructure projects, the cheaper credit available to governments needs to be weighed against possible inefficiencies in channelling funds through government."[8]

The notion that the government enjoys a lower cost of capital than private sector companies is misleading. While it is certainly the case that governments can borrow more cheaply than corporations and do not have to provide a return to shareholders, this does not imply that the total cost of capital is lower to governments than it is to the private sector. The lower interest rate paid by a government simply reflects the guarantee provided by taxpayers to lenders. In the case of private sector companies, the bulk of the risk presented by a project is borne by the equity-holders, who demand a correspondingly higher rate of return. A smaller part of the risk goes to the debt-holders, who bear the risk that the firm may default on its debt payments. In contrast, government debt is risk-free in nominal terms, a characteristic that is reflected in the low rate of interest on the debt. But the risk presented by the projects does not disappear when the project is financed by the government. If cash flows from the project are unexpectedly low and do not suffice to service the debt raised by the government to finance the project, the shortfall is met by taxpayers, who play a role similar to that of equity-holders in a private sector company (but without the benefit of limited liability). Indeed, because it seems likely that the capital markets share risk better than does the tax system, the cost of capital for the government could well be *higher* than for corporations.

We believe that the argument for transferring ownership as well as management revolves around the difficulty of writing contracts that ensure that managers maximize efficiency. We have described above how contractual arrangements provide in-

---

7. "Something Nasty in the Water," *The Economist*, 9 September 1995, page 32.

8. World Development Report 1994, World Bank.

EXHIBIT 3 ■ THE BENEFITS AND COSTS OF PROJECT FINANCE*

WHEN PROJECT FINANCE

MAKES SENSE

AGENCY EFFECTS:
- Specializes and decentralizes management.
- Makes possible the provision of separate incentives for project managers.
- Precludes the waste of project free cash flow.
- Increases the outside scrutiny of projects.
- Improves incentives for the production of information.

OWNERSHIP STRUCTURE:
- Permits joint ventures without requiring the exhaustive mutual evaluation of the creditworthiness of potential partners.
- Limits the liability of parents to projects.
- Limits the exposure of creditors to well-defined project risks.
- Allows project-specific debt ratios.

OTHER EFFECTS:
- Crystallizes project costs for regulatory purposes.
- Allows the provision of services to several companies rather than just to sponsors.
- Partially transforms a sponsor from an equity-holder in the project into a supplier to the project, thus improving the sponsor's priority ranking in case of default.
- May avoid double taxation.

WHEN PROJECT FINANCE

DOES *NOT* MAKE SENSE
- *There are complex interactions of the project with the rest of the firm.*
- *Default of the project is costly (lost coinsurance).*
- *The optimal leverage of the project is low.*
- *The costs of contracting for the project are high.*

---

*This exhibit, along with some of the arguments presented in this paper, adapt and extend arguments made by John Kensinger and John Martin in "Project Finance: Raising Money the Old-Fashioned Way," *Journal of Applied Corporate Finance*, Vol. 1 No. 3 (Fall 1988).

centives for efficiency by transferring risks to those best able to control them. At the same time, we have also argued that, because the vast majority of contracts are incomplete and imperfectly monitored, an exclusive reliance on service contracts is unwise. The ultimate incentive for project managers to maximize efficiency is for them to be made residual claimants who capture the benefits of any improvements they make. Thus, it is desirable to tie ownership and the provision of management services whenever it is difficult to specify *ex ante* the required level of services, or the acceptable level of costs, and to monitor them. This can be achieved through the use of project finance.

Rather than living off individual projects in order to attract private-sector funding and management expertise to a given industry, a government can do so by privatizing the industry. Indeed, it seems likely that the growth in privatization and in the use of project finance for infrastructure investments have both been prompted by the same concerns about the efficiency of government-owned enterprises and the appropriateness of government funding for large, risky investments. However, while the recent popularity of project finance and privatization may have similar causes, there are three reasons why project finance may sometimes be preferred to privatization. First, privatization is a more complex undertaking, particularly since it involves both existing and new plant. While project finance relies on a one-off set of contractual undertakings for each plant, privatization needs a regulatory framework for the entire industry. Second, there are a number of areas, such as health or education, where it may be possible to involve private funding for particular projects but where full-scale privatization is deemed inappropriate. Third, unless the industry is to be entirely foreign-owned, privatization requires a large local capital market, in contrast to project financings, which take place piecemeal and over a period of time.

HKU691

Poon Kam Kai Series

FREDERIK PRETORIUS

INFRASTRUCTURE FINANCE: THE SYDNEY CROSS CITY TUNNEL

In September 2000, the directors of Cheung Kong Infrastructure Holdings Limited (CKI) were excited about an unprecedented opportunity to invest in a transportation project in Australia. CKI had a vision to become an international infrastructure enterprise and was keen to extend its footprint beyond mainland China and Hong Kong. The group found that Australia, with its stable regulatory environment and sound economic prospects, provided an excellent environment for infrastructure investment. In 1999, CKI made its first foray into energy assets in Australia with the acquisition of a 19.97% stake in Envestra Limited, the largest natural gas company in the country. Envestra proved to be a prime asset and generated robust financial returns to CKI.

In 2000, CKI was vying for further opportunities to invest in transportation projects in Australia when the Roads and Traffic Authority (RTA) in New South Wales invited tenders for the Sydney Cross City Tunnel (CCT) Project [see **Exhibit 1** for the chronology of events]. CKI was particularly interested in tolled transportation investments because they were usually regulated under a finite-life concession period and carried relatively low political and regulatory risks. The nature of these investments usually determined that competition for the services generated by the assets was also limited, which meant investing in such projects could possibly provide stable and predictable returns to the group. Although transportation investments could entail significant construction and patronage risks, CKI believed that these risks were manageable and could be mitigated through careful planning and negotiation with the relevant government authorities. If CKI won the tender for the CCT project, it would be no small accomplishment, as the group's existing transportation assets were all located in greater China. Given CKI's strategy of globalisation, was the project too good to miss?

History of the CCT Project

Background

As in most big cities, road traffic congestion had long been a significant problem in central Sydney. In 1998, the minister for transport of NSW produced a manifesto entitled "Action for Transport 2010", which aimed to expand the road infrastructure and thus improve traffic flows in central Sydney. The manifesto was followed by a public consultation report prepared by the RTA in October 1998. The report proposed the construction of an east-west road tunnel that would cross under the heart of the Sydney Central Business District (CBD). The primary objectives of the CCT project were to relieve traffic congestion in central Sydney, improve the reliability of public transport and provide a safer environment and improved amenities to vehicles, cyclists and pedestrians. By removing east-west through-traffic on surface streets and reallocating road space for public transport and pedestrian use, the CCT was expected to provide a number of benefits to the Sydney community, including:[1]

- reduced congestion, as drivers could bypass 18 sets of eastbound traffic lights or 16 sets of westbound traffic lights on the old routes
- improved travel times, with estimated savings of up to 20 minutes during peak hours
- higher service reliability for buses through the introduction of bus priority measures
- improved access to and movements for pedestrians and vehicles
- safer and more pleasant environments with better urban designs, wider footpaths and the removal of intrusive through-traffic
- better air quality and reduced traffic noise levels.

In August 2000, following extensive environmental investigation and consultation, the RTA issued an Environmental Impact Statement (EIS) detailing the potential environmental impacts. After considering response from the community, the RTA made some amendments to the original design concepts. These modifications were approved by minister for planning in October 2001.

According to the construction plan, the CCT project comprised two stages. Stage One encompassed two east-west tunnels that spanned 2.1 km under the Sydney Central Business District and Darlinghurst/Woolloomooloo. The tunnels would run between the eastern side of the Darling Harbour and Kings Cross. Stage One works also involved the construction of associated tunnelled links to Sir John Young Crescent, the Cahill Expressway and the Eastern Distributor (see **Exhibits 2A** to **2D**). It was envisaged that Stage One works would be completed in 2004 or 2005.[2]

Most of the tunnel would be excavated using a driven tunnel method, a proven and widely used construction technology. This involved the use of tunnelling machines that cut their way through the underground rock mass. The remainder of the tunnel would be constructed using the cut-and-cover method, whereby rock was excavated and then covered with concrete beams or planks to form a tunnel.[3] No extraordinary construction risks were envisaged, though it was fully understood that this was a complex and risky project from site access, logistics and project planning perspectives.

---

[1] RTA (June 2003) "Cross City Tunnel Summary of Contracts".
[2] Parliament of New South Wales (February 2006) "Joint Select Committee on the Cross City Tunnel, First Report".
[3] CrossCity Motorway Pty Ltd, "Construction", http://www.crosscity.com.au/DynamicPages.asp?cid=7&navid=7 (accessed 30 August 2006).

advantage of the opportunities afforded by reduced traffic congestion. There would be improvements to surface roads, including new bus and bicycle lanes and other improvements to pedestrian facilities. **Exhibit 3** presents the different proposals for the CCT.

Public or Private Financing?

The NSW government considered a number of options for financing the CCT project. These included the utilisation of public funds or government borrowings. Alternatively, the NSW government could limit the commitment of public capital and finance the project through a public private partnership (PPP) arrangement [see **Exhibit 4**]. A privately financed project (PFP) was a specified form of PPP that involved not only private sector financing but also controlling ownership. Hence, PFPs differed from the outsourcing of infrastructure services or the procurement of design and construction services by the government. Under a PFP arrangement, the infrastructure would be created with a concession agreement whereby the private sector provided the capital to finance, construct, operate and maintain the assets for a specified contract period (the "concession period"). Such concession agreements typically formed part of the overall regulatory framework under which such investments were operated. When the contract period expired, the operation and maintenance of the asset would revert to public (government) ownership. While construction and operating risks could be transferred to the private sector through the use of a PFP arrangement, the market risk could still be shared by the government through an appropriate compensation arrangement. This essentially followed a project finance model where the assets were returned to the NSW government after the concession expired.

Although a number of infrastructure projects in NSW had been financed through public funds or other forms of PPP, the NSW government considered that PFP was the most appropriate method for financing the CCT project. This was largely because the NSW government was pursuing a debt reduction strategy at the time and thus, at least for the purposes of this project, imposed a budgetary constraint on itself.[4] If the project was financed through the use of public funds or government borrowings, the construction of the tunnel could be delayed due to competing demands for public funds and the Government could risk its AAA credit rating by increasing total state debt.[5] Alternatively, financing the project through PFP could avoid public debt altogether and result in early delivery. The RTA's total costs on the CCT project were expected to be AU$98 million.[6] The sum represented project preparation costs, work on utility networks and other ancillary works associated with the project and could thus be viewed as normal spending on infrastructure improvement. Furthermore, by allowing non-conforming proposals during the tender process, the government could possibly bring in innovative approaches from the private sector and find ways to recoup its project expenses. The ultimate objective of the government was to minimise its financial exposure, delivering the project at no cost to itself.

Cheung Kong Infrastructure Holdings Limited

Listed on the main board of the stock exchange of Hong Kong in 1996, CKI was one of the leading companies in the infrastructure sector in mainland China and Hong Kong. The group had a diversified portfolio of investments in energy infrastructure, transportation infrastructure and infrastructure-related business [see **Exhibit 5A** for a list of project assets of CKI]. In 1997, CKI acquired a controlling interest in Hongkong Electric Holdings Limited,

---

[4] Parliament of New South Wales (February 2006) "Joint Select Committee on the Cross City Tunnel, First Report".
[5] Standard & Poor's and Fitch assign bond credit ratings of AAA, AA, A, BBB, BB, B, CCC, CC, C, D. (see Wikipedia, "Bond Credit Rating, http://en.wikipedia.org/wiki/AAA_(credit_rating))
[6] "Cross City Tunnel Parliamentary Notice", http://www.lee.greens.org.au/campaigns/crosscity.htm (accessed 7 October 2006).

Hong Kong. The acquisition substantially boosted CKI's recurring revenue and strengthened its capital base. CKI and Hongkong Electric's investments in ETSA Utilities and Powercor made the group the largest electricity distributor in Australia.

With a turnover of HK$3.345 billion and net profits of HK$3.228 billion[7] in 2000[8] [see **Exhibit 5B**], CKI had a strong financial position and a good reputation for quality infrastructure projects. During the year, the energy division was the largest profit contributor, accounting for 78% of CKI's profit contribution. Investments in China and Hong Kong accounted for 86% of the group's overall profits, while investments in Australia, Canada and other countries accounted for the remaining 14%.

In 2000, CKI was actively seeking investment opportunities in three major infrastructure areas:[9]

- hedged electricity generation positions, wherein generation volume was contracted under a secure power purchase agreement structure
- near-monopoly transportation business, including toll roads, bridges, tunnels, airports and possibly sea transport facilities
- regulated monopoly network businesses, including electricity wires, gas and water pipelines.

In mid-September 2000, the RTA invited tenders for the construction, financing and 30-year operation of the Sydney CCT. The project presented an unprecedented opportunity for CKI to further achieve its global ambitions in transportation infrastructure project investment. In response to the invitation of Registrations of Interest from the RTA, CKI together with its major business partner, Bilfinger Berger Aktiengesellschaft (AG), decided to bid for the project in October 2000. Bilfinger Berger AG was one of the world's leading construction companies. Based in Mannheim, Germany, it had global operations in civil engineering and real estate, and had actively participated in privately financed build-operate-transfer (BOT) projects. With equity support from the minority superannuation trust investors, they formed the CrossCity Motorway Consortium (the CCM consortium) and obtained commitment to participate in financing from the Deutsche Bank AG, a major German bank. Bilfinger Berger AG and its wholly owned Australian subsidiary, Baulderstone Hornibrook Pty Limited, also played a sponsorship role for the tender. Baulderstone Hornibrook had a number of infrastructure projects in Australia, including the M5 East Freeway and Anzac Bridge in Sydney, the Western Link section of the Melbourne City Link and the Graham Farmer Freeway in Perth.[10]

The Bidding Process

In February 2001, the RTA short-listed three consortia out of eight competing for the CCT project. The CrossCity Motorway consortium was one of the three short-listed consortia for the final bid. The other two short-listed consortia were the E-Tube consortium (sponsored by Leighton Contractors Pty Limited and Macquarie Bank) and Sydney City Tunnel Company (sponsored by Transfield Holdings Pty Limited and Multiplex Constructions Pty Limited). All three selected consortia had to submit their detailed proposals for implementation on or before 24 October 2001. The proposals would be reviewed by an assessment panel from the RTA,

---

[7] AU$1 = HK$4.3673 on 31 December 2000.
[8] Per Cheung Kong Infrastructure Holdings Limited Consolidated Income Statement for the year ending 31 December 2000.
[9] Morgan Stanley (28 April 2004) "Cheung Kong Infrastructure".
[10] RTA (June 2003) "Cross City Tunnel Summary of Contracts".

panel would conduct a comparative value assessment against a public sector comparator (PSC). A PSC was a model of the hypothetical, risk-adjusted costs of delivering the project under a government-financed method. The panel would also evaluate the tender submissions based on various non-price determined criteria, which included:[11]

- project structure, participants and organisation
- design and construction
- initial traffic management and safety plan
- initial project plans for quality assurance, project management, environmental management, design, construction, operation and maintenance, community involvement, incident responses, occupational health, safety and rehabilitation management and project training
- operation and maintenance.

Preparing the Proposal

The CCM Consortium had to submit detailed proposals showing how it planned to complete the design, construction and operation of the CCT. According to the tender documents from the RTA, "business consideration fees" were potential areas that were available for further exploration if there was potential excess revenue over cost during the term of the concession. All short-listed consortia could nominate a business consideration fee to the RTA, which was intended to contribute towards RTA costs associated with the project.

The CCM Consortium was aware that the RTA was likely to prefer proposals that were consistent with its objective of delivering the project at "no cost to government".[12] Given RTA's policy, the CCM Consortium felt that the payment of a reasonable business consideration fee would be effective in meeting the objectives that the government had set. By putting forward a proposal that would focus their bid on the business consideration fee, the CCM Consortium was confident that its proposal could offer superior value for money over traditional methods of government delivery.

Since there was no mandatory requirement to submit a conforming proposal to meet all conditions set by the RTA, there was an opportunity for the CCM Consortium to bring in critical changes to the original project plan to reap maximum returns and recoup the costs incurred by the business consideration fee. For environmental and traffic reasons, the CCM Consortium considered that the length of the tunnel could be increased by 300 metres while the depth at the eastern end could be increased by 30 metres. Such changes would increase the tunnel's daily capacity by an extra 17,000 vehicles.[13] However, the extra work required for this "long 80 tunnel" proposed by the CCM consortium could result in an increase in construction cost of US$135.7 million.[14] The total projected construction cost would therefore become AU$680 million.

Valuing the Project

The value of the CCT project would depend principally on the revenues generated by traffic volume and tolls charged during the term of the concession. The CCT was comprised of two main tunnels. Both of the main tunnels would have two lanes, while the other entry and exit

---

[11] RTA (June 2003) "Cross City Tunnel Summary of Contracts".

[12] NSW Audit Office (2006) "Performance Reports 2006: The Cross City Tunnel Project—Executive Summary", http://www.audit.nsw.gov.au/publications/reports/performance/2006/cross_city_tunnel/execsum.htm (accessed 6 January 2007).

[13] "Cross City Contract Signed", (2003), *Tunnels and Tunneling International*, 35 (1), p. 15.

[14] AU$1 = US$0.5115 on 31 December 2001.

CCT had to purchase an electronic pass or hold a toll account and have a valid electronic tag. The CCM consortium felt it was necessary to apply a differential pricing scheme. Under this scheme, the toll charged would depend on the size of the vehicle and the route that that it took. Passenger vehicles such as motorbikes, sedans, station wagons, taxis and vehicles towing trailers were classified as Class 2.[15] Heavy vehicles were classified as Class 4.[16]

The CCM consortium considered that the initial toll charges for vehicles other than buses could be set as follows [see **Exhibit 6**]:[17]

- for vehicles using the main tunnels to and from Darling Harbour, including vehicles entering from or exiting to the Eastern Distributor, AU$2.5 for Class 2 passenger vehicles and AU$5 for Class 4 heavy vehicles (March 1999 prices, including GST)[18]
- for vehicles entering the westbound tunnel at Rushcutters Bay and then using the Riley Street tunnel to exit onto Sir John Young Crescent, AU$1.1 for Class 2 passenger vehicles and AU$2.2 for Class 4 heavy vehicles (March 1999 prices, including GST).

Buses providing public transport services were not required to pay tolls, but higher charges could apply to vehicles without electronic tolling transponders. The CCM suggested an initial administrative charge between AU$5 and AU$8 for each casual use of any of the tunnels on top of the standard tolls. In addition, higher tolls might be charged for traffic exiting from the westbound tunnel onto Harbour and Bathurst Streets, to help reduce congestion in the western CBD. The extra revenue collected could be used for public transport, pedestrian, cyclist, air quality and other amenity improvements.

The CCM consortium believed that it was imperative to secure the right to increase future tolls at its discretion. It therefore proposed a toll escalation scheme, under which the tolls could be increased in line with inflation or in line with minimum quarterly rates of increase equivalent to 4% per annum until the June quarter of 2012 and then 3% per annum until the June quarter of 2018.[19] From mid-2018, the maximum increases would be in line with inflation.

With advice from Hyder Consulting, the CCM consortium prepared traffic estimates for the CCT. According to the projections, the CCT would be used by over 90,000 vehicles per day by 2006 and over 100,000 vehicles per day by 2016.[20] By lengthening the tunnel, the consortium would be able to earn additional revenue of AU$10.98 million per year based on the traffic projections.[21] **Exhibit 7** shows the traffic forecast of the CCT. **Exhibit 8** summarises the results of the likely economic performance of the CCT project.

Under the Land Lease Agreement with NSW, the winning consortium would have to make rent payments for the first 12 months of the lease, each successive six-month period during the lease and then the final period of the lease, as follows:[22]

---

[15] Class 2: height less than or equal to 2.8m, length less than or equal to 12.5m.
[16] Class 4: height greater than 2.8m, length greater than 12.5m.
[17] RTA (June 2003) "Cross City Tunnel Summary of Contracts".
[18] RTA (June 2003) "Cross City Tunnel Summary of Contracts".
[19] RTA (June 2003) "Cross City Tunnel Summary of Contracts".
[20] RTA (August 2002) "The Cross City Tunnel Supplementary Environmental Impact Statement", p. 46.
[21] "Cross City Contract Signed," *Tunnels and Tunneling International*, 35 (1) , 15 January 2003.
[22] RTA (June 2003) "Cross City Tunnel Summary of Contracts".

- thirty-five percent of actual gross revenue—less any amount collected for GST or other taxes or government charges, other than income tax—from any non-toll business uses of the tunnels or the land leased, such as the use of the tunnels or land for telecommunications infrastructure
- if the actual toll and administrative charge revenue for the relevant period—less any amount collected for GST or other taxes or government charges—was more than 10% higher than that forecasted by the private sector participants' base case financial model for the project, a progressively increasing share of this extra revenue, as set out in **Exhibit 9**.

The CCM consortium considered that the toll escalation scheme could help to recover the business consideration fee. Therefore, in return for the RTA's granting it the right to undertake the project, the CCM consortium proposed payment of a business consideration fee in the sum of AU$100.1 million plus GST to the RTA.[23] According to the tender documents, the fee had to be over and above the costs associated with the project. The fee could be used by the RTA to cover its ancillary costs associated with delivering the project, including work on utility networks affected by the tunnel and cost recovery for project preparation costs.

Assessing Project Risks

The CCM consortium was aware that substantial risks would be transferred from the government to the consortium if it won the tender. The consortium had identified various risks associated with the project. These included:[24]

- risks associated with the financing, design, construction, operation, maintenance and repair costs of the project
- the risks that the tunnel might fail to deliver the anticipated traffic volumes or projected revenues
- the risks of over-estimation of the value motorists would place on the tunnel's benefits
- the risks that the capacity of the tunnel was not sufficient to allow for the projected traffic estimates
- the risks of overforecasting asset use—a study conducted by Standard and Poor's about traffic modelling on 104 international toll roads, bridges and tunnels showed that on average, across all toll roads, bridges and tunnels, forecasts overestimated traffic in the first year by 20–30%[25]
- income tax risks
- the risk that their works or operational and maintenance activities might be disrupted by the lawful actions of other government and local government authorities or a court or tribunal.

To minimise patronage risks, the CCM consortium proposed certain changes to the road network or the introduction of "traffic calming" measures. One of the major changes involved removing access to the Harbour Crossings from Sir John Young Crescent and Cowper Wharf Road. Nevertheless, such changes would restrict road users' choice and could affect residents of the affected communities. The CCM consortium would thus also require the government to pay compensation if any changes to the Sydney public transport system had a material effect on the amount of traffic traversing the toll road tunnel. A material effect would include

---

[23] The quantum of the business consideration fee changed over the course of the contract negotiations between CCM and the RTA. The original figure changed following the acceptance by the RTA of the consortium's non-conforming "long 80 tunnel" As a consequence of the differing minister's Planning Conditions of Approval, and later requirements imposed by more stringent air quality standards (the construction of a third tunnel for ventilation purposes, with estimated cost of $37 million) and through community consultation, CCM reduced the amount of the BCF to AU$96,859,688 they proposed to pay the RTA.

[24] RTA (June 2003) "Cross City Tunnel Summary of Contracts".

[25] "Cross City Tunnel Parliamentary Notice", http://www.lee.greens.org.au/campaigns/crosscity.htm (accessed 7 October 2006).

compensation could be computed based on the consortium's expected profits every year until 2035. This could amount to as much as AU$100 million annually.

To mitigate the risks of additional costs that could arise due to a change in the scope of works directed by the RTA, the CCM consortium would require the RTA to compensate it for the costs that reasonably arose from the change, including those associated with the contractors' overheads and profits and any delay costs or equity holding costs. If the RTA decreased the scope of works and subsequent operation, maintenance and repair obligations, the CCM consortium would pay to the RTA 75% of the direct cost savings.

Capital Structure

The Equity Investors

The CCM consortium had a complicated "Special Purpose Vehicle" structure that involved the use of trusts and corporate vehicles that were set up by the equity investors. A new company, known as CrossCity Motorway Nominees No. 2 Pty Limited (the trustee), was incorporated to serve as a trustee of the CrossCity Motorway Property Trust, which was established in October 2001. The Property Trust was held by CrossCity Motorway Nominees No. 1 Pty Limited, in its capacity as trustee of the CrossCity Motorway Holdings Trust, another unit trust set up in October 2001. In turn, all the shares in the trustee and the Holdings Trust were owned and controlled by CrossCity Motorway Holdings Pty Limited (CCM Holdings), which was owned by the following equity investors [see **Exhibit 10** for an overview of the structure of the CCT contracts]:[27]

- CKI City Tunnel Investment (Malaysian) Limited, a wholly owned subsidiary of CKI (50%)
- Bilfinger Berger BOT GmbH, a wholly owned subsidiary of Bilfinger Berger AG (20%)
- DB Capital Partners, a private equity arm of Deutsche Asset Management (30%). It invested in the project on behalf of a number of Australian superannuation funds, including Development Australia Fund.[28]
- All the units in the CrossCity Motorway Holdings Trust were owned in the same proportions by the same equity investors.

CCM Holdings set up a wholly owned subsidiary known as CrossCity Motorway Pty Limited (the Company). If the consortium won the bid, the trustee and the Company would be used as the vehicle to enter into the Cross City Tunnel Project Deed with the RTA.

The Contractor

The Contractor of the project would be the "Baulderstone Hornibrook Bilfinger Berger Cross City Tunnel Joint Venture", a partnership set up by Bilfinger Berger AG and Baulderstone Hornibrook Pty Limited.[29]

---

[26] Scott, S. and Allen. L (23 October 2005) "City Tunnel Contract in Doubt", *Australasian Business Intelligence*.
[27] RTA (June 2003) "Cross City Tunnel Summary of Contracts".
[28] CrossCity Motorway Media Release, 19 December 2002.
[29] RTA (June 2003) "Cross City Tunnel Summary of Contracts".

The Operator

The operation, repair and maintenance of the tunnel and its surface works would be undertaken by Baulderstone Hornibrook Pty Limited until reversion to public ownership.

The Borrower

Borrowings would be made by the CrossCity Motorway Finance Pty Limited, which was wholly owned by the trustee in its capacity as trustee of the property trust. The "borrower" would be the vehicle used to contract with the project's debt financiers.

Debt Financing Strategy

The total capital required for the Cross City Tunnel project was estimated to be AU$680 million. The consortium estimated that the project would be financed by AU$580 million debt, and the balance by equity. Under the proposed debt financing plan, one-half of the initial debt finance would be provided by Deutsche Bank AG and Deutsche Australia Limited (a wholly owned subsidiary of Deutsche Bank AG), the other half by Westpac Banking Corporation, with further loan syndicate participation expected to reduce this large concentrated debt requirement if the project proceeded.

Completion of the Deal

In late October 2001, the three short-listed consortia submitted their proposals to the RTA. The CCM consortium was the only proponent that bid on the business consideration fee. Two other bidders did not bid an upfront payment of a business consideration fee. During the evaluation process, the RTA relied on estimates of traffic flow prepared by traffic consultant Masson Wilson Twiney Pty Ltd, to compare the value of the proposals against the PSC. The forecast produced by the consultant showed that the "long tunnel" proposed by the CCM consortium would be used by 86,300 vehicles per day in 2006 and 101,700 vehicles per day in 2016. Such forecast figures were lower than the estimates prepared by the CCM consortium. **Exhibits 11** to **13** present the projected financial statements and the assumptions used by the CCT for the period from 2003 to 2008.

In February 2002, the RTA's assessment and review panel concluded that the proposals submitted by the CCM consortium represented better value for money than the PSC and the proposals submitted by the other two proponents. On 27 February 2002, the minister for roads formally announced that the CCM consortium was the preferred proponent. The submission from the CCM consortium was a non-conforming proposal that had incorporated various changes to initial concepts of the tunnel. As a result of the proposed changes, a number of additional environmental impacts would occur and a supplementary EIS had to be prepared. The execution of the project's principal contracts was completed on 18 December 2002.

The CCT project heralded CKI's first transportation project outside mainland China and Hong Kong. Under the plan, the tunnel components of the project would be operated, maintained and repaired by the CCM consortium until they were returned to public ownership after 18 December 2035 or for 30 years and 2 months from the completion of the tunnels, if their completion was delayed.[30] Analysts expected that the equity IRR[31] on CKI's investment in this green field project would be around 15%. With sufficient cash on hand and reasonably low

---

[30] RTA (June 2003) "Cross City Tunnel Summary of Contracts".
[31] IRR stands for internal rate of return.

2006, the CCT's annual contribution to CKI's bottom line would be HK$28 million.[32]

Project equity came from CKI (50%), DB Capital Partners (30%) and Bilfinger Berger BOT GmbH (20%). The CCM consortium completed the AU$580 million project financing after 16 banks joined the transaction with the initial senior debt financiers. These new banks included Australia and New Zealand Banking Group Limited, Bank of China, BOS International (Australia) Limited, Bank of Western Australia Limited, Credit Industriel et Commercial, Credit Agricole Indosuez Australia Limited, Credit Lyonnais (Hong Kong Branch), Dexia Credit Local, KBC Finance Ireland, Kreditanstalt fur Wiederaufbau, Landesbank Baden-Wurttemberg (Singapore Branch), Natexis Banques Populaires, Norddeutsche Landesbank Girozentrale (Singapore Branch), Sumitomo Mitsui Finance Australia Limited, United Overseas Bank Limited and WestLB AG (Sydney Branch).[33] The loan syndicate details were as follows:[34]

- Arrangers: Westpac Banking Corp lending AU$47 million and Deutsche Bank investing AU$39 million
- Lead managers: ANZ Investment Bank, Bank of Scotland, Credit Agricole, Credit Lyonnais, KBC Bank, Kreditanstalt fur Wiederaufbau, Landesbank Baden-Wurttemberg, NordLB, Sumitomo Mitsui Banking Corp and WestLB, with each manager taking AU$39 million
- Managers: Bank West, Dexia Bank and Union Overseas Bank, each lending AU$28 million, and CIC lending AU$20 million
- Purpose: Project financing for the construction of the AU$680 million CCT, with limited recourse to the equity investors[35]
- Size: AU$580 million
- Type: Seven-year term loan
- Margin: 150bp[36] over BBSY[37] (during construction)
- 160bp over BBSY (after construction)
- 170bp over BBSY (no rating)
- Fees for lead managers: 80bp for AU$50 million
- Fees for managers: 60bp for AU$35 million.

Project Outcomes

The CCT opened for traffic on 28 August 2005, less than two years and seven months after the commencement of construction. After opening, the CCT was often described as the "ghost tunnel", due to its low volume of traffic. Statistics released by the CCM in February 2006 showed that around 30,000 vehicles used the tunnel each day, well short of the projected 90,000 per day. Many road users considered the toll too high for a short journey of 2.1 km. They would rather use a free alternative public road, even though it might take longer to reach the destination. Although many road users wanted to avoid the tunnel, a number of "traffic calming" measures—which many observers and media commentators suggested merely functioned to funnel traffic into the tunnel—were introduced. Instead of relieving congestion,

---

[32] AU$1 = HK$6.1405 on 31 December 2006.

[33] RTA (June 2003) "Cross City Tunnel Summary of Contracts".

[34] Anonymous (28 January 2003) "Australiasia (Syndicated Loans)", *Euroweek*.

[35] Fislage, B. and Heymann, E. (10 June 2003), "Road Operation Projects: Lucrative for Institutional Investors", *Deutsche Bank Research*.

[36] Bp stands for basis point. 1% change = 100 basis points, and 0.01% = 1 basis point (see Investopedia, http://www.investopedia.com/terms/b/basispoint.asp)

[37] BBSY stands for bank bill swap yield.

disruptions. For instance, there were lane reductions at William Street and changes in light phasing at various intersections across the city. Road users also complained about misleading signage indicating the tunnel was the only route to reach certain destinations when in fact alternative public roads were available.

The huge upfront consideration demanded by the NSW government to achieve its "no-cost-to-government" objective also sparked public outrage. It appeared to the community that, in return for such consideration, the government allowed inflated tolls to be set by the operator, while it might have given assurances to the operators that sufficient traffic throughput might be achieved for the tunnel through traffic calming measures. Some analysts were also sceptical about the traffic projections derived by the CCM consortium. It was suggested that the projection method used by the CCM employed a "work back" (or implied) process, in which the projections were derived from an internal rate of return promised to equity investors. In other words, the traffic projections and tolls might have been financially reverse-engineered to provide the required toll revenue and the CCM had failed to consider land use and transport interaction factors properly. To increase patronage and public acceptance, the CCM introduced a toll-free period from 24 October 2005 to late November 2005 and also announced a freeze on toll increases for one year and a waiver-of-fee for casual users. In all, however, in its first six months of operation the Sydney CCT was operating at roughly one-third of projected throughput, nowhere near projected income and rumoured to be near financial collapse. It was also a public relations disaster, attracting significant negative media and political attention, and was subject to strong general-user resistance. In response to public pressure, in October 2005 the government released some contract terms to the public. A few days after the release, the head of the RTA stepped down due to his failure to disclose an amendment to the contract.

In February 2006, there was media speculation that the Sydney CCT was for sale and rumours of a "buy-out" by the NSW government began and persisted throughout 2006, despite denials that the CCT was for sale and that NSW was not a potential buyer. The rumoured price was over AU$1 billion. However, despite denials by the government and the CCM, NSW roads minister Eric Roozendal said that "any prospective buyers would be well advised to consider the cost of a trip through it", while NSW opposition roads spokesman Andrew Stoner said "taxpayers would be the ones to suffer most of if the government was forced to pay compensation to the tunnel operator".[38] It was clear that, in addition to being financially problematical, the CCT was starting to attract significant political interest and had the potential to severely embarrass the NSW government that championed it.

The bottom line was looking unpleasant. With the poor operating performance of the CCT project, it seemed inevitable that CKI and other partners of the CCM might have to incur a significant impairment loss in the next financial quarter. It further seemed that the Sydney CCT investment was rapidly turning into a liability for CKI, a prospect that was not comforting to a company that had in the past been highly successful in Australia, whilst remaining relatively low key.

---

[38] Hassett, S. (16 November 2006) "NSW Government Baulks at Tunnel Bid", *The Weekend Australian*, http://www.theaustralian.news.com.au/printpage/0,5942,20769578,00.html (accessed 6 January 2007).

Date	Event
22 Oct 1998	The premier (Mr Carr) and the minister of roads (Mr Scully) released an exhibition for comment on the initial concept (the "short tunnel") in a 16-page report titled "The Cross City Tunnel: Improving the Heart of the City". AU$2 toll is flagged.
April 1999	The City of Sydney Council released the Cross City Tunnel Alternative Scheme. This was a longer tunnel than the one proposed in the 1998 "Improving the Heart of the City", running to the eastern end of the Kings Cross Tunnel and included narrowing William Street.
15 Sept 2000	The RTA invited registrations of interest from private sector parties "for the financing, design, construction, operation and maintenance of the Cross City Tunnel project".
23 Oct 2000	Closing date for registrations of interest to construct and operate the tunnel
Feb 2001	The minister for roads (Mr Scully) announced that three consortia had been short-listed to prepare detailed proposals: CrossCity Motorways (CCM), E-TUBE and Sydney City Tunnel Company.
Oct 2001	Detailed proposals for implementation of the project were lodged by the three consortia and reviewed by assessment panel.
Feb 2002	The Budget Committee of Cabinet approved CCM to be selected as the preferred proponent and for the CCM "long 80 tunnel" option to be selected as the preferred proposal.
27 Feb 2002	The minister for roads (Mr Scully) announced that CCM was the preferred proponent. The tender submission from CCM incorporated changes to the approved activity that the minister for roads believed would provide more benefits and reduce construction related impacts on the community. As a result of the proposed changes, a number of additional environmental impacts would occur. A supplementary EIS was prepared.
14 Mar 2002	A letter was sent from the treasurer (Mr Egan) to the minister for roads (Mr Scully) stating "A key objective of the project has been its development at no net cost to government" and "it is not certain at this time that the project can achieve a 'no net cost to government' outcome. If the project cannot proceed without a government contribution, any such contribution would need to be funded out of the RTA's existing forward capital program".
16 Dec 2002	Approval was given by the treasurer (Mr Egan) to sign the project deed under the Public Authorities (Financial Arrangements) Act 1987.
18 Dec 2002	A contract between the CCM consortium and RTA was signed to finance, construct, operate and maintain the CCT. Differential tolling was set, AU$2.5 per car and AU$5 for heavy vehicles.
28 Jan 2003	Major works started on the AU$680 million Cross City Tunnel.
21 Dec 2004	The treasurer (Mr Egan) approved the RTA to enter into the Cross City Tunnel Project First Amendment Deed with the CCM under section 20 of the Public Authorities (Financial Arrangements) Act 1987. This deed included provision that "in consideration for the CCM's agreement to fund and carry out certain [changes if required by the RTA], CCM might increase the Base Toll to be collected from motorists on the terms set out in the First Amendment Deed".
23 Dec 2004	The First Amendment Deed was entered into by RTA and the CCM, enabling AU$35 million of additional works to be paid for through a higher base toll (increased by $AU0.15).
28 Aug 2005	The Cross City Tunnel opened.
Nov 2005	The Summary of Cross City Tunnel Project Deed was made public.
19 Dec 2035	The Cross City Tunnel was due to be returned to public ownership.

Source: Parliament of New South Wales (February 2006) "Joint Select Committee on the Cross City Tunnel, First Report".

EXHBIT 2A: THE CCT HORIZONTAL ALIGNMENTS

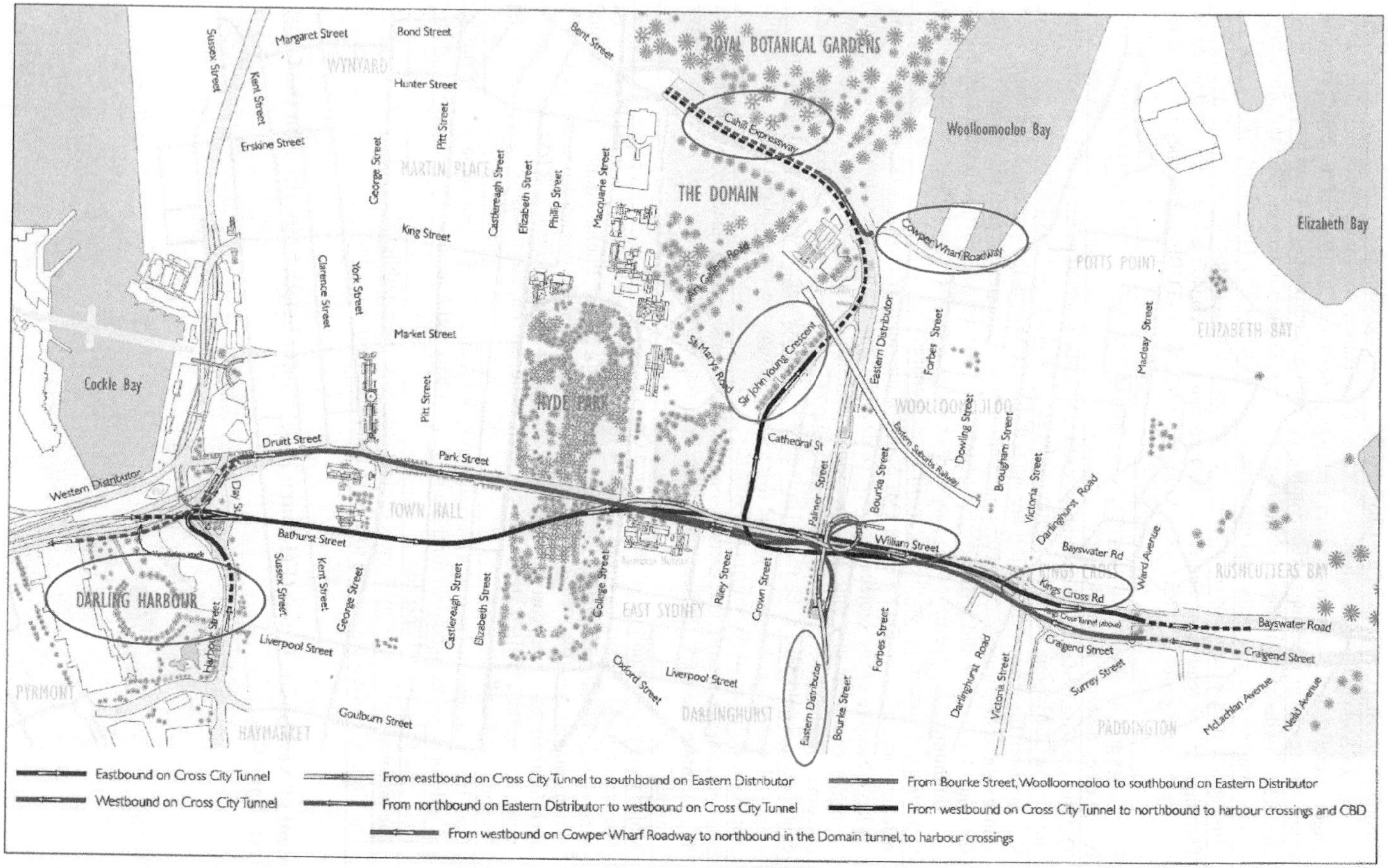

Figure 1. *Cross City Tunnel horizontal alignments.*

Source: RTA (June 2003) "Cross City Tunnel Summary of Contracts".

07/324C

EXHIBIT 2B: THE CCT ROUTE MAP

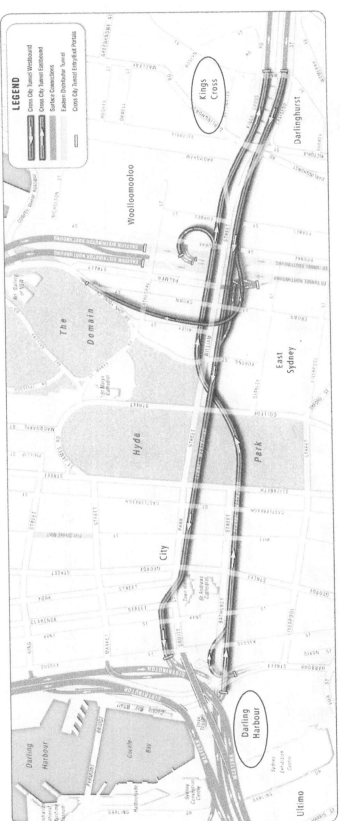

Source: CrossCity Motorway Pty Ltd, "Tunnel Route Map", http://www.crosscity.com.au/DynamicPages.asp?cid=81&navid=19 (accessed 2 October 2006).

EXHIBIT 2C: INDICATIVE VERTICAL ALIGNMENTS OF THE MAIN TUNNELS

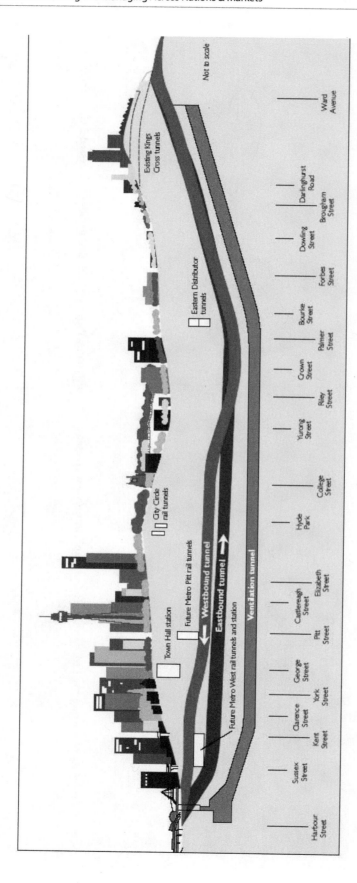

Source: RTA (June 2003) "Cross City Tunnel Summary of Contracts".

EXHIBIT 2D: MAP OF SYDNEY

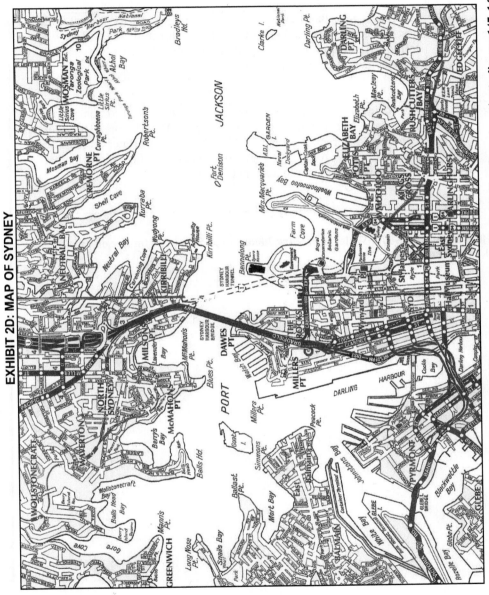

Source: *Sydney Compact Street Directory*, 10th Edition (1992), Gregory's Publishing Company: Australia, pp. 147–148.

Model	Details
The "short tunnel"	1.2km tunnel, exiting William Street near Museum of Sydney. Taking approximately 40,000 vehicles. Two way toll of AU$2. Cost estimated at AU$273 million. Published in "Transforming the Heart of the City" (1998).
The "long tunnel"	Approximately 2km tunnels exiting in the Kings Cross Tunnel to the east and connecting to the Western Distributor in the west. Two-way toll of AU$2.5. First described in the initial Cross City Tunnel Environmental Impact Statement (2000).
The "long 80 tunnel"	Approximately 2.1km tunnels exiting east of the Kings Cross Tunnel to the east and connecting to the Western Distributor in the west. Two-way differential tolling of AU2.5 and AU$5 (later increased to AU$2.65 and AU$5.3). First described in the Supplementary Environmental Impact Statement (2002).

Source: Parliament of New South Wales (February 2006) "Joint Select Committee on the Cross City Tunnel, First Report".

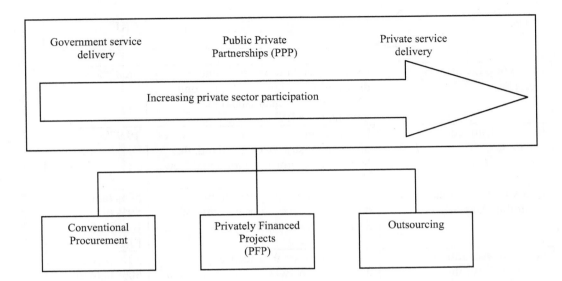

Source: New South Wales Government (November 2001) "Working with Government Guidelines for Privately Financed Projects".

Project	Business	CKI shareholding
Energy		
Hongkong Electric, Hong Kong	Exclusive right to generate and distribute electricity to Hong Kong Island, Ap Lei Chau Island and Lamma Island	38.87%
Envestra Limited, NSW, Australia	Distribution of natural gas in the states of South Australia, Queensland, the Northern Territory, Victoria and New South Wales	19.97%
ETSA Utilities, South Australia, Australia	Right to operate the electricity distribution network in the state of South Australia for 200 years	50% (another 50% held by Hongkong Electric)
Powercor Australia Ltd, Victoria, Australia	Right to operate the electricity distribution network covering an area of over 150,000 sq. km in the state of Victoria and retail operation in certain areas of Australia	50% (another 50% held by Hongkong Electric)
Fushun Cogen Power Plants, Liaoning, China	Operational	60% interest in the JV
Nanhai Power Plant I, Guangdong, China	Operational	30% interest in the JV
Qinyang Power Plants, Henan, China	Operational	49% interest in the JV
Shantou Chaoyang Power Plant, Guangdong, China	Operational	60% interest in the JV
Shantou Chenghai Power Plant, Guangdong, China	Operational	60% interest in the JV
Shantou Tuopu Power Plant, Guangdong, China	Operational	60% interest in the JV
Siping Cogen Power Plant, Jilin, China	Operational	45% interest in the JV
Zhuhai Power Plant, Guangdong, China	Operational	45% interest in the JV
Transportation		
Eastern Harbour Crossing Rail Tunnel, Hong Kong	Rail franchise period 1986–2008	50%
Changsha Wujialing and Wuyilu Bridges, Wunan, China	Operational	44.2% in the JV
Guangzhou East-South-West Ringroad, Guangdong, China	Operational	44.4% in the JV
Jiangmen Chaolian Bridge, Guangdong, China	Operational	50% in the JV
Jiangmen Jianghe Highway, Guangdong, China	Operational	50% in the JV

Jiangmen Jiangsha Highway, Guangdong, China	Operational	50% in the JV
Nanhai Road Network, Guangdong, China	Operational	49% – 64.4% in the JV
National Highway 107 (Zhumadian section), Henan, China	Operational	66% in the JV
Panyu Beidou Bridge, Guangdong, China	Operational	40% in the JV
Shantou Bay Bridge, Guangdong, China	Operational	30% in the JV
Shen-shan Highway (Eastern Section), Guangdong, China	Operational	33.5% in the JV
Shenyang Changqing Bridge, Liaoning, China	Operational	30% in the JV
Shenyang Da Ba Road and South-West Elevated Sections, Liaoning, China	Operational	30% in the JV
Shenyang Gongnong Bridge, Liaoning, China	Operational	30% in the JV
Shenyang Shensu Expressway, Liaoning, China	Operational	30% in the JV
Tangshan Tangle Road, Hebei, China	Operational	51% in the JV
Zengcheng Lixin Road, Guangdong, China	Operational	51% in the JV
Infrastructure materials and Infrastructure-related Businesses		
Anderson Asphalt, Anderson Asia, Hong Kong	One of Hong Kong's largest asphalt producers	
Asia Stone, Anderson Asia, Hong Kong	One of Hong Kong's four contract quarries	
Bonntile, Anderson Asia, Hong Kong	Exterior wall spray-coating system specialist	
Ready Mixed Concrete, Anderson Asia, Hong Kong	One of Hong Kong's largest concrete producers	
Green Island Cement, Hong Kong	Only integrated cement producer in Hong Kong	
Shantou Cement Grinding Plant, Guangdong, China	Operational	100%
Yunfu Cement Plant, Guangdong, China	Operational	67% interest in the JV
Siquijor Limestone Quarry, Philippines	Operational	40% interest in the JV
Polyphalt Inc, Canada	Developed and commercialised polymer modified asphalt technology, products and services. The company blended several of its asphalt technologies with plastics and rubbers, including recycled materials	63.7%

Stuart Energy Systems Corp., Canada	Developed and supplied hydrogen generation and supply systems through its proprietary water and electrolysis technology	12.9%
Shenyang LPG Business, Liaoning, China	LPG filling stations and vehicle conversion facilities	51% interest in the JV
Yueyang Water Plants, Hunan, China	Operational	49% interest in the JV
e-Smart System Inc, Hong Kong	Applications of the patented "Eyecon" microprocessor-based contactless smart card technology in the Asia Pacific region	50%

Source: Cheung Kong Infrastructure Holdings Limited (2000) "Annual Report", http://www.cki.com.hk/english/PDF_file/annualReport/2000/2000_AR_projectProfile.pdf, (accessed 2 October 2006).

YEAR ENDING 31 DECEMBER 2000

Figures in HK$ millions

	2000
Turnover	
Group turnover	2,567
Share of turnover of jointly controlled entities	778
	3,345
group turnover	
Other revenue	2,567
Operating costs	1,373
Finance costs	(2,819)
Operating profit	(621)
	500
Share of results of associates	2,413
Share of results of jointly controlled entities	588
Profit before taxation	3,501
Taxation	(288)
Profit after taxation	3,213
Minority interests	15
Profit attributable to shareholders	3,228
Dividends	(1,353)
Profit for the year retained	1,875
Earnings per share	HK$1.43

Source: Cheung Kong Infrastructure Holdings Limited (2000) "Annual Report".

EXHIBIT 6: PROPOSED TOLL CHARGES

	Eastbound Tunnel Darling Harbour to Eastern Distributor exit or Rushcutters Bay	**Westbound Tunnel** Rushcutters Bay to Darling Harbour	**Sir John Young Crescent Exit** From the east
Class 2	AU$2.5	AU$2.5	AU$1.1
Class 4	AU$5	AU$5	AU$2.2

Note: all tolls are inclusive of GST

Source: RTA (June 2003) "Cross City Tunnel Summary of Contracts".

Capacity	Eastbound 60,000	Westbound 60,000	Sir John Young Crescent 50,000	

Annual Average Daily Traffic (AADT)

Year ending	Eastbound	Westbound	Sir John Young Crescent	Total
31 Dec 04	30,041	36,626	22,433	89,100
31 Dec 06	30,713	37,597	22,796	91,106
31 Dec 11	32,433	40,137	23,695	96,265
31 Dec 16	34,250	42,848	24,629	101,727
31 Dec 21	35,507	44,409	25,315	105,231
31 Dec 26	36,811	46,027	26,021	108,859

Semi Annual Growth Rate

Year ending	Eastbound	Westbound	Sir John Young Crescent	Average
31 Dec 04	0.56%	0.66%	0.40%	0.56%
31 Dec 06	0.56%	0.68%	0.39%	0.55%
31 Dec 11	0.56%	0.67%	0.39%	0.41%
31 Dec 16	0.37%	0.36%	0.28%	0.34%
31 Dec 21	0.37%	0.36%	0.28%	0.34%
31 Dec 26	0.39%	0.39%	0.39%	N.A.

Annual Growth Rate

Year ending	Eastbound	Westbound	Sir John Young Crescent	Average
31 Dec 04	1.11%	1.32%	0.81%	1.12%
31 Dec 06	1.10%	1.32%	0.78%	1.11%
31 Dec 11	1.10%	0.92%	0.63%	0.82%
31 Dec 16	0.72%	0.72%	0.55%	0.68%
31 Dec 21	0.72%	0.72%	0.55%	0.68%
31 Dec 26	0.72%	0.72%	0.55%	0.68%

Source: "Cross City Tunnel Parliamentary Notice",
http://www.lee.greens.org.au/campaigns/crosscity.htm (accessed 7 October 2006).

ECONOMIC PERFORMANCE OF THE CROSS CITY TUNNEL

Taking account of initial and recurring capital costs, operation and maintenance costs, road user benefits (savings in vehicle operating costs, travel time savings and savings in accident costs) and pedestrian benefits, but not counting environmental externalities.

Discount rate	Present value of initial and recurring capital costs and maintenance costs	Present value of road user and pedestrian benefits	Net present value	Benefits:cost ratio		
				Benefits O&M D&C	Benefits D&C +O&M	Net present value/ capital cost
4%	AU$693 m	AU$2,754 m	AU$2,061 m	5.0	4.2	4.0
7%	AU$576 m	AU$1,689 m	AU$1,114 m	3.4	3.0	2.4
10%	AU$495 m	AU$1,102 m	AU$607 m	2.4	2.3	1.4

Source: RTA (June 2003) "Cross City Tunnel Summary of Contracts".

EXHIBIT 9: THE RTA'S SHARE OF ANY UNEXPECTEDLY HIGH REVENUES

(Generally over six-month periods, from tolls and administrative charges, including additional charges for "casual" tunnel users without electronic tolling vehicle transponders)

Actual revenue, as a percentage of forecast revenue	RTA's share of this portion of the actual revenue (to be paid by the trustee as part of its rent under the Land Lease)
Up to 110%	0%
110–120%	10%
120–130%	20%
130–140%	30%
140–150%	40%
More than 150%	50%

Source: RTA (June 2003) "Cross City Tunnel Summary of Contracts".

EXHIBIT 10: OVERVIEW OF THE STRUCTURE OF THE CCT

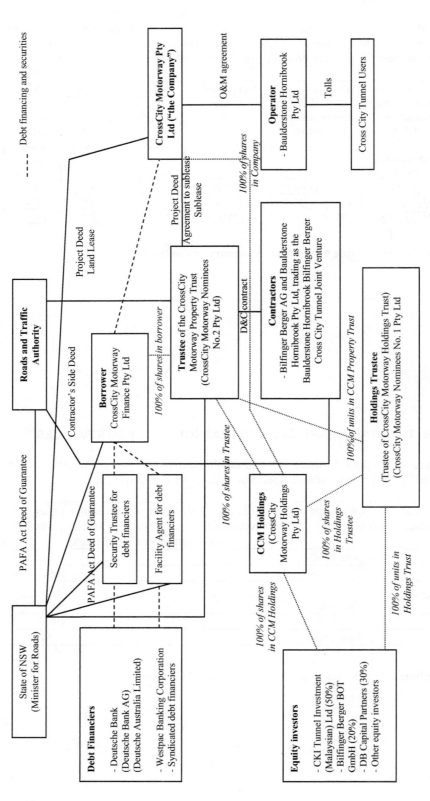

Source: RTA (June 2003) "Cross City Tunnel Summary of Contracts".

07/324C

EXHIBIT 11: PROJECTED CONSOLIDATED BALANCE SHEET (2003–2008)

Figures in AU$ millions

Six months ending	30/6/03	31/12/03	30/6/04	31/12/04	30/6/05	31/12/05	30/6/06	31/12/06	30/7/07	31/12/07	30/6/08	31/12/08
Period number	1	2	3	4	5	6	7	8	9	10	11	12
Assets												
Current Assets												
Cash on Deposit	–	–	–	–	–	–	12,528	–	–	–	–	–
Cash Balance in Equity Account	–	–	–	–	–	68	319	245	196	163	160	166
Accounts Receivable	–	–	–	–	–	–	25,169	25,169	–	–	–	–
Cash Balances in Ramp Up Reserve Account	–	–	–	–	–	–	–	–	–	–	–	–
Cash Balances in Major Maintenance Reserve Account	–	–	–	–	–	–	–	–	–	–	–	–
Cash Balances in Lockup Account	–	–	–	–	–	–	–	–	–	–	–	–
Cash Balance in Equity Holding Account	–	–	–	–	–	–	–	–	–	–	–	–
Cash in Debt Drawdown Account	–	–	–	–	–	–	–	–	–	–	–	–
Prepayment of Tax	–	–	–	–	–	–	–	–	–	–	–	–
Total Current Assets	–	–	–	–	–	68	38,016	25,413	196	163	160	166
Non-Current Assets												
Future Income Tax Benefit	1,338	2,869	7,602	12,623	18,895	33,902	36,260	37,829	39,373	40,965	41,903	42,842
Carrying Value of Fixed Assets	243,166	362,627	493,665	653,250	738,500	758,583	785,022	763,212	740,370	717,527	696,805	676,050
RTA Payment/Tender Process Allowance	95,392	93,925	92,457	90,989	89,522	88,054	85,587	85,119	83,652	82,184	80,716	79,249
Total Non-Current Assets	339,896	459,421	593,724	756,862	846,917	880,539	906,869	886,160	863,395	840,676	819,424	798,141
Total Assets	339,896	459,421	593,724	756,862	846,917	880,607	944,885	911,574	863,591	840,839	819,584	798,308
Liabilities												
Current Liabilities												
Accounts Payable	–	–	–	–	–	380	1,269	1,105	926	939	907	904
Provision for Income Tax	–	–	–	–	–	–	–	–	–	–	–	–
Total Current Liabilities	–	–	–	–	–	380	1,269	1,105	926	939	907	904

07/324C

Infrastructure Finance: The Sydney Cross City Tun...

Non-Current Liabilities												
Deferred Income Tax Liability	(110)	(282)	(519)	(849)	(1,261)	4,983	6,163	5,887	5,611	5,334	5,058	4,782
Senior Debt	176,235	291,608	439,782	608,229	704,139	756,191	579,992	580,000	565,016	565,016	565,016	565,016
Working Capital	–	–	–	–	–	–	–	–	–	–	–	–
Shareholder Loans	–	–	–	–	–	–	–	–	–	–	–	–
Capitalised RTA Payment	–	–	–	–	–	–	–	–	–	–	–	–
Total Non-Current Liabilities	176,125	291,326	439,263	607,380	702,878	761,174	586,155	585,887	570,628	570,350	570,074	569,797
Total Liabilities	176,125	291,326	439,263	607,380	702,878	761,554	587,424	586,992	571,554	571,289	570,981	570,701
Net Assets	163,771	168,095	154,461	149,482	144,039	119,053	357,461	324,582	292,037	269,550	248,603	227,607
Shareholders Equity												
Ordinary Equity - Original Equity	163,790	158,756	153,721	148,686	143,651	138,617	211,207	210,860	210,472	210,068	210,068	201,895
Ordinary Equity - Retail Equity	–	–	–	–	–	–	–	–	–	–	–	–
RPU	–	–	–	–	–	–	72,613	72,613	72,613	72,613	72,613	72,613
Bonds	–	–	–	–	–	–	90,000	68,015	44,017	28,474	9,989	–
Total Ordinary Equity	163,790	158,756	153,721	148,686	143,651	138,617	373,820	351,488	327,102	311,154	292,670	274,508
Retained Earnings												
Retained Earnings (Opening Balance)	–	(20)	339	740	796	388	(19,564)	(14,358)	(26,906)	(35,064)	(41,604)	(44,066)
Net Profit After Abnormals and Tax	(20)	359	401	56	(408)	(19,952)	5,205	(12,548)	(8,158)	(6,540)	(2,042)	(104)
Dividends/Distributions to Equity	–	–	–	–	–	–	–	–	–	–	420	2,732
Retained Earnings (Closing Balance)	(20)	339	740	796	388	(19,564)	(14,358)	(26,906)	(35,064)	(41,604)	(44,066)	(46,901)
Total Shareholders Equity	163,771	159,095	154,461	149,482	144,040	119,053	359,461	324,582	292,037	269,550	248,604	227,606
Total Liabilities and Shareholders Equity	339,896	450,421	593,724	756,862	846,917	880,607	946,885	911,574	863,591	840,839	819,585	798,308

Source: "Cross City Tunnel Parliamentary Notice", http://www.lee.greens.org.au/campaigns/crosscity.htm (accessed 7 October 2006).

27

EXHIBIT 12: PROJECTED CONSOLIDATED PROFIT AND LOSS STATEMENT (2003–2008)

Figures in AU$ millions	30/6/03	31/12/03	31/6/04	31/12/04	30/6/05	31/12/05	30/6/06	31/12/06	30/6/07	31/12/07	30/6/08	31/12/08
Six months ending												
Period number	1	2	3	4	5	6	7	8	9	10	11	12
Revenue												
Toll Revenue												
Eastbound Revenue	-	-	-	-	-	2,956	19,106	20,603	21,327	21,924	22,239	22,83:
Westbound Revenue	-	-	-	-	-	3,007	19,246	20,656	21,700	22,638	23,301	24,27:
Sir John Crescent Revenue	-	-	-	-	-	1,048	6,656	6,788	7,009	7,207	7,314	7,60
Total Revenue	-	-	-	-	-	7,011	45,008	48,046	50,036	51,770	52,854	54,72(
Sensitivity Revenue	-	-	-	-	-	-	-	-	-	-	-	-
Other Operating Revenue	-	-	-	-	-	-	-	-	-	-	-	-
Total Operating Revenue	-	-	-	-	-	7,011	45,008	48,046	50,036	51,770	52,854	54,72(
Operating and Maintenance Expenses												
Variable Operating Expenses												
Eastbound Operating Expenses	-	-	-	-	-	94	689	815	842	846	815	79:
Westbound Operating Expenses	-	-	-	-	-	95	692	813	853	870	851	84
Sir John Young Crescent Operating Expenses	-	-	-	-	-	66	481	563	588	597	582	57.
Casual User Variable Administration Fee	-	-	-	-	-	895	3,290	1,778	930	571	556	57
Total Variable Operating Expenses	-	-	-	-	-	1,150	5,152	3,970	3,213	2,884	2,804	2,78
Fixed Operating Expenses												
CCM Costs	-	-	-	-	-	1,498	4,576	3,547	2,811	2,927	2,721	2,69:
Finance and Administration	-	-	-	-	-	762	2,059	2,123	1,576	1,847	1,642	1,65:
Revenue Collection	-	-	-	-	-	39	120	123	124	126	128	13(
Operations and Routine Maintenance	-	-	-	-	-	835	2,550	2,596	2,588	2,632	2,677	2,72(
Other	-	-	-	-	-	-	-	-	-	-	-	-
Contingency	-	-	-	-	-	82	236	242	214	230	222	22:
Operator Margin	-	-	-	-	-	258	745	762	675	725	700	70:
Agency Fee	-	-	-	-	-	-	-	29	29	29	125	6(
Security Trustee Fees	-	-	-	-	-	-	17	17	17	18	18	1:

								35	38	6		
Tranche C - Bond Facility LC	-	-	-	-	-	-	-	-	-	-	-	-
Total Operating and Maintenance Expenses						4,624	15,437	13,444	11,285	11,424	11,037	11,00
EBITDA												
Depreciation/Amortisation	1,468	-	-	-	-	2,387	29,571	34,602	38,750	40,346	41,817	43,71
EBIT	(1,468)	(1,468)	-	-	-	23,722	23,727	24,314	24,314	24,314	22,227	22,22
Repairs and Maintenance - Expense	(1,468)	(1,468)	(1,468)	-	-	(21,335)	5,844	10,288	14,436	16,032	19,590	21,49
Income Tax Expense/Benefit on Operation	-	-	-	-	-	-	-	-	-	-	-	-
Bank Base Case Adjustment	-	-	-	-	-	(1,258)	6,895	8,430	9,674	10,144	11,238	11,79
Net Operating Profit Less Adjusted Taxes (NOPLAT)	(1,468)	(1,468)	(1,468)	(1,468)	-	(20,077)	(1,052)	1,858	4,761	5,888	8,351	9,70
Loss on Write Off of Assets	-	-	-	-	-	-	-	-	-	-	-	-
Distribution to RTA	-	-	-	-	-	-	-	-	-	-	-	-
Net Interest Expense	-	-	-	-	-	-	-	-	-	-	-	-
Interest Income												
Other Interest Income	-	-	-	-	-	-	-	613	884	297	194	23
Total Interest Income	-	-	-	-	-	-	-	613	884	297	194	23
Interest Expenses												
Interest Expense - Senior Debt		877	2,101	3,828	5,624	7,380	1,817	21,825	21,831	21,267	19,572	19,57
Interest Expense - RPU		877	2,101	3,828	5,624	7,380	1,817	3,451	3,451	3,453	3,451	3,45
Interest Expense - Shareholder Loans	-	-	-	-	-	-	-	-	-	-	-	-
Interest Expense - Bonds	-	-	-	-	-	-	-	-	-	-	-	-
Line Fee Expense	-	-	-	-	-	-	-	17	17	18	18	1
Refinance Fee Expense	-	-	-	-	-	-	-	-	-	-	-	-
Total Interest Expenses		877	2,101	3,828	5,624	7,380	1,817	25,293	25,299	24,738	23,041	23,04
Total Net Interest Expenses		877	2,101	3,828	5,624	7,380	1,817	24,680	24,415	24,441	22,847	22,81
Tax Shield on Net Interest Expenses	1,448	2,704	3,969	5,351	6,684	7,504	8,074	10,275	11,495	12,012	12,453	13,00
Net Profit after Tax (NPAT)	(20)	359	401	55	(408)	(19,952)	5,205	(12,548)	(8,158)	(6,540)	(2,042)	(104

29

Abnormal items after tax	-	-	-	-	-	-	-	-	-	-	(2,042)	(104)
Net Profit after Abnormals and Tax	(20)	359	401	55	(408)	(19,952)	5,205	(12,548)	(8,158)	(6,540)	(2,042)	(104)
Retained Earnings (Opening Balance)	-	(20)	339	740	795	388	(19,564)	(14,358)	(26,906)	(35,064)	(41,604)	(44,066)
Net Profit after Abnormals and Tax	(20)	359	401	55	(408)	(19,952)	5,205	(12,548)	(8,158)	(6,540)	(2,042)	(104)
Dividends/Distributions	-	-	-	-	-	-	-	-	-	-	420	2,73:
Retained Earnings (Closing Balance)	(20)	339	740	795	388	(19,564)	(14,358)	(26,906)	(35,064)	(41,604)	(44,066)	(46,901)

Source: "Cross City Tunnel Parliamentary Notice", http://www.lee.greens.org.au/campaigns/crosscity.htm (accessed 7 October 2006).

07/324C

EXHIBIT 13: ASSUMPTIONS USED FOR THE FINANCIAL PROJECTIONS

Base Case Financial Model

Assumptions book

Assumptions	value	Description
1. Transaction Parameters		
1.1 Analysis date	18 December 2002	Current model run date
1.2 Financial close	19 December 2002	Fulfillment of all CPs in loan documentation
1.3 Concession life	33	Years post financial close
1.4 Financial year end	30 June	Financial year end for Cross City Motorway SPV
1.5 Modeled entity	Op.co and trust	Entities which are modeled
1.6 Borrowing entity	trust	Entity that raises debt

2. Economic assumptions

General CPI assumptions

	value	Description
Last ABS published CPI	138.5	CPI index in last published ABS data
Date of last published CPI	30 September 2002	Date of last published ABS date
CPI in project deed base period	121.3	CPI index in the project deed base period
Project deed base period	30 September 1998	Base period specified in project deed
Long term national CPI forecast	2.50%	Long term national CPI forecast - assumed to be an effective rate

O&M Escalation		CPI%	AWE%	Description
Construction		16%	84%	As per the O&M contract
	31 December 2006	27%	73%	As per the O&M contract
	31 December 2007	41%	59%	As per the O&M contract
	31 December 2008	47%	53%	As per the O&M contract
	31 December 2009	50%	50%	As per the O&M contract
Thereafter		50%	50%	As per the O&M contract

31

07/324C

Replacement expenditure escalation

Average weekly earnings, trend, persons, total earnings, NSW	50%	Steady state proportion
All mechanical services - Sydney	50%	Steady state proportion
Blended rate	2.45%	Calculated rate based on the above proportions and rates

Repairs and refurbishment expenditure escalation

Average weekly earnings, trend, persons, total earnings, NSW	33%	Steady state proportion
All mechanical services - Sydney	67%	Steady state proportion
Blended rate	1.92%	Calculated rate based on the above proportions and rates

Back office admin fee escalation

Average weekly earnings, trend, persons, total earnings, NSW	79%	Steady state proportion
All mechanical services - Sydney	7.50%	Steady state proportion
Blended rate	13.50%	Steady state proportion
	3.57%	Calculated rate based on the above proportions and rates

3. Interest rate assumptions

Swap rate during construction	5.32%	Monthly rate used for swapped portion of base rate used during construction
Swap rate for first band of hedging post completion	5.99%	Semi annual rate used for swapped portion of base rate used during first hedging period
First hedge band - months	42	Month for first swap post completion
Ongoing swap rate - five year swap rate	5.29%	Semi annual on going hedge rate
Seven year swap rate - RPU	5.51%	Case assumed for RPU
Floating rate - during construction	5.03%	Three year monthly rate used for non-swapped interest rate during construction
Floating rate - post construction	5.08%	Three year semi annual rate used for non-swapped interest rate post construction

Hedging

% hedged during construction	95%	Hedging profile

% hedged in first band	75%	Hedging profile
% hedged in ongoing basis	50%	Hedging profile

Cost of swaps - pre-refinance

Liquidity	0.05%	Premium on swap cost due to liquidity risk, before refinance
Basis	0.05%	Premium on swap cost due to basis risk, before refinance
Credit	0.12%	Premium on swap cost due to credit risk before refinance

Cost of swaps - post refinance

Liquidity	0.05%	Premium on swap cost due to liquidity risk, post refinance
Basis	0.04%	Premium on swap cost due to basis risk, post refinance
Credit	0.09%	Premium on swap cost due to credit risk, post refinance

30 day BBSW	4.87%	30 day deposit rate

4. Construction parameters

Stage One construction

Stage One construction start	January 2003	First month of construction
Stage One construction period	34	Stage One construction period
Stage One completion	31 October 2005	Stage One completion date
Stage One D&C contract - trust - including contingency	453,830	Allocation of D&C price for Stage One construction - construction
Stage One D&C contract - op co - including contingency	119,771	Allocation of D&C price for Stage One construction - plant and equipment

Stage Two construction

Stage Two construction start	1 November 2005	First month of Stage Two completion
Stage Two construction period	8	Months of Stage Two completion
Stage Two completion	30 November 2005	Stage Two completion date
Stage Two D&C contract - trust - including contingency	34,511	Allocation of D&C price for Stage Two construction - construction
Stage Two D&C contract - op co - including contingency	0	Allocation of D&C price for Stage Two construction - plant and equipment

Total construction period	42	From financial close to completion
Stage One construction cost - including contingency	573,601	Summary of above costs
Stage Two construction cost - including contingency	34,511	Summary of above costs
Total construction cost - including contingency	608,112	Summary of above costs
Construction contingency allowed for	17,000	Contingency allowed by equity contributors
Construction contingency drawn	4,000	Amount of construction contingency assumed drawn
		Draw down on a pro rata basis according to the D&C contract
GST on D&C contract	10%	GST is payable on D&C contract. Payments are lagged 90 days and are Recovered in subsequent periods
		Commissioning tags provided by D&C contractor. Post this time provided through back office
Acquisition cost of tags	0	
SETA Equity contribution	1,200	One-off equity contribution to SETA. Contributed 30 June 2005

5. Tolling assumptions

Theoretical toll factor in modeled first period	138.89	Theoretical first operating period toll escalation amount as per project deed formula
Toll free months from Stage One completion	1	Number of months of legal toll free use
Differential tolling	yes	
Tolls		
Passenger		
Eastbound	2.5	Base tolls as per project deed, inclusive of GST
Westbound	2.5	Base tolls as per project deed, inclusive of GST
Sir John Young Crescent	1.1	Base tolls as per project deed, inclusive of GST
Commercial		
Eastbound	5	Base tolls as per project deed, inclusive of GST
Westbound	5	Base tolls as per project deed, inclusive of GST
Sir John Young Crescent	2.2	Base tolls as per project deed, inclusive of GST

Penalty fee charged to violators

First round	10	Penalty fee charged to violators (in addition to toll) following round 1 notice
Second round	20	Penalty fee charged to violators (in addition to toll) following round 2 notice
Third round - police infringement notice	115	Penalty fee charged to violators (in addition to toll) following police infringement notice

Penalty fee CCM receives from violators

First round	5	Dollar receipt to CCM (in addition to toll) following round 1 notice
Second round	5	Dollar receipt to CCM (in addition to toll) following round 2 notice
Third round	5	Dollar receipt to CCM (in addition to toll) following police infringement notice

6. Operating and maintenance cost

Variable opex charge

31 December 2005	0.12	Cost per tag variable charge
30 June 2006	0.12	
31 December 2006	0.12	
30 June 2007	0.12	
31 Dec 2007	0.11	
30 June 2008	0.11	
31 December 2008	0.1	
30 June 2009	0.1	
31 December 2009	0.1	
30 June 2010	0.1	
31 December 2010	0.1	
30 June 2011	0.1	

Upfront insurance cost	25,500	Upfront insurance premia

7. Working capital days

Accounts receivable	60	Days assumed for collection of 1st round penalty

07/324C

First round penalty	90	Days assumed for collection of 2nd round penalty
Second round penalty	120	Days assumed for collection of 3rd round penalty
Third round penalty		
Accounts payable		
Operating and maintenance expenses	30	Days assumed for payment of accounts payables

8. Key financial ratios

Minimum CLCR for a 33 year period	2.1	Concession life cover ratio
Period One minimum senior ICR	1.4	Debt sized off the minimum ICR in Period One
Period Two minimum senior ICR	1.5	Debt sized off the minimum ICR in Period Two
Period Three minimum senior ICR	1.6	Debt sized off the minimum ICR in Period Three
Minimum total ICR sizing test for RPU	1.45	Min total ICR for which RPUs are sized off
Date of minimum target for RPU sizing	31-Dec-07	Year of min total ICR for RPU sizing (3rd ratio date)
First ratio date	31-Dec-05	The first June or December 12 months post Stage One completion

9. Senior bank debt assumptions

Tranche A - equity bridge		
Facility size	253238	Peak facility size
Type of facility		Senior bank debt supported by guarantees or LCs provided by equity, refinanced by equity
		Injection on completion, drawdown prior to tranche B - project facility
Term (months)	42	Construction period
Facility available	1 January 2003	
Bullet	100%	Amount of principal outstanding at completion
Credit margin		
Construction	0.45%	Margin charged prior to completion
Operations	n.a.	Margin charged post completion (not applicable for this tranche)
Funding of interest during construction		Drawdown on the tranche A facility until tranche A facility limit is reached and then
		Drawdown on tranche B - project facility
Upfront fee	3.40%	Arranging/underwriting fee payable on financial close
Commitment fee (% of margin p.a.)	40%	Fee payable on undrawn facility balance prior to completion

Cost of LCs (%)	Fee payable to provider of LC by equity, if applicable	
Facility drawdowns	Commence when the construction account is reduced to zero	
Tranche B - project facility		
Facility use	Peak facility size	580000
Type of facility	Senior bank project deed facility	bullet
Term (years)	Term post financial close	7
Interest only period (years)	Number of interest only years post finance close	7
Margin during construction		
If rated BBB	Margin over bank bills/swaps charged prior to completion if project rated BBB	1.50%
If rated BBB-	Margin over bank bills/swaps charged prior to completion if project rated BBB-	1.50%
If unrated	Margin over bank bills/swaps charged prior to completion if project unrated	1.50%
Margin during operations		
If rated BBB	Margin over bank bills/swaps charged post completion if project rated BBB	1%
If rated BBB-	Margin over bank bills/swaps charged post completion if project rated BBB-	1.25%
	Margin grid over bank bills/swaps charged post completion if project unrated	
Assumed margins		
30 June 2006	Margin and period for which margin is applicable for	1.60%
30 June 2007	Margin and period for which margin is applicable for	1.60%
30 June 2008	Margin and period for which margin is applicable for	1%
Until first refinance	Margin and period for which margin is applicable for	1%
Margin post 1st refinancing	Margin applied to senior debt post first refinancing	1%
Commitment fees	Commitment fee payable on undrawn balances (% of margin)	40%
Upfront fee	Arranging/underwriting fee payable on financial close	2%
Assumed rating	Assumed BBB at year 3, post Stage One completion	BBB

Number of refinancings	4	The number of times the facility is rolled don the above terms
Upfront fee payable on refinance	1%	Upfront fee payable for refinance
Refinance debt term	5	
Amortisation profile	credit fancier	Basis for principal amortised in each period
Amortisation term	11	Term over which the facility is amortised after the last refinancing
Tranche C - bond facility - standby facility		
Tranche C - bond facility amount - construction	25000	Tranche c - bond facility amount during construction
Tranche C - bond facility amount - first 13 months of operations	5000	Tranche c - bond facility amount for 13 months post Stage Two completion
LC fee	1.50%	LC fee payable to tranche c - bond facility
10. RPU		
Amount	72613	Facility size
Underwriting fee	3%	Arranging/underwriting fee payable by equity underwriters out of equity underwriting fees at financial close
Base rate for coupon	5.50%	Seven year swap rate
Facility term	perpetual	Specified term of RPU
Bullet	yes	Repayment assumption for RPU
Margin-construction	n.a.	Margin during construction
Margin- operations	4%	Margin during operation
Refinance fee	1%	Refinance fee
Tax rate	30%	Corporate tax rate for the CCM

Source: "Cross City Tunnel Parliamentary Notice", http://www.lee.greens.org.au/campaigns/crosscity.htm (accessed 7 October 2006).

HARVARD | BUSINESS | SCHOOL

9-706-041
REV: OCTOBER 16, 2006

DEBORA SPAR

JEAN OI

China: Building "Capitalism with Socialist Characteristics"

We must not act like women with bound feet! If we want socialism to triumph over capitalism, we should not hesitate to draw on the achievements of all cultures. We need to learn from other countries, including the developed capitalist countries.

—Deng Xiaoping, 1992[1]

In November 2005, the Central Committee of the Communist Party of China issued its 11th five-year plan. As was typical for such pronouncements, the plan touched on many aspects of China's economy, including its fiscal situation, its current account surplus, and its desire to equalize rural and urban incomes. But the central theme was growth. China, the plan announced, would continue to grow at 8% a year between 2006 and 2011. It would also try to tilt its expansion away from exports and investment, and increase government spending to help the poor.[2]

Already, China was the fastest-growing country in the world, a position it had held, with only a few breaks, for nearly 30 years. Although a handful of other countries (Japan, Singapore, Botswana) had also sustained average growth rates of over 9% per annum for more than a decade, China's rapid-fire growth was longer-lived than its counterparts and showed no signs of slowing.[3] In China, moreover, growth was occurring across a population of nearly 1.3 billion, liberating millions of people from poverty and unlocking massive segments of demand. In 2004, China accounted for 12% of the world's total energy consumption and 15% of total fresh water consumption. It consumed 50% of the world's production of cement.[4]

Purely on economic grounds, therefore, China had become a phenomenon. It was the third-largest economy in the world and was frequently described as likely, within a decade, to surpass both the European Union and the United States in total GDP. Unlike these other countries, however, China was distinctly and explicitly a communist state. Under the leadership of President Hu Jintao, the Chinese Communist Party retained full control of the country's affairs and remained firmly committed to many of socialism's key tenets. All of the country's major banks, for example, remained tightly linked to the state, as did key sectors such as oil, petrochemicals, and steel. State agencies provided most of the country's still-limited financial services, and state-owned enterprises produced more than one-third of total output. Indeed, the state—and the Party—were central players in nearly all aspects of China's economy, guiding a development trajectory often labeled as "capitalism with socialist characteristics."

Professors Debora Spar and Jean Oi and Research Associate Chris Bebenek prepared this case. HBS cases are developed solely as the basis for class discussion. Cases are not intended to serve as endorsements, sources of primary data, or illustrations of effective or ineffective management.

It wasn't an obvious path to growth. But for nearly 30 years China had indeed been growing, thrusting its citizens into prosperity and its goods across the world. Between 1978 and 2005, China's per capita GDP had grown from $153 to $1284, while its current account surplus had increased over twelve-fold between 1982 and 2004, from $5.7 billion to $70 billion. During this time, China had also become an industrial powerhouse, moving beyond initial successes in low-wage sectors like clothing and footwear to the increasingly sophisticated production of computers, pharmaceuticals, and automobiles.

Just how long this trajectory could continue, however, remained unclear. According to the 11th five-year plan, China needed to sustain an annual growth rate of 8% for the foreseeable future. Only with such levels of growth, the leadership argued, could China continue to develop its industrial prowess, raise its citizens' standard of living, and redress the inequalities that were cropping up across the country. Yet no country had ever before maintained the kind of growth that China was predicting. Moreover, China had to some extent already undergone the easier parts of development. In the 1980s, it had transformed its vast and inefficient agricultural sector, freeing its peasants from the confines of central planning and winning them to the cause of reform. In the 1990s, it had likewise started to restructure its stagnant industrial sector, wooing foreign investors for the first time and channeling investment funds to the state-owned enterprises. These policies had catalyzed the country's phenomenal growth, but they could no longer be relied upon to propel the economy much further. Instead, China had to take what many regarded as the final step toward the market, liberalizing the banking sector and launching the beginnings of a real capital market.

This step, however, would not be easy. As of 2004, China's state-owned enterprises were still only partially reorganized, and its banks were dealing with the burden of over $205 billion (1.7 trillion RMB) in non-performing loans, monies that had little chance of ever being repaid. The country had a fixed exchange rate, and strict controls on both the current and capital accounts. Most importantly, it had a communist government that remained wary of loosening the reins of its control, even as protests by workers and peasants had become increasingly common. And thus the quandary remained: could China maintain its feverish growth rate without embracing full-fledged liberalization? And if it did choose to leap completely to the market, how could it ensure that the country's prized stability was not abandoned in the process?

Background: The Rise and Decline of the Middle Kingdom

Long before China emerged as an economic powerhouse, it had been a power in its own right and a force, albeit a quiet one, in the international arena. Chinese civilization first arose in the valley of the Yellow River around 2200 B.C. Because the soil of the valley was rich but the river treacherous, the people of the region developed sophisticated techniques of "permanent agriculture" that allowed them to control the volatile waters and cultivate high-yielding strains of rice.[5] On these agricultural foundations China's population boomed, and a unique and durable social structure evolved. The core of society was the extended family, several generations of sons who together farmed the family plot. Daughters traditionally moved into their husband's families and were subservient to their mothers-in-law. Above the family level, peasant farmers grouped themselves into villages, which existed as nearly self-sufficient units.

By 1120 B.C. the people of the Yellow River valley had gathered under the loose authority of the Zhou dynasty, a family of warrior priests who collected taxes and raised armies but otherwise stayed aloof from the life of the villages. Instead, the emperors and their bureaucrats devoted themselves to artistic and scholarly pursuits, nurturing a civilization that produced classic works of art and literature, as well as the great philosophers Confucius and Lao Zi.

When the power of the Zhou royal family at last declined in 403 B.C., wars broke out among some 170 feudal lords, throwing China into an era of political anarchy now labeled the Warring States Period. Chaos prevailed for nearly 100 years, until a single family managed at last to defeat the rival lords and bring China again under a common rule. The new emperor, Qin Shi Huang, then set out to establish a universal and everlasting empire. During his 11-year tyrannical reign, Qin killed thousands of Confucian scholars, divided the estates of other lords into smaller private plots, and undertook great public projects such as the reconstruction of the Great Wall of China. To ensure that his empire remained intact, Qin also established a formal system of government that linked the villages to central provinces and thence directly to the emperor. Between the emperor and the people he created an elaborate imperial bureaucracy that was to dominate China for the next two millennia.

Throughout this period, the core of China remained remarkably stable. It was largely an agricultural society, bound and nearly defined by Confucianism, a body of political and moral philosophy that taught the supreme importance of social stability. Starting at the level of the individual, it described a complex hierarchy of obedience, linking the child to its parent, the family to its ancestors, and the subject to his or her ruler. In all these relations, the patriarchal father was the center of authority, and filial piety was the most admired virtue. Because patterns of authority were repeated throughout the hierarchy, the emperor and his officials simply assumed the role of the father writ large. On a daily basis, meanwhile, order was maintained by the imperial bureaucrats, civil servants who were simultaneously a manifestation of the Confucian order and the physical means by which this order was preserved.

Not surprisingly, China's foreign policy also bore the imprint of this order. From the earliest days, the Chinese had considered their land the "Middle Kingdom," a seat of civilization surrounded on all sides by the "four barbarians." All non-Chinese people were deemed inferior, and the Chinese emperors—with a handful of exceptions—had no interest in exploring the world beyond their borders.[6] In their eyes, China was the center of the world and the Chinese emperor the link between heaven and earth. There simply was no reason to look elsewhere.

Eventually, of course, outsiders did come to China. The Mongols invaded in 1280, and the Manchus in 1644. Both of these foreign dynasties, though, ruled China much as the Chinese did, with a centralized hierarchy, an imperial bureaucracy, and a decided penchant for focusing their energies inward. For all practical purposes, therefore, China remained a closed civilization until the middle of the 19th century, when the barbarians came to stay.

Invasion and Revolution

Beginning in 1840, China's seclusion was dramatically shattered by a series of military defeats known collectively as the "Opium Wars." The ostensible source of these conflicts was opium, which British merchants had been smuggling to China in an effort to smooth their chronic trade deficits. When Chinese authorities seized 20,000 chests of British opium in Guangzhou, the British attacked to defend their rights of trade. The Chinese fought back and tried negotiating, but in 1842 the emperor reluctantly capitulated. China ceded Hong Kong to the British and agreed to open five additional trading ports. This was the first of what became known as the "Unequal Treaties."

Over the next several decades, Western powers entered China under the benign label of an American "Open Door" policy. Britain, France, Russia, Germany, and Japan together carved China into spheres of foreign influence and forcibly opened its coastal cities to foreign trade. In many cities, the foreign authorities went so far as to claim rights of extraterritoriality that made them effectively immune to Chinese law.

The success of the foreign powers dealt a tremendous blow to China's pride and complacency. In 1898, the young Guang Xu emperor launched a last-ditch effort at reform, hoping, like Japan's Meiji emperors, to change his country without destroying it. But he succeeded only in offending his enemies and was swiftly deposed by the Empress Dowager Ci Xi, who declared herself regent and rescinded all reforms. In the aftermath, China plunged again into chaos as reformers and reactionaries battled for control. When the Empress Dowager died in 1908, the power of the central government disintegrated, along with China's last vestiges of empire.

For the next 40 years, China was ostensibly ruled by the Kuomintang (KMT), a revolutionary party launched by Sun Yatsen and then led (following Sun's death) by General Chiang Kaishek. Throughout this period, the KMT's hold on power was exceedingly weak. Warlords controlled most of the outlying provinces, and the central government wielded little military might or political authority. In the countryside, meanwhile, a charismatic leader named Mao Zedong was building support for the Chinese Communist Party, developing tactics of guerrilla warfare, and encouraging peasants to turn the social order upside down—demanding land reform and fighting for socialism.

In 1931, Japanese forces invaded Manchuria, destroying any semblance of a unified Chinese state. The KMT and the communists continued their internal struggles, only reluctantly joining forces in 1937, when the Japanese launched a full-scale invasion. During the course of the subsequent fighting, KMT forces were pushed back into the western interior, where they established a capital in the once-sleepy town of Chongqing. By this point, however, the party had been significantly weakened by its relative lack of anti-Japanese fervor, and by the corruption that had become rampant among its officials. The communists, by contrast, were able to seize both the moral high ground and the military advantage. Their reliance on guerrilla warfare put Mao's troops in direct contact with the peasantry, who were impressed by the communists' discipline and quickly came to regard them as the country's defenders. When the Japanese surrendered in 1945, Mao's Chinese Communist Party (CCP), backed by militia forces and several million active supporters, expanded its control into the areas previously under Japanese occupation. By 1949, the communists had captured so much KMT equipment and recruited so many KMT soldiers that Chiang Kaishek had no option but to flee to the island of Formosa (Taiwan), taking with him the entire gold reserves of China and promising one day to liberate the mainland from the "communist bandits."

On October 1, 1949, Mao Zedong proclaimed the establishment of the People's Republic of China (PRC) and returned the country's capital to Beijing. The new government enjoyed wide support among the Chinese people, who were determined to recover their country after nearly a century of foreign invasion and internal chaos. China, it seemed, was once again poised to take its rightful place among nations.

The East is Red: China under Communism, 1949–1978

The proclamation of the PRC instantly transformed Mao and his followers from revolutionaries to administrators. With little experience in peacetime government or economic management, they faced two overwhelming tasks: to organize and administer the world's largest society and to rebuild an economy devastated by decades of war. Remarkably, both tasks were accomplished in the first five years of communist rule.

Membership in the Communist Party grew rapidly during this time, and, in a structure reminiscent of the old imperial bureaucracy, a hierarchy of party organs was extended from the top echelons of the CCP down to more than one million branch committees established in every village, factory, school, and government agency. The new government nationalized the country's banking system and brought all currency and credit under centralized control. It regulated prices by establishing trade associations and boosted government revenues by collecting agricultural taxes (the bulk of its revenues) in kind. By the mid-1950s, the communists had rebuilt and expanded the country's railroad and highway systems, boosted agricultural and industrial production to their prewar levels, and brought the bulk of China's industry and commerce under the direct control of the state.[7]

Meanwhile, in fulfillment of their revolutionary promise, China's communist leaders completed land reform within two years of coming to power. Party cadres visited local villages and incited the peasants in public "struggle meetings" to eliminate their landlords and redistribute their land and other possessions to peasant households. Shortly thereafter, the CCP encouraged rural households to form mutual aid teams, and then the agricultural producers' cooperatives which the government saw as the best means for increasing agricultural productivity.

Still not satisfied, Mao tried in 1958 to push China's economy to new heights. Under his highly touted "Great Leap Forward," agricultural collectives were reorganized into enormous communes where men and women were assigned in military fashion to specific tasks. Peasants were told to stop relying on the family, and instead adopted a system of communal kitchens, mess halls, and nurseries. Wages were calculated along the communist principle of "to each according to his needs," and sideline production was banned as incipient capitalism. All Chinese citizens were urged to boost the country's steel production by establishing "backyard steel furnaces" to help overtake the West. But while Mao believed that the politically directed outpouring of effort by China's vast population would result in economic development and miraculous production increases, the Great Leap Forward quickly revealed itself as a giant step backwards. Over-ambitious targets were set, falsified production figures were duly reported, and Chinese officials lived in an unreal world of miraculous production increases. Steel output did rise dramatically, but most of the steel was virtually useless. Even worse, it quickly became apparent that the peasants had made their steel by melting whatever metal they could find. By 1960, agricultural production in the countryside had slowed dangerously, and GNP declined by about one-third.[8] The people were exhausted, and large areas of China were gripped by a devastating famine. By 1960, the situation had become so grave that not even Mao could ignore it. Quietly and without fanfare, Mao stepped to the sidelines, and pragmatists within the CCP, including Deng Xiaoping, began to do what was necessary to restore incentives and production.

For the next several years, China experienced a period of relative stability. Agricultural and industrial production returned to normal levels, and labor productivity began to rise.[9] Then, in 1966, Mao reasserted his power and again launched a scheme that nearly brought China to its knees. Worried lest Deng and other bureaucrats pull China too far from the spirit of its socialist revolution, Mao proclaimed a Cultural Revolution to "put China back on track." Under orders to "Destroy the Four Olds" (old thoughts, culture, customs, and habits), universities and schools closed their doors, and students, who became Mao's "Red Guards," were sent throughout the country to make revolution, beating and torturing anyone whose rank or political thinking offended. Intellectuals were cursed as the "stinking ninth class," and any sign of "capitalism," such as wearing a necktie, was enough to condemn someone as a foe of the Communist Party. Deng himself was purged as a "capitalist roader" and sent to work in a tractor factory.

By 1969 the country had descended into anarchy, and factions of the Red Guards had begun to fight among themselves. Finally, Mao called upon the army to restore order and sent his young guards to the countryside, where many became an embittered, uneducated, "lost" generation. In 1973, Mao quietly recalled Deng Xiaoping to Beijing.

The Reforms of Deng Xiaoping

After Mao's death in 1976, power passed quickly to the reform faction of the CCP, led by Deng Xiaoping. Unlike Mao, Deng was a pragmatic man, known less for his ideological commitment than his slogan: "Who cares if a cat is black or white, as long as it catches the mice." Once he consolidated his power, he began to put his pragmatic policies to work, determined to bring China back from the devastation that the Cultural Revolution had wrought.

Phase One: Reform in the Countryside

When Deng came into office, China's vast peasantry was still organized in communes, work brigades, and production teams. Procurement prices were too low to cover even production costs, and ceilings were set on the amount of grain that producers could keep for consumption. Deng changed all that. He allowed farmers to produce on their own and sanctioned the sale of surplus production and other cash crops in newly freed markets. State procurement prices were raised, and prices for many agricultural goods were left to the dictates of the market. Beginning with the poor mountainous areas of Anhui and then spreading across the country, Deng and his officials broke up the communes established by Mao and replaced them with a complicated system of leases that eventually brought effective land tenure back to the household level (even though ownership of land remained collective). The Household Responsibility System allowed peasants to lease land for a fixed period from the collective, provided they delivered to the collective a minimum quota of produce, usually basic grain; they could then sell any surplus they produced, either to the state at government-set procurement prices or on the newly free market. They were also free to retain any profits they might earn. Within a decade, grain production had grown by roughly 30%, and production of cotton, sugarcane, tobacco, and fruit had doubled.[10]

Deng also attacked China's chronic food shortages by encouraging families to adopt a one-child policy. Always controversial, the policy was implemented with varying degrees of enthusiasm across China's provinces. Generally, all women were required to request permission for more than one child, and approval was given only if a first child had a birth defect or the mother had remarried.[11] Some provinces reportedly went even further, and reports of infanticide, forced sterilization, and third trimester abortions were widespread. As a result, China's rate of population growth slowly began to subside.

Along with these dramatic changes in the countryside, the early Deng reforms also began to open China up to the outside world. In 1979, China created four "Special Economic Zones" (SEZs) along its coast—three in Guangdong province next to Hong Kong and one in Fujian province across the straits from Taiwan. The SEZs explicitly welcomed investment and sought to attract potential investors with tax incentives, foreign exchange provisions, and a decided lack of regulation. Initially, investment in the SEZs took off somewhat more slowly than the leadership had expected: between 1982 and 1988, total foreign direct investment in the PRC amounted to only $8.5 billion, most of which came from Hong Kong–based clothing and textile manufacturers hoping to take advantage of cheap labor. And so the government, in the mid- to late-1980s, began to open its doors more aggressively. It made provisions giving foreign investors more direct control of factories, offered leases on land with 50- to 70-year terms, and introduced a system of dual exchange rates, permitting foreign enterprises (as opposed to their domestic counterparts) to exchange foreign exchange receipts at a market-based rate. China opened four coastal cities, including Shanghai and Guangzhou, to foreign trade in 1985; and in 1988 it transformed the island province of Hainan into an SEZ and then opened the country's entire 3,000-mile coastline to trade. By 1992, these stratagems had clearly paid off. FDI hit $11.2

billion, up from $4.4 billion the previous year, and foreign firms—from Nike, to Squibb, GE, and Honda—had established operations in the country.

Phase Two: Rural Industrialization and Enterprise Reform

As the reforms fueled production increases that surprised even the reformers, the scale of change grew bolder, and by the mid-1980s the party leadership had begun the more complicated and politically delicate task of transforming the country's cumbersome system of central planning and state-owned enterprise. Prior to 1978, enterprises were almost all owned by the state in one form or another. At the top of each sector were the State-owned Enterprises (SOEs), answerable to the national government. Below these were other enterprises reporting to provincial, municipal, or county authorities. Private enterprises, meaning family-run shops, were not allowed until after 1978, and even then they were limited to seven employees.[12]

China's SOEs were typical of large industrial firms in a centrally planned economy. Inefficient, overstaffed, and with outdated technology, they functioned not only as industrial units but also as social agencies, providing housing, daycare, education, and health care for the workers and their families. The largest enterprises included hundreds of thousands of employees, only a small proportion of whom were directly engaged in production. Despite their size, however, the enterprises enjoyed very little autonomy, since the state determined prices, input, and output and retained any profits that might accrue. The enterprises merely produced their allotted quota of output and passed it along to prearranged buyers at government-determined prices. Profit and loss were not meaningful, accounting was primitive, and profit maximization was of no consequence.

The upside of this system was that Chinese workers could expect both lifetime employment and an extensive, firm-based welfare system—the so-called "iron rice bowl." All welfare entitlements in this system were accounted for as costs of production and were deducted from revenues before the calculation of the profits that were to be remitted to the state. There was no national social security system because none was needed.

In 1983, however, the government decided to introduce a variant of the responsibility system that had worked so successfully in the rural areas. Under the Contract Responsibility System, the enterprise and its controlling ministry negotiated contracts that specified the enterprise's performance target, production quota, and financial obligation to the state—usually a combination of taxes and dividends. Aside from meeting these targets, the enterprises were free to run their businesses as they saw fit, including producing over-quota goods for sale at market prices. For the first time, managers could set wages, make investment decisions, and retain profits. Theoretically, after 1988 the enterprises were also subject to bankruptcy. In practice, though, they remained closely linked to the central authorities and somewhat beyond the usual confines of a market economy. Despite the reforms, they were still performing a wide variety of social functions and often sold at regulated rather than market prices. They were also able to get financing on the basis of local political ties—China's infamous *guanxi*—rather than on any real notion of creditworthiness. Nevertheless, they were clearly more market oriented than at any time in China's past.

An even greater push toward the market came with the establishment of township and village enterprises (TVEs), small manufacturing operations led frequently by local communist officials. While these TVEs were explicitly collective in terms of their ownership structure, they were also largely capitalistic; villages raised money in any way they could (from retained earnings, agricultural profits, and loans from local banks), and then used these funds to do everything from making local crafts to manufacturing industrial equipment.[13] They paid taxes to the state rather than producing any contracted output, and purchased their supplies directly from the market. Local authorities facilitated loans, but, lacking the deep pockets of the central government, tended to be less tolerant of losses. Over time, the TVEs grew fiercely competitive with each other, and, eventually, with the SOEs. They also became extremely successful, reinvesting their profits to fund growth. Throughout the 1980s, their output grew at an average rate of about 30% a year, and exports increased at a rate of 65%.[14]

Finally, the second phase of China's reform also attempted to move the country closer to a market-based system of pricing. Prior to this move, prices in China had gone unchanged for many years and bore only a vague resemblance to international prices or supply and demand. Although some prices were set by the free market, the majority were either state set or "guided," meaning that they floated within a predetermined range. After 1984, the state took a version of the dual-price system that had worked so well in agriculture and applied it to an ever-increasing number of industrial products. Enterprises were still required to sell their quota of production to the state at state-fixed prices, but they could now also sell any excess production into the open market. This dual track forced the SOEs to the market, subjecting their marginal investment decisions to the discipline of market forces. But dual prices also left the entire system vulnerable to corruption, since the easiest route to profits lay in using fixed-price inputs to manufacture goods sold at market prices.

Rebellion and Retrenchment

By 1988, China's economy was in full swing. Rushing to take advantage of the market inducements inherent in the reforms, China's nascent capitalists had pushed both agricultural and industrial production to new heights. Agriculture was growing steadily at 3.2% per year, while industrial production increased an amazing 20.7% annually.

As the economy surged, however, so too did inflation. During the first half of 1988, the consumer price index rose 19.2%, while prices in some cities increased by as much as 30%. Freed from the constraints of central planning, the SOEs were racing to bring their excess production to the open market, while TVEs were increasing local revenues, swelling the extra-budgetary funds that belonged exclusively to local governments. To fund their expansion, both SOEs and TVEs were borrowing heavily from local financial institutions, many of which were branches of the four state-owned banks and manned by local officials eager to extend credit to enterprises in their region. Meanwhile, to forestall any potential unemployment problems, the central budget continued to provide support for the many loss-making SOEs. As a result, SOEs could use state funds to support their expansion with virtually no downside risk. And in the process, inflationary pressures accumulated and financial authority slipped further from the center toward the provinces.

By 1989, with the economy on the verge of an inflationary spiral, the central authorities leapt suddenly into action, launching a wide-scale retrenchment that essentially froze credit issued by the state banks. Government agencies tightened administrative controls on imports and credit, cut state investment expenditures, raised interest rates, and devalued the currency by 21%. Almost immediately the economy cooled down, with inflation falling to 2% by 1990.[15]

Along the way, however, the "rectification" program unleashed a violent train of political events. When the leadership cracked down on the economy, it alienated some of its most vital constituencies: farmers received IOUs instead of cash for their products; fledgling enterprises lost their access to credit; and urban workers experienced a fall in their standard of living. This dissatisfaction erupted during the spring of 1989 in Beijing's historic Tiananmen Square. Upon the death of reform-minded General Secretary Hu Yaobang, students mobilized to express their support for the pro-reform wing of the party leadership. For nearly a month, hundreds of thousands of students demonstrated peacefully in the square while China's leaders argued privately about the most appropriate response.

In the end, the old guard triumphed. In the early hours of June 4, a convoy of 50 tanks stormed through the crowded streets leading to Tiananmen Square, and 10,000 soldiers advanced from the Forbidden City, randomly shooting protesters on sight. By the end of the day, hundreds and perhaps more than a thousand people had been killed (the exact number remains unknown). Unequivocally, the Chinese Communist Party had signaled that it had no intention of letting loose the reins of control.

Reform in the 1990s

The 1990s was a watershed decade that consolidated China's reform efforts and firmly set the course for a capitalist market economy, if still with socialist characteristics. It began on shaky ground in the wake of Tiananmen, when China briefly retreated into a period of isolation, and the international community condemned the CCP for having fired on its citizens. While reforms never stopped, there was a moment when the momentum could have shifted, and some leaders questioned the wisdom of moving forward. But reform was securely back on track after Deng Xiaoping's southern tour in 1992, when he gave his blessing to the newly established stock exchanges in Shanghai and Shenzhen.

Throughout the decade, the regime played institutional catch-up—updating or abolishing regulatory agencies and policies inherited from the Maoist era and creating new institutions for an increasingly market-oriented economy. The central government shored up its coffers and regained control of the ballooning funds that local authorities had managed to retain in the 1980s. They used monetary tools to squeeze the semi-official and informal credit associations that had emerged during the earlier stages of reform and began to tackle the problem of privatization, starting with the TVEs and then moving—slowly and more cautiously—to the SOEs. In 2001, Jiang Zemin, Deng's successor, even began to redress the ideological gap that still confronted his country: to the consternation of his more conservative colleagues, he argued that China's new capitalists be allowed to join the CCP.

One major piece of the government's strategy was to establish a new system for national taxation, one that would allow the center both to increase its revenues and enhance its control over provincial authorities. In 1994, it announced a "divided tax system" (*fenshui zhi*), which redesignated all categories of taxes as central, local, or shared (with revenues to be divided between the center and the localities). This classification effectively eliminated the category of extra-budgetary revenues and quickly increased the center's taxes. To ensure that taxes were properly collected, a national tax collection was set up alongside the existing tax bureau, which was left to collect local taxes. Around the same time, the government also began to adjust its dual exchange rates, a clunky arrangement that, since 1986, had allowed foreign firms to exchange their foreign exchange receipts at a "market" rate, while still requiring domestic enterprises to convert their foreign profits at the (nearly always higher) rate set by the central bank. In 1994, with the gap between the "official" and "market" rates growing ever wider, the government merged the two into a single exchange rate, with the market rate prevailing. In effect, the currency was devalued from 5.75 yuan to the dollar (the old "official" rate) to 8.7 (the "market" rate). Several months later, the exchange rate was officially stabilized at 8.28.

During this period, China accelerated the process of privatization as well. It auctioned off many TVEs—often to former factory managers or with local governments remaining as shareholders—and then, under the policy of "grasp the large, let go of the small," turned toward smaller- and medium-sized SOEs. In most cases, proceeds from these sales went to the localities that had previously controlled the enterprise.

In sharp contrast to Russia and parts of Eastern Europe, China's restructuring in the 1990s was gradual, in terms of both unemployment and change in form of ownership. Instead of following a big-bang approach, selling off assets and creating immediate stakeholders through insider privatization, China pursued more limited shareholding systems. Only a small percentage of firms were transformed to fully private entities in the 1990s, and the state remained a major shareholder in the largest and most important firms. In some cases, strong firms were nudged into corporate groups with more struggling entities. And in others, ancillary portions of old SOEs were spun off into self-sufficient entities, creating new "private" firms to compete in China's ever-growing market.

The Next Wave

In 2003, political leadership had passed seamlessly from Jiang Zemin to Hu Jintao, leaving the Communist Party with virtually uncontested control over China's affairs. Internationally, China was playing an increasingly important role. It joined the WTO in 2001, signaling its entry into the league of major trading players, and stood, by 2004, behind the United States and Germany as the world's third-largest exporter.[16] It was also emerging as an important diplomatic force in the Pacific and beyond and had brokered a deal during six-party negotiations in September 2005 that saw North Korea agree to end its nuclear efforts.[17]

In both economic and political terms, however, China was still very much a developing country. The banking sector remained inextricably tied to the state; the SOEs continued to produce a significant share of total industrial output; and capital markets were exceedingly thin. The state-owned banking system remained largely unreformed and continued to strain under a torrent of bad debt. In 2004, the four major state-owned banks together held over 1.7 trillion RMB in non-performing loans, an amount equal to roughly 13% of that year's GDP.[18] Unless these loans were written off or redressed in some fashion, China would still be without a functioning and vital banking sector, unable to proceed with the next phase of reform: financial liberalization.

Some of the obstacles to this reform, however, revealed deeper and more profound political gaps. Many of the non-performing loans, for example, had come from the banks' extending excess credit to the SOEs, which together still employed over 75 million Chinese citizens. If the non-performing loans were simply called in, many SOEs would cease to exist, and millions of Chinese would be suddenly unemployed. Such an outcome was still simply unacceptable to China's political leaders, committed as they were to the maintenance of social and economic stability.

Similarly, China was in 2005 facing increased pressure from the United States over its exchange rate, pegged since 1994 at 8.28 yuan to the dollar.[19] According to U.S. officials, the yuan was distinctly undervalued, contributing to China's persistent current account surpluses and its steady buildup of foreign exchange reserves. Yet Chinese officials had little interest in revaluation, since a higher yuan would mean tougher economic times for China's exporters and more downward pressure on employment.

What made this calculation particularly acute was the growing realization that growth in China was no longer evenly distributed. Indeed, as of 2005, China's Gini coefficient had hit .4, an unprecedented level for the country, and one that stood in sharp contrast to the leadership's still-socialist ideology. For nearly 30 years, China's explosive growth had been distributed relatively widely: although the rich had gotten richer, so, too, had the poor. But in 2005, for the first time, the World Bank reported that some of China's very poorest people had begun to see their incomes decline in absolute, as well as relative, terms.[20] For the leadership, this was troubling news. Since the time of Mao, after all, China's ideology had remained deeply committed to equity, and its strategy had depended on winning the support of the rural peasantry—the very people who were now arguably losing out because of the reforms. If the peasantry turned away from the cause of reform, the legitimacy of China's leaders would suffer. And if this disgruntlement gave way to unrest, it could potentially threaten China's most prized commodity: stability.

As the winter of 2005 approached, therefore, China's leaders found themselves grappling with a delicate set of issues. In order to generate continued growth rates of 8% per annum, they believed they had to proceed with the next phase of reform, liberalizing their financial sector and allowing a real capital market to emerge. At the same time, though, they had to ensure that liberalization of the financial sector did not let loose a chain of other, undesired, effects. They didn't want large-scale destruction of the SOEs, for example, or any large increase in China's unemployment rate. They didn't want inequalities to widen any further than they already had; and they, along with a growing chorus of external critics, were becoming increasingly concerned about the toll that growth was imposing on the natural environment.[21] According to the World Health Organization, for example, 80% of China's rivers were so polluted that they no longer supported fish, and women in certain industrial areas exhibited the highest rates of lung cancer ever recorded. As a result of industrialization, deforestation had averaged 0.7% a year in the 1980s; and, since 1949, the country had lost one-fifth of its agricultural land.[22] The CCP was also struggling to clean up corruption, which by all accounts was rampant, not least in the party's own ranks. In 2005 it unveiled a moral education campaign that promised to "preserve the advanced nature" of CCP members and planned to put some 44 million of its cadres through the program that year.[23]

Finally, although China in 2005 was a considerably more open society than it had been 20 or even 10 years earlier, it still was by no means a democracy.[24] With an active force of 2.3 million, the People's Liberation Army (PLA) was the biggest military force in the world, and one that, since the 1990s, had been avidly building its capacity for winning short-term, high-intensity wars along China's land and sea borders. Inside China, it also played an inordinately large role, running not only military-industrial enterprises but civilian ones as well, including mines and pharmaceutical factories.[25] More critically, selected groups with Chinese society, such as the Falungong, were still frequently, and sometimes violently, repressed. There were no national elections in the country, and Western-style political and civil liberties were largely absent. China's leaders were intent on maintaining their unique brand of political control and their hugely successful strategy of gradual economic reform. But would this combination work as well in the future as it had in the past? Or did a more open economy demand a more open political system as well?

Reforming the Banks

Ever since the launch of China's reforms, its banks had been something of an outlier. Without any of the liberalizing measures enacted elsewhere in the system, they retained nearly all the vestiges of central planning, with one bank—the People's Bank of China (PBOC)—performing the full array of monetary and financial functions. There were no independent investment banks in China, no credit rating agencies, and only a weak network of freestanding credit unions. Instead, the PBOC presided over a massive network of regional branches and local banking offices. The four major state-owned banks within this system—the Bank of China, China Construction Bank, Industrial and Commercial Bank of China, and Agricultural Bank of China—operated independently, but each focused on a particular segment of lending and was ultimately accountable to the PBOC. Each township had its own rural savings and credit cooperative, which extended credit to local farmers and TVEs.

During the early years of China's reforms, this system worked relatively well. The banks provided newly emerging enterprises with the capital they needed, kept cash flowing to the troubled SOEs, and turned a blind eye when loans went bad. Meanwhile, the PBOC worked with the Ministry of

Finance to manage the country's macroeconomy with considerable caution. Access to foreign exchange was sharply limited, and the yuan was tied tightly to the U.S. dollar.

Eventually, however, cracks in the system began to appear. The most obvious of these was the nation's steadily increasing toll of non-performing loans, the result of over a decade of easy lending to the SOEs. Linked to this, though, and in some ways even more troubling to the leadership, was the extent to which provincial banks, formally subordinate to the PBOC, had expanded their own realms of power, plying local connections to extend billions of yuan in what had quickly become bad loans. What made this situation particularly worrisome was the lack of any alternative to it: without a liberalized financial sector, and with deep-seated problems in the local banks, the only way for China to fund its growth was through the state-owned banking sector.

And so in the early 1990s, the state slowly started to reform the banks. The first steps, not surprisingly, were gradual. Relying on advice from the World Bank and major global investment firms, the PBOC began experimenting with monetary instruments like open market operations and interest rate controls. They eliminated all quotas on banking credit and restructured their own internal management systems. Then they turned to the provincial banks, replacing them—formally at least—with a new structure of nine "greater regional offices." These offices were staffed by bankers sent from Beijing, managers who had been trained in the PBOC's new way of thinking and who lacked personal links to the provinces. The PBOC itself got out of the direct lending market, and responsibility for banking supervision was vested in a new agency, the China Bank Regulatory Commission (CBRC).

These reforms went part way toward recentralizing power in the PBOC and pushing it closer to the market. But the reforms barely made a dent in the accumulating pile of non-performing loans (NPLs), which by 1999 stood somewhere between 1.65 and 1.8 trillion RMB.[26] At this level they posed a considerable threat, both to the internal stability of China's banking sector and to its external credibility with other financial entities. And so in 1999, the government took extraordinary measures. First, it borrowed 1.4 trillion RMB from the PBOC and state commercial banks, using the capital to purchase an equivalent amount of NPLs from the major state-owned banks. Then, in 2004, the PBOC took $60 billion out of the country's foreign exchange reserves and injected it, via a new institution named China SAFE (*Huijin*), directly into these banks. This latter tranche of money was used to write off a corresponding amount of the lowest-grade NPLs and to transform the banks—ideally—into listed companies, ready for foreign investment.

At the same time, the government established four new asset management companies (AMCs)—joint stock companies in which the government held 100% of the shares. These companies were given the 1.4 trillion RMB worth of NPLs that the government had recently purchased and were charged with the daunting task of restructuring or disposing of the debt that remained, creating in the process the makings of a modern capital market.

By 2005, Chinese officials reported that the AMCs were well on their way. They had disposed of an estimated 60%–70% of the NPLs they had received in 1999, and had restructured much of the rest.[27] In many cases, the AMCs had taken control of the assets that lay behind the NPLs, either selling them for cash or converting them into more profitable ventures.[28] As a result of these measures, coupled with increased regulatory scrutiny and tougher review of new lending, operating profits at the major banks had started to edge upwards: in 2004, both the Bank of China and China Construction Bank had increased their profits by 15% and seen their NPL ratios decline, respectively, to 5% and 3.9%.[29] Most of these NPLs were the result of new loans, extended in the period between 1999 and 2004.

Still, the market that China was building did not yet resemble its Western counterparts. Although one of the goals of banking reform was to sell shares of the cleansed banks to strategic, and particularly foreign, investors, steps in this direction were minimal. The AMCs were still fully owned by the state, and foreign participation in the banking sector, though growing, was slight.[30] The rural cooperatives remained deeply in debt, and many of the SOEs showed no signs of creeping, much less leaping, to the market. Chinese officials, though, insisted that this slow-but-steady reform was the only way to go. "The whole wisdom," asserted an official of the CBRC, "lies in striking a proper balance."[31]

Revaluing the Yuan

A second issue of financial liberalization concerned the yuan, still pegged resolutely to the U.S. dollar. Since 2003, the U.S. government had been complaining vociferously about this peg, arguing that China's currency was undervalued by some 30% to 35%, and that this undervaluation was contributing to China's burgeoning current account surplus with the United States.[32] U.S. officials also asserted that China's 2001 entry into the World Trade Organization meant that the country could no longer use its currency as a tool of trade policy: instead, like other major trading nations, it needed to remove its peg over time and let the yuan float.

China, however, showed no particular interest in embracing this logic. Instead, Chinese officials maintained that a fixed yuan was crucial to China's growth and economic stability, and that it provided indigenous firms with one of their few international advantages. Or as Premier Wen Jiabao explained, China would move toward a floating exchange regime based on "the principles of independent initiative, controllability, and gradual progress to independently determine the modality, content and timing of the reform in accordance with China's needs for reform and development."[33] Officials also noted that the United States was not really in a position to make such demands on China. As of 2004, China held $174.4 billion in U.S. treasury bonds and total foreign exchange reserves of $609.9 billion.[34] A tussle over currencies, therefore, was clearly not in the United States' best interest.

Nevertheless, in the summer of 2005 the Chinese made a minor concession. They let the yuan float briefly and then repegged it at 8.11 to the dollar, a small but noticeable increase of 2.1%.[35] Chinese officials described this move as a successful experiment, a step, once again, in their slow but steady advance toward financial liberalization. But the Bush administration was more circumspect. "Our views on this are by now well known," said Treasury Secretary John Snow during an October 2005 visit to Beijing. "China and the global economy will both benefit from greater currency flexibility."[36]

Dealing with Inequality

If China's leaders were relatively unconcerned about their currency regime, though, they were seriously worried by the growing issue of inequality in 2005, and by the extent to which development's gains no longer fell evenly.

In the 1970s, when reform began, China's Gini coefficient was generally in the range of .21–.24.[37] It was a very poor country during this period (private consumption per capita in 1970 was only $70), but also a relatively equal one. Some of this equality came naturally—the result, mostly, of small-scale agriculture performed under harsh conditions. But much of it was also enforced and reflected by the dominant ideology of Maoism, an ideology that preached equality above all else, and by a regime that practiced—often harshly—what it preached.

By 2005, however, three decades of explosive growth had eroded the equality that once prevailed. The country's Gini coefficient hovered between .4 and .5, and small segments of the rural poor were, for the first time in 30 years, experiencing a real decline in income.[38]

In other situations, these gaps might not have appeared either extraordinary or worrisome. Indeed, rising income gaps were a well-known accompaniment to economic growth and had likewise arisen as countries such as Korea and Taiwan underwent their own phases of development. In China, though, the persistence of communism made these gaps particularly tough to explain. China, after all, was still ruled by the Communist Party and still committed—in theory at least—to the creation of a socialist state that, in the words of President Hu Jintao, "integrat[ed] the fundamental tenets of Marxism with the concrete practices of our country and with the characteristics of the times."[39] Meanwhile, the political structure of communism in China also made these gaps difficult to redress. Because while power still ran unchecked from the center, the actual content of this power was often severely compromised by the time it reached the rural poor.

During the New Year's celebration of 2004, President Hu and Premier Wen Jiabao both made a point of being shown eating dumplings with peasants. They then announced the abolition of agricultural taxes and all surcharges for peasants. In theory, this should have served to redistribute income away from the wealthier and more industrial parts of China and toward the poorer interior regions. In practice, however, the effect was considerably more muted. Rural communities lost their major source of revenue and, strapped for cash, cut back on the services they traditionally provided their constituents. Efforts to redress these imbalances through transfer payments often proved unsuccessful as well, since local officials could easily reroute the payments for their own purposes.[40]

By 2005, therefore, central authorities in Beijing were determined to attack the problem of inequality with more potent tools. They planned to provide a basic standard-of-living allowance for low-income urban citizens and to create unemployment insurance for certain classes of employees. They intended to create health and pension insurance programs, and to revitalize the country's aging system of social security.[41]

How well these tactics would work, however, remained to be seen. The Communist Party was not willing to slow down growth to address inequality, or to leave the balance purely to market forces. They had to rely on local officials to implement their policies, but they were wary of ceding too much power to these officials, lest they begin to chip away at Beijing's careful strategy of controlled, top-down reform. China's policymakers were also unwilling to eliminate the country's infamous *hukou* system, which dictated where workers could legally reside. Labor mobility was not severely compromised, but many illegal migrants were ineligible as a result of their migration for any social services.

The upshot of these tensions was predictable: sporadic uprisings, scattered by the start of the 21st century across China. In 2004 alone, 74,000 incidents were reported.[42] Protests over the illegal seizure of land were particularly severe in 2005, and included violent demonstrations in Hebei province (in central China) and in Guangdong (outside of Hong Kong).[43] Each of these incidents was, by itself, relatively unimportant. Together, though, they suggested a rising level of popular dissatisfaction in China and a threat—albeit still distant—of political instability.

The leadership was well aware of this threat and fully committed to preventing it by whatever means possible. But these means, again, were not entirely clear. If China truly wanted to attack inequality, it would have to engage in a massive program of redistribution, building an administrative infrastructure along the way and almost certainly slowing growth in the process. If it wanted to spur continued growth, by contrast, and generate the millions of new jobs that the country required each year, it had to continue moving toward the market and accepting the inequalities that this movement was likely to perpetuate. In the past, China had balanced these pressures through a uniquely careful strategy of controlled reform, led and monitored by the unchallenged authority of the Chinese Communist Party. Could such a strategy survive the final phases of market reform? Or, in the end, would China need a democracy to make its market work?

706-041

Exhibit 1   Map of China

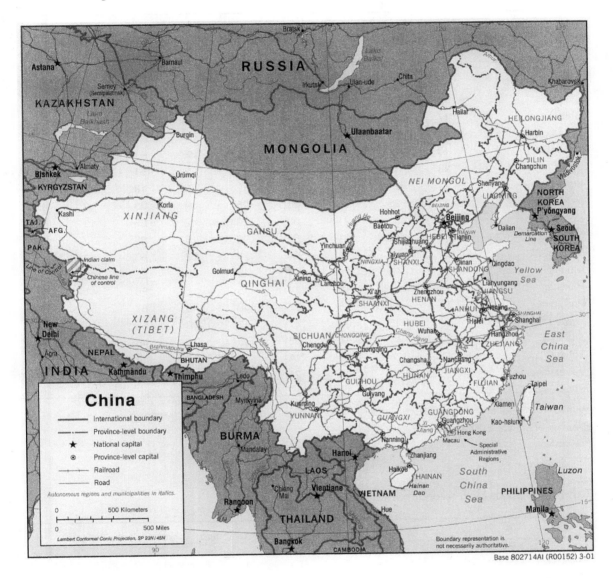

Source: University of Texas Perry-Castañeda Library.

China: Building "Capitalism with Socialist Characteristics"

706-041

Exhibit 2 China's Place among Developing Countries

	Investment as Percent GDP			Trade as Percent GDP[a]			Foreign Debt as Percent GDP		
	1985	1995	2005[b]	1985	1995	2005[b]	1985	1995	2005[b]
Argentina	17	18	21	9	10	23	57	38	78
Brazil	19	21	20	10	9	14	46	23	28
Chile	17	25	23	27	28	37	124	31	41
China	**30**	**35**	**44**	**11**	**20**	**39**	**6**	**17**	**13**
Colombia	18	23	20	13	18	22	41	27	27
Egypt	28	16	16	23	26	29	151	53	37
India	21	24	25	7	12	18	18	27	16
Indonesia	20	26	21	20	25	32	38	56	52
Korea	29	37	31	32	29	42	57	18	19
Malaysia	30	44	21	52	96	115	65	39	40
Mexico	NA	16	21	NA	29	32	50	58	19
Nigeria	10	16	24	14	43	50	23	142	39
Pakistan	19[b]	19[b]	15	14	15	18	36	41	36
Philippines	18	22	16	23	40	48	87	53	69
Taiwan	19	25	22	47	47	60	13	10	23
Thailand	27	41	31	25	45	72	45	60	29
Turkey	NA	24	19	NA	22	30	NA	44	46
Venezuela	18	17	20	21	24	30	59	46	30

Source: Compiled from Economist Intelligence Unit Country Data, http://www.eiu.com, January, 2006.
[a] Average of exports and imports.
[b] Estimated.

Exhibit 3 Major Macroeconomic Indicators, 1980–2004

	1980	1985	1990	1995	2000	2001	2002	2003	2004
Inflation rate (%)	NA	NA	3.1	17.1	0.3	0.7	-0.8	1.2	3.9
Lending interest rate (%)	5.0	7.9	9.4	12.1	5.8	5.8	5.3	5.3	5.6
Deposit interest rate (%)	5.4	7.2	8.6	11.0	2.3	2.3	2.0	2.0	2.3
Money supply (M1, billions RMB)	114.9	301.7	701.0	2,308.3	5,454.1	6,168.9	7,266.5	8,644.9	9,930.6
National savings rate (% GDP)	32.4	35.9	39.0	40.8	37.6	37.8	39.1	41.9	44.5
Unemployment rate (%)	4.9	1.8	2.5	2.9	3.1	3.6	4.0	4.3	4.2

Source: Economist Intelligence Unit Country Data, http://www.eiu.com, accessed February 2006; World Bank World Development Indicators; Asian Development Bank, *Key Indicators 2005*.

Exhibit 4A China's National Income Accounts: Gross Domestic Product, 1980–2004 (billions RMB, constant 1990 prices)

	1980	1984	1988	1992	1996	2000	2001	2002	2003	2004
Government consumption	93.6	143.6	199.6	305.2	395.3	583.5	645.0	690.2	728.4	773.6
Private consumption[a]	412.9	605.4	861.2	1,220.6	1,843.3	2,499.0	2,569.2	2,665.6	2,654.7	2,899.2
Gross domestic investment	281.7	391.9	666.6	787.2	1,416.9	1,764.3	2,009.8	2,277.2	2,735.6	3,107.7
Exports	106.3	158.7	233.7	408.9	614.6	1,216.6	1,333.7	1,726.0	2,188.2	2,748.2
Imports	131.3	180.5	244.6	408.9	690.0	1,206.6	1,336.6	1,704.5	2,126.6	2,761.3
GDP	763.2	1,119.1	1,716.5	2,313.0	3,580.1	4,856.8	5,221.1	5,654.4	6,180.3	6,767.4
GDP (billions 2006 US$)	188.2	256.1	307.2	418.2	816.5	1,080.7	1,175.7	1,270.7	1,416.6	1,649.3

Source: World Bank World Development Indicators Database, January, 2006; Economist Intelligence Unit Country Data, http://www.eiu.com, January, 2006.

[a]In 2000, the World Bank changed its method of reporting private consumption to account for statistical discrepancies in the use of resources relative to the supply of resources. Private consumption figures for 1980–1996 and 2004 are estimated to maintain consistency.

Exhibit 4B China's National Income Accounts: Gross Domestic Product, 1980–2004 (billions RMB, current prices)

	1980	1984	1988	1992	1996	2000	2001	2002	2003	2004
Government consumption	65.9	102.0	172.7	349.2	785.2	1,170.5	1,302.9	1,391.7	1,480.8	1,644.5
Private consumption	231.7	367.5	763.3	1,246.0	3,215.2	4,289.6	4,589.8	4,888.2	5,268.6	5,899.5
Gross domestic investment	131.8	212.6	462.4	831.7	2,333.6	3,262.4	3,681.3	4,191.8	5,130.4	6,235.1
Exports	27.1	58.1	176.7	467.6	1,257.6	2,063.4	2,202.4	2,694.8	3,628.8	4,910.3
Imports	29.9	62.1	205.5	444.3	1,155.7	1,863.9	2,015.9	2,443.0	3,419.6	4,643.6
GDP	426.6	678.1	1,369.6	2,450.2	6,435.9	8,922.0	9,760.5	10,723.5	12,089.0	14,045.8

Source: China Statistical Yearbook, 2005; China External Economic Statistical Yearbook, 2004.

China: Building "Capitalism with Socialist Characteristics"   706-041

Exhibit 5   Comparative Wealth, Size, and Growth of Selected Regional Markets in China, 2004

	Annual Household per Capita Income (US$)	Average Annual GNP Growth (2000–04)	Population (millions)
Shanghai City	2,234.50	11.5%	13.5
Beijing City	2,067.21	12.8	11.6
Zhejiang Province	1,918.07	14.4	45.7
Guangdong Province	1,805.96	11.9	77.6
Tianjin City	1,483.06	13.5	9.4
Liaoning Province	1,051.50	9.1	41.1
Guizhou Province	908.06	11.1	39.0

Source: *China Statistical Yearbook,* 2005.

Exhibit 6   Employment by Sector, 1978–2004 (as a percentage of total)

	1978	1980	1985	1990	1995	2000	2001	2002	2003	2004
Total employment (mils.)	401.5	423.6	498.7	647.5	680.7	720.9	730.3	737.4	744.3	752.0
Agriculture	70.5%	68.7%	62.4%	60.1%	52.2%	50.0%	50.0%	50.0%	49.1%	46.9%
Industry	17.3	18.2	20.8	21.4	23.0	22.5	22.3	21.4	21.6	22.5
Services	12.2	13.1	16.8	18.5	24.8	27.5	27.7	28.6	29.3	30.6

Source: *China Statistical Yearbook,* various years.

Exhibit 7   Value Added by Sector, 1978–2004 (as a percentage of GDP)

	1978	1980	1985	1990	1995	2000	2001	2002	2003	2004
Agriculture	28.1	30.1	28.4	27.0	20.5	16.4	15.8	15.4	14.6	14.6
Industry	48.2	48.5	43.1	41.6	48.8	50.2	50.1	51.1	52.3	50.8
Services	23.7	21.4	28.5	31.3	30.7	33.4	34.1	33.5	33.1	34.5

Source: *China Statistical Yearbook,* 2005.

706-041

Exhibit 8 Structure of Government Expenditure in China, 1980–2004 (as percent of total government expenditure)

	1980	1985	1990	1995	1999	2000	2001	2002	2003	2004
Government administration	6.1	8.5	13.4	14.6	15.3	17.4	18.6	18.6	19.0	19.4
National defense	15.8	9.6	9.4	9.3	8.2	7.6	7.6	7.7	7.7	7.7
Culture, education, public health	16.2	20.4	23.9	25.7	27.6	27.6	27.6	26.9	26.2	26.3
Economic construction	58.2	56.3	44.4	41.9	38.4	36.2	34.2	30.3	28.0	27.8
Other	3.7	5.3	8.9	8.5	10.5	11.2	12.0	16.5	18.9	18.7

Source: *China Statistical Yearbook*, 2005.

Note: Figures may not add due to rounding.

Exhibit 9 Central Government Budgetary Operations, 1990–2004 (billions RMB)

	1990	1995	2000	2001	2002	2003	2004
Total revenue	293.7	624.2	1,339.5	1,638.6	1,890.4	2,171.5	2,635.6
Tax	282.2	603.8	1,258.2	1,530.1	1,763.7	2,001.7	2,414.2
Nontax	11.5	20.4	81.4	108.5	126.7	169.8	221.4
Total expenditure and net lending	345.3	NA	1,616.6	1,914.3	2,227.2	2,483.3	2,836.1
Current	272.7	512.0	1,253.4	1,498.1	1,762.6	2,015.1	NA
Capital	72.6	NA	363.2	416.2	464.6	468.2	NA
Overall surplus/deficit	-51.6	NA	-277.1	-275.7	-336.8	-311.8	-200.5
Financing							
Domestic	9.4	151.1	415.4	448.4	566.0	602.9	671.9
Foreign	17.8	3.9	2.3	12.1	-9.5	12.1	14.5
Use of Cash Balances	24.4	NA	-140.6	-184.7	-219.7	-303.2	-486.0
As a Percent of GNP							
Revenue	15.8	10.7	15.0	16.8	18.0	18.5	19.3
Expenditure	18.6	NA	18.1	19.7	21.2	21.2	20.8
Overall surplus/deficit	-2.8	NA	-3.1	-2.8	-3.1	-2.7	-1.5

Source: Reproduced with permission from the Asian Development Bank from the ADB website, www.adb.org/Documents/ Books/Key_Indicators/2005/pdf/PRC.pdf. For more information on development in Asia and the Pacific, see www.adb.org.

Exhibit 10 Central Government Tax Revenue 1978–2004 (billions of yuan)

	1978	1980	1985	1990	1995	2000	2001	2002	2003	2004
Value-Added Tax	--	--	14.8	40.0	260.2	455.3	535.7	617.8	723.7	901.8
Business Tax	--	--	21.1	51.6	86.6	186.9	206.4	245.0	284.4	358.2
Consumption Tax	--	--	--	--	54.1	85.8	93.0	104.6	118.2	150.2
Tariffs	2.9	3.4	20.5	15.9	29.2	75.0	84.0	70.4	92.3	104.4
Agricultural and Related Tax	2.8	2.8	4.2	8.8	27.8	46.5	48.1	71.8	87.2	90.2
Company Income Tax	-	-	69.6	71.6	87.8	100.0	263.1	308.3	292.0	395.7
Other	46.2	50.9	73.9	94.3	58.1	308.7	299.8	345.7	403.9	416.1
Total Taxes	51.9	57.1	204.1	282.2	603.8	1,258.2	1,530.1	1,763.6	2,001.7	2,416.6
Taxes as Percent of Total Revenue	45.8	49.2	101.8	96.1	96.7	93.9	93.4	93.3	92.2	91.6

Source: *China Statistical Yearbook, 2005;* Asian Development Bank, *Key Indicators 2005.*

Exhibit 11 Changing Role of the State

	1978	1980	1985	1990	1995	2000	2001	2002	2003	2004
Output of SOEs as % of total industrial output	78	76	65	55	34	48	43	40	37	34
Output of collectives as % of total industrial output	22	24	32	36	37	18	13	11	9	8
Output of individual enterprises as % of total industrial output	-	-	3	9	29	34	43	49	54	58
Government revenues as % of GNP	31	26	22	16	11	15	17	18	19	19

Source: China Statistical Bureau.

Note: Figures may not add due to rounding.

706-041   China: Building "Capitalism with Socialist Characteristics"

Exhibit 12   Balance of Payments, People's Republic of China, 1990–2004 (millions of US$)

	1990	1995	2000	2001	2002	2003	2004
A. Current Account	11,997	1,618	20,518	17,401	35,422	45,876	68,659
Exports	51,519	128,110	249,131	266,075	325,651	438,270	593,393
Imports	-42,354	-110,060	-214,657	-232,058	-281,484	-393,618	-534,410
Trade Balance	9,165	18,050	34,474	34,017	44,167	44,652	58,982
Services: Credit	5,803	19,130	30,430	33,334	39,745	46,734	62,434
Services: Debit	-4,352	-25,223	-36,031	-39,267	-46,528	-55,306	-72,133
Income: Credit	3,069	5,191	12,550	9,388	8,344	16,095	20,544
Income: Debit	-1,962	-16,965	-27,216	-28,563	-23,289	-23,933	-24,067
Net Transfers	274	1,435	6,311	8,492	12,984	17,634	22,898
B. Capital Account	--	--	-35	-54	-50	-48	-69
C. Financial Account	3,255	38,673	1,958	34,832	32,340	52,774	110,728
Direct Investment Abroad	-830	-2,000	-916	-6,884	-2,518	152	-1,805
Direct Investment Inward	3,487	35,849	38,399	44,241	49,308	47,077	54,936
Portfolio Investment Assets	-241	79	-11,307	-20,654	-12,095	2,983	6,486
Portfolio Investment Liabilities	--	710	7,317	1,249	1,752	8,444	13,203
Other Investment Assets:							
Monetary Authorities	--	--	-7,261	-5,387	--	--	--
General Government	-116	-367	--	--	--	--	--
Banks	-	-	-21,430	16,800	-10,258	-15,733	2,959
Other Sectors	-115	-714	-15,173	9,400	7,181	-2,189	-979
Other Investment Liabilities							
Monetary Authorities	-115	1,154	--	--	--	--	--
General Government	3,129	6,021	3,153	1,124	40	-2,758	999
Banks	-2,315	-4,045	-8,281	-1,305	-1,725	10,269	13,375
Other Sectors	371	1,986	17,457	-3,752	655	4,529	21,554
D. Errors and Omissions	-3,205	-17,823	-11,748	-4,732	7,504	17,985	26,834
E. Change in Reserve Assets	-12,047	-22,469	-10,693	-47,447	-75,217	-116,586	-206,153
Exchange rate: RMB/$	4.783	8.351	8.279	8.277	8.277	8.277	8.277
Average Tariff Rate	43.9%[a]	35.9%	16.4%	15.3%	13.0%	12.0%	10.4%

Source: Compiled from *International Monetary Fund Balance of Payments Statistics Yearbook*, 1990–2004; Economist Intelligence
Unit Country Commerce Statistics, http://www.eiu.com.

[a]Estimated.

Exhibit 13 Chinese Imports and Exports by Major Commodity, 1985–2003 (as a percentage of total)

	1985 Imp.	1985 Exp.	1990 Imp.	1990 Exp.	1995 Imp.	1995 Exp.	2000 Imp.	2000 Exp.	2001 Imp.	2001 Exp.	2002 Imp.	2002 Exp.	2003 Imp.	2003 Exp.
Food and live animals	3.7	13.9	6.3	10.6	4.6	6.7	2.1	4.9	2.0	4.8	1.8	4.5	1.4	4.0
Beverage and tobacco	0.5	0.4	0.3	0.6	0.3	0.9	0.2	0.3	0.2	0.3	0.1	0.3	0.1	0.2
Crude materials, excluding fuels	7.7	9.7	7.7	5.7	7.7	2.9	8.9	1.8	9.1	1.6	7.7	1.4	8.3	1.1
Mineral fuels, etc.	0.4	26.1	2.4	8.4	3.9	3.6	9.2	3.2	7.2	3.2	6.5	2.6	7.1	2.5
Animal, vegetable oil, and fats	0.3	0.5	1.8	0.3	2.0	0.3	0.4	-	0.3	-	0.6	-	0.7	-
Chemicals	10.6	5.0	12.5	6.0	13.1	6.1	13.4	4.9	13.2	5.0	13.2	4.7	11.9	4.5
Basic manufactured goods	28.2	16.4	16.7	20.3	21.8	21.7	18.6	17.1	17.2	16.5	16.4	16.3	15.5	15.7
Machines, transport equipment	38.4	2.8	31.6	9.0	39.9	21.1	40.8	33.1	43.9	35.7	46.4	39.0	46.7	42.9
Misc. manufactured goods	4.5	12.7	3.9	20.4	6.3	36.7	5.7	34.6	6.2	32.7	6.7	31.1	8.0	28.8
Unclassified goods	5.8	12.5	16.9	18.7	0.5	-	0.7	0.1	0.7	0.2	0.5	0.2	0.3	0.2
Total (billions of US$)	42.3	27.4	53.3	62.1	132.1	148.8	225.1	249.2	243.6	266.1	295.2	325.6	412.8	438.4

Source: Reproduced with permission from the Asian Development Bank from the ADB website, www.adb.org/Documents/Books/Key_Indicators/2005/pdf/PRC.pdf. For more information on development in Asia and the Pacific, see www.adb.org.

Note: Figures may not add due to rounding.

Exhibit 14 Foreign Direct Investment in China, 1979–2004

	1979–82	1985	1990	1995	2000	2001	2002	2003	2004
Total utilized FDI (billions of US $)	**1.2**	**1.7**	**3.5**	**37.5**	**40.7**	**46.9**	**52.7**	**53.5**	**60.3**
Of which:									
Equity joint ventures	8.4%	35.0%	54.1%	50.8%	35.2%	33.6%	28.4%	28.8%	27.0%
Wholly foreign-owned ventures	3.4	0.8	19.6	27.5	47.3	50.9	60.2	62.4	66.3
Cooperative joint ventures	45.6	35.2	19.3	20.1	16.2	13.3	9.6	7.2	5.1
Other	42.6a	29.0a	7.0	1.6	1.3	2.2	1.8	1.6	1.6

Source: *China Foreign Economic Statistical Yearbook*; The U.S. China Business Council: China Statistics and Analysis, http://www.uschina.org/china-statistics.html.

aConsists almost entirely of joint oil exploration contracts.

706-041   China: Building "Capitalism with Socialist Characteristics"

Exhibit 15   Foreign Participation in Chinese Banking Sector as of September, 2005

Chinese Bank	Foreign Investor	Stake (%)
Bohai Bank	Standard Chartered	20.00
Nanjing Bank	IFC	15.00
	BNP Paribas	19.20
Hua Xia	Deutsche Bank	9.90
	Sal. Oppenheim	4.10
Hang Zhou City Bank	Commonwealth Bank of Australia	19.90
Jinana City Bank	Commonwealth Bank of Australia	11.00
Bank of China	UBS	1.60
	Temasek Holdings	10.00
	Royal Bank of Scotland	5.16
	Merrill Lynch and Li Ka Shing Foundation	4.84
Industrial & Commercial Bank of China	Goldman Sachs	6.00
	Allianz AZ	3.33
	American Express	0.67
Nanchong City Commercial Bank	German Investment and Development Co.	13.30
China Construction Bank	Bank of America	9.00
	Temasek	5.10
Bank of Beijing	IFC	5.00
	ING	20.00
China Minsheng Bank	Temasek	4.55
	IFC	1.60
Shenzhen Development Bank	Newbridge Capital	18.00
Xi'an Bank	Bank of Nova Scotia	11.50
	IFC	12.50
Bank of Communication	HSBC	19.90
Dialien City Bank	SHK Financial	10.00
Shanghai Pudong Development Bank	Citigroup	5.00
Industrial Bank	Hang Seng Bank	15.98
	GIC	5.00
	IFC	4.00
Bank of Shanghai	HSBC	8.00
	Shanghai Commercial Bank (HK)	3.00
	IFC	7.00
China Everbright Bank	Asia Development Bank	3.30

Source: Adapted from Laura Alfaro and Rafael Di Tella, "China: To Float or Not To Float (D)," HBS No. 706-031.

Exhibit 16   China's Population, 1970–2004

	1970	1975	1980	1985	1990	1995	2000	2004
Population (millions)	818.3	916.4	981.2	1,051.0	1,135.2	1,204.9	1,262.6	1,296.5
Total fertility rate[a]	5.8	3.4	2.5	2.2	2.5	NA	NA	2.0
Infant mortality rate (per thousand)	69.0	46.0	41.0	36.2	38.0	37.0	32.0	NA
Life expectancy at birth (for males)	61.7	64.8	66.9	68.5	68.6	NA	69.6	70.0
Total executions[b]	NA	NA	NA	135	750	2,190	1,000	3,400

Source: The World Bank, *World Tables*, 1983, 1991, 1992 and 1995; Amnesty International Annual Reports.

[a]Defined by the World Bank as the average number of children that would be born alive to a woman during her lifetime if she were to bear children at each age in accordance with prevailing age-specific fertility rates.

[b]Total number of executions *documented* by Amnesty International. Amnesty estimates that the true number is much higher.

Endnotes

[1] Jianying Zha, "Learning from McDonald's," *Transition*, no. 91, 2002.

[2] "China Leaders Push Economic Rebalancing," www.chinadaily.com.cn, November 29, 2005.

[3] Technically, Botswana still holds the record: 10.6 average GDP growth per annum for 36 years. Its tiny size, however, makes it an unfair comparison with China.

[4] Li & Fung Research Centre, "China Distribution and Trading," Issue 28, October 2005, p. 4.

[5] John King Fairbank, *The Great Chinese Revolution, 1800–1985* (New York: Harper & Row, 1987), p. 5.

[6] Two of the most important exceptions were the great Tang emperors, Taicong (r. 626–649) and Gaocong (r. 649–683), who established trading relations with Central Asia and Persia and intervened militarily in Korea and northern India. China's next great burst of adventurism occurred in the 15th century, when admiral Cheng Ho commanded immense expeditions to Southeast Asia, the Persian Gulf, and even the eastern coast of Africa. After the seventh expedition in 1430, however, China withdrew entirely from overseas exploration.

[7] Maurice Meisner, *Mao's China and After* (New York: Free Press, 1986), p. 60.

[8] This is only an estimate. See John K. Fairbank and Edwin O. Reischauer, *China: Tradition and Transformation* (Boston: Houghton Mifflin Co., 1978), p. 500.

[9] See Barry Richman, *Industrial Society in Communist China* (New York: Random House, 1969), p. 615.

[10] The World Bank, *China between Plan and Market* (Washington, D.C.: The World Bank, 1990), p. 152.

[11] Regulations were looser in the countryside, and when their first child was a girl, families were often allowed to try again.

[12] This limit was removed in 1988.

[13] There were some privately owned firms, but they were insignificant in terms of output and employment.

[14] *Economist,* "China Survey," November 28, 1992, p. 12. For a more detailed account of TVEs, see Jean C. Oi, *Rural China Takes Off: Institutional Foundations of Economic Reform* (Berkeley: University of California Press, 1999).

[15] Michael Bell and Kalpana Kochhar, "China: An Evolving Market Economy—A Review of Reform Experience," International Monetary Fund Working Paper, November 1992, p. 30

[16] "China Becomes World's 3rd Largest Exporter," *China Daily*, April 16, 2005. For a more in-depth analysis of China's decision to join the WTO, see Regina Abrami, "China and the WTO: Doing the Right Thing?" Harvard Business School Case No. 704-041.

[17] Joseph Kahn, "North Korea Says it Will Abandon Nuclear Efforts," *New York Times*, September 19, 2005, p. A1.

[18] "Experts Ponder Ways to Deal with NPLs," *China Daily*, December 20, 2004.

[19] For a more in-depth analysis of China's exchange rate situation, see Laura Alfaro and Rafael Di Tella, "China: To Float or Not to Float? (A)," Harvard Business School Case No. 706-021.

[20] Authors' interview with World Bank officials, Beijing, November 29, 2005. See also Shaohua Chen and Martin Ravallion, "China's (Uneven) Progress Against Poverty," World Bank Policy Research Working Paper 3408, September 1, 2004.

[21] See, for example, "Five More Years," *Economist*, October 13, 2005; Li & Fung Research Centre, "China Distribution and Trading," Issue 28, October 2005, pp. 1–8; and "China: Country Profile 2006," Economist Intelligence Unit, January 12, 2006, pp. 31–2.

22 See Cynthia W. Cann et al., "China's Road to Sustainable Development: An Overview," in Kirsten A. Day, ed., *China's Environment and the Challenge of Sustainable Development* (London: M.E. Sharpe, 2005), pp. 3–25; and *Clear Water, Blue Skies*, The World Bank, 1997.

23 "China: Country Report," Economist Intelligence Unit, September 15, 2005.

24 The bulk of China's citizens did, however, enjoy significantly greater realms of freedom than they had in the past. For a discussion of these trends and their implication, see Jean C. Oi, "Realms of Freedom in Post-Mao China," in William C. Kirby, ed., *Realms of Freedom in Modern China* (Stanford: Stanford University Press, 2004); and John P. Burns, "The People's Republic at 50: National Political Reform," *China Quarterly* 159 (September 1999), pp. 580–594.

25 U.S. Department of Defense, *Annual Report to Congress: The Military Power of the People's Republic of China, 2005*; and Frank O. Mora, "Military Business: Explaining Support for Policy Change in China, Cuba, and Vietnam," *Problems of Post-Communism*, November–December 2004, pp. 44–63.

26 These numbers are estimates. See Makoto Ikeya, "Chinese Banking System: Impact of Asset Management Companies," *R & I Rating Joho*, November 1999; and Guifen Pei and Sayuri Shirai, "The Main Problems of China's Financial Industry and Asset Management Companies," Keio University, February 5, 2004.

27 Authors' interview with Ministry of Finance officials, Beijing, November 29, 2005.

28 Great Wall, for example, was an AMC that received 1.3 billion yuan in NPLs from the Shanghai Agriculture, Industry and Commerce Group, an SOE that, at its peak, had 100,000 employees and over 100 subsidiaries. Over a two-year period, Great Wall closed many of these subsidiaries and consolidated the debt of the others. It then took control of the enterprise's most valuable assets: 15 million shares in two listed companies and land use rights for 17,000 mu (2,800 acres) outside of Shanghai.

29 International Monetary Fund, "Staff Report for the 2005 Article IV Consultation, People's Republic of China," July 8, 2005, p. 20.

30 In 2004, the number of Chinese banks with foreign strategic investors doubled, and reached 10. In June of 2005, the largest foreign deal was announced: the sale of a 9% stake in China Construction Bank to Bank of America. See International Monetary Fund, "Staff Report for the 2005 Article IV Consultation, People's Republic of China," July 8, 2005, p. 20.

31 Interview with authors, China Banking Regulatory Commission, Beijing, November 30, 2005.

32 See, for example, Nerys Avery, "China's Trade Surplus Widened to $10.3 Billion in July (Update 2)," Bloomberg, August 11, 2005, at http://quote.bloomberg.com/apps/news?pid=10000006&sid=aI6ubprxXtFM& refer=home.

33 Premier Wen Jiabao, quoted in International Monetary Fund, "Staff Report for the 2005 Article IV Consultation, People's Republic of China," July 8, 2005.

34 Mark O'Neill, "China's Reserves are a Growing Problem," *South China Morning Post*, November 29, 2004; U.S. Department of the Treasury, International Capital Data for December, 2004; and http://www.uschina.org/ statistics/2005economyforecast.html.

35 They also announced that the value of the yuan would henceforth be based on a basket of currencies, rather than on the U.S. dollar alone.

36 "Remarks by John Snow to the Securities Industry Association," U.S. Treasury Department press release, from http://www.treasury.gov/press/international.html, accessed January 2005.

37 Authors' interview with researchers at the Institute of Fiscal Science, Beijing, November 30, 2005.

38 Authors' interview with World Bank officials, Beijing, November 29, 2005.

[39] "Chinese President Hu Jintao Stresses Study of Marxism," BBC Monitoring International Reports, November 27, 2005.

[40] See the discussion in Jean C. Oi and Zhao Shukai, "Fiscal Crisis in China's Townships: Causes and Consequences," in Merle Goldman and Elizabeth Perry, eds., *Grassroots Political Reform in Contemporary China* (Cambridge: Harvard University Press, forthcoming, 2006).

[41] Authors' interview with officials at Ministry of Finance, Beijing, November 29, 2005.

[42] Howard W. French, "Land of 74,000 Protests (But Little is Ever Fixed)," *New York Times*, August 24, 2005, p. A4.

[43] "Turning Ploughshares into Staves; China's Land Disputes." *Economist.* June 25, 2005. For a discussion of the causes and consequences of civil unrest, see Jean C. Oi, "Realms of Freedom in Post-Mao China," in William C. Kirby, ed., *Realms of Freedom in Modern China* (Stanford: Stanford University Press, 2004).

A06-97-0014

Tianjin Plastics (China)

The surge in foreign direct investment spending is easing back from its 1994 highs as the authorities seek to channel funds into so-called priority areas—away from real estate and towards high-tech manufacturing production, infrastructure expenditure, energy and communications and, on a geographical basis, increasingly into the 18 inland provinces.

Recent guidelines, however, continue to fail to offer sufficient incentives for expanded participation in the infrastructure sector as far as foreign investors are concerned. Plans to attract US$20 billion into China's power sector by the year 2000, for example, are hampered by the ceiling of 15% put on investment rates of return.

"Struggling With Reform,"
Corporate Finance Foreign Exchange Yearbook 1995/96, p. viii.

It was May 1996, and Pat Johnson looked out the window at the seemingly perpetual New England winter. His recommendation regarding the financial viability of the Tianjin Plastics power plant project in China was due in two days. The recommendation would require a final evaluation of all financing options—project financing, as well as reaching contract closure with his joint venture partner, Tianjin Plastics/Chinese Ministry of Power Industry (MOPI). Pat was the project finance analyst for Maple Energy, a U.S.-based international power plant developer. The problems with the project as proposed were substantial. Pat was afraid that even if the basic financials could be structured to be acceptable to both Maple and MOPI, Maple would face substantial risks in getting its investment dollars back out of China. And it was snowing again.

Maple Energy

Maple Energy (US) was a wholly-owned subsidiary of Northern States Utilities. Since its inception in 1989, Maple has successfully completed power plant projects in Argentina, Costa Rica, the Dominican Republic, and the United Kingdom. Current project development focused on Asia, particularly India and the People's Republic of China (PRC).

Maple was truly a *developer* of power plant projects. Maple would structure the agreement for the construction of a power plant (usually a joint venture arrangement with a local partner), arrange the necessary financing, acquire and contract for all power sales once the project was fully operational, and subcontract to other firms the construction and actual operation. The power plant itself was a "turnkey EPC," an engineering procurement and construction contract in which the contractor designs, builds, and tests the power plant, so that the actual owners only have to turn the key to run it.

Most power plant projects like the one under consideration by Maple and Tianjin Plastics were undertaken as *project finance* ventures. Project financing is a method by which large stand-alone investments may be financed on the basis of their own assets and cash flows, with no substantial recourse to the assets of the equity holders themselves. Project financing is the primary method by which the massive infrastructure investment was taking place throughout southeast Asia, including China, Malaysia, Indonesia, the Philippines, India, Bangladesh, Pakistan, Laos, Thailand, Vietnam, and a host of other emerging economies. Pat, although well-versed in the intricacies of project finance (they were typically extremely detailed agreements requiring thousands of pages of documentation), was extremely uncomfortable with the problems posed by the Tianjin proposal.

Project Finance

Project finance was not new. Examples of project financing go back centuries, many of the earliest examples actually providing the financing of merchant trade with Asia. Trading companies such as the Dutch East India Company and the British East India Company financed their trade on a voyage-by-voyage basis. Each individual voyage's financing would be returned upon the return of the ship, from which the fruits of the Asian marketplace were sold at the docks to Mediterranean and European merchants, and the individual shareholders of the voyage paid in full.

In many ways little had changed about the financing needs of Asian investment. Although the investment was now for infrastructure such as electricity, water, railways, telecommunications networks, and resource-based industries like mining rather than for spices and silk, project finance was still the preferable approach. Pat knew that each individual project was different, but they all had a similar set of characteristics, listed in Exhibit 1, lending them (pun intended) to project finance.

In order to attract capital to a project, the lenders must feel secure that they will be repaid. Bankers are not by nature entrepreneurs, and they do not enjoy entrepreneurial returns from project finance. The banks are not providing venture capital and they do not accept risks that are more properly the responsibility of equity investors.[1] The problem presented by project financing lies in the balancing of the needs of the sponsor for total non-recourse financing with the needs of the banks, whose aim is to be assured of repayment either from the project, the sponsor, or some interested third party.

---

[1] The risks normally associated with project financing include: reserve or resource risk, operating risks, market risk, *force majeure* risk, political risk, foreign exchange risk, currency conversion risk, and completion risk. An essential element of the structuring of project financing is which party (bank, project sponsor, or offtake contractor) assumes the responsibility for each of the risks listed.

EXHIBIT 1   Characteristics of a Viable Project Financing

1. The project must be backed by a strong credit; the sponsor should be financially healthy to assure lenders that the sponsor will be around to build it and operate over its lifespan.
2. The risk involved relates to credit and not to equity or venture capital.
3. The project itself must be financially viable.
4. Supply contracts for the product must be in place at a cost consistent with the financial projections.
5. A market for the product must be assured at a price consistent with the financial projections.
6. The contractor who is to construct the project must be acceptable.
7. Financial capability and technical expertise must be available to cover cost overruns and complete the project.
8. The sponsor or the borrower must be capable of operating the project.
9. The project must not represent new/unproven technology.
10. There must be an appropriate equity contribution.
11. Adequate insurance must be available, both during construction and operations.
12. Any required government approvals must be available.

Qualitatively, the characteristics lead to a set of properties which are critical to the success of a *project financing*.

1. Separability of the project from its investors. The project is established as an individual legal entity, separate from the legal and financial responsibilities of its individual investors. This not only serves to protect the assets of equity investors, it provides a controlled platform upon which creditors can evaluate the risks associated with the singular project, the ability of the project's cash flows to service its debt, and assurance that the debt-service payments will be automatically allocated by the project, not by the complex decision making arising from the multinational firm.

2. Long-lived capital intensive singular projects. Not only must the individual project be separable and large in proportion to the financial resources of its owners, its business line must be singular, singular in its construction and operation at a set capacity. The capacity is set at inception, and is seldom, if ever, changed over the project's life.

Examples of project finance have included some of the largest individual investments undertaken in the past three decades: British Petroleum's financing of its interests in the North Sea (totaling $972 million in 1972); the Trans-Alaska Pipeline, a joint venture between Standard Oil of Ohio, Atlantic Richfield, Exxon, British Petroleum, Mobil Oil, Phillips Petroleum, Union Oil, and Amerada Hess (1978). Each of these represent capital expenditures which no single firm would/could attempt to finance.[2] Yet, through a joint venture arrangement, the higher than normal risks absorbed by the capital employed could be managed.

3. Cash flow predictability from third-party commitments. An oil field or an electric power plant produced a homogeneous commodity product which would produce pre-

---

[2] Project finance has been employed in many other industries and applications as well. For example, R&D Limited Partnerships (RDLP) were common in the 1980s, such as Cummins Engine's $20 million financing of a new form of diesel engine. Other firms (Genetech, Nova Pharmaceuticals, and Amgen) have utilized similar financing forms in which a finite project was financed with large proportions of non-recourse debt.

dictable cash flows if third party commitments to take and pay could be established. In addition to revenue predictability, non-financial costs of production needed to be controlled over time, usually through long-term supplier contracts with price adjustment clauses based on inflation. This predictability of net cash inflows through long-term contracts eliminated much of the individual project's business risk, allowing the financial structure to be heavily debt-financed (sometimes over 80% debt) but still 'safe' from financial distress.

The predictability of a project's revenue stream is essential in securing project financing. Typical contract provisions which are intended to assure adequate cash flow normally include the following issues: quantity and quality of the project's output; a pricing formula that enhances the predictability of an adequate margin to cover operating costs and debt service payments; a clear statement of the circumstances that permit significant changes in the contract such as force majeure or adverse business conditions.

4.**Finite projects with finite lives.**   Even with a longer-term investment, it is critical that the project have a definite ending point at which all debt and equity has been repaid. Because the project is a stand-alone investment in which its cash flows go directly to the servicing of its capital structure, and not to reinvestment for growth or other investment alternatives, investors of all kinds need assurances that the project's returns will be attained in a finite period. There is no capital appreciation, there is only cash flow.

Pat's checklist indicated that Tianjin seemed to meet all of the basic requirements. But the basic law of project finance was his paramount concern: the debt-service payments of any project finance proposal must match as closely as possible the ability of the project to generate earnings. The devil was indeed in the details.

The Tianjin Plastics Joint Venture

Tianjin was an important industrial and port city in Northern China under the direct administration of the central government. The 9.2 million inhabitants of Tianjin were among the first to enjoy the benefits of increasing openness towards foreign investment when the Tianjin Economic and Technological Development Area was established in 1984. This new economic zone became one of the most favored among foreign investors quickly. By 1995 over 156 foreign companies had established differing levels of activity in the economic zone, some of which were China's largest foreign investors such as Motorola (USA) and Samsung (Korea).

Tianjin Plastics was a government-owned enterprise which utilizes an extremely energy-intensive extrusion process for the production of a variety of raw industrial plastic products. The proposed power plant, a 140 megawatt coal-fired steam-electric plant, would provide all of Tianjin's power needs, with excess to spare—which would in turn be sold on the regional electrical power grid. Maple had already concluded the negotiation of the power purchasing agreement (PPA) with the Chinese Ministry of Power Industry (MOPI).[3] The

---

[3] Most power purchasing agreements state the specific amounts of power to be provided for the life of the contract as well as the price to be paid, normally based on an inflation-adjusted electrical rate structure.

most notable feature of the agreement was the provision for free coal feedstock for the life of the power plant (20 plus years).

The power plant construction and testing would require four years. If production could be started later, the power could start flowing to Tianjin Plastics by the summer of 2000, and the cash flows from operations could start flowing to Maple at the same time. The project was a build-operate-transfer (BOT) arrangement, where the Maple-Tianjin-MOPI joint venture would own and manage the plant for twenty years, at which time the plant would be turned over to the regional utility in Hebei province. So regardless of the productive life of the plant, the economic life of the project, from Maple's viewpoint, would end in the year 2020.

Project Economics

The *pro forma* financial statements on the project forecast an operating margin of 178,000,000 Chinese renminbi (Rmb) beginning in the year 2000, increasing 3% annually thereafter.[4] The project was to be granted a tax holiday for the first six years of operation, and would face a tax rate of 40% after that on corporate income. Interest and principal repayment would begin in the year 2000. The annual depreciation of plant and equipment was estimated to be Rmb98,000,000 per year for 10 years (which was already subtracted to arrive at the operating margin). The government of China required that 25% of annual depreciation charges be "reinvested" in operations. There would be no recapture of depreciation at the end of the investment. Operating losses incurred during the tax holiday could be carried forward seven years for tax purposes.

The joint venture would be split 49% Maple, 46% Tianjin Plastics, 5% MOPI, with Maple holding the controlling interest. This was the structure Maple generally preferred, so that it could maintain actual control of operations while its local partner could provide nearly equal financing and something more important than mere dollars or renminbi—local participation. The actual equity-stake in a project of this type ranged between 15 and 30% of total capital. In this case, equity would make up only 15% of the total $110 million in capital needed. The majority of the capitalization would come from bank financing—local banks, foreign banks, and international lending institutions with interests in economic development.[5] A diversified capital structure, both in equity and debt participation, was one of the keys to successfully developing a project finance venture. Lining up the bank financing, both public and private, however, was increasingly a problem.

But all was not well with some of the major lenders. The U.S. Export-Import Bank, a government-funded lender for the facilitation of U.S. exports to foreign buyers, had announced today that it would not participate in the funding of the Three Gorges Dam

---

[4] The Chinese currency, the *Renminbi*, is Mandarin, with an English phonetic pronunciation of "run-mean-bee."

[5] It is the participation of international institutions like the World Bank, the International Financing Corporation, the European Bank for Reconstruction and Development, etc., which reduces the risks associated with lending to emerging market countries, at least to a level at which private lending institutions are willing to participate.

Project in China. The project, with an estimated cost between $24 and $40 billion, was already underway on the Yangtze River east of Wuhan. Several major U.S.-based firms (Caterpillar, Rotec Industries) had openly campaigned for Ex-Im Bank support. The Ex-Im Bank's refusal to participate was based on the environmental repercussions of the dam, which would flood the historic Three Gorges Region of central China.

Maple's part of the deal would be its 49% of the $16.5 million in equity. The project size was standard for a medium-sized player like Maple, its projects typically ranging from $10 to $200 million in total capital employed. The average payback from Maple's projects was about 6 years after commencement of power plant operations, also normal for the industry.[6] The company's required hurdle rate was 15%, but would have to be higher to compensate for the additional risks posed by the Chinese market.

Maple, however, wanted this project to happen. The market potential for similar power plant projects in China was enormous. It was estimated that the PRC would need 21 gigawatts of new capacity each year for the coming decade. This was equivalent to re-electrifying all of southern California each year, a truly promising market opportunity. But for all of the needs of power plant development, the capital resources of China were obviously inadequate to meeting the task, and there remained considerable impediments to foreign capital stepping in to fill the gap.

Financing Arrangements

Total construction financing of $93.5 million (Rmb786.8 million) was provided through a combination of loans from the equipment vendors ($22.0 million), Tianjin Plastics ($7.59 million), Maple Energy ($8.085 million) and a bridge loan from a West Coast U.S. bank ($55.0 million). Upon completion of the project, all three parties would convert their respective loans into equity. MOPI's and Tianjin Plastic's loans were in renminbi as was 10% of the equipment vendors loan. The bank required completion guarantees from both Tianjin Plastics and Maple Energy. Local currency construction loans carried a rate of 14% while the U.S. dollar loans carried a rate of 9.0%.

The construction plan called for the funds provided by the project sponsors to be drawn down at the beginning of the first year, the bank loan to be drawn down equally over years two and three, and the loans from the vendors to be drawn down at the beginning of year four. Interest on the loans would accrue for the four years. At the end of the four years the interest earned by Tianjin, Maple, and the vendors would be paid out by the banks and capitalized in the project financing loan. In the case of the vendors, the loan principal would be taken out by the new project financing loan as well.

The post-completion financing of $117.4 million ($93.5 million principal plus $23.9 million in accrued interest) was arranged through a club syndication consisting of three banks which had experience with project financing in China, and by the Bank of China.

---

[6] Unfortunately, as a result of the extended construction period often experienced in developing countries, this translated into a payback of between 10 and 12 years after much of Maple's equity capital was put at risk.

A06-97-0014

The three foreign banks were the U.S. West Coast bank that provided the bridge loan, a large Canadian bank, and a well positioned Japanese bank. All three banks also had an *indirect* interest in the project: Maple was a good customer of the West Coast bank; a number of the vendors to the project were Japanese; and the Canadian bank was actively pursuing business in the PRC. The Bank of China loan of Rmb90.7 million (the equivalent of $10.9 million) was provided at a fixed rate of 13% for 12 years. Repayments of loan principal on the Bank of China loan and on the club syndication loan were to be made in equal annual installments.

The syndication loan was structured into two tranches, for $33 million and $57 million, respectively. The first tranche was a *project-sponsored/supported limited recourse loan*, and the second tranche was a *project-supported non-recourse loan*. The first tranche was priced at .95% over six-month LIBOR for six years (the average payback period for Maple). The second tranche was for 10 years and priced at 1.75% over six-month LIBOR (currently 5.75%).[7] The club syndication loan was denominated in U.S. dollars. The three banks were willing to accept the currency convertibility risk on both tranches.

Currency Impediments

A major problem for all foreign investors was the Chinese currency, the renminbi (Rmb). The renminbi was not currently freely convertible, so that any cash flows for either profit repatriation or debt-service repatriation would have to go through a government approval process. Requests for hard currency exchange and the opening of foreign exchange accounts must be submitted to the State Administration of Exchange Control (SEAC). Even with a reduction in actual restrictions in recent years, foreign investors in China must still obtain SEAC approval to buy or sell foreign currencies, as well as submit documentation evidence for each individual transaction.[8]

The renminbi had first depreciated with the abolishment of the dual currency system in 1994, but had stabilized since that time (although one must keep in mind that it was still a highly managed official currency value). The outlook for the value of the renminbi was uncertain; the Bank of China had set the year 2000 as the target date for full convertibility for currency transactions related to the current account (trade transactions), but no date was yet set for the more complex capital account (money and capital market transactions and investments). The Chinese government continued to control the amount of renminbi converted to hard currency with an iron fist in an attempt to manage the currency's value and the external impacts on the domestic financial economy through volatile exchange rates or imported inflation.[9]

---

[7] Non-recourse loans tend to be at a higher rate than either balance sheet loans or limited recourse loans.
[8] China utilized a dual exchange rate system up until January 1994, when it was abolished. The dual system was a result of the establishment of swap centres in 1988 to trade currencies outside the official exchange rate. Whereas the official rate was maintained at an overvalued official rate, the swap centre rates more closely followed the black market rates, reducing the degree of economic distortion for international payment settlements.
[9] In reality, even with governmental agreements or guarantees, international banks were not convinced that these agreements would be honored over the extended period of time a project finance venture such as this one requires.

As illustrated in Exhibit 2, however, the stabilization program for the renminbi's value was not always that successful. The renminbi was trading around Rmb8.32/$ in the first three months of 1996. Surprisingly it had actually appreciated slightly against the dollar in 1994 and 1995, but inflationary pressures were reigniting concern. Where it would be in one year, four years, or 20 years, was anyone's guess.[10]

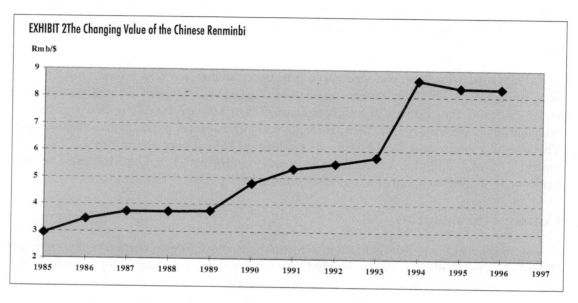

EXHIBIT 2 The Changing Value of the Chinese Renminbi

Barriers to Foreign Investors

The barriers to investing in China were substantial. First, the Chinese government was attempting to limit the return on investment (ROI) on projects of this type to 12%. After most power plant developers like Maple balked at such low rates of return, the Chinese government revised the target ROI to between 15% and 17% if the plant demonstrated outstanding efficiency.[11] Many analysts still considered that to be low, estimating that at least 18% was needed as adequate compensation for projects of this type.

Secondly, the Chinese government often refused to guarantee fulfillment of a contract such as this one, even though Tianjin Plastics was a state-owned-enterprise. This increased the level of risk as perceived by the bank lenders, and certainly was not helping the cause at the moment.[12] The fact that MOPI was a partner might have little impact on the performance of the Chinese government.

---

[10] The renminbi rate was allowed to float ± 0.3% from the official daily rate, which was itself fixed at the closing rate from the previous day's trade-weighted index value.

[11] The Chinese government revised its expectations only after a clear indication that power plant and other infrastructure capital investment was literally flowing away from China towards India as a result of the restrictions on investment returns.

[12] Many pro-Chinese developers argued that this was not a legitimate concern, pointing to the fact that most of the loans which eventually were either re-scheduled or actually defaulted upon by the Latin American debtors in the early 1980s were, with few exceptions, all guaranteed by the host government. The comparison, however, did not serve to make many of the potential lenders feel much better.

Finally, the Chinese government did not allow *registered capital*, the equity capital initially invested under the agreements of the project, to be repatriated. This meant that Maple would not be able to return to the parent company anything other than the profits, the dividends, which might or might not in actuality arise over the life of the project. There would be no re-payment of equity participation.

Repatriation of Equity Investment

It was in fact the last point which had bothered Maple's project evaluation team the most. Maple had always been able to repatriate, in one way or another, a large part if not all of its capital invested in a power plant project. A number of different proposals had been evaluated in order to find a way out. Proposals varied from back-to-back loans to dollar-indexed rate adjustment clauses to Rmb swaps.

The simplest solution from Maple's perspective was to have the power price paid by Tianjin Plastics indexed to the dollar. Given the relatively dependable revenue stream and the minor role of costs of production (remembering that the primary variable cost was coal, which was free, and the majority of fixed costs arising from capitalization) this would essentially guarantee earnings in the joint venture which would maintain their U.S. dollar value as repatriated. This would obviously please both the foreign creditors and Maple, but the Chinese pricing bureau of MOPI had ruled this out immediately as the revenue structure of Tianjin itself was purely domestic (renminbi based). MOPI was also opposed to this scheme because of the negative impact it might have on the returns on their invested capital in the project.

A method employed in China on several occasions in the last three years was the *back-to-back loan* (illustrated in Exhibit 3). Maple had identified another Western firm, Wintel (US), who already had an investment in China. Wintel had generated profits in renminbi but could not repatriate the earnings. Maple and Wintel had discussed a back-to-back loan agreement in which Wintel would loan the equivalent of Rmb70.018 million to Maple for six years at 10.5%, and Maple would in turn lend to Wintel $8.415 million at LIBOR plus 1.45% for the same six years. At the prevailing exchange rate of Rmb8.32/$, the loan amounts were equal in value. Instead of converting the dollars and making the equity investment in China, Maple would *borrow* the renminbi for the investment (from Wintel). Both loans were structured with bullet principal repayment at maturity. The renminbi loan would be serviced by Maple's share of the local currency profits in excess of Rmb70.018 million. Wintel was willing to enter into this structure because its registered capital was locked into renminbi and it could only make 8% on its liquid funds in China. Additionally, if it were to borrow the funds back in the United States it would pay a higher rate—LIBOR plus 1.80%— for the same six years.

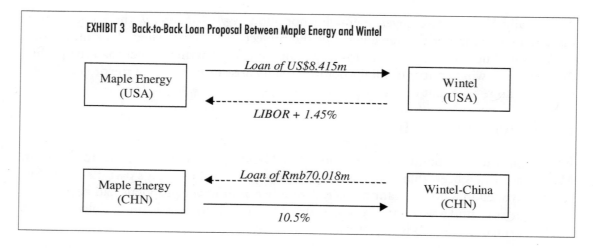

EXHIBIT 3 Back-to-Back Loan Proposal Between Maple Energy and Wintel

Currency Risk

A partially convertible currency posed special problems. Assuming governmental approval would be obtained for the conversion, the currency risk for such an extended period of time was unacceptable. Maple had worked with a number of the major multinational banks in evaluating a number of potential solutions. What made this currency risk different from any other long-term floating rate foreign currency denominated receivable was the lack of financial derivatives to hedge renminbi cash flows. All risk management derivative products relied upon access to money and capital market instruments in the subject currency, and those financial markets simply did not yet exist in China or in Chinese renminbi anywhere. This same principle applied to other suggested alternatives such as U.S. dollar—Chinese renminbi swaps.

The remaining solution of the greatest potential value was to finance the majority of the project in renminbi, that is, borrow locally. This would simply match the local currency inflows with local currency outflows—financing outflows—insulating the majority of the firm's cash flows from currency risk. Discussions with officials of the Chinese banking industry indicated that, with the proper approvals, a 10 year loan agreement at approximately 13% would be possible. But there was one catch: the renminbi loan would require 100% dollar-denominated collateral: the lenders for the Tianjin power plant project would put up a $101.5 million deposit with the Bank of China.[13] Although the deposit would not be required until operation startup in 2000, this seemed to be a rather expensive alternative. For example, similar 10 year loans in the U.S. dollar markets at this time were roughly 8%. (The basic arrangements for this dollar-deposit collateralization proposal are illustrated in Exhibit 4.) Pat made an additional final note regarding the dollar deposit, that the profits earned and repatriated to Maple (US) would still be exposed to currency risk.

Time was running short, and Pat was running out of ideas.

---

[13] The dollar security deposit would be drawn-down over time (Maple would be able to draw dollars out) as the principal of the renminbi loan was amortized and repaid.

A06-97-0014

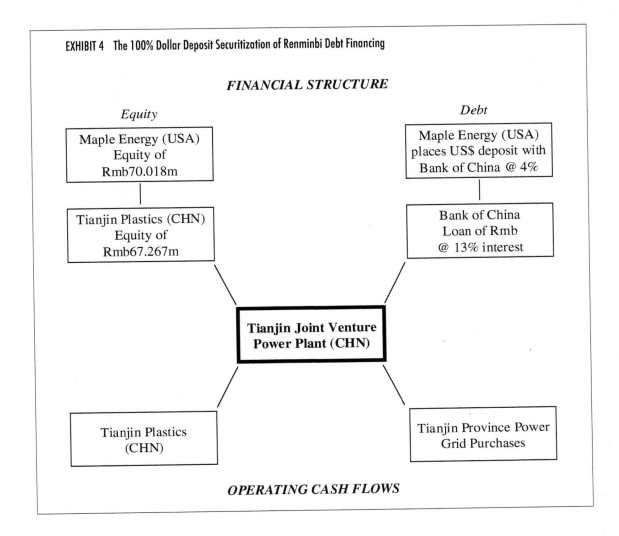

EXHIBIT 4 The 100% Dollar Deposit Securitization of Renminbi Debt Financing

FINANCIAL STRUCTURE

Equity

Debt

Maple Energy (USA) Equity of Rmb70.018m

Maple Energy (USA) places US$ deposit with Bank of China @ 4%

Tianjin Plastics (CHN) Equity of Rmb67.267m

Bank of China Loan of Rmb @ 13% interest

Tianjin Joint Venture Power Plant (CHN)

Tianjin Plastics (CHN)

Tianjin Province Power Grid Purchases

OPERATING CASH FLOWS

V. Mergers & Acquisitions

A06-98-0015

AGUAS MINERALES S.A. &
CADBURY SCHWEPPES PLC (A)

In February 1992, the mergers and acquisitions team of the Latin American department of Bankers Trust ("the Bankers Trust team") received the telephone call from Cadbury Schweppes plc: Bankers Trust was awarded the role of sole advisor in its attempt to fully or partially acquire Mexico's Aguas Minerales SA (AMSA). AMSA is the wholly owned mineral water subsidiary of Mexico City-based Fomento Economico Mexicano SA (FEMSA), a producer of beer, mineral water, and other beverages.

This would be one of the largest acquisitions of a Mexican business by an overseas company. The country setting and the fact that Cadbury Schweppes currently competes with FEMSA's soft drink business unit led the Bankers Trust team to conclude that valuation would not be easy.

FEMSA's Background

FEMSA was founded in 1890 by Isaac Garza and his brother-in-law, Francisco Sada as the Cuauhtemoc Brewery in Northeast Mexico. During the first quarter of this century, they expanded to other regions by opening new plants. During World War II Garza, Sada, and their heirs began manufacturing steel to ensure adequate supply of bottle caps. Around that time, they also expanded into financial services by acquiring Banca Serfin, the oldest bank in Mexico. In the 1970s, the brewery operation and Banca Serfin were spun off into a new group of family-owned companies called Valores Industriales SA (VISA). This group was led by Eugenio Garza.

In the second half of the 1970s, Garza, like many Mexican industrialists, got into financial trouble. During the boom years of the 1970s and early 1980s, VISA borrowed freely in order to diversify: it expanded into soft drinks and mineral water, as well as into unrelated fields like hotels, animal feed, and automotive parts. When the price of oil declined in 1982, so did VISA's businesses, which by then had accumulated over $1 billion in debt.

On top of this, President Lopez Portillo's administration nationalized Banca Serfin. Desperate to raise cash, Garza sold VISA's hotels and other businesses unrelated to its core beverage and packaging businesses. In the reorganization of VISA's capital structure, Garza included World Bank's International Finance Corporation, Mexico's state-owned development bank NAFINSA, and Citicorp as new lenders.

In 1988, VISA undertook a debt-for-equity restructuring. The restructuring eliminated three-quarters of VISA's $1.7 billion debt and gave its new creditors approximately 20% of the equity in a newly created, publicly traded beverage and packaging company called Fomento Economico Mexicano, SA or FEMSA. VISA retained 60% of FEMSA, and 20% of the shares traded on Mexico's Stock Exchange (Bolsa de Mexico). Grupo Proa, a private holding company (51% owned by Garza's family), owned around 80% of VISA (Garza's share is currently worth $550 million). The remaining 20% trades on Mexico's Bolsa. Grupo Proa also owns 60% of the insurance group, Valores de Monterrey, S.A. or Vamsa (Garza's share in this is currently worth $200 million). The rest of the shares are publicly traded (see Exhibit 1).

By 1990, FEMSA was Mexico's fifth largest company with 1990 revenues exceeding $1.7 billion and net income in excess of $120 million. It was the nation's largest beverage company, and the 13th largest brewery in the world. This rapid growth was achieved through the acquisition of additional beer (Superior, Dos Equis, and Sol), soft drink, and mineral water brands. FEMSA acquired the Mexico City and Southeastern Mexico Coca Cola franchises and the flagship mineral water brands, Penafiel, Aguas de Tehuacan, and Balseca. FEMSA had a leadership position in all the segments it competed: 51% share of the brewery market; 59% of the soft drink market; and 80% share of the flavored and unflavored mineral water market (see Exhibit 2).

In October 1991, VISA acquired 51 percent of Bancomer, the second largest bank in Mexico with $28 billion in assets, for $2.6 billion. The acquisition was financed with new stock issues worth $1 billion, debt worth $1 billion, and cash. To help finance Bancomer's acquisition, FEMSA announced that it would sell interests in its beverage operations.

FEMSA looked for investors with international beverage experience who could form a joint venture with them, provide marketing and operational expertise, and contribute significant potential for added shareholder value.

In any event, the first divestiture—it was not evident whether it should be a full or partial divestiture—would be FEMSA's mineral water business, AMSA.

AMSA

AMSA bottled and franchised five brands: Penafiel, Balseca, Etiqueta Azul, Catemaco, and Extra Poma. Penafiel was the largest selling mineral water brand in Mexico. Balseca was a strong regional brand in the south eastern Mexico and Etiqueta Azul a discounted regional brand primarily sold through FEMSA's Coca Cola bottling division. In 1991, Aguas Minerales made a pre-tax profit of $24.4 million (pesos 73.1 billion), on sales of $161.6 million (pesos 484.4 billion). AMSA was considered by industry experts to be a well managed company.

AMSA's product line included a portfolio of flavored and unflavored mineral waters positioned as "sourced from famous wells, intrinsically pure, and of high quality." The business owned five bottling plants with natural springs. In the Mexican mineral water industry, as opposed to the U.K. or France, waters are not required to be source-dependent. The law permits it to be sourced with high-quality water from wells anywhere in Mexico.

The Soft Drink Market

In 1991, the Mexican carbonated soft drink market was one of the largest in the world, with annual sales of 2.8 billion gallons (at a price of approximately $1.07 per gallon). Mexico's per capita consumption was 34 gallons per person per year. Colas represented 60 percent of total carbonates and flavored drinks accounted for the rest. Coca Cola and Pepsi had a 47 percent share and 17 percent share, respectively, of total carbonates. The market had grown at 9 percent per year from 1987 to 1990, and had a forecasted growth of 6 percent per year (including the population growth of 2 percent per year) until the year 2000. This indicated a per capita consumption growth of 4 percent per year.

The bottled water market was underdeveloped in comparison to other segments of the carbonates markets, representing only 5 percent of total soft drinks (142 million gallons). However, this market segment has been growing at nearly 12% percent per year since 1985.

Historically, prices for carbonated soft drinks in Mexico have been lower than world prices, and despite the large volume, both franchisers and bottlers experienced marginal profitability. However, there were significant price increases in the last three years.

The Bankers Trust Team's Financial Valuation Assumptions

As a first step, the Bankers Trust team drew up an estimated base-case income statement and balance sheet for AMSA for financial year 1991 (Exhibit 5). From a 1991 base, they assumed sales (volume) growth of 9 percent per year through 1995, 5% per year from 1996 to 2000, and 2 percent per year thereafter. They supported these assumptions with the following arguments:

Advertising: Since 1989, AMSA had supported its 80 percent market share of carbonated waters with national television advertising. In the past, no other Mexican water brand could afford such an investment.

New Products and Packaging: AMSA introduced Penafiel Light in 1990, and the Bankers Trust team believed that this flavored mineral water could grow without cannibalizing the rest of the product portfolio. They believed that plastic bottles would become a key factor in the Mexican carbonated soft drink industry, and saw significant capital expenditures behind this packaging Penafiel represented a major portion of the projected growth rate of 9%.

Pricing: Since 1988, Mexico's inflation had declined in part due to "el Pacto," an annual agreement among government, business, and labor. Price increases at the consumer and retail level were authorized nationally, and transportation services and energy were subsidized. In 1992, the Salinas' administration was expected to lower the IVA tax (value added tax) from 15 percent to 10 percent, which could support a net 4.6 percent price increase.

The Bankers Trust team expected revenues to increase by an achievable price increase. The valuation presumed a 28 percent increase in mineral water prices through December 1992. Assuming a small negative impact on next year's volume, it would increase overall revenues. During the longer term, they assumed price growth roughly in line with inflation. If the North American Free Trade Agreement (NAFTA) came to fruition, it was expected to close the gap between US and Mexican consumer prices, mainly in the beverage and cigarette industries (see Exhibit 6).

Capital Expenditures: Between 1992 and 1996, new capital expenditures would equal approximately 8% of sales. Thereafter, capital expenditures are expected to be at the same level as depreciation.

Currency: Given the considerable presence (and long-term plans) that Cadbury Schweppes had in the US, the Bankers Trust team felt that it would not be inappropriate to undertake the valuation in US$. Data on projected inflation and exchange rates for Mexico are provided in Exhibits 7 and 8.

Tax Rates: Corporate tax rate calculations are complicated in Mexico. There are two basic tax rates, consisting of a regular tax rate of 35%, and a "profit sharing tax rate" of 10%. Moreover, the Mexican government required firms to set up a pension plan from 1992, whereby AMSA would have to set aside 10% of the pre-tax income; however, this amount would be tax deductible. In addition to this, there is a "net asset tax" rate of 2% that is based on a complicated inflation-adjustment formula involving revaluation of fixed and current assets. The Bankers Trust team estimated the net result of these tax rules to be approximately 20% of the post-pension plan income per year till 1995, and approximately 30% per year thereafter.

Mexico's Economic Recovery

The severe economic setbacks of the 1980s—Mexico's "lost decade"—shocked it into abandoning the statism, populism, and protectionism that had crippled its economy since colonial times. Mexico's economic style of the 1980s was to build up infant industries protected with high tariffs (in order to achieve self-sufficiency), to discourage foreign investment seen as "imperialist," to disregard "experts," to allow fiscal deficits to grow, to nationalize near-bankrupt firms where jobs were at risk, and to borrow heavily from the only-too-willing foreign banks.

The cycle ended in August 1982. The administration of President Jose Lopez Portillo proposed a moratorium on the $19.5 billion of principal payments due in 1982 and 1983. His successor, Miguel de la Madrid, had little choice but to embark on a politically costly process of reform.

A06-98-0015

On December 1, 1988, Carlos Salinas de Gortari took office. He led the current Mexican economic recovery and built closer ties to the US. The reforms established by the Salinas administration were characterized by drastic restructuring of its external debt under the Brady Plan, entering into international trade agreements (joining GATT and negotiating NAFTA with the US and Canada), an aggressive privatization program, and support for Mexico's emerging private capital markets.

The consequence of the structural changes was an overall improvement in most economic indicators. In May 1989, the Salinas government unveiled its national development plan (Plan Nacional de Desarrollo) for 1989-94. The plan had two principal goals: (1) gradual increase in GDP growth from 1.5 percent in 1989 to 6 percent in 1994; and (2) gradual decrease in inflation rates to 9 percent by 1994 (see Exhibit 7). In addition to fiscal restraint, it was hoped that monetary and exchange rate policies would produce stable real interest rates and exchange rates (see Exhibit 8).

The renewed confidence in the Mexican economy meant that Mexican companies could now access international capital markets. Lowered inflation rates and nominal interest rates led to a narrowing of the spreads between eurobonds issued by Mexican companies and US treasuries of similar maturity—the average spread, reflecting country risk, was about 250 basis points (see Exhibit 9).

Mexican companies accessed equity financing not only through the domestic stock exchange (Bolsa de Mexico), and through equity issues in the US through American Depository Receipts (ADRs). By 1991, the P/E gap between US and Mexican companies had narrowed considerably (Exhibit 10). The recent economic reforms had also decreased the cost of borrowing for Mexican companies (see Exhibit 11).

Cadbury Schweppes plc

Cadbury Schweppes plc and its subsidiaries comprise an international group of companies engaged in the manufacturing, marketing, and distribution of branded confectionery and beverage products. Cadbury Schweppes was formed in 1969 through a merger of Cadbury Group Limited and Schweppes Limited. Cadbury was originally formed in 1831 as a family enterprise to produce cocoa and drinking chocolate. The Schweppes business was established by Jacob Schweppe in the late eighteenth century and was incorporated with the name Schweppes, Limited in 1897.

In 1991, Cadbury Schweppes' net sales were $5.6 billion (£3.2 billion, at the current exchange rate of $1.75/£), and operating income was $644 million (£362.5 million; Exhibit 12). The company employed over 35,000 people and its products were sold in more than 140 countries. Its brands included the well-known Schweppes, and Canada Dry lines of carbonated beverages. Other brands included Sunkist carbonated drinks, the Crush line of carbonated orange and other fruit flavors, Hires Root Beer, Sundrop, Pure Spring, and Old Colony carbonates. In the UK, a joint venture between Cadbury Schweppes (51 percent) and the Coca Cola Company (49 percent) bottled, canned, and distributed Coca Cola and Cadbury's soft drinks.

Cadbury Schweppes' subsidiary Cadbury Beverages International manufactured, bottled, and marketed its soft drinks in Europe. The subsidiary aimed to expand its market share in North and South America in both beverages and confections, through joint ventures and acquisitions (see Exhibit 13 for their recent past acquisitions).

Since the early 1980s, Cadbury Beverages International had achieved a healthy presence in Mexico's beverage market with its popular Orange Crush soda and its Canada Dry soft drinks. Acquiring AMSA would reinforce its Mexican presence and would be consistent with its growth strategy. AMSA's sales volume was larger than Cadbury Beverages International's businesses in France, Spain, or Australia.

Potential Synergies

The acquisition provided an opportunity for synergies through a shared distribution system. The key success factor in Mexico was aggressive distribution. With 30 percent of the population living in rural areas and low levels of car ownership even in urban areas, supermarkets played only a small role in soft drink distribution. Therefore, the main channel was the small grocery store and street vendors. Despite an area equal to one-third of the US, distribution channels were more dispersed and consumers more expensive to reach.

Orange Crush represented 77 percent of Cadbury Beverages International's 1991 volume in Mexico. The current Crush bottler network covered around 128,000 outlets out of Mexico's total 810,000 soft drink outlets. This network covered around 19 percent of the Mexican population. AMSA's brands were distributed through the same outlets and had 50 percent penetration. The company expected to increase its Orange Crush penetration up to AMSA's levels by 1996. The current market size for carbonated soft drinks is approximately 2.8 billion gallons, at an average price of $1.07 per gallon, and the casewriters' estimate of Cadbury Schweppes' current sales is approximately 50 million gallons. Further, the casewriters estimate that the net income margin in this business would be approximately 6%.

Considerations in Financing the Acquisition

Cadbury Beverages International was undecided as to how to finance the proposed acquisition. Issuing stock in the London Stock Exchange could have a dilution effect, and unknown signaling effects. The company was worried about the softness of the stock market following the news of the Labor Party's five point lead in the polls in March 19. On March 18, 1992, Cadbury's shares closed at £4.43 on the London Stock Exchange.

On the other hand, a stock issue in the US or London could attract investors looking to diversify their equity interests into the booming Mexican market (during the period 1985-1990, the correlation coefficient between total US$ returns on an index of Mexican stocks and the returns on the S&P 500 was 0.46).

The company had recently undertaken a leveraged recapitalization in order to defend itself against a possible unfriendly takeover by Philip Morris, and as a result, its net debt is expected to rise substantially.

The Bankers Trust Team's Final Concerns

Assessing the appropriate cost of equity for the acquisition presented something of a problem, since AMSA is not a publicly traded company. Firms in lines of business similar to that of AMSA in the US had asset betas[1] that ranged from 0.9 to 1.1. The question that troubled Bankers Trust was whether or not the cost of capital for AMSA should reflect an appropriate premium for country risk—after all, the bond markets reflected such a premium, so why not equity markets?

Cadbury's management was concerned about the possibility of new competition and about AMSA's source water quality. AMSA's biggest competitive risk would be that Coca Cola decided to launch its own mineral water brand in Mexico. Although Coca Cola was inexperienced in the mineral water market, the passage of NAFTA could be a factor.

Another major concern in selling AMSA to Cadbury was that FEMSA and Cadbury Beverages International competed in the soft drink business—this acquisition could help Cadbury Beverages International strengthen its brands in Mexico by cannibalizing FEMSA's sales.

Bankers Trust was also concerned that completion of the deal was subject to certain commercial and regulatory conditions in Mexico (and Mexican government approvals). Mexico's Foreign Investment Law allows 100 percent ownership of qualifying investments by foreign firms without prior authorization from the Foreign Investment Commission, but only if the investment does not exceed $100 million.

---

[1] The asset beta (β_A) measures systematic risk associated with the business risk of a company. The beta, in turn, is a measure of the percentage movement in the expected share returns of a particular company for each percentage move in the expected returns of a well-diversified portfolio of stocks. The asset beta is distinguished from the 'equity beta' (β_E) in that the latter includes the effects of *both* business risk and financial risks from financial leverage in a firm. If a firm's debt-to-market value of equity ratio is defined as D/E, then the relationship between the asset and equity betas is expressed as follows: $\beta_E = \beta_A(1 + [D/E])$.

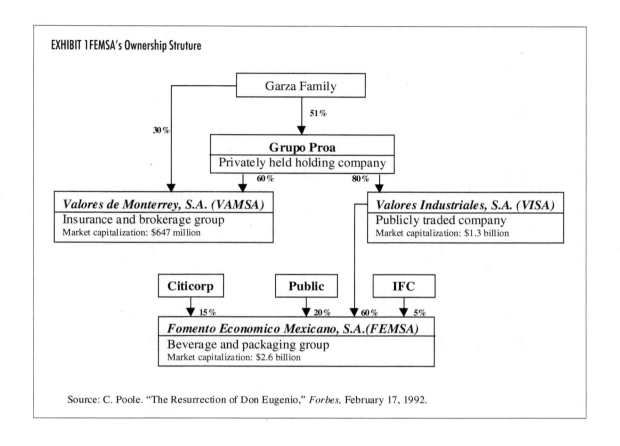

EXHIBIT 1 FEMSA's Ownership Struture

Source: C. Poole. "The Resurrection of Don Eugenio," *Forbes,* February 17, 1992.

EXHIBIT 2 FEMSA's Business Segments

	Activity	Main Companies	Main Products	Assets	Sales	Employ
Beer Division	Beer	Cerveceria Cuauhtcmoc, Cerveceria Moctezurria, Carra Blanca de Occidentc, Servicios Industriales y Comerciales	Carta Blanca. Superior, Tecate, XX Lager, Bohemia, Sol. Indio, and Heineken Beers	3,141	2,037	19,213
	Convenience Stores	Codicome del Sureste, Codicome del Centro, Cadena Comercial (Oxxo Stores) Vendo de Mexico. Anuncios y	Retailing of Convenience products	84	317	867
	Marketing Support	Servicios. Fornento Comercial.	Ice. Coolers, and Panoramic Advertising	32	50	500
	Cola and Flavoured Soft Drinks	Distribucion y Comer dc Hielo y Gas, Embotelladora de Tlalnepantla, Embotelladora del Istmo Refrescos dc Oaxaca, Embotelladora Sin Rival, Industria Embotelladora de Mexico	Coca Cola, Diet Coke, Sprite, Fanta, and Sin Rival Soft Drinks	424	529	5,605
Mineral Waters Division	Mineral Waters	Distribuidora de Bebidas del Valle de Mexico, Distribuidora Surena, Manantiales Penafiel, Extractora y Embotelladora de, Productos Balseca, Compania Exportadora de Aguas Minerales	Penafiel, Balseca, Etiqueta Azul, Extra Poma, and Dietafiel Mineral Waters	257	198	3,727
Packaging Division	Metallic Packaging	Fabricas Monterrey, Partes Industriales Mecanicas	Beverage Cans, Foodstuff Cans, Crown Caps, and Caps	407	361	1,889
	Glass	Silices de Veracruz	Glass Bottles and Silicious Sand	105	60	527
	Flexible Packaging	Grafo Regia	Labels, Laminations and Wrappers for Cigarettes, Soaps, Chewing Gum Snacks, and Milk	155	87	581
Celulosa y Papel de Xalapa	Cardboard and Paper	Corrugados Tehuacan	Corrugated Cardboard Boxes	25	44	379
	Plastics	Plasticos Tecnicos Mexicanos	Soft Drink Cases, Coolers, Containers, and Chairs	51	32	366
	Chemical Products	Quimiproductos	Detergents, Lubricants, and Adhesives	10	17	146

Note: All financial data is provided in billions of 1988 pesos.

EXHIBIT 3 FEMSA and Subsidiaries' Financial Statements (A)

Consolidated Income Statement
For the years ended December 31
(amounts in billions of pesos)

	_1989_	_1990_
Net sales	4,522	4,783
Other operating revenue	67	79
Total revenues	4,589	4,862
Cost of sales	(2.881)	(2,984)
Gross profit	1,708	1,878
Operating expenses:		
Administrative	(556)	(622)
Selling	(746)	(811)
Total operating expenses	(1,302)	(1,433)
Income from operations	406	445
Integral cost of financing:		
Interest, net	(235)	(231)
Foreign exchange loss, net	(133)	(68)
Gain on monetary position	212	278
Total cost of financing	(156)	(21)
Other expenses, net	(47)	(55)
Income before income tax, tax on assets, _and employee profit sharing_	203	369
Income tax, tax on assets, and employee profit sharing	(74)	(177)
Extraordinary credit derived from utilization of tax loss carryforward	24	112
Extraordinary income due to debt prepayment and other	135	39
Net income for the year	288	343

Source: FEMSA Annual Report.

EXHIBIT 4 FEMSA and Subsidiaries Financial Statements (B)

Consolidated balance Sheet
At December 31
(in billions of pesos)

Assets	1989	1990
Current assets:		
Cash and marketable securities	221	105
Accounts receivable:		
Notes	16	19
Trade	239	290
Other	39	47
Total accounts receivable	294	356
Inventories:		
Finished products and in process	150	174
Raw materials and supplies	608	708
Total inventories	758	882
Prepaid expenses	26	27
Total current assets	1,299	1,370
Investments and other assets:		
Shares and securities	26	8
Long-term notes	0	0
Other assets	1	0
Total investments and other assets	27	8
Property, plant, and equipment:		
Land	413	437
Buildings, machinery and equipment, net	4,606	4,874
Construction in progress	127	136
Total property, plant, and equipment	5,147	5,447
Deferred charges, net	38	52
Total assets	6,511	6,877

Liabilities and Shareholders Equity	1989	1990
Current liabilities:		
Bank loans	82	185
Notes payable	3	5
Current maturities of long-term debt	0	68
Accrued interest	22	16
Suppliers	202	291
Accrued taxes	117	107
Accounts payable, accrued expenses and other liabilities	80	115
Total current liabilities	506	787
Long-term liabilities:		
Bank loans and debentures	1042	879
Notes payable	20	10
Current maturities of long-term debt	0	(68)
Total long-term liabilities	1,062	821
Seniority premium and other liabilities	32	31
Stockholders' equity:		
Minority interest in consolidated subsidiaries	8	10
Majority interest:		
Capital stock	253	253
Additional paid-in-capital	2,995	2,995
Retained earnings	989	1,277
Net income for the year	288	343
Holding gain on nonmonetary assets	378	360
Total majority interest	4,903	5,228
Total stockholders' equity	4,911	5,238
Total liabilities and stockholders' equity	6,511	6,877

Source: FEMSA Annual Report.

EXHIBIT 5AMSA-Base Case (1991) Estimated Income Statement and Balance Sheet

Estimated Income Statement (all figures in US$ mn)		*Estimated Balance Sheet* (all figures in US$ mn)	
Cases sold (000s)	54,202	Surplus cash	8.00
Annual growth (%)	5.04	Cash for operations	3.50
Sales	161.60	Accts receivable: trade	6.60
Variable manufacturing cost	40.90	Inventories	6.00
Variable selling cost	42.80	Prepaids	2.00
Total variable cost	83.70	Accnts receivable: nontrade	21.00
		Total current assets	47.00
Gross Margin	77.90	PPE	113.50
Gross margin (%)	48.20	Deferred tax assets	
Marketing cost	8.30	Other assets	
Production: salaries	4.90	Total assets	160.60
Production: other	8.30	Short-term debt	2.00
Selling and dist'n: salaries	7.90	Payables: trade	4.00
Selling and dist'n: other	7.60	Affiliated creditors	4.00
Admin: salaries	7.20	Payables-nontrade	8.00
Admin: other	5.00		
Depreciation	4.30	Tax payable	5.30
Total Fixed Cost	53.50	Total current liabilities	23.30
Operating profit/sales (%)	15.10	Long-term debt	36.30
Interest expense	3.83	Common stock and paid-in capital	67.30
Interest income	1.83	Preferred stock	0.00
Pre-tax income	22.40	Retained earnings	33.70
Employee profit sharing*	0.00	Treasury stock	0.00
Taxable income	22.40	Total equity	101.00
		Total liabilities and equity	160.60
Income taxes	10.00		
Net income	12.40		

*Will be 10% of pretax income from 1992.

EXHIBIT 6Consumer Prices (in U.S. cents) in the United States and Mexico

Industry	*Price in Mexico*	*U.S. Price*
Cigarettes	59	200
Beer	32	58
Soft drinks	16	50
Mineral water	19	70

Source: Bankers Trust Company, March 1992.

EXHIBIT 7 Mexico's GDP and Inflation Rates

	Real GDP Growth/ Yr.	*Annual Inflation (%)*
1960-1970	5.5%	5%
1970-1976	6.2	13
1977-1982	6.0	42
1983-1988	-1.0	92
1989-1991	2.9-3.5%	20-25%
1992-1996 est.	5.3-6.0%	15% decreasing to 9%

Source: The Economist Intelligence Unit.

EXHIBIT 8 Mexico's Exchange-Rate Analysis (Note 1)

Year	*1985*	*1986*	*1987*	*1988*	*1989*	*1990*	*1991*	*1992*	*1993*	*1994*	*1995*	*1996*
Exchange rate (note 2)	371	923	2200	2320	2683	2948						
Exchange rate (note 3)	256	611	1378	2272	2474	2831						
Projected (note 4)							3025	3136	3210	3277	3339	3403

Note 1: All exchange rates in peso/US$.
        2: End of period. Source: International Finance Corporation.
        3: Average of period. Source: International Finance Corporation.
        4: Average of period. Source: VISA.

EXHIBIT 9 Major US Dollar Eurobonds Issued by the Mexican Government

Eurobond	*Due Date*	*Basis Point Spread (Note 1)*
2008 Aztec	31-Mar-08	406
Par bonds	31-Dec-19	277
Discount bonds	31-Dec-19	367
MYRA	16-Nov-06	461
Banobras 10.75%	16-Aug-96	282
BNCE 9.875%	24-Jun-96	208
NAFINSA 11.75%	02-Aug-85	276
NAFINSA 10%	14-May-96	217
NAFINSA 10.625%	22-Nov-01	259
Permex 10%	15-Mar-93	222
Pemex 11.625%	25-Oct-93	193
Pemex 17.75%	01-Jun-94	265
Pemex 10.25%	06-Oct-98	209

Note 1: Basis points over U.S. T-bonds of same maturity; the current U.S. T-bill rate is 6%, and yield on long-term U.S. government bonds is 7.9%.

Source: Bankers Trust Company, March 1992.

EXHIBIT 10 Price/Earnings Comparisons between Mexican and U.S. Firms

Industry	*Mexican Company*	*P/E*	*International Equivalent*	*P/E*
Packaged goods	Bimbo	21	Gerber Products	21
	Tablex	16	CPC	17
Retailing	Cifra	21	Kmart	12
	Commercial	17	Sears	13
Paper	Kimberly Clark	14	Kimberly Clark	15
Cement	Cemex	13	LaFarge	11
	Tilomex	15	Holderbank	12
Container	Vitro	13	Ball Corp.	17

Source: Bankers Trust Company, March 1992.

EXHIBIT 11 Cost of Debt for Mexican Companies

Company	*Due Date*	*Yield to Maturity (%)*
Apasco 10.25%	11-Dec-96	9.86
Barton 12%	20-Sep-93	8.29
Cemex 9.41%	21-May-96	10.00
Dynaworld 10.5%	17-Jan-96	9.88
Novum 12%	27-Sep-93	9.97

Source: Bankers Trust Company, March 1992.

EXHIBIT 12Cadbury Schweppes and Subsidiaries' Financial Statements

Consolidated Statements of Income
For the 52 weeks ended December 30, 1989, December 29, 1990, and December 28, 1991
(in £ millions except for share data)

	1989	*1990*	*1991*
Net sales	2,777	3,146	3,232
Cost of sales	(1,597)	(1,738)	(1,736)
Gross margin	1, 180	1,408	1,496
SG&A	(906)	(1,705)	(1,130)
Other operating income (expense)	0	1	(4)
Operating income	274	334	363
Equity in earnings of associated companies	3	3	11
Net interest expense	(31)	(57)	(57)
Inc. before taxes, minority interest, and extr. items (note 1)	246	280	316
Taxes on income	(70)	(78)	(88)
Inc. before minority interest and extraordinary items	176	202	228
Minority interest	(17)	(22)	(25)
Income before extraordinary items	159	179	203
Extraordinary items net of tax	14	0	0
Preference dividends	0	(3)	(9)
Net income for ordinary shareholders	173	176	194
Earnings per ordinary share	0.27	0.25	0.28

Note 1: Income before taxes, minority interest, and extraordinary items.

Sources: SEC; Cadbury Schweppes Annual Report, May 1, 1992.

Consolidated Balance Sheet
At December 29, 1990, and December 28, 1991
(in £ millions)

	1990	1991
Assets		
Current assets:		
Cash	63	85
Investments at cost	118	262
Acc. receivable and prepayments	554	579
Inventories	328	332
Total current assets	1,063	1,258
Long-term investments	17	34
Trademarks	304	308
Property, plant, and equipment (net)	979	1, 054
Total assets	2,362	2,655
Liabilities, Minority Interest, and Shareholders' Equity		
Current liabilities:		
Short-term borrowing and current portion of L.T. debt:		
Bank loans and overdrafts	60	72
Capital leases and others	76	66
Income taxes	78	95
Acc. payable and accrued interest:		
Trade creditors	272	275
Accruals and deferred income	255	275
Other taxes and social security costs	66	83
Customer deposits	50	33
Dividends proposed	61	67
Other payable 44	66	
Total current liabilities	962	1,033
Long-term debt, less current portion	408	542
Restructuring provisions	83	27
Deferred tax	(4)	(1)
Other long-term liabilities	29	65
Total liabilities	1,479	1,666
Minority interests	116	112
Shareholders' equity:		
Preference shares	0	0
Ordinary shares	174	176
Premiums in excess of par values	382	394
Revaluation surplus	96	100
Retained earnings	116	207
Total shareholders' equity	768	877
Total liabilities, minority interest, and equity	2,362	2,655

A06-98-0015

EXHIBIT 13 Major Cross-Border Acquisitions by Cadbury Beverages International

Year	Country	Company or Brands	Comments
1987	Australia	Beatrice Australia	
1987	United States	Taylor Food Products	Owns "Red Cheek" apple juice
1988	France	Chocolate Poulain SA	Confectionary manufacturer
1989	United Kingdom	Basset Foods PLC	Sugar, confectionery
1989	Spain	Chocolates Hueso SA	Chocolate, sugar, confectionery
1989	Canada	ED Smith & Sons, Ltd.	
1990	Belgium & Luxembourg	N.V. Gibeco	The Gini franchise
1990	France	Oasis, Atoll & Bali	Perrier's Noncola soft-drink business
1991	Germany, & Austria	Apollinaris Brunnen AG	Mineral water

Source: Cadbury Schweppes Annual Report, 1992.